The World of Art

The World of Art

ROBERT PAYNE

Doubleday & Company, Inc., Garden City, New York
1972

DESIGNED BY WILMA ROBIN

LIBRARY OF CONGRESS CATALOG CARD NUMBER 73-157615
COPYRIGHT © 1972 BY ROBERT PAYNE
ALL RIGHTS RESERVED
PRINTED IN THE UNITED STATES OF AMERICA

To the Happy Memory of
HERBERT READ *and* MAX RAPHAEL

Contents

INTRODUCTION: The World of Art   I

THE ROOTS

The Hunters and the Hunted   19

The Noons of Egypt   35

The Wounded Lions   57

The Splendor of Persia   69

THE FIRST FRUITS

The Elegance of the Cretans   85

The Experience of the Greeks   98

The Etruscan Tombs   121

The Roman Triumph   131

THE CHRISTIAN FLOWERING

The Holy Fire   147

The Face of Christ   162

Romanesque: The Humble Folk   179

Gothic: The Sumptuous Palaces   193

The Coming of Mohammed   209

THE ORIENTAL VISION

The Dreams of India   229

The Face of Buddha   246

The Landscapes of China   267

The Floating World of Japan   289

Fanged Jaguar and Feathered Serpent   303

THE FLOWER IN FULL BLOOM

The Florentine Renaissance   317

The Flemish Visionaries   339

The Magnificence of Venice   360

The Clarity of the Dutch   382

The German Agony   401

Michelangelo   419

The Dark Ones   437

RIPENESS AND DECAY

The Desperate Visionaries   459

The Awakened Eye   478

High Noon and Darkest Night   498

INDEX   514

Illustrations

HALFTONES

(Between pages 32 and 33)

Detail from great frieze at Lascaux
Wounded Lion from Nineveh
Relief from Palace of Darius
Gudea
Akhenaton
Nefertiti
Pre-Achaemenid Prince
Etruscan Chimaera

(Between pages 104 and 105)

Divine Maiden, 510 B.C.
Boy Carrying Water Jar, Parthenon
Apollo, Temple of Zeus
Poseidon or Zeus, 460 B.C.
Victory of Samothrace
Trajan Sacrificing to Apollo, Arch of Constantine
Augustus Caesar, Prima Porta
Tutelary Goddess of Vienne

(Between pages 176 and 177)

Seated Buddha from Gandhara
Buddha Delivering His First Sermon
Bodhisattva from Horyu-ji Temple

Wei Dynasty Bodhisattva from Yün Kang

Walking Buddha from Sukhothai

Buddha from Ayuthia

Buddha from T'ien Lung Shan Caves

Miroku, the Buddha of the Future

(Between pages 224 and 225)

The Pantocrator, Daphni

The Youthful Christ, St. Mark's

Christ in Majesty, Moissac

Christ, from The Tribute Money, Masaccio

The Crucifixion, Grünewald

The Crucified Christ, Donatello

The Risen Christ, Piero della Francesca

Christ Blessing, El Greco

(Between pages 296 and 297)

Siva as King of Dancers, South India

Buddha Holding Blue Lotus, Ajanta Caves

The Trimurti, Elephanta Caves

Wounded Horse, T'ang Dynasty

Toba Exiled, Hokusai

Pottery Tomb Figure of a Lady, T'ang Dynasty

Late Shang Dynasty Ritual Vessel

Wisteria, Ch'i Pai-shih

(Between pages 344 and 345)

The Annunciation, Martini

The Magdalen Reading, Van der Weyden

Portrait of a Young Man, Memlinc

The Madonna of the Small Trees, Bellini

Eve, Cranach the Elder

Bartolommeo Colleoni, Verrocchio

Detail from The Birth of Venus, Botticelli

Venus of Urbino, Titian

(Between pages 416 and 417)

Head of Lorenzo de' Medici, Michelangelo
David, Michelangelo
The Christ of the Last Judgment, Michelangelo
Portrait of the Artist's Father, Dürer
The Tempest, Giorgione
Abraham and Isaac, Rembrandt
Self-portrait by Rembrandt
The Conversion of St. Paul, Caravaggio

(Between pages 488 and 489)

Saturn Devouring One of His Children, Goya
From The Prisons, Piranesi
Nada. Ello Dira, Goya
When the Morning Stars Sang Together, Blake
The Italian Woman, Rouault
Tahitian Women with Mango Blossoms, Gauguin
Les Demoiselles d'Avignon, Picasso
Man Awaking, Henry Moore

LINE DRAWINGS

Schematic Drawing from Lascaux	26
Schematic Drawing from Cave of the Trois Frères	27
Archers, Morella la Vieja	29
Bushman Painting of Cranes	31
Schematic Drawing of Nude, Sefar	32
Schematic Drawing of Archer, Teruel	33
Egyptian painting at Hierakonpolis.	36
Schematic Drawing from Egyptian Relief	39
Gold Helmet 3500–3200 B.C.	61
Hagia Triada Sarcophagus	92
Cup Painted by Euphronios	102
Third-century Face of Christ	168

Sleeping Apostle by Villard de Honnecourt   190

Nôtre Dame de la Belle Verrière   201

Wood block redrawing from The Diamond Sutra
       Facsimile woodcut by Jung Pao-chi, 1960   263

Yang and Yin   268

Chinese Winged Dragon   269

Detail of a Bodhisattva by Wu Tao-tzu   277

Great Image from Chavín de Huántar   307

Aztec Calendar Stone   312

Illustration by Botticelli for The Divine Comedy   330

Head of a Woman by Matisse   510

Jaguar by Gaudier-Brzeska   513

There is no such thing as softness in art,
and everything in art is definite and minute.

WILLIAM BLAKE

INTRODUCTION

The World of Art

Art is a mystery, and we do not know why it affects us so deeply. A sculptor cuts into a stone, an engraver etches on a copperplate, a painter coats a strip of woven flax with a thin layer of color made from earth, pounded jewels, and the juices of plants and insects, and we find ourselves strangely moved and disturbed by the power of the artist to convey the illusion of a reality more compelling than the reality we see around us. The stone has the color of stone, but life seems to pour out of it. The needle of the engraver penetrates the copper plate only a hundredth of an inch, but the finished engraving may suggest an endless landscape. The paint on a canvas may be so thinly spread that the fibers of flax shine through, but the painter may have suggested the depth of the sky or the depths of the human soul. Something very strange takes place when the artist goes to work.

When we enter the world of art, we find ourselves in a strange topsy-turvy land where nothing is what it seems to be. There are few guideposts, the roads are treacherous, and there are no places of refuge. Here everything is very bright and still, and time has come to an end. We encounter people and civilizations which seem to be charged with vitality, but no blood flows through their veins and they do not breathe. If we put out our hands to touch them, they do not respond, and if we speak to them they do not answer. Men and women long dead appear to us in all the abundant colors of youth, and sometimes they seem about to open their lips and turn their heads toward us, but we observe that all these movements are illusory, for they are caught up in a timeless world of their own.

It is not our world, although we are permitted to enter it. We are the guests who attend the silent feast.

Soon enough we learn that in the world of art all the normal laws of human life and experience are held in abeyance, while entirely new laws, equally rigorous and demanding, take their place. Scale and proportion are whatever the artist desires them to be; he is the master of dimension. He may draw human figures no larger than postage stamps, like Jacques Callot drawing his soldiers and mountebanks, and infuse them with so much energy and splendor that they seem to be life-size. Or else he may design a portrait of Christ in mosaics forty feet high, like the Christ in the apse of the cathedral at Cefalù, and it becomes a perfectly credible portrait. And just as the artist may change the size of the human figure at will, so he may change its colors to please himself and set it in whatever landscape he chooses. He is not bound by the conventions of the world he portrays, nor is he bound to portray the world, for he is free to wander through all imaginable worlds. There are no limits to the reach of his imagination, and if he pleases he can invent worlds unlike any that have ever existed. All that is demanded of him is imaginative consistency, and the power to give relevance and meaning to his creations. He is a free agent, perhaps the only completely free agent still left in the world.

All creation is his subject, and if he wishes to draw a portrait of the entire universe on a single sheet of paper there is nothing to stop him. He is harnessed to the stars and to the raindrops; nothing great or small is foreign to him. What he attempts is nothing less than a recreation of worlds, of universes, of people. He brings the dead to life, and breathes into inert matter the power to suggest living form. He is the magician who can summon up the ghosts of the long-dead past or the far-distant future. He is the brother of the shaman and the prophet, for his task is to create magic spells and hold us within the concentrated circle of his own vision.

When we enter the world of art we must be prepared for conjuring tricks, sleights of hand, revolving mirrors. The artist is the splendid manipulator of deceptions. It is not only that he makes men an inch high and mysteriously recreates immense distances with thin layers of paint, but it is in the very nature of his craft that he must continually hoodwink his audience into believing that these inch-high men and thin layers of paint represent a reality greater than the reality we see around us. Not only the quality of his imagination and artistic skill are called into question. He must possess the gift of illusion. While he draws or paints, the process is nearly always continuous. He dare not pause, for the moment he relaxes the illusion perishes; and he must continually pour his own energy into his work in order to sustain the illusion. Not surprisingly many artists have been drained by this abnormal expenditure of energy, this pouring out of themselves on paper and canvas and stone.

The artist is a man set apart, drawing his strength from unknown reserves, possessing strange powers, curiously remote from society, which has often distrusted him. What purpose does he serve? According to the Muslims he serves no purpose except to take from God the power of creation. According to the Byzantine emperors before the reign of the Iconoclasts his purpose is to celebrate the glory of God. But when an artist is asked why he practices his art, he is likely to say that he does so because he must; some inner compulsion has led him to it, and he can no more escape from the world of art than he can avoid breathing. For him the world of art is the only reality, and he is content to spend his lifetime exploring it. Above all he is attracted by its timeless quality; he has only to walk up to his canvas or his drawing board, and he enters eternity.

Why did Van Gogh paint? The truth is that we do not know, and there are five hundred definitions of the nature of art to show that we are ignorant. To assert any single definition of the nature of art is to assert something so improbable that it is beyond all reason, and so it must be, since art by its very nature lies beyond the frontiers of reason. Every work of art demonstrates that reason is only one of many weapons for an understanding of the universe, and that imagination is a far more powerful weapon. The artist, in his own way, pushes back the darkness surrounding us, and like the scientist he is engaged in dangerous traffic with the universe. All through the history of art we shall see him exploring new territory, cultivating virgin land, and marching out into unknown wildernesses. He is the heroic explorer of the mind, exerting his domination over a world of sensations, colors, shapes, and ideas, and far too often for his own comfort he enters regions inhospitable to man. On the map of art there are many regions marked "Here are deserts" and "Here are tigers." These are the regions where he seems to be most at home.

Vasari tells the story of Piero di Cosimo sitting for hours and gazing at a wall in a hospital where sick men spat. For him this many-colored wall was among the most beautiful of creations. In his mind these stains, yellow, brown, black, and scarlet, resembled a canvas on which there were displayed, if only men gazed at them long enough, the shapes of fantastic cities, stupendous landscapes, and ferocious battles. When we speak of works of art we must take into account the spittle, blood, and phlegm spewed out by dying men.

Piero di Cosimo was following the example of Leonardo da Vinci, who described in a famous passage of his *Trattato della Pittura* how he would gaze at a damp wall and see "divine landscapes adorned with mountains, ruins, rocks, woods, great plains, hills, and valleys in great variety, and then again you will see there battles and strange figures in violent action, expression of faces, and clothes, and an infinity of things." No doubt he was thinking of the patterns left by rain or some curious stains on an old damp house wall. Piero di Cosimo was more daring, for his world was more violently colored and closer to the works of men.

It is worth pausing for a moment before that hospital wall, for it offers some clues to the nature of art. There was nothing especially novel in the artist's practice: we know that ancient Greek painters and the artists of the Sung Dynasty did exactly the same thing. Those strange stains had the power to release the imagination from its cage and send it winging away. The artist was not looking at nature, but at a fortuitous mess of shades and colors, which the imagination seized and refashioned into familiar shapes according to its pleasure. In a moment the imagination can change it. What had been a mysterious landscape can be instantly transformed into a battlefield full of waving banners and plunging horses, and this in turn can be transformed into a man leaning on his staff beside a summer pool while on the other bank a woman suckles a child and a house is struck by lightning. The images multiply, and there is no end to them. A smudge on the wall becomes a face, a hand, a flower, a goblin, a mountain with a small, heavily burdened man walking up a steep path, or an island in the sky. The restless imagination continually improvises, and this faculty of the imagination to see what is not there is fundamental to the artist and to art.

The invisible is visible, the absent is present, the far is near, the earthly is heavenly—these are the paradoxes of art. There are many more paradoxes, and indeed art is riddled with them.

There is, for example, the paradoxical relation of the artist to his finished work. What can he do with it? What purpose does it serve? Does he own it? In the days when painters and sculptors were employed by churches and temples, the answer was apparently quite simple. The works of art decorated the holy places and fulfilled a religious function. They belonged to the church or the community of monks and officiating priests who presided over the church. Zeus in his majesty, Buddha in his glory, Christ Crucified—all these were works of art, and at the same time they were regarded as divine presences, for the painted wall and the sculptures above the altar were impregnated with divinity by the very fact that they were representations of the gods. The artist had created divinity, and to that extent he was regarded as one possessing a special knowledge of the mysteries.

Until the time of the Renaissance the greater part of the world's art was concerned with the gods and the kings, who were treated with only a little less reverence than the gods. The artist's relationship to his own work was therefore circumscribed by his relationship to the Church and to the court. But even in those days he was not totally dependent on the Church and the court. He could, and did, practice his art for private profit. In China, for example, the painters of religious frescoes during the T'ang Dynasty would also paint frescoes for the houses of the wealthy. Similarly the sculptors who carved the colossal statues in the Buddhist caves would be employed privately to carve votive offerings, small images of Buddha which would take their place on the walls of the caves. A Greek potter would fashion enormous amphorae to be presented in the temples or to the winners at the Olympic games, and the same potter would sell his wares on the marketplace. But from the beginning the artists regarded their religious work as the more demanding and the more rewarding. Into this they poured their utmost energies, the fullest measure of their genius. Secular art provided a means of earning a living; religious art was the offering of themselves to the gods.

After the Renaissance, of course, secular art came into its own, and the artists turned increasingly away from the Church and the court. Now for the first time paintings hung in frames in the houses of the wealthy. Because paintings no longer needed to reflect the necessities of heaven and the royal courts, landscape and portraiture became acceptable to the merchant princes, who enjoyed seeing themselves in their finery and contemplating their estates through imaginary windows in their dining rooms, while reserving religious paintings for their bedrooms, where the more dangerous dramas of life took place. Gradually painting became secularized, until in the nineteenth century there was scarcely any religious painting of significance.

We usually forget how recent secular painting is. In the West it came into existence with Lorenzo de' Medici. Quite suddenly the dam burst open; the ordinary everyday affairs of men acquired an overwhelming importance, while divinity visibly receded into the background. The nude body of a handsome young athlete symbolized the awakened devotion to the human condition; richly embroidered stuffs suggested the new wealth pouring into the Florentine republic; the fall of Constantinople brought a revival of Greek learning to Florence, with Platonism taking the place of Christianity in the minds of the small elite who were the effective rulers of the republic. Not all the painters and sculptors surrendered to secular subjects. Except for the *David*, intended to represent Florence armed against tyranny, and for a few minor works, Michelangelo concentrated all his energies on religious art. It was simply that any other art seemed unworthy of his genius.

As far back as we can trace, we see the artist asserting his individuality, his independence, his right to see whatever he chose to see, to paint and sculpt whatever he pleased. He gave himself the right to see the gods in his own way, and no one could take this right away from him. He was a seer, a *vates*, one of those who were believed to have a keener vision than other men. In primitive societies he was sometimes set apart from other men, living in a happy isolation.

Artists were deeply conscious of their power, rejoiced in their creations, and were perfectly aware of their privileged place in society. Since they were engaged on intensely personal voyages of exploration, they made careful records of their journeys and did everything possible to ensure that their names would be remembered. Shang Dynasty bronzes, made nearly four thousand years ago, were signed by their makers. The Chinese painters not only signed their paintings prominently, but added poems and inscriptions relating the circumstances in which they were painted. Painted Greek pottery was signed by both the potter and the painter. Phidias signed his sculptures, and sometimes he would sign a carving by one of his own pupils after putting the finishing touches to it. After completing the colossal gold and ivory statue of Athena, he carved a portrait of himself on Athena's shield in much the same way that Velázquez and Goya, when painting royalty, included portraits of themselves. Artists sometimes refused to sign their work, perhaps in the assurance that their genius was instantly recognizable. Caravaggio signed only one of his paintings. This was *The Beheading of John the Baptist,* where the blood spilling along the floor from the nearly severed head of the Baptist forms the letters of his name. Michelangelo never signed a painting, and signed only one of his sculptures. This was the great *Pietà* in St. Peter's, which he completed when he was only twenty-three, writing his name in large letters on a ribbon falling across the Virgin's breast. Van Gogh signed many of his works with a large "Vincent," but this too was totally unnecessary. The style of the artist is his real signature, but when artists imitate one another, as they did during the early Renaissance, the absence of signatures brings confusion to art history. We simply do not know the names of the artists who painted many of the works attributed to Botticelli.

With the Renaissance came the concept of the museum, a building set aside for the display of works of art. No doubt something of the kind existed in ancient Greece and Rome, where collections of precious objects were formed in temples and sanctuaries. Wealthy Greek and Roman connoisseurs collected sculptures and paintings and built special galleries for them. Marcus Agrippa, the friend and confidant of Augustus, was the first to proclaim that art deserved a better fate than to vanish into the obscurity of rich men's villas; he asked that it should be shown to the public, because it was the heritage of the entire people. More than fifteen hundred years would pass before that cry was heard again. In the Renaissance, popes and princes showed their devotion to art by amassing huge collections, which differed from the collections of the ancients by embracing a far wider range. A Renaissance prince collected Roman statues, contemporary painting, rich embroideries, enamel reliquaries, gold and silverware, jewels, and illuminated manuscripts. Such collections were established for the prince's pleasure; no one was permitted to see them except by his invitation. Even the great papal collection at the Vatican was thrown open to the public only one day a year, on Good Friday.

No one remembered the words of Marcus Agrippa: art had become a private preserve. The first public museums came into existence during the last years of the eighteenth century. Significantly the impetus came from Florence, when Anna Maria Ludovica, Grand Duchess of Tuscany and the last of the Medicis, gave her great collection to the state of Tuscany at her death in 1743, but the doors of the Pitti and Uffizi palaces were not opened to the public until more than fifty years later. The first museum to open its doors was the British Museum, which was built on the collection of art objects sold to Parliament by Hans Sloane. It was opened to the public in 1759. In the following year William VIII of Hesse opened his Painting Gallery in Cassel to the public. In 1793, by a decree of the National Convention, the royal palace of the Louvre and all its treasures became the property of the state. These were the first museums; afterward they came in spate, with scarcely a year passing without another museum coming into existence. Except in Great Britain, where the royal collection still remains a private preserve, all the collections of the European monarchies have become accessible to the public. The wonder is that all this happened so late in the history of the world.

For obviously, from the very beginning of history, museums had a proper place in the affairs of a nation. One can imagine Marcus Agrippa as director of a Roman Museum filled with the arts of all the conquered tribes of the Mediterranean, and what a museum it would have been! When a civilization dies, all it can leave behind is its art. Today, when we are more than ever aware of the impermanence of civilizations, museums have come to occupy a special place in our affections. In the museums the past lives on, and we have only to walk through the galleries to see it unfolding before us. Museums have become the precious treasuries of nations, and their crowning ornaments.

Nevertheless museums are often misleading, for they convey the impression that they display the greatest works of art in existence. In fact, the very greatest works can rarely be seen in museums, because they are still in the places where they were first created. The Royal Portal at Chartres, the Sistine Chapel, the caves of Ajanta in India, and the Buddhist cave-temples in China are far beyond the reach of museums. To see works of art it is still necessary to travel across the world, for photographs can rarely suggest their scale and amplitude. The greatest works of art belong to the places where they were created, where they bathe in their proper light and are surrounded by their own landscape. Set up Chartres Cathedral in China and it becomes a monstrosity; set up a pagoda on a hill in America and it is totally out of place. The sky, the shape of the hills, the colors of the earth demand their own forms of art. Sculpture, removed from its original site, is especially vulnerable, and in a museum slowly bleeds to death.

All works of art belong to their time and place. Time eats into them like a disease; place restores them. It is as though they were living things, creatures of habit, hating to be uprooted and alienated, happy to be among their own. A Titian bathed in the blue and golden light of Venice is visibly healthier than a Titian transported to another continent. Achaemenian art breathes in the museum at Teheran, and breathes even more abundantly at Persepolis; its clean-cut opulence corrodes outside Persia. We must go to the

Acropolis Museum in Athens if we want to see the sculptures of archaic Greece, for scarcely any are to be found elsewhere, and for the same reason we must go to Kyoto and Nara to see Japanese sculpture. Even the Metropolitan Museum of New York, the richest and most prestigious in the world, the heir to all the civilizations of the past, can only hint at the splendors of oriental art.

For a few more years it will be possible to assemble great private collections, but by the end of the century the days of private collectors will be nearly over. The earth has given up most of its treasures: little remains to be found. Gradually all the truly great objects of art in private possession are making their way into museums, where they can be enjoyed by the public and shown under the supervision of experts. The great estates are breaking up; taxes, inexorably mounting, compel the sale of objects of art; and as each year passes there are fewer and fewer people who own authentic masterpieces. And this is as it should be: for the art of the past belongs to the future.

For a few more years it will be possible for a man of great wealth and cultivated taste to build a great collection. He will no longer be able to buy an authentic Leonardo da Vinci, for all are in museums, and it is doubtful whether he will be able to buy a Piero della Francesca, for nearly all are in churches or museums. Yet he may still, if he is lucky, buy one of the Raphaels still in the possession of the Italian princely families, or a Titian, or an El Greco. Let us suppose that he wants to build a representative collection which includes masterpieces from every great period of the world's art. He buys a Raphael, a Titian, an El Greco, a Chardin, a Goya, a Rembrandt, a Van Gogh, a Cézanne, noting ruefully that all the Caravaggios and Vermeers in the world have already been accounted for. Having a special liking for Italian primitives, he buys a Sienese Madonna by Duccio. Then he turns to the ancients, and buys a Roman copy of a Greek statue, a fragment of a Greek torso, a jewel-studded icon from Byzantium, and some Tanagra figurines. On a journey to the East he buys a head of Buddha from the temple-caves of T'ien Lung Shan, a Siamese Buddha gilded and crowned with majesty, the carved torso of a Khmer youth, a bronze dancing girl from southern India, a leaping horse from a

T'ang Dynasty grave, a painting by Chao Meng-fu showing the Emperor Ming Huang on horseback and another by the modern master Ch'i Pai-shih of scarlet persimmons. Turning to America, he buys a Chimu gold cup showing the stark and sorrowing faces of divinities and a jade mask of Quetzalcóatl, the Feathered Serpent, from Mexico.

He has now collected some twenty objects from many different regions of the earth, all of them by acknowledged masters. It is time to pause and arrange them in the room he has set aside for them. He observes that the apples painted by Cézanne are not altogether dissimilar to the persimmons painted by Ch'i Pai-shih, and that the torso of the Khmer youth will be perfectly at ease in the company of the Greek torso. On one wall he hangs the European masters of the Renaissance, for they possess a family resemblance. The modern European masters are hung together with the Chinese paintings on the facing wall, while the smaller objects, properly lighted, are arranged on tables below the paintings. When he has arranged them to his satisfaction, he steps back and contemplates these first fruits of his collection to hear what they have to say to him; and what is strange is that they appear to speak in one voice and it is as though they had come together of their own accord. There is no discordant note, for they reflect each other, balance each other, and speak directly to each other. The Buddha from T'ien Lung Shan springs out of religious concepts which have very little to do with Christianity, and yet this enchanting sculpture with the lowered eyelids and the ravishing smile speaks in a language which is recognizably the same language as El Greco's Christ—the language of divinity. The painting of the bearded nobleman by Titian recognizably belongs to the same order of things as Chao Meng-fu's painting of an aging emperor on horseback. The gold cup, once part of an Inca treasury, appears to be happy in the company of the jewel-studded icon from Byzantium. The room is alive with beauty beyond anything our collector expected, for each single work of art by its presence increases the beauty of the other works. In the mathematics of art there is only multiplication: beauty magnifies.

The collector hesitates, for it occurs to him that these paintings and statues are merely provisional ornaments brought together rather haphazardly, and in time there will be separate rooms for the Renaissance masters, for the Impressionists, for the Chinese works, and so on. He will secure the services of an adviser, and in due course everything will be arranged "in proper historical order to show the development." It is a pleasant thought, and gives him an excuse to add many more works to his collection.

A second thought occurs to him: Is there, after all, anything that can be called a development in art? Is the artist so much at the mercy of his predecessors that he must always develop out of them? The critics who analyze the epochs of art conclude, for example, that Post-Impressionism develops out of Impressionism, as though there had existed a body of attitudes, ideas, and techniques which developed into another body of attitudes, ideas, and techniques. No doubt in some technical matters Giorgione developed from Bellini, Titian from Giorgione, and Tintoretto from Titian, but what is chiefly important about these four masters is that they were totally different in spirit, were continually making discoveries of their own, and seemed to live in different universes, all of which were called Venice. We speak of the Impressionists, as though something called Impressionism had actually come into existence: instead, there were eight or nine men of vastly different temperaments who disagreed about everything except the supremacy of color, and if none of them had been born, art would have followed roughly the same course. We are told that Gandharan art developed out of Roman provincial art. Perhaps it did, but no one has ever succeeded in demonstrating the existence of Roman provincial sculptors in northern India, and even if it could be demonstrated, it would be the least important thing about Gandharan art. We can trace the changes produced over the centuries in the portraits of Buddha, but they do not so much develop out of one another as assume clearly identifiable national characteristics and attitudes, so that an early Siamese Buddha with a long upper lip, a slit mouth, and a receding chin, though ultimately derived from Gupta art, is essentially the creation of a new likeness of divinity, and in its powerful ruggedness is totally dissimilar to the graceful and intellectual Gupta original. The Siamese Buddha is a transformation, a sudden alteration, brought into sharp focus at a moment in time. It proclaims and gives shape to the faith; it is a statement about divinity uttered with grave finality. And when Rembrandt made statements about divinity, he uttered them with the same grave finality, without any thought of those who went before him and those who would come after him. Did Rembrandt learn from his teachers to become Rembrandt?

That finality, that sense of an ultimate judgment, which is implicit in all great works of art, precludes any theory which involves the history of art in summary derivations and influences. A work of art stands by itself, alone and tyrannically obedient only to its own laws, and what it has derived from the past is merely an inescapable acceptance of conventions. The artist paints on canvas, because such paintings are the convention of his time, but there is nothing to prevent him from painting on mahogany, as Rembrandt did from time to time. A Chinese painter refuses to paint shadows, seeing landscapes and portraits as shadowless, and this too is a convention which is acceptable and necessary to him, while Rembrandt, who loved shadows, could scarcely believe in a world where the shadows were not on parade. There are conventions for making portraits of Christ and of Buddha, but they answer the same human need and therefore we should not be surprised by the extraordinary resemblance in feeling between them. A great deal of the world's art consists of portraits of Christ and Buddha in the act of blessing.

When we look at Michelangelo's great *Pietà* in the Vatican, it seems to us that the sculptor is portraying Mary and the dead Christ in a conventional attitude. In fact, there had never been a *Pietà* resembling it in Italy. Michelangelo had borrowed a purely Flemish form, which answered to Flemish needs, and transformed it until it answered his own needs as a Florentine with a peculiarly Florentine vision of the world. In the process of transformation it was saturated with his own visionary feeling. It had become wholly his own, and existed in its own right by the divine grace of art, and what it owed to the Flemish was merely a convention.

So the collector decides against placing his works of art in proper historical order and assembles a collection which he hopes will be a miniature representation of the entire world of art. It will include African and Oceanic masks, Tibetan silk paintings, Japanese prints, Indian miniatures and Peruvian tapestry weaves, as well as ancient Greek sculptures and the Renaissance masters. He will learn that every age and every people have produced works of art, and there is no end to the art produced on this earth. He will learn, too, that the Renaissance masters are the brothers of the sculptors of African masks and that the artists of ancient Greece are coeval with the artists of T'ang Dynasty China, though more than a thousand years separates them. A single sun shines on the world of art, and a single energy radiates through it.

Sometimes when the collector contemplates his art collection or the imaginary museum which exists only in his mind, he will find himself wondering whether there exist forms of art in other worlds beyond his own. Beyond the galaxies there may be earths where even richer metals and a wider range of colors are available, where gold runs in rivers and temples are carved out of diamonds and men have seven eyes and their bodies are flames. Another sun may illuminate these earths or the sky may be bright with a thousand suns; but it is beyond belief that there will be no art. Bergson said that the universe was a machine for making gods, but it is more likely to be a machine for making artists; and the universe itself is a work of art.

Only in our own time have we been able to see the mysterious world of art in all its complexity and variety, as though it were a continuous landscape laid out before us. Snow-capped mountains, chasms, raging torrents, luxurious meadows, they are all there, and sometimes we are permitted to enter very close to the heart of the mystery. In this world of art the air is astonishingly pure, and the colors glow more vividly than on earth, and there is the only peace we are ever likely to know.

THE ROOTS

The Hunters and the Hunted

When we look for the first artists, we see them in places where we would scarcely expect to find them. They are standing on high scaffolding in the depths of limestone caves, sometimes two miles from the cave mouth, the darkness lit only by the feeble flames of oil lamps. They are painting the shapes of horses, wild bulls, bison, reindeer, mammoth, and rhinoceros on the craggy walls. They paint in brilliant colors, in wide sweeping strokes of amazing accuracy and authority, and there is nothing in the least tentative about their portrayal of these animals seen grazing quietly or racing across the prairies.

We shall never know the exact purpose served by these paintings in the minds of these artists of northern Spain and southwestern France as they huddled in their damp caverns so far from the sunlight. That the paintings answered some urgent need, that they represented in some way the divine forces of creation, and that they were conceived as objects of worship or reverence, like icons hanging on the wall in the glimmering light of oil lamps, all this may be true, but we have no way of knowing how the artist felt toward his handiwork. When the paintings were finished and when the artist stepped back to observe the composition, then he eludes us completely, for he vanishes into the shadows. Nevertheless, while he is in the process of painting, we can watch him closely. We know what paints he used, what shapes he favored, how he succeeded in gaining his effects. There is no mystery in his method, or even in his mastery. What is mysterious is his desire to paint the shapes of wild beasts in those nearly inaccessible regions where there was no danger of ever meeting them.

From the very beginning the cave artist gives every indication of knowing what he is doing. He is a highly sophisticated workman in full possession of the tools of his trade. He paints with brushes not unlike the brushes we use today, grinds his colors, mixes them, employs a medium, probably animal fat, to make the ground powder viscous, and spreads out his paint on a palette. He is equipped with scrapers for smoothing the rock and sharp flints for engraving the outline. He erects stages and ladders so that he can paint high up on the wall or on the roof of the cavern. There by the light of small stone lamps fed with animal fat and provided with a moss wick, he surrenders himself to the mysterious purposes of his art.

Strangely, his theme is severely limited, for he paints only wild beasts. These paintings are portraits of individual beasts seen in a moment of time and remembered in tranquillity, for there can be no more tranquil place than this sheltered cavern hidden deep within the earth. So from the beginning we find the artist painting far from the scene he describes, already established in his ivory tower. No wild beast has been dragged into the cave to serve as a model, yet his painting reflects minute and deliberate observation. He is in fact as far from the living beast as it is possible for him to go.

There are other strange things about this painter who stands on his high scaffolding and paints with such apparent ease. He sees the beasts always in profile. He tends to emphasize the weight and power of the animal's body, treating the head and especially the legs with an exaggerated delicacy. He knows how to suggest plastic form by shading, and he can suggest an astonishing range of textures, from the shaggy hair of the bison to the smooth pelt of a young reindeer. He rarely portrays dead or dying animals, and shows only a casual interest in their sexual organs. His art is essentially linear, and what delights him especially is the rippling line of the beast's back, the arching neck, the curve of the shoulder, the rounded haunches. Indeed, there is considerable evidence to suggest that this was the line he drew first, following it with the head and then the belly, and finally the feet. Throughout his aim was to represent the beast in its living wholeness, in the totality of its strength and beauty. He had already worked out an aesthetic and consciously followed established conventions.

In the past it was generally assumed that the cave painter served a magic function and possessed the priestly power of communicating with the vital *mana* of the wild beasts he painted. It was supposed that these paintings made men stronger and women more fertile, hunters more dexterous and the beasts more vulnerable. From the painted walls there streamed the power to dominate that small part of the universe which lay outside the mouth of the cave, that hostile predatory universe which they feared, placated, and conquered by means of magic rites.

But too much can be made of the theory of the magic power invested in the paintings. If these caverns were indeed centers where magic was practiced, then we would expect to find some evidence of the ceremonies performed and of the great feasts held there, and there would be dancing floors and altars of sacrifice where the masked and robed shamans celebrated their victory over the wild beasts, and at the very least there would be found the bone tips of spears and arrows. But strangely the caves are very nearly empty of any evidence of man's presence, and though a hundred caves have been discovered in southwestern France only one shows any evidence of a magical rite—the life-size clay bear at Montespan, which has been riddled with spear thrusts, with a bear cub's skull lying beside it. At Lascaux, where the finest of the wall paintings have been discovered, the caves appear to have been swept clean of anything which would suggest the presence of human life. There were no kitchen middens, no heaps of discarded bones, no altars, no dancing floors. Though the archaeologists searched carefully, they found in these huge caverns only a few bone splinters, the carbonized remnant of a rope which may have been used to erect the scaffolding, the sharpened antler of a deer which may have been used to outline a painting, and a number of shallow limestone bowls lying neatly together. The bowls still contained carbon deposit, and evidently served as lamps. In other caves thin bone flutes have been found, leading to the pleasant supposition that the Paleolithic artists, like Leonardo da Vinci, enjoyed painting to music.

Although we shall never be able to penetrate their minds, and we can no more follow them in their daily pursuits than we can follow the daily pursuits of long extinct animals, the paintings reveal a good deal about their way of looking at the world. We know, for example, that they looked at animals with grave tenderness and affection, even though they were hunters. The animal kingdom lay all around them, and their imaginative life was filled with the gleaming presences of the beasts who gave them fur and food and bone, sinew and hide and horn. So they painted them out of reverence and fellowship, with a deep compassion for them, knowing themselves to be sharers of the same kingdom. They did not paint them in orderly rows on the cave walls, but as they saw them: singly, or in massed herds, running free or at pasture, and they filled the walls with them because their minds were filled with them.

What is chiefly notable is the astonishing grace and accuracy of the paintings, which accomplish far more than a simple rendering of outlines. They gave weight and dimension to the animals. Heaviness of belly, strength of shoulder and breast, softness of fur, hardness of bone, all these are suggested by the use of conventions which they were the first to discover and which have remained intact through the ages. There are horses on the walls of Lascaux that could have been painted by a Chinese painter. The clean lines of the haunches, the shaggy underbelly, the flying mane, and above all the simple and decisive placing of the forelegs are depicted with power and feeling. They were not particularly handsome beasts, but the artists were more concerned with the magnificence of the animal than with formal beauty. A reindeer painted on the walls of the cave at Font-de-Gaume appears to have been painted with a deliberate regard for formal beauty, the softness of hide and the sweeping curve of antlers suggesting the conscious artist who has studied the reindeer patiently over a long period in order to reduce it to its simplest and most appealing form. Once again we are reminded of the Chinese artist laboring under the immaculate weight of his sophistication.

Such figures could be produced only by a sophisticated elite who spent more time at painting than at hunting, developing over the years an instinctive knowledge of their craft, until at last they could paint with the full resources of their genius. There is some evidence that there were regular schools for artists, and here and there among the rock paintings we come upon sketches which seem to be no more than the labored attempts of pupils corrected by their masters.

We come a little closer to the heart of the mystery when we see these walls as the prehistoric artists saw them. It is not enough to see them in the Abbé Breuil's admirable watercolor reproductions or in photographs which fail to render the rough texture of the rock, nor is it enough to go down to the caves and see them by electric light, with its steady, undeviating glare. The prehistoric artist saw them in the light of lamps of animal fat, with their ripe and lustrous glow. The flame was never still, winking continually and throwing a pulsating, rhythmical light on the objects it illuminated. The caves with their gnarled bosses and projecting shelves, seamed and veined, here a reddish brown, and here black or purple, possessed an organic form, rich in contrasts. In such a cave the artist of the immaculate reindeer would spend a good deal of time searching for exactly the right projection of rock, which would then be planed down before the shape of the reindeer was incised with a sharp flint. He could change the rock surface at will. He was not producing a painting only; it was a sculptured relief, with the shape of the rock working for him or against him, using him or being used by him. His mastery lay in a precise understanding of the material. So he was both painter and sculptor, molding the rock to the shape he desired.

As he stood there with his lamp in the immensity of the cavern, in the overwhelming solitude and loneliness of the place, seeing the shadows swirling across the walls and the sudden gleams of light leaping off the sharp points of rock, he was presiding over a mystery which was perhaps very similar to a mystery that is still being performed today. A man worshiping before a mosaic of Jesus in a Greek church will see the figure moving and pulsating in the flicker of the candlelight. The lips seem to move, the expression changes, the folds of the gown billow in an invisible wind, life and substance flow into the body made of colored stones. All this comes about because the stones are deliberately set at different angles and therefore continually reflect the light in different directions, so that there are continual subtle alterations. The effect is completely lost with electric light. So with cave paintings. In the light of an ancient lamp they would glow and pulsate with every flicker of the flame, and a man might wait until the flame died down before he had exhausted all the possibilities of movement in the animal. Indeed, the climactic moment might well have occurred when the flame died, for then he would see the animal in his mind's eye as richly colored and full of streaming life as when he was gazing at the painted wall. Then at last it would become his possession, to keep and to hold for ever.

But all this is speculation, and what we know for certain is so much less than we desire to know that we can never hope to penetrate very close to the heart of the mystery. We know no more about the artists than what they chose to reveal on the walls of the caves. Nevertheless, there are moments when they seem to be offering clues, as though they knew their work would survive for thousands of years and people would one day come and ask what they were doing.

Scholars and students who have spent long hours in the painted caves speak of the extraordinary sense of order and permanence that reigns in them. It is not in the least the sensation we associate with a return to the womb, but of entering an entirely different landscape, remote from the earth and all its cares. The only sounds come from a man's heartbeats and his breathing, and soon enough he discovers that the walls seem to breathe with his breathing and to pulse with his heartbeats. There is no sensation of fear, but on the contrary there is a sense of communion with the living rock. A cave becomes a place for uninterrupted meditations, where a man can calmly take stock of himself. Time vanishes; even place vanishes, for the familiar walls seem to be outside of space altogether. Sitting, thinking, meditating, he finds he has entered a kind of eternity. When he makes his way out of the cave, he is suddenly struck by the wild, jarring dissonances of nature, with all its formlessness and crudity. A little clump of grass at the cave mouth, waving in the wind, seems to him an intolerable affront and the glaring sunlight strikes him like a blow between the eyes. Suddenly he has left the world of eternity and entered the world of time.

The experience of these scholars and students who have been immersed for long periods in the caves tells us something of importance about the cave artists. We may imagine the caves as places where primitive man retreated not for safety but in order to claim a share in eternity, to meditate and to see visions. The caves were not unlike monks' cells, but far larger and more majestic. Just as Fra Angelico painted the walls of the cells of the Convent of San Marco with illustrations from the life of Christ, so the painters in these caves drew the outlines of the great themes of life and death. The wounded bison, dying in agony, was a subject for profound meditation, for the death of a powerful animal was an illustration of death's magnitude, and the procession of living animals was an affirmation of life. Life and death ruled over the caves, as they ruled over all men's lives.

These themes are so vast that nothing is permitted to obscure them. We see the spears and arrows that bring death, but only on rare occasions do we see the men who throw them. We see no landscapes, because the shape of the rock suggests landscapes, and there is no need to paint in the background, because it is enough to render the animals in the perfection of their being, in their silent majesty. The only additions to the paintings are some strange signs, dots, boxes, lozenges, which may be the artists' signatures. Sometimes they superimposed one animal on another, as in the great cave at Lascaux, where a fawn-colored pony is painted below the shoulder of an enormous white ox. The archaeologists have concerned themselves with the problem of these superimposed pictures, but the simplest explanation would seem to be that the cave artist was perfectly content to use all the available space and saw no reason why he should not paint as many animals as he pleased.

Of the great events which took place in Paleolithic times—the kingdoms won, the heroes slain—there is no trace in the caves of southwestern France. Almost man has vanished. When we see him for the first time, he is lying naked on his back with his arms flung out, in a state of erection, between a woolly rhinoceros and a dying bison.

This painting on the walls of a small deep crypt at Lascaux is startling in its haggard simplicity, but no one has succeeded in deciphering its exact meaning. It was perhaps the first time a story had been recounted in pictorial form, and as we might suspect, the story takes the form of a tragedy, the tragedy that was a commonplace in Paleolithic times, when the hunter was often hunted, and both man and beast died in the conflict. There is first the bison with its flanks pierced by a long spear or javelin, the belly ripped open and the entrails hanging in great loops, while it turns its head away from the man it has gored, its mane bristling, its strength ebbing away, and the artist has depicted admirably how it has

Man, rhinoceros, and bison. A schematic drawing from the cave painting at Lascaux, France.

been brought to a halt and cannot move backward or forward. Then there is the man lying prone, feet up, with a very small birdlike head, and close to his right hand is a bird on a pole, which may be the scepter of a king, or the emblem of his tribe, or the mask of a shaman. To the left the woolly rhinoceros goes calmly on its way, and we have no way of knowing whether it has anything to do with the tragedy.

It is a strange and disquieting painting, and not only because it leaves so many questions unanswered. A window has opened and for a few moments we are permitted to look at a tragedy which took place 20,000 years ago, and though we know, or think we know, what has happened, for the scene is depicted with remarkable sharpness and an air of complete verisimilitude, we can no more penetrate the mind of the artist than we can penetrate the minds of animals. Any interpretation of the scene ultimately depends on the interpretation of the bird on the pole. There are no clues, for nothing like this bird exists anywhere else in the caves.

The man in the Lascaux crypt is painted schematically, with only the barest indication of three-dimensional form, unlike the bison, which is given weight and substance. While the man is merely sketched out, the scene is deliberately composed and the taut relationship between bison, man and bird-pole is clearly shown with the spear and the fallen arrow giving emphasis to the composition. When we first see man in three dimensions, we would expect to see him masked and wearing the skins of animals, entering the animal kingdom in disguise, and so he appears in the Cave of the Trois Frères in the foothills of the Pyrenees. Once again we find him in an almost inaccessible crypt far from the cave mouth, and once again the outlines have been incised with sharp flints and painted in black. We see his human rump and human legs, but he has the tail of a horse, the erect ears and antlers of a stag, the eyes and whiskers of a cat, and the shaggy beard of a bison. He is painted in strong strokes, and there is no

Man masked and wearing animal skins. Two feet tall. A schematic drawing from the painting in the Cave of the Trois Frères, French Pyrenees.

doubting his fierce energy and assumption of unquestioned power, but there is considerable doubt as to what he represents. Is he sorcerer, or decoy? Is he priest, or king? It is possible that he is performing a dance of triumph over the animal kingdom, for thirteen feet below him in the same cave there is a painting of horses, bison, and bears, all wounded, with arrows in their flanks and what appears to be blood pouring out. Sorcerer, decoy, priest, or king, his position high up on the walls of the crypt denotes the masked conqueror, whatever his other attributes.

The painting has a precise structure, with the shapes of bones and muscle clearly delineated to express the utmost vitality and movement. The turning of the mask toward the observer gives a three-dimensional effect, while the position of the legs gives the necessary thrust. The figure, which is a little more than two feet high, is one of the supreme masterpieces of Paleolithic art.

Some ten thousand years later, in eastern Spain, we find a new concept of man. No longer is it thought necessary to paint a portrait. Man is schematized until he becomes little more than a bifurcated line with one waving arm and a tiny blob for a head. Men are not only fighting animals; they are fighting each other. A new and highly articulate vocabulary has come into existence: the vocabulary of pictographs with human bodies reduced to a few skillful and animated lines. We find pebbles with mysterious red lines painted on them; they are evidently words, or what passed for words in late Paleolithic times. By means of pictographs it becomes possible to describe events in time, and we are far from the timeless world of the caves.

In a narrow gully near Morella la Vieja, a few miles south of the Ebro River, an artist painted a skirmish between archers. The figures are painted in dark red paint, and each archer is about an inch tall. The artist has captured the thrust and counterthrust of combat by a schematic arrangement of planes of force. He has painted an abstraction of a skirmish, and at the same time he has painted the scene as though he were standing on a high rock and looking down. In much the same way these artists depict a woman who has climbed a cliff and disturbed a beehive high up on the cliff edge. We see her clinging to the swaying rope ladder, the

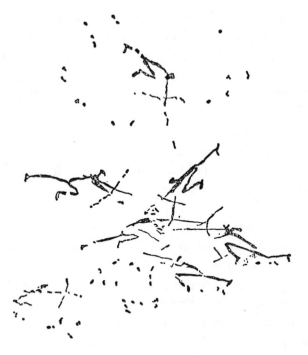

Skirmish between archers, in red paint, in a gully near Morella la Vieja, Spain.

bees swarming around her. The shape of the body is fleshed out a little, so that we see the haunches and thighs and are made aware of her strength and daring as she perches precariously on the topmost rung of the ladder, one hand in the hive of wild bees, the other clutching her basket. The story is told cleanly and neatly, but she remains a schematic representation, a little blob of red paint only a little larger than an ant. The swift and accurate linear rhythm conveyed an entire scene, and there was no need to add any details.

A new element had entered the world of art: the conceptual image, the sign-in-motion, so far removed from the eidetic images of the cave paintings that it was as though art had passed altogether from one form to another. The contemplative art of the caves was exchanged for a rhythmic calligraphy reflecting men's daily lives. There is the sense of history, of time passing, of man reduced to a line of force. In the light of these calligraphic designs the paintings in the caves assume an archaic grandeur, the images of the beasts being images of the divine, magnificently austere, not threatening or demanding, but answering the needs of the contemplative soul. The calligraphic designs answer the practical needs of day-to-day living.*

This calligraphic art was capable of endless variation and adaptation. Congealed into the letters of the alphabet, or elaborated in Egyptian hieroglyphics and Chinese characters, it takes the form of language. In time it will become mathematics and abstract design, and men will use conventional abstractions to convey their deepest thoughts. With the invention of the calligraphic line, civilization begins to emerge, for now at last men have taken possession of the tools of communication.

Throughout the primitive world the artists have always been concerned to paint the eidetic image. They painted with visionary eyes, seeing with astonishing power and delicacy, in full awareness of the beauty of form. The cave painters at Lascaux and Altamira did not reconstruct their horses and bison from separately apprehended parts, but as wholes. In the same way the Bushmen of Basutoland painted their white cranes as wholes. These two cranes, painted white against a gray rock background, with reddish crests and yellow legs, are evidently wading across a stream, but the Bushman artist saw no more reason to depict the stream than the cave

---

* The distinction between eidetic and calligraphic images can best be given in two parallel columns:

Eidetic	Calligraphic
eternity	time
legend	history
form	line
intensity	diffusion
sculpture & painting	drawing
innocence	experience
masses	lines of force
pronouncement	communication
centripetal	centrifugal
inaction	action
monumental	occasional
divine	human

Traffic between the two kinds of images occurs continually, but generally speaking, there has always been a concentration of eidetic images at great periods of art.

Drawing from Bushman painting of white cranes, Basutoland.

painter saw a reason to depict the wild grasses where his bulls and bison pastured. He saw the white cranes divorced from nature, outside time and place, living in the luminous world of art. At Sefar in North Africa, among the innumerable paintings dating from Paleolithic times discovered by Henri Lhote during his 1956 expedition through the Tassili N'Ajjer Mountains, there was found the portrait of a nude seated woman with flowers in her hair, holding another flower in her outstretched left hand. It is a portrait of quite extraordinary beauty, painted with the same visionary immediacy as the white cranes. Not far away there were found the swift calligraphic paintings of archers engaged in their eternal warfare against the wild beasts.

In the course of time these two aspects of the artistic vision, the eidetic and the calligraphic, would achieve a kind of compromise. We can see the process at work in a rock painting found near Teruel showing an archer proudly advancing with his bow and arrows. He still bears traces of his calligraphic origins in the thin waist and dot head, but his lower limbs have been fleshed out and there are ornaments attached below the knees. He comes toward you with the superb air of a conqueror, conscious of his dignity, determined to take possession of the earth and all that lives on it. He holds himself erect, his legs already parted in the posture of

Schematic drawing from painted nude, Sefar, North Africa.

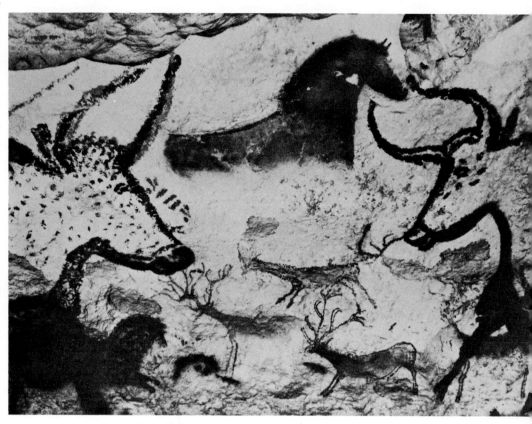

Aurochs, horses, and deer on great frieze at Lascaux.

Wounded Lion from Nineveh, about 650 B.C.
BRITISH MUSEUM.

Akhenaton, found at Karnak,
about 1360 B. C.
CAIRO MUSEUM.

Opposite, Gudea, found in Tello,
Iraq, about 2100 B. C.
BRITISH MUSEUM.

Nefertiti, found at Amarna, about 1360 B.C.

Opposite, a Pre-Achaemenid Prince,
about 3000 B.C.

Etruscan Chimera, about 500 B.C.
ARCHAEOLOGICAL MUSEUM, FLORENCE. ALINARI.

Schematic drawing from rock painting of archer near Teruel, Spain.

triumph that will become so familiar later, an arrow held nimbly in one hand while with the other he holds a bow and seven arrows, with the arrows forming a curving pattern to offset the curve of the bow. He wears earrings, and around his waist a belt of beads looped and swinging free. The figure is painted in red ocher and stands nearly three feet high. It is sophisticated art of a high order accomplished with a minimum of means.

The "Sorcerer" of the Cave of the Trois Frères had merely announced his conquest of the animal kingdom; the armed warrior of Teruel proclaims more dangerous conquests. He is idea and image, calligraphy and eidetic vision, the word "conqueror" and the conqueror himself. With him, modern man begins.

Throughout the history of art we shall find these two aspects of the artistic vision, and always with the great artist there is the striving for the eidetic image, the object seen in the luminous fields of eternity. Sometimes we shall find the eidetic and the calligraphic working together in harmony, as though it were possible to live simultaneously in eternity and in time, and sometimes we shall encounter arts that are entirely calligraphic, yet expressed with such power and conviction that they almost take on the aspect of eidetic vision. Like paradise, the full eidetic vision is rarely seen, for it is chiefly found among primitive people or in the early stages of a civilization, and it tends to vanish as civilizations become increasingly complex and artificial.

As the songs of innocence give place to the songs of experience, so we usually find these images at periods when men are still in close communion with the gods, before the gods have retreated into their mysteries and left the world to its conventions and traditions. They are the bright and glistening first fruits of the dawn, stored and treasured in the unconscious memory of peoples and races long after the sun has set. Sometimes there emerge artists with the power to recapture the lost vision and by prolonged study and meditation they produce works of art which have this immediacy and perfect assurance, but they are rare. At long intervals they appear, and there is always something miraculous in these rare appearances, for they bring with them intimations of the presence of the gods and an awareness we no longer possess.

The Noons of Egypt

In the calm light of Egypt, where the never failing sun rises every day like a glory and the Nile rises every year like a dependable blessing, the earth and the sky proclaim a sense of order. In that sheltered world ringed round and protected by mountain barriers, nature seems to have restrained herself in order to provide a gifted people with the fruits of the earth, an unhindered livelihood.

In the secure valley of the Nile everything that a man could normally need was provided for him. The river was power, which could be tapped at will; it gave life to the papyrus and the corn, to the game and the waterfowl, and to the animals which came to feed on its banks. They did not know why the Nile rose in June or July, but they knew it was so, and they were grateful for the prevailing winds from the north which allowed their ships to move against the current and for the reddish-brown mud which the Blue Nile washed down from mysterious mountains far in the south—a life-giving mud, almost the color of blood. The Nile was life and food and gaiety, color and taste and sweetness, a highway to the present and perhaps a highway after death, for it was inconceivable to them that they would not find it again after their deaths. They saw themselves as people who were born out of the Nile and went back to the Nile again; and the Nile spoke to them through the lips of their king, the pharaoh.

In that changeless civilization, interrupted only by occasional wars, an enviable people lived in harmony with the earth, the river, and the sun. There were no disasters that could not be foretold, no sense of yearning doubt before the forces of the underworld. Since the pharaoh was the divine mediator between a peaceful earth

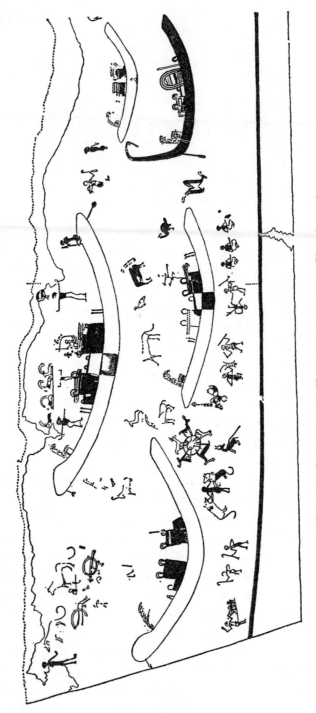

Schematic drawing from Egyptian painting at Hierakonpolis.

and a peaceful heaven, the orderly alignment of society and nature was complete and perfect. There was almost no sense of the past or the future, for both were implicit in the present. There was almost no history, for history involves change, and there was almost no discernible change. The same Nile rose and fell, the same stars rose in the heavens, while for three thousand years these people continued to live peacefully and gently. At no other period in history and in no other place has there been such a quiet, orderly civilization extending over so long a time.

Nevertheless changes took place: there was a beginning and an end. In the beginning, when we first see them in the Nile Valley, they have already developed many of the characteristics they would possess at the height of their civilization. They loved dancing, hunting, and drinking; they made fine clay pottery; they made wooden boats which were not remarkably different from the boats they built thousands of years later; they believed that the dead belonged to the community of the living. In the earliest Egyptian wall painting known to us, dating from about 3300 B.C., they assume postures and attitudes which are recognizably the same as those which will appear later, vastly magnified, in statues and painted reliefs on the walls of their temples.

These wall paintings were found in a subterranean tomb chamber at Hierakonpolis, an ancient predynastic capital near Edfu. The tomb belonged to a commanding general, whose triumphs are recorded in a calligraphy which would have been perfectly comprehensible to the artist who painted the dead man lying beside the wounded bison at Lascaux. We see the same dot head, the same thin oblong body, the arms and legs no more than expressive lines. Like the dead man at Lascaux he is sometimes shown in a state of erection. The general, who appears several times at the bottom of the painting, is sketched out in red with black dots representing the leopard skin which is the sign of his authority. He wields a mace as he stands in triumph over his enemies, and we shall see the same posture in the portraits of Tuthmosis III and Ramses II on the great pylons of the temples erected in the Eighteenth and Nineteenth Dynasties.

In the wall painting, the earliest painting known to have been made on a man-made surface, we see the solar barks carrying the heavy coffins to the mysterious lands of the West. Here and there we see women with arms spread wide apart in grief. An effort has been made to suggest a landscape where the deer browse and there is a halfhearted attempt to suggest the presence of chariots. On the lowest register the general proclaims his victories in a calligraphy which can be read in words, remembering that the Egyptians always represented "multitudes" by depicting the object three times, so that the three bound and kneeling prisoners on the far right indicate "a multitude of prisoners." Reading from right to left, the pictograms say: "I captured multitudes of prisoners and utterly overwhelmed the king, and from another king I received a tribute of leopard skins, and horses and many deer were brought into captivity. Twice I killed lions with my bare hands, and the multitudes of prisoners all bound together were presented by me to the two pharaohs." We cannot be sure of the five deer on the wheel or of the man between two lions, which may be a heraldic image, but there is not the least doubt that the general is proclaiming his victories and offering his prisoners to two pharaohs, both armed with the sacred crook of kingship. Since co-regencies were common in dynastic Egypt, we are not surprised that the conqueror should be confronting two pharaohs. What is surprising is that these tomb paintings are organized with considerably less care than the wall paintings at Lascaux, which may date fifteen thousand years earlier.

In the years immediately following these paintings Egyptian civilization took an immense step forward. The first hieroglyphs appeared, the gods acquired their familiar appearance, artists learned how to carve in relief, order was imposed on the visual field, the background was separated from the foreground, and for the first time the human figure was depicted realistically. Only three hundred and fifty years separates the tomb chamber at Hierakonpolis from the slate cosmetic palette found in the same city. The relief shows Narmer (c. 2950 B.C.), the first ruler to unite Upper and Lower Egypt, as he seizes one of the enemy kings by the hair and threatens him with a mace. The king is wearing the white crown of Upper Egypt; on the reverse of the palette he can be seen wearing the red crown of Lower Egypt. He is barefoot, but the presence

Schematic drawing from Egyptian relief, circa 2950 B.C.

of an attendant with a pair of sandals and a water pot will enable
him to wash the dust of battle from his feet. Below the king a
double line separates him from two more enemy kings, who perhaps fled the battlefield, and facing him is Horus, the falcon god
of the sky, who has threaded a rope through the nostrils of still
another king from the regions of the delta and now brings the
captive into the presence of the Pharaoh. On the topmost register
Hathor, the queen of the sky and wife of Horus, with the horns
and ears of a celestial cow, looks down on the scene of carnage.
All except the gods are given their proper names; even the boy
attendant, presumably a prince of the royal line, receives a name.
Significantly the name of King Narmer is written on the same level
as Hathor, for he belongs among the gods.

On this palette a series of extremely complex historical and
artistic statements has been made, relationships have been precisely
organized, and enduring traditions have been established. For the
first time we see the Egyptian figure in three dimensions, and we
note the delicacy of the modeling, the clean-cut lines, the contours
of muscles admirably conveyed, and the clarity of the composition.
There is no clutter. Everything is in its proper place. We are given
to understand that conquest is accompanied by order and the same
fate will be meted out to anyone who disputes the royal command.

The palette is about twenty-five inches high, but the Egyptian sense of monumentality is already in evidence.

Although each pharaoh was given a character of his own in monumental sculpture, there was always a family likeness, for there existed a conventional pharaonic face: austere and heavy-browed, with a look of unconquerable determination. All will wear the false beard of Narmer, and like him they will wear a bullock's tail hanging from their waistbands and kiltlike skirts. They will present themselves as larger than the gods, and they will represent their enemies as small and naked. They have the calm of the gods.

All this is already represented in the palette: the king's majesty, his communion and familiarity with the gods, the sense of order, the calm and deliberate design of space. Only in minor details will there by any additions to this portrait of the king in the years to come. Portraits of queens and women will have more variety, for the Egyptians delighted in the sensuous forms of women and portrayed them with perceptible excitement.

The monumental statue of Zoser (c. 2650 B.C.), the first ruler of the Third Dynasty, shows him seated, one hand resting on his knee, the other lying across his breast, the powerful face with the deep-set eyes made more powerful by the presence of a voluminous wig like a lion's mane. He seems to be lost in the contemplation of his own majesty, so proud and austere a figure that he appears to belong not to mankind but to another species altogether, half animal, half divine. It is inconceivable that he will move, that he will ever step down from his throne; he is at home in heaven among the changeless gods. Once he was painted in living colors, the face red, the gown white, with jewels set in the broken eyes, but the paint only rendered more vivid the enchantment of his majesty, in which all the mutable aspects of personality were abstracted. Aloof, imperturbable, he guarded his own tomb.

This nearly life-size statue, now in the Cairo Museum, was originally set up in a statuary chamber on the north side of the stepped pyramid erected for the king by his friend the great architect Imhotep, a man of such learning in the arts, medicine, astronomy, and magic that he was identified with Ptah, the man-headed god of Memphis, and in time the Greeks would identify him with their own god of medicine, Asklepios. It was not intended that the statue should be seen by mortal eyes. In the enclosed statuary chamber two eye-level holes permitted him to gaze at the pole star and the other fixed stars, which were his appointed home. His companions were more statues of himself, as though his vast residual powers could only be represented by multiplication, as a face is multiplied to infinity by parallel mirrors.

What is remarkable about the statue is precisely that magical quality which still adheres to it, all the more perhaps because the features have been ravaged by time and accident, so that he acquires the appearance of abstract power—the power emanating from the deep cavities of the eyes, from the shattered face, and from the body which, but for the squared shoulders and squared knees, would resemble a volcanic cinder; and from the squared knees comes the upsurge of majesty.

The six-staged pyramid at Saqqara rose to a height of two hundred feet. Once, with its facing of polished white limestone, it shone like a blinding mirror in the sun. It stood on the edge of the desert overlooking Memphis, the ancient capital of the empire, a perpetual reminder of the king's presence, dominating the city from afar. All round the pyramid and enclosed by a thirty-foot-high wall, palaces and pavilions, courtyards and colonnades were built for him. There were chapels and altars where the priests made their offerings. There was a pool where he could bathe, and trees were planted so that he could take shelter from the sun, though his body lay deep below the pyramid.

Today the pyramid is no more than a vast ungainly heap of reddish-colored bricks surrounded by the drifting sands, but the six stages can still be sharply distinguished. The proportions of these stages were carefully worked out to suggest immense controlled power. Imhotep had provided an abstract portrait of the king, and he was also suggesting the march of the king's progress toward the heavens and his eternal presence on the earth. Ambiguities abounded: he was present, and not present, visible and invisible. He was the brightness of the sun and the nakedness of power.

The Egyptians believed in the immortality of kingship. A dead king was a contradiction in terms: he could die, but remained deathless. As a man he died, as a king he was immortal, and as a god he reigned with the other gods. Yet he was most vulnerable as a god, since he was altogether lacking in the legendary and mythological aspects of the gods. Though he would present himself walking beside Horus, he was never quite the equal of Horus and never quite convincing when he called himself "the son of Horus." Hence, as time passed, there would be more and more portraits of the pharaoh in the company of the gods, and he would assert more and more boldly that "he was like unto a god; his form was that of a god; he did everything like a god; his splendor was that of a god." Hence, too, the proliferation of the gods and the extraordinarily complex mythologies which gradually evolved, subtly changing with every dynasty.

King Zoser's pyramid was essentially an abstract portrayal of the kingly majesty. The pyramids of Gizeh portray the divinity of the kings, for each side of the pyramid represented a ray of the divine sun. When these pyramids were built, they flashed fiercely in the sun and the air all round them shimmered and blazed with an unearthly light, for the smooth polished limestone facing acted like a mirror of the sun's rays. The pyramids of Gizeh therefore represented the pharaoh's claim to be united with the divine powers of the sun. It was a claim that went beyond mythology altogether, and the gods are notably absent in the pyramids.

They are absent, too, in the tombs of the nobles built in the shadow of Zoser's pyramid. In these tombs the walls are covered from floor to ceiling with painted reliefs brilliantly executed in limestone. We see the feasts and the ceremonies, the hunting of wildfowl in the pools, processions of cattle, the harvesting of figs, the building of ships, the offering of sacrifices, the boys naked, the men in their kilts, the women always clothed. All these scenes from daily life are depicted with freshness and a wonderful sense of rhythm, and though we sometimes come upon formal portraits of the gods, it is evident that the main concern of the dead man is to contemplate his life on earth, seeing himself hunting and fishing or attending the festivals of the seasons in the company of his wife and children. He stands there life-size, sometimes alone, sometimes with his wife beside him, and he gazes rapturously at the world he knew nearly five thousand years ago. For him, heaven is earth and his memories of earth, and we are far from the world of the gods.

These tomb chambers at Saqqara are the size of a small house, with many rooms, and many artists worked on the painted reliefs, for we can distinguish different styles. It was never intended that these scenes would be seen by the living, and perhaps this is why they are depicted with such intensity, such a delight in the flesh and the work of men's hands. Children, birds, and calves are rendered with a special feeling for their liveliness; young animals delight the sculptor; and when he sculpts a procession of cattle, they are all different. These carvings sometimes appear in sunk relief, a more difficult art, and they are always painted, like everything that was carved in ancient times. Sometimes the paint has flaked away, and we see the purity of these carvings in their austere whiteness, which is more pleasing to the modern eye.

Even though the tomb chambers resemble each other, for the life of one nobleman was very much like the life of another, the sense of individuality is present throughout. The long orderly scenes unfold like a Chinese scroll, one above the other, and one finds oneself reading them as one reads the lines of a newspaper. The sculptors knew how to break up the steady rhythm with a sudden interruption. The procession pauses, and we see a bemused donkey wandering alone or a wild goose flashing up unexpectedly from the marshes. In these serried lines order has been imposed on the universe.

The sculptures are seen best in the half-light of the tomb chambers, not in the flat light of the museums. In that setting, in the silence of the desert, the spectator has the feeling that he, too, is awakening into life, seeing the springtime of the world spreading out before him, calm and beautiful under the sun.

A prodigious vitality informs the art of the Old Kingdom. A people who had only recently been painting the haphazard scribbles at Hierakonpolis had reached the full maturity of their art. They had invented the fluted column, which first appears in the colonnades surrounding the pyramid of Zoser. They knew how to sculpt so that blood seems to flow through stone veins. There was no scene in the countryside which they could not render in a running frieze, no posture which they could not represent in clay or stone. With Mycerinus (c. 2525 B.C.) for the first time, we see the king standing in majesty, naked except for the loincloth, his left foot forward, his hands at his side, and usually he is in the company of the goddess Hathor or his wife. The seated pharaoh is the lawgiver; the standing pharaoh takes possession of the land and dominates men's lives.

Two thousand years after Mycerinus, the Greeks discovered this exact pose and imitated it in their portraits of the youthful *kouroi,* the only difference being that the *kouroi* are free-standing, unlike the pharaoh, who is always represented with the wall of his palace behind him. The archaic Apollos would be represented in exactly the same way. What is astonishing is that the *kouroi* give an impression of such freshness, although the pose is so old. The enduring style of the Old Kingdom deeply influenced the youthful art of Greece.

Egyptian sculptured relief was practiced with dazzling success, but never again with the power and simplicity of the reliefs in the Old Kingdom tomb chambers. In time the reliefs would cover acres of wall space, usually with the depiction of the victorious pharaoh in his chariot smiting his enemies. The spectacle of the pharaoh's triumphs finally becomes wearisome, and with this weariness comes the suspicion that the triumphal processions were sometimes celebrated to disguise defeats.

One innovation was provided by Mentuhotep III (c. 2035 B.C.), who reunited a divided country and established the Eleventh Dynasty. At Deir el Bahri, he built a funerary monument for himself on the edge of the Libyan cliffs. There were three vast courtyards planted with trees, one rising above the other, each courtyard reached by a ramp, and in the topmost courtyard he built a pyramid with its back to the cliffs. Four hundred years later Queen Hatshepsut built her own monument nearby, abandoning the pyramid and vastly increasing the scale, so that her courts stood out beneath the beautiful red cliffs and seemed indeed to flow from them. The effect, especially from a distance, is superb, for the entire landscape appears to be embraced and set in order by the white and gleaming terraces and columns designed by her architect Senmut, who was so proud of his achievement that he had relief portraits of himself inserted in the walls of the colonnades. For this act of *lèse majesté* he was apparently put to death.

The Queen's monument at Deir el Bahri is one of the wonders of Egyptian art, and not only because of the perfect proportions of the columns and the courtyards. The events of her life were carved in light relief along the walls, and in their freshness and elegance they might have been carved in the late years of the Old Kingdom. Among the triumphs of her reign was an expedition to the mysterious land of Punt, which was perhaps Somaliland. The reliefs record the events of the expedition in intricate detail, the five vessels sailing away with the products of Egypt and returning with a cargo of apes, incense trees, ivory, myrrh, and rare woods. The Prince of Punt pays tribute to the Queen of Egypt, accompanied by his stupendously fat and ungainly princess followed by a donkey, and the artist has added the inscription: "This is indeed a donkey," as though to bewail the fate of the animal that had carried so great a burden. Everywhere on these reliefs there is delicacy and grace, the sense of calm assurance. Thebes, the capital of her empire, four hundred miles south of Cairo, lay on the east bank of the Nile only a few miles away.

At Thebes the pharaohs of the Eighteenth Dynasty built the largest complex of temples ever built by man, stretching over sixty acres. The temples honored the pharaohs and the god Amon, bringer of victories. Originally Amon was an obscure local deity represented by a ram or a serpent. Self-created, he had entered the world at the beginning of time, married Mut, the goddess of heaven, and fathered Khonsu, the god of the moon. Under the name of Amon-Re he was to become over a long period the god who presided over the destinies of the nation.

In his honor an avenue of ram-headed sphinxes was laid out along the avenue to his temple, which successive pharaohs enlarged until it sprawled in vast profusion, one temple adjoining another, one forest of fat pillars encroaching on another, until at last it came to resemble a petrified forest in which you could recognize different species of trees and the signs of increasing age. An Egyptian temple has a simple design: an outer wall, a gateway, a colonnaded court open to the sky, and then a sacred enclosure crowded with columns, and finally there is the inmost sanctuary. To pass from the gateway to the shrine was to pass from light into increasing obscurity, into the place where the sacred mysteries were performed and the sacred relics were hidden from sight.

Imagine that every hundred years or so a king had conquered Rome and celebrated his conquest by adding yet another vast basilica to the Vatican. Imagine that he crowded his basilica with columns on which he depicted his god-given victories and in front of the basilica he set up a gigantic statue of himself. Imagine, too, that from time to time a conqueror would tear down half the columns of one of his predecessors' temples, erase the inscriptions and portraits and set them up in his own temple with new inscriptions and new portraits. Such was the great temple of Amon at Thebes. The conquering Arabs, who could make nothing of it, called it El Karnak, meaning "the fortress." A nearby temple on the banks of the Nile, built largely by Ramses II, comparatively simple but still resembling a petrified forest, they called Al Uqsur, meaning "the palaces." We know these two vast temple complexes as Karnak and Luxor.

Over the centuries the priests of Amon who presided in these two temples acquired such power and prestige that they threatened to become the real rulers of the empire. They possessed countless slaves, countless head of cattle, innumerable villages, orchards, and shipyards. Inevitably this concentration of wealth led to profound strains, and it needed no great gift of prophecy to know that attempts would be made to destroy the priesthood. The temples, however, were indestructible.

With the coming of Akhenaton to the throne, the age-old traditions were shattered and in their place there came a new kind of king, a new worship, a new art. Quite suddenly the accepted ways of looking at the world were discarded, and men saw with new eyes.

When Akhenaton was born, about the year 1392 B.C., the memory of Tuthmosis III, who died about fifty years before, was still fresh. The great conqueror had elevated Egypt to a position of supreme power among the nations, and his successors had consolidated the empire. Trade flourished; the people on the frontiers were quiet; there was no longer any need for armed expeditions to Asia; the successors of the conquering Pharaoh lived in unparalleled luxury and contentment. Akhenaton came to the throne when he was about seventeen. He was a visionary with a lean, ascetic face, fine eyes, a thin nose, full sensitive lips, and a heavy, rather pointed jaw. He had a thin neck and the rounded shoulders of a scholar, and there was about him an air of quiet detachment, as of one who broods patiently over mysteries. The early portraits show him in his early manhood, looking like a young and serious student, distinguished from the other young princes of his age only by a certain deliberate affectation of languor. Later, at his bidding, he would be represented in lively caricature: the long head made longer, the thin neck scrawnier, the belly more pear-shaped, the legs like sticks. These caricatures were more than the diversions of a scholar, for they satisfied his feeling for the truth which lay behind appearances, and he permitted and encouraged his sculptors to represent his beautiful wife Nefertiti in the same way.

From the moment he came to the throne Akhenaton determined to abolish the priesthood of Amon, which had grown wealthy and powerful on the spoils of conquest. The power of the priesthood could be felt in all the provinces of Egypt. The Church was ruled by ordered hierarchies, and the priests held the people in bondage, for they alone possessed the key to the sacred mysteries. To break their power Akhenaton decided to revive an ancient form of Sun worship, first taught by the philosopher priests of Heliopolis, the ancient city of On. According to these texts the Sun was a fiery circle radiating power, blessing and caressing everything it touched. It was the only god, supremely powerful, devoid of legends, with no encrustation of mythologies. The Sun had not died, and would never be reborn. Where Amon was "the hidden Sun," Akhenaton introduced the worship of Aton, "the Sun revealed," represented as a solar disk with long hands reaching to the earth and caressing it. Instead of the Sun of brooding power and majesty, he introduced the Sun of tenderness and gaiety, reigning peacefully over all the nations of the earth.

In the *Hymn to the Sun,* which he wrote in collaboration with his wife Nefertiti, he proclaims his devotion to a Sun, which is wholly without mythology, and in need of no sustaining ritualistic

prayers from a hidebound priesthood. He found the Sun everywhere: it was in the earth, in the faces of people, in the flowering
plants, even the cities were merely transformations of the energy
emanating from the Sun.

Lovely is Thy rising on the horizon of heaven,
O living Aton, Thou who givest life.
Thou risest in the eastern sky,
And all the land is colored with thy loveliness,
For Thou art splendid, mighty, and beautiful,
Being uplifted over all creation . . .

When the earth brightens, Thou risest on the horizon,
Thou shinest as the Aton of the daylight.
Thou drivest away the shadows.
When Thou sendest Thy rays,
The Two Lands rejoice,
Men awake and stand on their feet,
For Thou hast raised them.
They bathe their limbs, they put on clothing,
They raise their arms to adore Thy rising,
The whole earth goes to its work,
All trees and grasses turn green,
Birds flutter in their nests
And lift their wings to adore Thy energy.
All the cattle leap to their feet,
All flying and fluttering things come alive,
When Thou shinest upon them . . .

When the chick chirps in the egg,
Thou pourest breath within him
So that he may live,
And when Thou hast made him strong
To break through the egg,
He comes chirping with all his strength
And runs with his feet . . .

Thou art the Only God,
And no other possesses Thy power.
Thou has created the earth for Thy pleasure, Thou alone!
Men, and all cattle and herds,

All that walk upon the earth,
All that fly in the heavens,
And the nations of Syria and Kush and the land of Egypt.

To each Thou hast given a place.
Thou givest to each what he needs.
According to the length of his days
Thou hast provided his sustenance.
Men speak in many tongues,
And many are their forms and colors,
And Thou hast made the foreigners different from us . . .

Thou hast made infinite transformations of Thyself
In cities, villages, fields, rivers.
All eyes behold Thee in them,
For Thou art the Aton of the daylight . . .

This long hymn was far more than a simple prayer to the Sun; it was an act of war against the entrenched priesthood of Amon. The weighty formulas, the endless titles granted to Amon in the prayers spoken by the priests are absent, and the claim of the priests to be the mediators between man and the Sun are implicitly denied. The Sun is "the only God" and he reigns equally over the Egyptians and other races, spreading his universal dominion over everything that lives and breathes. The hymn also introduces a new aesthetic, for it celebrates all that is young and tender, gay and colorful. The newborn are seen to be especially under the government of the Sun; all that skips and leaps is blessed by the Sun. The Nile of the heavens—that mysterious Nile which no one has seen—flows equally over all lands, and blesses them. The entire earth lives in the loving embrace of the Sun.

So the artists in the court of Akhenaton depicted the earthly paradise, where everything is young, swift, and urgent with life, brilliantly colored, trembling with joy and adoration beneath the hands of the Sun. The stiff, hieratic patterns were abandoned, while the sculptors and painters produced works of enchanted naturalism. The Pharaoh no longer sat stiffly on his throne, portentous with power. Instead, he was represented at his ease, smiling and laughing, taking his wife in his arms, playing with his children, waving to the crowds outside his window. We see him at dinner munching a bone, or lifting one of his daughters and swinging her in his arms, or holding up the scepter with a look of happy mockery. In his temple at Thebes he was portrayed in a colossal statue which emphasizes his high cheekbones, flaring nostrils, flat chest, and flabby belly. The austere gravity of the earlier pharaohs was thrown to the winds. These sculptors and painters celebrated life as though they were intoxicated with it, as though a new and more life-giving blood had been poured into them.

In 1912 a German archaeologist, James Simon, discovered in Akhenaton's capital at Tell-el-Amarna, halfway between Heliopolis and Thebes, a portrait bust of Nefertiti made of painted limestone and plaster. She wore a blue crown, and except for two red ribbons at the nape of her neck and a painted necklace of beads and gold petals, she wore no decorations. She was found lying on the floor of an artist's studio, having fallen from a high shelf. A small portion of the crown had broken off, and the ears were slightly damaged, but she was otherwise unharmed. The German archaeologists, making their way through the ruined studio filled with plaster heads, life masks and unfinished portraits, realized that they had come upon a supreme masterpiece of the age of Akhenaton; and knowing that all the treasures they found must be shared equally between the Berlin Museum and the Egyptian State Department of Antiquities, they deliberately concealed it and smuggled it to Germany. In the nineteen-thirties, when discussions for the recovery of the statue were opened in Berlin, Hitler intervened. "Nefertiti," he declared, "must and will always belong to Germany."

He had every reason to want to keep her, for she is one of the great and enduring masterpieces of Egyptian art, and especially valuable because nothing comparable to this statue was ever found. In its psychological power it ranks among the greatest works ever made. The contraries meet in her. Arrogant, tender, cold, warm, with a melting softness, she confronts the world armed only with her splendor. She is certain of her femininity and of her imperial power, and perhaps also of her divinity, for as Akhenaton's Queen she takes her place among the gods. She knows she is beautiful, and the artist has expressed the self-consciousness inevitable in anyone so beautiful. He also expressed the changing, flickering pattern of her thoughts, so that we are aware of an intense inner life, of subtle and delicate meditations. The jeweled necklaces, the heavy blue crown, and even the slender neck are deliberately fashioned to frame her face, and just as a painting by Rembrandt acts on the spectator by giving him first a sudden, startling awareness of character, so that we are brought into immediate communion with the sitter, and only later are we made aware of the subtleties of that character, so here in the portrait of Nefertiti we see the Queen as power and beauty, and later we are made aware of depths upon depths in her.

She was no longer young when the sculptor made this image of her. It must therefore have been carved toward the end of her reign, when it was already becoming apparent that Akhenaton was in grave difficulties, not only because the priests of Amon were attempting to dethrone him, but also because the client kingdoms were no longer able or willing to pay tribute and the Army was disaffected. She gave her husband six daughters. One of them died, and there exists a relief showing Nefertiti clutching her husband's hand as they mourn over their dead daughter. On that face, so delicately formed, we may discern the beginnings of the tragedy that finally overwhelmed the family of the philosopher-king, who died, probably by poison, after a reign of barely twenty years.

In 1925 two colossal statues of the king were discovered at Karnak on the site of the temple he had erected to Aton. The temple had been destroyed, and the statues were found buried twenty feet below the earth. Though broken, they could be easily put together and they stand now in the Cairo Museum in the room set apart for the sculptures and paintings of his reign. The long, lean face, the narrow shoulders, the bony chest and the swelling belly are depicted as in the small reliefs, but now he stands twelve feet tall and the effect is all the more startling. Once these monumental statues stood at the entrance to the temple of Aton, and today they stand in a room not much larger than a dining room: there is no denying their strangeness. It is as though he was flaunting his physical deformities, insisting that he was not like other men, bony and bloated in the wrong places, the craggy face at odds with the swelling belly.

If the statue were placed in the sun, the impression would be altogether different. In the sunlight the sharp, simple planes would be strongly defined by shadows as hard and unyielding as the lead on stained-glass windows. We see this effect when the statues of Akhenaton are lit by floodlamps: the softness disappears, and there emerges the majestic figure of a king who is all the more majestic for possessing a recognizable human personality.

During Akhenaton's brief reign the workshops of the artists were kept busy, with the king himself supervising and teaching them. "I was taught by the king in person," wrote the artist Bak, who may have been the genius who composed the portrait of Nefertiti, and it is unlikely that he was exaggerating the king's expertise. The revolution in art stemmed from a single imagination and was colored by the philosophy of Sun worship and tenderness toward all living creatures announced by Akhenaton at the beginning of his reign. Everything we know about him suggests that he was perfectly capable of wielding the sculptor's chisel and the painter's brush.

At his death the throne passed to Smenkhkare, his son-in-law, whose reign was so brief that it left almost no trace on history. Smenkhkare was followed by another son-in-law, also of royal descent, called Tutankhaton, whose name means "Living Image of Aton," and almost nothing would ever have been known about him if Howard Carter and Lord Carnarvon had not discovered his tomb in the Valley of the Kings in November 1922. For the first time in history an Egyptian royal tomb was found intact. At first they found only hopeless disorder. There were boxes of preserved food, mummified ducks, bunches of flowers, dismembered gold-plated chariots, an armless dummy of a young man in a royal headdress. That was the outer chamber. It was not long before they penetrated the chamber where the king lay in a tomb of rose granite. Inside the tomb were three gold coffins, and in the four rooms which made up the king's mortuary chambers there were over seventeen hundred objects lying where they had been left during the hurried funeral. Tutankhaton, who died at the age of nineteen, had been buried in all the panoply of kingship, and every prayer had been said, and every offering which would help him to come to birth again had been prepared for him, but there was visible evidence that he had been buried in the utmost secrecy, on a dark night when the funeral cortege would pass unobserved.

Tutankhaton had reigned for a few years under his own name. Akhenaton was dead, the priests of Amon were in the ascendant, and to survive at all it became necessary for him to abjure the worship of Aton. His name was accordingly changed to Tutankhamon. Surprisingly, both names are recorded in the funeral chambers.

Never before or since has so much treasure been found in such a little space. The young king with the pensive features lay in golden luxury hitherto undreamed of. Thrones, scepters, shrines, statues, swords, all were of gold or covered with gold plate, and all these objects bore the demonstrable signs of Akhenaton's artistic revolution. They were clean-cut, powerfully evocative, sensuous, with the breath of life in them: the only stereotypes were the wall paintings in the tomb chamber. All that profusion of gold, alabaster, pearls, lapis lazuli, faience, wood, and stone was shaped with grace and tenderness. The slender golden goddesses who stand guard over the gilt shrines might have been modeled on Akhenaton's daughters. Skillfully engraved on the gold doors of the shrines are portraits of the young king in the company of his young wife, Akhenaton's daughter Ankhesenaton, as she nestles at his knees. We see her again on the back of the throne, leaning forward invitingly, one hand lightly touching the king's shoulder, and with the other she offers him a bowl of incense. Amid the confused splendor there is always this note of intimacy. The conventional august presence never appears; there is only the joy and the gaiety, the king at his ease.

Tutankhamon's mortuary chambers are reliquaries of that short-lived artistic revolution, which never completely died out, for although the dynasty perished and the worship of Aton was never revived, it left indelible traces on Egyptian art. At least half the objects in the tomb were the king's own possessions, while the rest were especially fashioned for his long journey into the land of the dead. His toys, the pearl-embroidered sandals he wore as a child, tiny ivory castanets, a small staff, a small bow, were there to remind him of his childhood, as his thrones and all the sumptuous articles of gold were there to remind him of his kingship. The boy's life and the customs of the royal court could be reconstructed from the possessions found in his mortuary chambers. By supreme good luck the archaeologists had found a treasure which represented Egyptian art at its crest, and only the discovery of the unplundered tombs of Tuthmosis III or Akhenaton himself would have yielded a more impressive treasure, for they reigned for longer periods and had more possessions.

Inevitably, when the dynasty came to an end, there was a reaction in favor of the austerity of an earlier age. The outlines grew harder, the weights of things became heavier, more and more columns sprouted in the great temples at Karnak and Luxor. Under the Ramessid pharaohs the heaviness becomes obsessive: always there is the striving for monumental power. The northern colonies were falling into the hands of the Hittites, the Nubians were restless, the marauding Bedouins were raiding the Nile Valley. Ramses II led an Egyptian army against the Hittites and after a dubious victory at Kadesh on the Orontes he returned to celebrate a prolonged triumph, which was solemnly recorded on the walls of his temples. A slim, athletic Pharaoh twenty feet high can be seen overwhelming his enemies in all his temples. He descends upon them like an avenging fury, the incarnation of outraged majesty, and in long hieroglyphic proclamations he attributes victory to himself alone with no assistance from anyone in the Army except his devoted shield bearer. No other pharaoh ordered so many statues of himself. Soon the traveler among Egyptian temples finds himself wearied almost beyond endurance by that look of frozen magnificence and pride, the long curving nose, the almond eyes. Ramses II, "Son of Re, Lord of Diadems," litters the landscape. One of his giant statues has been erected outside the railroad station at Cairo: it seems an appropriate place for him.

At Abu Simbel he ordered images of himself carved on a yellow sandstone bluff overlooking the Nile. Four identical images guard the temple, carved out of the living rock. He sits there enthroned, with his hands resting on his knees and his eyes gazing on the far horizons, his lips forming a faint smile of benediction, and quite clearly he is blessing himself. These are the largest human figures ever carved, being half as high again as the great bronze Buddha at Kamakura, but this was not enough to satisfy the Pharaoh's conception of his own majesty. He is made to appear grotesquely heavy, monumentally powerful, and this is brought about by providing him with an immense footrest and by giving extraordinary prominence to his powerful legs, which suggest enormous pistons beating down on the earth and crushing everything under them. These cliff sculptures testify to the Pharaoh's implacable determination to survive through all eternity, and when the new Aswan Dam was constructed recently, the temple was cut away from the living rock and lifted until it could be reassembled at the top of the cliff and thus saved from the floodwaters of the Nile. It was as though the Pharaoh's commands were being obeyed more than three thousand years after his death.

These commanding portraits of Pharaoh left many legacies. Greek art was deeply influenced by them, and in more subtle and indirect ways they influenced the Buddhist art of the Far East. The first formal portraits of Buddha derived from the Greek portraits of Apollo, and these in turn derived from portraits of pharaohs. The majestic calm of Ramses II evolved in the course of time into the majestic calm of Buddha. It was as though in the Far East sculptors who had never set eyes on Ramses II or his successors remodeled and recreated the Egyptian prototype, and one has only to set a small carved head of a pharaoh beside a head of Buddha to realize how much the Buddha derives from the Egyptian god-king, not only in the air of majestic repose and self-assurance, as of one who is in communion with the gods, but also in the shape of the withdrawn smile, the long pendulous ears, and all the sculptural elements that suggest disassociation with the ordinary preoccupations of mankind. In the deserts of North China there are Buddhas that derive in a long line of succession from the pharaohs of ancient Egypt.

Egyptian art endured longer than any other, because at a very early stage in its development wonderfully satisfying forms evolved, answering to the human and imaginative needs of the people. By the end of the Sixth Dynasty, c. 2160 B.C., they had invented nearly all they needed. The pyramid, the fluted column, the obelisk, the ground line, carving in the round and in light relief had all been invented, and the same essential forms recurred for generation after generation. Egypt suffered invasions from Libya, Ethiopia, Syria, Persia, Greece, and finally Rome, and foreign kings ascended the thrones of the pharaohs: paintings and sculptures always represented them as though they descended from Ramses II. Both Alexander the Great and Augustus Caesar appear in Egyptian temples in all the panoply of kingship; they have the Egyptian look, and they too are represented as kings who owe their power to the special favor of the gods. This long-lived civilization absorbed its conquerors until the coming of the Arabs; then at last, after an existence of nearly four thousand years, Egyptian civilization perished. The whirlwind out of Arabia destroyed the last vestiges of a settled life that had endured since the beginning of civilization.

While the greatest achievement of Egyptian art was to give artistic form to divine kingship, the Egyptian artists were the first to explore the world of human relationships. They learned very early to depict husband, wife, and children together and to suggest the devotion they had for one another; and loving domestic animals, they depicted them at play with an enchanting tenderness. They invested the ordinary lives of ordinary mortals with a grave dignity, and in no other ancient civilization, neither in Sumeria nor in China, did the artists celebrate the dignity of the human family. In the long noonday of Egypt this was perhaps the greatest triumph of all.

The Wounded Lions

We have seen how Egyptian art remained stable for more than thirty centuries, enclosed within its own boundaries, content with its superb conventions. The purity of the Egyptian eye remained constant because it was continually refreshed with the clarity of the air and the spectacle of the Nile enclosed within the desert and the mountains. At intervals there occurred small and sometimes imperceptible changes; then the hot wind would come out of the desert and the sands were smooth again. Only in a country as well favored as Egypt could such purity and refinement have maintained themselves for so long.

In Mesopotamia there existed none of the conditions of a stable art. Unlike the Nile, the Tigris and Euphrates are unpredictable in their rise and fall; the menace of the floodwaters struck fear in men's hearts; the world did not appear to be governed by unchanging order. For the Egyptians water was peaceful, beneficent, fructifying. For the Sumerians living on the banks of the Tigris and Euphrates it was fraught with danger. In the spring, when the snow melts in the Armenian highlands, the rivers overflow their banks, and at the same time the tides of the Persian Gulf may rise to a height of eight or nine feet, banking up the rivers. The floodwaters gave life, but they also destroyed. Harvests were uncertain, and wars were frequent, for those who lacked crops would fight those who brought in a good harvest. In these conditions of uncertainty, depending on the vagaries of nature, the Mesopotamians quite naturally came to possess an attitude to life and the gods radically different from that of the Egyptians. They lived in momentary fear, while the Egyptians lived in eternal hope.

The innumerable gods of the Mesopotamian pantheon governed the cosmos by consensus. Final authority rested with no single god, but with the divine community. There was no pharaoh walking the earth and pronouncing the verdicts of the heavenly Sun, "the eternal and enduring," for the community of the Mesopotamian gods was a replica of human society. There was no absolute authority in heaven, and none on earth. The earthly ruler derived his mandate from the consensus of the elders, and could not act independently. There was Anu, the god of the sky, who was only slightly more important than Enlil, the god of the storm, and Ea, the god of the watery deep, whose dwelling was in the abyss. They were gods of terrible aspect and portentous powers. The lesser gods included Shamash, the god of the sun; Sin, the god of the moon; Gibil, the god of fire; Ninhursag, the Lady of the Mountain, and Dumuzi, the god of the harvest, who becomes the lover and spouse of Ninhursag, and in the act of love brings about her death; to revive her he must sacrifice his own life. Ninhursag is the earth mother, and she is represented with a leafy crown on her head, her hair flowing behind her, as she holds the flowering branch of fertility in her hands.

The art of the Mesopotamians was nervous, crowded, curiously angular, like the wedge shapes of the letters they invented and engraved on clay. An impatient people, yearning for certainties, they portrayed the restless gods as they portrayed themselves, or in strange effigies composed of human bodies with birdlike beaks and enormous eyes. The cylinder seals, which came into existence at the end of the fourth millennium B.C., were carved with fierce vigor and incisiveness on small cylindrical stones; when they were rolled over clay, they produced a relief which hardened when the clay was baked in the sun. The cylinder seals came before writing, and led the way to the creation of letters and pictographs.

The early cylinder seals have a sinister quality, like the drawings of a demented child. It is not only that the space is crowded and filled with abrupt tensions, but they seem to have made an effort to crowd a multitude of direct experiences into an area less than an inch square. Like certain coins, these seals when magnified startle us with their monumentality and immense vitality. In time the

nervousness would give way to a calm sobriety: the wayward calligraphic figures would be filled out, becoming recognizable human
figures, no longer lines of force; and there would be a more orderly
arrangement of space. In the process the raw edges would be
smoothed away, until all the essential vitality was lost. Early Sumerian cylinder seals are among the most urgent carvings ever made,
and even though we can rarely understand exactly what is being
portrayed, they still have power to move us with their violence and
fury.

Thousands of cylinder seals have been unearthed by the archaeologists, and most of them are no larger than pebbles. Some of them
no doubt served as seals, and were stamped on the property of their
owners. Others, as we know, were offerings to the gods, for little
heaps of them have been found in the high stages of their temples.
These seals are the earliest known examples of portable art.

Although the cylinder seals were made deliberately small, the
Sumerians had no special attachment to miniature art. They built
their temples to their gods on a massive scale, and the *ziggurats*,
"the mountains of God," were conceived in vast proportions. It is
possible that the *ziggurats* developed from the watch towers erected
to enable them to see the advancing floodwaters. In the form in
which they have come down to us they were works of art, beautifully proportioned, conceived with an intense feeling for abstract
shapes of power. They took the form of stepped pyramids, with
huge bastions and buttresses and great processional stairways. The
core was mud brick, the outer wall was constructed of baked brick
mortared with bitumen, and the whole surface except for the terraces was coated with white plaster, so that the building gleamed
white under the hot Mesopotamian sun. The terraces were planted
with trees and flowers, like the greener coasts of paradise. At the
head of the processional stairway stood an ornamental gate and
another stairway leading to the sanctuary of the god. On feast days the
priests carried the statue of the god up and down the stairways
according to a ritual meant to ensure the fertility of the earth, of
flocks and of people.

The *ziggurat* was a far more public structure than the stepped
pyramid at Saqqara. It was not a mausoleum for a dead king and

had nothing whatsoever to do with death. It celebrated life—the life of the race, and the eternal life of the gods. Therefore it was built strongly like a fortress to last for eternity.

When Sir Leonard Woolley excavated the *ziggurat* of Ur-Nammu, which dated from about 2100 B.C., he was surprised to discover that in the whole building there was not a single straight line. The wall line from corner to corner had an outward curve, and a man sighting from the corner could see no farther than the center. The walls sloped inward, forming a subtle curve designed to mislead the eye in the same way that the entasis of a Greek column is designed to mislead the eye; the great mass of the building would have looked weaker if the lines had been straight. Wherever he looked he found carefully calculated curves, demonstrating that highly skilled and experienced architects had been at work.

So, too, with the heights of the different stages, the proportions of the masses forming the stepped pyramid, and the angles of the stairways. The sloping walls led upwards and inwards to the center. The principle stairway, which reached two thirds of the way up the building, was deliberately designed at a steep angle, to dramatize the approach to the divine sanctuary. On the outer wall it was still possible to observe long narrow slits carved at intervals in the brickwork; they proved to be "weeper holes," designed to drain off the water which seeped into the mud-brick interior during the torrential rains. Since the terraces were gardens, and the rain must of necessity pour through the soil, there was always the danger that the water would burst the walls asunder. They were canal builders with a considerable knowledge of hydraulic engineering; they knew the strange ways of water and how to cope with them. The "weeper holes" broke up the surface of the facade and provided appropriate decoration. The people who could conceive such imposing and monumental temples clearly possessed a high degree of organization, technical knowledge, and artistic skill. These shining man-made mountains with their hanging gardens were aesthetically satisfying. Here at last, stated in the simplest possible terms, was the abstract portrait of a people thrusting upward to the gods.

Like Schliemann in an earlier age, Sir Leonard Woolley was

one of those archaeologists who seem instinctively to find themselves in the presence of great hoards of treasure. In the winter of 1927 he uncovered in the royal cemetery at Ur the grave of the Sumerian general Mes-kalam-dug. There were gold bowls, gold swords, and gold beads, gleaming freshly as on the day they were placed in the grave. Most wonderful was a helmet of hammered gold which took the form of a golden wig, lying low over the forehead, the hair neatly curled above the decorative headband, while more curls like stylized wavelets fell to the nape of the neck and over the cheek pieces. An inscription on a gold lamp and on two bowls found in the tomb described Mes-kalam-dug as "the hero of the good land," and no doubt he was a soldier who had risen through the ranks to become a conquering general, for he was not buried with any of the attributes of royalty. It was a small grave, but heaped with treasure and the most splendid Sumerian accouterments seen up to this time. Sir Leonard Woolley was content. Even

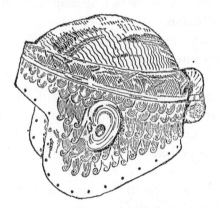

Gold Helmet of Mes-kalam-dug. 3500–3200 B.C. Baghdad Museum

if nothing more was found, there was now more than sufficient evidence to show that Sumerian art had reached an astonishingly high stage of development. The gold wig with the encircling diadem could only be the product of a sophisticated art that had been in progress for hundreds of years.

More and more treasures were found, all confirming the brilliance of the long vanished civilization. Startling discoveries were made in the tomb of Queen Shub-Ad, who had been buried with twenty-five of her red-robed ladies-in-waiting. The way they had met their deaths could be reconstructed without too much difficulty. They had walked alive into the grave pit, taken poison, and then quietly lain down with their hands cushioning their faces. They lay there in orderly rows, and the gravediggers then covered them with earth. Perhaps the Queen also took poison, for a gold cup lay close to her hands. But what chiefly excited the archaeologists was her crown of beech leaves and flowers intricately joined together and surmounted by a seven-pronged golden crest, each prong bearing a gold eight-petaled flower, while from the gold headband there fell four heavy gold earrings. The ladies-in-waiting wore similar crowns. Though all the crowns had been crushed flat by the weight of the earth, the veins of the beech leaves were still clearly visible. These wonderfully gracious crowns, which can be seen in the Baghdad Museum, make all subsequent crowns look meretricious. The Sumerians had invented a crown of unexampled magnificence at the very dawn of civilization.

But this was only the beginning. Cups, goblets, bowls, fibulae, all in gold, all exquisitely carved, came pouring out of the royal graves. In particular there was a gold wine cup six inches high, flaring up from a narrow base with wonderful energy, the flutings perfectly proportioned. It is quite simply the most beautiful cup ever made. The Queen's diadem was a ribbon set with lapis lazuli, on which there passes a procession of exquisitely fashioned gold stags, gazelles, bulls, and goats, with here and there golden trees and golden fruit. All the jewelry in the tomb had clear-cut lines and was strangely modern in feeling.

Among the treasures found in the graves was a ram, twenty inches high, fashioned of gold hammered over a wooden core, the fleece rendered in shell and lapis lazuli. The ram leans against a flowering shrub, from which he has devoured the leaves and most of the flowers. Sir Leonard Woolley was inclined to see the biblical "ram caught in a thicket," but it is just as likely that the ram was worshiped as an emblem of fertility. In the precision and delicacy of the ram there is the hint of a society which has already become too precise, too delicate. It is one of the very few objects found in the Middle East which could quite conceivably have been made by Fabergé.

But if the ram suggested too great a refinement, the so-called Standard of Ur, which was also discovered by Sir Leonard Woolley, was considerably more human and informative, for it brings the spectator into the immediate presence of the Sumerians. The art lies precisely in conveying that sense of immediacy, for we see the King and his councilors, his warriors, his servants, musicians, and singers, and we see the peasants with their animals, and the prisoners who have been stripped of their clothes and are forced to stand naked in the presence of the King. On those two small panels nearly a hundred people appear, all made out of little mosaics of gold-colored shell, mother-of-pearl, and red limestone set against a lapis lazuli background.

One of the panels is devoted to war, the other to peace. In the first we see the King confronting his prisoners, having just stepped down from his war chariot. Warriors in long cloaks and leather caps are herding the prisoners toward him, and in another scene we see the two-horsed war chariots advancing over a battlefield strewn with the dead. In each chariot there is a knight accompanied by his squire, whose task is to offer him a javelin at the right moment. The chariots are painted red and provided with defensive breastworks; there are large clumsy wheels, unpainted, without spokes; the horses are yoked together and provided with decorative collars. For the first time the artist has depicted a charge by showing the chariot advancing slowly, and then the same chariot is seen moving more rapidly, and finally it hurtles through the air at breakneck speed. The effect is rather like seeing an animated film. It was a bold and convincing way to represent movement, and nothing comparable with this technique appears in Egyptian reliefs or wall paintings. Nevertheless the Standard owed much to Egyptian artists, who were the first to show orderly processions marked out by ground lines. The Standard can be dated about 2650 B.C., and therefore comes long after the first Egyptian murals.

In the second panel we see the King, who wears an elaborately tasseled skirt, celebrating in the company of six of his councilors, all of them holding cups shaped like the fluted winecup found in the Queen Shub-Ad's tomb. They are all beardless, and have shaven heads. They recline on elegant chairs and they are clearly delighted to share in the King's celebration, while the servants stand around waiting to fill their cups. A musician plays on a harp and a girl sings with her hands folded over her breast in the conventional attitude of someone singing high notes. The councilors are homely, middle-aged men, with the overlarge heads and curious squat bodies characteristic of the Sumerian style of portraiture. They all have enormous ears. The artist has portrayed them with a casual matter-of-factness, as though he had been called in to make some quick sketches and immediately carved them out of shell. Depicting the King with his councilors, the artist has given himself elbowroom, and while all the other panels give an appearance of being crowded, this one is deliberately uncrowded, thus suggesting that they are at their ease.

Below the King we see the tribute bearers from the conquered countries or perhaps they are merely people from Ur bringing their offerings to the King. They march in stately procession: one leads a heifer, another a goat, another carries two large fish, and twice we see a man bent under the weight of a corded bale wearily mopping his brows. Here, too, the people in the procession are rendered in a casual, matter-of-fact way, as though the artist had run out into the street and made the simple, clear-cut sketches which could be immediately transformed into mosaics of shell.

These panels have considerable importance in the history of art because they show how the Sumerians grappled with the problem of representing reality in a narrow space, covering an area no more than nineteen inches by sixteen and filling it with an extraordinary variety of people and animals. If it lacks the refinement of Egyptian reliefs, the Standard has a warmth and rough good humor that are deeply moving. In the blue lapis lazuli background, made up of small chips of different sizes laid on a flat bitumen surface, the artists discovered a way to render the changing depths of space, while the figures carved out of shell are altogether more "alive" than figures carved out of limestone.

This vitality, this energy, is never absent from Sumerian art, and some four hundred years after the Standard was made, we find statues in the city of Lagash which are among the most accomplished sculptures ever carved, with a controlled strength and vigor never surpassed. These statues, all carved out of an intensely hard black or bluish-black diorite, are portraits of Gudea, governor and viceroy, a deeply religious man with a gift for large-scale trading expeditions. He was continually building temples, which would henceforth possess statues of him praying to the gods or sitting down with a plan of the temple on his knees.

The statues of Gudea may be compared with the earliest Egyptian statues, for they are deliberately constructed to suggest the surge of power rising within the figure. Where the Egyptians conveyed the sense of power by showing a naked and powerfully built pharaoh, the Sumerians conveyed the power of Gudea by enclosing him in a gown which was itself carved into shapes of power. In addition they employed two other techniques which were unknown to the Egyptians. They gave great prominence to the hands clasped fiercely across his chest and to the boldly carved round head. The statue resembles a bomb filled with an explosive charge. The pharaohs are calm, their inner violence completely under control. Gudea, though outwardly calm, is about to explode.

He was clearly a man who liked to see himself portrayed, for over thirty statues of him have been found. He was a short sturdy man with large eyes, full lips, a thick neck, and an underslung jaw, and he was sometimes represented with a round hat, which was evidently part of the uniform of his high office. The dark stone is highly polished, and the sculptors possessed an extraordinary sense of plastic form. Gudea lacks the imperious detachment of the pharaohs, for he is very much engaged in the business of this world.

A sharp man, a heavy man, an earthy man, a man to be respected, he was an early Lorenzo de' Medici, making a fortune by trade and cultivating the arts. No doubt if he had been a king he would have been portrayed differently, with all the appropriate symbols of divine power. But Gudea was not a king, and we are not invited to enter a royal presence. Instead, we are confronted with a penetrating intelligence, a manipulator of power, a lover of art; and what he demanded of men was their respect. In this sense he was the first modern man.

At least four different sculptors of the Gudea statues can be discerned, and all of them produced masterpieces. Those dark gleaming statues are heavy with mortality; unlike the pharaohs, he will never become a god. Nevertheless, by ordering so many statues of himself, he was attempting to achieve a kind of immortality.

The Sumerian genius for architecture and sculpture survived the conquest of Sumeria. The Babylonian and Assyrian conquerors brought with them a sense of urgency, a quickening, which did not, however, extend to the portraits of their kings. Gudea, earthbound and meditative, with his purely human intelligence, gave way to the archaic bearded kings holding the attributes of sovereignty, the battle mace and the sword. They are so ringleted and so heavily bearded that they resemble one another, and clearly it was the intention of the sculptor that they should do so, for they are not so much portraits as emblems of a continuing sovereignty. Gudea stood alone; these kings belong to the community of kings. As tall as trees, holding lions like lapdogs in their arms, they dominate the sacred enclosures and announce their permanence.

When these artists turned away from the contemplation of their kings, they demonstrated their independence from archaic forms. Animals especially delighted them. They sculpted animals in light relief with extraordinary tenderness, so that a relief of Sargon II holding an ibex gives the impression of having been done by two artists: the artist who portrayed every last archaic curl of the royal beard, and the artist who portrayed the alert and quivering ibex, which seems to know that it is being prepared for the sacrifice and is all the more alive because it is so close to death.

A strange blood mania drove these kings, who spent their days in war and sometimes contemplated their victories in the quiet of their palaces, where the walls were crowded with murals describing all the stages of a battle from the setting out to the successful conclusion. We see the King riding in plumed majesty, as large as or larger than the city he is attacking, and later we see the wretched prisoners being led into captivity, a small boy clinging to his father's hand, a woman clutching her few remaining possessions, and then at the King's pleasure we see these same prisoners being fed from the public granary so that they can take part in the trium-

phal march, and then again we see them being tortured and muti-
lated, flung down, trampled upon, left to the vultures. Or else
we see the King reposing on the royal couch, the Queen sitting
beside him, musicians playing, servants gathered around them, the
cupbearers bringing more and more wine. In a garden of palm
trees and creeping vines the King points with a pleased expression
to a severed head hanging on a tree and dripping blood.

A pitiless empire produced a pitiless art: the faces of all men
are alike. Individuality is reserved for the animals which appear
in the hunting scenes. The artists excelled themselves in depicting
wild horses, gazelles, ibex, hunting dogs, and lions, and gave them
the freedom denied to the human species. Wild horses and gazelles
are especially well rendered. We see them in all their moods; the
horses toss their manes, the foals gallop furiously beside them, the
young gazelles spring lightly across the invisible landscape, for there
is rarely any attempt to suggest the scenery. Among these animals
running free the King's chariot appears as an intruder from another
world. The King stands in his chariot, impassive and imperturbable, with every curl of his beard in place. In one hand he wields
a javelin whose pointed end is halfway down a lion's throat.

The most magnificent of these hunting scenes was carved out
of alabaster and set up in the palace of King Assurbanipal at
Nineveh about 650 B.C. Evidently the King's intention was to provide documentary evidence of his prowess at the hunt, his courage
and resourcefulness. In fact, he was so well guarded in the chariot,
and there were so many horsemen protecting him, and his chariot
was traveling so fast, that he was never in any real danger. He hurled
his javelins at the lions, and all of them hit their mark. It is all a
little too easy to be convincing. But how well the artist depicted the
wounded lions and lionesses as the blood pours out of them and they
roar with pain, their muscles tense in the agony of dying, as they
wearily attempt to lift their heads from the dust or turn to observe
the heavy arrows in their flesh, snapping at them, for they would
bite them off if they could. A wounded lioness with paralyzed hind
legs tries to drag herself along by the forelegs, and every curve of
the sagging back and belly, and every tendon of the forelegs sug-

gests the awareness of death, and all the sympathy of the artist flows to the lioness.

Nothing remotely comparable with the wounded lioness had ever appeared in Egyptian art, where hunting scenes were rare and always decorous. The Assyrians gloried in their triumphs over men and animals: the Egyptians had no blood lust and seem scarcely to have understood what death was doing in the world. The Assyrians were fascinated by the maimed, the wounded, and the terror-stricken. Significantly the portraits of the gods never appear in the Assyrian palaces, while an Egyptian palace is filled with them. No pharaoh walks without the gods by his side, but the Assyrian king with the face of a man, the body of a bull, and the wings of an eagle walks alone. He has no need of the gods, for he is himself the lord of the universe.

This terrible civilization, one of the most cruel that ever came to birth, left a profound legacy. They were the first realists, the first to see the world as it was without benefit of the gods. While their violence seems to have sprung from an essential indifference to the divine forces ruling the universe, their vigor was their own; and there is something to be said for an art where the dying lions are more living than the victorious kings.

Just as Greece laid the foundations for Roman art, so ancient Sumeria laid the foundations for the arts of Babylonia and Assyria. From Sumeria came certain archetypal forms: the immense fortress-like *ziggurats,* the clean flaring lines of Queen Shub-Ad's cup, faces with enormous eyes, heads a quarter the size of the entire body, animals standing adossed or confronting one another, an addiction to spheres and cylinders. They had mastered mosaics and light relief and the intricate working of gold. The Babylonians and later the Assyrians added swiftness and urgency and the sense of doom.

Out of these many arts there would come an art far superior to any of them. At some time between the reigns of Cyrus and Darius I there would come into existence an art which employed the archetypal forms of the Sumerians and utterly transformed them. In the art of the ancient Persians a new and hitherto unknown element entered the scene—the sense of human majesty.

The Splendor of Persia

In 1928 there began to appear on the Paris market some strange bronzes unlike anything that had yet appeared in history. A hitherto unsuspected culture, evidently having its origins in the Near East, had come to light, but without any exact provenance, and even today we cannot be certain where these bronzes came from. They were usually quite small, being about four to six inches long, and represented gods and mythological beasts or long-horned goats or deer. The vast majority were evidently bridle or harness pieces cast by the *cire perdue* process, but there were also swords, daggers, and talismanic figures of gold, silver, and hammered bronze. Few of these objects were beautiful, but they had a raw vigor and a harsh provincial elegance which made them peculiarly appealing to students of the Near East, for they seemed to represent the last surviving elements of a tradition which went back to Sumerian times. There was something abrupt, urgent, and commanding about these figures with enormous eyes and strained bodies. A highly inventive and imaginative people had made them, but no one knew who they were.

As the months passed, it became known that peasants in the Persian province of Luristan had been systematically excavating shallow graves dating from about 1200 B.C. In the course of two or three years some four thousand objects were excavated, and then the supply abruptly ceased. No excavations by trained archaeologists were made, and since the locations of the graves remained unknown and no written records were found, our knowledge of these Luristan bronzes remains fragmentary. Because the greater part of the discoveries consisted of rein rings, cheek pieces, and bits, it could be assumed that the bronzesmiths were nomadic herdsmen who traveled in carts and whose wealth consisted largely of horses, and because the art was related at a great distance to both Scythian and Sumerian art, it could be assumed that they were a people of mixed ancestry who had moved in a southeasterly direction until they came to settle, far from Scythia and Sumeria, in the upland meadows and grassy valleys of Luristan.

Even today we know very little about these people. Bronzes like these have not been found in any large quantities elsewhere, and indeed it is scarcely likely that they will be found: they describe an attitude of mind and a way of life which cannot have endured for more than two or three hundred years. There is almost no sense of development: the art appears and then vanishes completely. Yet it was to leave enduring traces on the art of Persia.

For what chiefly characterized the Luristan bronzesmiths was a certain harsh gaiety and a highly developed feeling for the sculptural properties of bronze. They do not seem to have been a deeply religious people: the urgency derives from their extraordinary ability to render real and mythological animals in muscular tension, with the suddenness of vision. The bits, of course, must have holes in the center, and the Luristan sculptors knew exactly how to balance the figure around the hole. So we find a winged monster with a human head and the rounded haunches of a horse, and from the head of the monster there emerges a horned tiara and from the tip of the wings there emerges a grimacing eagle which appears to be about to snap at the monster's head; and there is about this figure, with its crudity and its raw vitality, no suggestion of improvisation. This is what the sculptor has seen in his mind's eye, and having seen it, he shapes the bronze according to his vision in such a way that it becomes immediately compelling, credible, and satisfying. Even the hole in the center has its place in the general design; it becomes simply one more of the conventions inevitable in the sculptor's art.

If we compare the Luristan bronzes with the highly skilled bronzes which were being fashioned about the same time in the region of the Yellow River Valley in China, we find remarkable points of difference. The Chinese portrayed mythological power in the abstract: the forces of the universe became the masks of heraldic beasts resembling no beasts that ever walked the earth. The Chinese introduced a highly sophisticated art intimately connected with ritual. The Luristan bronzesmiths were concerned only to give appropriate decoration to their horses, carts, whetstones, and tent poles. Essentially it was an art unrelated to ritual and therefore little concerned with the gods. The bronzes were the ornaments of their nomadic life.

Above all there is a quality of alertness in Luristan art, all the more attractive because it is so rough, so earthy, so provincial, so determined upon reflecting the common life of the camp. There are no flourishes. The artists described the world they knew, and never went beyond. Their gods—on the rare occasions when they depict their gods—are always derivative, descending in direct line from Sumeria. When they depicted themselves, they were inclined to caricature, emphasizing their heavy arching eyebrows, long straight noses, small mouths, and puffed cheeks. They have the glow of health on them.

The discovery of the Luristan bronzes inevitably aroused scholars of Near Eastern art to search for their origins among the tribes known to have occupied these regions of Persia. Many theories were advanced, and many dates were discussed. One authority suggested that Hittite metallurgists had somehow entered Persia after the fall of Kassite rule in Mesopotamia, other authorities placed the date much later, with the invasion of Persia by the Scythians about 680 B.C. Yet there is overwhelming evidence that they belonged to a period about five hundred years earlier. Until the archaeologists discover new graves, it is unlikely that we shall learn very much more about their origins.

These Luristan bronzes, which came to light so recently, have a special importance in the history of Persian art, for they go some way toward explaining the intense vitality of Achaemenid art with its triumphant expression of monumental form. Achaemenid art seemed to grow out of a vacuum: it was so splendid, so fully formed, and came so suddenly that it seemed to have no ancestors. That royal and aristocratic art, which dominated the Persian Empire between 550 and 330 B.C., could be traced back at a great remove to ancient Sumeria, but always so tenuously that the line of descent seemed unreal. The Luristan bronzes revealed one of the many links in the chain.

Outwardly the Luristan bronzes and the Achaemenid sculptures in stone and marble have little in common. Achaemenid art is wholly monumental, designed to be seen from afar, impatient of privacy. It is public ornament on a scale which becomes possible only when great wealth and power are concentrated in the hands of an imperial dynasty possessing vast resources of refinement and good taste. Most of the Luristan bronzes are small enough to hold in the hand; they proclaim the poverty of their owners, and the wandering life. The Achaemenid emperors proclaimed on the contrary their wealth and their settled civilization. They carved out an empire which reached from Greece to India and from Egypt to central Russia. They were the first world emperors, and they rivaled the Egyptian pharaohs in their magnificence. The Luristan bronzesmiths, confronted with the carved lions or adossed bulls at Persepolis, would have relished the powerfully modeled forms, the sense of hard bone beneath the yielding skin, and they might even have approved the simplification and stylization which are demanded by monumental forms, for they were themselves adepts at simple stylizations, but they would have been puzzled by the vast size and dignity of these animals. You could not take a marble lion from Persepolis and make it into a cheek piece or a rein ring; it was not useful, and a man could not treasure it as he wandered about the land, and he could not give it to his son as an heirloom. The marble lion was remote from ordinary life, as the Achaemenid emperor was remote from ordinary life, for he was a priest-king whose acts were circumscribed by ritual. Yet between the nomadic Luristanis and the Achaemenid emperors there was a common bond: they had the same wild-eyed delight in animals, the same feeling for the vitality of animal life. The provincial nomad worked with a kind of deliberate crudity which reflected the crudity of his nomadic existence, while the sculptors attached to the emperor's household polished and refined their sculptures according to the demands of the court. The monumental forms mirrored the pride and majesty of imperial rule, and their only use was to suggest the infinite power of the emperor.

Although the Luristan bronzes supply one of the many links in the chain, the origins of Achaemenid art remain mysterious. From Sumeria, Assyria, Scythia, and Luristan came the influences which worked on the powerful Achaemenid imaginations, but we can only guess how these influences were assembled. One clue has survived in a bronze portrait head found in Azerbaijan and now in the Metropolitan Museum in New York. With its beautiful deep green patina, this superbly modeled head represents a prince or chieftain of one of the frontier tribes, gazing out at the world through heavily lidded eyes in a mood of profound contemplation. The lips are pursed, the beard is pointed, and along the cheeks there are basket-work patterns which evidently descend from the rigid curls of the Assyrian kings. The portrait has a compelling and immediate effect. The nobility and calm of the prince are completely convincing, but it is not a face of any great power, and indeed in his refinement and in the tragic intensity of his expression, he might be taken for the last of a long line of princes. It is precisely that powerlessness and intensity which give him such a singular appeal, so that he seems to be speaking directly to the beholder across the centuries. He hints at the decay and dissolution of empires. He is provincial and derivative, but these are the least important things about him, for he comes to us with his nobility and sensitivity unimpaired. The blood courses under his skin, the eyes peer keenly across abysses of time, and he welcomes us with the faintest hint of a smile. In any age this portrait would be regarded as a masterpiece.

Unhappily we cannot even guess the date of the sculpture, and the historians resign themselves to the uncertainties of "the second millennium B.C." We may hazard the guess that it was considerably later than the Luristan bronzes, but the date is not so important as the fact that these same features will be found again in Achaemenid art and something of that same delicacy and refinement is visibly present in all the works of the Achaemenid sculptors.

In the middle years of the sixth century B.C. a whirlwind came out of Asia. It took the form of a small and well-trained army led by a Persian chieftain called Kurush, whom we know as Cyrus the Great. The great-grandfather of Cyrus was a local chieftain called Achaemenes, a man of considerable fame in his own province, and it pleased the founder of the new dynasty to invoke the name of his great-grandfather when describing his own exploits. With Cyrus, whose army swept through Babylonia and Asia Minor, the age of the Achaemenid emperors began.

This empire, which survived for more than two hundred years until it was destroyed by Alexander the Great, was distinguished by an extraordinary refinement which achieves its supreme expression in the palace of Persepolis. The ruins of the palace remain, a few columns still standing, and the great sculptured doorways and stairways leading to the audience chamber of "the king of kings." Although part of the palace was fired by Alexander the Great, so much survives that we can reconstruct its most minute details, and every year the archaeologists are discovering new and important elements in the grand design.

The palace was built originally by Darius and his son Xerxes, and seems to have been begun about the time of the invasion of Greece, not long after the successful invasion of Egypt. Yet curiously there is little evidence of Egyptian or Greek influence, although Greeks were employed in the building of other Achaemenid palaces, and the great audience chamber at Persepolis, known as the Hall of a Hundred Columns, evidently derives at a great distance from the hypostyle temples at Luxor.

What distinguishes the palace at Persepolis from all other palaces is quite simply its grandeur. Lying at the end of a great plain, in the shadow of the low hills, the palace stood on a vast platform and dominated everything in sight. Huge painted columns soared heavenward. Five horses could ride abreast up the great stairway, where hundreds of figures were carved in low relief. It was more than a palace, for it comprised a complex of many palaces, halls, chambers, galleries, treasuries, harems, stables, and workshops, reaching up the slopes of the hills and spilling over into the valley below. Each emperor added his own palatial quarters, as though he felt an overpowering need to build anew on the foundations built by his forefathers. On the hills above, and in some other hills nearby, lay the tombs of the emperors carved out of the rock face.

Today we see the ruined palace reduced to its bare bones, the columns worn by time and wind and storm, the carved reliefs cracked by winter frosts, and only the figures carved on the stairway, long buried in rubble, remain unchanged, as fresh as on the day when they were lifted into place. In the days of the Achaemenid emperors all these were brilliantly, and even garishly, colored. The wooden beams and ceilings were intricately painted, the doors were plated with gold or bronze, tapestries hung on the outside columns, and, according to Athenaeus, they depicted "animals of every kind, beautifully executed." The reliefs showing the Emperor at war with the mythological beasts of the seasons were painted, and in addition he wore a headdress of hammered gold set with jewels, his beard was of carved bronze or gold or lapis lazuli, and he wore golden necklaces and bracelets. The figures on the stairway were painted, and so too were the columns and the adossed bulls which decorated the tops of the columns. Today when we see the marching soldiers and tribute bearers in low relief, we marvel at their grace as the processions move imperceptibly toward the throne of the Emperor. The outlines are chaste, carved in a gleaming gray stone which admirably conveys the texture of flesh, and we forget that this gray stone lay concealed under a layer of paint. Here and there traces of color can still be seen. From a distance the entire palace shone like a many-colored jewel.

Persepolis was a riot of color, and in this it resembled the Parthenon at Athens, which was equally gaudy and splendid. The sculptors of the Parthenon carved their great processional frieze high up near the roof of the temple, almost out of sight, while the sculptors at Persepolis carved their processional frieze in full view of everyone who approached the palace, for it decorates the stairway and the outer walls. Here there are no youths in chariots, no young and athletic boys riding bareback. The figures on the Persepolis frieze are always mature men, very masculine, very calm, and very conscious of their dignity as they approach the emperor.

Among those hundreds of figures there is not a single child or a single woman. There is a deliberate emphasis on masculine power.

Tribute bearers from twenty-eight nations are represented, and we recognize their distinctive features and dress, but all are given the same outward bearing as they march slowly, perhaps to the sound of drumbeats, into the royal presence. They bring gifts and offerings —bulls, camels, gold vessels, goblets. One would expect to see musical instruments, but there are none. In their expressions there is firmness, but not sternness; there is grace in the flowing draperies and gentleness in the depiction of animals. The Persians had accepted the religion of Zoroaster, who demanded gentleness toward animals, and consequently all the animals appearing on the frieze are depicted lovingly, in great detail, and in a close relationship with the men who watch over them—a servant or a tribute bearer will throw his arm lightly and caressingly over a bull's hump or he will rest his hand against a horse's neck, and every gesture conveys an astonishing depth of affection. The sculptors excelled in the portraits of animals. While the soldiers appear to be all alike— though on closer inspection each is seen to possess his own characteristic gesture and expression—the animals are depicted with clearly defined indentities. So, too, in the other great carvings of the Achaemenid period: there is always the sense of a slow, stately music, and a compelling masculinity and nobility. Where the Assyrians portrayed their captives in chains or on the execution ground, the Achaemenids contented themselves by displaying their peaceful power, their sense of perfect possession. The great frieze at Persepolis represents a civilization so powerful and so sure of itself that it must have seemed inconceivable that it would ever come to an end.

No other ancient empire has bequeathed to us such an insight into the characters, the costumes, and the appearances of the subject races. If these reliefs were placed together in a single row, they would form a panel about five feet high and nearly 1000 feet long. Here are people from all the regions of the empire, which extended from Ferghana in the north to Abyssinia in the south, from the Balkans to the great plains of India. These tribute bearers do not have the bearing of slaves; they are members of the imperial commonwealth. The more one studies the frieze, the more inescapable is the conclusion that it was conceived at a supreme moment in

Persian history—a moment when peace reigned from one end of the empire to the other, and the protection of "the king of kings" was granted equally to all.

Persepolis was more than a complex of palaces. It was the spiritual and political center of the empire, the seat of power, the shrine of the Achaemenid dynasty. Here were performed at the New Year the mysterious rites during which the emperor invoked the blessing of the gods, and especially of Ahura Mazda, on the people. Although no books of ritual have survived, we can guess the nature of the ceremonies from the reliefs and from the surviving fragments of the Zoroastrian scriptures. It would seem that in the spring, when the New Year was celebrated, all the nations of the empire brought their offerings, and while the priests intoned the sacred hymns, the emperor committed the whole empire into the hands of Ahura Mazda and received it back again. The great ceremony seems to have begun at dawn, when there was enacted the ritual slaying of the powers of darkness, with the emperor stabbing to death a lion brought to his throne, the blood being caught in a golden beaker and then dashed over the parapet to fructify the plain. Throughout the day the Emperor received the tribute bearers, and as the sun set over the lion-headed mountains the sacred flame of the empire was lit in all the temples in the neighborhood and carried by runners to the four corners of the known world.

As he is depicted in the reliefs, and most especially in the monumental relief now in the Teheran Museum, Darius was a man of grave beauty, with heavy eyes, thick lips, an expression of calm benignity. We never see him in the round, and we therefore cannot penetrate deeply into his character. He is usually shown seated on his throne, welcoming some high officer of state, a slender staff in one hand and a lotus, the symbol of royalty, in the other. He does not tower over his sons, who stand behind his throne, or the officers who have been summoned to an audience with him. He is of their size, and all are depicted in much the same way. They are calm when they confront the Emperor, and the Emperor himself is calm, and there is never any sense of strain.

Many years later, when the Achaemenid empire was little more than a memory, a new dynasty of conquerors came to the throne.

The Sassanian emperors clearly modeled themselves on the Achaemenid emperors, whom they regarded as their ancestors. Centuries had passed, but the traditions remained. Yet when the Sassanian emperors were depicted by their court sculptors, they nearly always appear on horseback, in violent movement, amid a swirl of windswept draperies, and there is something in the tilt of their bodies and the expressions of their faces which suggests the calculated recklessness of powerful men. A new eagerness and impulsiveness appears, concealing an inner weakness. They show themselves as intrepid warriors and hunters, slaying single-handedly their enemies or wild beasts. Darius had never any need to show himself in the act of destroying men or beasts, for his power was vast and undifferentiated. Maturity, vigor, and assured strength were the marks of his reign.

As more and more of the sacred city of Persepolis is excavated, it becomes increasingly clear that these palaces formed the powerhouse of the empire, and that the Persians regarded the palaces with awe and veneration. Some mysterious mana attached itself to this corner of the Mervdasht Plain, and when Alexander the Great led his armies across Persia he was compelled by the very nature of his invasion to destroy the source of Persian power. Plutarch tells the story of how Thais, a camp follower from Athens, suggested that the palaces be burned to the ground during a night of revelry and drunken riot. It is more likely that the decision was taken by Alexander himself long before he reached Persepolis. He burned the libraries and the sacred books, sacked the treasury, removed the gold plate from the doors, and sent a thousand carts laden with spoil back to Greece. Then Persepolis was abandoned, never again to become an inhabited place. In this way Alexander the Great took revenge on the Persians for their invasion of Greece.

Achaemenid art survived, subtly influencing the arts of the Middle East. Out of innumerable conflicting influences there had developed an art which was settled, composed, deliberate, and mature, an art of clear outlines, singing curves, and dazzling colors, created by men who had an instinctive feeling for the dignity of human life. To a quite extraordinary degree they shared these qualities with the Egyptians of the Eighteenth Dynasty, especially during the reigns of Tuthmosis III and Queen Hatshepsut. There is the same sense of controlled design, of nobility, of ease. The difference lies in Achaemenian vigor, which is apparent even when the subject is at rest. A thousand years separated the Eighteenth Dynasty from King Darius, but the artists drank from the same wellspring.

The Achaemenid empire went down to defeat before the armies of Alexander the Great, whose successors quarreled among themselves. A divided empire fell prey to Parthian invaders, who were more deeply influenced by Greek models than by the Achaemenians. They left some noble bronze statues of their princes wearing long curly hair, short tunics edged with leather, and shorts in the modern fashion, to which they would add leather leggings when they went riding. Perhaps it was from the Romans, with whom they were constantly fighting, that they learned the art of portraiture: a Parthian prince or princess in bronze or marble wears a recognizably human face, whereas the Achaemenian kings are scarcely more than symbolic representations of kingship. When the Sassanians overcame the Parthians, they deliberately modeled themselves on the Achaemenians, whom they claimed as their ancestors. The ancient empire was revived in all its glory, and with even greater panoply.

Sassanian art is characterized by vigorous movement, a love of ornate swelling forms, a deliberate avoidance of the austere line. It was a romantic rather than a classical art, feminine in its love of adornment and soft rippling lines, but wholly masculine in its celebration of force. Much had changed since Achaemenian times, and one of the principal changes was the rise of the goddess Anahita to a place of influence and power in the minds of the Persians. She was the virgin goddess of streams and rivers, flocks and herds, wearing a cloak of beaver skins to signify her affection for all the living things inhabiting water, but above all she was the goddess of the springs, of the beginning of things. She had been a comparatively minor deity in Achaemenian times; now she was almost the rival of Ahura Mazda, god of the holy light, and there would come a time when Sassanian kings would be shown receiving the sacred emblem of investiture from both the god and the goddess decked in their

most sumptuous apparel. Anahita appears to have answered the
same need which brought about the veneration of the Virgin Mary
in twelfth-century Europe.

A new tenderness entered Persian art. Horses, elephants, deer,
and wild boar were depicted lovingly and in astonishing detail; and
when the king was shown hunting or receiving on horseback the
greetings of the god, the horse was given special prominence. In
one of the greatest of Sassanian rock carvings we see Shapur I on
horseback receiving the homage of the conquered Roman emperor
Valerian, and although the artist has caught the moment of supreme
victory and supreme abasement, and the air is electric with the passions of the moment, yet we remember chiefly the massive beauty
and calm of the horse, silent and unmoving in the midst of turmoil.
Valerian has suddenly knelt down in the presence of the Persian
king, and his cape billows up, and his hands stretch out in the immemorial gesture of a man pleading for his life. The Roman emperor
has a coarse, peasantlike face, while Shapur has features of great
refinement. As he gazes down at his enemy, a smile plays about his
lips, and one hand rests on his sword hilt while the other is raised
in triumph. Waves of anger, fear, resentment, triumph, and despair move between the two actors in the drama, and for the first
time in Persian art we are introduced to a sculptor with keen
psychological insight. But it is the superb, gaily caparisoned horse
which ultimately gives meaning to the scene carved out of the
honey-colored rock.

Among the glories of Sassanian art are the engraved silver
salvers showing the kings at the hunt. No doubt there were once
many salvers made out of gold, but they appear to have been melted
down, for none survives. The engravers evidently delighted in making these salvers, for they are always filled with an intense vitality.
About two thirds of the circular space is given over to the horse
and the rider, while the rest shows the wild animals in the enclosed
hunting field which the Persians called "paradise." The animals
are lions, cheetahs, stags, wild boars, deer, and rams. The king has
stretched his bow, the animals are in full flight, all running pell-
mell away from the king. There are no servants, no beaters. Very
rarely do we see any animals killed, and there is not the least trace

of any morbid delight in the death agonies of the victims. These hunting scenes describe the joy of the chase, and the engravers rejoice in depicting the leaping joy of the horse. At Taq-i-Bustan, on the walls of the grotto showing Chosroes II receiving his investiture from the hands of Ahura Mazda and Anahita, there are sculptured reliefs of the King at the chase. The artist, no longer circumscribed for space, carved on the living rock a portrait of the "paradise" in minute detail. We see the King being ferried across the marshes in a boat filled with female choristers. He stands in the bow with his stretched bow, shooting at the wild boars crowded at the edge of the marshes, while behind him on dry land come the lumbering elephants on whose backs the slain boars will later be thrown. On another wall we see the same King accompanied by his retinue as he hunts deer, and once more we are made aware that the sculptor carves the animals with considerably more feeling than he carves the huntsmen.

In all the Sassanian reliefs there is the sense of an unfolding and continuing narrative. A story is being told, and we are being urged to follow its development. The element of time has been introduced; we are no longer in the timeless world of Persepolis. It was a period when the Persians were deeply concerned with all the manifestations of time, both finite and infinite, and much of Sassanian art and architecture may be regarded as an extended commentary on *zurvan*, "endless time," which became an obsession during this period. The soaring archways of Sassanian palaces seem to reflect this passion for the infinite; and while the ruins of the palace at Ctesiphon testify to the magnificence of the Sassanian emperors and the genius of their engineers, there is also the sense of an immense striving for the unattainable.

The ruins of the palace at Ctesiphon cover an area of nearly thirty acres. High above them there rises the great Taq-i-Kisra, the archway of Chosroes, a vault 110 feet high and eighty-three feet wide, the widest and highest single-span vault of unreinforced brickwork in the world. But it is not so much the size of the arch as its grace and dignity which give it a place in the history of art. While the Achaemenian palace was supported on a forest of pillars which almost concealed the emperor from mortal eyes, the audience chamber at Ctesiphon permitted a full view of the emperor sitting high on his jeweled throne, while a golden crown let down from the roof hovered an inch above his head.

In June, A.D. 637, the Arab invaders stormed the palace and captured it intact. They found vast stores of silver and gold, costly robes, chests full of amber and musk, a horse made of gold with teeth of emeralds, a ruby mane, and trappings of gold. They also discovered the great carpet in the audience chamber, a carpet unlike any other carpet because it was made of jewels. Emeralds and rubies formed the flowered borders, pearls formed the running streams, laced with gold and silver thread. It was over eighty feet wide, and a torn corner of it might have kept a large town alive for generations. The invaders wanted to cut the carpet to ribbons and distribute it among themselves, but better counsels prevailed. It was sent to the Caliph Umar, the father-in-law of the Prophet, who received it in Medina and divided it among his own captains. Less than a hundred years after Chosroes had built the palace on the Tigris, it was converted into a Friday mosque. The Arabs conquered Persia, and the last Sassanian king died at the hands of one of his own countrymen at Merv.

Today the ruined palace still possesses a remote majesty, the great archway like an enormous brown eye peering eternally across the Mesopotamian deserts.

In the course of time the Arab invaders were absorbed by the Persians, whose art and culture remained virtually intact. They built mosques of surpassing magnificence and beauty, with designs derived from Achaemenian and Sassanian ideas, and they never lost their awareness of peculiarly Persian forms: the splendor of the springing line, and the rich colors of the Persian land. Changing and yet unchanging, the ancient Persian traditions were maintained against all their conquerors.

THE FIRST FRUITS

The Elegance of the Cretans

All the ancient chroniclers were agreed that the island of Crete was especially well favored. There were wide and fertile plains, many winding streams, vines, olives, and figs in abundance, and great stands of forest timber. Fish, octopus, and mollusks abounded off the coast. Deer and the ibex wandered in the hills, and ducks and geese were plentiful in the marshlands. Flocks of sheep and herds of horned cattle grazed in the pastures. The ancient Greeks, who lived in a more barren land, always regarded the Cretans with envy and also with a feeling of reverence. They remembered that for many hundreds of years before the Dorian invasions there had been great emperors ruling from Crete, and their power and influence was felt over the eastern Mediterranean. In the age of Theseus, the Athenians paid tribute to a mysterious emperor in Knossos who demanded an annual gift of seven youths and seven maidens. When they reached Crete, they were devoured by the Minotaur, half man and half bull. The Greeks remembered too that Zeus himself was born in a cave high in the Cretan mountains. Everything about the island seemed to them beautiful, desirable, and strangely menacing.

Until the beginning of this century the arts of ancient Crete were unknown, the Minotaur was an inexplicable figure, and the historians knew only the barest outlines of Minoan civilization. Today, thanks to the patient work of archaeologists in some thirty sites on the island, we are beginning to know a people living in the second millennium B.C. more intimately than we know many people living today. Their astonishing paintings speak to us directly; their palaces, their delicate jewelry, their ivories, their vases, their clay votive offerings all have a bewildering modernity. The visitor to the museum at Heraklion, where most of the treasures of Minoan Crete are preserved, goes away with the feeling that the ancient Cretans saw more vividly and keenly than any other people of their time. For a brief space they achieved an art remarkable for its quiet intensity and directness of vision, its nobility and unhampered freedom of expression; and then, very suddenly, the art perished. We see them at work and play on a brightly lit stage, and then the curtain is rung down. Plague, earthquake, tidal wave, invasion—all these have been suggested to explain the abrupt ending of Minoan civilization, which appears to have perished in a single tragic day.

When Sir Arthur Evans began digging at Knossos, a mound of olive trees lying a few miles inland from the seaport of Heraklion, he had no idea that he would spend the rest of his long life working on the same site, or that most of his considerable fortune would be exhausted in these excavations. His interests were mainly literary: he had hoped to discover the language of the ancient Cretans, for he had been collecting the delicately engraved seal stones, which sometimes showed recognizable letters in an unknown language. He learned to know Minoan civilization well, but as long as he lived he never learned what language they spoke, although he amassed a huge quantity of their writings. Ironically the language was deciphered a few years after Evans' death by a young architect, Michael Ventris.

Evans chose well, for once the olive trees were uprooted, Knossos began to come to life almost immediately. There was only a light covering of earth. Among the first frescoes to come to light in the great hallway of the palace was the noble portrait of a vase bearer, a youth of great beauty, naked except for a ceremonial orange-colored loincloth patterned in quatrefoils, with a silver ornament at his ear, silvers rings on the arms and neck. Blue, white, and red cloud bands trail above his head to indicate that he is in the open air. His body is painted a deep reddish-brown, following the precedent of Egyptian portraits, and the waist with its silver belt is characteristically slender. He holds his head erect, showing a profile of almost classical beauty, the nose very straight, the dark hair clustered with curls, only the lips are somewhat full. With one hand he grasps the bottom of the tall conical vase, with the other he grasps the green curving handle. Such youths with narrow waists had been seen already. They were carved on seals, less than an inch in height, the agile bodies rendered to good effect, but the faces were unrecognizable. Now for the first time the true portrait of a Minoan youth emerged from his native soil, life-size, and recognizably belonging to a race of conquerors. As the years passed, more and more portraits emerged, until it seemed possible to re-create all the people, from the kings to the lowliest servant, who had once inhabited the palace.

In due course there emerged a painted stucco relief, much damaged, but still retaining its original colors, of another and even more regal youth. His crown, his chest, his right arm bent so that his clenched fist rested over his heart, part of his left arm, and a considerable portion of his left leg survived. In addition there was a brilliantly colored butterfly hovering beside him, and some traces of waist-high irises. He wore a necklace of pink lilies, his dark hair rippled over his shoulders, and there were bright blue and red bracelets at his wrists. The crown, though fashioned in the shape of springing lilies, suggested metalwork painted over, and from it there rose rainbow-colored plumes. Evans called him a "priest-king," and believed he was Minos, the legendary ruler of the Minoan empire.

The "priest-king" was, of course, an even more dazzling discovery than the youth with a vase. If the youth showed an astonishing degree of sophistication in the elegance and beauty of his bearing, the "priest-king," equally elegant, seemed to suggest the utmost panoply of power. Naked, except for a small sheath-shaped loincloth, of which traces could be seen on the firmly rounded buttocks, he was nevertheless appareled in majesty, and that extraordinary crown of blue and white lilies with the rainbow-colored plumes hinted at a delight in decoration wholly at variance with the practice of the pharaohs. Here was the first crowned head known to have lived on European soil, and it was strange and delightful that he should wear a crown of lilies.

As Evans dug deeper, and more treasures were discovered in

outlying areas, it became evident that a hitherto unknown and un-recorded art was coming to light, remarkable for its grace and color, its sense of movement and formidable power. A people unknown to written history, remembered only because the Greeks recorded some strange legends about them, they began to emerge as a race charged with vitality, possessing a highly developed civilization, and Evans found himself sometimes wondering whether any race had ever lived in such quiet dignity. They gave the impression of a people wholly at peace with themselves. They had no great guardian gods to terrify an awe-stricken populace. They were warriors—for swords were found in their graves—but they never wore armor. They were colonizers, who established outposts on the coasts of Asia Minor and on the shores of the western Mediterranean, but they never seem to have regarded themselves as conquerors, for they never showed any interest in depicting hordes of prisoners. They built three- and four-story houses provided with light wells and water towers, and they possessed in Knossos a drainage system superior to anything known in Europe until the middle years of the reign of Queen Victoria. The men were depicted naked or with em-broidered and patterned loincloths, the women wore great flounced many-colored skirts and gaily decorated sleeves, and their breasts were bare. They worshiped at altars filled with flowering shrubs, and their athletes, both girls and youths, fought with bulls not in the Spanish manner, but in a fashion which was altogether their own, for the aim was not to kill the bull but to grasp the bull's horns and swing lightly over its back. Their dancing floors were fields of lilies, and their hymns were sung to the goddess of the wilderness, whose emblems were the serpents she held in her out-stretched hands. There were no temples, no fortifications, no blood sacrifices except on the rare occasions when a bull might be sacri-ficed to the memory of a dead hero. Again and again the archaeolo-gists came upon three objects which at once delighted and puzzled them, for their exact significance could not be determined: they found double axes sometimes ten feet high, and sometimes they were delicately worked in gold and only an inch high; they were evidently symbols of sovereignty, but it was not clear whether they had a religious significance. Then there were the horns of consecration carved out of stone, which sometimes appeared on altars, and these might be three feet high or two inches high. Often the horns and the double axes were found together. Finally they found clay tablets, cigar-shaped or in the shape of palm leaves, with writing scratched into them before they were baked. Evans spent many years puzzling over them, determined to wrest their secrets. When they were finally deciphered by Ventris, they proved to be little more than tallies describing the objects kept in storerooms or the number of people engaged in various occupations. They were singularly uninformative. The Minoans spoke louder in their paintings than in words.

The frescoes and painted reliefs were always fragmentary, but there was usually enough to permit a good artist to fill out the missing spaces. Just in front of the vase bearer a square inch of colored fresco survived, showing a portion of an armband at exactly the same level as the armband of the vase bearer. This was enough to suggest a procession of vase bearers, and accordingly the artist was able to reconstruct the entire figure of the second bearer, five feet eight inches high, from a square inch of color. It was a daring method, but surprisingly successful.

One of the strangest and most delightful discoveries occurred in the "throne room," where a high-backed gypsum chair was found standing against a wall painted with a frieze of griffins. The chair was small and unpretentious, unpainted, remarkable only because no other chair was found at Knossos and because the back was carved in a wavelike pattern. The griffins were far more remarkable, for they looked like creatures which had strayed out of fairyland. Large portions of the frieze remained, and there was no question of reconstructing them from a few square inches of paint. They had the heads of eagles, the bodies of lions, the tails of serpents, and they were not in the least ferocious. They were the heraldic guardians of the gypsum "throne," brilliantly colored and perfectly at ease as they lay down among the pale blue reeds against a Venetian red sky. The tails were blue, the bodies tawny, the eagles' beaks were orange, and from the eagles' heads rose rainbow-colored crests not unlike the crested crown of the "priest-king." But if this soaring crest was surprising, still more surprising were the exuberant green whorls, blue wedge shapes, and red petals on the griffin's breast. Where the griffin's heart would be, there was a blue flower, and round its neck, hanging very low, was a necklace of small blue lilies. The haunches and the shadowed undersides were indicated with cross-hatching; it was the first known example of shading in the history of art.

Naturalism and the purest fantasy were combined in this superb griffin which raises its head so proudly, as though perfectly aware of its beauty. Nothing like it had ever been seen before, for although the Egyptians rendered griffins with the heads of hawks and the bodies of lions, and gave them wings, they were always represented as creatures of ferocious power; but this griffin was calm and peaceful, at ease among flowering reeds. It is as though the artist had told himself: "I shall depict the plenitude of power, not the power that exalts itself and strives for domination, but the power that has no need to exalt itself or to strive for any domination whatsoever. I shall depict a power which is so sure of itself that it has no need to exert itself."

That ease, that calm appear in all the surviving frescoes. There are no battles between men and gods, no giants, no terrifying monsters. Most of the frescoes depict the men and women of the court, or animals at play, or flower gardens. In 1903, three years after the excavations had begun, Evans discovered in the great "sanctuary hall" of the palace a fresco depicting priestesses sitting face to face on stools and ritually passing to each other a sacred goblet. Among them was an elegant young woman seen in profile with an enormous eye, neatly curled dark hair, bright red lips, and a small arrogantly tilted nose. When the workmen saw her, they christened her "la Parisienne," for she seemed to belong to the present day, and her elegance and impertinence seemed more appropriate to Paris than to Knossos. Although the artist has deliberately exaggerated the size of her eyes and the red paint has been spread altogether too richly over her lips, the effect is not one of caricature but of sophisticated art. Quite suddenly, across the centuries, there appears a pert and gracious young woman quivering with vitality and the desire to please. The painting can be dated about 1500 B.C.

Although many Minoan portraits survive in those fragmentary frescoes, "la Parisienne" holds pride of place as a deliberate attempt to portray a full and rounded character. We know this young woman well. There is something generalized about the portrait of the vase-bearer, who is scarcely more than the silhouette of an idealized youth, the epitome of all the handsome youths of Crete. There is nothing generalized in "la Parisienne," who is a person in her own right.

Here and there, in different areas of the palace, Evans came upon frescoes all demonstrating to a pervading gaiety and a vivid delight in people, flowers, animals, and birds. Dolphins cavort in peaceful seas, octopuses spread their elegant tentacles around vases, pheasants emerge from the high grasses, and monkeys wander through fields of saffron flowers. Always the gentleness and quietness, the gaiety, the ardent celebration of life.

In Minoan art all the fragments fit together like a mosaic. A lovely baby lion, sleeping with his muzzle resting on his forepaws, is of a piece with the Harvester Vase with its procession of happy farmers celebrating a successful harvest, some marching serenely, others bawling at the top of their lungs, and one so drunk that he falls and clasps the thighs of the man in front, and this too is of a piece with the wonderful painted coffin of Hagia Triada which shows in brilliant colors the offerings paid calmly to a dead hero.

This limestone coffin, or sarcophagus, is an extraordinary work by any standards, but what gives it compelling power is the sense of immediacy which enables us to enter the ceremony and partake of the rituals attending the death of an ancient hero. All four sides are painted in fresh madders, rose pinks, delicate blues, scarlet, and tawny orange. Within a pattern of blue and white suns wheeling across the heavens, each sun with its little kernel of red flame, we see the sacrifices and offerings to the dead hero as he emerges from his tomb. A bull is roped to an altar with brilliant red scarves; its throat has been cut and the blood spurts into a basin, while a flautist plays on a double flute and two calves resting below the altar watch imperturbably. There follows a bloodless sacrifice, as a priestess places a basket of fruit and a jug of wine on an altar set before an immense double ax of hammered

One side of the Hagia Triada Sarcophagus

bronze, and beyond this altar lies another and greater altar crowned
with the horns of consecration and a flowering tree. A priestess in
a blue and red gown blesses the slaughtered bull, and we observe
without surprise that she wears the same crown of lilies as the
"priest-king," but this time it is made of hammered gold.

On the other side of the coffin we watch the three priests
wearing sheepskin skirts bringing gifts to the dead hero—two
brindled calves and a boat which has evidently been carved out
of an elephant's tusk. These priests have an Egyptian air about
them, for such tribute bearers to the dead are often seen on the wall
paintings of Egyptian tombs. But these are no ordinary priests,
for they come out of the darkness, out of the square of blue-painted
background which separates them from the brightness falling on

the dead hero. In this stately fashion they march solemnly to a stepped altar and a flowering tree; beyond the tree stands the dead hero.

Elsewhere we see the crowned priestess again as she bears the basin filled with the bull's blood in the direction of a blue urn standing between two more double axes of hammered bronze. Sacred birds perch on the double axes, and a musician plucks the strings of a lyre with a plectrum. Everywhere there is solemnity, but there is also a quiet joy in the expectation of deliverance from death. While the priests betray an Egyptian influence, the women are wholly European, robust, high-breasted, swinging their heavy skirts. The sun of Europe shines on the scene, and we are far from the East.

The calm exuberance of Cretan art suggests a people unfailingly at peace with themselves. Unlike the Egyptians, who insisted too emphatically on the redeeming presence of the gods, they are a people perfectly content to live out their lives with the barest minimum of ceremonial worship and in no fear of death. The Harvester Vase found at Hagia Triada shows twenty-seven men on their way to harvest olives or grain. They are led by an old, long-haired man in a voluminous cape, evidently the owner of the farm, while among them someone shakes a sistrum and four men are singing to the rhythm of the sistrum. The man holding the sistrum is singing so lustily that he is in danger of bursting his lungs. The entire procession, as it revolves around that small black steatite vase, has a warmth and humanity which lift it out of its time and bring it into the present. Once the vase was covered with gold leaf, thus more effectively suggesting the flesh colors of those nearly naked harvesters.

The Harvester Vase is a masterpiece of compression, for it is less than five inches in diameter and yet conveys a long procession in which all the participants have recognizable features. With unerring skill, the artist conveys a sense of lively movement, the glint of rippling muscles, the joys of harvesting. The sculptor uses broad impressionistic strokes to suggest the tempo of the procession: the harvesters are running vigorously. Not even on the Egyptian tomb friezes do we find such an affirmation of purely human vigor. Here for the first time we see the ordinary farm laborers as they were, lusty and venturesome and totally unself-conscious, and we are far removed from the motionless painted figures of the princes of the Minoan court, splendid in their elaborate elegance, quivering with self-consciousness.

Nevertheless the Harvester Vase is the product of court artists, like all the other artifacts found at Hagia Triada, where the great officers of state had their villas overlooking the Mediterranean. Hagia Triada is only a few miles from Phaestos, the great Minoan palace dominating the majestic plain of Messara. Phaestos appears to have been the southern capital of the Minoan empire, a huge and thriving citadel built on a scale commensurate with its position dominating all the surrounding plain, in sight of the sea. Evans found a small stairway at Knossos, and called it the Great Stairway though it was only about five feet wide. There is a processional stairway at Phaestos forty feet wide, and no one has ever troubled to give it a name.

The power and majesty of the Minoan empire can be felt at Phaestos. There is spaciousness and a sense of abundance; it has none of the triviality of Knossos, which overlooks a much smaller valley. Yet strangely very few artifacts have been found in the southern capital. There are no paintings of youthful priest-kings in their finery and no royal thrones have been found. The Phaestos disk, inscribed with delicate characters in an unknown language, each character being separately stamped on the clay before it was fired, remains one of the few important discoveries made on the site. Only the broken walls testify to the greatness of the citadel, which once ruled all the seas of the eastern Mediterranean.

The Minoan empire came to an end about 1400 B.C. Exactly how it came to an end, whether by plague or by earthquake or by the explosion of the volcano of Santorini or by invasion, is a question which scholars have endlessly debated without coming to any satisfactory conclusion. We know now that empires die quickly: in the space of a few years the British and French empires perished, offering almost no resistance to the aroused colonies. Something very similar may have happened in Minoan Crete. Quite suddenly the colonies may have rebelled and a naval battle may have put an end to Minoan dominion of the seas. All we know is that the palaces were fired and a thousand years later men had almost forgotten that they ever existed.

Minoan art did not perish. In some way still unknown it reached the mainland of Greece and deeply influenced the sculptors and metalsmiths attached to the court of Mycenae. The shaft graves discovered by Heinrich Schliemann were filled with works that betrayed their Minoan origins. It was not only that inlaid swords and jewels found in the graves resembled those of Minoan Crete, but the cult objects also seemed to have come from Crete, and the Mycenaeans worshiped the Cretan gods. At Mycenae, too, there have been found inscriptions in the same language which was spoken at Knossos. It is certain that the palace at Knossos existed long before the palace at Mycenae, and it would appear that Mycenae was one of the colonies that rebelled.

Yet the art of Mycenae differs in some important respects from the art of the Minoans. There was an emphasis on power and on death totally lacking in Minoan Crete, which was so powerful that it felt no need to advertise its power. The shaft graves at Mycenae suggest an overwhelming obsession with mortality. The dead kings were laid out in all their royal panoply, in robes studded with gold and jeweled ornaments, thin golden masks on their faces, their weapons and their most valuable possessions beside them. Like the Egyptians they believed in or hoped for a resurrection, and in all this they were unlike the Minoans, who lived for the present and paid scant tribute to the deathly kingdoms. No doubt those golden masks derived ultimately from Egypt, where the embalmed pharaohs were provided with elaborate masks of wrought gold, but the Mycenaean goldsmiths possessed none of the expertise of the Egyptians and did not aim for naturalism, with the result that the masks found by Schliemann in the grave shafts have a strange abstract beauty as though they were not so much masks of the dead as of death itself. The artist has not attempted a portrait of the dead man; the eyes are slit circles, the nose is a hollow wedge, the mustache and the shape of the mouth are sketched in with a sharp instrument, and the workmanship is of the most elementary kind, but the total effect is breathtaking. The goldsmith has produced a

simple statement on the nature of death and the very simplicity of
the method makes it completely convincing. Nothing comparable
with these masks has been found anywhere in the Near East. For
the first time we are presented with the abstract forms of death.

Into the forms derived from Crete the Mycenaeans poured a
new energy. They were warriors in league with warriors, fighting
across the narrow valleys of southern Greece, armed with long
swords, short daggers, and man-high shields, leaving evidence of
their conquests in all the cities they occupied and plundered. "Mycenae, rich in gold," said Homer, but the gold came from conquest.
The arts of Mycenae flourished because the royal treasuries were
filled with gold.

Gold cups and beakers of exquisite shape were found in the
shaft graves. They are never slender or vase-shaped like the gold
cup of Queen Shub-Ad, but well-rounded and capacious, as befitted a people who drank heavily. Even when they are quite small,
these cups give an impression of monumentality. Sometimes they
are decorated with the heads of greyhounds or falcons with spread
wings, but more often they are unornamented. Two gold cups found
at Vaphio in Laconia, dating from about 1500 B.C., show scenes
from bull hunting embossed on the outer surface. On one we see
a bull captured and tethered with the help of a decoy cow, on the
other we see a bull caught in a net after it has charged a hunter
and a huntress, both dressed in Cretan costume, wearing little more
than heavy belts round their narrow waists. One lies sprawling on
the ground, quivering in agony; the other, caught in the bull's horns,
spins fiercely in the air. The theme is Minoan, the goldsmith may
have been Cretan, but the energy of the composition derives from
Mycenae. This gold cup has an explosive violence. The artist comes
to the scene freshly, and he records accurately the outflung arms
of the hunter and the coiling hair of the huntress as she is flung
into the air.

For perhaps five hundred years the barbaric Mycenaean civilization dominated the mainland of Greece. Then, about 1100 B.C.,
the fair-haired Dorians descended from the north, settling finally in
the Peloponnese, but not before they had created havoc in all the
Mycenaean kingdoms. The plunderers were plundered, and Greece

became a desert. Out of that desert there gradually arose the civilization we associate with classical Athens, where once there had
been a Mycenaean settlement.

There was no complete break in traditions: even in classical
Athens we can observe the influence of ancient Mycenae and the
still more ancient influence of the artists of Knossos. The Minoans
loved the gay curling S line, introducing it everywhere, in flowers
and tendrils and waves and wheeling stars, and this became in time
the characteristic Greek meander. The same bulls we see on the
Vaphio cup are seen again on the Parthenon frieze. It was as though
the Athenians combined the gaiety of the Minoans and the harsh
energy of the Mycenaeans, and out of that conflict produced their
formidable empire, their philosophy, and their art.

The Experience of the Greeks

There are few moments in the history of art which can be said to be completely revolutionary. The great discoveries are made slowly, over many years, by many artists standing on one another's shoulders. There is nearly always a gradual development, the senses following the known ways and then thrusting deeper and deeper into unknown territory, into the dark and hitherto unimagined landscape where new forms, new methods of representation, reveal themselves, at first shadowy and diffuse, and then with increasing clarity and sharp outlines, a multitude of artists asking themselves what the new forms mean, examining them as though they were in the depths of a mine, and scarcely understanding them until they are brought into the light of day, and even then, such is the strangeness of these discoveries, many years pass before they become the accepted conventions of an age. So an ancient miner, tunneling through a mountain, might discover a seam of gold, and then a nest of emeralds, and then a layer of coal, and would not know what to do with them. It is a familiar process which accompanies all explorations: the blind thrust into the dark, followed by the unveiling of new forms, new apparitions, new shapes of life, which in turn give new meaning to life as it is lived on earth.

We see this process at work about 540 B.C. in Greece, when there appears to be a phenomenal change in the direction of art. Quite suddenly, and for the first time, we see marble statues which give the appearance of being alive, the lungs filled with air, the skins gleaming, the muscles quivering, the human body rejoicing in its youthful strength. The traditional hieratic attitude is absent; the statue is not enclosed in stillness, but seems about to move and speak; almost we hear the footfalls. Nothing quite like this had appeared before. It is as though man had discovered the fullness of life, and the sculptor had set about carving the shape of a man in his human glory. A new and unforeseen element has been introduced: the living flesh.

In 1936 there was discovered in Anavyssos in southern Attica the statue of a youth, which is now among the treasures of the National Museum in Athens. He stands six feet high, but gives the impression of being larger than life. One leg is only a few inches in front of the other, but he seems to be striding boldly and powerfully across a landscape in which he is sovereign. His hair is curled over his forehead, and falls to his shoulders in closely knit braids; the faintest of archaic smiles plays on his lips. He has a firm chin, a broad chest, powerfully muscled arms and thighs. We know his name and how he died, for there is an inscription carved on the pedestal:

Stand and mourn at the tomb of the dead Kroisos,
Whom furious Ares snatched from the field of battle.

There is nothing in the inscription to suggest that this is an actual portrait of the dead warrior, though it may have borne a cursory likeness to him. The statue is a memorial figure, and fulfilled the same purpose as a statue of Christ or of an angel in a Christian cemetery, for this was his tomb set on the battlefield where he fell; and while the sculptor has presented the portrait of a man in the magnificence of his youth, warm-blooded and rich with color—for the eyes and hair were painted, as we know from the traces of paint still remaining, and no doubt the whole body was painted—this is more than a youth and more than a man. It is in fact the portrait of a god as he majestically surveys his empire, serene in life and in death, which he has conquered by his gift of divinity. If he has any name, it is Apollo.

With this statue the abstract hieratic element which had been present in Greek art from the beginning finally comes to an end. At some period about 540 B.C. the sculptors of Attica turned away from the contemplation of mythologies and portrayed the gods in the likeness of men, while giving them more splendor and radiance than men have ever possessed. The youthful Apollo of Anavyssos, standing on the hillside, drenched in the Attic sunlight which dramatically emphasized the exquisite shaping of curls and braids, and the broad curving planes of his torso and limbs, has finally torn himself free from the stiffness of archaic art. He belongs not to the temple or to the museum, but to the open air.

The process of bringing him to birth was a long and complex one; a multitude of subtleties is concealed in his powerful simplicity. The stance, the braids, the wide-eyed gaze, the very thrust of the head, and the squared shoulders derive from Egypt, and in particular from the very early days of Egyptian sculpture. There are portraits of Mycerinus dating from 2525 B.C. which have exactly that stance, with the fists clenched in exactly the same way, and indeed those statues of Mycerinus carved out of slate are very close in composition and feeling to the statue from Anavyssos carved out of Parian marble. What is lacking in the Egyptian statue is the sense of the swirling air, of untrammeled freedom of movement, and of the living breath. If you cut Mycerinus, you will find slate. If you cut the Apollo of Anavyssos, you will almost certainly find blood.

But if the Anavyssos statue derives across twenty centuries from an Egyptian original, he derives also from sources closer to the mainland of Greece. The purity of outline of the Cycladic statues, the naturalism and freedom of the reliefs of Knossos, and the energy of Mycenaean art are implicit in that heroic figure, but what chiefly appears to have brought him into being was the new spirit of inquiry introduced by the Ionian Greeks centering in the city of Miletus. Rejecting all traditions, they examined the world with fresh eyes, their inquiries culminating in the triumphant discovery that "man is the measure of all things." The philosophers had tunneled through the mine and discovered the most dangerous and useful of all the jewels embedded in it.

This was new, and the far-reaching implications were soon being studied by philosophers all over Greece. The gods were seen in a new light, no longer creatures of terrible aspect. In the past when the Greeks portrayed the gods, they gave them power, authority, and dignity in a conventionally stylized form. Apollo might be represented as a column of bronze with head, hands, and feet attached, or Athena would be represented by a rudely carved xoanon of olive wood, which only hinted at her features, or Demeter would be represented as a monster with a horse's head, as she was in Phigalia. Stones, rocks, or meteorites would represent the presence of a god. The strangeness, elusiveness, and violence of the gods were emphasized, and their remoteness was an article of faith. To represent them as men and women demanded an attitude to life which permitted men and women to partake of divinity, to be very nearly gods. People were no longer slaves of incomprehensible forces, but sharers in a divine communion.

In this way, at first hesitantly and then with astonishing ease and mastery the Greeks entered their heroic age of sculpture and painting, when everything they touched seemed to be infused with nobility and divine grace. The most important collection of these sculptures is to be found in the small Acropolis Museum, which contains among other treasures the fourteen smiling goddesses discovered by Panagiotis Kavvadias on January 25, 1886, a red-letter day in the history of Greek archaeology, for this was quite simply the greatest single discovery of ancient Greek sculptures ever made.

These smiling goddesses, who once stood between the columns of the Parthenon—not the present Parthenon but the one built in the sixth century B.C. and later destroyed by the Persians—carry themselves with grace and refinement. Nearly all of them wear richly embroidered mantles, and on some of them there are rich traces of polychrome. One, known as the Peplos Kore, has flowing braids of red hair falling over her breast, and her red lips are formed into the most enchanting half-smile. The sculptor Phaidimos is believed to have been responsible for this statue, and he almost certainly carved the figure known as the Rampin Horseman, a youth with intricately curled hair who rides on horseback in naked magnificence. The same style can be detected in a well-known statue of a bearded man with a calf flung over his shoulders. Smooth powerful planes, clarity, and simplification are the marks of this style; the marble sings, the taut flesh is alert, and there is an intense life flowing through the marble veins. Phaidimos was perhaps the first of the great Attic sculptors.

A cup Painted by Euphronios Showing a Young Horseman Wearing a Chlamys

About the same time these sculptures were being made, the vase painters began to experiment in a new technique. For generations there had been black-figured vases with the designs painted almost in silhouette, the dark gods and goddesses parading across the rounded surfaces. These paintings had lightness and elegance, but they did not have the colors of life. Around 530 B.C. the figures were left in the color of the fired clay, and the background was filled in with a black glaze. Now they stood out sharply in deep orange red, seeming to project forward where previously they tended to recede, and this sudden alteration in technique represented a triumphant advance in the power to suggest three dimensions. Weight could now be given to the flesh, and gestures could be suggested with greater subtlety now that the bodies were given the colors of life from the orange-red clay. The painters reveled in the new technique, which permitted great strength and the utmost delicacy, together with an immense variety of forms. It was as though a lens had opened wide and granted them a vision of the whole of life, not only of the dark gods revolving around the vases.

A new and hitherto unknown range of expression led them to paint with extraordinary vitality. The marketplace, the bedroom, drunken riots, dancing girls, soldiers leaving for battle, soldiers returning on their shields, the ways of courtesans and young lovers, all these were painted on vases in such a way that the observer is brought intimately into their presence. The artists painted with a clear-cut mastery, and they were not in the least oppressed by the difficulties of the task. They cheerfully vied with one another and offered friendly challenges to one another. "Euphronius could never do this," wrote Euthymides on a red-figured amphora showing drunken revelers.

Greek wall painting emerged out of vase painting, and we hear of large frescoes adorning the walls of temples and houses, and of painted scenery set up on the Greek stage. Agatharchus of Samos was the first to depict scenery in perspective, and the plays of Aeschylus were provided with backdrops, which gave the illusion of Persian palaces or the vast ranges of the Caucasus. Only a few fragments of Greek wall painting survive. According to Pliny, the Greek painters adopted the convention of using only the same colors employed in vase painting, and their paintings were limited to the colors black, white, yellow, and orange. The mosaic known as *The Battle of Alexander*, found in the House of the Faun in Pompeii and evidently copied from a late Hellenistic painting, does in fact use only these four colors, but with so many subtle modifications that it suggests the entire spectrum. Although the convention appears to have been largely maintained, especially in formal compositions, there must have been many exceptions, for neither the sky nor trees could be reproduced with that limited palette. The names of many Greek painters have survived, and we have ample descriptions of their wall paintings. But while the descriptions tell us how the figures were arranged on the walls, they tell us nothing about the quality of the paintings. Of Apollodorus, Agatharchus, Zeuxis, Apelles, and all the rest, we have only literary accounts and whatever information we can extract from surviving Roman paintings.

With the Greek victory at Plataea in 479 B.C., and the end of the long war against the Persians, there occurred an inevitable change. A heroic art was needed by a people conscious of their heroism. The statues of the gods, especially those held responsible for the victory, were carved with great power and authority. Poseidon, the god of the sea, was clearly implicated in the victory, and the heroic bronze statue found in the sea off Cape Artemision and now in the National Museum in Athens celebrated the triumph of Greek arms and the liberation of the Greek spirit. No more dramatic representation of human majesty has ever been conceived. Poseidon stands with his legs apart, one arm pointed toward the enemy, the other poised to hurl an invisible javelin; and there is about that naked bearded figure, so calm in his divine savagery, an authority surpassing any surviving statue of this time, or of any time. Poseidon is at once a man of transcendent beauty and a divinity with human features and a human body, and we shall not see his like again until Michelangelo carved his David for the Florentines.

Again and again the Greeks celebrated their triumph over the Persians, their coming to full maturity, as though they were perfectly conscious that they had changed the course of history. The heroic theme reappears throughout the second quarter of the fifth century B.C. It is present in the statue of the Omphalos Apollo, which survives in a Roman copy in Athens, and in the statue of the tyrannicide Aristogeiton, which survives in a Roman copy in Naples, and most of all it is present in the Charioteer at Delphi and in the Apollo on the west pediment of the Temple of Zeus at Olympia, who commands silence and obedience with his outstretched arm. In the posture of Apollo there is far more than a commanding presence; nor was it necessary that Apollo should stretch out his arm or crook a finger, for he asserted his divinity, and therefore his power, simply by being there. The towering chryselephantine image of Zeus designed by Phidias at Olympia did not command. He sat on his throne and calmly ordered the universe; and it was a tribute to the genius of Phidias that he could portray a Zeus so imperious and so noble that he carried immediate conviction. In time his portrayal of Zeus would influence the portrayal of Christ.

Divine Maiden, about 510 B.C.
ACROPOLIS MUSEUM, ATHENS. MELETZIS.

Boy Carrying Water Jar, from north frieze of the Parthenon, about 440 B.C.
MELETZIS.

Opposite, Apollo,
from west pediment of the Temple of Zeus
at Olympia, about 460 B.C.
MELETZIS.

Poseidon or Zeus, found in the sea off Cape Artemision, about 460 B.C.
MELETZIS.

Victory of Samothrace, about 200 B.C.

Trajan Sacrificing to Apollo,
relief medallion from the Arch of Constantine in Rome, about A.D. 125.

Tutelary Goddess of Vienne.
LYONS MUSEUM. J. CAMPONOGARA.

Zeus, Apollo, and the Charioteer are all unmoving, silent figures. The power wells out of them; they possess the imperturbability of the gods in their most commanding aspect; and not one of them could have been fashioned without the victory over the Persians. But the mark of a heroic age is its delight in action, and in the Parthenon in Athens Phidias would show the gods and the people of Athens in delighted awareness of their activity.

When about the year 452 B.C. Pericles began to prepare the rebuilding of the temples on the Acropolis destroyed by the Persians, he had at his disposal the entire treasury of the Confederacy of Delos, which had been removed for safekeeping to Athens, and the services of a people willing and determined to build a monument for their own age and all the ages to come. Quite deliberately and self-consciously he set about the creation of temples so beautiful that they would bring eternal renown to Athens. No expense would be spared, no art would be left untouched, no science would be permitted to avoid paying tribute to these gleaming temples which seafarers would see long before they set foot on Attica. The creative activity of a whole people would be bent to a single aim—the splendor on the Acropolis.

In this mood the Athenians set about the creation of the single masterpiece which towers over all their other masterpieces. The Parthenon, meaning "the house of the Virgin," would dominate the Acropolis, but there would be smaller temples clustering around it to reinforce its beauty. Treasuries, shrines, museums, guardrooms, a vast gateway, statues, and altars would all have their place on that crowded rock, reflecting in their orderly and complex arrangement the order and complexity of the Athenian mind. Today we see the Acropolis in its stark simplicity, but as the temples rose one by one in the fifth century B.C. there was an effect of magnificent confusion. A forest of marble rose on the bare, scalded rock.

At the beginning the general design was left to a very small group of men: Pericles himself, the architects Ictinus and Callicrates, and the sculptor Phidias, originally a painter. Ictinus and Callicrates appear to have limited themselves to the architectural framework, while Phidias was given charge of the ornamental detail, which included the huge sculptures of the pediment, the cult statue of Athena, and the reliefs. In time Phidias appears to have taken command of the entire project and to have stamped his own aesthetic sense on every part of it. There were, however, some ultimate decisions which were not and could not be made by him, for it is recorded that he originally planned to carve a colossal cult image of Athena in marble, but was outvoted by the Assembly, which insisted that the image be made of ivory and gold, as being more in keeping with the dignity of the goddess. When after lengthy preparations the work of building the Parthenon was begun in 447 B.C., Phidias was forty-one years old, and in the full possession of his genius. He was exactly the same age as Michelangelo when he completed the *Moses*.

In the spring of that year, when the first stones were laid, Athens took on the aspect of a city transformed into a workshop. Everyone, or nearly everyone, was pressed into service. Plutarch has left a picture of the sudden whirlwind of activity which descended on the city and the many skills and occupations involved in the making of the temples. He wrote:

> The materials were marble, bronze, ivory, gold, ebony and cypresswood, and the arts and trades which wrought and fashioned them included smiths, carpenters, masons, braziers, goldsmiths, painters, embroiderers and turners. The conveyance of them by sea involved merchants, sailors and ships' master, and by land cartwrights, cattle breeders, wagoners, ropemakers, flax spinners, leather cutters, paviors, iron founders, and miners. Every trade was, as it were, commanded by a general with the lower ranks arranged in an orderly fashion under him, these consisting of journeymen and laborers who acted as the instrument and body for the performance of the service. And because all these trades were represented, wealth was distributed among people of every class and condition.

In this way, working against time, with the artisans and sculptors continually at work, the Parthenon was built in the incredible space of nine years, although another six years passed before the last of the sculptures and friezes were lifted into place. The timing was fortunate, for in the following year the energies of the Athenians were needed for another purpose—the disastrous war against Sparta and her allies, known as the Peloponnesian War, had begun.

The Parthenon which the Athenians saw on the day when it was finally completed was strangely different from the Parthenon we know today. Today we see the ruined bones of the temple, which the Greeks saw fully fleshed, radiant with color. We see it reduced to its bare essentials, while the Greeks saw it exuberantly decorated in blue and scarlet and gold. They would not have understood our passion for a ruin, and they would have wondered at our pleasure in seeing the sky through the columns. We see it as a whole, dominating the crest of the Acropolis, but the unimpeded view was not possible in antiquity, when large areas of the Acropolis were cluttered with other buildings and the courts of the goddess were littered with statues. For us the Parthenon possesses a superb unity, crowning the Acropolis, while for the ancient Athenians it was merely the dominant structure in a whole complex of buildings, each of them playing a role in the worship of the goddess. The Parthenon was not even the most sacred building. The most sacred was the Erechtheion. On the site of that smaller temple the battle between Athena and Poseidon had taken place, and there people were shown the marks of the trident which Poseidon hurled to the ground, and there too was Athena's sacred olive tree, her serpents, and her image, the xoanon, carved in wood.

The ancient Athenians came to the Parthenon along the winding processional way which started in the Outer Cerameicus and proceeded through the Inner Cerameicus and across the Agora to the cliffs of the Acropolis. They did not come daily or weekly, as we go to church, but only on the high feast days of the goddess, and then always in orderly processions bearing gifts. This was the palace of the goddess, and no one entered except by her invitation. It was also the site of the well-guarded Athenian treasury, of many cult objects, and of the weapons captured in wars. Here Athena reigned, and from here she would sometimes descend to lead the Athenians in their battles.

When the ancient worshiper had climbed the steep pathway and passed through the Propylaea, the great carved gateway which served as the goddess's gatehouse, he would cross a small square to another gate let into the surrounding wall of the temple. It was only then, when he was already very close, that he saw the Parthenon in its entirety, in all its blinding colors. Everything gleamed. The honey-colored columns were washed lightly with saffron and wax; the huge figures in the pediment were brightly painted, the skin in flesh tones, the hair, eyebrows, and lips in deep red, and the background in blue. Probably Athena wore a golden gown on the pediment, as she did inside the temple. The metopes, the reliefs set into the entablature between the triglyphs, were in flesh tones against a red background, while the triglyphs were blue. The frieze of alternate metopes and triglyphs therefore formed a gaily colored fringe below the roof extending all the way round the temple. The continuous frieze which ran along the length of the temple and above the inner columns of the east and west porticoes was also brilliantly colored, with gleams of gold bridles and helmets and perhaps the golden robes of the gods. This must have been even more highly colored than the metopes, for the direct rays of the sun could never reach it. Only a diffused light from between the columns and from the marble pavements shone on it. The great processional frieze of the Panathenaea, on which the sculptors worked with prodigious energy over many years—for it extends to 525 feet and includes an enormous number of separate figures—was seen only in shadow, and then only by craning the neck and looking high up.

Yet this frieze was perhaps the single greatest achievement of the Athenian artists, the one work which preserves the character of an entire people in the years of their triumph. About half of the frieze depicts young horsemen and charioteers, the remaining half depicts the elders of the city, the maidens bearing baskets and sacrificial vessels, the sheep and heifers who will become sacrificial victims, musicians, magistrates, boys carrying jars of wine for the offerings, and the great gods themselves. The west frieze, probably the first to be carved, shows the young horsemen and their attendants as they prepare to take part in the procession; some fasten their boots, others groom their horses, or merely stand in attitudes of quiet expectancy or self-absorption. They are calmly self-conscious, aware of their beauty within the greater beauty of the procession. Then they move off slowly, the horses high-stepping to

music, until at a turning of the road corresponding to a corner of
the temple they are met by a marshal, who checks their impatience
with an upraised arm.

Some of these youths wear wreaths, some wear cloaks which
fall loosely from their shoulders, some wear crested helmets and
leather cuirasses over short tunics, and others are naked, rejoicing in their nakedness. They all appear to be between the ages
of thirteen and twenty-three, and they are all beardless. There
are no stirrups, no saddlecloths. No doubt the reins and bridles were
sometimes represented by painted bands, but here and there the
holes for the gilded bronze attachments are clearly visible. The effect is of a display of massive youthful energy, of controlled power,
and of great calm. This is the procession which moves from the
city up to the heights of Athena's palace in the early morning of
a day in late summer, the youths coming first, because they are
the chief guardians of the goddess and the pride of Athens.

Then come the chariots, those ceremonial two-wheeled chariots employed only on parades, for in classical Athens no one any
longer drove a chariot to war. Each chariot is drawn by four horses,
the driver wearing a long pleated ceremonial gown like the Charioteer of Delphi, and he is always accompanied by a soldier wearing
a crested helmet and carrying a shield, who amuses himself by
leaping on and off the chariot in full career. The pace quickens.
Here and there the chariots are bunched together, only to separate
again as the marshals, the traffic police, bring more order to the
cavalcade. Then abruptly the procession of charioteers comes to an
end, and we are in the presence of the city elders walking with
slow steps—they have already climbed the Acropolis and are now
preparing to make their offerings to the goddess. Then we come to
the magnificently proportioned *canephori*, bearers of the baskets
containing salt, meal, chaplets, and sacrificial knives which will
be used to cut the throats of the spotless white heifers and the
sheep. One of the *canephori* holds a torch, and another a scroll with
the words of the hymn sung to the goddess; and there is in their
stately march, the ease and splendor of their young bodies, and in
the rippling folds of their garments such a perfection of beauty that

they take pride of place over the youths and the exquisitely carved horses.

Finally over the east portico we see the gods and goddesses on their thrones. They are very grave, absorbed in their contemplations or in one another, for the high point of the ceremony has already taken place—the presentation of the *peplos*, the brilliantly colored robe woven each year afresh by the priestesses of the Acropolis—and they have little to do until the sacrifices outside the Parthenon are over. They, too, are perfectly at ease. Zeus sits on his ornamented throne beside Athena, who proudly displays the *peplos*. The twelve gods are not always identifiable, because the faces have sometimes been cut away We see Athena in conversation with Poseidon, while Asclepius, Apollo, and Artemis sit together in one of the best-preserved fragments. The god of war, Ares, lounges insolently beside Demeter, whose hand touches her chin in the ancient gesture of sorrow, as she mourns for the lost Persephone. It is a happy and beautiful confrontation: the god of destruction beside the goddess of all fruit and flowers. The style of these portraits of the gods is homogeneous: only one sculptor can have carved them, and that one must be Phidias, who also carved the great pediments.

We know the original appearance of a great part of the frieze from the careful drawings of Jacques Carrey of Troyes, an artist in the service of the Marquis de Nointel, French ambassador to Turkey, who visited Athens in 1674. Thirteen years later a Venetian army besieged the Turkish garrison on the Acropolis, and one of the besiegers' shells fell on the Turkish powder store. In the explosion the center of the Parthenon was destroyed, but the great pedimental figures, although weathered by time, still stood in place. Francesco Morosini, the captain-general of the Venetian forces, decided to remove the central figures of Athena and Poseidon together with the accompanying horses. Athena had lost her head and Poseidon his arms, but they are still monumental figures of elemental power, and in Morosini's eyes they were meant to decorate St. Mark's Square in Venice. Accordingly he erected a platform, brought up blocks and tackle, and prepared to carry them away. He miscalculated their weight—Athena and Poseidon were both eleven feet tall and each weighed four or five tons—and when the tackle collapsed, all the figures fell to the ground and were shattered. In the following year he sailed back to Venice, leaving the Turks in possession of the Acropolis. He had gained nothing and destroyed much. He had destroyed the most precious figures of the Parthenon, the first the worshipers saw as they climbed the long road to the Acropolis.

The shattered fragments of Athena, Poseidon, and the horses remained where they had fallen. Some fragments were buried in the neighborhood, to be unearthed many years later. So it happened that when Lord Elgin, the British ambassador to Constantinople, arrived in Athens in the early years of the nineteenth century and removed most of the surviving fragments of the east and west pediments to London, he discovered a portion of the torso of Athena buried on the Acropolis. This vigorous torso, with one beautiful and thrusting breast, now stands among the treasures of the Lord Elgin Room of the British Museum.

The west pediment represented an act of conquest. By the sacred olive tree Poseidon brandishes his trident and Athena waves her spear, while the other gods and goddesses look on in attitudes of terror, not knowing which way the battle will go. By a supreme grace Poseidon is given equal space with Athena. His powerful body is drawn back a little, to give a greater thrust to his trident or perhaps because he is in terror of Athena. What is happening at the middle of the pediment is an explosion of divine energy, and like waves this energy pours out toward the ends of the pediment, and then recoils toward the center. In fear and trembling some of the gods huddle together, while others lean forward in astonishment, dazzled by an event whose significance is beyond their understanding, and there is one who gazes calmly into space as though unaffected by the war in heaven. The west pediment presents a drama which occurs in a single moment of time, and it is this heroic drama of a battle between two gods which the worshiper first saw when he entered the sacred courtyard of the goddess. Here Athena proclaims herself triumphant, exercising all her powers, in command of Athens and its destinies.

The east portico was the principle entrance to the Parthenon, for it led to the cella containing the huge chryselephantine portrait of the goddess. But the east pediment was curiously lacking in drama, even though it showed the birth of Athena, fully clothed and fully armed, from the head of Zeus. Hephaestus with his ax—the ax that split open the skull of Zeus—was depicted, but he was shown holding the ax loosely in his hand. There is no action, no fierce confrontation of forces. Athena appears in all her glory, and it was evidently an easy birth; the day she was born was also that of her maturity. The surviving sculptures suggest that Zeus is presiding over a reception attended by the gods, who welcome the newborn goddess with no excessive demonstrations, quietly, as though they had long expected her. Zeus is enthroned on his majestic throne, Dionysus rests languidly on his panther skin, Demeter and Persephone sit together, while at the other end of the pediment a sumptuous Aphrodite reposes on the lap of her mother Dione. Victory crowns Athena. It is the moment of calm that follows a birth. The world is reborn in the presence of the new goddess, and the fresh winds ripple the luxurious garments.

What is especially remarkable about these pedimental sculptures is their monumentality, the richness of the carving, the superb elegance of the gestures, their heroic size and dignity. As we see them in the British Museum or in the small museum on the Acropolis where some fragments are preserved, they give an impression of astounding completeness. They were not made for an age, but for all ages; and they glow with health, although time has scrubbed their colors away. So much vitality flows through them, there is such a fierce rippling of their garments, and they hold themselves with such proud awareness that they seem to be intensely alive.

There are two horses' heads at the angles of the pediment. They are the horses of the sun and the moon, the sun's horse youthful and arrogant, rearing his arched neck, while the moon's horse sinks down in exhaustion and fatigue. But it is important to observe that these horses are not rendered naturalistically: the natural forms have been rethought and reshaped to present them in powerful well-defined masses, with gaping nostrils and bulging eyes; they are the huge elemental horses which gallop across the fields of heaven.

We do not know who carved these monumental figures, though

here and there we may detect the hand of a recognizable master. Phidias, famous for his figures of majestic calm, was almost certainly responsible for the east pediment. Myron, who was renowned for the tension he imparted to his figures, may well have carved the west pediment; his statue of Marsyas, a satyr leaping back in surprise when Athena presents herself to him, was remarkably similar in form and feeling to the statue of Poseidon on the pediment. Alcamenes, too, must have worked on the pediments; here and there in those richly robed figures of goddesses we can discern a stateliness which appears again on the east pediment at Olympia. The metopes are curiously uneven, some of them appearing to be the work of apprentices, but here too we can sometimes discern the hand of Alcamenes, with his studied grace, his gravity, his delight in the interplay of limbs.

From Plutarch we learn that Phidias was in supreme control, and it is therefore likely enough that he would reserve for himself the most superb and dominating compositions. He was a man of strong character, who could impose his vision on others, with the result that a single breath seems to pour through the whole. In the pediments a soaring boldness of conception; in the frieze a sustained delicacy of arrested movement; in the metopes the agonized struggle with the forces of darkness, that struggle which has come to an end with the emergence of Athena to power. All these give the impression of having been ordered and molded according to the commands of a single imagination; and just as a Michelangelo does not permit others to do his work for him, so Phidias seems to have insisted upon keeping control of the entire design, making all the preliminary designs, and himself executing as much of the sculpture as was humanly possible.

Only one figure was demonstrably by a single sculptor: this was the immense chryselephantine statue carved by Phidias which appeared within the temple. It was thirty-nine feet high, and therefore grazed the roof of the temple. Athena appears in majesty, with all her instruments of majesty about her. Her shield, her spear, her gown were all plated in gold. Gold, too, were her sandals and her helmet. The mysterious *aegis* rested against her breast, her divine serpent appeared from behind her shield, on which Phidias had carved the war between the Greeks and the Amazons, including a portrait of himself, bald and wrinkled, bringing a huge stone down on the head of a defenseless Amazon, and Pericles also appeared on that shield, which measured fifteen feet in diameter. The goddess stood in the half darkness of the cella, illuminated only by the light from the doorway and perhaps from sheets of alabaster let into the roof. She gleamed among shadows, too large and too awesome to be fully comprehended at a glance. There were a few minutes at dawn when she became a blaze of gold, for the temple faced the east and she caught the sunrise. Then for the rest of the day, and through the night, she would appear in a mysterious darkness lit by small lamps.

This statue of Athena has long since vanished. The gold plates were stolen by the tyrant Lachares, who also removed the gilded shields hung below the east and west pediments by Alexander the Great. The theft by Lachares occurred about 300 B.C., but the gold must have been replaced some time later, for when Pausanias visited Athens in the reign of Marcus Aurelius, during the second century A.D., Athena still glowed in majesty. The statue vanished altogether, apparently in a conflagration, about A.D. 450.

Eleven years after the completion of the Parthenon, in a lull during the Peloponnesian War, work was begun on the Erechtheion, the delicate and exquisitely beautiful palace on the northern shore of the rock. Like the Parthenon, it was built on the site of an earlier temple destroyed by the Persians. The sacred relics included not only the xoanon of Athena, the original cult image which had descended from the skies or at least from remote antiquity, but also the images of the former gods who once ruled over Attica. There were images of Erechtheus, the god-king with the serpent tail, and his brother Butes, both being the sons of Poseidon, and Cecrops and his daughter Pandrosus, which means "sprinkled with dew." These divinities, though superseded, retained a kind of vestigial sanctity and power, and Athena therefore kept them under her protection. Out of her mercy she provided them with a room in her royal dwelling.

The Erechtheion is the classical example of the "divine repository" which exists in nearly all religions. Here, in order of rank, the ancient gods were assembled, placated, worshiped, and provided with proper nourishment for their ghostly souls. Their own priests still attended them, and from time to time they received the honors due to their high estate. Athenians still swore by Cecrops and regarded him with affection, though he belonged to another dispensation. The Erechtheion may be compared with the Baptistery at Florence, where the Baptist is represented by a fountain, and the golden doors and the mosaic ceiling are largely concerned with the ancient past, before Christ entered the scene. The Caryatids, who support the roof of the Erechtheion, are also supporting the weight of the ancient past.

It is characteristic of the "divine repositories" that they should be small, ornate, and extremely complex buildings designed to answer many pressing needs. They were jewel boxes and treasure chests, relic chambers and archives. They were very small in comparison with the great temples, but they contained all the gods and were therefore granted respect and reverence out of all proportion to their size.

For the Greeks the ancient gods were very close, perhaps even closer than the gods of Olympus. Zeus, Hera, Demeter, Apollo, Dionysus, and Athena loomed large in their imaginations, but the gods of the woodland, the streams, and the pastures were more beloved. In the Greek colonies of Sicily and Asia Minor the finest coins represented the local heroes, or sea nymphs, or the angelic goddesses who presided over fountains; no coins ever made exceed in beauty the Sicilian coins honoring Arethusa, Terina, and Hyele. Apollo, wearing the features of local heroes, appears on innumerable coins stamped with his beauty, intelligence, and power.

When the Peloponnesian War came at last to an end with the ruin of Athens and Athenian power, a subtle change could be observed working on the minds of the Greek artists. While the gods continued to be depicted with monumental grace, they gradually assumed the graces of personality. Where previously they were motionless, seen as though in a flash of lightning while performing an act of benediction or summary judgment, now they were like people moved by conflicting impulses, restless in a restless world. The Apollo at Olympia performs a single act of majestic authority, standing in an attitude of inflexible determination. No doubts have ever assailed him, and nothing so inconsequential as personality has ever touched him. The gods of the fourth century no longer possess this commanding and monumental presence, and no longer inhabit the high heavens. They come down to earth.

The process, as we watch it emerging from the hands of the sculptors, was gradual, tentative, curiously sporadic. The greatest gods continued to be depicted in the manner of Phidias right down through the Roman period, but the lesser gods assumed the recognizable characteristics of humanity. So Hermes and Aphrodite, though remaining godlike in their beauty and their waywardness, take on the colors of the human race and reveal themselves as flesh and blood. The veils drop from Aphrodite; she shows herself in her nakedness, and her modest gestures suggest that she is vulnerable. Hermes gazes at his son with a peculiarly human tenderness. Even Athena, her eyes aglow with divine intelligence, the deadly *aegis* at her breast, appears in the wonderful statue recently discovered at Piraeus as nothing more than a high-born Athenian maiden who will soon step down from her throne, remove her helmet, and shake out her curls. She has played too long at being a goddess, and it is time she returned to the comfort of her home.

We see the process at work throughout the fourth century as the hieratic frontal view is gradually abandoned and the statues themselves appear to generate movement. The restless gaze of the artist invokes a corresponding restless gaze in the spectator, who finds himself compelled to move around the sculpture in order to see it in its totality. For the first time there appeared a deliberate sensuality. At the end of the fifth century Aphrodite was still being depicted in thin rippling drapery; Praxiteles of Athens tore the drapery away and showed her stepping out of her bath only too aware that she was being observed. With Praxiteles the flesh becomes softer, the muscles more rounded, the bones more brittle. His Hermes, now in the museum at Olympia, suggests the languor of sexual exhaustion in a body of such palpable and effeminate beauty that it might almost belong to a hermaphrodite. Indeed, all the statues attributed to Praxiteles have a peculiarly sexual quality, inviting the spectator to dwell on the luxuriance of the flesh. The

generous thighs, the ample breasts, the full buttocks, and the softness of the arms are invitations to license, and it is not surprising
that his Aphrodite was once the victim of indecent assault.

Nor was it surprising that the canons of physical beauty invented by Praxiteles should have served as models for the sculptors
of funeral steles, who carved in deep relief portraits of the dead
visited by their grieving relatives. The dead are usually decently
clothed; the living offer their nakedness as a gift to the shades. The
dead rest on chairs and gaze upward at these visitors from another
world, who flaunt their nakedness as though they knew no other
way of insisting that they still belonged to the world of the living.
It was a strange convention, but it evidently satisfied the Greeks,
for these funeral steles were produced in great quantities by craftsmen who took pleasure in suggesting the beauty of the flesh even
on gravestones.

The influence of Praxiteles was prodigious, and continued
down the centuries, to be revived whenever men felt the need to
celebrate the flesh. Inevitably so much luxuriance produced its opposite, and with Lysippus a sterner code emerged. Working with
athletes as models, resolutely refusing to depict women, he cultivated a more ascetic and heroic ideal. He made the head smaller, the
body harder, less responsive to the touch. Insisting on realism, he
was especially noted for his treatment of the hair, which the earlier
Greek sculptors regarded as scarcely worthy of their attention. He
was said to be the first to use life casts. His figures—as we discern
them through the marble forest of Roman copies—have a springing
tension and eagerness, with no trace of languor and without an
inch of fat. The *Apoxyomenos,* a young athlete scraping oil from
his forearm with a strigil, survives in a Roman copy in the Vatican.
One arm points forward, the other sweeps across the chest in a gesture of grave authority: the young athlete resembles an emperor
announcing a conquest rather than a man merely scraping the oil
from his skin. Lysippus gave him nobility, ease of movement, a sense
of conscious superiority. Alexander the Great, recognizing the greatest artist of his time, made him his own personal sculptor, refusing
to permit anyone else to make portraits of him. All these portraits
have perished, for Lysippus worked only in bronze, which conquer-

ors have habitually melted down. Yet the pale copies in stone still suggest the clean-cut vitality of the lost originals.

With Lysippus there began the long and strenuous final efflorescence of Greek sculpture. There was never any failure of nerve; and the sculptors of the second century B.C. labored with the same sense of conscious triumph as the masters of the classic age. The *Victory of Samothrace*, the *Venus de Milo*, the *Laocoön*, the *Belvedere Torso*, and the gods and giants on the Great Altar of Pergamon all date from the second century B.C., when in the normal course of evolution the classic tradition should have reached a stage of exhaustion. But in fact the tradition survived intact, and what distinguishes these statues from those of an earlier period is precisely their greater vitality, as though the blood were speeding more quickly through their veins and as though they possessed a greater eagerness for movement.

The *Victory of Samothrace* was originally set up on the prow of a stone ship surrounded by water, and the unknown sculptor deliberately carved the great wings in such a way that they would reflect the rippling lights of the water, and these reflections and all the other reflections on the swirling garments of the goddess would only increase the illusion of movement. She belonged to the sea and the rocks and the open air and the full sunlight. In her present setting in the Louvre, set against a gray wall at the top of a flight of stairs, she is altogether out of her element, being landlocked and artificially elevated, like an angel dancing on the summit of a mountain, when in fact she demands to be seen at eye level, and only then do we become aware of the thrust and power of her athletic body, the superb motion of the draperies, her sudden plummeting from the skies. She has lost her head and her arms, but we might not love her any more if we possessed them. What remains is the purest image yet conceived of divine grace hurrying to earth to offer her protection and blessing to men.

The Great Altar at Pergamon belongs among the strangest of architectural monstrosities, but is saved from tedium by the genius of the sculptors who portrayed the battle between the gods and the giants on the outside walls of the altar. The battle is a real battle: this is no formal engagement of chivalrous opponents performing a war dance. Zeus hurls himself into the fray, taking on three serpent-footed giants single-handed; Athena seizes a giant by the hair; the sudden appearance of Apollo silences the enemy for a moment, but the battle continues unabated elsewhere. Too often these sculptures have been described as restless and tormented, befitting a tradition in decline, but there is not the least evidence of decline. Power streams from these more than life-size figures, all brilliantly executed, so that even now we are made aware of the tumult of the battle, the sweat and the agony; and in their proportions and gestures they rival the art of the classic age. Michelangelo would have recognized these unknown sculptors as his masters. Today we can see them reconstructed in the East Berlin Museum, badly lit, strangely cold and unconvincing, enclosed within a vast hall, where formerly they illuminated a hilltop in Asia Minor. Yet even in the worst of settings they speak with authority, the brooding gods and the divine heroes, all wonderfully in command of themselves, at war with the giants who are doomed to certain defeat.

The Great Altar was erected about 164 B.C. by Attalus II, the owner of the greatest library of his time. Thirty years later Attalus III bequeathed his kingdom to the Romans, and no more sculptures were ever made in Pergamon.

Greek art came to an end with the Roman conquest, but even the Romans could not stamp out this perfect and fragile beauty. The mark of a great art lies in its wholeness, its power to create a world of comprehensible forms so complete that no other is conceivable; and in their time, and for many centuries to come, Greek forms dominated the arts of Europe. So powerful was the thrust of form that even a small fragment of a Greek torso can convey the whole figure. A fragment of a Hellenistic torso of a nude woman conveys the presence of the whole woman. On the island of Thasos there survives the gateway of a temple to Apollo, and this gateway, by its proportions, by the color of the stone, and by its appropriateness to the chosen site, becomes the whole temple. Never before or afterward has any people fashioned an art where the parts were so nearly equal to the whole. It was as though the Greeks had foreseen the inevitable ruin of their art and charged it with so much energy that it would endure through all disasters, even the ultimate disaster of being broken into fragments.

When we climb the steps leading to a Greek temple, let us say the ruined temple at Lindos overlooking the dark blue seas of Asia, we see only a few ruined columns set on the edge of a vast jagged cliff, and we can scarcely imagine what the temple looked like when the pilgrims came here to worship Athena. What attracts us is the beauty and brilliance of these columns, which have weathered so many centuries, their absolute rightness in this setting testifying to the prodigious power of architecture to move us deeply even when only the bare skeleton of the temple remains. Time, by reducing the temple to a few white and perfect bones, has made it even more immaculate, even more incorruptible, and thereby divested it of all that was extraneous and contemporary. In this way the Greek temple enters eternity.

The Etruscan Tombs

Herodotus tells a strange story about the beginning of the Etruscan people. They were originally Lydians from Asia Minor, he tells us, and they were the first to use gold and silver coinage, and the first to engage in trade. A luxury-loving people, they amused themselves by playing endless games of dice, knucklebones, and football during a prolonged drought. At last, unable to endure their hunger any longer, they drew lots and half of them set sail from Smyrna to discover a more fertile land overseas. So they came to Etruria, the land on the western coast of Italy which lies between the Arno and the Tiber.

As Herodotus tells the story there is no suggestion that he is relating an old wives' tale. He speaks confidently and authoritatively, as of a matter well known to him. When he relates his discoveries in Egypt, he is on his guard against false impressions, but he feels no need to be on his guard when he discusses the adventures of the Lydians. Smyrna, after all, was not very far from his birthplace in Halicarnassus.

Though some modern scholars have disputed the claim that the Etruscans originally came from Asia Minor, there seems to be little doubt that they came from the East and were already well equipped with artistic skills and were proficient in working metals and building defense works. No doubt they intermarried with the original Italic tribe whose lands they conquered, for almost from the beginning an Italic strain can be observed in them. But their habits and modes of thought were oriental. Herodotus tells us that the Lydian prostitutes, merchants, and artisans vied with one another to produce the money needed to build a great funeral mound for the father of King Croesus, and the prostitutes paid the most. From this we learn that the Lydians built funeral mounds and supported a large number of prostitutes; and we find funeral mounds and prostitution among the Etruscans. There are other marks of similarity between the Etruscans and the Lydians, which are to be found in their paintings, the splendor of their accouterments, and their beliefs.

When we see them first on Italian soil, they have conquered most of the lands between Florence and Rome, and their fleets are sailing into the Tyrrhenian and Ionian seas. They are freebooters and pirates ravaging the coasts of the western Mediterranean, with a taste for finery and hard living. They have established colonies and trading centers in Corsica, Sardinia, and the Balearic Islands, and Elba with its rich lodes of iron ore is securely in their possession. A recently discovered inscription on thin gold plates, written in Carthaginian and Etruscan, shows them to have been on friendly terms with Carthage. By 700 B.C. they have already formed a recognizable and valid culture, distinguishable by a certain austere joy and a robust inventiveness.

Although we know very little about their history in the early years of the settlement, for none of their records have survived, the archaeological finds show them to have been as good soldiers as they were seamen. They reached out across Italy to the Adriatic, where they colonized the city of Spina; they turned south and sank their teeth into Rome, which they conquered with the help of a Corinthian adventurer. From them the Romans inherited an enduring taste for luxury, having observed the splendid state in which their conquerors moved. The historian Diodorus Siculus said the Etruscans were "the authors of the dignity that surrounds rulers"; and while the Etruscans could not vie with the pharaohs in panoplied dignity, at least they were the first on Italian soil to make a cult of panoply. Their priest-kings, the *lucumenes,* passed through life with the calm and measured dignity of gods, aware that their smallest gestures possessed significance. They rode in gilded chariots drawn by four snow-white horses and wore embroidered robes adorned with palms, which perhaps proclaimed their oriental heritage. They wore gold crowns and gold breastplates, trumpeters heralded their approach, they sat on ivory thrones. The symbols of their power were double-headed axes bound with scarlet rope. Their colors were white and gold, and they blazed with splendor.

About the time of the conquest of Rome in the latter half of the sixth century B.C., we begin for the first time to see them in brilliant perspective. The mists fall away, and they present themselves in their frescoed tomb chambers in the colors of life. The largest accumulation of these frescoes lies in the hills above Tarquinia, the ancient Tarchuna, where the Etruscans, according to tradition, first settled in Italy. There on the windswept heights, among the thistles and red poppies overlooking the modern town, the tomb chambers can be found simply by stepping down a few steps and entering the gates. Some of the chambers have not changed in twenty-five centuries, and the paint seems to have been applied only yesterday. There is no feeling of death's gloom: there is gaiety and an airy spaciousness, a calm and joyful solemnity. The Egyptian tomb chambers, depicting in three or four formal registers the lives of long dead farmers and their attendant slaves, have none of this spontaneity. There is always movement and stirring life on these walls crowded with banqueters and dancers, with processions and games, mythologies and legends.

The colors are apple green, sky blue, red, orange, yellow, white, the colors of spring. The hair is black, the bodies are painted in red, sometimes they wear pointed beards. But what is chiefly noticeable about the frescoes is the extraordinary immediacy of the paintings as the dancers tumble or play on their double flutes or lead their horses to water or recline at the banqueting table. Just as the artist seems to have left the chamber only a few moments ago, so the people he depicted seem also to have left only a little while ago, and we can almost hear their voices, their footfalls, and the rustle of their garments.

A flute player strides across a wall, his patterned blue and red bordered cloak swirling behind him, knees and arms bare, a vine wreath round his curling hair. He does not walk solemnly, but with youthful vigor. Etruscan youths on the tomb frescoes fling their legs apart, make wide gestures with their hands, show off their athletic limbs. They ride their high-stepping horses with ease, tumble and

turn cartwheels, wrestle and throw the discus, and drive their
chariots with happy abandon. It is evidently a masculine civilization,
for men appear far more often than women; and since the male
genitals are rarely represented, it may be assumed that they felt no
need to emphasize their masculinity. Sometimes at the banqueting
tables we see the lovers caught in an eternal embrace, but more
often they recline side by side, the men naked to the waist, the
women chastely dressed. There are occasional scenes of solemnity,
as in the Tomb of the Augurs, where among flowering plants and
hovering wildfowl, the surviving sons of the dead man stand like
sentinels before the blood-red gates of death, but such depictions of
grief are rare. Sometimes, too, there are strange masked men with
blue faces who preside over executions or tragic deaths, but these
are also rare, and the most famous of them occur in the François
tomb, which belongs to the first century B.C., when the Etruscan
empire was in full decline. For the most part the frescoes depict
scenes of quiet joy, so that you leave those underground chambers
with the impression of having lived among a people who were content with life and in love with vigorous joys.

To ascribe a ritual meaning to these vivid paintings is to mis-
understand their purpose, which was to keep the dead warm with
memories of their life on earth. Not only do the tomb chambers
assume the form of an Etruscan house with painted roof beams and
couches laid along the walls, but they are so constructed and painted
that they reflect the precise individuality of the owner; the personality—the word comes from the Etruscan *phersu,* a mask—remains. To enter an Etruscan tomb is to be aware of a unique person whose ashes have long since melted into the earth, yet there is
a continuing sense of his presence, his awareness. No tombs are
the same. The funeral steles of the Greeks and the crucifixes in
Christian cemeteries have a terrifying sameness. The Etruscans rejoiced in their differences and took their separate personalities with
them to the grave.

They were a ceremonial and highly cultivated people, living
in quite extraordinary luxury. They were not a people weighed
down by a sense of guilt, and they were noted for their sexual freedom. The Greek historian Theopompus, writing in the middle of

the fourth century B.C., remarks that the Etruscan women appeared in public naked and "were common to all men." At banquets they drank with whatever man pleased them at the moment, and they enjoyed drinking. Few children knew their fathers. Sexual relations were conducted openly, without shame. Men enjoyed the same liberties as women, and Theopompus notes that "though the men approached the women with great pleasure, they derived as much pleasure from the company of adolescents and of boys." Aristotle observes that in Etruria a man and a woman would dine together on the same couch "with a common mantle over them."

This tenderness between them is clearly visible in the paintings, especially in the banqueting scenes, where the wives nestle against their husbands, caressing them. The lovers gaze into each other's eyes, lost in adoration. Sometimes we see a myrtle-crowned husband offering his wife an egg with one hand, and with the other a phial containing oil, or else he offers her grapes in his cupped hands. So too, in the life-size terra-cotta figures showing husband and wife reclining on the same funeral couch, we are aware of the tenderness in the half-formed embrace and in the lingering smiles. The Greeks and the Romans regarded the Etruscans as inveterate wantons, given to lascivious pleasures. There was some substance in the charge, for puritanism was absent from the Etruscan code. Those sturdy men and beautiful women—Theopompus informs us that Etruscan women were famous for their beauty, a fact borne out by the tomb paintings and the figures on the terra-cotta sarcophagi—embrace with such an exquisite tenderness that it would seem that the Greeks and Romans felt for them a kind of wistful envy. No other civilization has produced so much evidence of tenderness between men and women.

These terra-cotta sarcophagi are among the marvels of Etruscan art. Usually the man, bare to the waist, has one arm resting lightly on the shoulders of the woman, clothed in her finest garments and wearing her most sumptuous jewels. They gaze intently at one another, as the wife points to her husband with one hand, and with the other extends a gesture of farewell. What is chiefly remarkable about these funereal figures is their humanity, their decorum, their quiet affection and silent enjoyment of one another's presence. The gestures are stylized, and all the tomb figures resemble one another in their general proportions, but how much individuality the artist has given to their features! How cunningly he has suggested the waves of affection flowing between them! There is nothing in the least decadent about these people who gaze on death calmly, with wide-open eyes and the hint of a smile. Perhaps the closest to these figures are the medieval knights lying beside their ladies on Gothic tombstones, but what a difference there is! These knights and their ladies lie with their eyes closed, their hands folded in resignation. They do not smile, and it would never occur to them to embrace. They lie there in the promise of paradise; the Etruscans see themselves persuasively in paradise.

Our knowledge of Etruscan art derives as much from chance as from the patient explorations of the archaeologists. In 1533, in the high noon of the Renaissance, there was discovered in Arezzo, the capital of one of the Etruscan princely states, a bronze Chimaera now in the Etruscan Museum in Florence. The mythological beast has the muzzle of a lion, the tail of a serpent, and from its back there rises a strange horned birdlike animal. This bronze, which dates from the fifth century B.C., is about two and a half feet high, but fills the whole gallery with its formidable power. At first sight it would appear to have nothing in common with the banqueters and dancers in the Etruscan tomb chambers, but on closer observation there may be detected a close affinity of style, a certain sleekness and suppleness and stylized grandeur. The spring is coiled, there is a sense of power and residual energy waiting to be unloosed. The Chimaera is wounded, and crouches there with unrelenting ferocity, and will not yield. Alertness, naked energy, suddenness are its attributes. There is nothing in Greek art to equal this image of pure ferocity, sculptured in an age when the Etruscans were at the height of their power; and indeed it could only have been sculptured in such an age. The mythological animals of Greece dream their lives away; the Etruscan Chimaera is piercingly awake.

So is the She-wolf in the Capitoline Museum, also an Etruscan work of the same period, though two Renaissance cherubs representing Romulus and Remus were added to it so that the founders of Rome could be shown suckling. With outstretched neck, snapping jaws, and blazing eyes the She-wolf springs from the same powerful imagination that produced the Chimaera: no living she-wolf could ever look so savage. She is not jolted into savagery by a sudden awareness of danger, but is savage by nature, by inclination and desire. This, too, could have been produced only during the fifth century B.C., when the Etruscans were still in possession of an empire, though knowing that it was threatened by the Greeks and the Carthaginians.

Such creations of ferocity are rare in art, for extreme violence is not normally within the compass of a sculptor. Compared with the Chimaera or the She-wolf the carvings in Romanesque and Gothic churches depicting the torments of the damned at the mercy of strange mythological animals are merely playful. The Chimaera is not playing. When you see it for the first time, you are likely to step back in mingled respect and fear.

While the Etruscans were capable of expressing the purest ferocity, by far the greater number of surviving works express great charm and tenderness. The life-size *Apollo of Veii*, now in the Villa Giulia Museum in Rome, expresses kindness and a bewildering sweetness, the curve of his body forming a benediction as he leans forward, and the winged horses of Tarquinia, also of terra cotta, announce themselves as angelic messengers. There is in Florence a terra-cotta statue of the Mother Goddess, protectress of the living and the dead, holding a naked child in her arms as tenderly as the Virgin holds her son, and there is about that statue, now lost in a dark corner of the Museum, a quiet and brooding majesty and monumentality. It belongs among the very greatest of surviving works of Etruscan art, and like the winged horses of Tarquinia is only a meter high.

The Etruscans looked at the world through eyes that were never jaded. There is always movement and excitement in their small bronzes; they rejoiced in depicting life as free, strong, and glowing. They were the first great sculptors in metal. Constantly developing, they learned to make bronze obedient to their will until it could record even the subtle movements of the soul. The *Brutus* in the Capitoline Museum is a portrait in depth, and like the life-size *Orator* in Florence it celebrates undeviating intelligence. Power married to intelligence marks this art, which has a peculiarly modern quality; and the weary visitor to museums finds himself walking more lightly when he comes face to face with the images of long-dead Etruscans.

So it was in all their arts, even in their delicate jewelry, the engraved mirrors, the *cistae* with their bronze handles in the forms of gods, soldiers, and acrobats and the round surfaces inscribed with engraved designs out of mythology. They were continually expressing power in a little space: most powerful of all, perhaps, are the thin, drawn-out, Giacometti-like figures of soldiers who seem, even when enclosed in a glass case, to be striding over immense landscapes. What led them to make these drawn-out figures seems to have been the search for an ultimate form representing the dignity and pathos of the soldier's existence: he becomes the blade of the spear. Soldiers, augurs, and priests are represented in this way, but by far the greater number of them are soldiers. Nothing quite like this deliberate return to geometric form is found in Greece.

Greece, however, deeply influenced Etruscan art, and there were few things which delighted the Etruscans more than Greek vases. In fact we owe the greater part of our knowledge of Greek painted vases to the massive collections found in Etruscan tombs. Some twenty thousand vases have been dredged out of the sea on the site of Spina, the ancient Etruscan seaport on the Adriatic. They rejoiced in possessing the finest vases, regarded them as their greatest treasures, and were buried with them. These graves were found when the sea was driven back during extensive reclamation projects beginning in 1922 and still continuing. Entire new chapters in the history of Greek vase painting have been opened out, and we know now that trade in works of art during the fourth and fifth centuries B.C. was far more extensive than we had imagined.

The Greek colonies in the south of Italy also traded extensively with the Etruscans. The influence of Greece on Etruria came in successive waves, and sometimes it is difficult to know whether a small bronze statue of an athlete or an engraved mirror found in an Etruscan grave is Greek or Etruscan, for there comes a point when the two civilizations fuse together. From literary sources we learn that Corinthian and Ionian artists were employed in Etruria, while nearly all the pottery found at Spina has a recognizably Greek ancestry. The Etruscans were so deeply impressed by Greek art that they surrendered to its enchantment, imitated it willingly, adopted the Greek gods into their pantheon, and the Greek canons of proportion were carefully obeyed. Yet to the very end something of the Etruscan character remained in all their art. They had a more profound sense of character than the Greeks, a springing strength, a knowledge of fatality. They were augurs and prophets, famous for their power of divination, handing down to the Romans their prophetical books known as the Sibylline Oracles. Above all, they possessed a sense of life's majesty, which they celebrated with oriental panoply.

Before the end of the fifth century Etruria was beginning to lose her empire, and during the fourth century the Romans succeeded in making their first inroads into Etruscan territory, destroying the temples and enslaving the people. The long sporadic war ended with the capitulation of the Etruscan cities, but not before the Romans themselves adopted so many of the customs and manners of the Etruscans that Roman culture became scarcely distinguishable from Etruscan culture. The first temple on the Capitoline Hill had been built by Etruscans; Roman worship derived from Etruscan worship; the shapes of houses and walls and viaducts, the methods of government, the processions, the horse trappings, the uniforms, the standards, and even the orders of battle derived from the Etruscans. The Romans wore the toga, and this too derived from Etruria. They had one great advantage over their enemies: a total ruthlessness. They were determined to conquer the known world at whatever the cost, and the Etruscans were their first victims.

At first the Romans seem to have been content with booty and slaves. They dismantled the Etruscan temples, but had too high a regard for the Etruscan gods to destroy them and instead carried them to Rome. In 264 B.C. they carried off two thousand bronze statues from the conquered Etruscan city of Volsinii, and the process was repeated so often that Roman temples must have been crowded with Etruscan gods. As more and more cities fell, the Romans increasingly suffered the influence of Etruscan culture. In this way the victors were vanquished.

This process might have gone on indefinitely if the Roman dictator Sulla had not decided that Etruscan culture penetrated too deeply into Roman life. He gave orders for the extermination of the remaining Etruscan cities: the buildings must be destroyed, the records burned, the statues thrown down, the walls razed. Fiesole was leveled, and in its place he built a military colony known as Florentia, and he would have done the same with Arezzo if Cicero had not protected it. Volterra resisted the Sullan army for two long years and suffered the same fate as Fiesole. Sulla deprived the Etruscans of the right to exist by denying them a share of the public lands, and his forty-seven legions settled on the lands once owned by Etruscan princes. By the time of Augustus even the language of Etruria had become little more than a memory.

Only the indestructible survived. Etruscan culture lived on in Roman culture, just as Minoan culture lived on in Mycenae and later in Athens. Men, houses, temples, statues could be destroyed, but the indestructible elements of art continued to work on men's imaginations and to resist mortality. Certain shapes and forms, certain ways of looking at life, certain concepts of dignity and power, once brought into being, seem to enjoy a life of their own. Fifteen hundred years after the death of Sulla there would emerge in Florence a new art essentially Etruscan in its origins, recognizable by its energy, its elegance, and its understanding of human character. Sulla's military camp, once inhabited by Roman legionaries and Etruscan slaves, became Florence, the artistic capital of Europe.

The Roman Triumph

Horace wrote of the Romans that they were like oaks shaped by the ax, drawing life from the very steel, and perhaps in all of history there was never a people so rapacious, so determinedly hard-bitten, so adamant for conquest. The Roman poets gloried in the violence of the Romans and spoke approvingly of the endless wars which reduced all the lands bordering the Mediterranean, from Judea and Egypt to Spain and Mauretania, to the status of slave states. It was as though the Romans felt themselves driven by some power greater than themselves to stamp out every culture except their own, and at the same time they were obscurely aware that they possessed no culture of their own.

From the earliest beginnings Roman art was strangely derivative, and therefore formal. The Etruscan temples with their rich and gaily painted ornaments were transformed into somber edifices intended to suggest power and domination, and there were no Roman tombs filled with brilliantly colored frescoes. The Italic tribes conquered by the Romans all left indisputable evidence of their affection for the arts; the conquerors seemed indifferent, borrowing on occasion, distrusting the creative artist with his spontaneity and his desire to elaborate on traditional forms. Spontaneity was not a characteristic of the Romans and they possessed no traditional forms.

The art of the Italic tribes is known to us only from their tomb paintings. The Samnites, who fought the Romans for three centuries, left wall paintings of great elegance, totally different in style from Etruscan paintings. We see the Samnite warriors in white tunics, gleaming armor and horned helmets marching to battle under bright banners, not unlike the brilliantly colored banners of medieval Florence and Siena, and there is about these warriors, who were so often victorious in battle, a singular dignity and composure. The historian Livy, who chronicles the interminable wars between Rome and Samnium, remarks on the contrast between the uncouth legionaries and the splendidly accoutered Samnites, whose wealth and power had become proverbial. The Romans hated the Samnites for the same reason that they hated the Etruscans: they were civilized. The Samnites were finally conquered during the last years of the Republic and their cities were leveled.

Of the surviving Italic frescoes the most magnificent is the fresco known as *The Mourners,* though it is possible that it has nothing to do with mourning. It shows a group of women dancing and linking hands, all dressed in costumes of identical shape though of different colors. It is a stately dance performed to the sound of a lyre. The women wear long headdresses, mantles, and heavy skirts, which sway to the music. Altogether there are thirty-six women, and the artist has succeeded in giving each of them an individuality of her own, and to prevent the frieze from becoming monotonous he had deliberately broken it up in three places, first by showing one of the women facing the opposite direction, then by inserting two youths in the ceremonial dance, and finally by including a young lyre player together with a woman. The effect is to bring variety and new colors at exactly the right places. The frieze, which is eighteen feet long, is now in the National Museum at Naples. It was found in Apulia and evidently dates from the fifth century B.C. when the wars with the Romans were only beginning.

Because the frieze was discovered in a tomb, it was generally assumed to be a mourning dance, yet there is nothing about the dancers to suggest mourning. It may be a dance of triumph, or a stamping dance, or even a dance in honor of an unknown god, or perhaps it is simply a dance to rejoice the soul of the man buried in the tomb. In much the same way the Etruscans painted dancers in their tombs. Nevertheless the lighthearted Etruscan dancers are far removed from these stately women, who seem to incarnate the energies of a lost civilization.

There are no frescoes of dancing Romans, and there is perhaps some significance in the fact that the earliest art which can be said to be specifically Roman derives from the death masks of important personages. Not the living dancer but the dead politician or soldier; not the youthful body filled with energy but the mask of an old man of forbidding aspect: such was the beginning of Roman art. Originally, as we learn from literary sources, the Romans made death masks of wax, which were carried in procession during the funeral rites and later preserved in a special shrine. Since the wax tended to disintegrate, the funerary masks were later carved out of stone, without any effort to suggest the psychological qualities of the dead man, the sculptors merely copying the wax masks. The Romans wanted accurate, topographical representations of the dead man and they were not in the least concerned with the living man. They saw in the stark, severe lineaments of death an answer to their unspoken needs.

There survives from the last century of the Roman Republic an entire gallery of portraits of grim, weather-beaten men with brutal mouths and sullen eyes. They have the look of men who ride roughshod over opposition, deliberate and purposeful, accustomed to killing. Most of them were officers during the period when the Romans were engaged in a protracted civil war, when the air was thick with treachery and murder. They have the look of engines of destruction. One cannot imagine them smiling, and it is beyond belief that they ever showed mercy. No portraits of women or children have survived from Republican times.

Portraiture entered Rome through the death mask, and something of that severity would remain throughout Roman history. The patrician Roman liked to see himself represented as a grim, iron-willed *paterfamilias*, unconsoled and unconsoling, and unconcerned with psychological subtleties. This lack of psychological substance is all the more surprising because Hellenistic art was widely known to the Romans, and hundreds, perhaps thousands, of Hellenistic statues had been carried off to Rome by conquering generals, to decorate the suburban villas and town houses of the new nobility.

Not until the age of Augustus would Hellenistic art find merit in Roman eyes. Then the floodgates opened, for the art of the Augustan age was essentially Hellenistic art with some necessary modifications.

From the earliest times until about 150 B.C. Greek sculpture survived as a continuous living tradition. It was the misfortune of the Romans that they encountered Greek sculptors when the tradition was already dying, and the Greek artists who came to Rome seem to have spent their days making copies of great works of art, working mechanically, producing statues which seem oddly lifeless, as though they had entered upon a conspiracy to destroy the life within the statue in order to make it more appealing to their patrons. The world's museums are full of Roman copies of Greek originals; they are copies of copies of copies; and sometimes we can only guess at the beauty of the lost masterpieces.

A more vigorous art survives in the coins of the Republic with their harsh portraits of consuls and military leaders. They are sketched out in metal by men who might have been trained as caricaturists, and they are full of life. Julius Caesar appears more lively in the coins than in his statues, his thin-lipped arrogance and sensuality being wonderfully expressed in a portrait an inch wide.

With the coming of Augustus to power after the battle of Actium in 31 B.C., Greek influence on the Roman arts became predominant. There had been a small temple to Apollo at Actium, and Augustus came to believe that he was under the benevolent protection of a god who had blessed him with victory. Accordingly he built on the Palatine, not far from his palace, a white marble temple to Apollo with two wings containing two immense libraries, one of Greek books, the other of Roman, as though to symbolize that the two cultures should henceforth exist in equilibrium. Outside the temple he built a colossal bronze statue of Apollo, who looked remarkably like Augustus himself. The Greeks portrayed Apollo naked; Augustus, more modest, portrayed him in a long flowing gown, with a harp in one hand and the *patera*, the sacred bowl, in the other.

That Augustus should have elevated Apollo to such high rank

among the gods meant that a profound change had taken place in the attitude of the Romans toward Greece, and especially toward Greek art. The process of assimilation now went on at a rapidly increasing pace, encouraged by Augustus, who sometimes seemed to regard himself as more Greek than Roman. He sent scholars to study the laws governing the architecture of Greek temples, and set the sculptors to work on Hellenistic models. The Roman temples, which had been abandoned and uncared for during the civil wars, now rose again with high Corinthian and Ionic columns. Greek sculptors were imported to carve the cult statues. Greek painters and poets served in his court. The image of Apollo was stamped on his coins. Fourteen years after Actium, when Augustus was firmly in the saddle, he decided to put into effect his long cherished plan to dedicate the city of Rome to Apollo, the god of the divine intelligence, of the sun, of medicine, of architecture and the arts. In much the same way Akhenaton had dethroned the old gods and elevated a new god to a position of supreme power thirteen centuries before.

The occasion was the celebration of the centennial games in 17 B.C. These games, following an ancient Etruscan tradition, were held every hundred and ten years. The poet Horace was commanded to compose the centennial hymn, which opens with an invocation to Apollo and to his sister Diana, the queen of the forests, calling upon them to bless and protect the city. Addressing Apollo and Diana, the poet proclaims: "Rome is your handiwork" —*Roma si vestrum est opus*. And it was from these gods, not from Jupiter, that the poet begged the boon of "virtue and learning for the young, peace and quiet for the aged, and for the race of Romulus wealth and offspring and all glory."

The centennial games continued for three days and three nights, with vast processions moving through the city. At night, under the full moon, there were torchlight parades, and in the presence of Augustus, a choir of youths and maidens sang the centennial hymn in Apollo's temple on the Palatine. A new age had begun. Under the rule of Apollo and his divine sister the long promised centuries of peace were to be ushered in.

In this way Rome fell heir to the Hellenistic East, and the

idealized sculptures of the Augustan age show an Apollonian grace scarcely distinguishable from the graceful forms of the age of Alexander the Great. Roman sculpture, which had derived from the death mask, though on occasion it had felt the influence of Etruscan vitality and maturity, now came to springing life, and there survives a portrait gallery of Julio-Claudian princes and princesses who might have been Greeks. They are charming, temperamental, civilized, obviously intelligent; they have character and nobility, and they are far from gazing grimly on a world to be conquered; on the contrary, they gaze pleasantly on a world already conquered. In Republican times the sculptors rejoiced in depicting the massive folds and wrinkles of embittered faces, but these faces reflect the calm beauty of Augustus, serene and imperturbable. Greek culture had at last conquered Rome.

The statue of Apollo on the Palatine is lost, and we can only guess at its majesty from the rough sketches which appear on coins. But in its general effect it cannot have been very different from the superb over-life-size statue of Augustus found on the estate of the Empress Livia at Prima Porta, just outside of Rome. The statue is now in the Vatican Museum, set against the wall with perhaps fifty other statues in the same gallery, but it was clearly intended to be seen alone, on a high plinth, and in a commanding position. Seen thus, it would have dominated the landscape. Augustus appears in a cuirass ornamented with scenes from mythology. We see the sky god opening wide the sky, while Phaëton drives the chariot of the Sun against the fleeing shades of the night, and the Earth Mother pours out her plentiful cornucopia. Apollo rides a griffin and brandishes his lyre, while Diana rides her stag, one hand caressing the stag's proud neck. So calmly, blazoned in mythology, Augustus presents himself on the cuirass as the child of the gods, descended from Apollo, and blessed with prophetic foresight, for prophecy too was one of Apollo's gifts. He announces himself as the Prince of Peace, divinely regulating the world into the paths of peace. In this way he enters the chambers of the gods.

The Prima Porta Augustus is one of the towering achievements of the Augustan age, a work of the finest quality and authority. It was sculpted by a Greek deeply influenced by early Hellenistic models, but he has achieved an effect which is wholly of his own time. Augustus is depicted barefoot, as the Greek gods and heroes were depicted, lightly touching the earth, and in the Greek manner the statue was once painted in brilliant colors, and traces of them remain. But no Greek had ever been represented in quite such an attitude of imperious majesty, so disdainful of his own powers, so absorbed in the contemplation of his own divinity. We know from many records that Augustus possessed a delicate beauty and was inordinately proud of his brilliant eyes, but in the Prima Porta statue he passes beyond human beauty altogether and assumes the self-absorbed beauty of the gods.

The statue must have been carved about the time of the centennial games. Eight years later, when the reign of Augustus was half run, an altar to the Augustan peace was dedicated on the Campus Martius. The design was very simple, based on the Altar of the Twelve Gods in the Agora in Athens. It is a small building, about thirty-five feet broad and thirty-eight feet deep, and could therefore be fitted into a fairly large room. But the smallness of the building was quite deliberate. It was in Augustus's power to erect a monument as large as the Parthenon or larger. He chose to build a sumptuous jewel box.

According to the plan, the altar was to be surrounded with a marble wall decorated on all four sides with reliefs; four steps led up to the altar; carved on the entrance wall were scenes representing the foundation of Rome, and on the back wall there would be the same mythological scenes which appeared on the cuirass of the Prima Porta Augustus; on the side walls there would be the procession of the *flamens,* the fire priests, and the dignitaries of the court attending the dedication of the altar. The altar was therefore an intensely self-conscious and contrived work, for the reliefs on the side walls depicted a precise moment of time—the dedication of the altar—while the front and back walls enclosed all of Roman history from its foundation by Aeneas to its fulfillment in the peace of Augustus. Peace is represented as a goddess of grave beauty seated amid flowering fields with her babes around her. But it is along the side walls that the formidable power of Augustus is revealed, not by means of idealized portraits, but by emphasizing

the priestly role of the Emperor as he moves quietly and purposefully, accompanied by the entire imperial family, toward the accomplishment of his own destiny, to that apotheosis which is
symbolized simply by the lighting of his own flame on his own
altar.

The procession moves with slow steps, deliberately and pon-
derously, a little crowded—for every member of the imperial family
must be included—and some look over their shoulders to see that the
rest are in line, and one pauses to fondle one of the imperial
children. We recognize Augustus and Agrippa, Livia and Julia, but
the faces of many of the others have been reworked and we cannot
always give names to them. The Athenian sculptors have carved on
those crowded panels the slow and stately march of power, as on
the Parthenon more than four hundred years before they carved
the quick, excited march of the Athenian cavalry, the youthful
power of the young Athenian state. But on the altar of the Augustan peace there is no excitement: only the slow, deliberate unfolding
of a drama which embraced Augustus, his family, and all Roman
history.

This jewel-box altar was once brilliantly painted, and we must
imagine the flesh tones and the brilliantly colored gowns. So it
shone in the sun, very small and quiet, in the Campus Martius,
not far from the place where triumphant generals set out on their
journey to the Temple of Capitoline Jupiter to lay the laurel crown
of victory on the lap of the god. But in the altar to the Augustan
peace there is no god, or rather Augustus is communing with his
own divinity. In its quiet way the altar makes claims as vast as those
made by the Parthenon, for it celebrates the apotheosis of a god.

How deeply personal the altar was, and how greatly Augustus
cherished it, may be seen from a rarely noticed detail hidden at
the base of the wonderfully rich floral decorations which support
the frieze. At first sight this immense convolution of fantastic
flowers, leaves, vines, and grapes swarming with a multitude of
insects, butterflies, birds, and lizards appears to be out of keeping
with the severely vertical ceremonial procession. These great wheels
of curling leaves and petals suggest high noon, the riot of summer,
the hot and fecund earth displaying its wealth of vegetation. The

symbolism is deliberate: the flowering earth has been brought into existence by the Augustan peace. Swans settle on the acanthus flowers, suggesting once more the presence of Apollo. And deep down, at the very roots of the immense spreading acanthus, we see a serpent gliding up to a nest filled with fledgling swans soon to be devoured. One stronger than the rest has escaped, and this is evidently Augustus himself, the survivor of so many treacheries and the ultimate avenger. In this characteristic way Augustus describes the strongest motive which drove him through the long years of his reign.

The Roman emperors who followed Augustus never built small monuments to themselves. Nero built a gilded bronze statue of himself 120 feet high in front of his Golden House. The still surviving columns of Trajan and Marcus Aurelius testify to the emperors' admiration of their own exploits, their belief that future generations would find them equally admirable. Today these columns have been worn down by centuries of storm, and they have long ago lost the last remnants of color, but in their prime they glowed like jewels. Flashing with brilliant color, inescapably present, they dominated the great gathering places called *fora* and testified to the permanence of the imperial tradition. Gilded statues of the emperors graced the tops of the columns, but the popes, who had little sympathy for emperors, replaced them with gilded statues of St. Peter and St. Paul.

These spiral columns carved out of marble have no known ancestry, for previously all reliefs were placed in architectural settings. These reliefs revolve around the column, defying all logic, for to understand what is being depicted, it would be necessary to walk round the Trajan Column twenty-three times in an effort to follow the continually evolving story of his campaigns in Dacia. Some new and hitherto unsuspected element had entered Roman art. It was as though time and space had suddenly changed their meaning and acquired new directions, with time revolving around itself and space seen in continuous ascent. Within the newly established convention the sculptors labored as though they had been born to it, and the patient student of Trajan's Column finds himself bemused by the brilliance of the sculptors who conveyed in some two thousand figures and thirty shifting scenes the drama of being an emperor in a time of battle. We see the legionaries pitching camp, attacking and defending, and butchering at their leisure, and we see them in hard-fought campaigns. The sculptors had evidently traveled with the army, for they depict the mountains, rivers, and forests of Dacia, and the wild boar roaming. At intervals we see the Emperor receiving embassies, conducting sacrifices, or addressing his troops, imperturbable in the midst of carnage. The theme is the heroism of the conqueror, whose ashes were laid within a golden urn inside the column, and perhaps the design of the column may be explained as a kind of marble winding-sheet enclosing the mortal remains of the Emperor. But no simple explanation serves to explain this extraordinary column, as full of complexities as the Emperor himself. Michelangelo, who lived in its shadow, pronounced favorably on the quality of the sculpture, the most skillful ever produced by the Romans.

The Column of Marcus Aurelius in the Piazza Colonna was erected in A.D. 193, and therefore some eighty years after the Trajan Column. Much had changed in the interval, and perhaps the greatest change was the fact that it had become possible for a philosopher to come to the throne. The sculptors no longer depicted a continuing campaign, but broke it up into small and comparatively disjointed episodes; there is almost no background; space vanishes, and the people stand out as though they were being violently projected by some power within the column itself. On nearly all of them there is the look of strain and exhaustion: we are no longer in the presence of imperturbable conquerors but of men who are passionately aware of suffering and anguish. Again and again the sculptors depict faces filled with grief and horror. The outlines of the figures are carved deeply enough to suggest that the sculptors were deliberately creating deep shadows, and for the first time we see the ordinary men and women of the captured tribes possessing personalities of their own; and from the faces of old men about to be massacred Christian sculptors would learn how to portray martyrs.

The column of Marcus Aurelius seems scarcely to be concerned with history, or even with the Emperor; it is far more concerned with the human condition. No doubt the sculptors had carefully studied the great temple at Pergamon, for occasionally we can recognize a conscious imitation of a defiant gesture or a posture of despair. Quite suddenly a warm sense of sympathy and understanding of human suffering had entered Roman art.

Nevertheless the theme of the pitiless conqueror survived to the last days of the Roman Empire, which was built on brute force and therefore needed to celebrate force at the expense of any civilizing mission entrusted to the emperors. The triumphal arches, deriving ultimately from the huge yokes under which prisoners were made to pass, continued the same theme. The most impressive of these triumphal arches was built at Beneventum to honor the Emperor Trajan and the many aspects of his personality: the conqueror, the colonizer, the mediator between the gods and mankind, the chief participant in the supreme sacrifices, the philanthropist who instituted doles for poor children, the man who brought a few years of peace to a warlike empire. On the panels of the archway, between imposing Corinthian columns, the sculptors depicted the real and legendary incidents of a life completely devoted to governing the empire. In these panels, and most especially in the panel under the archway showing the Emperor attending the sacrifices, we are made aware of a man who cared deeply. The Emperor wears a veil, as always when he attends sacrifices, and there flows between him and the people surrounding him an extraordinary sense of trust and affection. It was as though the sculptor was trying to catch one of the supreme moments of human history, the moment when the Roman people discovered that it could place all its trust in an emperor and not find him wanting.

There were very few emperors who cared deeply, though many made the appropriate gesture of caring. Some emperors, Trajan among them, built immense bathhouses, which served also as shopping centers, art galleries, amusement parks, and places of assignation. These bathhouses were the size of cathedrals. The Baths of Caracalla, a mile in circumference, were deliberately designed to be the largest single structure in Rome. Immense vaults dwarfed the naked bathers below; and among those acres of mosaics and millions of marble tiles, among the statues lining the colonnades and the huge granite columns, so vast that it seemed impossible that they had been carved out of the living rock by human hands, the Romans lived at ease in the secure knowledge that all their physical needs were being attended to. These bathhouses were gigantic engineering feats designed to grant full satisfaction for all the cravings of the flesh, and if the bather felt the need to read and study, this also was attended to, and if he wished to worship, he could go to the small cult temples with their attendant priests. The Baths of Diocletian, considerably smaller than the Baths of Caracalla, now serve to house both the Church of Santa Maria degli Angeli and the National Museum, and these two buildings occupy only a corner of the original baths.

Magnificence, "the making of bigness," had become endemic in imperial times. Hadrian's villa was far from being a villa; it was an immense sprawling estate, an entire city devoted to the pleasure of an Emperor who consoled himself after the death of his young favorite Antinoüs by ordering innumerable statues of the Syrian boy whose beauty once pleased him, and when he wished to be alone he would resort to a marble study set in the midst of a small lake. Yet the same Emperor was responsible for the construction of the Pantheon, the noblest of all Roman buildings.

If all the Roman buildings except one were swept away, the one survivor would have to be the Pantheon. The details are exquisite; the whole is a marvel of grace and nobility, which appears to have sprung from the imagination of a single man. Of all the architects who might have designed it, the most likely is Hadrian himself.

The Pantheon was built on the site of an earlier temple erected by Marcus Agrippa, the son-in-law of Augustus. Hadrian tore it down, but deliberately retained the inscription recording the erection of the earlier temple. Agrippa's temple celebrated Neptune, the sea god, who had granted him the naval victory that decided the fate of the empire. Hadrian's temple celebrated all the gods worshiped by the Romans, and he therefore devised a temple shaped like a great sphere open to the heavens. In columned niches the statues of the gods stood in a great circle, and each in turn would be touched by the light flowing from the sky.

Hadrian seems to have been fascinated by the circle and the square. The porch forms an exact square, the floor plan is a perfect circle. Though from the outside the temple appears curiously robust, it is in fact constructed with great delicacy, and the austere circle is deliberately broken by coffered panels diminishing in size as they ascend, until finally at the very summit they meet the circle of light that crowns the entire edifice. Nothing so pure had ever been attempted by the Romans, nor was any similar building erected again. Almost it might have been designed by Pythagoras, who believed religion to be intimately associated with mathematics.

Such perfect simplicities are rare in Roman art. Increasingly the Roman tendency toward the grandiose and the magnificent manifested itself. In painting, too, we come upon strange illusionistic decorations representing colossal edifices, one springing out of another, until the mind boggles before the accumulated weight of so many cloud-capped palaces. The vast and the monumental even invaded the imperial coinage, which succeeded in suggesting the illimitable power of the emperor within the compass of a copper coin.

When Constantine came to power, monumentality on a colossal scale had become commonplace. The Emperor, who was later to embrace Christianity and to call himself *isapostoles,* "the equal of the apostles," thus establishing his right to a spiritual as well as an earthly empire, followed the habits of earlier emperors and placed in his own basilica a colossal statue of himself. The head and some fragments of a hand and legs survive, and are now in the Palazzo dei Conservatori in Rome. The head alone is eight and a half feet high and weighs about nine tons. Nor was there anything particularly excessive in such magnificence, for other emperors had made even larger statues of themselves.

Yet the art of sculpture was visibly dying, and the proof lies in the Arch of Constantine, powerfully built and magnificently placed, but devoid of any sculptures of his own time worthy of him. There are friezes which might have been carved by a primitive craftsman in some remote provincial town, without grace or authority. It is woodcutter's work, and you can almost see the marks of the ax. The designers were concerned with the absence of any effective decoration, and so they simply removed sculptures from existing monuments from the time of Hadrian, Trajan, and Marcus Aurelius.

On Constantine's triumphal arch the most beautiful decoration derives from the eight medallions from the time of Hadrian, who died two hundred years before Constantine was elevated to the throne. Of these the loveliest are the medallions depicting a boar hunt and an offering at the altar of Apollo, who appears in all his beauty among the laurel trees.

Roman art surrendered to grandiosity and paid the inevitable price. We become aware of the price in the remote valley below Monte Mangone in Sicily, where the Emperor Maximian, Constantine's father-in-law, built a hunting lodge as large as Hadrian's villa and laid down an immense carpet of mosaics, which has recently been discovered. There are acres upon acres of mosaics recounting the adventures of the Emperor, his battles, his hunting parties, his participation in a great round-up of African beasts which would later be displayed in Rome. There are vintage scenes and erotic improvisations, and records of feasts. There are girls in bikinis and parades of soldiers and there is even a portrait of the young Constantine attending a barbecue. Sometimes the mosaics display an intense vitality, as in the scenes showing the labors of Hercules, but just as often there is a quality of feverish improvisation and disintegration. Sometimes a face looms out of the whiteness of space, just such a face as a man might see in a high fever. The world is falling apart, men move aimlessly about, one scene follows disjointedly on another, there is no order or logic in the designs. There is no air, no scenery, no purpose. The Emperor has amused himself by creating the largest sheet of mosaics ever made, and the ultimate effect is to chill the onlooker at the thought of all this waste of artistic energy.

Chaos had come again. The Roman Empire was drawing to an end, and in a few more years Rome herself would be no more than a provincial city ruled by Constantine from Byzantium.

THE
CHRISTIAN FLOWERING

The Holy Fire

"I am the light of the world: he that followeth me shall not walk in darkness, but shall have the light of life." The Johannine text, and there are many similar ones, appears to have suggested very early that a Christian church should not be a place of gloom, but one shining with singing light. In some mysterious way an enclosed space with solid walls and roof must convey the impression of the otherworldly light in which Christ lived; light must flame along the walls and fill the spaces of the church.

There were in existence no churches which possessed this quality during the reign of Constantine, when for the first time vast sums of public money could be spent on the building of churches. Traditionally the pagan temples were dark and gloomy places, almost sepulchral, the cult image emerging out of the shadows and giving the impression of a superbly powerful but indistinct force confronting the worshiper. This was true even in the great temples on the Acropolis and at Olympia. We hear of stone pools filled with water lying in front of the cult statue, and no doubt the water acted as a mirror and reflected the light upward on the carved features of the god, and because the water was never completely still, there would be a faint trembling of the light and a quivering of the air. But in general the interior of a Greek temple was deliberately conceived as a place where the worshiper communed with the god in the half-darkness. However brilliant and beautiful the exterior, the interior resembled and derived from the Neolithic and Bronze Age cave with the cult object set in the remote interior.

The Christian church, evolving from the Greek temple and

the Roman basilica, was flooded with light by the simple process of filling the wall space with mosaics and by introducing oil lamps and candles on an unprecedented scale. The art of mosaic making was well known and had a respectable ancestry. Mosaics were used to decorate floors, or the bottom of a bath might be inlaid with mosaic fishes or aquatic birds, which would appear to be alive in the rippling water. More complex mosaics like the great *Battle of Alexander* which survives in the National Museum at Naples were clearly the reproductions of paintings, but the art had reached such a high standard of achievement that it is scarcely conceivable that there were not mosaic masters who worked directly on the *tesserae* after drawing up their cartoons, for mosaic making obeys its own laws, which are not the laws of painting. Few Alexandrian mosaics have survived; they are reputed to have been of great complexity and beauty. The earliest surviving wall mosaic comparable to the mosaics of Christian churches is to be found in a rich wine merchant's house in Herculaneum, dating from about A.D. 50. The merchant had exquisite taste, and converted a small courtyard behind his shop into a *nymphaeum* with a decorative fountain and a pool to honor the nymphs. Around the walls were mosaics. Two walls survive intact, and on one of them there are vines and running deer, on the other Neptune stands beside Amphitrite against a golden sky. Neptune is gray-bearded, but has the body of a youth, bronzed and muscular, giving an impression of formidable power. A blue scarf, representing the sea, winds around his arms and shoulders. Already in that portrait of the naked Neptune we have a foretaste of the magnificently commanding Christ who will appear on the walls of Byzantine churches.

The wine merchant lived in a thickly populated quarter of Herculaneum, where space was at a premium, and the small courtyard evidently served as his place of recreation. By building a pool to reflect the sky and by gilding the walls with gold mosaic, he increased the space. The gold wall, made out of thousands upon thousands of small cubes of glass fused with gold leaf, would reflect every ripple of the water flowing into the pool. Across this small space, light continually leaped and danced, and the figure of Neptune, caressed by the continually moving reflections from the water, would give the illusion of being in motion. In much the same way, with the gleam of candles replacing the glint of water, the mosaics in the churches leaped from the walls.

The earliest surviving Christian mosaics are to be found in the Church of Santa Constanza in Rome, about A.D. 360, and in the Rotunda of St. George in Salonica, about A.D. 395. Both churches are circular. The first, a small and wonderfully delicate baptistery, was later transformed into a mausoleum for Constantina, the sister of Constantine, while the second, originally a vast domed mausoleum erected by the Emperor Galerius, was converted into a Christian church by Theodosius the Great. The baptistery has a quiet, jewel-like beauty, the dome supported by a perfect circle of double columns, the ambulatory vault covered with gay mosaics which obviously derive from pagan sources: a tangle of vines, birds, hay wains, and handsome youths. Two semicircular mosaics in the apses show Christ offering the key to Peter, and Christ between Peter and Paul. They are amateurish works crudely fashioned by an artist who evidently believed that a mosaic was simply a fresco made out of colored stones, and they are out of place in the enchanted circle of the baptistery.

The mosaic artists who worked on the giant Rotunda of St. George confronted far more difficult problems and succeeded beyond any reasonable expectations. They knew exactly how to set the mosaics and were not under the illusion that a mosaic performed the functions of a fresco. Their task was a stupendous one, for it was nothing less than to illuminate with mosaics the entire expanse of a beehive-shaped rotunda which has an inner diameter of eighty feet and a height of ninety feet. The dome showed a mosaic of Christ in eternal glory surrounded by angels, and this is now lost. The mosaic designs on the walls are also lost. What remains is a mosaic frieze about eighteen feet deep below the dome, showing twelve saints in prayer against the background of the heavenly Jerusalem, golden palace rising above golden palace, with archways, colonnades, and arcades ornamented with glittering columns. The saints stand facing outward, their hands uplifted in adoration, and their shimmering embroidered vestments, plum-colored, purple, aqueous green, and gleaming white completely cover their bodies. The faces of the saints are depicted with extraordinary refinement, and they were evidently modeled on the princes and high dignitaries of the court. This is the earliest of the great Byzantine mosaics. In power and refinement it was never excelled in the thousand years of mosaic making that followed.

Earthquakes have left cracks and fissures spreading like tongues of flame across the heavenly city; birds nest in the rotunda, and their wings brush against the small tesserae until they fall away; and no doubt in a hundred years' time there will be even less of the heavenly Jerusalem and of the twelve majestic saints. But for our generation those who wish to see the art of the mosaicist in its most exquisite form must go to the Rotunda of St. George in Salonica. On that sumptuous ribbon of gold, gleaming like an immense crown below the shadowy dome, the miracle has been accomplished.

The masters who worked these colored stones and nuggets of glass fused with gold leaf made a profound study of the effects of light, of refraction and reflection, the varying angles of incidence, the peculiar properties of mosaics on curved apsidal surfaces. They studied the properties of surfaces, and knew how deeply light penetrates some stones; and they were able to calculate the angles at which the stones should be set. They recognized the fluidity of light, and the extraordinary way in which light pulsates. Employing many different techniques, they were able to illuminate the walls with shapes which seemed to have three dimensions and which seemed to advance bodily out of the walls. They accomplished what might have been thought impossible, for their aim was to convert temporal space into divine space, to transform a church with four walls and a roof into a place of vision and enchantment. The light of a Byzantine church is not of this earth; it is almost palpably the light of heaven.

Unfortunately we know very little about the lives of the mosaicists, who never signed their work and left no records of their craft. An edict in the reign of Diocletian informs us that the *pictor imaginarius* received 175 sesterces, the *pictor parietarius* received seventy-five sesterces, while the workmen who embedded the stones in the plaster received between fifty and sixty sesterces. The *pictor imaginarius,* working with the architect, designed the original cartoons and superintended the construction of the mosaics. Whole walls or whole churches would be entrusted to him, and he provided the creative force. The *pictor parietarius* was the draftsman and mechanic; presumably there were also foremen who supervised the work of the setters. It was an intricate and highly specialized craft, and there is evidence that some setters concentrated on heads, others on gowns, others on backgrounds, others on ornamental borders. There is some evidence, too, that the guild of mosaicists was closely guarded and under the protection of the imperial court. Whole palaces in Constantinople were covered with mosaics from floor to ceiling. The palaces have perished, but many of the churches survive.

Salonica has the largest collection of mosaics still standing on the church walls. A small mosaic of Christ in glory attended by Ezekiel and Habakkuk stands in the apse of Hosios David, once a monastic church, now just one more derelict building in the working-class district of Salonica. Christ rides the rainbow, the holy rivers of paradise flow at his feet, the bull and the lion guard him, strange shapes hover in the shadows, but what is most remarkable about the mosaic, which dates from about A.D. 450, is the face of Christ, very gentle, very feminine, so feminine indeed that the artist seems to have deliberately followed the tradition reported many years later by St. John of Damascus that he resembled his mother. The mosaic was lost for centuries, being found under a coating of plaster only in 1921; and though it lacks the brilliance and sophistication of the mosaics of the Rotunda of St. George, it must be counted among that small group of mosaics, numbering perhaps ten or eleven, which can be regarded as supreme masterpieces.

At the considerably more famous Basilica of St. Demetrius, built on the traditional site of the synagogue where St. Paul preached, only a few mosaics remain. The original church was destroyed by fire about A.D. 630, and the surviving mosaics date from about this time, for the basilica was immediately built on its ruins. The basilica was burned again in 1917, and it was after this fire that some of the most precious mosaics, long hidden and preserved by Turkish plaster, came to light. They show the youthful St. Demetrius, the patron saint of the city, placing a protective hand on the shoulder of the bishop, and there are others showing the saint protecting the founders of the church and blessing children. We see the jeweled and shimmering gown of the saint, modeled on the gowns worn by high officials of the Byzantine court, but he has the face of a boy of fourteen or fifteen, very quiet and reserved. It is the face of a young acolyte, and does not suggest power.

In the Church of Hagia Sophia in Salonica the immense dome is ringed with portraits of the apostles in attitudes of grief-stricken wonder as they watch Christ vanishing among the clouds of heaven. Some twist their heads, others gaze sorrowfully into the distance, and only the Virgin, who stands among them, remains unmoved by the spectacle of the Ascension. Once again the mosaic masters have contrived to represent a moment which is almost beyond the powers of anyone to depict, for that dome succeeds triumphantly in conveying the portrait of divinity vanishing before men's eyes.

At all times the cost of making mosaics was high, and only bishops and emperors with an ample treasury could afford them. The Emperor Justinian acquired vast treasure from his conquests, and in addition he was well served by the Nika riots, which destroyed large areas of Constantinople, thus providing him with an excuse to build new churches and to embellish them with sheets of mosaics. At no time in history was so much money spent in building churches. The poet W. B. Yeats described these mosaic workers and illuminators as though they were almost angelic presences gifted with a kind of unconscious awareness of the splendor they were creating, impersonally absorbed in their tasks. He wrote:

> I think that if I could be given a month of antiquity and leave to spend it where I chose, I would spend it in Byzantium a little before Justinian opened St. Sophia and closed the Academy of Plato. I think I would find in some little wine shop some philosophical worker in mosaic who could answer all my questions, the supernatural descending nearer him than Plotinus even, for the pride of his delicate skill would make what was an instrument of power to Princes and Clerics and a murderous madness to the mob, show as a lovely flexible presence like that

of a perfect human body. I think that in early Byzantium, and maybe never before or since in recorded history, religious, aesthetic and practical life were one, and that architects and artificers— though not, it may be, poets, for language had been the instrument of controversy and must have grown abstract—spoke to the multitude and the few alike. The painter and the mosaic worker, the worker in gold and silver, the illuminator of Sacred Books were almost impersonal, almost perhaps without the consciousness of individual design, absorbed in their subject matter and that the vision of a whole people.*

It was not a fantastic claim to make for the workers of Byzantium in the age of Justinian, for never before or since—not even in the time of Pope Julius II—was so much treasure expended by a monarch on the arts. In this age the production of great designs became a commonplace, and among a multitude of churches Hagia Sophia rose to prove that stupendous splendors could be achieved by human hands.

Of the mosaics ordered by Justinian in Constantinople scarcely anything remains except a palace floor crowded with some astonishing disconnected scenes: an eagle coiled in a serpent, a girl carrying a heavy amphora on her back, a boy offering hay to a donkey, which looks away with an air of complete detachment. The mosaics show an advance in technical mastery, but suffer from a curious irrelevance. No one has given a satisfactory explanation for these separate designs scattered over a white floor, and the most rational explanation seems to be that they were decorations for the courtyard of the imperial children.

Justinian built churches with a fierce prodigality, for he loved God nearly as much as he loved luxury. On the ruins of a church destroyed by his rioting subjects, he built Hagia Sophia in the short space of five years, and there is no reason to disbelieve the legend that on the day the church was consecrated, he cried out in triumph: "Glory to God, who has judged me worthy of accomplishing such a work as this. O Solomon, I have outdone thee!" In its time it was the largest church in Christendom, measuring 250 feet long and 235 feet wide, the crown of the dome being 182

* W. B. Yeats, *Pages from a Diary written in 1930* (Dublin: Cuala Press, 1945), p. 2.

feet above the floor. On that massive scale the architects Anthemius of Thralles and Isodorus of Miletus attempted to create a vision of paradise large enough to embrace the entire population of Constantinople.

Erected to the glory of God, Hagia Sophia glorified man as the glorifier of God, and it especially glorified Justinian, whose monogram, interlaced with that of the Empress Theodora, is carved all over the church. No expense was spared to make this the most sumptuous church of its age, and it was confidently predicted that no church would ever rival it. By order of Justinian the columns supporting the dome came from all the temples of the known world. Eight porphyry columns, the gift of a rich widow, were dispatched from the Temple of the Sun at Baalbek; eight more came from the Temple of Diana of the Ephesians; columns of rose-red marble were imported from the mountains of Phrygia. Sparta sent emerald-green marble, and from Numidia came marble the color of yellow crocuses, while the Lydians provided columns of white translucent marbled veined with red. At the end of the astonishing catalogue of the marbles sent to decorate Hagia Sophia written by Paulus Silentarius, we hear of marble from the Celtic mountains which shone "like a wealth of crystals, like milk poured here and there on a flesh of glittering black."

The Byzantines made the best of both worlds, and there was more than a hint of sensuality in the ripeness of the richly decorated interior and in the swelling of the dome, that huge dome which seemed in some mysterious fashion to hang suspended over the church rather than being supported by the walls and buttresses, an effect achieved by the row of small windows at the springing of the dome, which throw a diffused curving light into the dome itself. Originally the dome appears to have been filled with flowerlike stars in mosaic. "Whoever shall raise his eyes to the lovely heaven of this dome," wrote Paulus Silentarius, "dares scarcely gaze upon it; all the stars are there; and from the green marble below there springs, so it seems, the flower-bordered streams of Thessaly, and budding corn, and groves of trees, and there are leaping flocks also, and tortured olive-trees, the vine with green tendrils, and the deep blue peace of summer seas."

Vast areas of the church were decorated with mosaics, but of those designed during the reign of Justinian nothing remains except a few small decorative fragments. The surviving mosaics come from a later age, but even in their broken form, for scarcely a single mosaic is complete, they suggest the dazzling prodigality of colors which once flooded the entire church. In the time of Justinian it was lit at night by immense candelabras of hammered silver, some in the form of ships, others resembling flowering trees, with jets of flame taking the place of flowers. Today Hagia Sophia gives an impression of shadowy immensity except on the brightest days; the weathered stone has lost its color; and there is something cavernlike in the huge echoing interior. In its heyday there was a tumultuous riot of flaming reds, peacock blues, and purple greens, with white, gold, and green predominating. In addition to the mosaics there was an immense silken tapestry showing Christ in a tunic of shimmering gold flanked by Peter and Paul clothed in silver. The effect must have been of an unparalleled splendor, with deliberate clashes of intense color. Procopius noted the beauty of the reflections of the gold mosaics on the marble floor and columns.

If it was a deeply religious age, it was also an age of great conquests, of political disorders, and of material satisfactions. Constantinople stood at the center of an empire reaching out across Italy, North Africa, and a large part of the Near East. The entire empire was laid under tribute to supply materials for Justinian's churches and palaces, where whole rooms were decorated with mosaics depicting the victories of his reign, with here and there a portrait of the protecting Savior. Yet there were few portraits of the Savior in Hagia Sophia, according to Paulus Silentarius, who mentions the many mosaics of the Virgin, "nor have the workmen forgotten those who spent their early days among fishing nets and baskets." Indeed the great silken tapestry appears to have been hung behind the altar as a reminder that the church was after all dedicated to Christ under the aspect of Holy Wisdom.

Mosaics of the reign of Justinian are preserved in brilliant profusion in the Church of San Vitale at Ravenna. It is a small church which would be lost in the immensity of Hagia Sophia. Begun in A.D. 526, when Ravenna was still occupied by the Goths, and completed in A.D. 548, eight years after the reconquest of the city by the Byzantines, it took four times as long to build as Hagia Sophia. All the mosaics were designed during the period when the church was under the direct patronage of Justinian, who is shown in the company of his retinue on a mosaic panel set in the side wall of the apse. In this majestic portrait the artists flattered him by including him among the saints, for he wears a halo of scarlet outlined in silver, which has now faded. That he should be represented with the halo is not surprising, for he regarded himself as the vice-regent upon earth of a transcendent God. A triple tiara of pearls, emeralds, and rubies indicates his earthly rank, and the power and splendor of the Emperor are reinforced by the wide purple gown and the red buskins, the egg-sized ruby worn at the shoulder and the enormous gold offering bowl, a present to the church, which he carries in his hands. He is portrayed as a man of middle age with a fleshy face and steely eyes, thick eyebrows, and curly black hair brushed forward in the traditional manner of a Roman emperor. An intelligent voluptuary, skilled in the enjoyment of power, he is superbly aware of his own dignity. It is not a strong face, for there is a weakness about the mouth which the artist has underscored with small puffy shadows, and there is more than a hint of ill temper and petulance. The artist has composed a portrait of great psychological subtlety, and he has evidently studied the Emperor closely.

The brilliance of the mosaic panel lies in the subtlety of the portraits and the cunning arrangement of the figures, with the Emperor in the foreground and the rest forming a half-circle behind him, so that the entire design follows a recessive curve, emphasizing the forward motion of the Emperor, who appears to be on the verge of stepping out of the mosaic altogether. The faces of Justinian and his retinue are outlined against a golden heaven, but their feet walk on the green and springing earth.

On the opposite wall the Empress Theodora, the daughter of a bear keeper, appears in the company of her household. She, too, wears the purple robe and the triple tiara and carries a gold offering bowl, indicating that she is a benefactress of the church. She is festooned with jewels—strings of pearls hang down from the tiara, she wears a necklace of emeralds, a breastplate of jewels and pearls, and there are more jewels rising from the crown of her tiara. Her thin face is almost drowned in the prodigal display of her jewelry, as she moves forward like a sleepwalker oppressed by some nameless burden. It is a strangely empty face, thin-boned, nervous, solemn. She died six weeks after the church was dedicated, and the artist has conveyed the remoteness and fragility of a woman who has been slowly dying for a long time. The portrait of Justinian shows him in all his fleshly majesty, while Theodora is already a wraith.

In the history of Christian mosaics these two panels have a quite special importance, for nowhere else have imperial portraits been found in such a high state of excellence. These mosaics at San Vitale are among the supreme masterpieces of Byzantine art. Although they portray an Emperor and an Empress attended by their retinue, they are not secular works, for they are informed with Christian feeling and they express the medieval Christian concept of government, with the emperor as the divine mediator and therefore arbiter of human destinies. Justinian and Theodora are the vice-regents of God, and so they have been depicted. In that exalted station neither needs to show any humility, and they would regard it as a betrayal of the divine economy if they were shown kneeling. They have taken possession of the kingdom, and only death will separate them from it.

Only a few yards away from the Church of San Vitale there stands the small and exquisitely beautiful mausoleum of the Empress Galla Placidia, which was built about a hundred years earlier. For a quarter of a century she had ruled unopposed as the supreme authority of the Western Roman Empire. She, too, had built a great basilica which was as much in her own honor as in honor of God. On the walls of the basilica she had recounted in mosaics her miraculous rescue from shipwreck, but in the mausoleum which she built for herself and her family there are no portraits of her. If any monument can be humble, this was humble. The mausoleum consists of a small blue cave, about forty feet deep, faintly lit by a honey-colored light from the thin sheets of alabaster serving as windows, with flowerlike stars wheeling overhead, and the shapes of Christ, the apostles, and the Cross loom through the midnight blue of space.

In the mysterious submarine light of the mausoleum, in the flickering of candles, the visitor seems to have entered another dimension of space. Except for the reddish-yellow marble floor, the entire interior is encrusted with mosaics. Three sarcophagi stand in the three cruciform arms of the interior. Above them a beardless Christ reclines among his lambs, his gray-blue eyes gazing toward the west. Because Galla Placidia was a Roman Empress, Peter and Paul, the apostles chiefly connected with Rome, are also represented in snow-white garments and in attitudes of adoration; they resemble ghostly clouds floating across the blue of heaven. Two deer are seen drawing near to a pool, and they are festooned with flowering vines, and while the pool signifies the divine water of life, the vines clearly signify the abundance and beauty of earthly life. In this blue mausoleum everything is strangely appropriate and curiously tentative. Of all the mosaics ever made, those in the mausoleum of Galla Placidia have the greatest purity.

By the time of Justinian the foundations had been truly laid, the iconography had been worked out, and it needed only artists of genius to assemble the little cubes of glass and colored stone in their proper order. The art flourished, changed direction, acquired definite characteristics under each changing dynasty, and remained the same. It was always an art of the court or of rich endowments, and the very expense of covering walls with mosaics prevented it from becoming a popular art.

Although it was essentially a static art obedient to fundamental formulas, so that it is sometimes difficult to date a mosaic within a period of two hundred years, nevertheless there can be discerned a continuing development. Gradually over the centuries the stiff hieratic forms are fleshed out, the muscles become visible, the shape of the limbs can be detected beneath the robes, and movement appears with increasing frequency, not only the movement of the limbs but the movement of emotion and religious feeling. The art of the mosaic, which was ideally suited to portray the grandeur and unapproachability of divinity, is transformed into an art capable of portraying the minute details of human expression or the most delicate folds of a garment. There are whole stretches of mosaic at St. Mark's in Venice which have the appearance of paintings, and we are not in the least surprised to learn that they were executed from cartoons by Tintoretto. After the earthquake in 1511 many of the mosaics in St. Mark's were damaged, and the question arose whether they should be repaired or entirely refashioned in accordance with contemporary designs. The Venetian artists, including Titian, lent their weight to the renovators who wanted to refashion the mosaics in the modern idiom, with the result that Renaissance mosaics stand side by side with mosaics of the eleventh and twelfth centuries. The effect is as garish as if one placed a painting by Cézanne next to one by Leonardo da Vinci.

In the twelfth century there came a new tenderness. Just as in the West the rigidity of Romanesque gives place to the fluidity of Gothic, so in the East there can be felt a softening and a freshening. The winter had passed, spring was coming in—a brief spring, for soon it would be high summer. What is known as the Palaeologian Revival was already taking place a century and a half before the Palaeologi came to the throne. A new humanism, a new immediacy, enters all Byzantine designs. Already, by A.D. 1100, when the church at Daphni was built, we see the human figure becoming softer and rounder. The mosaic of the Baptism shows the influence of classical Greece: the youthful Christ has the long legs and deep chest of a runner in the games. Lithe and pure, he seems to be about to rise out of the Jordan toward the descending dove, and there is in his posture, one hand at his side and the other blessing the waters, the suggestion of exquisite tact. So again in the mosaic of the Crucifixion he clearly derives from an ancient Greek kouros. The freedom of the past has been revived, and behind the hieratic Byzantine masks we see the features of the ancient Greeks.

The small church of Daphni near Athens is the turning point. All the mosaics designed previously have the stiff, hieratic postures. Nearly all the mosaics of Salonica, all at Nea Moni on the island of Chios, and all at Hosios Lucas near Delphi have these stern, unyielding postures. Afterward there comes the new Christ, who walks and breathes and shows himself to his disciples and his worshipers as though he were made of human flesh and blood, beautiful and kingly, but nevertheless belonging to the human race.

At the same time there appeared a greater understanding of

psychological forces. The artists portray a much greater range of expression, they are more daring in their juxtapositions of color, they invent new shapes and new mythologies. Yet it was not by accident that the most powerful image of the Pantocrator ever made, an image of awesome profundity, should appear in the small dome of the church at Daphni at the same time that Christ was being represented in his human aspect. No doubt the Pantocrator derived ultimately from the Zeus of Olympia, but he derived even more directly from the avenging Jehovah. Almost it is a portrait of abstract power: the eyes are stern, the beard craggy, the hands gnarled, and there is nothing in the design which does not add to the overwhelming image of power, limitless and unconstrained. Here at last the *tremendum Dei* is expressed with the force of genius.

Many of the greatest mosaics of the Palaeologian Revival have been rediscovered in recent times. The great *Deesis* in Hagia Sophia and the fabulous wealth of mosaics in the Church of the Monastery of the Chora were all covered with plaster by the Turkish invaders. We owe their rediscovery to Dr. Thomas Whittemore and Dr. Paul Underwood, who patiently uncovered them, using the most delicate modern instruments and spending long hours on dangerous scaffoldings. They belong to the high summer of the art of mosaics. We see a gentle and kingly Christ walking through a world which is recognizably the world as we know it. The Church of the Monastery of the Chora dates from about A.D. 1320 and contains as many frescoes as mosaics; and already the mosaics are almost indistinguishable from the frescoes.

It was the end, or very nearly the end. The Byzantine emperors, threatened by the Turks, the Venetians, and the Genoese, ruled over a small and fragmentary empire. The Venetians, who sacked Constantinople in 1204, removed all the movable treasure, but they could not remove the churches, which were the greatest treasure, nor could they take from the city its pre-eminence as a generator of artistic power. When Michael VIII Palaeologus came to the throne in 1261, it was as though there had been no interregnum of Frankish and Burgundian princes, and Byzantine art continued as before. It was still developing, still seeking new ways of expression, when the Ottoman Turks seized Constantinople in

1453, and at the order of Sultan Mohammed II Hagia Sophia became a stable for Turkish horses and the crescent replaced the cross on the dome.

Byzantine civilization perished, but did not entirely perish. In countless different ways it continued to influence the arts of Europe, most notably in Russia, where the designs of the churches, the liturgy, the mosaics, and the holy icons followed faithfully on Byzantine patterns. In ivories, illuminated manuscripts, painting, sculpture, weaving, and the minor arts the Byzantines had demonstrated their mastery, endowing them with aristocratic and imperial forms. Survivors from the Turkish sack of Constantinople reached Florence, and at the court of Lorenzo de' Medici they found the refuge denied to them in Rome. In this way Byzantine vigor flowed into the mainstream of European art, for the Florentines owed much to Constantinople. A certain aristocratic impersonality, a litheness, a love of splendid color, a sense of majesty—these remained. Imperial Rome had crossed the sea and taken up residence on the Bosphorus, on the shores of Asia, and now the arts returned to Italy. If all the churches and palaces of Constantinople had been razed to the ground, it would still have been possible to reconstruct that ageless civilization, for they had left their traces in Florence, Venice, Ravenna, Athens, Salonica, the islands of the Aegean, and the cities of Asia Minor. Byzantine art was visibly present in all the churches of Russia and Macedonia. In Palermo and Cefalù in Sicily, and in Rome itself, imperishable mosaics reminded men that art was for the ages to come, not for the evanescent moment. These artists were the "artificers of eternity" who gave a new splendor to art and also to man.

The Face of Christ

In the history of the world's art two faces have been predominant —Christ and Buddha. They have been represented by countless artists in countless thousands of paintings and sculptures in order to evoke an image of divinity in the eyes of worshipers. Tenderness, compassion, power, beauty, majesty, all these were suggested in the lineaments of the faces, and in addition it was necessary to suggest the supreme judge, the ruler of the universe, the author of a code of laws determining the lives of all men living on the earth. The task was almost beyond human accomplishment, for it demanded of the artist a knowledge he could never possess. With his own eyes he had never seen divinity, and he could therefore only hint at its immaculate perfection, its absolute grace.

Strangely, the portraits began to emerge about the same time in the Middle East, and were both deeply influenced by Hellenistic tradition. The portrait of the bearded Christ derived ultimately from Zeus, the portrait of Buddha derived ultimately from Apollo, but neither Zeus nor Apollo provided more than the essential framework on which the imaginations of the artists would play for many centuries. As Buddhism spread across the East and Christianity across the West, the portraits would acquire the special coloring of time and place, and there was never any moment when they were given a final, undeviating form. Even in Byzantium, where for a thousand years the Church insisted on determining what it conceived to be a fixed portrait with exactly calculated proportions, there were continual subtle changes. So, too, at various times the Buddhists developed canons of proportions for the figure of Buddha, and yet these proportions were in a continual state of flux.

The difficulty, of course, lay in the nature of the task. In the eyes of the worshipers Christ and Buddha were not simply the lords of the universe; they were lords who had come to earth in historical time, had wandered, taught, suffered, and died the physical death that comes to all men, whereupon they were translated to their thrones in heaven, ruling the world from their heavenly kingdoms. They were of the earth and of heaven; and it was necessary that the artist should somehow convey their divinity while giving them human form. Inevitably the earthly body would be secondary to the divine face, and the artist would attempt to convey divine power in the expression of the face. Piercing eyes, a broad forehead, a strong nose, a majestic beard for Christ, and for Buddha clean-shaven features of immaculate calm, with the eyelids gradually lowering over the centuries. In both faces the eyes were intended to hold the gaze of the worshipers, and the body was no more than the scaffolding supporting the face.

Since no authoritative description of the persons of Christ and Buddha had survived, it became necessary to invent them, as a blind man will invent the features of someone who is dear and familiar to him. Traditions could be used to build up a portrait which would be all the more recognizable because it contained evidence of the contradictions inevitable in a man who was also a god. Thus one portrait would be "married" to another, or a tradition would be discarded and another substituted. Since the words and acts of the god were known, the completed portrait would have to have a close relationship to the worshiper's knowledge of him, even though this knowledge did not extend to the god's features.

At some very early period icons showing the face of Christ were worshiped and we hear of *acheiropoietoi*, portraits not made by human hands. One icon, known as the Edessa portrait, has a certain claim to credibility. St. John of Damascus, the saintly theologian who was once the Prime Minister at the court of the Umayyad Caliph Abd-al-Malik, passionately espoused the cause of images at a time when the Byzantine emperor Leo III was determined to destroy them. St. John of Damascus was an authority on images, and not likely to fall widely astray when he discussed a particular image said to have been fashioned by Christ. He tells this story:

> It is known by an ancient tradition that Abgar, King of Edessa, having heard the wonders that were told about Jesus, sent envoys to beg him to honor him with his presence. If this could not be achieved, at the very least they should bring him a portrait of the Nazarene. And the story says that as the painter sent by Abgar failed to produce on canvas the likeness of Christ because of the splendor of his face, Our Lord took a cloth, applied it to his divine and life-giving face and sent it to that king who desired it so much.

St. John of Damascus tells the story in good faith, neither quite believing nor disbelieving. Elsewhere he says he had seen the portrait and marveled at its beauty. He was not the only authority who claims to have seen it, for Moses of Khorem, the father of Armenian history, who lived in the fifth century, also claimed to have seen it when he was staying in Edessa. According to Moses of Khorem, the portrait was painted by Ananias, the court painter of King Abgar. The king reigned from A.D. 13 to 50, and the letter he wrote to Christ and the reply are quoted by Eusebius in his *Ecclesiastical History*. Whether or not he possessed a portrait of Christ, King Abgar was a historical personage who lived at the time of Christ and was just such a man who could be expected to ask for a portrait. Eusebius attributes the portrait to a divine origin, Procopius wrote that it had been rediscovered in his own day among the treasures which had belonged to King Abgar, and Evagrius adds the further information that the rediscovery took place in A.D. 545. According to the Byzantine historians, this portrait, believed to be a wonder-working image, was captured by the Emperor Romanus I Lecapenus and brought in triumph to Constantinople on August 15, 944. He was one of the greatest of the Byzantine emperors, but a few months later he was dethroned by his own sons.

The Edessa portrait remained undisturbed for more than 400 years. When the empire was in full decline, it came into the possession of a Genoese captain-general who had allied himself with the Byzantine Emperor against the Turks. Finally, it came to the

Church of St. Bartholomew of the Armenians in Genoa, where it remains to this day.

The Edessa portrait has some importance in the history of the transformations of Christ's face, for it is clearly one of the very earliest icons and has a recorded history going back to the fourth century. The face has a dark reddish tinge, almost wine-colored. The forehead is smooth and rounded, the eyes are deep-sunken under wide semicircular brows, the nose is long and thin, the upper lip very short, the corners of the mouth are turned down, and the long soft black beard is forked. The left eyebrow is a little higher than the right, and this helps to give vitality to a face which is otherwise very grave and strangely lifeless. Byzantine artists almost invariably raised the left eyebrow in the same way.

When we see the Edessa portrait today, with part of the hair and the beard concealed by a heavy gold frame, the features melting in a kind of reddish haze, the shadows of the face losing themselves in the long shadowy beard, we can still recognize its power and authority. Painted on fine, closely woven canvas, it is clearly the work of a Syrian painter of a period long before Constantine inaugurated the Byzantine Empire. It is as though one had traveled back in time and found the original springs of Byzantine art in a small kingdom on the edge of Syria: for here is hieratic Christian art in its most simple and commanding form.

In the early years of Christianity, when men still looked forward to the Second Coming, there was very little interest in the physical appearance of Christ. Later, as the Second Coming appeared to become more remote, Christ began to be seen in historical perspective. In the course of time apocryphal traditions emerged, and in this way there came into existence precise and detailed descriptions of his appearance. Lentulus, the Roman governor of Judea, was said to have written a long account of Christ to the Roman Senate, describing his features in careful detail as though he had set eyes on him and remembered him vividly, even to the color of the eyes and exactly how the hair grew above the ears:

> His hair is the color of wine, and golden at the root, straight and without luster, but from the level of the ears curly and glossy, and divided down the center after the fashion of the

Nazarenes. His forehead is even and smooth, his face without
wrinkle or blemish, glowing with a delicate bloom. His beard is
full, of the same hazel color as the hair, not long, but forked. The
eyes are deep blue and intensely brilliant.

Although this description of Christ apparently derives from
ancient traditional sources, it first appears in the manuscripts of St.
Anselm of Canterbury in the twelfth century.

The tradition of the beautiful Christ had a long ancestry, but
it was not shared by all the Fathers of the Church. Some believed
that he was small, frail, dark-skinned, with an ugly twisted body,
and perhaps a hunchback. It was remembered that when a crowd
formed around him, he could not be seen. In the apocryphal *Acts
of Peter* he was described as both beautiful and ugly—*"formosus
et foedus."* Clement of Alexandria said he had "no comeliness nor
beauty, but was insignificant, inferior to the beauty of men, a man
of stripes and toil, who knew how to endure pain." Irenaeus said
more simply that he was weak and without any marks of splendor
—*"inferior et ingloriosus."* The belief that Christ was ugly was
common among the Fathers of the Eastern Church, for they were
more accustomed to seeing prophets and saints suffering from violent
infirmities of the flesh and of the spirit. Jerome spoke of Christ's
"starry face and eyes," but added no further description. St. Augustine said categorically that no man could know the appearance of
Christ, and this was because he was beautiful to those who imagined him beautiful and ugly to those who persecuted him. As for
the real face of Christ, it was beyond all knowing.

So perhaps it was, but the artists were not bound by theological concepts and they painted him according to the various traditions.
In the Roman catacombs he was rarely represented. It was enough
that he should be shown through his symbols, and the early Christians, impatiently awaiting the Second Coming, saw little reason to
draw the portrait of one who would soon appear to them in all his
majesty. In the catacombs he appears as a beardless youth surrounded by the apostles, who are equally young and no more handsome or remarkable than their teacher. In the catacomb of St.
Domitilla, of the fourth century, Christ sits among them with a

scroll open on his knees, while two servants hold up a purple cloth behind him, and only the presence of the cloth distinguishes him from the others. Once or twice he is represented as a young shepherd with the lambs gamboling at his feet while another lamb is slung round his shoulders. More often he is seen sitting at table with the apostles. There is no dramatic confrontation with Judas, and indeed Judas is never present: what is being represented is a Communion service performed quietly, calmly, in the knowledge that the divine presence held no mystery for them. The apostles are shown at ease in the presence of their youthful priest. There is no straining after majesty, no attempt to show him as the Lord of the Universe, for in his earthly life he was a man like other men. As for the all-powerful King, *Rex tremendae majestatis*, this was beyond the range of their imaginations.

The youthful beardless Christ, first seen in the catacombs, appears to have arisen spontaneously among the Roman Christians. He has no known literary origins; no theologians ever disputed over the age at which he shaved his beard. They saw him as a young man because the faith was young, and perhaps because they were themselves accustomed to being shaven. Certainly in their eyes he bore no relation to Jupiter, the hoary-headed ruler of the Roman pantheon. Christ had dethroned Jupiter: he had not taken on the likeness of the god he had dethroned.

Even when Christianity became the official religion of the Roman Empire, the tradition of the youthful Christ survived. For centuries he was represented in the West as a youth of about eighteen, usually with a rather round face, large dark eyes, small lips, the dark hair flowing down to his shoulders and combed low over his forehead. Sometimes the hair is red and is heavily curled, as we see him in the fifth century mosaics in the mausoleum of Galla Placidia at Ravenna. All these portraits have a family relationship. With minor modifications it is always the same round, appealing, faintly Semitic face, very calm, showing not the least presentiment of the agonies he will undergo. He feeds his sheep, confers crowns of martyrdom on the blessed, bathes in the River Jordan, or walks by the Sea of Galilee to watch the fishermen hauling in their nets. Sometimes he is clothed in purple with a golden stripe running down the length of his tunic, but just as often he wears the simple tunic worn by the people. In the ivory casket at Brescia, dating from the fourth century, he is scarcely more than a boy, while he appears in his early youth in the gold-glass fragment of the third century now in the British Museum:

Third-century Face of Christ

The change came drastically when Christianity became the official religion of the empire under Constantine. Then for the first time the portrait of Christ is invested with imperial grandeur, solemnity, and power. The boy vanishes, and is never seen again. Instead, there is the father image, the great bearded figure appareled in the vestments of an emperor, the expression of the face and the curling of the beard deriving from the great chryselephantine statue carved by Phidias for the temple of Zeus at Olympia. This temple was still standing, and the huge statue had suffered no damage. In the reign of Theodosius it was removed bodily from Olympia and set up in Byzantium.

The Greek orator Dio Chrysostom, who saw the statue in the first century, was overwhelmed by it. "It is the most beautiful image on earth, and the dearest to the gods," he wrote. "Let no one who has drained the cup of sorrows and from whom sleep is banished refuse to stand before the statue: he will forget all his griefs and all the troubles that encumber the paths of men." The statue made by Phidias did not merely represent the superb lord of creation in his power and majesty; there was also a superb benignity. He summoned the lightning, but he also blessed. It was only necessary to remove the oak wreath to present Zeus as Christ.

Other elements went into the fashioning of the new portrait.

According to St. John of Damascus, writing in the eighth century, Constantine commissioned paintings and mosaics of Christ's human visage from the artists who flocked to his court, and sent expeditions to Palestine to collect icons. The Edessa portrait, or one of the many similar Syrian icons, fell into his hands. The portrait of Zeus was subtly modified to include the Syrian elements. The power and majesty were retained, but there was an increasing tenderness, the lips were fuller, the eyes more gentle. From another source altogether—from Sassanian Persia—there came the golden nimbus or halo, the sign of his divinity. The Buddhists at Gandhara had already adopted the halo two centuries earlier from the same source.

In the court at Byzantium all influences met. The Byzantine emperor spoke in Latin, and all his pronouncements were published in Latin. He attended divine service in churches where the liturgies were chanted in Greek. When he gave private audiences, or delivered judgment in his robes of state, he wore the emblems of a Persian emperor, and like them he spoke from behind a jeweled veil. The Persians invented majesty; nowhere else were kings and emperors attended with such panoply; and that particular veneration which had been accorded to the Achaemenian and Sassanian kings was now given to the Byzantine emperor and still more to the portraits of Christ.

An old invention, now revived, added a new dimension to the portraits of Christ. It was not enough that he should be represented in paintings, in ivory, and in bronze, but the domes of the churches, or the half-domes, must be filled with his presence. Under Justinian the domes grew so vast that they seemed to enclose the whole sky, and to this day the dome of Hagia Sophia in Constantinople remains as a testimony to the Byzantine desire to bring heaven down to earth. Justinian wanted the interior of the church to be covered with mosaics. In the light of the oil lamps the rich glitter of the mosaics would produce a strange, otherworldly light, and the worshiper would find himself immediately translated into a heaven of bright colors.

A mosaic portrait of Christ filling the half-dome of a church, the face perhaps thirty feet high, has not the same effect as a small portable icon. The light is continually moving in waves across the hollow surface; refraction throws out a myriad splinters of light; the gold shimmers and moves forward; the blue recedes and trembles. There is the effect of light radiating out from the mosaic while simultaneously pouring back. Small chips of marble, stone, glass, silver, gold, turquoise, ruby, and emerald compose the face, which may be a hundred feet above the floor of the church. This dazzling creation has a single purpose: to bring the worshiper into the presence of Christ. Hallucinated, he cannot escape from Christ's gaze. His dreams and his waking hours will be filled with the memory of that beautiful face, which seems to breathe and utter commands and whisper words of blessing.

Nothing so splendid as the interior of a Byzantine church has ever been conceived by man. Imagine a sky composed of rainbows, yet of a deeper and more intense color than rainbows, and then set them in motion, and place in that sky a face of grave majesty and composure with searching eyes and an air of measureless authority, and you will have something of the experience of a worshiper at Hagia Sophia in the age of Justinian, when the church was lit with thousands upon thousands of lamps and candles, the walls streaming with bright color, and brightest of all was the face of Christ within the surrounding halo.

The artificers did their work well. They not only studied the properties of glass, metal, stone, and jewelry, but they worked out a way of rendering the portrait of Christ within the curved space of the apse without distortion. They gave depth and perspective to the face and shoulders looming in the heights of the church. There was no body, for the church itself was the body of Christ, but the hands could be seen holding a jeweled book or a scroll which often read: "I am the light of the world."

Light indeed had become the essential element: Christ was transmuted into streaming color. He had emerged from the darkness of the catacombs to become a vivid, brilliantly lit presence towering above his own altar in the company of his angels, disciples, prophets, and saints. Below him the priests performed rituals and chanted hymns appropriate to the events of his life on earth and in heaven, but though they wore richly embroidered gowns and sparkled with jewels and achieved a certain pomp and magnificence, they were so small in comparison with the vast overarching portrait of Christ that they might have been puppies playing about his skirts.

That Christ should be so large and dominant was essential to the new conception of his divinity, and so too was the fact that the worshipers saw only his face and shoulders. At Torcello we see the Virgin standing full length within the golden mosaic hollow of the apse, a slender and beautiful figure robed in blue, holding the Child in one arm, and with the other blessing the world. Such a figure was possible for the Virgin; it was not possible for Christ, who could not be represented at full length in the apse because his divinity was absolute and therefore he possessed no physical body. He filled the universe with his presence, that presence which was revealed by the contemplation of the divine face.

At Hosios Lukas the Byzantine craftsmen contrived an image of Christ's face with all the highlights transformed into shadows, so that it resembled a photographic negative. The intention was clear: they would emphasize the ghostly, otherworldly aspect of Christ by showing him *in reverse,* and therefore outside time and space. As far as we know, the experiment was never repeated, but it is not difficult to imagine such a face gazing down from the apse of a cathedral, so strange and yet so familiar that it would have a hypnotic effect on the worshiper, who would find himself deeply moved by the reversal of all the accepted canons of portraiture.

The Byzantine handbooks described the appearance of Christ in exact detail according to established conventions. But inevitably there were subtle changes. The immutable became mutable: consciously or unconsciously every artist added his own experience to the portrait. The stern, heavily bearded Byzantine Christ, the descendant of Olympian Zeus and Syrian icons, would soften or grow harder; he would assume an appearance of exaltation or triumph; or a fleeting smile of tenderness would appear at the corners of his lips. At Monreale he appears in all the stern dignity of the Pantocrator, while only a few miles away, at Cefalù, he wears the expression of kingly triumph and youthful exaltation. The Christ at Cefalù is among the greatest portraits of him that were made by Byzantine artists, but it is no longer a Byzantine portrait. The conquerors of Sicily were Normans, and the Christ of Cefalù more closely resembles a Norman prince than a Byzantine world emperor.

Dignity, power, superb intelligence, and beauty—all these are displayed by the Christ of Cefalù, who peers down from the conch of the apse in brilliant blue and gold vestments. He has power to move men's souls and to lead them to salvation, but he has also the power to summon them to battle. One could imagine him stepping down from the apse and commanding armies. He is no longer the absolute imperial lord of all men's destinies, but the tribal god of the Normans, so beautiful that he takes the breath away, so august that he inspires the utmost reverence, and yet one can imagine him flesh. The great Pantocrator at Daphni, just beyond the suburbs of Athens, had never been flesh; he had always been power.

The mold was breaking, and had indeed been breaking ever since Christianity traveled westward. Each nation, each culture, would refashion Christ in its own way and in its own image. By-zantine tradition would hold firmly to Christ as Pantocrator, the all-powerful and unyielding judge. In Rome there would appear an-other Christ altogether. Instead of the judge there would appear the exact opposite: the condemned. Christ Crucified played only a minor role in the Byzantine Church; in the Roman Church he would play the dominant role. On every altar, in every bedroom, there would appear the crucifix.

Into the portrait of the Crucified the artists would pour all their knowledge of suffering and grief. They would explore the shapes of death, and invent abstract designs of agony and impose them on the body of Christ. Cimabue's great painted crucifix at Arezzo shows a livid green Christ on a black cross outlined in heavy gold. The fingers are like thin spikes, the head is thrown awk-wardly against the right shoulder, the enormous chest has ex-panded almost to bursting, the stomach has swollen up like a balloon, and the thin legs feebly support the weight of the body. Every-thing in the design contributes to the sense of agony. The bunched scarlet loincloth is like an explosion of blood, and the immensely long arms resemble the branches of a withered tree. Yet that tor-tured body still conveys a sense of majesty and power; the face is still a Byzantine face, and there is even that strange tonguelike shape between the eyebrows which appears on the chalk-white face of the Daphni Pantocrator.

We know from Vasari that Cimabue studied under Byzantine masters, but it is certain that his masters did not come from the Byzantine court. Most likely they came from the Balkans, and his teachers were provincial artists lacking the refinement of the court artists. In Daphni, the Crucifixion was painless: Christ seems to sleep on the cross. In Arezzo, Christ is in agony until the end of the world.

Vasari said of Cimabue that he "resurrected painting from the dead." By this he meant that the artist had broken free from Byzantine models and established a new tradition. It was not quite true. What Cimabue did was to give Byzantine art a savage twist and then pour new energy into it. His pupil Giotto was the first to break the mold of Byzantine formalism. As Vasari observed, forgetting that he had already given the palm to Cimabue: "Through the grace of Heaven, Giotto alone, though born at a time of incompetent masters, resurrected the dead body of art and raised it to such a perfection that it could be called excellent. It was truly the greatest of miracles that so coarse and bungling an age could attain to such creative skill, in the person of Giotto, that the art of painting, of which people at that time knew little or nothing, once more came to take a definite part, through him, in our lives."

Giotto painted with an extraordinary sense of drama: not the intense, expansive drama of a Tintoretto anxious to transform every text into a theatrical scene, but the quiet drama of everyday life. He was a student of gesture, of the way men communicated with one another by faint movements of the head, the hands, and the feet, and of the way they walk. When he depicts Christ, there is nearly always a Byzantine stiffness in the features, but the body is set free. Giotto's *Crucifixion* in the Scrovegni Chapel in Padua shows no agony: there are no violent distortions; the bearded face is bent, almost hidden; and the naked body might be that of a youth, delicately and accurately painted. The drama is not in the suffering, but in the bending of the head.

Duccio, his contemporary, showed less understanding of the power of gesture and many of his figures derive from Byzantine illuminated manuscripts. When he paints a Crucifixion, he shows a chalk-white Christ writhing on the cross while the blood pours down in torrents. Duccio was a Sienese, possessing a mystical fervor and a love of shimmering colors. Giotto, a Florentine, with a more ample and sober imagination, with a greater sense of sculptural form and no predilection for mystery, painted the world as it was, a world inhabited by people close to the earth, aware of the weight of their bodies and in need to communicate with one another. All Florentine art sprang from an essential sobriety. A Florentine Christ is likely to be a heroic figure of flesh and blood, distinguished from other heroes by a vaster dignity. From Greece and Etruria classical forms fed the Florentine stream. Giotto painted a young Apollo on the cross; Cimabue, a shattered Zeus; while Duccio painted a distant descendant of the Byzantine Christ.

When the Flemish master Jan van Eyck introduced painting in oils, he brought about an innovation in art as revolutionary as the invention of mosaics. Giotto painted in tempera, which necessarily permitted little modulation in color. Oil painting immensely increased the spectrum of color, gave depth and resonance to shadows, and a strange intensity to reds and greens especially, though any color could be made to gleam with an intense luminosity at the pleasure of the painter, who could now fuse one color with another, or overlay one with another, or devise the most brilliant contrasts. The atmosphere could now be trapped within the painting: the paint itself seemed to soak in air and light. Tempera painting had always been curiously flat, but now the sharp edges of things could be given their proper prominence, so that a sword would appear to project outward. Oil painting could not do what the immense mosaic portraits of Christ had done; it could not fill a church with a fierce, glittering, otherworldly light. The place for an oil painting was on a rich man's walls or in the narrow space of a chapel or behind an altar, where it would gleam in candlelight.

With the introduction of oil painting the portraits of Christ acquired a new dimension. Oil painting admirably reproduced the most subtle textures of flesh, the most subtle curve of the lips, the most subtle smiles. Christ could be portrayed in depth, life-size, seeming to come toward the beholder or to be standing close to him; the eyes would seem to be alive, and the wounds to bleed. Oil painting could suggest an unearthly stillness, the calm of deep lakes. So lifelike were the people depicted that one could almost hear them speak, and the beholder would find himself gazing at a painting of Christ for long periods while lost in meditation or asking questions which seemed to be answered. The Byzantine icon had served the same purpose, but it never conveyed the illusion of being flesh and blood.

One of the most haunting oil paintings of Christ was made by Antonello da Messina. The *Salvator Mundi*, now in the National Gallery in London, shows a dark brick-red face, red beard, red hair, features of great power and solemnity but also of a strange gentleness indicated by the delicacy of the lips and a certain youthfulness. He stands behind a ledge, one hand resting on it while the other blesses; and in that ruddy face, given depth by the presence of the ledge, which precisely calculates our distance away from him, there is the hint of flames as though he were gazing upon the end of the world. Against the dark background he seems to have emerged suddenly, at once palpable and ghostly, but more ghostly than palpable, the dark eyes haunting the beholder with their depth and magnificence. A man might drown in those eyes. Quite deliberately Antonello da Messina has given them depth upon depth and concentrated his utmost energies in depicting them. In much the same way the great Byzantine masters exerted themselves to give depth and magnificence to the eyes of the great Pantocrators.

Oil painting could suggest the living and the dead Christ with equal fidelity. The colors of death and corruption were more readily found in oil painting than in fresco or tempera. But while oil painting could accomplish a far greater range of colors and suggest a far greater range of human and spiritual experience, it could only very rarely convey the presence of an absolute divinity. The absolute Christ, Lord of all Worlds, Light of all Lights, vanishes with the Renaissance.

Instead, there is the divine hero mercilessly exposed to the calumnies of his enemies, reviled, tortured, crucified. We see him naked, bleeding, crowned with thorns, dead or dying, in agony or in the exhaustion of death. Around the year 1460, that is, shortly after the first oil paintings were being produced, we begin to see him as he appears in Rogier van der Weyden's *Dead Christ* at Bruges, blood still gushing from his wounds, arms folded, head bowed, the drawn face reflecting weariness and despair: even in death he is suffering. He is the Man of Sorrows, and quite suddenly he has assumed primacy over all the other figures of Christ. In statues, in paintings, in woodcuts we are confronted so often with these portraits of the dead or dying Christ that we can only assume that they answered the needs of people who had seen too many wars and too many plagues to believe any longer in Christ triumphant. It is the time of the Avignon Pietà, of the woodcuts of the dances of death and the Ecce Homo, of the innumerable sculptures of Christ seated on a rock in Calvary, an unspeakable weariness filling his half-closed eyes as he waits to be crucified. Not even at the time of the Black Death in Florence, more than a century before, had there been such portraits of misery and dejection. Byzantine art emphasized his miracles and his pervading presence; the Gothic artists saw him as the teacher and the kingly majesty; it was left to the fifteenth century to see him in hideous agony.

The agony reaches its height in the Grünewald altarpiece at Colmar, where the lacerated gray-green body of Christ has become no more than a vehicle for pain. All dignity has gone; there is only a suppurating corpse which can still feel the horror of dying and the terror of death. The archaic tragedy has been played out to the end, and all that can be hoped for is that the earth will cover him, the surrounding darkness extinguish him. Grünewald went further than anyone had gone before to depict Christ separated from the hands of God and therefore damned.

This, too, would pass. Already the Christ of terror and corruption was giving place, even in the most haunted regions of Germany, to the Christ who promises salvation from pain and death. Indeed, on the very same altarpiece, Grünewald had painted Christ rising in glory, free of all mortality, his face transparent in the rays of the heavenly sun, blessing the world and offering his peace. Just as no one had previously painted Christ in such agony, so no one had ever painted him in such peace, or in such blinding colors.

While Grünewald was painting the *Isenheim Altarpiece*,

Seated Buddha from Gandhara.

Buddha Delivering His First Sermon.
SARNATH MUSEUM. INDIAN TOURIST OFFICE.

Opposite, Bodhisattva from Horyu-ji Temple, Nara.
GOVERNMENT OF INDIA INFORMATION SERVICE.

Walking Buddha from Sukhothai.
PRIVATE COLLECTION. ALEXANDER ARTEMAKIS.

Opposite, Wei Dynasty Bodhisattva
from Yün Kang, Shansi.
MUSÉE CERNUSCHI, PARIS.

Buddha from Ayuthia.

Buddha from T'ien Lung Shan Caves.
PRIVATE COLLECTION. ALEXANDER ARTEMAKIS.

Miroku, the Buddha of the Future.
CHUGU-JI TEMPLE, NARA. ASUKA-EN.

Raphael, Leonardo da Vinci, Giovanni Bellini, and Albrecht Dürer were at the height of their powers. None of them painted the agony. Leonardo saw a Christ who resembled the lords of the earth, detached and remote, possessing an exquisite nobility. The new humanism demanded a Christ who was philosopher and prince. In Leonardo da Vinci's *Last Supper* we see the princely philosopher sitting at table in the cool of the evening, unmoved by the waves of treachery and fear crowding around him, silent and commanding. His unearthly calm, his beauty, his silence have become drama; there is no hint that Gethsemane is only a few hours away. Almost it is as though Christ had become pure intellect.

In Michelangelo's *Last Judgment* Christ becomes once more the youthful Apollo, heir to the powers of the Greek gods, the superb artificer of destinies, only too evidently exulting in the beauty of his immortal body. The power is not in the eyes but in the violence of the gesture, and it is unthinkable that he should ever be calm. Michelangelo never painted a Last Supper or a Crucifixion, perhaps because his genius could not be confined to a formal composition. The *Last Judgment* portrays the splendor and energy of God, while the three Pietàs carved during the last years of his life portray God's despair and agony.

The two traditions coexisted side by side. There was the Christ robed in splendor, his eyes opened wide as he surveys his earthly kingdom, immaculately beautiful, and there was the other Christ, reduced to the dimensions of death, in mortal anguish, the eyes closed and the sweat running down his face. One portrait reaches out to the heights of man's understanding of divinity, the other to the depth of his understanding of mortality; and both answered men's needs.

The sculptures, paintings, and mosaics of Christ are among the supreme achievements of Western art. From the heavy Romanesque carvings of Christ in glory to the last attenuated Pietà of Michelangelo, from the earliest red chalk sketches in the catacombs to Rouault's fierce jewel-like icons of the Man of Sorrow painted in our own time, from the earliest tentative mosaics to the great glittering sheets of mosaics at Venice and Monreale, we are made aware of a constant and unremitting probing into the nature of divinity and the nature of man.

Often the artists saw more clearly than the theologians. Some special gift seemed to have been given to them to portray Christ unfalteringly. They placed him where he could be seen, and they gave clear outlines to the faith, which was otherwise clouded in sterile dogmas. And when men looked too hopefully at the splendor and radiance of Christ, blessing all men from the heights of heaven, there was always the dead Christ, who gave no blessings, to remind them of their mortal conditions.

Romanesque: The Humble Folk

When the Roman Empire foundered in the fifth century, the traditions which had been growing and gaining strength continuously from the days when the Romans built their first small empire on Italian soil did not perish completely. The empire had been destroyed by the Goths and the Vandals, becoming no more than a scattering of principalities, but the memory of the great imperial power which had once reached from Scotland to North Africa and from Spain to Persia was not forgotten. It was as though a great ship had foundered in a storm, the ribs and spars, the treasure in the holds, and all that was contained in it, strewn across the shore. In the years to come people would patiently attempt to assemble the broken remnants and to reconstruct the ancient glory.

So the artists and sculptors found themselves poring over ruins and inscriptions, at a loss to understand the whole, but perfectly prepared to use the fragments for their own purposes. Here and there a Roman monument survived intact. The Trajan Column survived unharmed and still bore on its summit the gilded portrait of the Emperor. This column was wholly Roman, both in feeling and in execution, and showed almost no dependence on Greek design. In long winding bands it showed men working and fighting, always active and in vigorous movement. The emphasis was on human labor, whether it was the labor of building a camp or of massacring the barbarians, of making a bridge of boats across a swollen river or of subduing an enemy city. Because the emphasis was on work, the backgrounds were sculptured out of all proportion to their real size, and when Neptune was portrayed he was shown rising vast and mysterious in an enclosing wave. The survivors of the Roman

Empire could see themselves in this column. They were the soldiers hard at work, bringing order to a barbaric country, but they were also the barbarians suffering at the hands of merciless oppressors; and indeed there appear on the Trajan Column portraits of barbarians in their dying agonies which have the terrible poignancy of medieval sculptures of the dying Christ.

The Roman passion for realism survived into medieval art. So, too, did that convention which Henri Focillon has called *homme-arcade,* where the figure and the frame it occupies form a single aesthetic unit, a convention which is seen at its best on Roman triumphal arches. On stone sarcophagi Christian sculptors in the years following the fall of the Roman Empire would imitate the clustered groups on the Roman arches. On the Ludovisi Sarcophagus, made for some unknown third-century emperor, and now in the National Museum of Rome, the figures jostle one another so violently that sometimes there can be seen only the head or the limbs or part of the torso of some wounded warrior; and that feeling of constraint, of crowded and agonized movement, also appears in the Christian sarcophagi.

The Trajan Column was a wonderfully characteristic monument of an age and after the Pantheon the most remarkable single achievement of Roman art; but the Christian communities after the breakup of the Roman Empire had neither the technical knowledge nor the intellectual ability to recreate the Pantheon until the coming of the Renaissance, and it was the Trajan Column which left the most profound traces on the medieval imagination. The huge Neptune would become Christ rising in majesty; the soldiers and barbarians would become disciples and faithful followers of the Church; and the detached scenes—for a man standing on the ground sees only detached scenes framed by the sky and by the waving bands winding up the length of the column—would be mirrored in the decorations of churches. There is no sense of time in the Trajan Column. Events flow into one another, like streams flowing into a river. There is almost no sense of space, for there is almost no sky and almost no earth for a man to stand on. And all these conventions, which seem anomalous and ambiguous to us, served to kindle the medieval imagination. It would have been perfectly possible for a medieval Christian sculptor to tell the story of Christ's mission on earth in the same style as the Trajan Column, beginning with the Annunciation and ending with the Resurrection. In fact, such a column, beginning with the Baptism and ending with the Entry into Jerusalem, appears in the cathedral at Hildesheim, though it belongs to a much later age. But it was not at all necessary for the medieval sculptors to carve great columns in honor of Christ: the story could be told in disconnected fragments around the doors of the church. In this way the column, broken down into its separate parts, became a gateway.

The medieval imagination lacked the Greek sense of form. Many years would pass before Christian sculptors were able to portray Christ as the Greeks represented their gods, their sensuous beauty displayed in life-size statues. No more than the sculptors of the Trajan Column were the medieval sculptors interested in accurate proportion. For them it was right that Christ should tower above the disciples, and that the disciples in turn should tower above the saints, and that all of them should tower above the pitiable race of men. Space, time, proportion, perspective, order— all these were abandoned in the cultivation of an art designed to glorify Christ, who stood outside space and time, and who needed neither proportion nor perspective in order to establish his power over this world and all the worlds to come.

The conquerors, the restless Goths and Vandals who had sacked the cities of Italy, France, Spain, and North Africa, were themselves the possessors of an artistic imagination which was to influence the Christian artists. Their art ultimately derived from the Asiatic steppes, depicting an animal life of bewildering variety and energy, with the forms of animals stretched out in tumultuous displays of carnage. They divide and subdivide, eat one another, acquire two heads on one body, or melt into the forms of many animals simultaneously. Out of the tiger's body there grows the head of a reindeer, whose antlers become crowing cocks. It was an art which derived from nomadic huntsmen, and it has left deep traces on the peasant art of Russia and Scandinavia. To the artists of Western Europe these intricately interlaced animals and mythological creatures could be made to serve the purposes of Christian symbolism.

So we find them decorating the pages of the Book of Kells, written in Ireland in the eighth century, the strange Asiatic shapes winding around the massive and delicate capitals—those capitals which in their beauty and intricacy are unlike any capitals ever made. Gone is the noble simplicity of Latin capitals, never more superbly carved than in the inscription below the Trajan Column. In the Book of Kells the capital is drowned in a panoply of jewel-like inventions formed from the shapes of monsters. Goblins peer out from behind coiling tendrils, and the strange beasts of the Asiatic plains appear on the margins. The Irish priests who copied these manuscripts had never confronted lions or elephants, but their imaginations were haunted by them; and they were at ease in landscapes they had never known.

We find the same goblins, monsters, and savage animals in the Romanesque churches, where they peer down at us from the capitals. The Romanesque imagination borrowed from every available source, from Roman, Byzantine, and Islamic sources, but it was rooted in a still more ancient past. Sometimes we encounter faces with sharp profiles, enormous eyes, thin necks, and we wonder where we have seen them before: was it in Mycenae, or in Babylon? There is the sense of the long dead past coming slowly to life, or rather uncoiling as a snake uncoils after a long hibernation. The Romanesque sculptors and painters had many things to say about Christ, but they had nearly as much to say about the pre-Christian world which lay very close to them, a fire raging a little below the surface. It was as though in their attempt to understand themselves they had gone deep into their own buried past, down galleries and corridors of stone, into the dark and unfamiliar world where they could recognize only the dim shapes of flame and shadow. When they looked closely they saw the outlines of wild beasts which no longer inhabited the earth and rituals no longer practiced. Sometimes when they penetrated deep into the mines, they were hurled back by the raging flames.

When we look into the Romanesque world, we see that the artists have not yet made their peace with Christianity. There is the sense of strain and uncertainty, of something not yet completely understood, and this is reflected in their turbulent wall paintings and in those strange compressed images of people who seem to be crushed by the weight of stone and to have become stone. In Byzantine art the flesh of Christ has become myriad points of light; in Romanesque art the flesh has withered away and become bone covered with a thin envelope of skin. A Romanesque relief figure seems to be simultaneously forcing himself out of the frame while being hurled back into it by invisible forces. We are very far from the casual paintings in the catacombs with their quiet self-assurance. A Romanesque painting is a continual striving against impossible odds, for the painters were only too well aware that the mystery could not be rendered adequately with the available resources, and could not in fact be rendered adequately with any resources. They painted with a kind of despair, ill at east except when they were simply copying Byzantine forms from a copybook, and they were never more magnificent than when they painted in the full knowledge that the task was hopeless and beyond their powers.

All over France, Spain, England, and northern Italy there survive the fading relics of Romanesque paintings on ancient church walls. In another hundred years almost nothing will be left of them, and it must be accounted a miracle that they have survived so long, for there exist no societies for the protection of Romanesque paintings. They are not finished works of art in the sense that a Giotto fresco is a finished work of art; their chief claim to our affections lies precisely in their unfinished, unresolved character, their adventurousness, their awkwardness. They were asking questions, while Giotto was offering answers.

Take, for example, the Virgin and Child in the crypt of the Romanesque church at Montmorillon. She sits on a low Byzantine throne elegantly adorned with swan-neck armrests, within an oval rainbow-colored frame. Her gown is painted in red ocher, her skirts are green. She holds the Child in one arm, and she takes his hand with the other and presses it to her lips. It is a gesture of exquisite tenderness, and it appears nowhere else. The Romanesque artist was inventing his own iconography, introducing an entirely new and unsuspected element in the portrait of the Virgin and the Child. He has also introduced something astonishingly new in his attempt to paint the Virgin's gown, which assumes the form of breaking waves, foaming cascades, swirling fold upon swirling fold, spray and spindrift. The Virgin's face is calm, but the gown has become an abstraction of tumultuous power. The design is based at an immense distance on the characteristic whorls employed by Byzantine artists, but the Romanesque painter has used these whorls for his own purposes and demonstrated an extraordinary capacity to imagine the unimaginable—the soaring, tumultuous power of the Virgin combined with her human tenderness.

It is not strange that the Virgin of Montmorillon should be the only one in the history of Christian art who is seen kissing the hand of the child. What is strange is that no one so far as we know ever thought of developing the same theme in wood, stone, or ivory.

So, too, when the Romanesque artists paint angels, they give them the familiar faces of children, not the sweetly impassive faces of good children, but the round-faced, sulky, excited faces of the children they saw around them. When we see the Archangel Gabriel announcing the good news to the Virgin, there is no holy reticence, no hovering ten yards away from her. Instead, the Archangel throws his arms around the Virgin impulsively and they gaze fondly at one another.

Much of the charm of Romanesque art lies in the absence of a settled iconography. The Byzantine copybooks were not always available, nor was there any reason why the copybooks should be followed. One of the greatest of all paintings of the Crucifixion appears in the Chapel of the Holy Sepulchre in Winchester Cathedral. The nails have been removed from Christ's hands, but his feet are still fixed to the cross. His body slumps forward into the arms of St. Peter, while an old man, who may be Nicodemus, leans forward and pulls at the last remaining nail with a pair of pincers as long as a man's arm. In the swirl of the draperies there is something reminiscent of the Virgin of Montmorillon, and there is also something else to remind us of Montmorillon—the Virgin has taken Christ's bleeding hand and lifts it tenderly to her face.

Even the best preserved of Romanesque paintings are flaking away, but most of the statues survive intact. Originally they were brightly colored, but these colors have to be imagined. When we see the great tympanum over the portal of a Romanesque church, we must imagine Christ robed in blue and gold, with a halo of gold, with a face more white than flesh-colored, the eyes and lips painted in, and sometimes there would be painted shadows around the nose, and the saints are shining in brilliant colors. Such painted statues are not to our taste, but we would be mistaken if we did not accept the Romanesque vision of brilliantly colored heavens inhabited by saints in gaudy raiments.

In the small town of Moissac near Montauban in the south-west corner of France there is a church dedicated to St. Peter, founded, according to the legend, by King Clovis in A.D. 507, but rebuilt many times. In its present form it was completed by Abbot Ansquitil about A.D. 1115. According to the chronicles he had ordered "a most beautiful gateway" (*portale pulcherrimum*). The unknown sculptor gave him what is probably the most beautiful gateway in all Christendom.

The royal gate, protected by a deep archway, portrays Christ in majesty at the Last Judgment. It is the moment described in a stupendous passage from the Revelation of St. John:

> Behold, a throne was set in heaven, and one sat on the throne. And he that sat was to look upon like a jasper and a sardine stone: and there was a rainbow round about the throne, in sight like unto an emerald. And round about the throne were four and twenty seats: and upon the seats I saw four and twenty elders sitting, clothed in white raiment; and they had on their heads crowns of gold. And out of the throne proceeded lightnings and thunderings and voices: and there were seven lamps of fire burning before the throne, which are the seven Spirits of God. And before the throne there was a sea of glass like unto crystal: and in the midst of the throne, and round about the throne, were four beasts, full of eyes before and behind. And the first beast was like a lion, and the second beast like a calf, and the third beast had a face as a man, and the fourth beast was like a flying eagle.

On the tympanum at Moissac the vision is carved in stone with great power and authority. Many different elements have come together in the sculptor's imagination. The central figure of Christ clearly derives from Persian sources, the small squat elders enclosed within their narrow frames might be the work of Gallo-Roman sculptors, the general design owes much to an illumination in a manuscript by Beatus of Liebana called *A Commentary on the Book of Revelation,* and this illumination by a Spanish artist was clearly derived from Islamic sources. The twenty-four elders are all kings wearing elaborate jewel-encrusted crowns; they have heavy beards, wide-open eyes, and prominent ears, and they all have a resemblance to Christ, being members of his body, and each holds a viol and a perfume cup, so that his praises can be sung to music and the incense will rise before him. The lion, the calf, and the eagle are all elaborately distorted, bent and twisted so that they can peer up at Christ, and the beast with "the face as a man" is similarly bent and distorted, but there is nothing in the least repellent in these deliberate distortions. The sculptor has subordinated all the elders and evangelical symbols to the imperious presence of Christ, who stands out from among them as though they were no more than his proper decoration. Everything is seen as in a vision, with Christ glowing at the white-hot heart of the mystery.

The tympanum stands as the single most powerful masterpiece of Romanesque carving. Here all the strangely discordant elements have been fused together into a portrait of divine majesty which is wholly satisfying and wholly convincing. The same unknown artist is responsible for the central pillar supporting the tympanum with six crossed lions and lionesses, mouths agape, ready to devour anyone who enters the church. *"Libera eas de ore leonis,"* says the offertory of the Mass for the Dead. "Deliver them from the lion's mouth, that hell swallow them not up, that they fall not into darkness . . ." The lions are heraldic beasts with exquisitely curled manes, but the muscles of their necks are stretched taut and they are ravenous with hunger. On the sides of the pillar the sculptor has portrayed St. Paul and Jeremiah. Like the great tympanum these sculptures must be included among the masterpieces of Romanesque sculpture.

They loom there in the shadows, not immediately visible, for a man entering the church is first aware of the tympanum and then of the lions and lionesses, and only when he has come past the pillar is he aware of the two immensely elongated figures of Jeremiah and St. Paul, who seem to be floating in midair, their beards, hair, and draperies all flowing in the winds of heaven.

They are strange sculptures, because they seem to inhabit an even more rarefied world than the Christ of the Last Judgment. They seem to be about to melt away, to become lost in the flowing wind, and at the same time they have an extraordinary intensity. They are the prophets of two dispensations, equally venerable, guardians of the royal gate, enemies of the perpetual lions, and so the sculptor deliberately represents them with great force, since they are more than prophets—they have been summoned to keep death at bay. Jeremiah's legs are crossed and his head is bent like a man in dazed meditation, while at the same time he seems to be dancing before the Lord. He is not the Jeremiah who vents his curses on sinners and proclaims the downfall of great cities, but the precursor and the prophet of the new dispensation. Almost he might have been fashioned in China during the Wei Dynasty, when it was customary to show the Maitreya, the Coming Buddha, with legs crossed and all the undulating folds of his garments in careful disarray.

St. Paul is a more somber figure, advancing with one hand raised, not in warning or in blessing, but in the attitude of a man proclaiming the New Law. With the other hand he holds the Gospel. He walks sedately, while Jeremiah lives within the violence of the dance. The sculptor is clearly the same person who carved the great tympanum, and we see his work again in the nearby Abbey of Souillac, where a wonderful Isaiah dances even more splendidly than Jeremiah and once again there is a pillar carved on three sides with extraordinary beauty and authority. Where at Moissac there were simply the six crossed lions and lionesses, here there are strange four-footed vulturelike birds as well, and we see them at work as they tear into the flesh of a man, a dove, a dog, and a gazelle. Evil is triumphant, and man is pathetically weak against the ravenous beaks and the lions' teeth. The fury of the design is equaled only by the astonishing energy in the individual sculptures: they are all vividly, terrifyingly alive,

even though the total effect is to emphasize the hopelessness of
the human condition. But on the side of the pillar the sculptor
offers another aspect of the human condition—the grace of God.
Abraham is about to kill Isaac when an angel comes hurtling down
from heaven to stay his hand. The angel, falling vertically, occupies nearly half the column. Abraham is clinging to Isaac, the
angel is clinging to the ram, the sculptor has carved the very
moment when Abraham passes from anguish into the utmost relief,
and there is the sense of destinies unfolding, of worlds coming
to an end and new ones being born. The elongated figures do not
belong to our world: they are outside time altogether, legendary
and almost inhuman, though recognizably possessing human energy.
Into that narrow carving the unknown Master of the Moissac
Tympanum has portrayed another aspect of the explosive visionary
world where he is at home.

In the church at Beaulieu a few miles away the same
sculptor portrays the new dispensation in all its glory, for on the
tympanum we see Christ triumphant, sitting in majesty with his
arms spread out to form a cross, while behind him the angels
crowd around the jeweled cross, and below him the sinners writhe
in eternal agony. The wide-spreading arms embrace the world, and
Christ is simultaneously the Judge and the Crucified. It is a dazzling
invention, and it is possible that it owes its origin to a passage in
a contemporary work by Honorius d'Autun. "How shall we see
Christ on the Day of Judgement?" a disciple asks, and the priest
answers: "To the elect he will appear as when he stood on the
mountain, and to the sinners he will appear as when he was
crucified." When the Abbot Suger built the first Gothic cathedral
at Saint-Denis, he employed the same general design and once
more we see Christ sitting in majesty with his arms wide-spread,
but this time they lie against the cross. The design has become
formal, and there is no longer any weight of passion. The Master
of the Moissac Tympanum would have been out of place in Gothic
France, where visionary intensity was no longer demanded of the
sculptor. He was one of the greatest of artists, and one of the least
known.

Gislebertus of Autun, who carved his own name beneath the

feet of Christ in the great tympanum he carved for the Cathedral of St. Lazarus, lacked the superb fire of the Moissac master. Where the Moissac master aims for the heights, depicting the overwhelming power of God and the absolute terror that awaits sinners, Gislebertus was content to portray a more humble vision. His Christ is more merciful, his people move about in a world which remains dear and familiar to them, and often they are smiling. The mood is lyrical, as though set to music, and as he portrays a child pulling at the skirts of St. Peter or an angel lifting another child into the arcades of heaven, or when he shows Mary and Joseph riding on donkey-back to Egypt, or the three magi sleeping under a single coverlet when the angel announces the birth of the Savior, then we become aware of a distant music of pipes and kettledrums. For the most part his devils are charming grotesques, and even his reptilian Satan, who finds himself to his extreme indignation confronting St. Michael, is scarcely more than an absurd bogeyman, all gaping mouth and flaming hair. But just as a lyric poet will sometimes convey the ultimate horror with a greater anguish than the epic poet, so on that same tympanum we see one of the sinners startled out of his wits because an enormous hand has appeared from nowhere to clutch him by the throat, and there is more poignancy in that single startled face than in all the other naked sinners lamenting their fate. The sculptor has carved a hand of exquisite beauty, but instead of fingernails there are claws.

The style of Gislebertus is intensely personal and easily recognized. He concentrates on the face, which is always very large in relation to the body, and he marries the posture of the body to the expression of the face with an uncanny accuracy, so that, from the body alone, one can almost guess what the expression will be. Intimacy is not usually a quality which a sculptor can convey on a capital or on a tympanum, but Gislebertus always succeeds in depicting the intimate relationships between people, and he fills the space between them with affection and tenderness. When the three magi come to greet the infant Christ, they show a brooding tenderness as they offer their gifts, and one of them claps his hand to his jeweled crown in his excitement. The Virgin has the round full face of a peasant girl. The infant Christ, sitting

The Sleeping Apostle, from the Sketchbook of Villard de Honnecourt. Circa
A.D. 1235.

on her knees and wearing an embroidered gown, has a look of quite extraordinary intelligence, and indeed Gislebertus is preeminently a sculptor of intelligence, planning his compositions according to a generous and loving mathematics. Besides the tympanum, he carved more than fifty capitals, and there is never any sense of failure. Happily, he did not have to share his work with anyone. The whole work is his, and he seems to have had no assistants, or else they were trained so well that they could imitate his style to perfection.

He seems to have learned his art at Vézelay, for some broken statues found there are certainly by his hand, and at Saulieu there are carvings which appear to have been made by him before he became a master. He may have designed the tympanum at Cluny, which has been destroyed, and his influence can be felt in the great tympanum at Vézelay, which he may well have designed, while leaving others to complete the work. The Christ of Vézelay is conceived in exactly the same position as the Christ at Autun, with a gentle spreading of the hands, but what is most beautiful about him is the design of his gown, which cascades as fiercely as the gown of the Virgin at Montmorillon, but with a disturbing elegance. Elegance, indeed, was to become the watchword of Gothic art. All the rough edges would be smoothed away, and instead of an art designed for humble folk, there would come into existence an art of the aristocracy and the royal courts.

Romanesque churches are dark and humble, concerned with mortality, the sins of the flesh, the hope of paradise; a just and inexorable God rules over them; with sorrow and pity the priests dispense God's judgment on the human condition. To enter a Romanesque church is to become aware of the sacramental quality of all sorrows: one thinks of the dying, of women in childbirth, of grief and loss, and man's utmost hope of a region beyond the stars where he may be at peace, where there is no suffering, and where God's presence is perpetually manifest. The Romanesque church answered to human needs; the Gothic church was an expression of human pride, man's soaring magnificence, his desire to create on earth the semblance of a palace fit for Christ and the Virgin, heaven brought down to earth, man raised to a heavenly stature. Neither Gislebertus nor the Master of the Moissac Tympanum could ever have thought in those terms. They thought of the *Rex tremendae majestatis* and man's gentle and sorrowful journey through life, and they created sculptures to reflect their peculiarly Romanesque vision of God and man.

Although Gothic art was directed toward different purposes and reflected a new concept of the universe, it never completely divorced itself from the preoccupations of Romanesque art. Here and there in the Gothic cathedrals we come upon authentic Romanesque images. The superb elongated figures guarding the royal portal of Chartres derive ultimately from the Master of the Moissac Tympanum; they had survived the burning of the earlier Romanesque cathedral, and were regarded as worthy of the place of honor even though the cathedral no longer needed them, because they clashed with the general design. To the very end Gothic would conserve these elements of the Romanesque imagination, as though to remind itself of a glory long surpassed and a beauty it could no longer express.

In this way Romanesque flowed into Gothic and found a humble place in the most sumptuous palaces ever built.

Gothic: The Sumptuous Palaces

It happens very rarely in the history of art that we can associate great innovations with a single person and a single date. The currents of art move mysteriously like the wind, and sometimes the boughs bend where no wind flows, and winter flowers bloom in high summer. Art does not follow the orders established in textbooks; it moves according to its own obscure rhythms and impulses, and sometimes returns along the same path it had pursued many centuries before. True innovations are rare, and when they occur they are surprisingly long-lived. Gothic art which was to endure in various forms for more than eight hundred years, was very largely the invention of Abbot Suger, who consecrated the sanctuary of the first Gothic church on June 11, 1144.

The great innovator was born in 1081, the son of poor parents of Saint-Denis, the small town outside Paris where he was later to rebuild the Carolingian church built over the relics of the patron saint of France. He entered the church school at the age of ten, and there met the young prince who was to come to the throne as Louis VI. At the age of twenty-five he became secretary to the abbot, and in the following year he was made provost of the coastal town of Berneval in Normandy. Thereafter he received a succession of high appointments, and for a brief period was employed as an ambassador to the Holy See. He accompanied young Prince Louis on his mission to Aquitaine on the occasion of his marriage to Eleanor of Aquitaine. For a while he was Prime Minister of France, and for the laborious cultivation of the royal interests he received the title of *pater patriae*, "the father of his country." He was a historian, an architect, a connoisseur of jewels, and a consummate politician. As he appears in a stained-glass window in the apse of his church at Saint-Denis, he was a small, heavyset, powerful man with his monkish hair cropped neatly in a straight line across his round forehead, with large and widely spaced eyes, a small nose, determined mouth, and firm jaw. In the portrait he lies barefoot in an attitude of prayer at the feet of the Virgin, but one can imagine him sitting sternly in the seat of power.

In 1122, when Suger was forty-one years old, he was elected abbot of Saint-Denis, an honor rarely accorded to commoners. Large benefices attached to the abbey church, and it is recorded that as abbot he was charged with the administration of three towns, seventy-four villages, twenty-nine manors, no fewer than a hundred parishes, many chapels, fifteen forests, and extensive lands, and all these paid rent and tribute to him. Possessing the wealth and power of a great feudal lord, and with excellent connections at court, he decided that his church needed to be renovated on an enormous scale. At first he decided to remodel, or at least to re-paint, the interior of the Carolingian church which had been consecrated by Charlemagne in 775 and was now in a state of disrepair. His first task was to summon painters from all over France to paint the walls "with gold and precious colors," but the effect was merely to inflame him with the desire for more substan-tial alterations. One of the treasures of the Carolingian church was the porch sheltering the tomb of Pepin the Short (the father of Charlemagne), who thought himself unworthy of being buried inside the church. Suger tore down the porch and erected a new facade eighty feet westward. Four massive buttresses rose up, to support the three doorways with their lavish carvings of the Last Judgment, and scenes from the life of St. Denis, martyred in Montmartre at the orders of the Roman governor. It was a powerful and wonderfully contrived facade, but it remained essentially Ro-manesque. It was dedicated on June 9, 1140, and five weeks later Suger began work on the sanctuary.

While the facade gives an overwhelming impression of sturdy strength and regal power even though little remains of its original decoration, Suger's boldest and most brilliant concepts were reserved for the sanctuary. Neither power nor domination nor sturdy strength seemed to him appropriate for the bones of St. Denis. He saw the whole of the sanctuary as a jewel-studded reliquary drowned in the mysterious light of heaven flowing through stained-glass windows. There was nothing new in stained-glass windows; they were known in Roman times and were common in Romanesque churches. What was new was the concept of the sanctuary blazing with light, the altar itself thickly encrusted with jewels and mysteriously reflecting the light pouring from the windows. A man walking slowly up the nave would find himself entering a light which was not of this world. In this way he would be led "from the material to the immaterial," *de materialibus ad immaterialia.* Dazzled and half blinded, he would come at last to the place where the relics reposed among golden crosses on fire with jewels and cabochons, among plates of solid silver, and multitudinous sheets of gold. When he looked up in order to escape the shattering fire, he would see the rainbow-colored windows, and in this way he would be transported out of himself, lost in the play of immeasurable lights.

Suger was a profound student of light, and he was well aware that a man can gaze upon jewels, and more specially a cluster of jewels, and soon find himself in a kind of hypnotic trance. His first thought was evidently to collect all the jewels he could find in order to adorn the altar containing the precious relics, and from this it was an easy step to the batteries of stained-glass windows which would have the effect of oil poured on the fiery altar. He had seen the jewels in the royal collection and in the collections of the dukes and princes: what better use could be made of them than to set them as ornaments in the crown of the martyr? So he borrowed all the jewels he could lay his hands on, and bought many from church funds. He found abundant confirmation for his belief in the virtue of precious stones from holy texts. Quoting the text: *Every precious stone was thy covering, the sardius, the topaz, and the jasper, the chrysolite and the onyx, and the beryl, the sapphire, and the carbuncle, and the emerald,* he comments:

> Thus, when—out of my delight in the beauty of the house of God—the loveliness of the many-colored gems has called me

away from external cares, and worthy meditation has induced me
to reflect, transferring that which is material to that which is
immaterial, on the diversity of the sacred virtues: then it seems to
me that I see myself dwelling, as it were, in some strange region
of the universe which neither exists entirely in the slime of earth
nor entirely in the purity of Heaven; and that, by the grace of
God, I can be transported from this inferior to that higher world
in an anagogical manner. I used to converse with travelers from
Jerusalem and, to my great delight, to learn from those to whom
the treasures of Constantinople and the ornaments of Hagia
Sophia had been accessible, whether the things here could claim
some value in comparison with those there, and they acknowledged
that these here were the more splendid ones.

In this way, like a jeweler absorbed in the contemplation of
the jeweled light, he stepped out of this world altogether into a
simulacrum of heaven.

It followed that in the apse there would be none of that
heaviness which characterized the facade. Slender columns would
support the weight of the painted windows. Ribbed vaults, introduced from Armenia or perhaps from Persia, solved the problem
of elevating the walls to immense heights without the need of
continuous buttressing. Within this delicate framework Suger placed
the fourteen towering windows of the ambulatory, reserving the
most important window for the Virgin in her blue robe, himself in
his brown habit lying at her feet.

When Suger came to describe this innovation, he spoke of the
"lux continua," the unbroken light, which bathed the sanctuary
in its glow. With these two words he announced the beginning
of the style we know as Gothic. Henceforth the walls would be
vehicles of light, and the solemn darkness of Romanesque would
give place to a continuous radiance.

In different places in the church he set up thirteen bronze
tablets, invoking the blessings of Christ, the Virgin, St. Paul, St.
Denis, and the angelic hosts, begging them to intercede for him
for a place in paradise, and proclaiming his desire to bring the
heavenly light down to earth:

Whoever seeks to exalt the honor of these gates,
Let him not marvel at the golden treasure but at the
      workmanship.
Bright is the noble work: this work shining nobly
Enlightens the mind so that it may travel through the
      true lights
To the True Light where Christ is the True Door.

In his eyes Christ was the entrance to the True Light of Heaven, and it was the task of the church to render that light as nearly visible as it can be on earth. *Nobile claret opus* . . . Bright is the noble work . . . So he will play with all the words connoting the properties of light, and he will never permit himself to forget that light is his continuing theme. *Splendor, claritas, lux* are words that appear again and again in his bronze verses. He was drunk with light.

In an astonishing short space of time the ribbed vaults and the stained-glass windows were erected. From crypt to roof the sanctuary was completed within four years. Suger had no illusions about the importance of the day of consecration, when the relics of St. Denis were translated from the crypt to the reliquary tomb. The young King and his Queen, Eleanor of Aquitaine, reached the abbey church on June 10, 1144. Nineteen prelates, led by the archbishops of Reims, Sens, Rouen, Bordeaux, and Canterbury, arrived for the celebrations, and there were so many nobles and knights that, so Suger tells us, they were beyond counting. The king, bearing the reliquary containing the relics of St. Denis, led processions of monks and prelates through the cloisters while choirs chanted and the lesser reliquaries were heaped before the greater relics of St. Denis. On this day Abbot Suger reached the pinnacle of his earthly career. He lived on for another seven years, spending the last months of his life in a small cell devoid of all ornament and especially of all jewels, as though he no longer felt the need to bathe in the light of heaven. He seems to have known that he had started a movement which would long outlive him.

The sanctuary at St. Denis was the beginning. Soon the *lux continua* would be observed in all the new cathedrals rising in France and England, and the new feeling for light would change the nature of the church and of worship. No longer were men content to pray in the dark and humble Romanesque churches; instead, they would demand palaces where the light poured through glass walls, coloring the marble pavements. The crabbed Romanesque Virgins would give way to the Virgin of exquisite gentleness and mercy, radiant in the beauty of motherhood: not the crucified Christ but the gentle Mother would dominate these palaces with their painted glass, soaring columns, and steeples which seemed to reach up to the foothills of heaven. Romanesque was masculine; the new churches were essentially feminine. Where Romanesque spoke of a man's urgent striving for salvation, his fear of hell, his dread of death, the new churches offered the spectacle of the earthly paradise in the likeness of the heavenly paradise, and hell and death were granted no tenure. Sin, too, found itself outlawed in those gracious palaces intended to celebrate the holy light and the beneficence of God.

Although Gothic art evolved out of the imagination of Abbot Suger, he would not have recognized the word "Gothic," and indeed he would have been surprised by it. In his eyes "Gothic" meant "pertaining to the Goths," the half-barbarian tribesmen who ravaged Europe for centuries and finally destroyed the Roman Empire in the West. The term was invented by Raphael, who had no sympathy with the art and little understanding of it. Raphael regarded these cathedrals as foreign elements imposed upon Europe by the descendants of the Goths, and the word was meant as a term of abuse. Not until the nineteenth century was the word used respectfully to describe a powerful art which mirrored a powerful upsurge of the human spirit.

In the twelfth century the weather of the soul was rapidly changing. Warm winds were coming from the East, where the Crusaders were learning from the embattled Saracens the arts of luxury. Travel had become safer, and men went on longer and longer pilgrimages. Arab learning was entering Europe; and Aristotle, translated sometimes from Arabic translations, was quickening the minds of philosophers and theologians. The starkness and heaviness of Roman tradition, which Romanesque art preserved, was giving place to a soaring inventiveness.

On June 10, 1194, exactly fifty years to the day after the consecration of the sanctuary of Saint-Denis, the ancient cathedral of Chartres suffered the worst of its conflagrations. The whole building went up in flames; molten lead from the roof poured on the altar; and the most sacred of all the relics belonging to the cathedral, the veil of the Virgin, was thought to be consumed in the flames. The veil was subsequently found intact, a fact that was ascribed to the intercession of the Virgin. When at last the flames died down, there remained only the crypt and the west front, which had been re-erected some sixty feet away in preparation for an extensive enlargement of the nave. So it happens that the west front, built in the time of Abbot Suger, recreates as it were the west front of Saint-Denis, while the rest of the cathedral, rebuilt after the conflagration, recreates on a more massive scale the jeweled perspectives of the sanctuary of Saint-Denis. Chartres was Saint-Denis writ large: altogether more massive, more magnificent, and more splendidly illuminated, but belonging to the same order of things. Although Abbot Suger died long before the new cathedral was erected, there is a sense in which Chartres is his greatest invention.

In the eyes of the French the cathedral at Chartres was preeminently the palace of the Virgin. It was her private residence, her royal court, her playground. That the Virgin had taken up her abode in the cathedral became an article of faith, and it was therefore appropriate that there should be placed in it the head of St. Anne, the mother of the Virgin, after the Crusaders found it in 1204 among the relics preserved in Constantinople, and that it should have been presented to the cathedral "in order that the head of the Mother should repose in the house of the Daughter." There were now two relics of incalculable power in the possession of the cathedral, and all France flocked to see them.

Chartres was wealthy, civilized, sophisticated, and almost pagan. If we forget for a moment the ancient kings and queens of Judaea and the Christ in judgment who preside over the royal portal—those emblematic presences filled with deep religious feeling and fashioned in an earlier age—and if we enter by the north portal, so that we are not immediately confronted by the high altar, we seem to be in a vast and richly ornamented palace given over to secular affairs. Those vast courts seem to be intended for processions of noblemen in sumptuous garments, for audiences with the King, and for the reception of embassies. Caparisoned horses could come prancing between the columns, and one would not be greatly astonished to see a royal messenger jump down from his horse and present a report on a distant battle to a high officer of state. Everywhere there is a thirteenth-century elegance, an almost excessive refinement. Only with the great stained-glass window known as *Nôtre Dame de la Belle Verrière* on the south wall, shining with the blue frosty light of winter dawns and the deep golden blue of summer seas, do we come once more into the presence of true religious feeling, but this great work of art, perhaps the greatest stained-glass window ever executed, belongs to the same age as the royal portal, having been executed about 1150. It was evidently taken down just before the conflagration of 1194 and, like the Virgin's veil, survived by a miracle.

Nowhere else in the cathedral, not even in the sculptured figures of the great portal, is there anything to compare with her in majesty. The great rose window, called the *Rose of France*, dedicated to the Virgin and offered to the cathedral by Louis IX, glows and crackles like a great wheel of fire, but it is set so high up, and the details are so small, that it has the effect of decoration. The jewel-like colors are refined and aristocratic, but the rose says nothing to the heart, while *La Belle Verrière* speaks abundantly. In that crowded design the blue-robed Virgin is seen against a ruby-red sunrise, the censing angels at her side, a dove descending from the jeweled gates of heaven. She sits on a throne which is only sketchily indicated, for she fills the greater part of the frame and has no need of the great Persian bolsters and decorated armrests visible in so many of the mosaics of the Virgin. Yet she derives from Byzantine mosaics, and there is about her something of that deliberate stiffness and hieratic composure which comes directly from Byzantium, while at the same time she possesses a peculiarly French grace. Her head is inclined a little to the left, and as she presents her son she glows with a peculiarly French pride.

As she sits there, she is wholly at ease, splendid in her grace

Nôtre Dame de la Belle Verrière

and sweetness. To her worshipers she appears as a living presence throbbing with light. In the enveloping swirl of her blue gown they found their peace.

When the cathedral was finally reconsecrated in 1260, the choristers intoned a Mass especially written for the occasion. "This is a place of awe," they sang. "Here is the court of God and the gate of Heaven." It seemed no more than the truth.

But while the Cathedral of Chartres continued to be regarded as the supreme achievement of Gothic art, there were artists and architects prepared to reach out even farther into the unexplored regions of the *lux continua.* Could not a whole church be made of the heavenly light? A whole church might be built out of glass with only a thin spidery webbing to keep it in place.

Such a church was built at the orders of King Louis IX to house the most precious treasure which ever came into the possession of a French king. The veil of the Virgin and the head of St. Anne were small treasures in comparison to those which were being offered for sale by the Emperor of Byzantium in 1237. That the Emperor was a usurper, with no legitimate claim to the throne of Byzantium, was not a matter which disturbed the King. Baldwin II was in desperate need of money and prepared to sell the Crown of Thorns, which had been in the possession of the Byzantine emperors for many centuries. He had already borrowed heavily on it, and while a price was being negotiated it reposed in a *coffre-fort* in the warehouse of Nicola Quirino, the leading Venetian merchant in Constantinople. Finally a price of 177,300 livres, amounting to about $4,000,000 of our money, was agreed upon, and the Crown of Thorns was brought to Paris with all the appropriate ceremony. Two years later Baldwin II sold the French King a large portion of the True Cross, and it was at this point that Louis IX decided to build a glass chapel to serve as a reliquary for the precious relics. It was to be known as La Chapelle de la Sainte Couronne et la Sainte Croix, and it was built on the Ile de la Cité in the shadow of the Cathedral of Nôtre Dame.

For Louis IX the possession of the Crown of Thorns was vastly more important than the possession of the True Cross. In the Crown of Thorns he saw the ultimate representation of divine kingship, the supreme emblem of earthly authority and power. He felt that his own kingly authority was immensely magnified by the possession of the Crown, and therefore the relic must be enshrined in a chapel of unearthly beauty. It is likely that Pierre de Montreuil, famous for his work at Saint-Denis and the refectory and Lady Chapel of Saint-Germain-des-Prés, was called in as architect. Unlimited sums of money were placed at the disposal of the masons and the makers of stained-glass windows, and the jewelers of Paris were set to work making sumptuous reliquaries. Altogether 100,000 livres were spent on the reliquaries: this was more than twice the cost of building the entire chapel.

By the time the chapel was completed in 1248, Louis IX was well on the way to becoming the foremost relic hunter in Christendom. He acquired the Nails, the Reed, the Purple Robe, the Sponge, a portion of the Napkin used by the Magdalene to wash Christ's feet, a vial of the Virgin's milk and another of the Precious Blood, a stone from the Holy Sepulcher and the inscription that surmounted the Cross, together with the blue mantle of the Virgin and the swaddling clothes worn by Christ in the manger. He went on to acquire the staff of Moses, or rather a small part of it, which he enclosed in a crucifix. As a setting for these sacred objects he devised a palace which was essentially simple in form, although infinitely complex in its details.

Although the Sainte-Chapelle gives the appearance of airy grace and light, it is in fact a building of tremendous solidity. Six powerful buttresses support each side, and the vast windows, which seem merely to nestle between the buttresses, are themselves elements of strength within the total design, for the architects have cunningly introduced substantial iron bars across the windows to provide lateral support. The light curls round the bars, and they are almost invisible. What appears to be a single flare of colored light is an intricate network of lead, iron, and glass.

These stained-glass windows contain no single masterpiece comparable to *La Belle Verrière*, and at no time was there any effort to design a single figure occupying a great expanse of glass. The details are subordinated to the whole. Those immense fields of crimson, blue, yellow, russet, and green glass seem at first to have been molded out of pure color, and we are not immediately aware that the whole history of the earth from the Creation to the day when the relics came to the Sainte-Chapelle is being recorded in minute detail, in an orderly fashion, by craftsmen who were as deeply interested in presenting their own interpretation of history as they were interested in forming cascades of jeweled light.

Since Louis IX regarded himself above all as a kingly Crusader, there is a notable emphasis on kingship and on battle. Wherever possible, the coronations of the kings of Israel are introduced, and the battles of the Israelites, seen as forerunners of the Crusaders, are given pride of place. Moses and Joshua are the King's heroes; his heroines are Esther and Judith, the solitary avengers. Indeed, Judith and Esther occupy so much space on the windows that he seems to have regarded them with a special reverence. One entire window describes the history of the relics and how they came at last to the quiet of the Sainte-Chapelle. Although the windows suggest the calm and quivery light of heaven, a surprisingly large number of the medallions show acts of atrocious violence.

Of the fifteen hundred square feet of stained glass, a little more than two thirds have survived intact. At the time of the French Revolution the relics were dispersed and nothing now remains of the Holy Lance, the Reed, the Seamless Garment, the Holy Shroud, the vial of the Virgin's milk, and most of the other relics collected so assiduously by the King. One relic, however, survives: the Crown of Thorns. This is kept in the treasury of Nôtre Dame, while a single Thorn has been placed in a reliquary at the very top of the steeple of the Sainte-Chapelle, riding high over Paris.

The Sainte-Chapelle was Gothic art carried to an ultimate extreme: the church transformed into light. Such churches were immensely costly, and the experiment was never repeated. Nor would it have been possible to build a great cathedral on the same model. Nôtre Dame, though largely designed by the same architects, suffered from its immense size, and not even the great rose windows on the transepts could flood it with light. Instead, the architects concentrated on the facade crowded with sculptures in honor of the Virgin, flashing with golden halos and brilliantly painted saints. Nôtre Dame, as we see it today, has little outward resemblance to the plan conceived by its architects, who designed great steeples rising high above the quadrangular towers. They accepted the fact that it would be dark inside, because it was narrow, shaped like a long Viking ship, and the light from the high windows would necessarily strike the opposite wall rather than fall across the paving stones. The facade, however, was intended to be a riot of color.

Other Gothic cathedrals conveyed the same barbaric delight in color. At Chartres, too, there were brilliantly painted sculptures, the blue mantle of Christ was edged with gold, his hair, eyes, and lips sparkled with color, and there were jewels in his crown. The serried ranks of the saints were painted in contrasting colors, so that they were entirely lacking in the gray uniformity that characterizes them today. Violent contrasts and unexpected colors did not disturb the worshipers. In one of the stained-glass windows at Chartres Christ lies on an emerald cross and St. John lifts his crimson hands in prayer.

Wherever possible the stone was painted. A visitor to Chartres would have been dazzled by the prospects within and without, for wherever he set his eyes he would be met by explosions of color. Indeed, the aim of the architects and designers was to produce a state of enchantment in the worshiper. A cathedral was the palace of the Virgin, but it was also a fairy palace.

The Romanesque churches had been places where the human drama of Christ was re-enacted every Sunday. The Gothic cathedrals were so vast that the human element was dwarfed in the contemplation of the spiritual drama. The very height of the cathedral was an essential part of the enchantment: the higher the building, the closer it came to the walls of heaven. We hear of worshipers being "terrified" by the sheer mass of Nôtre Dame, which seemed not to have been built by human hands but by God himself. So there came about what Henri Focillon has called "the age of the colossal." The cathedral builders were vying with one another to create ever more imposing buildings. The height of the original spire of Chartres cathedral was nearly 350 feet from the ground. The height of Nôtre Dame to the vaulting was 107 feet; Chartres was 118 feet; Amiens was 138 feet; Beauvais was 157 feet. Not surprisingly, Beauvais collapsed about forty years later, but this did not prevent the architects from building a new cathedral.

Nearly all the great Gothic cathedrals of France and England were begun in the early years of the thirteenth century. Coutances, Amiens, and Salisbury were all begun in 1220. Reims was begun in 1211, and Beauvais, the most daring of all, the fruit of the most advanced design, was begun in 1247. It was the time of St. Francis of Assisi, St. Dominic, and St. Louis, the *Roman de la*

Rose, St. Thomas Aquinas's *Summa,* the works of Albert the Great and St. Bonaventura, and the *Speculum* of Vincent of Beauvais, that encyclopedic mirror of the universe in which all things known to man were recorded from the smallest fish to the three persons of the Holy Trinity. Prodigious advances were being made in knowledge and speculation; and the great *Summa* was just as much an architectural monument as the cathedral of Chartres. "Everything," said St. Thomas Aquinas, "is ordered toward God." He was wrong. Everything was being ordered toward the Virgin.

In the eyes of the people of the thirteenth century the Virgin occupied a special place. It was not only that so many cathedrals were being erected in her honor, but she represented in her own person the beauty, grace, and courtesy which people were craving for. She was the Queen of Heaven, the Queen of the Earth and of the Underworld, but she was also—and more importantly—the familiar presence whose name was on everyone's lips and whose special gift was that she gave a gentle dignity to life. She was hope for the living and assurance for the dead. Quite suddenly she had become the divine Empress of all the universes, past, present, and to come.

Since she was so beloved, it was proper that she should be represented in her beauty. We see her for the first time about the year 1250 on the north transept portal of Nôtre Dame. She might be taken for a beautiful, serene, and purposeful lady, who enjoys showing her child to the people. Her features have an exquisite refinement, and as she stands there, her weight falling on one foot, her body swaying a little, her long mantle following the curves of her body, so that we are made aware of her femininity, she is simultaneously goddess, mother, and queen. The folds of the gown no longer conceal, and we are made aware of the delicacy of the fabric enclosing her breast and shoulders. Twenty years earlier, at Strasbourg, an unknown artist had depicted a blindfolded woman representing the Old Testament, her long gown clinging to her. The female form was being discovered anew. Now even the Virgin was permitted to possess a human body, and soon there would be the eager, smiling *Vierge Dorée* of Amiens and countless others. It was the time of the smiling Angel of Reims, the

Beau Dieu of Amiens, and the Foolish Virgin, all grace and modesty, of Strasbourg. Because the Virgin smiled, fear of damnation was expunged, and there are no convincing Last Judgments carved by Gothic sculptors. The Last Judgment carved at Bourges is made totally unconvincing by the presence of a smiling angel who seems to be amused as he weighs the virtuous and the damned in his scales, and we are far from the thunder and lightning which explodes over the Romanesque tympanum of Moissac.

Generosity had returned to the faith: kindness and gentleness were being celebrated; the harsh doctrines were being purged in the radiance of the Virgin's presence. In the stone flowers carved on the portals we see the leaves bending back and the flowers bursting into bloom. Gothic cathedrals spread all over France, England, Germany, and northern Italy, testifying to the nobility of the human spirit, promising peace. The peace however was short-lived. In 1339 a dynastic quarrel between England and France led to the Hundred Years' War, and in the devastation of continual wars the Spirit of Gothic perished.

The Gothic cathedral, the most beautiful architectural form created by the Western mind after the eclipse of the Greeks, has long since gone the way of all created things. Once it was a living organism, radiating power and energy, a world in itself seemingly remote from the accidents of history and decay. The Gothic cathedrals we see today are pale replicas of the brilliantly decorated originals, the windows glowing with stained glass, the statues gleaming with paint, the candlesticks gleaming with gold, the wealth of the community placed at the service of the cathedral, as though there were no better use for wealth than to glorify Christ or the Virgin. The cathedral was alive with color, dignity, and immaculate beauty. Here, if anywhere, was the paradise men dreamed of.

Time, which plays strange tricks on stone, has given a new shape to the surviving cathedrals. Because the statues are gradually wearing away, and the stones are moldering, the cathedral, intended to proclaim the immutability of divinity, has come to share our common humanity. The more worn the stones the more human it becomes. We rejoice all the more over the smiling Angel of Reims because she has lost a hand and a wing; the kings and queens standing in the royal portal at Chartres are no longer regal presences, for time has rubbed away most of their distinguishing features and robbed them of their dignity, only to grant them a greater humanity. Today the once smooth columns are chipped and pitted, and more and more they come to resemble the enormous tree trunks from which all architectural columns are derived. Century by century the cathedrals have suffered the violent ravages of age, until at last they come to resemble the face of an old priest who has worn himself out in the service of God. Time has despoiled their immaculate beauty, and given them something even more precious.

The Coming of Mohammed

Almost immediately after the death of the Prophet Mohammed a whirlwind emerged out of Arabia. At first it was a very small whirlwind, and the Byzantine rulers in Damascus and Alexandria and the Persian Emperor at Ctesiphon scarcely noticed its appearance. Even if they had been warned, they would not have been afraid. For twelve hundred years Persia had been ruled by a succession of emperors, for three hundred years Byzantium had ruled over the lands bordering the eastern Mediterranean. They were great powers rooted in ancient traditions, and they possessed vast armies, immense treasure, and formidable allies. Why should they fear the small raiding parties emerging out of Arabia?

Within six years the Arabs conquered all the lands between Alexandria and Ctesiphon. In a series of daring raids their small ill-equipped armies took them from Arabia to the mountains of Central Asia. All the Christian cities of Palestine, including Jerusalem, fell to them; and places which had been great centers of civilization for thousands of years were sacked by marauding Arabs, who could scarcely read or write, and who resembled wanderers from another planet as they sauntered along the marble-pillared streets of Alexandria or beside the great arched palace at Ctesiphon.

These Arab conquerors had not been instructed to conquer the world by Mohammed; neither the Koran, nor the Hadith, the traditional sayings of the Prophet, gave them leave to destroy or uproot whole populations. They came out of Arabia with no carefully constructed plan. They wanted booty, not conquests, but when they found that nothing could stop them, that even the best-defended

cities with the most powerful armaments were easily conquered
by them, they knew it was too late to withdraw.

When the small black-bearded Amr ibn-al-As was scorching
Egypt and preparing to hurl his tattered army against Alexandria,
the Caliph Umar, the successor of the Prophet, wrote to him and
asked for a brief description of the country he was about to conquer.
Amr ibn-al-As wrote back:

> O Commander of the Faithful, Egypt is no more than a
> desert with two ranges of hills, the one in the west resembling
> sand dunes, the other like the belly of a lean horse. Between
> these hills flows the Nile: blessed are the morning and evening
> journeys. For the Nile has its seasons of rising and falling, fol-
> lowing the courses of the sun and the moon, and causes milk
> to flow, and gives abundant life to cattle. When the springs and
> fountains are let loose, then the swelling waters flood the fields
> on either side, and all the villages are cut off from one another
> so that the villagers must travel in coracles or frail boats or
> shallops bright as the evening mist. And when the river has risen
> to the full, it sinks back again, and that is the time when the
> people who have learned to plow the earth so well gather the
> fruit of their labor; and their labor is very light. So the crop is
> grown, and the water is the source of the nourishment. Therefore,
> O Commander of the Faithful, you can understand how Egypt is
> sometimes the color of a white pearl, and then like golden amber,
> and then like a green emerald, and then like a carpet of many
> colors.

From Amr ibn-al-As's letter we learn a good deal about the
Arab imagination in the very early years of the conquest: lyrical,
sensuous, sharply pictorial, with an affection for the rich earth and
a kind of wonderment that it should be so fertile and so easily
possessed. It was an earthy imagination, colorful, clear-edged, very
passionate, in love with simple things—the glitter of bridles and
saddles, the silken gleam of a horse, the shining faces of girls. Pre-
Islamic Arabic poetry was filled with a joyous enthusiasm for the
gifts of war, women, and wine.

Mohammed during his brief years of domination over the
Arabs—he died in A.D. 632, only two years after Mecca fell to his

army without a fight—succeeded in bringing about a puritan revolution which has endured with little change through the centuries. It is in fact one of the very few puritan revolutions that have been successful. He forbade wine absolutely, refused to permit fighting between the tribes, and severely limited the permissible number of women a man might have in his harem. He did not specifically forbid the making of images, and there exist no injunctions against painted and sculptured portraits of living beings in the Koran. Not long after his death a traditional saying was recorded: "A house which contains images is not entered by the angels." The story was told that Mohammed's wife Aisha bought a coverlet embroidered with pictures, and when he saw it from the doorway he refused to enter the house. Asked why he delayed, he answered: "The makers of these images will be punished and they will be told: Make alive what you have created." There is another hadith which speaks of the fearful punishment to be visited on the makers of images on the Day of Judgment. The effect of these traditional sayings, which may never have been spoken by the Prophet, was to produce an art in which the representation of the human figure or of any living creature was absolutely forbidden. No man, no woman, no horse, no camel, no bird, no dog might be represented. Trees and flowers might be painted, but nothing that could move of its own volition could be reproduced in any form. Mohammedan art was deprived of the living flesh, the ornament and glory of all other arts.

It was not to be hoped for that the injunction would be obeyed everywhere and at all times. The palaces and hunting lodges of the Umayyad kings, who reigned from Damascus, were provided with brilliant frescoes and mosaics showing men and women at play, and deer cavorting. One of the most brilliant Umayyad mosaics was discovered near Jericho in the winter palace of Caliph Hisham, who ruled the Arab empire from Spain to India. The mosaic floor, made about A.D. 740, shows a magnificent fruit tree: on one side two gazelles graze calmly in the shade while a lion springs upon another gazelle on the other side of the tree. The mosaic chips are unusually small, the colors are finely shaded, and the design has been accomplished with extraordinary refinement.

The walls of the room were decorated with carved horses and partridges and human faces all made out of stucco and lavishly painted. The Caliph of Islam had no intention of following the injunction against making images of living things.

But in the Great Umayyad Mosque in Damascus the injunction was religiously observed, and the mosaics take the form of an immense panorama of Damascus, with walls, towers, bridges, and orchards all clearly portrayed with not a single person walking among them. It is as though one had come upon the city at the first dawn before anyone was awake. The mosaic, which covers the wall for a length of 115 feet, was evidently made by Byzantine craftsmen. Indeed, the mosque had originally been a Byzantine cathedral dedicated to John the Baptist, whose head still reposes there, and it is possible that some of these mosaics were made before it was transformed into a mosque. Most beautiful of all are the great springing trees rising between the arches, the branches curving with the curve of the arch, the green and silvery leaves flashing as though trembling in the wind. These mosaic trees give an impression of vigor and movement oddly at variance with the ghostly, uninhabited city. Neither the mosaics of the Great Umayyad Mosque nor those of Caliph Hisham's winter palace were known until recent times. The mosaics of the mosque were discovered by a French archaeologist in 1928, when the whitewash was removed from the walls; the palace mosaics were discovered in 1937. At first the archaeologists thought the palace was a Christian church; in fact they had discovered the most sumptuous Umayyad palace in existence. The great Umayyad palace in Damascus, close to the Great Mosque, had long since perished.

The stern pietistic creed of Islam scarcely survived the passage to Damascus, a Hellenistic city set in a fertile valley, with magnificent avenues, shops, aqueducts, and caravansaries. The city was a center of sophisticated luxury, and inevitably the luxury of Damascus confronted the privileged poverty of Mecca, and emerged triumphant. Muawiya, the first Caliph to rule Islam from Damascus, seized power by fraud and violence: he came into possession of an empire which stretched from Persia across North Africa to the Atlantic Ocean. His successor, the Caliph Abd-al-Malik, built the

Dome of the Rock in Jerusalem, thus ensuring that he would be remembered as the author of the single most beautiful building in Islam.

The Dome of the Rock was a staggering achievement. There was nothing especially remarkable about the design, which was based on established Byzantine tradition. What was staggering was the decision to place the small temple on the vast platform which occupies about a sixth of the total area of Jerusalem, isolating it on an immense platform of rock and hewn stone, thus giving it the appearance of a single jewel set in space and floating above the city.

The problem was to build a temple around a small, rough, rocky promontory fifty feet square, reputed to be the place where Abraham had intended to sacrifice Isaac, and where Mohammed, according to tradition, leaped on his favorite horse and was taken up into heaven. Innumerable legends accumulated around the rock, and it was believed by the Mohammedans that paradise lay just below it and that the Last Judgment would take place on it. The temple built by Abd-al-Malik was a shrine for the rock.

The design was simple, being merely an octagonal wall surmounted by a dome; the working out of the design was infinitely complicated. The precise dimensions of the arcades and ambulatories were carefully worked out, and sheets of mosaics depicting angels and the heavenly palaces were created by Byzantine artists. These were later replaced by abstract designs of leaves and flowers even more vigorous than those in the Great Umayyad Mosque in Damascus. The outer wall was a continuous expanse of gold leaf and polychrome mosaic, which survived until the sixteenth century, when the mosaics were replaced by delicate blue, green and yellow tiles. According to contemporary chroniclers the Dome of the Rock was designed by the Caliph himself, and the small Dome of the Chain was the preliminary model for the temple. The Dome of the Chain still stands beside the Dome of the Rock like a small daughter in her mother's shadow.

Time has dealt kindly with the Dome of the Rock. Invasions and earthquakes have left it unharmed. The Crusaders conquered Jerusalem, converted the temple into a church, which they called

Templum Domini, and substituted the Cross for the Crescent above the dome. When Saladin reconquered Jerusalem, it became once more a Mohammedan sanctuary. The Dome of the Rock we see today is the same building erected by the Caliph Abd-al-Malik.

There are other wonderful things on that stone platform in Jerusalem and perhaps the most wonderful of all after the Dome of the Rock is the Fountain of Qait Bey. It is an enclosed fountain with a gaily decorated dome, resembling an elegant saltcellar but so perfectly proportioned in its relationship to the nearby Dome of the Rock that it possesses the special quality of being entirely appropriate, and if it were removed, it would be necessary to replace it. Yet it was designed seven hundred years after the Dome of the Rock at the orders of a Mamluk sultan in a style which relies heavily on geometrical ornamentation. Ornate simplicity and geometric grace encounter one another and ennoble one another, and in their confrontation there is only peace.

When Mohammed was asked what was the greatest gift a man could give to another, he answered: "Water for the thirsty." For the desert dweller water is life, abundance, solace, and he dreams of a heaven filled with running streams. Islamic architecture reserves a special place for fountains. The general plan of a mosque in the early days of Islam was a courtyard with a sanctuary facing Mecca, arcades to protect the worshiper from the sun, a minaret to summon the faithful to prayer, and a fountain, which was nearly always in the middle of the courtyard. One wall of the mosque, known as the *qibla* wall, was marked with a niche, which indicated the direction of Mecca, and there was a *mimbar*, or stepped pulpit, where the prayer leader delivered a sermon every Friday at noon. The niche and the pulpit, both introduced during the eighth century, were often decorative, but otherwise the mosque remained austerely simple. Islam had come out of the desert, and in the early years it retained an essential simplicity.

But not for long. The capture of Islam by the Abbasid caliphs ruling from Baghdad brought essential changes to the structure of the mosque, which became increasingly ornate. The Great Mosque at Samarra was ornamented with mosaics, and the minaret took the form of a spiral staircase of impressive proportions. The

Mosque of Ibn Tulun in Cairo was also provided with a spiral staircase. Although the proportions are austere, and the great court-yard oddly resembles a parade ground, the sanctuary was brilliantly decorated and the effect is one of grandeur with a hint of luxury. The mosque was gradually becoming a work of art, obedient to its own emerging laws. Luxury was in the wings, waiting to play its part.

Luxury, of course, was already playing its part in the lives of the Mohammedan rulers of the empire. Ibn Tulun, a Turkish slave promoted to governor of Egypt, inlaid his palace doors with gold. The Caliph Mutawakkil employed Greek artists to decorate his palace with paintings, and we owe to him the first recorded Islamic portrait. It was a medal bearing his effigy and shows him as a man with deep-set eyes, a powerful nose, and a long two-pointed beard, wearing a richly embroidered robe. Later, at least among the Islamic rulers, the injunction against making portraits was simply disregarded. Mutawakkil's grandson was represented on medals in full regalia, sitting cross-legged, with a cup of wine in his hand.

No doubt luxury on an extreme scale was already prevalent in the courts of the caliphs, but it had not yet imposed itself on the mosque. The first sign of the coming abundance appears in the small mausoleum of Ismail Samanid, built in Bokhara about A.D. 907 by an unknown architect of genius. Made entirely of fired brick arranged in a delicate basketwork pattern, surmounted by a dome, the mausoleum gives an impression of sumptuous elegance even though no costly materials have been employed. The mauso-leum is only thirty feet wide, but it has a monumental dignity and great purity. Magnified, this design would be used for the great domed sanctuaries of the Persian mosques. The mosques of Isfahan, Shiraz, and Mashhad, with their brilliant blue tiles and cascading sheets of color, are all descendants of the mausoleum of Ismail Samanid.

When the Seljuk Turks stormed out of Transoxiana in the early years of the eleventh century, they brought with them an architectural style peculiar to themselves, characterized by an ex-treme purity of line and a superb effrontery. Having conquered

Persia and been converted to Islam within the space of a few years, they sought to build a new kind of mosque which would reflect their own sense of dignity and accomplishment. In front of the mosque stood an immense porch resembling an arch of triumph decorated with brilliant tiles. Within the porch, in the mysterious half-light, cascades of stalactites curved down to the entrance of the dome chamber, where the faithful worshiped and listened to the Friday sermon. Within this sanctuary, slender columns and arched vaults gave an impression of towering height. Cross-arches supported the dome, and the intricate design involved a sweeping ascent so powerful that the worshiper was not conscious of the intricacy of the details. The Seljuks had evolved a complex structure which conveyed both the intensity of their newfound faith and their own soaring pride. The north chamber of the Masjid-i-Jami in Isfahan, built about 1088, within fifty years of the Seljuk conquest, represents Seljuk art in its utmost refinement.

This dome chamber has still another claim to our affections: here for the first time we see the working out of the principles of Gothic art, for there is abundant evidence that Gothic art derived from oriental sources, and most especially from this dome chamber. Soon the Seljuks would be meeting the Crusaders on the battlefield; prisoners would be taken; knowledge about the buttressing of vaults and domes, cross-arches, the strength of columns, and the design of mosques would find its way to the West, where Arab prisoners are known to have worked, for we occasionally find Arabic inscriptions in the churches of France. In the dome chamber at Isfahan the columns were made of fired brick; such columns would be made of stone in the Gothic cathedrals, for stone was more plentiful in the West. A new and dazzling architecture had evolved in Persia, and France together with all the countries tributary to the Gothic idea benefited immeasurably.

Seljuk civilization was marked by piety, luxury, clarity, clean springing lines. The mausoleum of a Seljuk king took the form of a tomb tower, fluted, with a conical cap, all made of fired brick, springing to a height of more than a hundred and fifty feet. There were inscriptions in Kufic characters, but otherwise the tower remained undecorated. One of these towers in a perfect state of preservation, known as the Tower of Qabus, is generally regarded as the supreme masterpiece because its lines are at once delicate and severe, and it has about it, like the dome chamber of Isfahan, that look of freshness which comes when a monumental concept becomes a reality for the first time. Some fifty of these towers survive, but most of them have lost their pointed caps or domes. The Tower of Qabus was built in 1107, about twenty years after the dome chamber of Isfahan.

The Seljuks were accomplished weavers and potters: the embroidered silks and satins worn by the Seljuk kings and nobles are among the most sumptuous ever made. The pottery of Rayy and Kashan rivaled all other ware in sheer opulence. The gold and golden-brown lusterware of Rayy, now a township in the suburbs of Teheran but in those days an imperial city, was especially opulent and memorable. The Seljuks evidently had no patience with the injunction forbidding images of men and women, for what is chiefly remarkable about these colored plates and bowls is the simple delight of men and women in each other's company. We see them sitting together and holding hands, riding together, or walking together. There are polo players, horsemen, hunters with their cheetahs and falcons, lute players and dancing dervishes, kings sitting in state or listening to minstrels. Above all, there are the painted plates with the princesses riding unattended on their caparisoned horses, their faces lit with enchanted smiles and the horses mettlesome. The vigor and deftness of these plates belongs to the highest art and we are immediately transported into the presence of these long dead princesses with their impudent glances. The Seljuks must have had some Mongol or Chinese blood, for many of them have almond eyes and the characteristic pear-shaped cheeks admired during the T'ang Dynasty.

The Seljuk Empire in Persia perished at the end of the thirteenth century with the coming of the Mongols, but Seljuk influence continued to shape the art of the invaders, and could be felt centuries after they had vanished from the scene.

Although Seljuk power in Persia was shattered, there were other Seljuk princes who had invaded far into western Asia, establishing an empire of their own in Asia Minor and threatening

Byzantium. If the art of the Western Seljuks was neither so rich nor so extensive as the art of the Persian Seljuks, nevertheless they built memorably, and their fortresslike caravansaries testify to their strength. Their art is massive, elaborate and concise. In the fourteenth century the Ottoman Turks swept into Asia Minor and the Western empire perished.

The history of Islam was one of continual turmoil. No dynasty lasted more than a hundred and fifty years, and most dynasties were much shorter. A new dynasty coming to power would sometimes breathe fresh energy into Islamic art, and then during a period of twenty or thirty years the energy would be dissipated, squandered by excess of luxury or simply because there was nothing left to say.

In Egypt a Mamluk, or "Slave," dynasty assumed power in the thirteenth century. It was the time of the Mongol invasions, when kingdoms and empires were being butchered into extinction. To Egypt fled the refugees from Persia, Afghanistan, and the countries of the Near East. Suddenly a new art, compounded of all the arts of the East, began to flower. The original Mamluk dynasty perished in blood, and was followed by another composed of descendants of Circassian slaves, fair-haired and blue-eyed. Barquq, the first of his dynasty, was the son of a peasant from the Caucasus, but the tomb mosque he built in his lifetime breathes an air of meditative repose, wholly Mohammedan. Qait Bey, whose fountain stands near the Dome of the Rock in Jerusalem, was another murderous Caliph. He was originally a Russian, born on the Volga, but was kidnapped as a boy and sold in the slave market of Cairo. He was fifty-five when he came to the throne in A.D. 1465, and one of his first acts was to build his tomb mosque, completed four years later in red and white stone. The minaret rises in tier after tier, each more ornamented than the other, almost destroying itself by an excess of magnificence, resembling a very slender palace rising high in the air.

An earlier Circassian Mamluk, Caliph al-Muayyad Shaykh, erected a mosque with two minarets. The mosque has perished, but the minarets survive. The Caliph was a notorious drunkard and murderer, who cared nothing for the people he ruled over, but he was an impressive benefactor to the arts. At the top of each minaret there is a small pavilion with slender columns, delicate and fragile, almost as though a Greek temple had sailed through the air and improbably taken up residence high above Cairo. These ornate minarets resemble the young shoots of strange flowers striving and thrusting into the sunlight, and everything about them is delightful, unexpected, and vigorous.

The supreme achievement of the Mamluk sovereigns of Egypt was their victory over both the Crusaders and the Mongols, thus saving the Near East for Islam and preventing Europe from becoming a Mongolian colony. In the reign of Sultan Al-Nasir Mohammed both these feats were accomplished within the space of a single year, for the last Crusaders were expelled from the island of Arwad off the north coast of Syria in 1302 and a few months later the Mongol invaders were destroyed in battle near Damascus. The Mamluks kept the East and the West at bay.

The Mongols claimed descent from a blue wolf, and no one ever doubted that they were rapacious and murderous to an extraordinary degree. The most rapacious and the most murderous was Timur i Leng (Timur the Lame), a great-great-grandson of Genghis Khan. Timur's father, a Buddhist, was converted to Islam. When Timur went into battle, it was as though he was himself the avenging Lord of Hosts, for he liked nothing better than to reduce cities to flaming ruins. His armies conquered Persia and Afghanistan, overran Mesopotamia, invaded Russia, and three years later he was standing before the walls of Delhi and ordering the massacre of its inhabitants. Later he swept into Syria, defeated the Ottoman Turks in Anatolia, and was about to invade China when to the relief of nearly everyone he died in A.D. 1405, having destroyed more cities and put to death more people than any conqueror until recent times.

Like all conquerors, Timur was obsessed with the idea of building monuments to his own glory. At Kesh, south of Samarkand, he built for himself a palace which resembled an enormous mosque with an archway 165 feet high. There was a large reception hall with a ceiling of gold and enamel tiles, and there were galleries and storerooms and offices six stories high. It was by far the largest and most splendidly ornate palace built up to this time, and the

ruins of the great portal survive to testify to the conqueror's megalomania, while his beautiful blue-domed mausoleum at Samarkand
testifies to his exquisite taste. It is one of the loveliest buildings in
the world, made all the more beautiful by the bulbous swelling of
the dome and the curious lobed arrangement of the tiles. The lines
are clean-cut, with the soaring strength one expects during an age
of conquest. The tomb was designed by Mohammed al-Isfahani,
and throughout all the conqueror's buildings in Samarkand and
Bokhara the Persian influence is manifest. Isfahan remained the
artistic capital of his vast empire, which stretched from Anatolia to
the borders of China.

Persia indeed conquered all her conquerors. There was nothing
new that Timur could bring to art except his megalomania and his
determination to be served by the greatest living artists. His workshops were full of Persians working on Persian designs, so that
Samarkand might have been taken for a suburb of Isfahan or Shiraz.
Here and there you would find Indian workmen making intricate
wooden carvings for balconies or mimbars, and Syrian metalsmiths,
and Chinese tile-makers. Once Timur ordered a palace to be erected
in twelve days, and it was done. Since he inspired the utmost fear,
it might have been done equally well if he had ordered it to be built
in a single day.

Under Timur's successors, Shah Rukh and Baysunghur, both
ruling from Herat, the arrogance of the conqueror gave way to the
contrived exuberance of talented voluptuaries. Their greatest works
were not palaces but illuminated manuscripts, brilliantly colored,
sometimes only a few inches high. Under the conqueror's descendants illuminations became a fine art with their own carefully wrought
conventions, which owed much to China and more to native Persian
traditions. Now for the first time there came the convention of the
high horizon, which gave more space to the multiple foreground.
There was no middle ground or background, and a man standing
on the horizon would be exactly the same size as a man standing
close to the bottom edge of the painting. A scene may show rivers,
mountains, palaces, and flowering forests, and yet a horseman who
is evidently half a mile away might be even larger than the woman
gathering faggots in the foreground. Usually there is only a small

patch of sky, and most of it will be taken up with an inscription. The convention defies any reasonable perspective, but makes for a more egalitarian world: a man is not penalized for being in the distance.

In their beginnings these Persian miniatures resembled jeweled ornaments. The air is rarefied, the colors sumptuous, the postures always graceful, the expressions always empty of emotion. A man wielding a sword in the midst of battle looks as unconcerned as a king sitting on a throne. Clumps of grass are as tall as dwarf trees, and the artists have a peculiar fondness for showing people looking over the edges of distant mountains. Gold helmets, gold sands, gold rivers, gold heavens—there is gold wherever the artist can find an excuse for it. The rocks are coral or turquoise blue, the robes are rainbow-colored. The artists painted with brushes made from the throat hairs of two-month-old white kittens. It was an art of exquisite delicacy and sophisticated refinement, and it was in danger of going nowhere. Ja'afar Baysungkuri, the head of a school of forty painters and calligraphers organized by the grandson of Timur, breathed some life into his paintings, but it was left to Bihzad some fifty years later to transform the delicate figures on the gold or flowered ground into people endowed with blood, muscles, and emotions; and in his majestic paintings, and in those of his school—for the artists rarely signed their work—the sense of proliferating life pours off the gold-flecked paper, for the painter has accomplished the miracle of perfection. He will paint an attack on the city, and we are brought physically up to the blood-soaked walls, or he will paint four dancing dervishes, old men with waggling beards, and make us share their joyful dizziness. The colors of Bihzad are more jeweled than ever, the outlines as precise as ever, the horizons as distant as ever, but the air has suddenly become sharp and keen, as though there was frost on it, and the blood tingles.

When Shah Isma'il conquered Persia, thus providing the country with an authentic Persian monarch for the first time in eight hundred years, Bihzad, who had been working in the court of one of the Timurid princes, was summoned to Tabriz and placed in charge of the Royal Library. The Shah's royal edict has survived, and since great painters are rarely honored by their monarchs, a small portion of that immensely long and flowery decree should be quoted:

> We command that there should be assigned and entrusted to him the office of the control and the superintendence of the staff of the Royal Library and of the copyists and painters and gilders and margin-drawers and gold-mixers and gold-beaters, connected with the occupations above mentioned, throughout our guarded territory. All the enlightened Amirs and incomparable Wazirs and the secretaries of our world-protecting threshold and the envoys of our heaven-like court and the functionaries of royal business and the officials of our ministries—in general—and the staff of the Royal Library and the persons mentioned above—in particular—must recognize the above-mentioned Master as the director and the superintendent. They must submit to his control and administration all the activities of the Library, and pay due consideration to all his administrative measures authorized by his seal and signature. There must be no disobedience or neglect of any orders or regulations he may make for the control and conduct of the business of the Royal Library. Everything connected with the above-mentioned business they are to regard as belonging to his special province. He, for his part, must draw and depict upon the tablet of his heart and the page of his enlightened conscience the image of integrity and the form of uprightness. He must set out upon this office by the way of righteousness, shunning and avoiding all partiality and dissembling, and not swerve or decline from the highway of truth and virtue. Let all men pay heed hereto and accept these credentials as soon as this royal decree has been honored and adorned by the stamp of the seal of his exalted Majesty.*

In this way the first Shah of the Safavid Dynasty commended his first painter.

The new dynasty, which lasted for nearly two and a half centuries, was to have an extraordinary influence on the artistic life of Persia. It was as though the floodgates had been opened and now at last all the forms that lay hidden in the Persian imagination

---

* Sir Thomas W. Arnold, *Painting in Islam* (New York: Dover Publications, 1965), p. 151.

were allowed free play. In mosques, caravansaries, carpets, paintings, book illustrations, tapestries, and pottery the Persian genius re-asserted itself. Into the Islamic mold they poured new colors, new forms, new ideas. The splendor of the Achaemenian, Sassanian, and Seljuk periods was eclipsed by the splendor of the Safavids, who built as though their dynasty would endure forever, with that assurance which comes only to those who know themselves to be the unchallenged masters of their country and fear no foreign in-vaders. At Isfahan there arose the Masjid-i-Shah, the Mosque of the Shah, the huge dome colored with blue and gold tiles and so proportioned that it seems to possess a glowing life of its own, thrusting upward with an effortless grace and a soaring pride. The dome rises behind two arched portals of immense size, one set at an angle to the other, so that the entire building has the appearance of an improvisation. The dome, the two portals, the vaults, the fountain, the flower patterns of inlaid faïence on the walls, all these seem to have been designed to convey the presence of a divine blessing, and in the mysterious blue light of the mosque it is easy to believe in the eternity of peace, God's offering to mankind.

The Masjid-i-Shah was constructed between 1612 and 1638, and is therefore contemporary with the Taj Mahal, built by Shah Jehan in honor of the Empress Mumtaz Mahal. But where the Taj Mahal rises delicately and almost plaintively, the Masjid-i-Shah gives an impression of triumphant power. No other mosque in Persia compares with it in majesty and grace. Nearby, on another side of the great square, stands the Masjid-i-Shaykh Lutf Allah, with a smaller dome and an altogether more modest appearance, but equally compelling, for while the greater mosque proclaims the peace and majesty of God, the smaller one, being of a more human size, proclaims God's affection for mankind. This mosque was built by the Emperor Shah Abbas in honor of his saintly father-in-law and served as his own private oratory. His palace, which faces it on the square, possesses a deliberate simplicity to offset the superb decorations of the mosques: the slender columns of the palace rise above a fortresslike gateway, and their very slenderness proclaims the Emperor's power.

There is no other square in the world so brilliantly designed as the *maydan* at Isfahan. If one could imagine the Piazza of San Marco in Venice with a palace on one side and a Byzantine church of the utmost elegance on the other, with the great basilica in the distance, then one might approximate to the magnificence and beauty of this square in Isfahan, where the Persian architects excelled themselves.

The early Safavid emperors cultivated artists on a scale rare among oriental emperors. Persian carpets, designed by the most famous artists, display the same elegance as the mosques, and indeed the greatest of these carpets were two-dimensional portraits of mosques. The Ardebil carpet, now in the Victoria and Albert Museum in London, has a central sunburst which represents the dome of the mosque, and there are two delicately fashioned mosque lamps beside it, while the rest of the field forms a tumultuous garden of flowers set against a background of midnight blue. The vitality and majestic luxuriance of this carpet, made for the shrine of the founder of the dynasty, have given it pre-eminence, and it should be studied as a painting is studied, for all the intricate and rich details which continually reflect and react upon one another. No greater carpet was ever woven in Tabriz, or anywhere else. The master weaver, who was also perhaps the designer, was Maqsud Kashani, who worked in the royal carpet school at Tabriz and completed the carpet in 1537. He signed his masterpiece, and wove into it the inscription:

I have no refuge in the world other than Thy threshold,
My head has no protection other than Thy porchway.

A deep religious feeling fills that immense carpet which simultaneously portrays a mosque, the fields of heaven, and faith in God. Other carpets of great beauty and complexity continued to be woven in the Safavid workshops, but there is only one other carpet which can be spoken about in the same breath as the Ardebil carpet. This is the perfectly preserved carpet which once belonged to the Duke of Anhalt, dating from the early years of the sixteenth century, with a scarlet sunburst breaking on a brilliant yellow field, and with a most intricate scarlet border. Although intended as a medallion carpet to be laid in a mosque, it is essentially a carpet prepared to

The Pantocrator.
CHURCH OF THE LAURELS, DAPHNI.
HARISSIADIS.

The Youthful Christ
ST. MARK'S, VENICE.
OSVALDO BÖHM.

Christ in Majesty.
CHURCH OF ST. PIERRE, MOISSAC. ROGER-VIOLLET.

Christ, from The Tribute Money, by Masaccio.
CHURCH OF THE CARMINE, FLORENCE. ALINARI.

The Crucifixion (detail), by Grünewald.

The Crucified Christ, by Donatello.
CHURCH OF SAN ANTONIO, PADUA. ALINARI.

The Risen Christ, by Piero della Francesca.
BORGO SAN SEPOLCRO. ALINARI.

Christ Blessing, by El Greco.
TOLEDO MUSEUM.

delight an earthly king, and where the Ardebil carpet proclaims the joy of heaven, the Anhalt carpet proclaims the joy of earth.

In the time of Shah Abbas there came the vase carpets with flowers exploding over them, and sometimes the vase was omitted, but the explosion continued. There were hunting carpets with intricate designs of leopards, falcons, lions, and songbirds, and there were Polonaise carpets, which were really tapestries woven with gold and silver thread, and many others, but all of them demonstrated the characteristic Persian delight in sweeping curves and bold juxtapositions of color, and all of them in their different ways presented abstract portraits of paradise, whether on earth or in heaven.

There was a time when Islamic art reached across the greater part of the known world, from the Mohammedan provinces of China to southern Spain. Always it was an art of geometrical forms and brilliant renderings of color, as though color itself had become an abstraction. Sensual, calm, humble, magnificent, it was an art reflecting the intricate beliefs of Islam, which saw God as the whole, but simultaneously delighted in the divine particulars, and was therefore torn between unity and diversity: an art of many forms all moving toward the formless transcendence of an all-merciful God whose power reached down into the inmost hearts of men. It was a stern religion, and the art tended toward an uncompromising sternness and sobriety. Happily, artists are not by nature sober; and the Mohammedans reveled in an art which remained strangely chaste while permitting the utmost license to the imagination.

One cannot imagine Christian art without the naked Christ on the Cross, without the Virgin, the apostles, the miracles, and the Resurrection. Islamic artists contented themselves by necessity with an art which was largely impersonal. Mohammed rarely appears, and when he appears he is veiled. He has no apostles, no mother weeps over him, the only miracle is his flight to heaven from Jerusalem, and there is no Resurrection. In Islamic art he belongs to no time or place, and effaces himself so that God may be more readily made known. It is an art without legends and without human proportions: an art for the worship of God, and God alone.

For more than a thousand years Islamic art flourished, taking on the coloration of all the lands conquered by Mohammedan arms, absorbing the ideas of conquerors from Central Asia, and reaching its utmost perfection in Persia, a country which succeeded in preserving its ancient Zoroastrian traditions while accepting the new faith. By about 1750 Islamic art had run its course. No more great artists arose; there were no more memorable mosques, or paintings, or illuminated manuscripts. As suddenly as it rose, it perished. It was as though all over Islam the lights went out one by one. The mystery of the death of Islamic art is as insoluble as the mystery of its beginnings.

THE ORIENTAL VISION

The Dreams of India

Some five miles from Bombay there is a small thickly wooded island, with cliffs rising sheer from the sea, and there are only one or two places where a ship can be berthed. The island has had many names, and legends were told about a princess in the age of King Banasura who lived there under a vow of perpetual chastity and was rewarded with a shower of heavenly gold; hence the name Shantipore, the City of Gold. But no gold was ever found there, and today it is known as Elephanta from the two stone elephants found at the entrance to the caves.

The traveler climbing the steep winding path which leads to the caves sees only the shingly beach below, the small farms looking out to sea, and the desolate forest; and even when he has rounded a jagged crag and entered the forecourt leading to the cave temples, there is nothing to suggest the splendors that lie within. The forest has taken possession, and the square columns cut out of the living rock, seeming to support the whole of the mountain that rises above them, are almost hidden by the trees. The rain falls; green pigeons flash among the palms; and there is the smell of dampness and decay.

Once inside this complex of man-made caves, the aspect changes into one of honey-colored magnificence. An immense courtyard, 130 feet square, opens out to reveal a palace once covered with deep-cut reliefs of the gods. Many of these reliefs depict the majestic presence of Siva performing the *tandava*, the world-shaking dance. Over-life-size, the god is represented as a youth dancing in ferocious abandon, and with each step centuries and millenniums pass and the worlds are reborn. He has six arms, but the sculptor has so arranged them that they do not crowd one another and do not disturb the rhythm of the composition. On one of those walls we see him with his elephant-hide cloak tossed back, his sword uplifted, and from his neck there descends the famous necklace of skulls which is the sign of his empire over mortality. He has the new moon crest, a third eye in the center of his forehead, his hair is matted, and with one of his many hands he rings a bell, summoning the other gods to join in the dance. This sculpture of Siva is a thing to wonder at. In the West the gods are presented in attitudes of great calm, or dying, or dead; here a god is presented in an attitude of unrestrained energy and violence, breaking out of the enclosing rock, beautiful in his youthful vigor and in the serenity of his features.

Except in the massive portrait of the *Trimurti*, the gods in the cave are never seen in repose; all are dancers, and even those figures which seem to be momentarily in repose are informed with the spirit of the dance. Parvati, the bride of Siva, lies in bed, but in a moment she will leap away and run to his arms, or we see her standing beside her lover naked except for her transparent gown; it is the moment of separation after an embrace; they sway dizzily; and in their swaying there is the beginning of the dance.

On these walls where even now there are faint traces of color and where once there were enormous wall paintings, the ancient Hindu conception of whole worlds and universes coming into existence at the bidding of a divine dancer achieves its triumphant expression. Power streams down from the walls; it leaps from one relief to the next, and is never oppressive. There is an astonishing gaiety in the dance, and there is even impudence in the slow undulating curves of the belly, the downcast eyes, the playful half-smile, as of a dancer who knows that he is seductive and wholly beautiful, and is aware that he is being admired. Absorbed in the dance, he still demands our adoration.

But if Siva in his many manifestations conjures up visions of universes wheeling away or being formed at every moment when his feet strike the ground, exultant in the enjoyment of divine energy, the Hindu sculptors were able to convey that divine energy in more subtle ways. They could deprive him of his limbs, his torso, his beauty, his youth, his impassioned violence, and still they were able to create an image of a god who creates universes. The heroic *Trimurti*, standing at the back of the cave, dark and mysterious in the shadows, belongs almost to legendary art—that art which, even when you are standing in front of it, seems to belong to an ideal world beyond the powers of any artist to create. Here finally, in the three-headed god whose huge shoulders rise out of the living rock, the abstraction of infinite power has been made concrete, the inexpressible has been expressed.

There is no body; only the three heads and the shoulders carved by an unknown master during the seventh century in the afterglow following the decline of the Gupta Empire. The three-headed god is Siva in his threefold aspect of Creator, Destroyer, and Preserver. The Creator is seen full-face; his eyes are closed, and he wears a towering crown like a cascade of jewels. There is in that face, calm as eternity, so much power, so much majesty, so much thought, so much enchantment, that it cannot be approached except with awe. It is a face of great fullness and roundness, like a ripe fruit, absorbed in dreams. He dreams of worlds to come and worlds which have passed away, and by his dreaming he shatters them or brings them into existence. He knows all things, has brooded over all things, and is about to speak. Beside him on the left, cut in profile on the rock, we see the Destroyer: a stern face helmeted with skulls and cobras, and on the right there is the heavy face of a woman who is also lost in dreams. She is the Preserver. Her rounded headdress is studded with jewels, and her eyes are sealed more tightly than the eyes of the Creator, so that we feel she will never awake, and has no need to awake, for all her work is accomplished in an eternal sleep.

The twenty-three-foot-high *Trimurti* is one of those sculptures which have the power to haunt for a lifetime. It stands alone among the great monuments of Indian art in conveying the immensity of divine power, the heart of the mystery. One can believe that the worlds are formed out of the dreams of this strange three-headed god and that universes are born whenever he takes a breath. Beyond this it is almost impossible for sculpture to go.

The source of the *Trimurti* goes far back in Indian history and mythology, but that particular quality of serenity and majesty was the gift of Gupta art to medieval India. It was an age when Hinduism was absorbing those elements of Buddhism which it needed for its own purposes. Remove the Preserver and the Destroyer, and you have a monumental portrait of divinity which can be traced back through the ages by way of Gandharan art to the first statues of Apollo, for Greek art subtly influenced the shapes of the Indian gods.

The Cave of Elephanta is so filled with images of Siva that it is as though the sculptors were attempting to portray him in all his disguises. On a side panel near the *Trimurti* we come upon Siva riding a bull, his six arms summoning the demons and the angelic *apsaras* out of the air. Again he sleeps, and again he wears an expression of divine contentment, remote from the things of the world. With one hand he grasps the horns of a bull, with another he shakes a tambourine. So he rides, making his triumphant progress across the familiar earth, and it is not in the least strange that he should have one enormous breast and the rounded hips of a woman, for in this cave, and in this context, such things are to be expected. The androgynous gods appear in nearly all religions, and they are especially plentiful in the teeming Hindu pantheon.

Only a few steps separate the *Trimurti* from the dancing Siva, the one so calm and contemplative, the other caught up in the frenzy of the dance. From the extremes of silent self-communion to the wildest outpouring of physical energy the Hindu passes with ease, for these are the polar opposites of his faith. For him the Siva sunk in contemplation is only another aspect of the Siva who dances the dance of the worlds; and in the realm of the gods the divinity seemingly lost in his meditations may be exerting greater power and authority than the dancer exerting his utmost vigor and shaking the universe.

In no other country is there quite this sense of the polarity of life, the visionary extremes continually meeting. The Indian imagination is at home among vast concepts which send the Western imagination reeling; their gods are as vast as the Himalayas, and when they stamp their feet millions of years pass into oblivion. Their gods, of course, are the dreams of the race, the fulfillment of

their most cherished desires, the gleaming presences who give substance and meaning to the ceremony of life. Unlike the gods of
Greece and Rome the Indian gods are always strangely remote
and inaccessible, too large and too powerful altogether to be ac-
commodated easily in the imagination. The head and shoulders of
the *Trimurti* rise from the depths of the cave, suggesting that his
vast limbs reach down to the bowels of the earth; and all over India
the gods are portrayed as giants, so much larger than life that they
escape altogether from the ordinary world of men. Those august,
majestic presences tolerate no familiarity. They speak as the kings
speak, from the heights of their unapproachable thrones.

For the artist, and especially for the sculptor, such a mythology
makes extraordinary demands on his skill. To represent the gods he
must construct forms so powerful that they threaten to become caricatures, and so large that they are in danger of collapsing under
their own weight. Possessing a formidable knowledge of his art, the
Indian sculptor took pleasure in formidable tasks. If it had been
possible, he would have carved the shapes of his gods on the Himalayas.

At Ellora in the Deccan, near the ancient city of Dalautabad,
no fewer than thirty-four caves were carved out of the cliffs, gouged
out of the sloping sides of the mountain, or—in the case of the
most magnificent of all—the sculptors set armies of excavators at
work, digging down from the top of the rocky spur until they
reached the level of the base of the hills, carving huge monolithic
shapes of temples and shrines. The courtyard of the Kailasa temple
is 276 feet long, 154 feet wide, and 107 feet deep. There is a great
porch where every square inch has been carved with the shapes of
lions, elephants, and mythological beasts, while above this, immensely higher, stands the somber mass of the temple itself, hol-
lowed out into chambers and vestibules for the worship of Siva and
his sacred bull Nandi. The exterior of the temple was coated with
white plaster so that it resembled snow-capped Mount Kailasa, Siva's
birthplace in the Himalayas. The interior of the temple was brilliantly painted. Here in the torrid heat of a Deccan summer Siva
might find a cool and shining resting-place to remind him of his
holy mountain.

This temple is by far the most sumptuously adorned of the many temples of Ellora. But we see it today under conditions which have changed its appearance. The white temple is now a greasy black, and the courtyard, rubbed smooth by the footsteps of generations of worshipers, is a uniform leaden gray. The brightness has gone. The high cliffs, the crowded carvings, the huge mass of the temple have the effect of dwarfing the observer, who finds himself lost in a dark maze with no way of escape. There is no perspective from which the whole can be seen. The dancing Sivas, the *lingams*, and the bulls, the sculptured lovers at their play and the huge stone cenotaphs engraved with the names of the forgotten kings who built this temple, are like sea wrack cast on the shore. Everything seems to be in convulsive turmoil except for the life-size stone elephants who guard the entrance. But it is precisely this turmoil which the Indian sculptors have attempted to recreate, for Mount Kailasa was nothing less than the Mountain of Creation, and it was here that Siva hammered out the shapes of men and women, of fables and mythologies, of universes and eternities.

After a long while the wanderer in the courtyard finds himself gradually forming a picture of the whole. He realizes in the end that this is not so much a temple, or even a representation of the holy mountain, as a portrait of the Indian mind. The flying buttresses, the legendary lions, the *apsaras* in full flight along the cliff wall, all the thousands of reliefs on the temple and all the sculptured gods in the tunneled galleries, all these are subordinated to a single central theme—the power of generation. In the highest chamber of all there is the lingam, the white stone phallus gleaming with the oils and butterfat which have been poured on it for more than a thousand years. It is a small chamber, but well lit, for it stands at the summit of the holy mountain. For a hundred years men hacked a mountain to pieces in order that a place of honor should be given to a small chamber and a white stone.

The Indian imagination is fertile in invention and capable of endless improvisations. An Indian seeing a petal immediately improvises a basket of fruit, flowers, leaves, a tree, an orchard, a forest of orchards. So in the Kailasa the stonework is drowned in ornamentation, and every invention leads to another. Finally, all these inventions come into focus with the white stone.

At Ellora there are eighteen Hindu, twelve Buddhist, and four Jain temples, most of them constructed between the fifth and ninth centuries A.D., although there are a few which may be earlier and at least one which dates from the tenth century. The Buddhist temples are the earliest, and they usually take the form of pillared galleries carved deep into the hills. At the end of the gallery we see Buddha seated on a throne in an attitude of meditation, while in the shadowed porticoes the guardian gods stand in adoration, sinuous and slender, and sometimes the whole gallery will be lined with these gods, who are themselves the manifestations of Buddha. These dark gods, magnificently modeled, are like waves lapping at the feet of the Buddha enthroned in glory. Here and there are sculptured friezes telling the Jataka stories, those stories which were told about the early Buddhas who preceded him.

Under King Asoka, who came to the throne more than two hundred years after Buddha's death, Buddhism became the official state religion, and the King himself ordered the construction of the immense decorated mounds called *stupas,* which preserved his relics. There were as yet no images of Buddha, whose presence was indicated by a vacant throne, a pair of footprints, or the Wheel of the Law. The first images appeared around the beginning of the second century A.D., about the time of the schism between the "Great Vehicle" and "Lesser Vehicle" (Mahayana and Hinayana). Buddha himself had opposed the making of images. In his lifetime he had expressly disclaimed divine birth or supernatural powers, and inveighed against those who claimed to perform miracles. From his disciples he demanded that each should seek salvation by his own efforts: no gods and no prayers would help them. Buddha had set himself against the gods, and inevitably after his death he became a god. While Hinayana Buddhism remained relatively austere and restrained, Mahayana Buddhism introduced a characteristically Indian proliferation of gods, and soon there were as many gods in the Buddhist pantheon as among the Hindus. The legends, too, proliferated. He was given a divine birth, and could perform miracles at will. He had become not one god, but thousands of gods.

When the Chinese monk Hsüan Tsang visited India between
A.D. 630 and 644, he read deeply in the Buddhist sacred
writings and sought out the still surviving relics of Buddha, noting
that they all gave out a very bright light which only the devout
worshiper was able to see. He noted, too, that there was conflict
between the Buddhists and the Hindus, and there were signs that
Hinduism was already in the ascendancy. The Buddhist and
Hindu cave-temples at Ellora were therefore being carved at a time
when the two religions were in mortal combat. It was perhaps in
the nature of things that the imagination which could produce the
violent and dramatic Kailasa would triumph over the more reserved
and reticent imagination which produced the Buddhist temples.
By the eleventh century Buddhism had vanished from the place
of its birth and had taken up its home in Ceylon, in the Himalayas,
in Tibet, in China, and in Southeast Asia.

In those last years when the struggle between Hinduism and
Buddhism was keenest, the arts flourished. Rivalry, indeed, seems
to have acted as the spur to intense artistic creativity between
about A.D. 700 and 750; and while Buddhism went down to defeat,
some of the loveliest Buddhist art dates from the period when it was
already in decline.

The caves of Ajanta lie half a day's journey from Ellora, in a
beautiful gorge filled with feathery oleanders. Until recently tigers
roamed along the gorge and drank at the pool, and the caves were
in fact rediscovered after centuries of neglect by some English army
officers on a tiger-hunting expedition in 1819. A half-wild Indian
boy minding some buffaloes pointed up the hill to some caves, saying the tigers' lairs were to be found deep in the hillside. The officers made their way up the slope, cut through the undergrowth in
front of one of the caves, and entered through a large doorway of
carved stone. They found no tigers; instead, they found a square
temple with a huge figure of Buddha smiling mysteriously in the
gloom.

As the years passed, more and more visitors came to the caves,
but no effort was made to protect the caves or to record what was in
them until Major Robert Gill of the Madras Army was sent to
Ajanta to make faithful copies of all the paintings on the walls of the

caves. For twenty-two years he worked on the task in complete isolation. His complete collection of paintings was exhibited in the Crystal Palace in London in 1866, and there in December all except four or five perished in a fire. What we see today is only a remnant of the brilliant frescoes which Gill copied so patiently over so many years.

There are twenty-nine caves at Ajanta, dating from the second century B.C. to the seventh century A.D. As one might expect, the earliest ones are the simplest, with no representations of Buddha. By the fourth century A.D. the Buddhist artists were giving free play to their imaginations, carving gentle erotic scenes on the columns and painting over immense areas the real and legendary stories of Buddha. At some time in the second half of the sixth century an unknown artist painted in Cave I a superb portrait of Buddha Padmapani, "he who holds the lotus." He is not the historical Buddha, but the successor who came into existence at the moment of Buddha's death, to bless and protect the worlds, renouncing his own Nirvana until all have received blessedness. According to the Mahayana canon he possesses a divine charity and infinite compassion and solicitude for all created things.

As the artist has created him, he is a young prince who leans forward a little, dreaming of blessedness, smiling imperturbably. He holds a blue lotus in his uplifted hand. A little larger than life-size, he stands at the left of the doorway leading into the inner sanctuary, as though he were beckoning the worshiper deeper into the mystery. Naked to the waist, his skin a light gold, his jeweled headdress of a darker gold, with a necklace of pearls falling across his chest, he emerges from a red-walled palace, while palm leaves blow in the wind and blue swans fly overhead, and there is about him the delicacy and grace of the highest gods, and he moves in a more rarefied and tender world than ours.

What is extraordinary is the reality with which the Buddha Padmapani is invested. He is about to move, about to speak, about to smile, and about to dance, and yet he does none of these things. Though he wears the colors of flesh, he is almost pure spirit. The mystery is how the artist has been able to convey so much power and authority with such simple means.

In portraying the Buddha the artist has merely followed the established tradition. The eyes are like lotus petals, the eyebrows follow the shape of the Indian bow, the face is egg-shaped, the shoulders are curved like the dome of an elephant's skull. The artist has painted in flat colors, and there is almost no shading except on the face where two gray stripes run along the nose, and there is a touch of bright pigment on the tip of the nose and on the chin, and some reddish pigment to suggest the curve of the jaw. The jeweled headdress is made deliberately flat, without depth. There is no suggestion of muscles in the youthful torso, but the body is depicted in subtle curves, and it is from these sinuous curves that it derives life and the sense of movement. The flat colors are deliberate, for the unbroken planes convey an abstract perfection of form, while the triple curve, derived from the posture of the Indian dance, permits the Buddha to glide out of the wall. Today a guard will flash a portable electric light on the wall, and we see the colors more starkly than they were seen in the past, when white cloths or mirrors outside the cave projected a diffused sunlight within. No candles can have been permitted in this painted chamber, for the low roof is covered with paintings.

Near the Buddha two priests are seen praying, one clothed in blue, the other in gold. Behind him a girl goes running into a garden, and by his side a dark princess kneels, gazing into the distance. Who is she? No one knows. She comes again and again in these frescoes, perhaps eight times altogether, and always she wears a look of exquisite detachment mingled with sorrow. The walls are crowded with processions, with musicians and dancing girls and plump pink elephants and festoons of flowers. The cave has the gaiety and liveliness appropriate to the antechamber of a king, and in fact the throne room is only a few steps away. Here, too, there must have been paintings, but they have all perished, and there is only a stone Buddha of no particular distinction. Elsewhere in the caves there are carved stone Buddhas of monumental power, but it is not in sculpture that the Ajanta artists excelled so much as in painting.

The Buddhist monks had studied the court paintings of the time, and they had watched great embassies arrive and seen the young princes and princesses at their ease. So on the walls of the cave they painted the paradise they knew as a foretaste of the greater paradise to come. They painted with vivid earthy pigments: scarlet and green and brown and bright blues and yellows. All is ripeness and tenderness. Look, for example, at the bullfight in the same cave as the Buddha Padmapani. It is remarkably similar to a bullfight found at Knossos. The shoulders of the opposing bulls are deliberately exaggerated to give an appearance of massive strength, their tails lash, and you can sense the quivering of the tendons; and below these bulls there is a frieze of sunflowers and poppies. Or look at those ambassadors in heavily embroidered costumes, at once arrogant and humble, laden with jewels, as they pass before the full-bosomed beauties of the palace, golden-brown, naked except for their jewels and small strips of silk, smiling at the strange foreigners who wear bonnets with colored ribbons, and the ribbons glint and flash like petals.

So it is in all the painted caves at Ajanta: the exuberance, the deftness, the splendor, the sense of a world at ease and aware of its beauty. Never again would Indian painting achieve these heights.

The Gupta monarchs and princelings reflected a civilization in which men lived in harmony with their gods. About the same time in Ceylon, in an almost inaccessible gallery carved within the Lion Rock at Sigiriya, artists trained in the Ajanta tradition were painting the light-skinned ladies of the court together with their dark-skinned attendants, and both the ladies of the court and their attendants wear towering hair ornaments, bracelets, earrings, and necklaces. These portraits are cut off below the waist, and there are wavy lines indicating that they are wading through water or through clouds. By their beauty, and by the fact that they are all carrying flowers with the same delicacy as the Buddha Padmapani, we know they are at once divinities and human beings; they are goddesses bringing flower offerings to the Tusita heaven, and at the same time they are princesses or court ladies with recognizable features and characters, all leaning forward a little, intent upon the rituals of worship, caught up in the languor and excitement of the procession. Probably they were intended as guardians of the rock, which was surmounted by the white palace of the reigning mon-

arch. This huge rock resembles a crouching lion, and dominates the
countryside for many miles.

What is chiefly extraordinary about these processions of bare-
breasted divinities is precisely their humanity: they have the human warmth of the Ajanta frescoes, but being isolated figures, set
in space, without any background, there is all the more need for
them to assume a compelling reality. The artists succeed in endowing them with a life of their own by deliberately emphasizing their
femininity, their heavy breasts, the folds of their stomachs, the
smoothness of their arms, their beguiling smiles and inviting gestures. In this way the beholder enters the world of divine gaiety,
knowing that very soon the formal procession will be transformed
into a dance.

In the seventh and eighth centuries the canons of Gupta art
still retained their force. The Pallava princes ruling in the coastal
area south of Madras, enriched by trade with the Orient, built
temples by the seashore which remain virtually unchanged to this
day. The Pallavas were Hindus, but the youthful angels who
guard the temple gates might be taken for youthful Buddhas standing in meditation. They have a human grace and dignity, and an
unearthly beauty; like the women of Sigiriya they belong equally
to this world and the world of heavenly beings. They are guardian
presences, and it is not expected of them, naked and weaponless
as they are, that they will drive out any invaders by force of arms:
their mere presence is enough to safeguard the shrines.

Among the glories of Pallava sculpture is a rock eighty-five feet
long and thirty feet high, with a great multitude of figures carved
in high relief. The carving depicts nothing less than the birth of
the world, which came about as a result of the prayers and austerities
of the hermit Bhagiratha, who is seen praying at the temple where
the god Siva stands in the shadows. He is old and bent, no more
than skin and bone. Then the eye moves up the rock face and we
see him again, but this time he is dancing and his hands are waving, while the god Siva, twice life-size, gazes upon him with ap-
proval. It is the moment of triumph, for the world has just come
into existence, and everywhere the angels and the holy men, lions
and tigers, deer and elephants, demons and serpent princes, and

ordinary human beings, come flocking toward Siva and the hermit
to pay them homage. The visible sign of the earth's coming into
existence is a cleft in the rock representing the holy Ganges, which
springs from heaven and brings fertility to the earth and the breath
of life to men and beasts. In this cleft the serpent kings take their
places under canopies of hooded cobras and quietly rejoice.

Elsewhere the rock is clamorous with excitement. All are dancing as they come running toward Siva and the hermit. The elephants dance; so do the potbellied baboons; so do the princes and
princesses, who seem to be wearing nothing but their high crowns.
A deer rests and scratches its muzzle with its hoof, and some monkeys
amuse themselves by picking nits out of their hair, while a cat takes
its place among the ascetics in order to deceive the unsuspecting
mice. There is a joyous humanity in the rock carvings, which were
evidently conceived by a single sculptor of genius.

While this rock carving at Mamallapuram, "the city of heroes,"
represents the finest flower of Pallava culture, there were many
other sculptures along the seashore which are equally powerful,
lively and graceful. Altogether there are fifteen carved temples along
the seashore, and there may be many more beneath the sea. Most of
these temples were carved during the reign of the Pallava prince
Mahendra I, an accomplished musician and poet, and his son
Narasimha I. With the death of Narasimha I in A.D. 670 the
great tradition came to an end. For a few more years the Pallavas
continued to build their temples by the sea, but the beauty and
urgency had gone from them.

The movement of Indian sculpture had been toward the East.
The beginnings were in the West, in Afghanistan, along the shores
of the Arabian Sea, and in the Deccan. After the decline of the
Pallavas, the movement was carried up to Bengal, where in the Pala
and Sena dynasties sculptors learned to carve a peculiarly hard
bluish-black slate, giving to the original Gupta forms a strange
tightness, as though the very effort of carving the stone was felt by
the figures. It was a monumental art practiced for over five hundred
years, and curiously lacking in tenderness. The gods have become
stern again. Yet out of this art there emerged a goddess of surprising
and delicate beauty: Tara, born of the tears of Buddha, full-breasted

and with a slim waist, seated cross-legged in an attitude of meditation, the gentlest of smiles hovering about her lips. She arose for
the first time among the Bengalis, a people devoted to mysticism
and love songs, and thereafter her influence spread steadily north-
ward, for she became the favorite goddess of the Nepalese and later
the Tibetans. In Tibet she assumed two forms: the White Tara was
modeled on the features of a Chinese princess, the Green Tara
wore the features of a Nepalese princess. Both were saviors, dis-
pensers of mercy, their very beauty putting to shame the forces of
evil. Like the Virgin Mary and the goddess Kuanyin in China,
Tara reigned supreme in her own heaven.

The fertile land of India demanded fertile ornament, and
every temple was thickly encrusted with statues. Even the Buddhists,
outwardly so reserved and dispassionate, erected immense temples
covered with innumerable statues of Buddha. At Bodh Gaya, where
Buddha received enlightenment, the multiplication of his image
achieves astounding proportions, and in the Hindu temples of the
Hoysala kings, the gods and goddesses, their attendants and worshipers fill the vast walls of pyramidal temples. The endless intricate carvings nearly always show people taking part in a sacred
dance, but we are far from the caves of Elephanta, where the dance
was conceived as an act of divine creation, bringing the worlds
into existence. So the hermit had danced at Mamallapuram when
the heavenly Ganges flowed down to the earth, and so had Buddha
danced at Ajanta. But when walls a hundred and fifty feet high
were covered with sculptures of people dancing, the effect resembled an endless chorus line and little was gained.

Yet those immense temples answered to the needs of the Indian imagination, which is obsessed with fertility. At Khajuraho
the Chandellas, Rajput princes claiming descent from the moon,
built a complex of eighty temples during a period of about a hundred
years, from about A.D. 900 to 1000. Each temple was intended as a
foretaste of heaven: there was a portico, a vestibule, a sanctuary,
where the god reposed in magnificent state, and around this an
ambulatory. The worshiper who penetrated the sanctuary came into
the presence of the god, but if he walked outside and merely gazed
up at the carved towers with their hundreds of statues he was also

in the presence of the god, for heaven was displayed there in all its complexity. Many of these friezes show lovers accompanied by their attendants, but it is not only love between men and women that is represented here: a young hero caresses a lion, a woman crouches under a lion's jaws, another embraces the elephant-headed god Ganesha, and all things on earth are seen in amorous embrace. Sometimes the sculptor carves his loving couples with extraordinary tenderness, but just as often the carving is wooden and mechanical. The Gupta forms are no longer seen. The faces are generally too heavy for the weight of the bodies, the legs are improbably long, and the poses too deliberate. Ultimately the exuberance of the sculptors tends to produce drowsiness in the onlooker. There are altogether too many gods, too many crocodiles and serpents, handmaidens and celestial nymphs, and loving couples. There is no plan: only an endless variation on the theme of fertility.

At Konarak on the seacoast of Orissa, another King Narasimha, who claimed descent from the sun god Surya, devised a more brilliant and daring temple in honor of his ancestor. It took the form of the Sun's chariot drawn by seven horses. The chariot rode on twenty-four immense wheels. The tower, which has now fallen, reached a height of 230 feet. But it is in the working out of the details of the chariot that the artists excelled themselves. The intricately decorated wheels, the plunging horses, the thrust of the columns decorated with dancers and lovers, all testify to the coordinating imagination of the chief architect, whose name, Sibai Santra, has survived. Even without the huge tower, the temple gives an impression of majesty and purpose. Built about A.D. 1250, the temple is also an abstract portrait of the determined King Narasimha, who won victory after victory over his Hindu neighbors in Bengal and against the Mohammedan armies which were overrunning India. The Sun Temple of Konarak was the last major achievement of Hindu sculpture.

All that was magnificent in Indian art comes to a focus in the Sun Temple, where the statues are more than life-size and there is a sense of serene splendor. Only Surya, the sun god, remains motionless, his eyes half closed as he waits for the moment when he will shine with the sun's glow, while everywhere else the figures are caught up in intense movement. There are altogether three statues of Surya in green chlorite, and they have been so placed that each one will shine at the appropriate hour: sunrise, noon, and sunset. There is the illusion that the sun actually inhabits this vast stone chariot facing the Bay of Bengal and that at any moment the seven horses will leap into the air and the wheels will start spinning.

Islam drove across northern and central India, and soon it was no longer permissible to indulge in these fantasies. A sultan reigned in Delhi, and Khajuraho was given over to a few holy men who guarded the sacred flame in secrecy; the forests grew round it; and nothing more was heard of these temples until they were rediscovered in the nineteenth century. But Islam, though making many converts, failed to extirpate the Hindu gods, who lived on in the remote villages and returned to the cities when Islam grew more tolerant. The Mohammedans believed it was a crime to create images of the gods, and the Hindus reveled in creating them.

Above all, they created two images of surpassing beauty and power—the image of the deeply meditating god, whether Buddha, Vishnu, or Surya, and the image of the god dancing in triumph as he celebrates the creation of worlds. These images were made in stone, bronze, and wood, in gold and silver, in the base metals, and in clay. In bronze especially they showed a prodigious feeling for movement, and they were adept at catching the fleeting movements of dancers—the high-flung arm, the grace of a turned heel, the body held in the *tribhanga*, the triple twist which so delighted the Indian sculptors that they repeated it endlessly. In this way, even when they were standing motionless, a man and a woman seemed to be dancing.

Dancing, indeed, lay very close to the fiery core of their faith, and they saw themselves as perpetual dancers around the thrones of their gods. Siva Nataraja, the divine dancer, represented the highest expression of divinity. Within a ring of celestial flames, he danced through all the ages of the past and all the ages to come. In his headdress he wore a skull, a cobra, a lotus, a crescent moon, and a poisonous dhatura plant. In one of his four arms he held a drum, in another flames, with another he made the gesture of offering protection, with another he beat time to the rhythm of the dance. With the drum he summoned worlds into existence, and with the flames he reduced the worlds to sparks flying away into the distance until they were lost in the surrounding darkness. Lord of the dance, lord of all worlds, of all heavens and all earths, he was at the same time a very human dancer, delighting in his own beauty and prowess. He was a youthful god, and his face shone in the light of the flames. His beauty and energy were affirmations of the splendor of the god, but they also affirmed the splendor of man.

The Indian imagination luxuriated in depicting the gods and making them credible. Nobility, majesty, energy, and grace were all granted to them, and they were given stupendous palaces in which they could live at ease. So vast are these temples that when you enter them you have the feeling that even the gods must be bewildered by so much immensity, so much determined splendor. But at the heart of the mystery there were two images of extraordinary simplicity—the dancer and the dreamer. When the dreamer gazed into the brightly lit depths of his own soul he saw the eternal dance.

The Face of Buddha

When the first Christians painted Christ in the catacombs, they were still looking forward to the Second Coming, and there was therefore no need to depict the drama of Christ's life, which had little significance compared with the drama about to befall the universe. The Second Coming would be accompanied by fire and earthquakes; the heavens would open; Christ would appear in majesty, and all life as men had known it would come to an end. So they depicted the symbols of Christ's presence—flowers, fruit, the vines, the lamb, the fish, the bread—and sometimes they would depict the Last Supper, but this too without drama: there were only some young men sitting at table. There are no crucifixions in the catacombs, there is no agony in the garden of Gethsemane and no angel sits by the empty tomb. All this would come later, in the full flowering of Byzantine art; in the beginning there was the sense of something about to happen, whereas later there was the sense of something that had happened long ago and needed to be recorded before it vanished from human memory. The early Christians were caught up in the breathless hush of expectation of seeing Christ appearing in the heavens, and there was no need to depict his earthly life, and even less need to depict his sufferings.

So it was with Buddha: for centuries after his death there were no representations of him. He taught an ascetic philosophy calling upon men to detach themselves from the physical world and to master their desires. At a very early period his followers were forbidden to paint the monastery walls with the figures of men and women, but they were allowed to paint creepers and wreaths of flowers, perhaps because it was felt that the bare monastery cells were too inhuman to permit the flow of meditation. "Beauty is nothing to me," Buddha says in the *Dasa Dhamma Sutta*, "neither the beauty of the body, nor that which comes from dress." Ironically, the most beautiful works of art in Asia record his legend and his life.

Long after his death a legend was invented to explain the existence of a sandalwood statue carved by an unknown sculptor of Kosambi. It was said that when Buddha had ascended to the Tusita heaven in order to preach to his mother, the King of Kosambi, Udayana, despaired that he would ever return to earth and therefore sent thirty-two craftsmen to the disciple Maudgalyayana, begging him to permit the craftsmen to enter heaven and record his appearance. Maudgalyayana did so, and the sandalwood statue was installed in the Jetavana Garden in Sravasti, where it remained for centuries. The "Udayana portrait" appears to have been carved early in the first century.

The early sculptures display only his symbols: a footprint, a wheel, a throne, a pillar encircled by flame, a turban, a tree. These symbols are very different from the symbols of Christ, for each of them refers to an event in Buddha's life—the pillar encircled by flames represents his death and cremation at Kusinagara, the tree represents his meditations under the bo tree at Bodh Gaya, which ended with his enlightenment. In these early sculptures his horse goes riderless, and even in domestic scenes, where he is obviously the center of attention, he remains invisible. He was born in Nepal, south of the Himalayas, but when we see him first it is on a gold coin minted in what is now Afghanistan, a thousand miles from his birthplace and six hundred years after his death.

On this small coin, inscribed with his name in Greek letters, he appears in a form which scarcely varies in all the subsequent ages. A slender figure wrapped in a monk's robe, with a heavy lock of hair rising from the crown of his head, and with long pendulous ears, he raises his right hand in the gesture of one granting protection, and his left hand lies open at the level of his waist, granting whatever favors the worshiper demands. He is barefoot, wears a halo, and there is another halo enclosing his body. But what is most memorable about this small coin is the monumentality of this figure of Buddha, no more than half an inch high, which will later assume towering proportions, for we find in Bamiyan in Afghanistan a very similar figure 175 feet high carved out of a mountainside. When he first appears, Buddha is already completely formed. There must have been statues of him, carved in perishable wood, long before the gold coin was minted during the reign of the Kushan Emperor Kanishka about A.D. 150.

Originally the Kushans were Scythian tribesmen inhabiting what is now Kansu in northwest China. Marching westward, they conquered a vast region of central Asia stretching from the Aral Sea to the Ganges, including the greater part of modern Afghanistan, western Pakistan, and northern India. The small kingdoms built up by Alexander the Great's successors fell to them, so that these conquerors with their roots in China inherited the traditions of Hellenistic Greece. Quite suddenly and unexpectedly Greece encountered Buddha, and out of that confrontation there arose an art so dominant, so powerful that it endured down the centuries. Once more an improbable confrontation produced great art.

Many elements went to make up the art of the Kushans. Chinese, Persian, Indian, and Afghan influences were at work; and every region of the far-flung Kushan Empire would add its own increment of form. But essentially the art was compounded out of Scythian vigor and Hellenistic grace. Thousands of statues of Buddha were fashioned in the northern capital of Gandhara, often in a black smoky schist, with Buddha always assuming heroic proportions, resembling a warrior who has laid down his weapons to contemplate the carnage of the world. Huge-chested, rather stiff and heavy, seen always frontally, wearing the gown of the Hellenistic philosopher, with features ultimately deriving from a Hellenistic Apollo, with long pendulous earlobes and a third eye in the center of his forehead, he sometimes appears as a *chakravarti*, a world emperor, who orders the world by the massive power of his thought. In the earlier statues there is little compassion; no smile of benediction softens the powerful features. A figure of stupendous power, he stands in an attitude of authority or sits cross-legged on the throne of the world.

In time this Buddha will suffer many changes, but the essential elements will remain. The gown will fall away, the eyelids will gradually close, the lips will form a mysterious smile, and in Japan and Indonesia he will assume the characteristic features of a Japanese or a Javanese. But all the Buddhas subsequently made, however remote in time or space, will echo the stern beauty of the Apollonian Buddha of Gandhara; and the more he changes, the more he will be the same.

In the city of Mathura, the southern capital of the Kushan Empire, there arose about this time a school of sculptors who adapted the Apollonian figure to the demands of a more sensual tradition. The clothing with its innumerable folds would be stripped away, or suggested lightly; the flesh becomes soft and warm; a smile begins to play at the corners of the lips; the body becomes longer, lither, quivering with life. The starkly delineated art of the cold uplands is exchanged for the softer art of the warm lowlands. Since Mathura was the winter capital of the Kushan kings, Mathuran and Gandharan sculptors were soon influencing one another, the squat figures of Gandhara gradually became elongated, and the stiffness went out of them.

Indian sculptors reveled in movement, and they were never more masterful than when depicting the gods and goddesses in their violent dances. The sinuous leap, the sudden parting of the legs, the head tossed back while the arms fly in the air, all this they could suggest with a perfection unequaled by any other sculptors. These gods were naked except for loincloths, but they danced under the weight of immense crowns, chains of jewels, garlands, bracelets, and anklets; and in fact the swinging of their jewels added a spaciousness to their dances. During the reign of the Gupta emperors, who swept the Kushan generals back into Afghanistan, the art of Indian sculpture reached its greatest heights. All of northern India lay at peace, and all the arts flourished.

The portrait of Buddha now underwent a further refinement. The middle-aged world conqueror became a dreaming youth, almost a boy. Grace and delicacy, almost effeminancy, touch his face when he sits in meditation, but in the reliefs based on the legends of his life and his many previous lives, the Indian sculptors give full play to their delight in movement. A rich and cultivated aristocracy courted the artists, who succumbed to the temptation of por-

traying Buddha as a young prince and his companions as princelings.
Ever since the first Gandhara portraits Buddha has been growing
progressively younger, as though the film of his life were being run
backward. Yet in the great seated Buddha at Sarnath, where the
Gupta genius acquires its most perfect expression, we see a delicate
youth with downcast eyes and hands raised in the *mudra* of teaching, and he still preserves a kingly majesty, though he is naked of
any adornment. The heavy Gandhara gown has vanished: indeed
he wears no visible gown. Vanished, too, is the world conqueror's
weight upon the throne, and there is only the faintest hint of his
stern purposes. The face is framed in an immense decorative halo,
which takes the place of his royal insignia. But what is especially
noticeable is that his gesture no longer commands; instead, it en-
chants the worshiper to obedience. He is not so much Buddha as
Prince Siddhartha in all his legendary and breathtaking beauty.

In Cave I at Ajanta, which is contemporary with the seated
Buddha at Sarnath, we see the young prince again, wearing all his
regalia, a gold crown studded with jewels, a necklace of pearls,
heavy earrings, armbands, and bracelets, and twisted strands of pearls
hang round his neck. The long dark hair falls softly to his shoulders, which are well-rounded and gleam like fruit. Surrounded by
the women of his court, he seems lost in dreams, his eyes gazing
downward compassionately.

Today the visitor to Ajanta sees only the head and torso of
the young prince. The paint has flaked away from the gaily striped
cloth that once hung from his waist, and nothing remains of his
feet, so that he seems to be floating in the air. The delicacy and
languor of the face contrasts with the powerful body, the shoulders
broad and thrusting. Such an imperious figure could only be
fashioned by a court artist, and no doubt there is some remnant of
an idealized portrait of one of the reigning princes of the time.

In Cave XVII, which belongs to an earlier period, dating from
about the middle of the fifth century, we see Buddha under another aspect altogether. As tall as the heavens he moves through
the world, robed in his simple monk's gown, his begging bowl
held out toward a woman and a child, perhaps his wife, the Princess
Yasodhara, and their son Rahula. This grave, monumental figure

speaks of the majesty of saintliness. There are no ornaments, no suggestion of a physical body is permitted to appear, and only the bent head, austere and commanding, gives any indication that he had once belonged to the world of human suffering. This is perhaps the greatest of all the paintings of Buddha seen as a divine personage, and it was never imitated. Henceforth, although he reigned in all the heavens, he would never look more godlike.

After a period of over two hundred years the Gupta Empire fell into an inevitable decline, and once more the armies marched across northern India. Yet the power of the Gupta artists was such that they were able to construct an image of Buddha which would endure through the centuries. There would be innumerable subtle changes, and every nation would mold the image closer to its own conceptions of physical beauty. The wheel set in motion by the original Kushan artists, and then refined during the Gupta Empire, would gather speed and roll across Asia until it reached Japan and the islands of the East Indies.

All this happened with astonishing speed, for Indian influence was spreading across the known world. Buddhism was the religion of the merchants who sailed across the Indian Ocean and the South China Sea or journeyed indefatigably along the roads of Central Asia. The most audacious of these travelers were the Ceylonese, who sailed their ships to the coasts of China. Indeed, according to the T'ang Dynasty historians, they were the undisputed masters of the sea and all the merchant ships trading between China and India sailed under Ceylonese captains with Ceylonese crews.

Buddhism came early to Ceylon, so early that it escaped altogether from the dominance of the Mahayana creeds which were widespread in northern India. The Ceylonese believe that Buddhism was introduced to the island about 250 B.C. by Mahendra, the son or the younger brother of King Asoka. To this day Ceylonese Buddhism follows the Hinayana tradition, simpler and more austere than all the other traditions and therefore closer to the original.

Out of that austerity the Ceylonese fashioned their rigorous and monumental image of Buddha, who commands and does not entice. He stands with his arms close to his body, one hand raised in blessing, the other lying against his robe, and always he is barefoot and one shoulder is bare. The features are carved with no great delicacy. This is Buddha reduced to the essentials, a commanding figure standing firmly on the ground, and magnificently endowed with the weight of mortality. Sometimes the gown is softened by innumerable rippling folds, as though a summer wind were playing lightly over it, but these ripples only accentuate the hard body beneath the gown. The Buddha of Ceylon has walked endlessly over the interminable pathways of India, and he has large feet to show for it.

The Ceylonese Buddha is far removed from the art of the Gupta period. He is intensely masculine, and if he offers blessings, he demands at the same time the utmost from his worshipers. At Polonnaruwa, the ancient Buddhist capital of Ceylon, there is a recumbent Buddha carved out of granite, fifty feet long. He is lying on his deathbed in the lion posture, one hand pillowing his face, one arm lying against his body. Lying there, he resembles nothing so much as a wave about to hurl itself on the shore with immense power. Power, authority, dominion, all these are suggested by the Buddha as he falls into his last sleep.

Nearby, carved out of the same granite outcrop, are other Buddhas equally commanding. One, twenty-three feet high, stands beside the recumbent Buddha with his arms folded across his chest. No other Buddha was ever shown in this attitude, and for many years it was thought that the statue represented Ananda, the beloved disciple, standing grief-stricken beside his master. Grief might explain the folded arms, but cannot explain the triumphant expression on the face, the look of majesty. Within a few yards are two more Buddhas, both seated, one in the open and the other in a cave. They, too, have this same unornamented, ascetic appearance, the extreme simplicity which is the characteristic of Ceylonese art.

Not that the Ceylonese were addicted to a puritanical faith. In that tropical island the Buddhist ceremonial life was notoriously gay and improvident: vast sums were spent on processions and feasts, on temple building and the painting of the shrines. The Ceylonese possessed a relic of the Buddha, a tooth three inches long, which they regarded with awe and veneration: the possession of this tooth was the stimulus for artistic creation. In addition they possessed a collarbone and an alms bowl, of somewhat greater authenticity. Yet it was the sacred tooth which became the sacred palladium, the one object which must be in the possession of the king if his reign was to be propitious. Extraordinary ceremonies were held in honor of the tooth, and the Chinese traveler Fa Hsien, describing them in the fifth centery A.D., was reporting on scenes which can still be observed today. The ceremonies went on for days; trumpets sounded; dances were endlessly improvised; the processions wound in and out of the temples; and Buddha's tooth was celebrated as though it was the most holy object on earth.

In Ceylon the image of Buddha remained unchanged through the centuries. In China there were as many images of Buddha as there were dynasties. In Thailand, at some period in the thirteenth century, an altogether new image emerged. This portrait of Buddha, owing very little to earlier portraits, showed him walking with an exquisite grace, one hand raised in blessing, the other falling by his side. His eyes are closed, and he is lost in dreams.

This extraordinary portrait belongs among the great inventions of oriental art. Although the Chinese scholar and traveler Hsüan Tsang spoke of bringing from India to China a sculpture showing Buddha making his daily rounds with a begging bowl, no trace of such a Buddha has ever been found. The walking Buddha, seen in the round, never appears, for the excellent reason that he has become a divinity of stupendous power, and it was unthinkable that he should be seen walking the earth. But the sculptors of the northern kingdom of Sukhothai in modern Thailand solved the problem in a remarkable way. They showed him walking, but not as a man walks. They showed him gliding like a god through a dream of the world.

There are no statues of Christ walking. He stands always in profoundly dramatic attitudes, blessing or suffering, and simply by being motionless he becomes emblematic of power. The Sukhothai Buddha walks, and still the power gathers around him, and still he blesses.

The Sukhothai sculptors fashioned a Buddha of almost inhuman grace, flowerlike. They gave him a diaphanous robe, broad shoulders, a deep chest, a fullness around the hips, and long taper-

ing legs, so that he resembles a strange plant that has grown out
of the earth. Everything about him suggests something from the
animal kingdom or the world of plants. The sculptors had evidently
consulted the ancient Pali texts, in which Buddha's physical
characteristics are described at length. They wrote that the shape
of his head was like an egg, his chin like a mango, his nose like
a parrot's beak, his eyebrows like drawn bows, his hair curled like
the stings of scorpions, his hands like lotus petals. His legs were
those of a deer, and his arms were smooth and rounded like the
trunk of an elephant, and his thighs resembled the stems of banana
trees. All these improbable details were fused together by a sculptor
of genius to form a Buddha who was anatomically impossible, although imaginatively credible.

With his long lean narrow face the Sukhothai Buddha gives
an impression of unerring intelligence; the beaked parrot nose, the
clear-cut lips, and slightly jutting chin suggest a human personality,
whom we would recognize in the streets, but no one has ever seen
a body like this. The arm is so long that it reaches beyond the
knee, and it is precisely the flowing quality of this arm, reflected
in the flow of the body, which is so convincing, not as something
seen with human eyes but as something observed with the eyes of
the imagination. This is not the humble Buddha with the begging
bowl, but the Buddha who comes gliding into our lives unan-
nounced and almost unseen.

The Thais played many variations on the theme of Buddha,
and they were especially successful in presenting him in his royal
aspect in gilt bronze, crowned, with a faint smile on his lips, the
eyes nearly closed, the eyelids like swollen petals mysteriously
quivering. Almost they invented a new iconography, for they were
the first to depict flames issuing from the top of his head, and
sometimes when he sits cross-legged he is shown with flames issuing
from his knees and his shoulders as well, and there are more flames
curling around his ears. Most of their Buddhas were gilded, the
gold being especially pure and therefore with a reddish tinge.

Only a people with a delighted awareness of the world around
them could have been so inventive in the arts, or so full of admiration for their artists. We hear of sixteenth-century kings of Thailand

who went to war for no other purpose than to capture a painter
or a sculptor. Buddha in their eyes was always youthful, with a
youthful sweetness and composure. One of the most enchanting
of the Thai sculptures shows a round-faced walking Buddha, who
cannot be more than ten years old. He wears a thin gown embroidered with stars and carries a water jug over his shoulder, and
so that there should not be the least doubt about his Buddhahood
he wears the little hooks on the lower edges of his gown which
are the insignia of his divinity. He has a wonderful negligence and
innocence, and one might, but for the star-studded gown, take him
for a cowherd whistling down a country lane. But he is no cowherd,
nor is he intended to represent the historical Buddha. Instead, he
is Maitreya, the Coming Buddha, the Lord of the Worlds, carrying
the promise of the future in his water jug.

Thai Buddhism, as seen in these superbly youthful statues, re-
joices in the world and takes delight in the colors of the flesh
and all living things. A Thai temple is a fantastic playground. The
roofs curve playfully, the columns leap, the spires parade their
magnificence, and every wall is filled with chips of glass and porcelain to catch the glints of moonlight or the flash of the sun. The
brooding heaviness of India is far away; all is lightness and grace.
Essentially it is an aristocratic art, for nowhere else is Buddha robed
in such jeweled garments. He is always the young prince ruling
the world by continual acts of munificence, never the sage.

As Buddhism spread across eastern Asia and the islands of
the East Indies, it carried with it a certain delicate sensuality.
The youthful and naked Buddha of the Gupta period, sitting cross-
legged with his hands in the gesture of teaching, resembled an
earthly prince sitting on his throne, distinguished from other princes
by the grace and beauty of his presence. Only the hands suggested
the teacher: the grave smile was at once a benediction and an
invitation to mysteries. He sat there in perfect composure, watching
and blessing. His power—his dominion over the world—was emphasized by the vastness and splendor of his temples, but there was
no more than a hint of it in the youthful figure of Buddha himself.
Perhaps there would be a halo, a circle of shining stone, or a
backrest of sculptured flames, but just as often there was nothing at

all. Beauty and grace were his divine attributes, and he needed no
others.

About the year A.D. 825 there was constructed in the plains of
north-central Java a vast monument to the youthful Buddha. An
emperor of the Sailendra Dynasty, which had only recently come
into prominence, commanded the erection of a stone mound of
massive proportions and intricate design, at once a stupa to contain
the holy relics of Buddha, a temple where he was worshiped, and
a cosmological pattern of all the past worlds and the worlds to
come. There was nothing unusual in attempting so much in a
single monument, for a Christian cathedral is also a reliquary, a
place of worship, and a place where an entire cosmology is exhibited in the wall paintings and the stained-glass windows. The
cathedral tells the story of the universe from the day of Creation
to the very last day. So, in the great temple of Borobudur, which
is open to the sky, the worshiper passes through many galleries
and observes the story of Buddha in his many previous births,
and passes on to the historical Buddha, and beyond this the Buddha
of the future and of the worlds to come. Altogether there are
eleven stages, and the worshiper walks through all of them until he
reaches the stupa, which crowns the summit of the stone mountain.
Within this stupa, though invisible, were the holy relics and the
Supreme Buddha, who is the eternal lord of all the universes.

Nothing like Borobudur exists in India, where the stupas are
always small, three or four times the height of a man. Borobudur
is over a hundred feet high, but is so designed as to give the
impression of being much higher, for there were gilded pinnacles
at all the turnings of the galleries and each stage in the ascent
is recessed and decorated in a subtly different way. The entire
concept seems to have sprung fully formed from the mind of a
Javanese architect of genius called Gunadharma, about whom
nothing whatsoever is known.

A single unifying spirit breathes through the Borobudur, and
it can be said of Gunadharma, as of Phidias, that he alone was
the builder of the temple. On the sides of the galleries the reliefs
are displayed in two registers. Altogether there are nearly three
miles of reliefs, and one imagines the worshipers moving very

slowly in procession, "reading" the reliefs as they walk along the galleries. In the Western churches the history of the universe from the Creation to the Last Judgment was displayed in mosaics high up on the wall, but here the reliefs are carved at a man's height and the effect is one of great intimacy. No doubt these reliefs were painted in brilliant colors, but all trace of color has long since faded away. Each scene has been enclosed within its own panel, and happily they have survived down to the present day.

Although little known, these reliefs are among the supreme achievements of Buddhist art. The grace and delicacy of the carving, the tempered flow of movement, the enjoyment of the artists in depicting the bodies of women and children in almost every conceivable attitude, the lightly carved landscapes in the background filled with trees and animals, palaces and peasants' hovels, superbly convey the spirit of the legendary world in which the Buddhas move and have their being. A soft and dreamy atmosphere settles upon those figures, rarely more than eighteen inches high. About two thirds of them are young women: they are seen dancing, or giving alms, or sitting quietly attending to their own affairs, not smiling and with no desire to attract attention to themselves. They are the silent, ever present observers whose presence gives meaning to the high dramas enacted before their eyes.

All these carvings betray the influence of the Gupta style, designed to preclude all sensuality from the naked body, transforming it into an object of tenderness and veneration. There is therefore nothing in the least cloying in these scenes which unroll before the spectator's eyes like a film or an immensely long series of still photographs. The story is told clearly and simply, with no excess of ornament. We see the young Prince Siddhartha leaving his palace accompanied by his attendants with the air of a joyous conqueror, and we see him lying beneath the sal trees on the day when he entered Nirvana, and there are a hundred separate incidents between the two events. Even when he is not seen, even when the sculptor is depicting obscure stories from the Jataka fables about the previous Buddhas, his presence can be felt, for what is most notable about these reliefs is that they celebrate a dreamlike youthfulness, the springtime of the world. In much the same way the Florentines in the age of the Medicis depicted an eternal springtime, when everyone was young.

So, too, when you reach the circular platforms at the top of Borobudur, you find once more the youthful Buddha sitting cross-legged, life-size, a little more stylized than the smiling, contemplative Buddha at Sarnath, and with broader shoulders. He is still recognizably the product of the far-reaching Gupta tradition, but some of the gentleness and delicacy has gone from him. These figures—altogether there are seventy-two of them arranged around the circular platforms—are notably more heroic and less delicately fleshed than the original Gupta figures. They do not breathe the air of the earth. A transcendent spiritual quality invests them with a superhuman dignity, for they have not been born and they will never die. Though they wear the appearance of youthfulness, they were never young. They represent Buddha in his eternal aspect, eternally radiating the light of his understanding, at peace with himself and offering peace to the world.

Those surprising and enchanting statues set at the top of a low hill in central Java deserve to be seen carefully. There would be many other Buddhas, and in China especially a vast number of shapes would be invented to suggest the presence of the supreme lord of the universe. The seventy-two statues of the curly-headed boy at Borobudur, deriving from a long process of subtle change from a Gupta original, suggest the ultimate majesty, and nothing created afterward quite equaled them. They must be counted among the most superb works of sculptural genius ever made.

Though these sculptures were made in Java, they remain essentially Indian and possess a peculiarly Indian energy. Once more Gupta art had carried everything before it. In the history of art only classical Greece offers the spectacle of a similar projection across time and space, the canons invented by its artists being obeyed hundreds of years later in countries the Greeks had never dreamed of. In the same way Gupta art would influence the sculptors of China, Korea, and Japan.

Buddhism entered China along many roads, at many different times, and in many forms. Like a wave breaking on the shores of China, then falling back, then advancing again, Buddhism gradually swept across the whole country. We hear of Buddhist mission-aries carrying sutras to the court of the Han emperor about the time of the birth of Christ, but apparently they made little impact. Historians record that in A.D. 66 the Emperor Ming Ti dreamed about a golden image somewhere in the West, shining with such splendor that it could only be the image of a god. He sent messengers to India to discover more about the god, and the messengers re-turned in the company of Buddhist priests with gilded statues. But although Buddhism had its imperial converts—we hear of a Han imperial prince ruling over a district at the mouth of the Yangtze River and protecting a small Buddhist community about the same time that the Emperor Ming Ti was celebrating the arrival of the statues—there is no evidence that it had deep roots among the people. Travelers went to India and returned with more sutras during the following century. Buddhism spread slowly among the aristocracy and the literati, who were inclined to regard it as a theological *divertissement*.

In the Northwest, around the regions of Lake Baikal, the T'o-pa tribesmen, of mixed Mongol and Turkish blood, were carving out an empire for themselves. In A.D. 386 they invaded northern China, conquered it, established their capital at Tatung in the shadow of the Great Wall, and founded a new dynasty. The T'o-pa emperor assumed a Chinese name, surrounded himself with Chinese ad-visers, retained the existing bureaucracy, and ruled as though he had been the descendant of the great Han emperors. Buddhism, as practiced by the T'o-pa tribesmen, of the Wei Dynasty, was thereupon introduced to the Chinese. It was no longer a *divertisse-ment*: it became one of the arms of state power.

Under the Wei emperors gigantic works projects were in-augurated. At Yün Kang, some thirty miles from the capital, five enormous Buddhas were carved on the face of a high cliff over-looking a winding river. They were strange figures to find on Chi-nese soil, for none of these figures looked in the least Chinese. No doubt they looked like the T'o-pa tribesmen, rather ponderous, full-cheeked, with staring eyes and thickset bodies, almost ex-pressionless. The sculptors evidently came from Central Asia, and these statues, which were over fifty feet high, had much in common with the huge Buddhas of Bamiyan, though their ultimate source was to be found in Gandhara. They look like enormously magnified dolls. The cliff was honeycombed with monks' cells, and everywhere there were figures of Buddha in the same stiff, rigid, unyielding posture. They were such figures as might be created by a conqueror who desires to stamp his features on the landscape. Since the five colossal statues were carved in honor of the first five emperors of the Wei Dynasty, they presumably reflect some elements of the features of the emperors.

Chinese Buddhist art begins with the art of the invaders from Central Asia, but very soon the invaders began to be assimilated by the Chinese, with the inevitable consequence that the faces in Buddhist sculpture begin to acquire characteristically Chinese features. The shoulders slope down, the body becomes more delicate, finely boned, and the large square hands become flowerlike, as soft and expressive as petals. The eyes are no longer wide-open, but closed, or nearly closed, in meditation. At Yün Kang and in Lung Men, another series of caves cut into the cliffs at the orders of the Wei emperors, there begin to appear Bodhisattvas of extraordinary spiritual authority, bearing not a trace of Central Asian influence. Most of them are portraits of Maitreya, the future Buddha, as he sits in the Tusita heaven waiting for the moment of his earthly incarnation, seemingly exalted at the thought that he is about to exchange heaven for earth. He wears a vast crown, the symbol of his authority, and sits with his legs apart and his ankles crossed, in a posture which derives ultimately from that of Sassanian emperors on their thrones.

This Chinese Maitreya is among the most wonderful creations of Buddhist iconography. The first appearance of this Bodhisattva may be dated about A.D. 480, a hundred years after the T'o-pa invasion; by A.D. 700 the sculptors had exhausted all the possibilities of this form, and no more were made. These sculptures coincided with the belief that the future Buddha was about to descend to earth, for the Chinese believed that a thousand years had passed since the death of Buddha and that he was about to appear in the Maitreya form. The profound spirituality of these statues reflects a messianic hope. In niches in the cave walls thousands of these Buddhas were carved by unknown craftsmen, who seemed to be caught up in the same messianic hope, for they never faltered in their carving of these complex figures.

Most of the figures were quite small, no more than ten or eleven inches high, but occasionally they would be four or five feet high. No colossal images of the cross-legged Maitreya were made. Almost they are abstractions, the bodies flattened and distorted as in Romanesque sculpture, and indeed there are Romanesque sculptures in exactly the same position, the same crossed legs, the same downward tilt of the head, the same thin waists and narrow shoulders, the same careful elaboration of the folds, the same suggestion of vast reserves of spiritual energy. It is almost beyond belief that the Romanesque sculptors could have invented this form independently, and it is at least possible that churches in southwestern France could have been influenced by cave-temples in northeastern China. In the T'ang Dynasty there was constant traffic between China and the Near East, and over a period of five hundred years at least one cross-legged Maitreya could have reached France.

The great complex of caves at Yün Kang and Lung Men was only the beginning. All over North China the cliffs were being honeycombed with caves, monastic communities were settling in them, and sculptors were being trained. At Mai Chi Shan, three hundred miles to the east of Loyang, which had become the capital of the Wei emperors, the statues were modeled out of clay, because the rock was too friable to carve. Here Chinese Buddhist art finally shook itself free from Central Asian influences. Vigorous, naturalistic images appeared, and among the gaily colored goddesses and triumphant Bodhisattvas the pilgrim, wandering up the steps carved on the rock face, could believe himself in paradise. The cliff at Mai Chi Shan with its thousands of painted Buddhas was a center of Buddhist pilgrimages from the sixth to the thirteenth century. Then, mysteriously, it fell into eclipse and was completely forgotten. In 1953 it was rediscovered by Chinese archaeologists, who were delighted to find thousands of sculptures intact in a perfect state of preservation, for most of the other cave-temples had been despoiled by the antique dealers who broke off the heads

and sold them to the world's museums and the few collectors who
could afford to pay for them.

When the T'ang Dynasty arose early in the seventh century,
a new influence was felt. Gupta art, whose entry into China had
been so long delayed, now came to China in the form of images
carried by Indian and Chinese missionaries. The new faces of
Buddha remained Chinese, while the bodies showed the influence
of Gupta modeling. The attendant Bodhisattvas were dressed in
ornate ceremonial garments that derived partly from Indian sources
and partly from the garments worn by high officials of the Chinese
court with a plethora of necklaces, girdles, and pendants, and with
long scarves looping down from the shoulders. Buddha was depicted in a simple robe. A colossal Buddha, erected at the orders
of the murderous Empress Wu at Lung Men shows Buddha sitting
cross-legged on the lotus throne, and he is recognizably the four-
teen-year-old boy from Sarnath grown to manhood. For the carving
of the statue, which is fifty feet high, the empress contributed
20,000 strings of cash from the fund set aside for buying cosmetics
for the royal family.

T'ang art was largely Buddhist art, dreamlike and naturalistic,
spiritual and earthy, the extremes meeting in harmony. A T'ang
Buddha gives the impression of being simultaneously flesh and
spirit. Some of the most superb Buddhas come from the caves of
T'ien Lung Shan, halfway between Yün Kang and Lung Men,
where many hundreds of them are carved in the living rock. Serenely
indifferent to the world yet strangely attached to it, they offer their
benedictions with stupendous grace, while the Bodhisattvas smile
dreamily beside them. The smile of a Bodhisattva is capable of
melting the heart of the most determined demon. Usually the eyes
are closed, and the weight of those leaf-like eyelids emphasizes his
dreamy remoteness and spiritual authority, while the curving lips
have the eagerness and brilliance of a child's sudden smile of greet-
ing. It is the most ravishing of smiles, and the wonder is that it
could be depicted so unerringly and so often. The Bodhisattvas of
T'ien Lung Shan are nearly always life-size, they wear the jewels
and ornaments of Indian princes, the hair is gathered in a topknot

with the aid of a jeweled clasp and this gives them the appearance
of being crowned.

It was the time when thousands of monasteries were being
built, and most of them were decorated with frescoes. None of
these frescoes survive. We know that they depicted scenes from the
life of Buddha and were crowded with the figures of monks and
saints, angels and demons. In the world's oldest printed book,
The Diamond Sutra, published in a Chinese translation in A.D.
868, there is a wood block showing Buddha sitting in state and
conversing with the monk Subhuti, who is seen kneeling in the
left-hand corner. Lions and demons protect the Buddha, a royal
sunshade keeps the sun away, monks with shaven heads crowd
around him, and there are ministers of state dressed in formal
costume. The scene is evidently based on an immense fresco which
once decorated a monastery wall, and as we might expect there is a
sense of vigorous movement even though nothing is happening
except that Subhuti has entered the assembly, thrown his upper

Redrawing of wood block illustration from The Diamond Sutra, A.D. 868.

robe over his shoulder, knelt with his right knee on the ground, and leaned forward with clasped hands, saying: "How, O Lord, shall a man take command of his thoughts?" To the Chinese Buddhist it was a moment of grave significance, for *The Diamond Sutra* was to him the most appealing of the works translated from the Sanskrit, the one book he was certain to know by heart.

From this woodcut we can reconstruct the original fresco with a fair degree of accuracy. As always, Buddha occupies the center and he will be painted in brighter colors than the rest. Since the conversation takes place in a garden, the background will be filled with flowers. The robes of the monks will be orange, the demons scarlet, and the lions tawny. In the crowded composition there will be sharp juxtapositions of bright color, with green and orange, the favorite colors of the T'ang Dynasty, predominating. Although the frescoes painted on the walls of the monasteries have perished, the frescoes painted by provincial artists in the Tun-huang caves survive, and we see the same neat, crowded, brilliantly modulated figures, and we note with some surprise that they were painted straight onto the walls without any preliminary outline of the figures.

Landscape painting had been practiced in China from an early period and was already fairly developed in the Wei Dynasty. There are landscapes in the Tun-huang caves. Far away, beyond the green fields and the blue hills, we see the red ball of the setting sun, and in this light a Buddhist priest is meditating. The priest is not looking at the sun but at the reflection of the sun on the surface of a small pool. When finally the sun sinks below the horizon, he will enjoy a foretaste of Nirvana while gazing at the darkened water.

Although the figures in the Tun-huang caves are nearly always composed in pure colors without outlines, the frescoes of the Buddhist monasteries were essentially linear. Wu Tao-tzu was not noted for his coloring but for his sweeping line. Until recently it was still possible to see twelve wall paintings executed in tempera on the walls of a Buddhist monastery dating from the T'ang Dynasty. They were to be found in the Golden Hall of the Horyu-ji monastery at Nara in Japan, and they were painted about

A.D. 720 by Chinese artists or perhaps by Japanese artists profoundly influenced by Chinese traditions. On panels ten feet high the various incarnations of Buddha were depicted in purely linear form, with only the crowns, the lips, the jewels and some of the delicate folds of the gowns lightly touched with color. The power and delicacy of the drawing speak of an age of consummate faith, and if the statues of the Borobudur must be counted as the finest achievement of Buddhist sculpture, these linear paintings at the Horyu-ji monastery must be counted among the finest achievements of Buddhist painting. In 1949 the monastery burned down, and today there remain only a few scorched remnants of these twelve panels on which a great and unknown artist recorded his vision of Buddha in Paradise.

Both the Borobudur and the Horyu-ji monasteries date from the eighth century, a period when Buddhism, already dying in India, swept like a flame through eastern Asia. Never again would Buddhist art reach these heights, yet it is important to observe that there was never any sense of decline. In different ages and in different countries there would arise artists who possessed imaginative force capable of portraying Buddha in new and hitherto unsuspected ways. Each country would preserve its own conception of Buddha and concentrate on certain characteristics. So the Nepalese Buddhas were remarkable for the suggestion of power springing up from the narrow waist and for expressions of the purest joy rather than serenity, while the Cambodian Buddhas were strangely heavy of body with all the power residing in the face, without any suggestion of joy. The Cambodians portrayed the grave features of a universal monarch aware of his responsibilities as the ruler and guardian of an imperishable empire. The Koreans went to the other extreme. They gave him a youthful face which derived ultimately from Gupta sources, but filled it with an expression of sweetness and charm, so that we have the impression that, although lost in dreams, he will soon awake and smile divinely at his worshipers. The most beautiful of these boyish Buddhas is a camphorwood statue which shows him sitting with one leg crossed over the other, one hand raised delicately to touch his dreaming face.

The statue, which has grown dark with age, stands in the Chugu-ji nunnery in Nara.

For two thousand years the Buddhist sculptors and painters have been attempting to portray a face they have never seen. They have played endless variations on the face, and if, for example, you placed Cambodian, Korean, and Nepalese Buddhas side by side, you might think that they belonged to entirely different religions. Each nation, each group of artists, saw what they wanted to see, and nearly always they were able to express a sense of his divinity. They saw him as a dreaming boy, as an emperor, as a god descended from legions of divine beings, and as the lord of the universe, and sometimes they succeeded in fusing all these into a single portrait of incomparable beauty, majesty, and calm.

The Landscapes of China

The Chinese land shaped the people and their art. The misty gorges, the terraced fields, the tiger-headed rivers and the haunted lakes deeply influenced the forms of their art. For century after century flood, drought, famine, and misery were the companions of the Chinese peasants. They were a strong, purposeful people, but the land was almost too much for them. So they venerated it, placated it, and made offerings to it; they studied the forces that moved within it, and the heavens that moved over it, seeing themselves as minute specks wandering between a mysterious earth and an even more mysterious sky. Their art was therefore an impersonal art, concentrated upon the world of nature, and the artist felt no overwhelming necessity to include himself in the carving or the painting. They were a people with an immemorial modesty, and they had no illusions about their power to order the universe.

In all this the Chinese imagination stood at the sheer antipodes of the Indian imagination. The Indian saw the universe mirrored in his own divine image and portrayed the gods as celestial youths, naked and marvelously enticing; the Chinese found no comfort in youth and saw no divinity in the human body. Their art was almost sexless and dispassionate, aiming at harmony, an enduring stability. Their earliest gods, as depicted on Shang Dynasty bronzes, were the majestic beasts of the forests, tigers and leopards, but reduced to abstractions. From the earliest times their written language was formed from pictographs which tended to become abstractions, and they were at home among abstract ideas. They regarded the earth as feminine, heaven as masculine; and the two principles, the female *yin* and the male *yang*, were not in opposition, but on the contrary they supported, penetrated, and enclosed each other. *Yin* was cold, wet, soft, dark, mysterious, and shadowy. *Yang* was warm, dry, hard, bright, steadfast, and transparently clear. This subtle and satisfying concept was expressed in a pictograph of great simplicity:

Yang *and* Yin.

The weighted, teardrop-shaped curve would appear in innumerable variations in Chinese designs. There was also another shape which the Chinese aesthetic sense found immensely satisfying: the square with the rounded corners. These shapes appear on the early Shang Dynasty bronzes, dating from about 1750 B.C. to about 1100 B.C.

The paintings of the Shang Dynasty are lost, but enough bronze ceremonial vessels, sculptures, and oracle bones remain to give us a general idea of a complex civilization. About thirty kinds of bronze ritual vessels have been recovered from Shang tombs: wine beakers, cooking vessels, goblets, serving dishes. Some are four feet high, and these evidently served as memorials of special occasions, but the majority are about fourteen inches high. Originally burnished until they shone like gold, they have now acquired a rich sea-green patina. The green color however is misleading, for they were meant to gleam and flash, their broken surfaces breaking up the light and scattering it.

The most characteristic decoration was the mysterious winged dragon which later came to be known as *t'ao-t'ieh*. It had enormous wide-open eyes, fangs, claws, feathers, a crest, and a curling tail. Seen head-on or in profile, broken down into its constituent elements, the *t'ao-t'ieh* becomes a shape of abstract power, and at first the observer finds it difficult to associate it with a dragon. But if he looks first for the eyes and then the claws, he will usually make

The Chinese winged dragon, t'ao-t'ieh. Schematic drawing from bronze vessel. Freer Gallery, Washington, D.C.

out the shape of a mythological beast intended to represent the divine, generative powers of the universe. There was no standard form, and the artist could put the basic elements together in any way he pleased. What was demanded of him was that he should produce in a small space a monumental figure charged with divine power; and he succeeded so well that his bronzes even now seem to quiver with energy and to possess a life of their own. For pure concentration of energy, the Shang bronzes have never been equaled.

The same impulse toward vivid abstractions can be seen in the development of Chinese calligraphy. In the Shang oracle bones the calligraphy has an erratic, uneven quality which comes from scratching with a sharp knife. Once the characters begin to be engraved on the bronze vessels they acquire weight and solidity and a grave beauty. By the beginning of the Chou Dynasty the essential forms of many characters had been worked out, and a Chinese scholar today has little difficulty reading an inscription engraved inside a bronze bowl made three thousand years ago. Usually the inscriptions refer to victories, marriages, and deaths, and invoke the blessing of heaven.

By the time the Chou Dynasty finally came to an end in 255 B.C., Chinese art had already acquired a settled vocabulary of forms, and all the great classical books associated with the names of Lao

Tzu, Chuang Tzu, Confucius, Mencius, Mo Tzu, and Han Fei Tzu were already in existence, together with vast collections of histories, poems, and descriptions of the proper rites to be observed on all important occasions. Shih Huang Ti, the first Emperor of the conquering Ch'in Dynasty, ordered the destruction of all existing books, but succeeded in destroying very few. A few years later the former bandit Liu Pang overthrew the Ch'in Dynasty and introduced the dynasty which the Chinese regard as the greatest of all their many dynasties. The Han Dynasty endured for four hundred years.

China was now an empire, a world power, with vast wealth accumulating in the imperial capital. Tribute bearers came from distant Yunan, Korea, Mongolia, Turkestan, and Tibet. Inevitably the influence of foreign cultures was felt and a new vitality can be observed in the arts. Han wall paintings filled with remarkably vigorous figures survive, and Han tombs were decorated with stylized figures in low relief. We see two-wheeled chariots bowling along at breakneck speed, dragons soar to the heavens, peasants plant rice with unfailing energy, and vast feasts are set before the mourners. For the first time pottery figures begin to appear in the tombs, and they can be distinguished from the T'ang Dynasty tomb figures by their vigorous clean-cut lines, their sinewy strength, and controlled violence. The painters had developed a facility for composing portraits with a few deft lines of the brush. Modeling in clay showed quite extraordinary dexterity, so that a horse's head seems to possess an urgent life of its own and to be as powerful as the t'ao-t'ieh carved on the Shang bronzes.

Only a few authentic Han paintings survive on tomb tiles, and we know scarcely anything at all about the Han artists. The first great painter of whom we have abundant records is Ku K'ai-chih, born about A.D. 345, a man known for his boisterous temper and his wit, for his innumerable acts of folly and for his genius. His talents were quickly recognized and he was given a sinecure post as secretary to a general, dying at the age of sixty-two with the title of Attendant-in-Ordinary to the Light Cavalry. One of his most famous paintings, *The Admonitions of the Imperial Instructress*, has survived in a very early copy now in the British Museum. The roll of silk is thirteen feet long and ten inches wide, but does not tell a consecutive story. There are separate scenes depicting life at court, and each scene is announced by an apothegm like: "Fulfill your duties calmly and respectfully: this will win you honor and glory." Not unexpectedly, Ku K'ai-chih turns the apothegms around and uses them for his own purposes, and when the Imperial Instructress commends the court ladies to avoid frivolity and idle chatter so as not to incur the distrust of their bedfellows, he paints a connubial scene of a husband shuffling off his shoes as he gazes merrily at his wife in bed. In another scene we see the same husband and wife in the company of their children, one of the boys protesting loudly because his hair is being combed. Other scenes show young women primping their hair, a hunter stalking a tiger, and the Imperial Instructress writing down her admonitions. The elegance and refinement of the painting foreshadow the even greater elegance and refinement of the T'ang Dynasty.

According to traditional Confucian morality, art must always serve a moral purpose, and Ku K'ai-chih had obligingly permitted morality to have its say, while outrageously perverting it. Amused, cynical, without the least trace of malice, and with a subtle psychological understanding of the people he portrayed, he had depicted the life of the court in all its happy tedium. He was the contemporary of Tao Yuan-ming, the great poet who wearied of official life and retired into solitude to sing about chrysanthemums and peach-blossom fountains.

Seven brief dynasties followed the fall of the Han Dynasty, but with the founding of the T'ang Dynasty in A.D. 618 the incessant wars came to an end and stability was restored. The T'ang emperors ruled over a massive, well-ordered empire stretching from the Pamirs to the Pacific and from the forests of Siberia to the South China Sea. Once more, as in the early years of the Han Dynasty, there was a sudden surge of the arts.

Ch'ang-an, the capital, was the largest city on earth, with a population of two million. The emperor's three palaces dominated the northern section of the city, and each palace was a small city filled with pavilions, temples, audience chambers, and gardens, where the streams and artificial lakes were crossed by intricately carved marble bridges. Orchards grew close to the palace walls, which were covered with enormous frescoes. The ceilings and pillars gleamed with gold and vermilion lacquer. Silk hangings embroidered with rubies, jade, pearls, and sapphires hung over the entrances. The court lived in an atmosphere of stupendous luxury.

The city formed a great rectangle measuring five miles from north to south and six miles from east to west. A wide processional avenue led from the palaces in a straight line to the south gate. This avenue, called the Way of Heaven, divided the city so effectively that the eastern and western parts were virtually separate cities with their own habits and customs, and with their own separate marketplaces. In the northeast corner, between the East Market and the imperial palaces, were the theaters and the prostitutes' quarters, and here too were the jewelers and the goldsmiths. Along the Way of Heaven came caravans laden with merchandise from the Near East, from Persia, India, Tibet, and the kingdoms of Indochina, and from all the regions of South China.

The caravan routes to the West had been opened and were now guarded by Chinese garrisons. Along the Silk Road stretching across Central Asia came the endless trains of camels and horses driven by men from all the tribes and nations of Asia: Soghdians, Khotanese, Uighurs, Mongols, Turks, Kuchanese, Jews from Syria, Armenians from the Black Sea, all bringing their produce to the Chinese capital for sale in the two great marketplaces. And with the caravans came ideas, religions, customs, the shapes and forms of arts hitherto unknown in China. Buddhism, which had so often rolled like a wave across China only to fall back again, now received imperial favor, and nothing in the history of Chinese Buddhism was so remarkable as the reception given to the monk Hsüan Tsang when he returned from sixteen years of travel in India to the capital, bringing with him some 600 Buddhist scriptures and about ten small statues of Buddha gathered from all over India. He was a tall, well-built, rather stern man with penetrating eyes notable for their brilliance, and as he appeared in the streets of Ch'ang-an he was greeted as though he were a reigning prince. Thousands of people came out to meet him, banners were flown, tapestries were laid out on the streets, incense urns filled the air with perfume,

and flowers were scattered before him. There was such a crush of
people that the procession was halted until order could be restored.
The great scholar was returning to China in the midst of unexampled
panoply.

Buddhism entered the court of the Emperor T'ai Tsung like a
triumphant army, and a vast monastery, known as the Great Goose
Monastery, was built in the southeastern quarter of the city, and to
this there was later attached a pagoda nearly two hundred feet high
to house the manuscripts brought back from India with so much
difficulty. The iconography of Chinese Buddhism was enriched by
the new statues, in silver and sandalwood, brought by Hsüan Tsang.
These included a copy of the standing Buddha said to have been
made at the orders of King Udayana of Kosambi, contemporary
with Buddha, and also an image of Buddha "making his daily
round for alms at Vaisali." To the Chinese these statues came as
a revelation. Quite suddenly Buddha was seen in the round, hu-
manized, a living presence; and from these statues all the subsequent images and paintings of Buddha were ultimately derived.

The return of Hsüan Tsang took place in the spring of A.D.
645, not many years after the founding of the T'ang Dynasty and
only four years before the death of the Emperor T'ai Tsung. It
therefore coincided with the period when the newly established
empire was at the height of its influence and vitality. The quality
of that vitality can be measured in the monumental reliefs designed
by Yen Li-pen for the tomb of T'ai Tsung. Six life-sized horses,
the Emperor's favorite chargers, guarded the approaches to the tomb.
Each horse stands alone, except for one which is having the arrows
embedded in its flesh removed by a cavalryman. The saddles are
empty, and the stirrups hang free; the six horses appear to be
weighed down with grief over their master's death. But in the
simple perfection of these horses there is so much controlled power,
so much tenderness, and so great an intelligence that it is as though
the artist was attempting to provide a kind of abstract portrait of the
Emperor.

Yen Li-pen was a skilled and subtle portraitist, as we know
from the large scroll representing thirteen emperors from the Han
to the Sui Dynasty, now in the Museum of Fine Arts in Boston.

The painting, which may be an early copy, gives a precise individuality to each of the emperors. Yen Li-pen was attached to the T'ang court, where he was employed to make portraits of foreign ambassadors and tribute bearers, and sometimes he painted the strange animals they brought in their train.

It was a warlike age, and T'ai Tsung, a choleric heavyset Emperor, spent a large part of his life mounting campaigns against his enemies. He even asked Hsüan Tsang to accompany him in his wars, hoping that the presence of a venerable monk who knew all the secrets of the universe would help to bring him victory. Hsüan Tsang gently refused the request, but he appears to have had no illusions about the reasons why he was held in such high favor. Henceforth Buddhism would become one of the powerful arms of the state.*

The luxury brought about by the unparalleled prosperity of the people led to an enrichment of the materials used by artists. The long tradition of monochrome painting was virtually abandoned, and with new pigments introduced chiefly from Persia and Indochina the way was open for wide-scale use of color, sometimes muted, at other times blazing violently. Li Ssu-hsün, the grandson of a nephew of the first emperor of the T'ang Dynasty, and known as "the first great painter," was credited with the invention of "green and blue landscapes," showing the abrupt, craggy mountains around Ch'ang-an with fragile palaces perched on the cliffs, while tiny wayfarers and horsemen make their way along the valleys. Cliffs and mountains were always a bright gleaming blue, as though rain had just fallen, and there was about those delicate landscapes, even when they were very large and covered an entire wall, something that suggested the miniature artist. No certain examples of Li Ssu-hsün's work have survived, but there are enough reputed copies and more than a sufficiency of literary references to show that he established a tradition and painted with astonishing versatility within his chosen range. He saw the world in green and blue, and refined

* Buddhism could be made to serve the state in many different ways. In A.D. 690, forty-five years after Hsüan Tsang's return to China, the Empress Wu ordered that a new translation of *The Great Cloud Sutra* should be made. Inserted in the text, at her orders, was the prophecy that China would be ruled by a great empress who would be the living embodiment of Maitreya, the future Buddha.

it into a kind of fairyland. Sometimes there would be brilliant red guardrails or a yellow pennant, or a chestnut-colored horse cavorting over the landscape; and this sudden momentary blaze of color would have the effect of deliberately destroying the quiet submarine appearance of his paintings. He was famous for his paintings of lakes and waterfalls. Once he was invited to paint some screens for the Emperor Ming Huang, who later summoned the artist into his presence. "From the screens you have painted, sir," said the Emperor, "I have heard the sound of water coming at night. Yours is a mastery that partakes of the divine, and your landscapes take first place in the dynasty."

Li Ssu-hsün was a painter of extraordinary delicacy and refinement, who would spend many months working on a single painting. His contemporary, Wu Tao-tzu, worked in a completely different manner, for it was said of him that he would complete a painting in a few seconds, as though in a trance.

Chinese critics of all periods are agreed that he was the greatest master of all. In Chinese eyes Wu Tao-tzu is regarded as occupying the place which is reserved in the West for Michelangelo. There was no branch of painting at which he did not excel, and nothing in heaven or hell that he had not painted. He possessed to a full degree that *terribilità* which is characteristic of Michelangelo. When he painted a demon, the people ran for their lives.

He lost his parents when he was very young, and spent his youth in dire poverty. He must have been about twenty-five when he was summoned to Ch'ang-an to accept the post of tutor to the court ladies, a pleasant and not especially onerous occupation, which left him time to paint. Soon his spirited paintings caught the attention of Prince Ning, whom he accompanied on a long tour of inspection in the distant province of Szechuan. The story was told that both Li Ssu-hsün and Wu Tao-tzu were commanded by the Emperor to paint the wild scenery of the Chialing River, which flows into the Yangtze at Chungking. Predictably, Li Ssu-hsün spent many months on a vast scroll, which included all the improbable mountains and gorges he had seen on the journey. Equally predictably, Wu Tao-tzu painted the scroll in a single day. Since the Emperor could not give Li Ssu-hsün, his kinsman, a lesser prize, he announced that both paintings were equally good and should be rewarded equally.

Innumerable stories were told about Wu Tao-tzu, who became a legend in his own lifetime. Invited to paint an eminent general, he journeyed to the general's camp, set down his painting implements, and simply stared at the general, doing nothing. "No doubt you are contemplating," murmured the general. "No, I am waiting for you to begin your sword dance," Wu Tao-tzu answered. The general, who desired to be immortalized, immediately went into a ferocious dance, and by the time it was over Wu Tao-tzu had completed the painting, having performed as energetically as the general.

Sometimes, when he was asked to paint murals on the walls of Buddhist temples and monasteries, a crowd would form and press around him. Then, as though drawing energy from the crowd, he would suddenly hurl himself at the wall, his arms moving "with the force of a whirlwind," whole figures appearing in the space of a few minutes, while the crowd gaped.

There was reserved for Wu Tao-tzu a strange immortality. His vivid presence survives in the legends and traditions associated with his name, but of his work nothing survives except some copies engraved on stone, and there are no more than three or four of these. They spoke of the extraordinary power of his line and how he would build up a living body by the swirl of draperies, but they also spoke of his extreme delicacy and refinement. He would paint with a brush as large as a cabbage, and with this same brush he produced a line as thin as a razor edge. Something of that power and delicacy can be discerned in a stone rubbing of a Bodhisattva, copied from a painting made by him. The controlled vigor of the folds of the long gown suggests vast reserves of power, and the hands are drawn with an exquisite delicacy. There is the same delicacy in the flowers adorning the headdress and in the soft lines of the hair.

The Chinese were disturbed and delighted by Wu Tao-tzu's volcanic energy. He was a master of the broken line, the explosive drapery, the sudden illumination. He painted as though he were a sculptor, and a Sung Dynasty critic said that "when he paints a face,

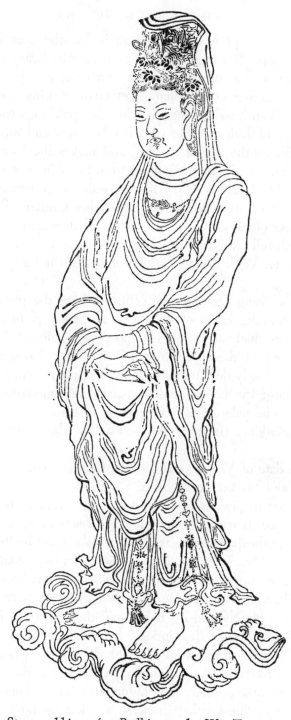

Stone rubbing of a Bodhisattva by Wu Tao-tzu.

the cheek-bones project, the nose is fleshy, the eyes hollow, the cheeks dimpled. But these effects are not got by heavy ink-shading. The shape of the features seems to arrive spontaneously, yet inevitably." Another critic, Chang Yen-yuan, writing about seventy years after Wu Tao-tzu's death, when his paintings could still be seen, spoke of him as "one who bends bones and swords, draws pillars without the use of a ruler, and makes the hair and beard stand out alive and moving, issuing from the skin with a great deal of force." He felt that Wu Tao-tzu could be compared with the famous butcher invented by the philosopher Chuang Tzu. With a single stroke of his knife the butcher could slice open an ox so that all the flesh fell away from the bones. Wu Tao-tzu could do exactly the opposite. With a single stroke of his brush he gave life to a painting.

In the Sung Dynasty five centuries later the painter Mi Fei observed that he knew of only four authentic paintings by Wu Tao-tzu that had survived. The poet and painter Su Tung-p'o possessed one of these paintings, but it was so faded that only a single marvelously delicate hand could be clearly seen. Of the three hundred large frescoes painted for palaces and monasteries nothing remained. The palace frescoes went up in flames during the wars, and the Buddhist frescoes perished when the monasteries were sacked.

The date of Wu Tao-tzu's death is unknown, and nothing is known about his last years. Since a man so revered could scarcely be permitted to die obscurely, a story was invented to explain his disappearance. It was said that when he was working on one of his immense landscapes on the walls of a palace, he invited the Emperor Ming Huang to see it the moment it was completed. He pointed to a corner of the painting where a cave stood beside a temple. "Inside the holy cave there is a spirit, Your Majesty," the painter said. He clapped his hands and the cave opened. "The interior is lovely beyond description," he went on. "May I show you the way?" Saying these words, he entered the cave, beckoning the Emperor to follow. But the Emperor hesitated, the door of the cave closed behind the painter, and gradually the entire landscape began to fade away. The startled Emperor was left facing a white wall.

Wu Tao-tzu belongs half to legend, while Wang Wei, his exact contemporary, belongs to history. Some of this history is recorded in his poems, in which he describes the passing events of the day and his affection for the mountains and streams near his country house just outside Ch'ang-an. He was a doctor, a musician, a granary inspector, a censor, a *bon vivant*, a practicing Buddhist, but above all he was a painter and a poet, the only man in China who ever achieved supreme excellence in both fields. His paintings, which we know only from copies and rubbings, resembled his poems, being landscapes seen through an exquisitely lyrical temperament. This was an aristocratic art pursued with wonderful clarity and depth. In the history of Chinese painting he is regarded as among the three or four greatest artists.

Some even regarded him as the greatest of all. Su Tung-p'o, writing in the eleventh century, spoke of visiting a temple where the last surviving murals of both Wu Tao-tzu and Wang Wei were still preserved. He arrived at the dark hours before dawn, and surveyed the paintings by the light of a guttering candle. Wu Tao-tzu had painted the scene of Buddha's Parinirvana, his death and escape from the wheel of existence. His followers weep and beat their breasts, and the goblins crowd round to watch the death of the only man who has power over them, their strange tortoiselike heads adding a necessary note of horror to the scene. Wu Tao-tzu's painting had "all the violence of a storm at sea," according to Su Tung-p'o. Wang Wei's painting showed the aged Buddha in the Jetavana Garden among disciples sorrowing because their master has only a few more months to live. Su Tung-p'o described the disciples: "They were as thin as cranes; in their hearts all passion and desire were dead and could not be rekindled." It was a winter scene, as so often in the paintings of Wang Wei, and Su Tung-p'o remembered especially the two frosty bamboos standing before the garden gate. "I saw the two paintings, and both were stupendous, both divine," he wrote. "But I bowed in silent awe only to the painting of Wang Wei, only to his painting."

Of all Wang Wei's paintings the most highly regarded in his own time was a seventeen-foot-long scroll depicting the landscape near his country house on the edge of the Wang River, as seen by an eagle swooping at a height of about two hundred feet. The painting was much copied; it was engraved on stone; and on at least one occasion it was unrolled for the benefit of a sick man, who immediately recovered his health. Shortly after the painter's death it passed into the possession of a Buddhist monastery, and a hundred years later it had vanished without a trace.

The painting was a lyrical evocation of a deer park, islands in a river, lonely shrines and kiosks in the mountains, steep pathways and forbidding crags. In all those miles of country there are scarcely more than five or six people to be seen.

A generous and kindly man, Wang Wei was always looking out for young talented artists to encourage. Han Kan was a pot boy, serving wine in a tavern, when Wang Wei encountered him drawing with his finger in the dust and encouraged him. A few years later Han Kan was presented at court, being already famous for his paintings of horses. The Emperor, who admired him, suggested that he should study the old masters. "Why should I?" Han Kan replied. "My masters are the horses in the imperial stables." They said of him that through long study he had "become a horse." From the few surviving copies of his paintings it is obvious that he showed a prodigious mastery. Never again, not even in the Yüan Dynasty, when the painting of horses was officially encouraged, were they painted with such elegance and such deep feeling. When he painted a horse and a rider, he gave the horse far more intelligence than the rider.

The T'ang Dynasty was a period of intellectual excitement and studied grace, of a gradual inpouring of influences from abroad. Across the Silk Road came Hellenistic vases and silver Sassanian plates, which the artists studied and transformed into recognizably Chinese objects. Persian influence was widespread, for the Sassanian Empire had fallen to Arab conquerors and streams of refugees poured into Chinese Turkestan. Indian influence was felt strongly in the south of China, for Indian ships sailed up the Pearl River to Canton. We hear of embassies from Byzantium, and many from the Near East. All the frontiers were breaking down, and for long periods the world was at peace.

Thanks to the grave robbers we know exactly how the Chinese

lived during the T'ang Dynasty. Thousands upon thousands of small glazed and unglazed pottery figures have been found in the graves, vividly portraying the people and their occupations. Slim-waisted dancing girls wave their long sleeves, soldiers go out to war, merchants preside at their counters, and farmers bring their bullock carts to market. All these miniature figures, intended to comfort the dead, proclaim the vitality of the race, and no foreign influence can be detected in them. Most of them are glazed with reddish-orange, lemon yellow, or spinach green glazes: the colors of the earth and of leaves. Horses, bullocks, and camels are rendered in precise detail by craftsmen who evidently enjoyed their work and sometimes introduced deliberate distortions. Semitic traders from the Near East would be given enormous noses, and the tribesmen on the frontiers would be rendered like country bumpkins. The best were the horses with their lean heads and quivering flanks.

Every stratum of society is represented in these tomb figures, which were sometimes three feet high. When great officers of state were buried, they would be accompanied by their beautiful high-stepping horses, their graceful long-necked wives, their concubines, and dancing girls, whose long sleeves still seemed to be whirling in the air. In addition there might be guardian demons, no more ferocious than pug-dogs, and menservants to wait upon them. These funerary figures grew so large that sumptuary laws had to be introduced: and the middle classes went down to their graves without benefit of any figures more than a few inches high.

No doubt most of these figures were cast in molds, for there existed a mass market. Never was a mass market so bountifully provided with small masterpieces. The delicacy, vigor, and beauty of these objects, never intended to be seen by human eyes, surprised the Chinese when the tombs were opened: they had not guessed at such a harvest. The figures were not minor works, but majestic invocations of living people, calm and joyous, possessing a strange and enviable assurance as they went about their daily affairs. A popular art assumed the dimensions of great art. Something very similar happened a thousand years later in Japan, when wood-block prints became fashionable.

The Indian influence on Chinese art was crucial, but left few traces. For a brief while the Buddhas and the Bodhisattvas were represented in the Indian fashion, nearly naked, the clothes following the curves of the body, but traditional Chinese modesty prevailed. Almost they denied the existence of the body, and it is significant that no naked goddess of love ever appeared in the Chinese pantheon. They took from India the smile of the Buddha, certain postures, a delight in ritual and prayers offered to gods with strange foreign-sounding names. Thus Buddha conquered China, but was himself conquered; and when the Chinese recreated Buddha in their own image he became even more powerful and more mysterious than before.

The T'ang Dynasty ended in interminable civil wars, which drained the substance of the country and left whole provinces depopulated. By about A.D. 900 the glory had departed. The city of Ch'ang-an was reduced to rubble, but the memories and imaginations of the Chinese continued to play on the most splendid epoch in their history. For over two hundred years there had been, save for some brief and terrible intervals, a settled way of life and a sense of purpose, a renewed respect for man, a new energy pulsing through the nation. For centuries they would look back on the accomplishments of the painters and sculptors of the T'ang Dynasty with very much the same excitement as the Europeans looked back on the accomplishments of ancient Greece. Never again would they know that serenity and self-assurance.

Great painters continued to emerge, but little more would be heard of the Chinese gift for sculpture, which was now channeled into ceramics, ivories, and jade. During the three hundred years of the Sung Dynasty (960–1279) art flowed through the end of a brush.

By the time of the Sung Dynasty Chinese painting had acquired a settled vocabulary, a certain deliberate way of representing the world. Not until the twentieth century would there be any large and deep influences from abroad, and there were no more abrupt changes of course. The T'ang Dynasty was a time of brilliant color, unbridled emotion, and sweeping experiment: now the excitement had passed, and the task of the painter was to consolidate the victories won long ago.

In this sense all Chinese painting after the T'ang Dynasty resembles a long autumnal flowering, the flowers fading, winter setting in. Painters of prodigious sensibility and inventiveness would arise, but they would continue to work within an established tradition, filling out some unexplored regions of knowledge and adding here and there some new colors, new experiences, but never changing the course of the flashing stream.

Mi Fei, who lived from 1051 to 1107, detested the court and reserved his most barbed remarks for the collection of paintings amassed by the Emperor. An accomplished painter and an exacting connoisseur, he possessed what was probably the last authentic collection of T'ang masterpieces, including an angel painted by Ku K'ai-chih and six snow scenes by Wang Wei, together with four flower pieces by Hsü Hsi and Han Kan's famous *Training Horses*. He was continually copying the T'ang masters, propping them up beside his bed so that he would see them the moment he awoke. A wildly erratic man, in love with the past, arrogant and obstinate, he poured his whole life into painting, as though nothing else could possibly matter, and he introduced what in his time was regarded as a revolutionary technique. Abandoning line altogether, he built up his mountains with thousands of little dots, very much as Van Gogh builds up a vast cornfield with thousands of little scratch lines growing smaller in the distance. This came to be known as the "Mi-dot" technique, and in less capable hands it was clearly dangerous.

Mi Fei, with his rages and his bitter tongue, his air of absolute authority, always drunk with painting and in fear of pollution from the world, so that he was continually washing his hands and taking baths, was a psychological phenomenon. For him, painting was an act of conquest. A scene must be dominated by sheer willpower or by the strength of one's emotions, and there was no humility in him. A famous painting called *Gathering of Scholars in the Western Garden* shows the three greatest painters of the time amusing themselves in the garden of Prince Wang Shen. Su Tung-p'o and Li Lung-mien are seen busily painting at tables in the foreground, while Mi Fei stands far away, and at first it is not at all clear what he is doing. He stands in the attitude of a conqueror, one arm outflung, his face in profile with the down-curling mustache giving him the look of a tribal chieftain from Central Asia. Then we see that he is painting characters on a rock. In that crowded garden, filled with concubines and servants, he dominates everything.

They called him "mad Mi" because he had a passion for strange, gnarled rocks, and once coming upon a superb rock of intricate shape, he knelt before it and embraced it, calling it "my elder brother." He delighted in wearing the costumes worn during the T'ang Dynasty, and in spite of his distaste for the court, he enjoyed its favors and rose to become Secretary of the Board of Rites and even served as a military governor.

His close friend Li Lung-mien was an archaeologist, a poet, a critic, famous for the realism of his paintings. He painted the Emperor's horses so well that he rivaled Han Kan, whom he regarded as his master, and was warned by a friendly Buddhist priest that if he continued to paint horses he would doubtless become a horse in his next reincarnation, a fate which would not cause him to lose any sleep. Like Mi Fei, he was also known for his brilliant calligraphy. Unlike Mi Fei, he was intensely religious and spent the last years of his life painting Taoist and Buddhist themes in a vast profusion. Hundreds upon hundreds of arhats, Bodhisattvas, genii, and Taoist fairies streamed from his brush.

Su Tung-p'o, who also attended the party in the Western Garden, was more famous as a poet—indeed the greatest of the Sung poets—than as a painter. He excelled in deft paintings of bamboos and seems to have been the inventor of a kind of shadow-graph painting, the sprays of bamboo leaves being seen as though they were shadows thrown on paper. He never painted standing trees, but was fascinated by the dancing life in the leaves. Employing the richest available ink, the tone changing from pearly gray to the deepest black, he is said to have painted hundreds of bamboo sprays. No authentic painting from his hand survives, but a large number of copies testifies to his endless skill. These meditative paintings assume the shapes of a strange and urgent calligraphy: the leaf is speaking. His own calligraphy was masterly, controlled and abrupt, yet filled with a dancing life. One can tell from his calligraphy that he was a man who enjoyed the play of the wind and the swirl of waters.

Sung painting was T'ang painting writ large, expanding beyond the confines of the court into the world beyond the vermilion walls. If most of the famous painters were also courtiers, this was only because the court offered the sole avenue to preferment and because the most acute intelligences of the time gathered in the capital. Intrigues were common, and a man might find himself banished to a remote island for having written a line that displeased a powerful official. So Su Tung-p'o found himself banished to the island of Hainan after being governor of Hangchow.

Something of that "fullness" or "plenitude" which was the mark of the Sung painters can be observed in their writings. Mi Fei wrote a history of painting, Su Tung-p'o left many scattered notes, and most of the painters left their views on other painters, for they were all highly opinionated. Kuo Hsi, a formidable painter of mountains, wrote an enchanting essay called "The Great Message of Forests and Streams," which was edited by his son, also a painter of talent. The son describes how his father would set about painting as though he were attending a religious rite. He would sit down at a clean table near the window, burning incense to right and left, choosing the finest brushes, the most exquisite ink, washing his hands and cleaning the inkstone, waiting till his mind was calm and undisturbed, as though he were waiting for "a visitor of rank."

This visitor was not a human visitor: he was waiting for the majesty of Nature, who in her own time would enter the sparsely furnished studio. He spoke of her coming as of a visitation. Here he described his favorite subjects—mountains and pines:

> A great mountain serves majestically as the ruler over the many lesser mountains grouped in order around it. Lord of the hills, the forests and ravines, far and near, small and large, it has the demeanour of an emperor majestically enthroned and receiving the homage of his subjects and courtiers, who never dared to show the slightest disrespect or an easy-going attitude.
>
> A tall pine rises straight into the sky, the leader of all other trees. It is lord over all the vines and creepers, grass and trees, like a master commanding those who cannot support themselves.

Its demeanour is that of a gentleman of honorable rank, commanding the services of the common people, who dare not show the slightest sign of anxiety or discontent.

Kuo Hsi was in no way subscribing to the pathetic fallacy: he did not imagine that the mountain was an emperor or the pine tree a gentleman of rank. There was an orderly universe, and mountains and pines possessed exalted rank, worthy of respect. Power poured out of them, and if it was not the same power that was exerted by men in commanding positions, nevertheless it was a power that the painter could recognize and perhaps convey in his paintings. The mountain was sovereign, and the men who crawled along the narrow pathways were merely its pathetic and ephemeral servants.

Yet Kuo Hsi was not quite certain why he painted landscapes, and he would give many reasons. He would say he painted as an act of homage to Nature, or again because he felt the need to understand the secrets of Nature, or again because he wanted in the mysterious way common among artists to take possession of them. First, an artist should permit himself to be charmed by them; then he would study them diligently; then he would wander among them; then he would feast his eyes on them until they were satiated; finally he would arrange his impressions in order and wait for the moment of inspiration. All these were stages of a necessary discipline, not unlike the stages through which a deeply religious man passes before he reaches ecstasy. "Having accomplished all this, his eyes unconscious of the silk and his hands unconscious of the brush and the ink, he paints the marvellous scene with perfect freedom and the boldness to make it his own."

Sometimes his notes resemble the fragmentary notes left by Leonardo da Vinci. He was passionately fond of water, for it provided sustenance to nature and gave to landscapes their living quality:

Water is a living thing; hence its aspect may be deep and serene, gentle and smooth; it may be vast and ocean-like, winding and circling. It may be oily and shining, may spout like a fountain, shooting and splashing; it may come from a place rich in springs and may flow afar. It may form waterfalls rising up against the sky or dashing down to the deep earth; it may delight the fishermen, making the trees and grass joyful; it may be charming in the company of mist and clouds or gleam radiantly, reflecting the sunlight in the valley. Such are the living aspects of water.

The flow of water, the flow of landscapes, the flow of branches and flowers: these were the things that continued to absorb the Chinese painters. It was as though the essential Taoism of the Chinese held sway, and no trace of Confucianism or Buddhism remained. Some of these painters were monks belonging to the Ch'an Buddhist sect, but their Buddhism was overlaid with a purely Taoist feeling for nature. Mu Ch'i, a monk who had once insulted the Prime Minister and had to flee for his life, seemed to paint in a trance, stabbing at the paper with his brush, performing miracles of ecstatic improvisation in thick, dark ink, incapable of producing a line out of place. Arthur Waley said that in his famous *Six Persimmons* "passion has congealed into a stupendous calm," but it would be more accurate to say that these persimmons, painted in startling monochrome, have somehow acquired the permanence of the fixed stars. He painted birds, monkeys, peonies, landscapes with the same unerring visionary ease. He lived long enough to see the advance of the Mongols into China and the establishment of a new dynasty, and in old age he seems to have come under the protection of the court painter Chao Meng-fu, famous for his paintings of horses, while his landscapes and bamboos are undeservedly forgotten.

There was nothing new, of course, in the sudden leap of the brush in the hand of a master absorbed in concentration. In paintings on Han tomb tiles we find a face, a whole character, expressed in perhaps four brushstrokes executed with power and authority. When Mu Ch'i paints a peony, it is unlike any peony ever seen except with the eyes of vision. More than three hundred years later Pa-ta Shan-jen, another monk, would paint with the same springing line. With incredible ease he would paint a bird on a lotus stalk: the stalk a single stroke of the brush, the bird four splashes of ink. In the same way he would paint a spider, a chick pecking at grain, or a school of fish. He was a prince of the Ming Dynasty, who turned away from the life of the court because he suffered from dumbness, but he spoke aloud in his paintings of chicks and spiders as well as in his vast landscapes.

His contemporary Kung Hsien stood at the opposite extreme, for where Pa-ta Shan-jen painted with a dazzling lightness and grace, the thing seen becoming instantly transformed into a painting, Kung Hsien labored extravagantly over dark and ominous mountains as heavy as death. He painted mountains as though they were decayed teeth ten thousand feet high, and no one ever painted such sinister landscapes. Grief and doom hang over those stark paintings which simultaneously reflect a passionate horror and a pure delight in his own craftsmanship.

The tradition of the great scholarly landscape painters survived, but the sudden visionary paintings were closer to the heart of the Chinese genius. The contemporary master Ch'i Pai-shih (1863–1957) would sometimes paint landscapes and strangely shaped rocks, but neither the landscapes nor the rocks were convincing. Yet when he looked out of his window and saw a branch of flowering wisteria or a clump of narcissi or grapes or an old pine, then he would paint them with the ease and spontaneity of Mu Ch'i and Pa-ta Shan-jen, but with his own peculiar delicacy. He was born in Hunan to a family of poor farmers, and until he was forty years old made a living as a carpenter. Then for more than half a century he painted exuberantly, never at a loss for a subject—if he looked up and saw a broom in the corner of the studio, he would say: "The broom wants to be painted," and immediately he would discard whatever else he was doing. Like Pa-ta Shan-jen he had a passion for chicks and schools of fish. Unlike the earlier masters, he rejoiced in color. When he died in 1957, it was as though an age had died with him.

Chinese culture was charged with an enduring energy and exuberance. Like the Egyptians, the Sumerians, the Greeks, and the Indians of the Gupta epoch, the Chinese created forms that spread out far beyond their own boundaries. Each civilization lit a delayed fuse, and the powder went on burning down the ages. Not the least of these procreative cultures began in the Shang Dynasty, reached its height during the T'ang Dynasty, and continues into our own time.

The Floating World of Japan

The Orient has its own laws of color and perspective, its own shapes and contours, which are not the shapes and contours of the West. In the Orient men wake to whiter dawns and see more flaming sunsets than anywhere else in the world, and their sensibility to color embraces a wider range. In Japan, spun off from the coasts of Asia, at the furthest reaches of the Orient, sensibility to color reaches an extraordinarily high pitch. Over countless generations the Japanese have trained themselves to a precise awareness of the most delicate and subtle shades, and where most cultures are remarkably consistent in their preferences for color, the Japanese seem to have taken over the entire spectrum for their own.

Geography, history, climate, the shapes of the land all powerfully affect the artistic imagination, and Japanese art was essentially the art of islanders living near the seacoast or in small valleys never far from the sea. Earthquakes were commonplace; so were hurricanes; and their restlessness and the more somber aspects of their culture arose from the knowledge that they were continually at the mercy of unpredictable forces. A secluded village in the heart of the mountains might vanish overnight in an earthquake or be torn to matchwood in a hurricane or be burnt to the ground if a thunderbolt fired the surrounding forests. In their wood-and-paper houses life was precarious and likely to be short. There was no sense of a divinely sustained order ruling the universe, and because catastrophes were continually taking place, there was scarcely any feeling for history.

Of Japanese history before A.D. 538, when the first Buddhist missionaries arrived from Korea, very little is known: legends and myths abound, but they vanish or melt into one another under the scrutiny of scholars. Kings of unknown dynasties lie under great mounds, with their bronze swords and mirrors beside them, and in their tombs are stone beads carved in the shape of bears' claws. Among the treasures found in these ancient tombs are remarkable pottery figures of ships, horses, houses, monsters, and men and women at play. These *haniwa* figures have clean lines, and the modeling is wonderfully direct and simple. There are warriors in full armor portrayed with a casual eloquence, and the clay houses sometimes have two stories. The shapes of these houses are essentially the same as those of farmhouses today and the faces are recognizably Japanese faces with their smooth planes, small eyes, and firm chins.

With the coming of the Buddhist missionaries, the floodgates opened. The Japanese welcomed the new religion eagerly, for it offered them consolation against all disasters and provided them with colorful ceremonies. When Prince Shotoku became regent in A.D. 593, Buddhism became the established religion of the court and the wealth of the royal treasury went to support the sixty-four temples erected during his reign. These Buddhist temples resembled feudal manor houses with hordes of servants, retainers, and tradesmen living on the outskirts. The greatest and most enduring of these temples was the Horyu-ji at Nara, the capital. This temple came under the special protection of the court, the young prince taking part in the ceremonies wearing the costume of a monk. When he died in A.D. 622, it was believed that he had ascended to the Buddhist heaven and he was therefore represented standing beside Buddha in a bronze commemorative statue which is still one of the treasures of the temple. He has a lean nervous face with high cheekbones and a smile of great sweetness, but what is chiefly noticeable about him is the look of penetrating intelligence. In the course of time many statues and paintings of him were made, and the artists took care to suggest his high birth, sanctity, and graciousness. The princely saint left an impress on Japanese Buddhism which survives to this day.

The Chinese had alternately welcomed and resisted Buddhism, and there would come a time when the monks were proscribed and the temples were razed to the ground. But in Japan there was never any doubt that Buddhism had come to stay. Quite suddenly and effortlessly the new religion conquered Japan, but it was not the religion known to the ascetic monk who founded it in northeastern India a thousand years earlier. It was Mahayana Buddhism, the "Greater Vehicle," with its scriptures composed long after Buddha's death. Moreover, it was permeated with Chinese feeling and Chinese concepts. By embracing Buddhism, the Japanese found themselves under the cultural domination of the Chinese.

These islanders had little in common with the Chinese, who cultivated a land as large as a continent, behaved as though they owned the whole world, and regarded all visitors from abroad as tribute bearers. The Chinese were stable, settled in their ways, aware of possessing an immemorial culture, having no fear of the elements. Earthquakes and hurricanes were unknown to them. They did not have to fight for survival, for their survival was assured. Immense spaces lay open to them, and the earth was their servant. For the Japanese space was always small, jagged, flame-shaped, or cut into fretted patterns like their own shores. They saw the world in brilliant fragmentation, sharp as the edges of things; and where the Chinese thought in wholes, the Japanese contemplated the parts, one after another or simultaneously. They loved the curves of things, especially the curve of a flame, a woman's arm, flowing silk, a petal seen in an instant, in a lightning flash. The most exquisite thing of all was a petal glowing in its own light, superbly aware of its evanescence. "The world is fleeting," says the Japanese poet. "It can never return." The Chinese poet answers: "The world is here, and endures for ever."

So there was a strange abyss between the Chinese and the Japanese, unfathomable. Having accepted Chinese culture with open arms, the Japanese immediately set about refining it for their own purposes. They adopted the clothes worn by the Chinese, but not Chinese furniture. They adopted the Chinese system of government, but not the Chinese language. From the abundance of Chinese poetry they would take what was most suitable to their own peculiar vision, so that we find Lady Murasaki quoting endlessly from Po Chü-i, a comparatively minor poet, while rarely if ever quoting from the major poets. Having learned from the Chinese how to cast bronze statues, the Japanese studied the process until they had acquired a technical perfection that surpassed that of their mentors. They adopted Chinese architectural styles and then refined them, giving them lightness and grace. The Chinese pagoda, a solid shaft, became a thing of aerial beauty, with eaves like wings, lightheartedly climbing into the sky. The Japanese pagoda, delicately thrusting heavenward, is one of the most miraculous structures conceived by the human mind.

To the Japanese the monumentality of the Chinese was an offense to the eyes. When, for example, a Chinese built a pagoda, he made it of stone to last forever. The Japanese preferred to make it of wood, well knowing that it would almost certainly be struck by lightning and burn down. They kept careful plans, and the day after it was destroyed they would set to work building it again.

It was not only that the Japanese mind was concerned with the impermanence of things, for other cultures, notably in India, have been obsessed with impermanence, but they had an attitude of their own toward impermanence. They rejoiced in it. The petal fades, the edges fray and curl up and change color, and soon the fragrant petal becomes hard and brittle as a flake of old paper until finally nothing is left except a tiny heap of ash. The Japanese do not weep over death. Throughout their lives they have an awareness of the pathos of existence, that trembling quality of the mind which they call *mono no aware*. Life is forfeit; it has gone almost as soon as it occurs; and what remains is the memory of a sudden splendor.

Instead of a monumental art the Japanese concentrated on producing an art that was fragile, restless, exquisitely refined, explosive. Flame patterns are everywhere. A Japanese scroll will be slashed with diagonal lines of great boldness, space is deliberately contorted, and even the blank spaces give an impression of restlessness. Garments stream out in long articulated folds, as though exploding from the body. Since the folds themselves are of many colors, the effect of an explosion of color, a trajectory of fireworks, is reinforced. The settled gravity of the Chinese, and their earthiness, is absent: in the Japanese painting nothing is settled, nothing is still. The winds of time blow through the world, and everywhere

there are turbulent eddies and whirlpools. Even when gravity and
serenity are demanded by the subject matter, for Buddha in his
glory or a Buddhist priest at worship should not be seen in a state
of fragmentation, the Japanese artist infuses the painting with his
own inner restlessness. The deservedly famous *Amida Rising above
the Mountain* by an unknown artist of the Kamakura Period shows
Buddha blazing in the light of the full moon, being himself the
moon, serene and tranquil in the heavens, and so the artist has
painted him against a smoky violet sky and a moon like an immense
opal. But the calm of the Buddha is destroyed by the restless waves
of the mountains and by the vivid presence of two enormous deities
who have come to worship him, gliding on silver streams which
resemble silver serpents, and the foreground is littered with worshipers and goblins. There is no peace, for the eye is immediately
led away from the Buddha to the shadowy, contorted world below.

The Japanese painters delighted in sharp angles, sudden improbable juxtapositions, the deliberate lack of balance. The earliest
surviving Japanese paintings appear on a lacquer shrine in the
Horyu-ji temple at Nara and depict in eight panels the wonders of
the Buddhist heaven. In the most memorable panel we see Buddha
in one of his early incarnations offering himself as food for a starving tigress and her cubs. We see him calmly removing his shirt and
hanging it on a tree, then we see him diving into a dark ravine with
his arms outstretched as though diving into the sea, finally we see
him lying peacefully on the ground while the tigress rips him apart
with her fangs and the starving cubs wait patiently for their share
of the meal. The grisly scene is painted with the utmost delicacy,
Buddha and the tigress both glowing in salmon pink against a
vitreous green background of ferns and flowers, and the artist has
shaped the cliff wall with broken curving lines like scattered bones,
The effect is to bring the spectator into the painting, these broken
lines guiding him deeper and deeper into the mysterious ravine.
In the serene violence of the painting we see a purely Japanese
imagination at work.

Sometimes the Japanese found great difficulty in resisting the
pervasive influence of China, and the early Buddhist sculptures
are largely derivative. The heavy, jowly Buddha exuding power

sometimes gives place to the youthful contemplative Buddha with a finger poised on his cheek as he follows a thought to its conclusion, and it is altogether evident that the power comes from China and the contemplation comes from Japan. The Japanese learned that it was not easy to refine and reshape a monumental art, and some of their greatest sculptures, like the *Daibutsu* at Nara, are even more oppressively heavy and massive than their Chinese originals. The *Daibutsu*, which towers to a height of more than fifty feet, was intended by the Emperor Shomu to serve as the palladium of the nation and was therefore endowed with extraordinary power and majesty. Other statues abound in the Todai-ji temple, but none has its energy. A million pounds of copper, tin, and lead were employed in making it, and just after it was completed the timely discovery of a new gold mine permitted the Emperor to order that it should be covered with gold leaf. Today, bereft of its gold, patched and repaired until little of the original statue is left, it remains brutally intimidating, and the worshiper is cowed before its massive splendor.

In time the Buddhist monks at Nara became so powerful that they threatened the government of the state, which was in danger of becoming a theocracy. To escape from the monks the entire court moved in A.D. 794 to a new capital at Kyoto, built on the model of Ch'ang-an in a huge square with high protecting walls and great gateways. Kyoto became the center of an elaborate artistic life enjoyed by a cultivated nobility whose power rivaled the power of the emperor. The aristocracy of Kyoto was dominated by the Fujiwara family, which intermarried with the imperial family and produced so many regents and chancellors that it gradually acquired the power to appoint emperors at will. About the same time that Kyoto was founded, new Buddhist sects came into existence with the result that a hundred new divinities, new aspects and manifestations of Buddha, came to be worshiped; and the painters and sculptors were kept busy reproducing the features of hitherto unknown divinities. Many of these divinities resembled the terrifying guardians of Chinese temples, with flaming hair, bulging eyes, and beetle brows, their swords drawn to protect the temples from the intrusions of heresy. Sometimes these divinities would appear to the monks in visions, and they would then faithfully record what they had seen. So the Red, Blue, and Yellow Buddhas came to haunt the Japanese imaginations with their teeth like tusks and eyes like burning coals. They were intended to terrify and they succeeded only too well.

But the main current of Japanese belief passed by these perverse and exotic inventions. In the tenth and eleventh centuries a gentler form of Buddhism prevailed. This was the Pure Land Buddhism, which proclaimed that merely by reciting the name of Buddha without any doubt in his mercy and with complete faith one would be born again into the Land of Perfect Bliss. In theory such a belief should have put an end to worship: there is no need for temples, paintings, and sculptures when a man has only to repeat the holy name to enter heaven.

During this period Lady Murasaki, herself a member of the Fujiwara clan, was writing *The Tale of Genji,* the world's first major novel, describing the adventures of the Shining Prince among the women and the treacheries of the court. The novel breathes the spirit of Buddhism with its heartfelt pieties and acceptance of the brevity of life. Soon the court painters would be vying with one another in recording the prince's adventures on long scrolls. To the Western eye there is something baffling in those paintings in delicate shades of green, salmon pink, purple, and orange, where everything is seen from above, as though by someone sitting in the rafters, the bold diagonal lines of walls, curtains, and balconies slicing nervously across the page, while as often as not the main incident to be described lurks in an unsuspected corner.

These twelfth-century paintings deserve to be studied carefully, because they reveal a great deal about the Japanese artistic mind. Those broken diagonal lines can and do suggest complex psychological states, while the oblique view from above gives the artist extraordinary possibilities for maneuvering his subjects. Faces are never defined: Prince Genji's features are represented by a round white blob with thickly painted eyebrows, a tuft of beard, the merest suggestion of a nose and a mouth. From the novel we know he was beautiful, but the spectator must imagine the beauty for himself. In one famous painting we see him dressed in voluminous flowered purple robes, cradling his wife's bastard son, and he resembles a purple cloud hovering somewhere to the northeast, while below him two serving women of the court, dressed in many-colored costumes, look on, and we scarcely see their faces and each one resembles nothing so much as a heap of brilliantly colored silk. More than three quarters of the painting depicts billowing curtains overlooking a balcony and a patch of barren earth. But it is precisely these curtains that tell the story, their agitation reflecting the agitation in the prince's heart. In Japanese paintings we find large areas of empty space, but this emptiness is crowded with psychological implications, subtleties, melodramas, the soul's anguish.

An equally famous painting concerning Prince Genji was made by Sotatsu in the seventeenth century in the form of two painted screens. By pure chance the prince has arrived at a barrier between two provinces at the same time as the Lady Utsusemi, with whom he was formerly in love. Now she is a governor's wife riding in an ox carriage, which must make way for the prince's carriage. So we see the two carriages in an imaginary landscape of gold foil and green umbrella-shaped trees, and we see nothing of the prince except a red sleeve trailing from his carriage window and of Lady Utsusemi, enclosed within the narrow walls of her carriage, we see nothing at all. Yet in the vast golden spaces between the two carriages the artist has suggested the sorrow of that chance meeting, which was really no meeting. Once more the view is obliquely from above and the empty spaces tell the story. The companion screen describes another meeting between Genji and one of his former loves on the seashore, and this too was full of sorrow, umbrella-shaped trees, gold spaces, and little groups of retainers waiting for something to happen.

In such paintings we are aware of a peculiarly Japanese spirit, even a peculiarly Japanese sense of appropriate disorder. This traditional attitude to composition continued, while simultaneously the Japanese showed themselves to be masters of the Chinese forms of painting, being especially adept in the impressionist techniques of the Sung masters Liang K'ai and Mu Ch'i—those paintings which accomplish an entire figure and a whole atmosphere in a few deft brushstrokes. The Japanese were so happy with these paintings

Siva as King of Dancers, from South India.

Buddha Holding the Blue Lotus.
AJANTA CAVES.

The Trimurti, Elephanta Caves.

GOVERNMENT OF INDIA
INFORMATION OFFICE.

Wounded Horse, from the Tomb of the Emperor T'ai Tsung, T'ang Dynasty.

Opposite, Toba Exiled, by Hokusai.

Pottery Tomb Figure of a Lady,
T'ang Dynasty. The painted
figure is nearly four feet high.

Late Shang Dynasty Ritual Vessel.
METROPOLITAN MUSEUM OF ART:
ROGERS FUND 1943.

Wisteria, by Ch'i Pai-shih.
PRIVATE COLLECTION.
ALEXANDER ARTEMAKIS.

that they collected them assiduously, with the result that the Chinese themselves are scarcely aware of them, because nearly all these paintings have entered Japanese collections and even the great Palace Collection now in Formosa has only a single example of Liang K'ai's work and none of Mu Ch'i.

Employing the "splashed ink" technique, the Japanese showed themselves to be absolute masters. With a flurry of brushstrokes the Zen priest Sesshu could produce a landscape with trees and huts at the foot of a cliff and vast mountains looming through the mists beyond. With a few jagged strokes he painted a winter scene so cold that even now, although the paper is cracking and the ink fading, one feels the icy wind against one's face. In the Chinese manner he painted a scroll over fifty feet long, every scene filled with precise detail, and almost he should be counted among the Chinese masters. He lived to a great age, dying at last in a monastery in 1506, and there remain today about thirty paintings authentically by this hand. Tohaku, who died about a hundred years later, followed the same tradition, and his painting of pine trees seen through the mists of summer have the same extraordinary quality. Accomplished within a few moments, they remain forever memorable. Another painter, Musashi, more famous as a swordsman, painted a shrike on a long slender branch with a nervous intensity which owed much to his skill in swordsmanship. The painting may have taken perhaps twenty seconds, but the lean swinging branch is alive and the shrike will be seeking for its prey throughout all imaginable eternity.

With the development of the wood-block print and the color print known as the *ukiyo-e* or "Floating World Picture," a new element entered the scene.

In the closing months of 1764 some designers, wood-block cutters and printers, working in Tokyo, discussed the possibility of making prints in four or five, or even more, colors. There were no overwhelming difficulties: the colors were available, and the same methods used for printing in two colors could obviously be used for printing in a wide range of colors. The real question was whether the people of Tokyo were in a mood to buy prints in all the colors of the rainbow.

Once the idea of polychrome prints had been established, there was no turning back. The people of Tokyo delighted in these prints and began to forget that they had ever taken pleasure in any other kind. The first artist to produce these prints was Harunobu, then forty years old, having spent most of his life as an undistinguished designer of books. He had five more years to live, and in those five years he produced some of the most dazzling prints ever made.

In the long and impressive list of Japanese woodcut designers Harunobu stands among the three or four who share the topmost place. It was not so much that he drew with incomparable delicacy and refinement, and could suggest the atmosphere of a place to perfection, so that we are aware of the air and of the shadows swirling round his slender women, as that he invented a strangely quiet, permanent, elaborately detailed world where all the characters seem to be taking part in a solemn rite and all are beautiful. His elegant women are small-boned, with sloping shoulders, narrow hips, thin arms, thin legs, and tiny hands, and they wander in enchanted landscapes with looks of luminous intelligence, in love with classical poetry, which they are endlessly quoting, the verses appearing on the print. This intelligence, this exquisite artificiality, are not the sign of decadence: these are the first shoots of the flowers that will flourish during a long summer. In some mysterious way Harunobu has anchored and rooted these adorable women to the earth, given them a curious monumentality, and sustained them with his own passion.

At first sight his models would seem to be all ladies of the aristocracy. In fact they were the courtesans of the Yoshiwara, the prostitutes' quarters, and some working girls well known to him. At the Yoshiwara the prostitutes paraded behind wooden bars in brilliant silks, with attendants dressed just as sumptuously; the visitor found himself in a kind of royal court, where these women, dressed like empresses, received the tribute of their admirers. Harunobu's models included a toothbrush vendor, a temple attendant, and a girl who kept a small tea and cake stall outside the fox shrine at Kasamori. Her name was Osen, and her beauty was so well known that people came on pilgrimage to see her. It was a quiet, reserved, very gentle beauty, and predictably she did not remain a working girl for long. She married a wealthy samurai, and lived well into the nineteenth century.

It happens very often that a man who comes at the beginning of a great new invention in the arts exhausts nearly all its possibilities. So it was with Harunobu, who invented scenes which were to become the commonplace of the *ukiyo-e* artists, devised a vast range of colors and tones which would be used by his successors, and invented *gauffrage*, the delicate embossing of the paper in patterns corresponding to the patterns of a dress, or of waves, or of anything he pleased. He liked to use sudden splashes of vivid color, while generally using subdued tones. He mixed white face powder with powdered sea shells, and this curious mixture would be stirred into the paint to give it warmth and depth—with unfortunate effect, for paint so treated tends to oxidize and grow darker over the years. He chose new colors appropriate to his designs, the spectrum ranging from a pearly glistening white to the darkest and most mysterious black. His plum colors, blues, emeralds, grays, and smoky yellows have an extraordinary intensity, giving a shimmering vitality to his portraits of women. He especially liked to paint them dressed in rainbow colors against a mysterious midnight black, so rich and luminous a black that it seems to belong to moonlight.

Harunobu established the tradition, and his successors enlarged on it, filling out some of the regions he left unexplored for lack of time. Kiyonaga, who sometimes imitated his designs, painted women with rounded cheeks and flesh on their bodies, taller and even more elegant, with a more spacious presence. The lean, nervous intensity of Harunobu is replaced by the most enchanting gaiety. His courtesans descend in direct line of succession from the paintings of Wu Tao-tzu. In the lift of their heads, in the dazed happiness of their expressions, and in the swirl of their garments they are recognizably descendants of the T'ang Dynasty.

With Utamaro, who was briefly Kiyonaga's pupil, a new and unexpected element enters. Using only line and the flat washes of color applied by the printmakers, he was able to suggest the tenderness of the flesh, the glow of a woman's skin, the mysteries of touch. No one ever drew women with such tenderness, such an overwhelming sense of intimacy. In print after print he showed himself to be the master of a pure sensuality, his line endowed with some mysterious quality evoking the charm and waywardness of women. Naked or lightly clothed or in full ceremonial costume, they come to us with a startling immediacy.

Like all *ukiyo-e* artists, Utamaro was limited to a minimum of means. The face was only an outline: a curving cheek, two thick eyebrows, eyes like small slits, a mouth like two small buds, all this the work of a few seconds. The character of the woman was suggested by her bearing, the intricate folds of her many-patterned dress, the elaborate and skillfully organized hairdo, and perhaps above all by the petal-like hands which were always too small. Having spent most of his life watching women and carousing with them in the Yoshiwara, he was able to see them through their own eyes and he knew all their secrets. He therefore drew them with an effortless precision and an uncanny self-assurance, being the one artist of genius who has entered fully into the world of femininity.

Hokusai, who outlived Utamaro by more than forty years although they were born within a few years of one another, possessed a severely masculine temperament. He depicted women with relish, but he was happiest painting the vigorous world of men and nature; he could not paint a tree or a mountain without infusing it with his own energy. His bamboos crackle with energy, his waves roar, his mountains leap with joy. He lived strenuously for his art, disdained all creature comforts, and was often in great poverty. Once, very early in his career, he painted a portrait of Buddha on a sheet of paper 200 yards square; he rejoiced in great spaces and most of his designs look as though they were intended for much larger pages. He was about seventy-six years old when he wrote as an epilogue to his *Hundred Views of Mount Fuji* a concise account of his life and philosophy:

> From the age of six I had a mania for drawing. For fifty years I produced innumerable pictures, but really nothing I did before the age of seventy was of any value at all. Only when I reached the age of seventy-three did I begin to understand how to represent birds, fish, animals, insects, trees and grasses. When I am eighty I shall have made a little more progress, and at ninety

I shall have really mastered the art. When I reach a hundred my work will be truly sublime, and at a hundred and ten I shall be able to endow every line and every dot with life.

He signed these words with a name that delighted him: *The Old Man Mad about Drawing*. He was nearly ninety when he died in 1849, having produced over thirty thousand drawings and paintings, or about one a day for every day of his working life. He was quite simply the most prolific artist who ever lived.

By his own account Hokusai spent eighty-three years practicing his art; Sharaku spent ten months. From May 1794 to February 1795 he produced an extraordinary series of actor prints numbering altogether about 136, nearly all of them blazing with demonic energy and seeming to penetrate into the very soul of the actor: pride, meanness, ruthless brilliance, all the poisonous and pleasant intoxications of the stage. The characteristic Sharaku line was bold to effrontery, his coloring was superb, his psychological gifts were direct and baffling, and it was as though the gods had endowed him with everything a man could possibly desire to become a great artist. For those ten months the fountain flowed with astounding energy and then stopped. Nothing more was ever heard of him. We do not know when he was born and when he died and what trade he practiced. Utamaro said that "his portraits depict the least attractive of human traits." It was not true. Sharaku pictured actors as they are, and his prints are works of consummate genius.

Hiroshige belonged to a gentler and more indulgent tradition which sought to render landscape with luminous intensity and brooding affection. Born in 1797, the son of a fireman, he became famous for his scenes of the landscape between Tokyo and Kyoto, and having produced one book of these scenes he went on to produce at least twelve more books. If we compare his landscapes with Hokusai's, we see two totally dissimilar worlds, one gentle and compassionate, the other strenuous and almost merciless in its judgment on mankind. A famous print by Hokusai shows the Chinese poet Tu Fu departing into exile in the midst of a snowstorm. A tree laden with frost hangs over him, the narrow road is sharp with stones, and the snow falls like bullets. In Hiroshige's winter scenes

—there must be at least a hundred—the snow enfolds the earth like a garment, and we are aware of its silence, its tenderness and composure, the white countryside transformed into a foretaste of paradise. He was the master of the luminous atmosphere, and he was especially adept at depicting the coming of storms, the moment when the earth prepares itself for violence. The pelting rains, the spring winds in the trees, the winding roads glistening in the evening under summer skies, all these he represented so naturally that it was as though he had breathed the scene onto paper and watched it growing before his eyes. He had the Buddhist temperament, and shortly before he died in 1858 he entered a Buddhist monastery. A few days before his death he composed a farewell poem:

> I leave my brush in the East
> And set forth on my journey.
> I shall see the famous scenery of the Western Land.

Hiroshige was the last of the great Japanese printmakers, and the easiest for the Western mind to understand. It was as though it were given to a single man to express all the graces of Japanese feudal society and none of its violence. In the year of his death the first commercial treaty would be signed by Japan and the United States, and within ten years of his death there would be the Meiji restoration, designed to bring the nation into the current of modern industrial states. Hiroshige produced the last fanfare, a sound as soft and gentle as the falling snow.

Fanged Jaguar and Feathered Serpent

There is a sense in which Chinese civilization, like the Egyptian civilization, remained strangely stationary. New ideas and new forms emerged over the centuries, but they resembled the leaves of a tree, falling and renewing themselves each year. Every leaf was different, and every leaf was the same. A design fashioned in the remote Shang Dynasty closely resembled a design fashioned under the Chinese Communist empire: the same soil and the same people had formed them. They had not that restless desire to create new forms which characterized the European artists; they were content with themselves and with their art.

So it was in the two Americas, where for nearly two thousand five hundred years there existed an art of prodigious power and endurance. This art was continually changing and continually renewing itself, but nearly always we are aware of a formidable continuity, a formidable sameness. A fanged jaguar carved high up on the eastern slopes of the Andes about 1000 B.C. resembles even to the abstract designs painted on its sleek sides a fanged jaguar carved in what is now Mexico City in the early years of the sixteenth century before the city fell to the Spanish conquerors. Neither of these carvings resembled a living jaguar. If they had been naturalistic sculptures based upon acute observation of the living creature, then we might expect to see an inevitable correspondence, and we would not be in the least surprised by the similarity of form. The two artists, living at a vast distance from one another in time and space, had not been carving a living jaguar so much as an archetypal jaguar, the product of the ageless memory of the race, seen, felt, and minutely observed in the artist's imagination.

If we go on to compare the fanged jaguar carved in the region of Chavín de Huántar in the northern highlands of Peru with a fanged tiger modeled in bronze by a sculptor of the Chou Dynasty in China, we see another correspondence. The ancient Chinese sculptors see animals in much the same way. They are four-square, low to the ground, immensely powerful, the round eyes wide open, the fangs only too evident. The Chinese sculptors are not in the least interested in the musculature of the animal's legs, or its hairiness, or its physical strength. We never see the animal leaping and its mouth is never open. It is very quiet, very still, and this is as it should be, for the sculptors were interested in the animal as the vehicle of spiritual forces. A Chinese *t'ao-t'ieh* mask would have been immediately comprehensible to a Peruvian highlander, who fashioned similar masks, even more convoluted, even more abstract, breaking up the elements of power in the animal's features and rearranging them until they expressed almost the abstraction of power. The sculptor working on the shores of the Yellow River was the brother of the sculptor working in the Andes.

The people who wandered out of Asia during the eleventh and tenth millenniums B.C., making their way across the Bering Strait, then descending the western coast of the Americas, belonged recognizably to the same stock as the tribesmen who settled about the same time in northern China and later formed the confederation of Chinese states. They were a dark-eyed people with high cheekbones, springing black hair, rather flat noses, and characteristically Mongoloid features, graceful and small-boned, living in small tribal communities. There seems never to have been a time when they were gathered together in massive migrations. They spilled slowly out of Asia into America, and thousands of years passed as they inched their way down the coast. They lived by hunting, and their gods were always represented by animals.

They brought with them certain traits of character and certain imaginative concepts hammered out during the long years of settled existence before the folk wanderings began. Like the Chinese, they generally enclosed the shapes seen in their imaginations within rounded squares or oblongs, worshiped at stepped temples, regarded all the animals they hunted as belonging in some mysterious way to the human community, and delighted in powerful abstractions which permitted them to bring the forces of the universe within their comprehension. When for the first time we see them clearly, about 1000 B.C., they already possess complex rituals and a well-developed art characterized by extraordinary energy and precision.

We find the first American artists in places where we would scarcely expect to find them: they are clinging to the slopes of the Andes ten thousand feet above sea level and standing in the swamps and tropical jungles of the Gulf of Mexico. They are already masters of their art, carving with superb daring. The Olmecs in the lowlands were carving colossal heads out of basalt in places where no basalt existed, floating the stone some 350 miles by water to the places where the heads were finally erected. These sculptures have a breathtaking intensity, as befits the representation of a supreme god whose head appears to be emerging from the ground, gazing upon his creation with an expression of extraordinary calm, at once triumphant and disdainful, with a high domed forehead and deeply cut, penetrating eyes, a heavy chin, heavy lips, and a small flattened nose which gives him a faintly Negroid appearance. It is a portrait of a god such as a man might have seen in his dreams, startlingly alive, instinct with energy and intelligence, resembling the central figure in the portrait of the *Trimurti* at Elephanta in its massive, otherworldly power.

The Olmec lord of creation is represented naturalistically: the god has the face of a man, though this face is ten feet high. In the Chavín culture, arising among the headwaters of the Amazon, the gods have a completely different aspect, being formed out of the abstract countenances of condors, serpents, and jaguars, representing the spirits of the air, the underworld, and the earth. The stele known as the Great Image, from the temple at Chavín de Huántar, solemnly erected in the holy of holies, shows a human figure with one arm stretched high above his head. Nearly fifteen feet high, it is one of the very few Peruvian cult images still in the place where it was first erected, about 800 B.C. The human figure wears the mask of a fanged jaguar with the beak of a condor, and there are serpents coiling round his head. His left arm falls to his side, his right arm is flung up in a gesture of command and carries the emblems of authority graven on it—a serpent coiling up the arm, fangs, and watching eyes. Essentially the Great Image resembles the Alaskan totem poles, which often show two arms raised above the heads of mythological creatures, but the Alaskan poles have none of this intricately abstract portraiture. The god wears ear pendants, a necklace, a chain of faces forming a girdle at his waist. He is the jaguar god, lord of the earthly realms, one hand pointing to the sky and the other pointing to the underworld.

The geometric intricacy of Chavín art, with its whorls and serpentine loops, often broken up by the appearance of sharp curving fangs, is something to wonder at. The Chavín artist will portray a giant condor with the same elaborate geometric patterns, with every feather curved to express the utmost power, every talon tensed. More than a thousand years later the same themes will be employed by the sculptors of Tiahuanaco in the uplands of Bolivia, but by this time the loops and whorls have given place to a kind of mechanical fretwork. The famous "Gateway of the Sun," built so squarely on a vast plateau thirteen thousand feet above sea level, derives from ancient Chavín designs, but is totally lacking in conviction. The jaguar has been tamed, the condor's fretted wings could never fly in the air, and the serpents are no more than meander patterns. Chavín culture vanished about 200 B.C., perhaps as a result of earthquakes. When we see great artists again, they are working along the northern and southern coasts of Peru, at Moche and Nasca. The jaguars, condors, and serpents have not been forgotten, but the artists have become deeply involved with the human body and with human personality.

About the same time that the Greeks were raising the art of painted pottery to its greatest heights, the artists of Moche and Nasca were beginning to experiment with painted pottery bowls and water jugs with stirrup spouts all based on the assumption that it was perfectly possible to translate them into completely human terms. They did not simply paint the jugs; they modeled each jug so that it became the portrait of a person or an animal, with a recognizable head, a heavy body, and a spout. It was something the Greeks sometimes attempted, but without any notable success. The

Schematic drawing
of the Great Image,
from Chavín de Huántar.

artists in the northern regions around Moche produced hundreds and thousands of these painted jars in every conceivable shape, their imaginations triumphing over all difficulties. Mochica ware is human, all too human. No gesture, no turn and twist of the human body escaped them. They designed jars with extraordinary virtuosity, painted them in warm colors, and gave the breath of life to all of them, with the result that we know more about these people, their way of life, their habits and features than any other ancient people in South America.

Mochica ware scales the entire range of human experiences. We see them at their noblest: old men with the look of wisdom engraved on their faces, young heroes with expressions of extraordinary audacity, and then again we see chained prisoners, the sick, the infirm, the starving. Nothing human was alien to them, and you will come across water jugs with figures in strange sexual embraces. The Mochica artist will model a terrible deformity or paint in the running sores on a leprous face. There are water jugs in the shapes of ducks, pelicans, and owls, and the owls are fashioned with a special understanding of their form, perhaps because it was believed that they were especially sacred, for we find the priest-king holding a scepter surmounted by an owl. There are water jugs in the shape of houses with all the windows and stairways clearly shown; or else the artists will simply paint a battle scene on a gourd-shaped jug.

Never again in South America would artists take so much delight in humanity. After the Mochica culture perished, about A.D. 1000, a strange aridity descended upon Peruvian art. Their successors, the Chimu and the Inca, lacked their gift for seeing cleanly. The Chimu were virtuoso metalsmiths, who shaped gold cups with flaring rims and hammered out gold masks with a deep feeling for metallic shapes, but without any feeling for people. The world, formerly owned by men, was given back to the gods.

The Inca, settling in Cuzco about A.D. 1200, showed an astonishing gift for architecture, building fortresses, palaces, and temples with huge megalithic blocks, each many-sided block fitting into the next with mathematical precision. The towering fortress of Sacsaihuamán above Cuzco might have been designed by Titan princes.

They were conquerors, and their hard, geometric art was curiously unpleasing. We hear of immense gold plaques hanging in the palaces of the priestly rulers of the Inca Empire, but we know nothing about the designs engraved upon them. On rare occasions the Inca made small figures of animals in gold and silver, but the outlines are hard and they were incapable of breathing life into them. Even their woolen tapestries and ponchos employed hard shapes of geometric color. No large-scale Inca sculpture survives, and it seems likely that none ever existed.

The Inca conquest of the Chimu seems to have taken place about A.D. 1460. Less than seventy-five years was given to them to enjoy the fruits of their conquest. In 1532 Francisco Pizarro, accompanied by a handful of Spanish adventurers, captured the entire empire. Thirteen years earlier Hernán Cortés entered Tenochtitlán, the capital of the Aztec Empire of Mexico, and soon all of Mexico had fallen to his pathetically small army.

If we can judge the strength and validity of a civilization by its art, Hernán Cortés must be accounted a greater conqueror than Francisco Pizarro. The art of the Aztecs was vividly alive, without shadow of decadence. The monolithic sculptures, the stepped temples, the pottery figurines, the earthenware cups, even the wooden war drums, pulsated with vigorous life. On the evidence of their carvings and paintings the Aztecs had reached an astonishingly high stage of civilization without losing that essential fortitude which is necessary for survival. Few nations have reached these heights, and few have fallen so tragically in their prime.

Like the Incas, the Aztecs were latecomers on the scene, for they founded the city of Tenochtitlán in A.D. 1325. No one knows where they came from. According to the legend, they had come from the northwest at the urging of a prophet who said they would found a great empire when they reached a place where an eagle was poised on a cactus with a serpent in its talons and where there were white willows, white frogs, and white fish. This place they found on the shores of Lake Texcoco, and here they established themselves, at first taking service under foreign masters. Gradually they conquered or allied themselves with all the chieftains around them, and from what is now Mexico City sent out their armies to the shores of the Pacific and the Atlantic.

Tenochtitlán, in the days when Cortés first set eyes on it, possessed an enchanting beauty and monumental grandeur. Bernal Díaz del Castillo, who fought beside Cortés, remembered his first glimpse of the teeming city. "We were amazed," he wrote, "and we said it was like the enchanted things related in the book of Amadis because of the huge towers, temples, and buildings arising from the lake, and all of masonry. Some of the soldiers even asked whether the things we saw were not a dream." What they saw was a city floating on a lake, reached by a causeway, with an immense central plaza ornamented with palaces, altars, and temples, all brilliantly painted and richly designed. The plaza was dominated by the soaring temple dedicated to Tlaloc, the rain god, and Huitzilopochtli, the god of the sun, with shimmering white stairways leading to the twin sanctuaries. The roof of Tlaloc's sanctuary was decorated with giant seashells, for the rain god also presided over the fortunes of the sea, while the roof of Huitzilopochtli's temple was ornamented with huge butterflies, symbols of the sun and of fire. Both temples were provided with giant intricately painted combs, thus adding a further dimension of splendor. The proportions of the buildings in relation to one another had been worked out by architects of genius. Nothing comparable to this plaza existed in Europe, or indeed anywhere in the world.

The Aztecs were in full possession of an art of exquisite refinement and power. They were sculptors, painters, poets, learned in complex mythologies. The sculptors carved magnificent portraits, but they also enjoyed carving brilliant representations of fruit, grasshoppers, rattlesnakes, and small dogs. But it was in their sculptures of the gods that they demonstrated their greatest mastery. When they depicted Quetzalcóatl, the feathered serpent, the lord of light and flowers, they showed him in majesty, armored with feathers, with serpent fangs and blazing eyes; and they carved the stone until you could almost see the rippling of the feathers. Or when they depicted Coatlícue, the mother of the gods and of mortals, the wearer of the serpent skirt, she becomes an abstraction of power, a colossus shaped to express the power that moves the universe.

There are many images of Coatlícue, but there is one in the museum in Mexico City which must be counted among the supreme masterpieces of sculpture. Human hearts and hands, serpent fangs, the claws of jaguars, skulls, and the flayed bodies of men have been brought together into a single image of divinity, and somehow, by the sheer intensity of vision, that headless monolith acquires a superb and terrible dignity. Nothing like it exists in the Western world. The student must put aside all his ideas about anthropomorphic gods; he must forget all the accepted canons of art, and he must abandon the idea that the supreme gods are in any way concerned with morality. Coatlícue is beyond morality, beyond the reach of human thought or imagination. The Aztec artist has depicted death, imperturbable and final, and at the same time he has depicted the womb generating abundant life. Not the human imagination but the dreams of an entire race seem to have brought about this visionary image of the ultimate divinity, the terror at the heart of terror.

The Aztec world is so foreign to us that we need to enter it gradually, step by step, without impatience. The Aztec logic is not our logic; their symbols are not ours, and their way of life was strangely ceremonial. But once we have entered into their world a little way, then we find all the pieces beginning to fit together, displaying a civilization so rounded and complete that we can only envy them.

The Aztecs did not invent this art. They were the heirs to many kingdoms, and to a great treasury of artistic experience. They borrowed their forms and legends from Toltec, Mixtec, and Mayan sources, but so fused them together that they created a civilization which existed in its own right. In much the same way the Japanese fused together the elements that came to them at different times from China to produce a civilization which was singularly Japanese.

Some thirty miles northeast of Mexico City lies the ancient city of Teotihuacán, "the place where men become gods." When the Aztecs came to power, Teotihuacán was already a city of the dead, abandoned and half forgotten. A thousand years had passed since the rulers of Teotihuacán had stood at the apex of their power, their influence extending as far as Guatemala. They had

Aztec Calendar Stone. Anthropological Museum, Mexico City.

built the most superb pyramids ever built by man, of such awesome proportions that at first the mind refuses to accept their reality. They are stepped pyramids, one of them a hundred and thirty-eight feet high, the other more than two hundred feet high, but it is not their size which commends them to us. The pyramids are built in tiers so cunningly arranged that they express vigor and vitality, as befitted the thrones of the gods. Like Coatlícue, they are abstract designs of divine power and authority. The Aztecs believed that the larger pyramid was dedicated to the Sun and the smaller to the Moon, but in fact we do not know what gods presided over these pyramids. Not far away there stands the smaller pyramid known as the "Citadel," dedicated to Tlaloc and Quetzalcóatl. There is not the least doubt that the rain god and the feathered serpent were worshiped here, for the slopes of this pyramid are patterned with the images of these gods—the thrusting serpent head ringed with feathers, the fanged rain god with the two hollow eyes through which the rain falls.

But even more wonderful than the temples themselves is the architectural unity which unites them, so that they give the impression of reinforcing and echoing each other. There is the springing energy of the individual pyramids, but there is also the energy arising from the subtle relationship of one to the other. The pyramids of Giza are scattered over the desert in confusion, but the pyramids at Teotihuacán exist in a close and living companionship.

A few paintings from the small palaces at Teotihuacán survive —there is an especially engaging painting of a jaguar singing at the top of its lungs—but the chief glory of the city lies in those breathtaking pyramids, which even now give the appearance of being mysteriously quickened with the forces of life, unlike the Egyptian pyramids, which celebrate the forces of death. Just as the Parthenon is an abstract portrait of the goddess Athena, so these pyramids were abstract portraits of the living gods.

By about A.D. 600 the civilization of Teotihuacán was already declining, and by A.D. 950 it had perished, leaving only its monuments behind. For a period of about a thousand years it had been the capital of an empire, supporting perhaps a quarter of a million people. No one knows why it perished: earthquake, fire, famine, invasion, disease, all the conventional catastrophes put forward to explain the extinction of empires, fail to carry conviction. We do not know what happened, and we cannot guess.

So, too, with all the other empires of Mexico. The Mayan cities in Yucatan and the Zapotec city on Monte Albán near the modern Oaxaca rose to great heights of power and influence during the first millennium of the Christian era, and all perished about the same time. For hundreds of years painters, sculptors, and architects erected monuments of extraordinary grandeur and authority, and the priest-kings ruled amid panoply that no Western king has ever rivaled. There is the sense of an enduring majesty, a grave calm, a quietness that can come only from deeply held beliefs, in the stepped temples at Palenque, Uxmal, Labná, Sayil, and twenty other places in the Yucatan peninsula. Always there are stairways leading up to the habitations of the gods, but the proportions of the stairway, the platforms, and the palaces are always different, the architects subtly adapting the proportions to the demands of the landscape. Only one temple, at Palenque, has been found to contain a mausoleum, the relics of an unknown priest-king, and all the ceremonial trappings once heaped upon his body. Here, too, the temples celebrated the forces of life.

They carved in the round or in light relief with an exquisite feeling for the shapes of stone; they painted murals; they worked out immensely complicated calendars and studied the nature of time, inscribing the all-important date on all their monuments, while forgetting to include the name of the artist or the name of the priest-king who appears on the monuments in all the glory of an immense feathered headdress, one priest-king after another, so that sometimes we have the illusion that it is always the same priest-king, just as the Egyptian pharaohs become one pharaoh. But their art was not always monumental. They would make clay toys, and sometimes you see the faces of ordinary people. In the region of Vera Cruz there was a period when they modeled in clay with the same warm humanity as the Mochica craftsmen, and smiling children take the place of the austere gods.

These students of time produced a timeless art, which seems to escape out of history altogether. The millenniums pass, the same stars look down on the earth, and the same artists are at work. The alterations, the sudden changes of directions, which simultaneously plagued and exhilarated the artists of the West, were not for them. It was an art without restlessness, superbly humble toward the gods, so rounded and complete within itself that it is as though they had enclosed the world of men and of gods within a magic circle. We, who come after them, find ourselves standing outside this world of enchantment, wishing we could enter it and knowing that it has gone forever.

THE FLOWER
IN FULL BLOOM

The Florentine Renaissance

The Italian genius for the arts reached its height in Florence. The three hundred years between the birth of Giotto and the death of Michelangelo saw a renaissance of the arts such as no other city has ever enjoyed; for the fountain seemed to flow effortlessly, perpetually renewing itself. Great artists came hard on the heels of great artists. Goldsmiths, painters, sculptors, architects, and poets arose in dazzling profusion. Florence was so charged with artistic energy that it might have been the capital of an empire. So it was at Luxor, Tell-el-Amarna, Babylon, and Byzantium: the arts flourishing, the cities becoming works of art. So it was in Athens and perhaps in Herodian Jerusalem, but of Athens in its glory we have only ruins and nothing remains of Herodian Jerusalem except the Wailing Wall and the wildly ornate Corinthian columns beneath the Al Aqsa Mosque. Florence, sheltered by Brunelleschi's rose-red dome, still lives among its treasures.

In all the world there are only a few ancient cities crowded with works of art, being themselves works of art. Kyoto and Nara with their glowing temples, Peking with its golden roofs, Isfahan with its colored domes, Venice with its palaces, Florence with its statues and paintings. All these cities were capitals of empires, even if sometimes the empires were very small. They all possessed in common the resolve to produce their own works of art in a style appropriate to themselves, and they shared a common determination to endure. They regarded their cities as treasure chests, and they believed they would endure all the longer because they were filled with treasure.

One of the proudest boasts of Augustus Caesar was that he

found Rome made of brick and left it marble. He, too, had hoped to build a city which would survive as a work of art, but Augustan Rome owed too much to Hellenistic Greece to acquire a recognizable style of its own. It was imitative and disorganized, with twenty centers and as many circumferences, at the mercy of its seven hills. Venice, originally a pirate's lair sheltered by lagoons, shaped by the men who drove the piles into sandy soil, was at the mercy of nothing, not even the tides. Florence, built on the site of an obscure Roman camp, possessed none of these safeguards and advantages, for it was well situated to be at the mercy of invaders. In its vulnerability lay its strength.

A visitor to Florence about A.D. 1260 would have found a small walled city living luxuriously but without visible means of support. The soil was stony, patched with scrub and occasional cypresses and clumps of pine. Some of the hill slopes supported vines and olives, but the grudging soil demanded almost more labor than it was worth. The visitor would have observed that the inhabitants were exceedingly well dressed and were ruled by their own elected officials, for the city was a free commune. The real power lay in the craft guilds, and no one was allowed to vote unless he was a member of one of the twenty-one guilds. Of these guilds the most powerful was the wool manufacturers', for the wealth of Florence, such as it was, derived largely from the manufacture of woollen cloth. The Florentines were cloth makers and dyers to the world, and they imported wool from as far away as Spain and England. Indeed, in A.D. 1273 an eighth of the total English wool export, some 4,000 sacks altogether, went to Florence. As for their dyes, these were imported from still farther afield, from Africa and Asia Minor, where they also found the alum to fix the dyes. Having no resources of their own, the Florentines had made a virtue of necessity. They became entrepreneurs on a massive scale, traders in far countries, experts in rates of exchange, bankers to everyone who could afford their services. They minted their own coinage, the golden florin, and within twenty years it had become the common currency of Europe.

These merchants, bankers, lawyers, craftsmen understood the power of money, cultivated the finer points of speech, took care to study foreign languages, and quickly developed a taste for luxury. At the Jubilee of 1300 Pope Boniface VIII observed with some surprise that all the ambassadors of the Christian powers assembled in Rome were Florentines, and remarked that the world consisted of five substances—earth, air, fire, water, and Florentines.

But wealth, intelligence, and a taste for luxury are not enough to create great art. There was the desire to excel, the determination to accomplish greater works than Rome or the other city-states could accomplish. Above all, there was the innate sense of human freedom shared by all Florentines, who regarded themselves as the inheritors of the republican tradition of ancient Rome. There was still another element of incalculable importance—the Tuscan light. It is a light that gives pure and clear outlines to things, not quivering like the light of Flanders, but very still. A slender cypress tree climbs clean into the air as though cut in metal, while olive trees stand against the blue hills as though their one desire was to be painted accurately. Florence, the center of the world's trade in dyes, had no difficulty in acquiring paint. As for marble, there were quarries near at hand. If great painters and sculptors arose, Florence was ready for them.

Cimabue, which means "Ox head," was the first to break through the traditional hieratic forms derived from Byzantium. Although his fame was soon eclipsed by Giotto's, he was a painter of astounding powers of invention. His portraits of St. Francis and St. Clara in the Lower Church at Assisi have both a human grandeur and a spiritual eloquence; they live and breathe and glow in the radiance of divinity. "Ox head" was a name probably given to him for his stubbornness, but what one remembers most is his profound sensitivity to character in the portrait of St. Francis and the tenderness of his Madonnas. He died about 1300. With him Italian painting begins.

It might have begun in an entirely different way if Cimabue had studied the work of his contemporary, the sculptor Giovanni Pisano, one of the greatest creative spirits who ever carved in stone. The son of a well-known and rather academic father, Giovanni Pisano single-handedly moved sculpture out of the classical tradition and endowed it with a fierce energy. He worked in wood,

ivory, gold, and marble, but none of his figures in gold or wood
has survived, and one can scarcely believe that he made the ivory
crucifixes ascribed to him. He detested the conventional, inventing
new scenes in the life of Christ, and he showed that it was perfectly
possible to carve forms of an inspired naturalism while at the
same time giving them monumental dignity. In the Church of
San Andrea at Pistoia he carved a Nativity which abruptly rejects
all preceding Nativities. Quite suddenly the scenes are alive with
movement. In a single panel we see the Angel of the Annunciation
elated with stupendous joy as he confronts the Virgin; we see the
Virgin flinging a protective arm over the cradle; we see her preparing
to wash the Child, dipping her hands in the water to test the tem-
perature; and in the corner Joseph sits hunched and watchful, like
a coiled spring which will uncoil with terrible effect if anything
should happen to his son. The shepherds watch and the angels
hurtle across the sky. Forty years before, his father Nicola had
carved a Nativity for the Baptistery at Pisa which contained the
same essential ingredients, but with what a difference! Nicola
carved a sarcophagus, the son carved a scene filled with the breath
of life.

In the summer of 1306 Dante is said to have arrived at
Padua during his wanderings. There he would have seen Giovanni
Pisano carving a crucifix for the Arena Chapel, while his fellow
Florentine Giotto was painting the walls of the same chapel with
scenes from the life of the Virgin and of Christ. The greatest poet
of his time, the greatest sculptor, and the greatest painter may
have stood together in the church built at the orders of Enrico
Scrovegni, the son of the greatest usurer in Italy.

By a miracle Giotto's paintings in the Arena Chapel have
survived intact, the design unaltered, the colors seemingly as fresh
as on the day they were first painted. In some fifty panels Giotto
invented a new world of form which owed much to Giovanni
Pisano and more to his own sense of lucidity and order, deriving
from a peculiarly Florentine intelligence. The sense of movement,
the coiled spring, derives from Giovanni Pisano; the clean-cut edges
come from the shapes seen under Florentine skies; the brilliance
of the compositions comes from Giotto alone. To have painted those

fifty panels, all of them alive with emotion, was a staggering accomplishment. For the first time in European painting we become aware of the weight of human bodies and the air in their lungs, and we almost hear their voices. When Judas embraces Christ, we are aware of the pressure of his arms. When the innocents are being massacred, we are aware of the straining muscles of the executioners and the strangled cries from the dry throats of the women. The human gestures are observed with perfect accuracy and at the same time Giotto's sense of the dignity and monumentality of the human form permits him to endow his figures with such power that we do not question their divinity.

A new element has entered painting—intelligence. In Giotto's work the mind and the body are in movement.

As he grew more famous, Giotto appears to have acquired a multitude of assistants. He would sketch out the designs and permit others to complete the painting, which he would then review, adding some masterly touches. There is scarcely a passage in the Arena frescoes which is not authentically his, but in all the subsequent work attributed to him we come upon magnificent figures side by side with inferior work. The *Ognissanti Madonna*, with her glance of piercing intelligence, comes from his hand, but almost any practiced painter could have produced the surrounding angels. Most of the frescoes on the life of St. Francis in the Upper Church at Assisi were designed by him, but only a few were painted by his hand. As for the innumerable Madonnas attributed to him by the curators of the world's museums, it can be said with assurance that most of them were painted by the followers of his followers.

Giotto was the first of the long line of Florentine artists who were simultaneously painters, architects, and engineers. He was called upon to design the fortifications of Florence and the bell tower of the unfinished cathedral, and since he was a practical man he was made foreman of works and superintended the constructions he had designed on the drawing board. He died in 1337 and was very properly buried in the cathedral he had adorned. Just as Giovanni Pisano had changed the entire course of European sculpture, so Giotto had changed the course of painting.

Yet his contemporaries in Siena, only a short distance from

Florence, remained strangely unaffected by the revolution he had brought into being. Duccio, Pietro Lorenzetti, and Simone Martini were still painting in the tradition of Cimabue, the stylized figures usually silhouetted against a golden sky, with just enough weight of body to distinguish them from Byzantine icons. Only the extraordinary sensitivity of the Sienese artists saved them for preciosity. They painted in intricate, brilliantly colored patterns, with the precise opulence of Persian miniaturists. In Simone Martini's *Annunciation* a patterned Virgin confronts a patterned Archangel before a golden screen, itself so patterned that it threatens to dominate the painting; and although the effect is glorious and although we find ourselves believing implicitly in the Virgin and the Archangel, it is a belief that cannot be sustained for long, for the painting gradually dissolves into its fret of patterns. So, too, when he painted the conqueror Guidoriccio da Fogliano riding on his patterned horse—it was the first equestrian portrait in Western painting—the brilliance of the patterns obscures the character of the conqueror, who might be riding off to attend a wedding instead of attacking a city. There is no trace of intellectual vigor in Sienese painting. Only in the works of Barna da Siena, who plunged from the high scaffolding in the Collegiate Church of San Gimignano to his death, is there any demonstrable tension. He alone had studied Giotto and could infuse a scene with drama. For the rest, the Sienese painted with a grave sweetness and serenity, and none ever rivaled them in expressing the Virgin's tenderness for all living creatures. It was essentially a feminine art, which found no place for God's majesty and power.

The seed planted by Giotto did not lie dormant. Ninety years after his death a visitor to Florence would have seen it in full flower. Never before or since have no many great artists been assembled in a single city. In 1427 Masaccio was twenty-six, and had already completed all the works for which he would be remembered. Paolo Uccello was thirty, and Fra Angelico was forty. The sculptors Luca della Robbia and Donatello were twenty-seven and forty-one respectively. Ghiberti was forty-nine and Brunelleschi was a year older. With them the second wave of the Florentine Renaissance had begun. With the exception of Masaccio, who died suddenly and inexplicably during the following year—Vasari hints that he died of poison—they all lived long and fruitful lives, and were thus given time to develop their ideas to their highest potential and to enjoy the fruits of their fame. Only Uccello, who died at the age of seventy-nine, fell into great poverty, and we find him writing not long before his death: "I am old and without means of support, my wife is ill, and I can no longer work." He was a shy, solitary man, in love with animals and a prodigious student of mathematics and perspective, afflicted with melancholy, a disease rare in Florence. His real name was Paolo di Dono, and he adopted the name by which he is known out of a consuming love for birds (*uccelli*).

These seven masters were all great innovators, and there is a sense in which they were harbingers of the same innovation. All in their different ways were obsessed with perspective and proportion, but these words were merely the keys to a determined study of reality divorced from mythologies. Their aim was to represent the world as it was, in depth and color, in form and nature, with the encompassing atmosphere and the starry heavens. Heaven, purgatory, and hell were real to them, but the earth was more cherished. The new sense of reality implied an understanding of structure, of anatomy, and all the sciences.

Masaccio, painting his great frescoes in the Church of the Carmine in Florence, was not simply expressing a new sense of sculptured space and a new feeling for human dignity, but he was also triumphantly solving a host of technical problems which had proved to be particularly intractable. Masaccio rooted his figures in space more firmly than they had ever been rooted; he gave them air to breathe, a credible landscape to walk in, and like Giotto he gave them movement and intellectual energy. Masaccio painted Adam and Eve escaping from paradise as tragic figures, their minds and flesh bruised by the knowledge of evil. In *The Tribute Money* we see the disciples and a servant gathered around Christ; they are discussing how they will pay the tribute money when none of them has any money; and as they look at one another with expectation and a curious uneasiness, their thoughts and surmises echo from one to the other, gather force, and mount to a crescendo. Each figure in the large group has his own individuality. They seem to exist in their own right, not by dispensation of the gospel story alone. They possess both human and divine power, and they possess human and divine intelligences. Masaccio has liberated their energies, and thus presented them as living presences. It was as though Giotto had played a simple melody, and Masaccio had taken this melody and transformed it into a symphony.

The artistic sensibility was Masaccio's, but the science belonged to his time. The perspectives and proportions had been carefully worked out by Uccello and Brunelleschi, who were obsessed by the problem of rendering spatial depth. Foreshortening and the uses of chiaroscuro were not the inventions of Masaccio: he was merely employing them with greater authority than anyone else. How much he was influenced by the prevailing theories of perspective we know from the huge fresco of *The Trinity* in the Church of Santa Maria Novella in Florence, where the Crucifixion takes place not on the barren rocks outside the walls of Jerusalem but in an imaginary vaulted arcade deep within the church walls, and the patterned vault is conceived in strict mathematical perspective. In *The Tribute Money* the mathematics of the design are based on a section of a cylinder; in *The Trinity* the vault is constructed in true mathematical form and we can, if we wish, calculate the exact distance between the Cross and the vault. In both paintings the mathematics are subservient to the artist's sensibility. It is one of his tools, but he has many more.

In 1403 the sculptor Lorenzi Ghiberti began to design the twenty-eight bronze panels on the north door of the Baptistery at Florence. Twenty-two years later he would begin work on the ten bronze panels of the east door, and twenty-seven years would pass before they were completed. He devoted nearly all his working life to these thirty-eight panels, and we can watch his growth step by step from the erratic and inconclusive beginnings to the full maturity of his genius.

The first set of panels embraced twenty scenes from the life of Christ, together with four evangelists and four doctors of the Church. The scenes are uneven, perhaps because they had to be enclosed within a complex quatrefoil, which demanded the utmost ingenuity in massing the figures around a central axis. These small figures, only two or three inches high, owe much to his experience as a working goldsmith: they are intricate, brilliantly detailed, accomplished with extraordinary finesse, but there is no sense of the inevitability of the composition. A two-inch-high shepherd shades his eyes from the blinding apparition of an angel, and while we marvel at the accuracy of the gesture we are not convinced that the gesture is appropriate or adds anything to the Nativity. The shepherd could be detached and labeled: "Shepherd at Sunset." Similarly, when Ghiberti shows Christ riding to Jerusalem, we see some fifteen people, mostly graybeards, observing him or taking part in the procession, but there is no emotion running through the crowd, no apprehension or delight, no sense of a community alive with thoughts and emotions such as we find in Masaccio's *The Tribute Money*. Throughout these panels Ghiberti has played the goldsmith's game. When he came to make the east door with its ten large panels, he played another game altogether.

This time he was in full command of a medium much closer to painting than to conventional sculpture. Ghiberti's knife bites no more than an inch into the bronze, but he conveys the heights of heaven, entire cities, immense palaces, whole landscapes. In a single panel God creates Adam, Eve soars out of Adam's rib, the serpent tempts them, the doors of paradise close on them, and hosts of angels roam across the heavens, while another angel keeps watch on the fugitives, her wings sharp as the edges of a sword. In the center of the panel God blesses an Eve as immaculate as Venus rising from the sea-foam. She is a figure of majestic serenity and beauty, well aware that she possesses a singular attraction for Adam, who is already weighed down by the knowledge of his tragic destiny. Other panels tell the stories of Cain and Abel, Noah, Abraham, Esau and Jacob, Joseph, Moses, Joshua, David, and Solomon, who receives the Queen of Sheba in a temple which seems to be at least a hundred feet deep and is crowded with nearly a hundred separate figures. Each panel is a square measuring thirty inches by thirty inches.

With extraordinary ingenuity and accuracy Ghiberti sets up his multiple stages, defines the landscape, models the shapes of palaces or the leaves of the trees, and yet this is the least of his accomplishments. With these panels he establishes a living relationship between the figures, so that they are all in communion with one another, as Masaccio's figures are in communion with one another. Nothing can be detached, and all the figures are part of a whole. The melody has again given place to the symphony.

Ghiberti was aware of the immensity of his achievement. "This work of mine excels all my other works," he wrote. "I labored over it with the greatest ardor and technical proficiency, completing it with every possible artistry, sense of proportion, and knowledge of the arts." Michelangelo, standing in front of the doors, said: "They are so beautiful that they might be the Gates of Paradise."

But this, too, was goldsmith's work: the modeling of intricate planes on a surface only a little thicker than a coat of paint, the embroidery which permits whole cities to come into existence at the summons of the engraver's needle, the extraordinary manipulation of space in all its depths and in all its grandeur—nothing like this had ever been seen before, and its like was never seen again. Ghiberti invented a technique and exhausted its utmost possibilities, with the result that in the history of art the Gates of Paradise stand alone, immaculate and perfect.

Donatello, whose name sounds like a thunderous ring of bells, belongs to another dispensation altogether. Where Ghiberti might carve the face of God on the head of a pin, Donatello would have preferred to carve the same face on a block of marble fifty feet high. He had the sense of spaciousness: vigor expanding and overflowing, the nobility of the subject demanding the utmost nobility in the execution. He learned much from his studies of antique Roman sculpture, having traveled with Brunelleschi to Rome for the sole purpose of examining the antique statues which were beginning to erupt out of the soil like overripe vegetables. But if we examine the proportions of his heroic figures—the lithe *David* in the Bargello at Florence, the *Penitent Magdalen* in the Baptistery, or the *St. John the Baptist* in the Duomo, perhaps the most magnificent of all his figures—we realize that they are far from the classical canons of ideal beauty. These are Florentine bodies seen by an imagination that was peculiarly Florentine. The famous *Zuccone*, so called for his gourdlike bald pate, is just such an old, bleary-eyed, visionary priest as may still be seen wandering through the streets of Florence, and in fact it was a portrait of a man well known to him; yet Donatello has added his own sense of vigorous spiritual exaltation. Vasari says that Donatello would sometimes gaze at the statue while he was still working on it and say: "Speak, damn you, speak!"

One believes the story, for Donatello alone seemed to have the power to create heroic figures possessing gifts of intelligence and understanding. If Michelangelo's *Moses* spoke, it would be in a language no one has ever fathomed. If Donatello's *St. George* spoke, it would be in the clear and precisely enunciated Italian of his time, for he is no more St. George than Michelangelo's *David* is David. *St. George* is the embodiment of all the heroic virtues of Florentine youth, and is Florentine to the core. Indeed, all Donatello's sculptures have a family resemblance. His young *St. John the Baptist* will grow up to become *David,* who in turn will grow up to become *St. George,* who becomes in middle age the conquering *Gattamelata* in Padua. Donatello created majestic presences armed with an intense spirituality; and if the *St. Francis* in Padua resembles no other St. Francis known to man, for it is entirely improbable that St. Francis ever wore a severely ecclesiastical expression, nevertheless Donatello has once again accomplished something almost beyond the power of any man to accomplish—in a single portrait he has fused together heroism, intelligence, and spirituality.

Donatello's influence was far-reaching, for in different ways he profoundly influenced Pollaiuolo, Verrocchio, Leonardo da Vinci, and Michelangelo. He had established the new canons not only of physical beauty but of intellectual beauty. The *Gattamelata,* the first equestrian statue erected since ancient times, was not only an achievement of stupendous daring, but also—and this is perhaps even more important—the first portrait of modern man, coldly destructive, possessed of incalculable reserves of energy, determined upon conquest. In its authority and magnificence it may be compared with the great Apollo at Olympia, who also stood at the turning of the ways. Gattamelata is riding out of the Middle Ages into the modern world.

Of Donatello it is related that Cosimo de' Medici gave him a red cloak and Piero de' Medici gave him a vineyard, and he returned both of these, saying he did not know what to do with them. He lived for his art, and of all the world's great sculptors he alone possessed unfaltering mastery.

With the exception of Masaccio all his contemporaries seemed to belong to an earlier dispensation. We have only to compare Uccello's heraldic horses with the powerful, deep-chested horse of the *Gattamelata* to realize how great a chasm separated the two artists, both working in the same city at the same time. Fra Angelico and Donatello were born in the same decade, and might, for all their understanding of the arts, have belonged to different centuries, for Fra Angelico still worked in the tradition of the ancient miniaturists. No one ever rivaled him in the sheer splendor of his colors or in the intensity of his vision of heaven, but no one was less aware that the world of legend was giving place to the world of scientific inquiry. We realize with a shock that he was born long before Masaccio and long outlived him.

Into this new world created by Donatello there came three painters all born within his lifetime who possessed indisputable qualities of genius and seemed outwardly very dissimilar. They were Piero della Francesca, Antonello da Messina, and Botticelli. What they had in common, apart from the fact that each produced an unbroken series of masterpieces, was a certain relentless spirit of inquiry and the desire to probe into unexplored regions of the soul. They were all masters of line, employing warm and powerful colors. Botticelli, absorbing the humanism of the court of Lorenzo de' Medici, Piero della Francesca writing his treatises on the nature of painting, Antonello wandering across Italy and Flanders and leaving scarcely any trace of himself although his profoundly intelligent features seem to be present in all his paintings—all these were men of extraordinary spiritual and intellectual energy. Botticelli spent all his life in Florence, Piero della Francesca lived in the small town of Borgo San Sepolcro in the Florentine domains, and Antonello da Messina seems to have lived everywhere except in Florence. They never met, but in the history of art they march together like three companions in arms bound by a common faith and a common aim.

The Birth of Venus by Botticelli has become such a commonplace of our lives that we can no longer see it in its original purity and freshness. Set it beside Piero della Francesca's *The Risen Christ* now in the Pinacoteca Communale at Borgo San Sepolcro, and we realize how much the paintings have in common in authority and austerity, and how much they derive from the same sources that produced Donatello. Indeed, the Venus of Botticelli as she comes floating across the pearly ocean is very close to Donatello's Virgin of the Annunciation at Santa Croce in Florence. There is the same bemused expression, the same hand on the breast, the same bent knee, and the same astonished languor, as of someone who simultaneously reveals and is revealed, suffers a revelation and is herself the revelation. Piero's risen Christ has the august splendor of Donatello's saints, urgent, abrupt, utterly demanding. If we isolate the figures—the naked Venus clothed in her golden hair, the naked Christ clothed in his rose-red shroud the color of the dawn— then it becomes still easier to recognize their common line of descent: the springing litheness, the almost casual grace and magnificence we associate with Florence. These paintings are both resurrections, and there is perhaps some significance in the fact that they were made within a dozen years of each other at a time when the young Lorenzo de' Medici commanded the destinies of Florence.

Few visitors go to Borgo San Sepolcro or to the little cemetery church at Monterchi with its strangely powerful *Madonna in Childbirth,* standing in august majesty, her gown split open, as though by lightning, to reveal the swollen womb. The Virgin full of grace was never so explicitly expressed, and it was precisely this capacity to express "the fullness of the creature" which distinguishes Piero from his two great contemporaries in the art of painting. For this purpose he employed a palette made of the colors of the springtime, and a line so severe that it might have been modeled on the cracks in ice. An extraordinary inner tension animates those figures with their apparent calm, their deliberate remoteness. In the twenty frescoes in the Church of San Francesco at Arezzo he tells the story of the True Cross from the moment when the seed of the tree was planted in the mouth of Adam to the moment when it was discovered by St. Helena, but what we see on the walls has little enough to do with the True Cross. Angelic presences move across the walls in stately procession, pause, and move on again; and where they are going and what they are doing is beyond the knowledge of men. All the faces have a strange similarity. They are round as an egg, with full lips, lowered eyelids, and expressions of grave serenity, resembling the Buddhas of the T'ang Dynasty. They are creatures to be contemplated, themselves absorbed in contemplation, so remote that they are almost beyond the reach of love.

An Illustration by Botticelli for The Divine Comedy.

Botticelli, too, was haunted by the enduring masks of divinity, and the same austere and perfect features appear again and again in his paintings. His Madonnas are the daughters of Venus, the eternally youthful daughter of the sea, while his heroes and saints, even the sleeping Mars in the National Gallery in London, possess a resilience and power which the artist does nothing to conceal. Botticelli was totally without morbidity; there is a springing life in all his paintings, a calm urgency. In his last days he illustrated Dante's *Divine Comedy* with a line so austere that it might be made of hammered steel.

Leonardo da Vinci, six years younger than Botticelli, rose to such heights that he seemed even in his lifetime to dominate the universe which we call Florence. He incarnated all the Florentine virtues: elegance, a love of splendor, the remorseless spirit of inquiry, the springing line.

The legendary qualities which make Leonardo da Vinci so appealing and so powerful a figure in the history of art are precisely those which he would have most deplored. We see in him mystery, chiaroscuro, the inner turmoil of a troubled spirit, a strange fragmentation of talents. We remember him as a man who never completed anything he began because he was too detached from the world, and too indifferent to his own fame, to care whether a work was finished or not. We are told that he was the possessor of an exquisite sensitivity, a lover of boys, effeminate and strangely retiring, continually immersed in his own sensations, a man whose eyes turned inward to illuminate the vast chambers of his thought. The red chalk drawing of an old man with hooded eyes, melancholy lips, and long rippling white beard is presented to us as a self-portrait, an authentic likeness of the master composed in 1512, when he was sixty. This drawing has entered the legend, for we can see in it if we wish the features of an immaculate sage. In fact there is no authority whatsoever for believing it to be a self-portrait, and it is only one more of the many sketches he made of old men.

The legend of Leonardo da Vinci began in his lifetime. What men knew, and sometimes feared, was his fierce intellectual energy, his pride and audacity. He was no recluse, but walked about the world like a king, on an equal footing with kings. He was splendidly equipped, for he combined great physical beauty with a towering intelligence. He was so strong that he could bend a horseshoe as though it were lead. He was proud of his legs and deliberately wore a short tunic in order to show them off, and of his fine beard, which was curled in ringlets and reached to the middle of his chest. We know him as the painter of some thirteen finished and four unfinished masterpieces and as the author of an immense notebook in which he recorded in mirror writing the thoughts of his long life, but in his own time he was known chiefly as a musician, a sculptor, and an engineer. The greatest of his works was an equestrian statue of Francesco Sforza, the tyrant of Milan, over which he labored for sixteen years. It measured twenty feet from head to foot, and was therefore twice as large as the equestrian statue of Colleoni by Verrocchio, who had been his teacher. It was in fact the largest and most brilliant equestrian statue ever made. It was completed in clay and ready to be cast in bronze when war broke out. Leonardo fled from Milan, and the French soldiers in the army of occupation amused themselves by shooting at the clay statue until it was torn to shreds.

It was his fate to see many of his greatest works destroyed. For the conference hall of the Palazzo Vecchio in Florence he produced a large cartoon of the Battle of the Standards, which took place in 1440 at Anghiari during the wars between Florence and Pisa. It was the most important commission he ever received from the Florentine government. We know the painting today from fragmentary copies. The battle horses are butting one another with their chests, biting each other, rearing up on their hind legs, and quivering with ferocious vitality. Leonardo kept a stable and was especially proud of his knowledge of horses; and like the Greeks, who saw in the battle between the Lapiths and the Centaurs a display of cosmic energy, a revelation of the divine forces which moved the universe, the artist was concerned to show the divine vigor and energy of the Florentines at a time of resurgence of national power. His horses were heroic and legendary creatures infused with heroic and legendary strength. "In rage, hatred and revenge," wrote Vasari, who saw the completed painting, "they are the equals of the soldiers."

Neither the equestrian statue nor the fresco of the *Battle of Anghiari* testify to a mind immersed in troubled introspections. Instead they testify to a colossal outpouring of vital energy.

While working on the battle painting, Leonardo executed a portrait of Lisa del Giocondo, the wife of a Florentine merchant. The portrait survives, but it is far removed from the portrait as Leonardo painted it. Vasari describes it in some detail, and we would be hard put to recognize in his description the painting which hangs in the Louvre. He wrote:

> The eyes are bright and moist, and around them are those pale red and slightly livid circles seen in life, while the lashes and eyebrows are represented with the closest exactitude with the separate hairs drawn as they issue from the skin, every turn being followed and all the pores exhibited in the most natural manner. The nose with its beautiful and delicately red nostrils might easily be believed to be alive. The mouth, admirable in outline, is rose tinted in harmony with the carnation of the cheeks, which seem not painted, but of flesh and blood. He who looks earnestly at the pit of the throat must fancy he sees the beating of the pulse. It is a marvel of art. Mona Lisa was very beautiful, and while he painted her, he employed persons to sing or play to her, or to amuse her with jests, to avoid that look of melancholy so common in portraits. This painting has so pleasing an expression and a smile of such sweetness that it appeared more divine than human.

In this way Vasari describes a painting which time has changed, for the rosy mouth, the carnation cheeks, the springing hairs of her eyebrows have all vanished, and no one looking at the shadowy pit of her throat expects to see the beating of a pulse. She was young, but now appears middle-aged. The presence that rises before us is sedate and matronly, her mysterious smile suggesting unfathomable experience. She hides behind a soft blue patina like a veil, her folded hands suggesting acquiescence and habits of reserve. Behind her lies a frozen landscape of fantastic mountains, seen as in intense moonlight rather than by the usual light of day, and there appears to be a correspondence between the cold and distant mountains and the languor of her smile. Glamour, we are told, comes from an Icelandic word meaning "the gleam of ice," and it is this icy quality of glamour which we recognize in Mona Lisa.

Time, which has divested the Parthenon of its bright colors, and given to ancient bronzes a ripe green patina, has worked on her face a strange transformation, making her more imperious than she was in life. He had painted a young rosy-cheeked woman with a sidelong glance and an enchanting and lingering smile, but as the years passed, she assumed the aspect of a Virgin of the Snows. Time, rather than Leonardo, worked the miracle. Indeed, he painted her twice—the second time naked, and in this painting, which has survived in copies, it is evident that all mystery is stripped from her. Plump, full-breasted, with a rosy nacreous skin, she resembles those paintings by François Clouet which show the aristocratic ladies of France emerging from their baths, and in fact Clouet derived the theme directly from Leonardo. If the Mona Lisa were cleaned, we would find it glowing with a jeweled brilliance.

The fate of the *Last Supper*, painted on the rear wall of the refectory of the Convent of Santa Maria delle Grazie in Milan, was far more tragic, for while Time alone is responsible for the gradual ruin of the colors of the *Mona Lisa*, many other forces have been at work to ruin the *Last Supper*. Today it gives the appearance of being covered with a film of broken glass; the colors have a curious chemical look about them; all that was definite and deliberate has been diffused and rarefied. Seven different restorers working during the last hundred years have patiently retouched the whole surface, so that there is scarcely a single square inch of paint which can be ascribed to Leonardo. The ruin is very nearly complete.

What survives is the cartoon: the shapes and outlines before the subtleties of color were imposed on the surface, the waves of power generated by the twelve disciples, the grandeur and isolation of the central figure. We know the painting so well that it is difficult to appreciate its originality in its own time. Many paintings of the Last Supper had been composed, but they were always static and solemn. Leonardo is concerned to paint a moment in time which is unlike any other moment. Jesus has just said: "Behold, the hand of him that betrayeth me is with me on the table." (Luke 22:21) The disciples express horror, consternation, doubt, defiance, abject misery, despair. Some leap from the table, others look with expressions of bewilderment and indignation. Thomas raises his index finger, that finger which will later be laid in the wound. Peter presses urgently forward, John leans languidly back, being the only one of the disciples who knows that under no dispensation whatsoever can he be implicated. Philip sweeps forward like a ship with all his sails flying, and Matthew stretches his arms wide in a gesture of mute appeal. So it is throughout the painting—all the energies of the disciples released by the words of Jesus. They know, for they have just been told, that they are engaged in a war to the death, and so they rear up like the horses in the *Battle of Anghiari,* and they have the grace and dignity of those monumental horses. Waves of power move backward and forward across the painting.

Even today, though we see the painting through a strange misty screen of melting colors, something of that immense vitality remains. The restorers have reworked whole figures, and Judas, whose features were menacingly invisible when painted by Leonardo, who deliberately portrayed him with his head turned sharply away from the spectator, is now seen in clear profile. Yet the total effect is still one of extraordinary authority. This, one tells oneself, is how it was and how it had to be, in a room with windows overlooking a quiet countryside, beside a long table littered with bread and fruit, in the evening as the sun is setting. There is a new psychological understanding, and a new dramatic order with fierce and unresolved tensions suddenly erupting.

Only a few years earlier Ghirlandaio had painted a Last Supper for the refectory of the guest room of the Convent of San Marco in Florence. Christ sits at the center of a long table, while St. John leans against his breast, and the remaining disciples look on, calm in their meditations and with a decent space between them. Only Judas, insisting on his singularity, sits on the near side of the table, gazing calmly at Christ. Through the windows there appears a typical Tuscan garden with cypresses, fruit trees, and palms. A peacock settles on a window ledge, and a kitten waits to be offered a fish head. Everything about that large painting, which is almost the first a visitor sees at the Convent of San Marco, is decorous, genteel, and therefore frivolous. It might be a board meeting of a company of tax assessors.

With Leonardo's *Last Supper* a centuries-old tradition was broken. He threw the windows open and gave free rein to human passions at a moment of supreme tragedy. He painted it in the intervals of designing his heroic twenty-foot-high horse, and we have a record by an eyewitness, the novelist Matteo Bandello, describing how he would leave the Corte Vecchia and walk to the Convent of Santa Maria delle Grazie nearly every day to work on the painting, or to add a few touches here and there, or simply to gaze upon it. In this way he swung like a pendulum between two heroic tyrants, the earthly lord and the lord of the spirit.

Time has dealt unkindly with Leonardo, who had every reason to hope that his sculptures would be his most enduring works. A man of superb vigor, deliberate and fiercely exacting, he acquired over the years the reputation of a man who suffers from a disease of the will, hesitant and self-defeating. Because his notebooks are fragmentary, it is assumed that he thought in fragments, and because he traveled incessantly, it was believed that he never set himself a single, clearly thought-out goal. He lived in a time of continual civil wars; his princely patrons might be at the height of their power one day, murdered or in exile the next. He was continually on the move because there was no other way for an artist to survive. There was nothing reserved or hesitant about his affection for princes; he served under the infamous Cesare Borgia, for whom he designed monstrous war machines, with the same competence as he served the Medicis and the Sforzas. His aims were high: to be the equal of kings, to be the creator of new worlds.

Raphael, who was for a brief period his pupil, possessed an essential humility which saved him from the punishments of pride. Where Leonardo moves strenuously from one discovery to another, like a conqueror continually enlarging the territory in his possession, Raphael gives the impression of a man content to walk within the confines of his serene experience, with no desire to capture heaven by storm. In his short life—he was born on Good Friday, 1483, and died on Good Friday thirty-seven years later—he painted at least twenty Madonnas, and there is scarcely one which does not express a serenity raised to the height of a pure passion. From the *Madonna della Sedia*, filled with calm circles enclosed within a larger circle, to the dramatic *Sistine Madonna,* seen suddenly amid green curtains and the heavenly clouds, and beyond these to the enraptured *Madonna of Foligno* calmly gazing at her Son while nestling in the flames of the sun, we are aware of an intelligence probing into all aspects of his own serene vision; and just as all the Madonnas of Piero della Francesca look alike, for the vision once seen is never forgotten or surpassed, so do the Madonnas of Raphael. The Madonna stands at the center of all his works, and we are aware of her presence even in the vast Vatican frescoes, where she is never permitted to appear.

While Rome was tearing itself apart and Florence after the death of Lorenzo de' Medici was at the mercy of communal factions, Raphael pursued his study of serenity as though the world were settled in perpetual peace. In *The School of Athens* the philosophers of all ages walk with unhurried calm through the vast porticoes of thought. When he paints *The Betrothal of the Virgin* in the setting of the forecourt of Solomon's Temple, there is once again the sense of unhurried meditation, and even the presence of a youth snapping a stick across his knee merely reinforces the atmosphere of calm. The stick will never break, the ring will never touch the finger, the Temple will never fall. The calm is so pervasive that the spectator inevitably succumbs to it. It is as though Raphael had invented silence.

Yet it was not for nothing that he was an adopted Florentine, and therefore in possession of the tiger's claw. When he painted portraits they were remarkably severe and impassive: he knew exactly what shape to give to a blaze of a blood-red tablecloth to illustrate the character of a pope, and how to penetrate the mazes of Baldassare Castiglione's character. Pride he must have had, for over the doorway of the Temple in *The Betrothal of the Virgin,* he inscribed his own name, although in general he never signed his paintings, nor was there any need for him to do so. He concealed the tiger's claw, but the very possession of it gave him his strength. It was not his fault that his paintings should be reproduced so badly that his Madonnas seem to suffer from a melting sweetness. He, too, possessed the Florentine austerity.

When Raphael died, Michelangelo had nearly half a century of fruitful work before him. Then, finally, as though in sullen rage, with all his claws unsheathed, the last great Florentine artist would assert his supremacy over the world of art, and neither Florence, nor Rome, nor the Western world, would ever be the same again.

The Flemish Visionaries

We have seen how the great periods of art nearly always come when peace is secure, when the barriers of trade are thrown down, and when there are great accumulations of wealth. Art has its seasons of famine and plenty; it flourishes under gifted and wealthy patrons, and languishes under tyrants. It withers away if it cannot breathe the air of the outside world, and it is the first victim of wars. So in the Periclean age it was the peace imposed by Pericles and the capture of the treasury of Delos which permitted that sudden flowering, and in the T'ang Dynasty it was the peace imposed by the armies of the T'ang emperor and the opening of the trade routes to Persia and India which brought about a vast expansion of the arts. The superb art of the Augustan age sprang out of the Pax Romana. The Gothic cathedrals could only have risen in a country at peace and when the limitless treasury of the kings of France was placed at the service of architects, goldsmiths, and the makers of stained-glass windows. Just as art needs to be free of restraint, so that the artist can gather his influences from every source that pleases him, so it needs wealth. Wealth is the manure, the forcing ground; without it art perishes.

In the early years of the fifteenth century the richest country in Europe was the Duchy of Burgundy, which stretched from its capital in Dijon, south of Paris, over most of the territories which we know today as the Netherlands, Belgium, Flanders, Picardy, Luxembourg, Alsace, Lorraine, and large parts of northern France. The reigning duke, Philip the Good (1396–1467), was a man of exquisite taste and formidable knowledge of the arts, and it was largely due to him and to his Chancellor Rolin that the golden age of Flemish art was ushered in. Dijon in Burgundy, Bruges and Ghent in Flanders, and Brussels in Brabant, became the centers of artistic achievement which were to influence the course of European art.

It was an age of peace and increasing comforts, with the bourgeoisie in full control of trade, eagerly acquisitive, deeply religious, in love with the surface of things: the gleam of jewels, the textures of brocades, the colors of flesh. They were a people who slept in overstuffed beds, weighed their money carefully, raised their children in the fear of God, and hoped for paradise, humble and proud by turns, always faithfully observing the ordinances of the Church. They ate well. They enjoyed great processions and festivities, which Duke Philip provided in abundance, but they especially enjoyed their own intimate daily lives, the calm procession of the days. Living in small rooms cramped with possessions, the narrow windows open to let in the sound of the cobbled streets, their families gathered round them, rich food on the table, and fine linen spread below the silver drinking vessels, these burghers seem to have known a contentment we can only envy. Their days were full, and they died peacefully.

Among those who served in the court of Duke Philip was the painter Jan van Eyck, who was born about 1390 at Maeseyck in the province of Limburg. His title at court was *peintre et valet de chambre*, which meant that he was on intimate terms with the duke, a member of the ducal household, performing whatever services were demanded of him. We learn that on three separate occasions he was sent out on confidential missions. The best known of these missions took place in 1428, when he was sent as a member of an embassy to the King of Portugal to arrange a marriage between the duke and the King's daughter Isabella. Jan van Eyck was under orders to paint the portrait of the princess and to send it secretly to Dijon. The embassy proved to be highly successful, for in the following year the marriage between the young princess and the thirty-three-year-old duke took place.

Of Jan van Eyck's life we know very little. No documents written in his hand, no anecdotes, no self-portraits have survived. A letter written by the duke to his paymaster, protesting too great a delay in paying the artist's pension, survives, but it tells us only what we knew before: that the duke regarded him as one of the great adornments of the court. It is an angry letter, and the duke was clearly afraid of losing the services of his favorite painter. We know even less about Jan's brother Hubert, who is described on the frame of the *Ghent Altarpiece* as "the greatest painter who ever lived." We do not know how much of the altarpiece he painted. He died in 1426, and Jan completed the painting in 1432. There is nothing in that supremely beautiful altarpiece to suggest a collaboration: one idea, one vision runs through all its elements.

The vision was essentially the same which led Abbot Suger to create the Gothic cathedral. The splendor and beauty of God could be conveyed through rich adornments, brilliant vestments, the fire of precious jewels. The central figure in the altarpiece is Christ resplendent in a scarlet gown, wearing the triple white and gold crown, the hem of his gown blazing with jewels. There are more jewels clustered on his breast, and at his feet there is another crown, like a gold nest ornamented with egg-sized rubies and emeralds. Christ is not a powerful figure; indeed he looks like a burgher who has abandoned his business and entered upon a life of good works. But is was not power which the artist intended to convey: purity, benignity, majesty, all these are present, and in addition there is a very human grace.

Altogether there are twenty separate panels to the altarpiece, which, when opened out, is nearly fifteen feet long and ten feet high. At the left and right hand of Christ stand Mary and John the Baptist, both dressed in jeweled gowns. Beyond them stand the choiring angels, also wearing sumptuous vestments, and then dramatically at the very wings Adam and Eve confront one another in their nakedness. It is the flesh of earth, the landscape of ruined hope. They stand there awkwardly, gazing at one another across the spaces of God's majesty, weighed down with cares, conscious of their human dignity. Here the Gothic vision meets the awful reality; and in the pathos of Eve gazing sadly at the apple of corruption the artist demonstrates his power to convey the rawness of the flesh and the solitude of the spirit.

But it is not for those marvelous renderings of our first ancestors that the *Ghent Altarpiece* is chiefly remembered. The scene below, spread across five panels, depicts the *Adoration of the Lamb* on the flowering meadows of the earthly paradise. The subject is taken from the Revelation of St. John: "I looked, and lo, a Lamb stood on Mount Zion." There, on the meadow, with the sun at high noon, the blessed dead come to worship the white Lamb, standing in superb isolation on an altar of cherry-red damask, while the blood spills from its heart into a golden chalice.

Never before had the *Agnus Dei,* the Lamb of God, been given such prominence in a painting, and never again was it to be painted so convincingly. This plump and mild-eyed Lamb set on a decorative throne comes to us like an image in a dream, at once beyond belief and totally credible in that mysterious landscape of forests and rosebushes, churches and strangely shaped rocks. Toward this Lamb, as though propelled by some force greater than themselves, come the rich and the humble, the knights of Christ and the holy virgins; and in their movement, and in the way they hold themselves, there is a kind of quiet relish, as though they knew themselves to be blessed. Indeed, in all his paintings Van Eyck betrays a certain self-consciousness and pride. He is preeminently the painter of what St. Jerome called *sancta superbia,* a sacred pride.

The altarpiece attempts the same task that Michelangelo attempted in the Sistine Chapel: to convey the entire compass of human history from Adam and Eve to the final vision of Christ at the world's end. We see Cain and Abel, the Sibyls (who resemble Flemish housewives), the prophets, and the angelic hosts, but we do not see the damned. In Van Eyck's imagination there can be no place for damnation.

So it is throughout his paintings and those of his immediate successors: heaven lies close at hand, the angels are eternally present, and the evil spirits are banished so far away that they are never seen. For him the earthly and the heavenly are one and indivisible, as he demonstrates in the *Rolin Madonna* in the Louvre, where the great Chancellor in his sumptuous brocades is seen kneeling before a Virgin in her sumptuous red gown, and one cannot tell whether the scene is laid in some palace in heaven or on earth.

The Chancellor has the features of Caesar; and if he is humble and devout, it is only because he is in the presence of the Virgin and the Child, and when his prayers are ended, he will be the Duke of Burgundy's ruthless and unscrupulous Chancellor again. As for the Virgin, she was no doubt modeled on one of the women of the court. The sense of divinity comes from the heavenly glow bathing the entire scene, a crystalline light which permits everything to be seen in sharp and perfect focus, while at the same time producing an effect of dreamlike unreality. The very air is sumptuous as ripe fruit, and no golden sun ever cast so golden a light.

In the portrait of Arnolfini and his wife in the National Gallery in London there is the same air of sumptuous elegance and refinement. The wealthy merchant lightly clasps the hand of his wife, who is seven months pregnant and will soon be seeking the protection of St. Margaret, who presides over childbirth and is seen carved on the high-backed chair in the background. The chandelier is so intricately and brilliantly fashioned that it resembles a heavenly crown. Jan van Eyck himself appears in the mirror, and so that there should be no question about his presence there is an inscription: *Johannes de eyck fuit hic 1434.* "Jan van Eyck was here 1434." He is not saying that he made the painting; he is announcing his presence, and indeed he fills the whole room with his presence. That painting, filled with so many subtleties of color and proportion, with so much that was essentially medieval, remains the first modern masterpiece. Here for the first time we see the realistic full-length portrait in a setting made credible by an exacting sense of perspective. But while it is realistic in the modern sense, possessing an astonishing depth and structure, we should be under no illusions about the light that bathes the painting. It is not the light of earth but of heaven, and Arnolfini is not simply clasping the hand of his wife: he is performing a sacrament.

With Jan van Eyck we are in the presence of indisputable genius, for he opened up the new way, perfecting a technique which was to endure until the present day. He invented atmosphere, he was the first to grant realistic landscapes a major role in his compositions, and he was the first master of naturalism. Nevertheless the world he painted, except for his rare head and shoulder portraits, is the world of the supernatural.

The vision of Jan van Eyck dominated Flemish painting for a century, and his immediate followers, Petrus Christus, Rogier van der Weyden, and the Master of Flémalle, seem in retrospect to be little more than his superbly gifted imitators. The golden, otherwordly light fades away; the Virgin and the angels shed their divinity; and the cold light of earth gradually replaces the visionary light of the heavenly sun. It was not that they lacked the sense of the divine; it was simply that they could not reproduce it. The hallucinatory visionary quality of Jan van Eyck's world has vanished.

Rogier van der Weyden, born in Tournai, appears to have studied sculpture when young, for all his works are sculptural. He paints with intelligence and insight, and as a portraitist he is the equal of Jan van Eyck, but when he paints a Descent from the Cross or an Annunciation we are never convinced of the reality of the vision. Jan van Eyck could paint the Virgin wandering with a look of enchantment through her own church, or set her on a throne alone or in the presence of attendant saints, and we believe in her. She walks with assurance into her paintings, and it is precisely this assurance which is lacking in the Virgins of Rogier van der Weyden. His *Descent from the Cross* in the Prado is dominated by the figure of the fainting Virgin supported by St. John, the figures arranged with a purely sculptural elegance. As for the Virgin, she resembles a plump housewife who has fainted at the sight of some rats in her closet. Though the artist's superb intelligence is everywhere present, the scene defies belief: there is only a painted waxwork. Rogier van der Weyden had all the gifts except the gift of vision.

Hans Memlinc and Dieric Bouts were far less accomplished painters than Rogier van der Weyden, but they were more convincing, perhaps because they were absorbed in the art of painting as a continuing act of devotion. They painted with a raw and kindly eloquence. A characteristic Memlinc painting shows a man or woman set against a landscape bathed in a soft evening light. We see only the face and the shoulders, which sag a little, and the clasped hands. The faces are careworn, hushed, and reverent.

The Annunciation, by Simone Martini.
THE UFFIZI. ALINARI.

The Magdalen Reading, by Rogier van der Weyden.
NATIONAL GALLERY, LONDON.

Portrait of a Young Man, by Hans Memlinc.

The Madonna of the Small Trees, by Giovanni Bellini.
ACCADEMIA, VENICE. AFI.

Opposite, Eve, by Lucas Cranach the Elder.
THE UFFIZI. ALINARI.

Bartolommeo Colleoni, by Andrea Verrocchio.

VENICE. OSVALDO BÖHM.

Detail from The Birth of Venus, by Sandro Botticelli.
THE UFFIZI. ALINARI.

Venus of Urbino, by Titian.
THE UFFIZI. ALINARI.

All passion is spent in his sitters, who are waiting quietly for the revelation which is always about to come, but never comes.

When Memlinc painted a Virgin and Child in close-up, with a glimpse of an evening landscape seen through a window, he was in his element. It was a scene he painted many times, and never more successfully than in a diptych now in the Hospital of St. John at Bruges. The Virgin in blue and scarlet is offering a red apple to her Son; and in her gesture, in her air of calm absorption in her task, and in her brooding love, she is wonderfully eloquent of maternity, but she is not divine. She has been touched perhaps with a feather of the Archangel, but she is far from possessing the absolute divinity we demand from her. Memlinc gave her almost the same hushed and reverent expression he gave to the wealthy sitters who flocked year after year to his studio in Bruges.

Dieric Bouts was a somber painter with a far greater range of expression, and his *Entombment* in the National Gallery in London must be counted among the masterpieces of Flemish art. Mysteriously a stone coffin has appeared in a field in Flanders. There are no crosses on the horizon, Jerusalem is behind us or is so far away that its existence is irrelevant, and somewhere a lazy river wanders among poplars. Into the stone coffin Joseph of Arimathea lowers the emaciated body of Christ; St. John watches, and the women mourn. The Virgin's hand covers the wounded hand of Christ: the gesture is so quick and tender that it might pass unobserved. Everything about the painting suggests a mood of elegiac tenderness. There is no drama, no straining for the heights. The very quietness of the painting illuminates it. For a moment we are bathed in the holy light.

For the moment, but no longer. Dieric Bouts was a memorable painter, but he was lacking in the quality we demand of the great masters: he lacked power. Jan van Eyck possessed power in abundance; he spent his days painting scenes virtually beyond the reach of any painter. Dieric Bouts painted only what he knew: careworn faces, the fields of Flanders, the open skies. For him the Entombment could only take place in a field of Flanders on a day when no birds flew and the air was strangely silent.

Hugo van der Goes also possessed power in abundance, but

it drove him to the edge of madness. He painted an altarpiece for
Tommaso Portinari, an Italian merchant in Bruges, agent of the
great banking house of Medici and a formidable connoisseur of the
arts, and like Jan van Eyck's altarpiece of the Holy Lamb at Ghent,
this work resembles a vision seen with the utmost clarity, and the
observer is, as it were, sucked into the painting and finds himself
walking about in it, even though there is no real perspective and no
space as we understand space.

This enormous painting—it is nearly twenty feet wide and
more than eight feet high—is ostensibly an *Adoration of the Shep-*
herds, but it is also very much more. We see the blue-robed Virgin
praying over a diminutive Child lying in the golden straw, and if
this were all, the painting would still be one of the great masterpieces of Flemish art. Around the Virgin, in huge concentric circles,
the artist has arranged some sixteen red-haired angels, all of them
very small and doll-like, totally out of proportion to the Virgin or
the massive figure of Joseph, who is also praying as he leans in-
congruously against a superb Corinthian column. The architectural
components of the painting—the manger, the church, the gray
Corinthian column—are brutally emphasized, as though the artist
were desperately attempting to create a sense of space around the
Virgin. Space is fragmented, bending in different directions. Joseph
lives in one kind of space, the angels in another, the buildings in still
another, and the Christ child scarcely exists in space at all. The
painting is ultimately held together by the presence of the three
shepherds who come crowding in from the left, and so powerful
are those uncouth, exalted figures, so humble and so ecstatic, that
they seem to be more possessed by the spirit than the very angels.
Together they provide the thrust of adoration that knits the scene
together, while separately they provide the most penetrating studies
of humanity that the Renaissance had yet seen. Men of flesh and
blood, they have entered a world of enchantment.

Those three shepherds would have been unthinkable in the
world of Jan van Eyck, just as it is unthinkable that he would ever
have crowded a painting with so many theatrical angels. The shepherds come with the force of an irruption, a blow between the
eyes. Caravaggio would have recognized these gnarled, unruly,

purposeful men, but more than a hundred years would pass before they would be seen again. Quite suddenly modern man had entered a Flemish painting.

The Florentines who crowded round the painting when Tommaso Portinari presented it to the Hospital of Santa Maria Nuova were fascinated by the energy and virtuosity of the artist, whose powerful will had drawn so many disparate elements together. He had obviously studied nature out of doors. Equally obviously he was immersed in traditions going back to the time of the Romanesque cathedrals. From Jan van Eyck he had learned nothing except how to paint rich brocades, and the very presence of those swirling brocades tended to split the composition apart. Nevertheless a new and hitherto unknown vitality poured through the painting. If they had asked what had happened to the artist, they would have learned that he had taken refuge in the convent of Roode Kloster just outside of Brussels where, though he continued to paint, he became increasingly subject to fits of melancholia. During his lucid intervals, according to a chronicle written by a novice in the convent, he would drink wine, receive important visitors like the Archduke Maximilian, and conduct himself like a famous painter who rejoiced in worldly rewards. The evidence of these mental disorders is to be found in his paintings with their prodigious sense of strain, the uncompromising will at war with spiritual things.

When Hugo van der Goes died in 1482, apparently in early middle age, Hieronymus Bosch was enjoying the full maturity of his strange and startling genius. His grandfather, father, brothers were all painters, and therefore he entered painting with no sense of strain and with no willfulness. He seems to have painted as easily as he breathed, and like Jan van Eyck, but in an altogether different direction, he painted scenes which would appear to be altogether beyond the scope of painting. No greater creator of fantasies has ever existed. He possessed a wonderfully accurate sense of space, and he enjoyed peopling credible landscapes with the incredible creatures of his imagination.

Bosch stands alone outside all known traditions. His fantasies sprang out of an ordered imagination; satire and caricature were the least of his weapons. Having invented some perfectly preposterous devil intent on plaguing the generations of men, he would paint it with the care of a miniaturist, with exquisite refinement and brilliant colors. One of his more somber inventions was a broad-bladed giant knife, supported on two human ears, which goes berserk, and while the knife slices the damned, the ears crush them like chariot wheels. When he paints hell, he fills it with totally unexpected instruments of torture, and there is a staggering proliferation of dark inventions represented with an enchanting gusto.

In his four great triptychs, *The Hay Wain* and *The Garden of Earthly Delights* in the Prado, and the two *Last Judgments*, one in Vienna and one in Bruges, he paints man's journey from paradise to ultimate doom with a casual delight in human folly. He depicts the shapes of fear, the artifices of temptation, and the most exquisite joys as though no one had ever painted them before. Each triptych is a morality play in three scenes. First, paradise; then the human carnival in the large central panel; then hell. Paradise is green and spacious, and Christ walks with Adam in the morning of the world. The human carnival is crowded with Adam's jostling descendants hopelessly entangled in their love play and their senseless ambitions. Hell, smoking with volcanic fumes, belching with flames, rewards them with an intricate damnation.

The themes were simple, but they were worked out with fantastic elaboration and delicacy. Bosch was incapable of the simple statement; it was not enough to proclaim that we are all revelers wasting our lives away, but he must show a hundred figures engaged in their fatal revelry. In *The Hay Wain*, the least elaborate of the four triptychs, we see a great hay cart being pulled across a summer field with an escort of cheerful, ribald countrymen absorbed in their pleasures. The great men of the earth, emperors and clerics, follow the cart, lovers cavort on the hay, the fortune-tellers are at work, the fat priest is attended by nuns who offer him sheaves of the precious hay. And then, as though there had been a sudden shift of focus, we observe that all these figures are demented and not in the least what they seem to be. People are quarreling murderously for a few straws, peasant women are falling under the wheels of the hay cart, and strange demons with the heads of giant rats and the bodies of fishes are leading the way. Everywhere we look the bright summer day is filled with menace.

Yet it is the mark of Bosch's extraordinary gifts that he can portray this menace with a kind of tenderness, and in *The Garden of Earthly Delights* the menace is scarcely apparent. Once more it is summer, and we are in the open fields among lakes and streams, but the coarse villagers of *The Hay Wain* are absent. Instead, there are hundreds of lithe naked figures, all without exception youthful and well proportioned, their bodies gleaming like white pearls. They ride on panthers, bathe in the lake, dance in the presence of immense gaily colored birds and cavort merrily among strawberries, puffballs, pomegranates, huge fish, and enormous oyster shells. *The Garden of Earthly Delights* is like a fairground, and the strange buildings fashioned out of blue rock and pink coral, sprouting with vegetation, only add to the illusion. Modern commentators have exercised their wits in explaining the sexual symbolism, which needs no explanation. It has been suggested that Bosch belonged to the sect of Adamites, who enjoined an innocent and mystical delight in the flesh, but it is far more likely that the artist was giving free play to his imagination. His naked lovers shrouded to the waist in petals or enclosed in glass bubbles, eating strawberries, flogging one another with roses, and eagerly examining the bright seeds spilled by immense fruit, derive from a single imagination operating at white heat, and it is beyond belief that he attached "meaning" to their love play. In the land of Cockayne everything is permitted; and Bosch moves through this landscape with ease and a happy astonishment, painting himself many times, so that at intervals we find him gazing out of his own painting with a look of bemused enchantment.

He delighted in painting *grylli*, his especial contribution to the art of the grotesque. These were human heads directly attached to feet, without the intervention of bodies, or with only the suggestion of bodies. He paints a self-portrait, his own head gazing searchingly at the spectator, with two legs shaped like withered trees fused into a carapace formed of the splintered half of a giant egg. The feet are shod in awkward-looking boats floating on a murky sea. Within the broken egg, we see three naked revelers sitting at table with a single goblet between them, while nearby an old bent ale woman turns the spigot of a wine barrel. On the man's flat white cap there rests an obscene pink bagpipe with a human-footed bird and a mitered bishop parading around it. Not far away is the broad-bladed knife charioted on two human ears.

Bosch's self-portrait is one of his supreme achievements. Smashed egg and desiccated tree form the simple ingredients, but he has arranged them with such art that they acquire the shapes of vision. So a man might find himself at the end of the road, all passion spent, devoid of grace or hope of grace, crumbling into powder but still intent on gazing searchingly around him with all his remaining intelligence. We may regard this self-portrait as a companion piece to the Arnolfini portrait: one is the anatomy of man devoid of grace, the other is the anatomy of a man only too well aware of being among the elect.

Bosch could be savage when the mood was on him. When he painted an *Ecce Homo,* or a *Christ Carrying the Cross,* or a *Mocking of Christ,* we are shown faces of extraordinary bestiality, while the face of Christ is represented with the utmost gentleness. He painted the *Mocking of Christ* twice, and though the compositions are entirely different, both of them show an iron stump raised against Christ. The iron stump gleams, and all the world's malice seems to be concentrated in it.

Bosch was far from being only a painter of grotesqueries. His range of invention was enormous, and he was a phenomenal landscape painter, a superb designer, and perhaps the most brilliant colorist of his generation. At ease in the world of fantastic demons, he was equally at ease in the ordinary everyday world. He would paint an *Adoration of the Kings* and set it outside a ramshackle cottage in a summer field, with the peasants peering through the cracks in the wall or climbing on the sagging roof in order to see better. The kings are clothed in splendor and bring magnificent presents: a huge emerald, a crown of white gold, a marvelous golden bird on a silver globe. But these are the jeweled offerings inevitable in an Adoration of the Kings, and not entirely credible. Far more credible are the peasants peering through the cracks in the rotting walls.

Pieter Bruegel the Elder, who followed him three decades later, might have been his son. It is not that they painted in the same way or that they shared the same enthusiasms, but they possessed in common a certain rough humanity, adored the flesh, and could as easily cast it aside and enter visions, and these visions were always intimately concerned with the human condition. Neither of them continues the mood of the early Flemish devotional paintings; they are as far away from Jan van Eyck as it is possible to be, and it is inconceivable that they would ever have painted the Virgin robed in sumptuous brocades. They belonged to a more troubled time, and were more concerned with the earthly life than with splendid visions of paradise. Van Eyck could bring the light of heaven to earth: Bosch and Bruegel sometimes painted by the light of hell's flames.

Bruegel's early works *The Fall of the Rebel Angels* and *Dulle Griet* derive straight from Bosch and borrow from his menagerie of diabolic insects and animals, but where Bosch paints them with the care of a miniaturist, Bruegel, more impulsive and more violent, sketches them hurriedly, thus granting them a turbulent momentum. The rebel angels have been transformed into bloated lizards, gaping fish, strange headless creatures all arms and bellies, with the result that the archangels, wearing their brilliant robes and even more brilliantly colored wings, have no difficulty in subduing them. In *Dulle Griet* (Mad Margaret) the battle is joined on more ambiguous terms. Mad Margaret, according to the legend, was a giant of a woman who stormed the gates of hell armed with the sword of righteousness, a breastplate, a battered helmet, a money box, and a sack of kitchen utensils. She is an extraordinary creature, sharp-faced, vulgar, half crone, half heroine, and Bruegel invests her with tremendous power. Hell gapes before her, and behind her the village women wage war against the obscene demons erupting from a dank river, and there are no men in sight. Mad Margaret dominates the scene, but not far away from her, in conscious tribute to Bosch, Bruegel has created his version of the apocalyptic portrait of a man made of an eggshell, a rotting tree trunk, bagpipes, and a human face, with a boat supported crazily on his head, where previously it served as a boot. The apocalyptic man is evidently in league with the demons, for out of his cracked-egg buttocks spill coals eagerly gathered by the village women, and some of them are more intent on gathering coals than fighting demons with broomsticks. *Dulle Griet*, with its ominous scarlet sky, is a ferocious and feverish masterpiece. As he grew older, Bruegel became quieter, and the fever left him.

In the works of his maturity, and especially in the great series of *The Seasons*, he seemed to weary of those canvases filled with crowded figures at horseplay. Gradually the figures become less obtrusive. *The Fall of Icarus* shows the Strait of Messina, which Bruegel had once visited, on a calm sunlit evening. A solitary plowman follows the plow; a ship sails across a glassy sea; and all we see of Icarus, who has plunged from the sky, is a pair of wildly kicking legs as he plummets down to the bottom of the sea. These legs occupy so small a place on the canvas that the spectator has some difficulty in finding them.

Bruegel painted the five panels called *The Seasons* when he was forty, but they might have been painted by an old man who had known all the world's foibles and come at last to a mood of profound acquiescence, with no desire to record the grotesque joys of men. In these panels men almost vanish; there is only the fruitful and dying earth, which will be fruitful again when another year has passed. Winter is an icy prison; spring storms snatch the boughs from the trees; the dull gold of early summer turns to the molten gold of harvest; in autumn the cattle come down from their summer pasture amid the jeering of the crows. The atmosphere is painted in so subtly that we scarcely realize that it is the main subject of the painting. The five panels are scattered, with three in Vienna, one in Prague, and another in New York. This is a pity, because they belong together and reflect each other, forming one extended painting.

Bruegel had always had a feeling for the earth, but never was it more superbly expressed than in these paintings where men are shown as earth's creatures, almost earth's victims. We see a man moving laboriously through the summer wheat, thirsting for water, women crouching over the willow twigs they will make into baskets, huntsmen plodding wearily through the snow, carrying their pikes as though even pikes are burdensome; and in the starkness of these scenes there is no comfort, nor is there any sorrow. He has torn the veils apart and seen the world as it is.

The Hunters in the Snow, The Dark Day, Haymaking, The Harvesters, and *The Return of the Herd* are the prodigious achievements of a man who seemed incapable of painting anything but masterpieces. Not until the Japanese woodcut artist Hiroshige produced his great series of snow scenes would there be such a feeling for the raw coldness of snow, the bitterness of endless stretches of ice. But to have accomplished this was perhaps the least important thing about *The Hunters in the Snow.* What obviously mattered very deeply to Bruegel was that he had accomplished a scene so real, so actual, that almost it had become vision.

Others came after him, for the traditions of Flemish painting were firmly rooted and capable of thrusting out branches in all directions. Not the least of his successors were his sons Pieter and Jan, born during the last years of his life. Pieter followed in his father's footsteps, and his winter scenes have an uncluttered beauty of their own. Jan, who was twelve months old at his father's death, became a miniaturist and a painter of flowers so marvelously glowing that they seem not to be flowers but some new and hitherto unknown forms of life. Jan became Rubens' assistant, thus establishing a living link between two of the greatest of Flemish painters.

In any other age Peter Paul Rubens would have been extraordinary; in his own age he was regarded as a force of nature, a man so superbly endowed with genius that he could not be expected to behave like an ordinary mortal and was permitted to live as flamboyantly as he pleased. Robust, sensual, addicted to all the pleasures of life, capable of fantastic powers of concentration so that on one occasion he completed a huge altarpiece in six days, he seemed to be living six lives at once. Painter, art collector, secret agent, ambassador to the courts of the most powerful kings in Europe, scholar, linguist, he was all these, and he was also very much more.

He was born at Siegen in Westphalia in 1577. His father, Jan Rubens, a well-known Antwerp lawyer, was then serving a five-year sentence of exile in this small German town. The reason for his exile was a curious one. While serving as secretary and legal adviser to the Princess of Orange, the wife of William the Silent, he committed adultery with her, was arrested, brought to trial and sentenced to death, a sentence later commuted to exile. A daughter was born to the Princess of Orange, and there was not the least doubt that Jan Rubens was the father. Peter Paul Rubens was born when his father was in total disgrace.

Jan Rubens died when the boy was ten years old, and he was brought up by an indulgent mother. At thirteen he decided to be a painter, at fifteen he entered the studio of Adam van Noort, at twenty-one he was admitted as master painter in the Guild of St. Luke in Antwerp, at twenty-two he set out on a grand tour of Italy, and he was in Venice a few days after his twenty-third birthday when a chance encounter with an agent of the Duke of Mantua led to his employment in the Mantuan court. His destiny was now settled. For the rest of his life he would be found in the centers of power, conversing with kings and princes, accepting commissions from them, at the service of painting but also at the service of foreign courts.

Vicenzo Gonzaga, Duke of Mantua, possessed a genuine feeling for learning and the arts. He had corresponded with Galileo, rescued Tasso from imprisonment, encouraged and supported Monteverdi, and continued to add new paintings to the vast collection he had inherited with his dukedom. Rubens was employed as a painter and copyist, and he was perfectly content to study the Mantegnas, Titians, Peruginos and Raphaels in the duke's collection, to make copies and paint his own paintings, while living comfortably in the duke's licentious court. He sometimes objected to painting the court beauties—Vicenzo Gonzaga was a notorious collector of women—and the constant atmosphere of intrigue was so suffocating that he decided quite early to spend as much time as possible in traveling about Italy. He traveled so extensively that he came to know every important city in Italy, and every private collection. Venice, Genoa, and Rome especially attracted him. He was in Rome when Caravaggio's great painting *The Death of the Virgin* was being publicly exhibited after being rejected by the church for which it was intended. Rubens bought it for the duke's collection.

He also bought the paintings of Adam Elsheimer, his close friend, who had been a friend of Caravaggio.

In 1603 Rubens was sent to Spain with a small fortune in gifts for the Spanish King. Since much of Italy was under Spanish domination, the Duke of Mantua was anxious to be on good terms with Spain. The gifts consisted of a carriage, perfumes, crystal vases, and paintings. When he learned that some paintings were damaged, Rubens simply restored them or quickly replaced them with his own. The Duke of Lerma, chief minister of the King, was favorably attracted to him, and he painted a wonderfully precise portrait of the aging duke on horseback. He studied the Spanish court at close quarters, and his studies were to prove very useful. He also found time to make copies of some of the Titians in the royal collection.

He returned to Italy, Rome, the Mantuan court, commissions for altarpieces, commissions for paintings to decorate ducal bedrooms. He had found his style: violent curves, intoxicating colors, the design formed on concentric and intersecting circles, the sense of life communicated by means of a sustained and ferocious energy. He posed his nudes in the full sunlight. He painted them in full bloom, full-bosomed, with broad hips and soft enveloping arms. When he painted *The Three Graces*, he painted the same body in three different poses. He could communicate the excitement of the flesh like no other painter before or after him: even Renoir, who is closest to him, fails to suggest the palpable flesh. And when Rubens painted altarpieces, his innate sensuality is always evident. One of his most extraordinary paintings is *The Fall of the Rebel Angels*, a cascade of tumbling naked bodies plunging helter-skelter into the flaming pits of hell. Wherever he looked, on earth, in heaven, or hell, he found the naked flesh.

When he returned to Antwerp in 1609, he married Isabella Brandt, daughter of a town dignitary who was a famous humanist and a man of considerable wealth. She was dark, with a small, pointed, intelligent face, and did not in the least resemble the full-fleshed women of his paintings. She was eighteen, and he was thirty-two. She gave him three children, and died seventeen years later.

Rubens made a portrait of the bridal couple sitting in a honeysuckle bower. They wear their finery, clasp hands, smile languidly, and rejoice in their happiness; the artist who so convincingly represented glowing flesh now represents the glow of their spirits, and while he is less successful in presenting a psychological portrait of himself, he succeeds wonderfully in suggesting the character of his young wife, amused, tolerant, level-headed, not at all bewildered by the thought of being married to a fashionable painter. He painted portraits of his children with the same depth of penetration, and just as Rembrandt would paint Titus decked up in oriental costumes, so Rubens would paint his sons in the most elaborate finery, his joy and affection stimulated by seeing them dressed like princelings.

Success left him unharmed. He woke long before dawn, attended Mass in his private chapel, and painted throughout the day. Sometimes there would be three easels before him and he would go from one to the other according to his mood. He built an Italian palace for himself in the center of Antwerp: the palace still exists, though heavily restored. He kept a stable of pupils and assistants, who were often permitted to paint the figures he had sketched, leaving him to provide the finishing touches; and if he worked on these paintings for half an hour, they became authentic Rubens.

Commissions seemed to pour in daily. The most extravagant commission came from the Queen of France, Marie de Medicis, the widow of Henri IV. She demanded twenty-one immense canvases for the Luxembourg Palace in Paris. The theme was her own life, her glory, and apotheosis. Since she had lived a comparatively uneventful life, and was fat, Rubens concentrated on her glory and apotheosis. Although he provided himself with an army of assistants, he worked so brilliantly on these canvases that even today they have power to move us. The gods of Greece, the Christian saints, bishops, and water nymphs, all attend her majestic progress through life. Honor, Fame, Fertility, and the Virtues assume well-fleshed proportions, voluptuously decending from heaven to greet and commend her, and Rubens even finds an occasion to present her to the Three Graces, who are permitted to occupy the greater part of a canvas. Scarlet robes swirl, the naked flesh appears in all its abundance. Nothing could be more ludicrous than the apotheosis of Marie de Medicis, but individual figures are so superbly achieved that the Queen, though appearing in all the paintings, seems to acquire the special quality of being invisible. When she rides a white horse, we marvel at the beauty of the horse, and when she arrives from Italy in Marseilles, we admire the three luxurious sea nymphs cavorting in the water. The parts are greater than the whole.

Begun in 1622, these paintings were completed three years later. Rubens received a fee of 20,000 ducats, a fortune at the time. In the following year the newly acquired fortune could have meant very little to him, for his wife died and left him inconsolable. Six months later, as though he wanted to divest himself of all the useless luggage he had accumulated during his life, he sold his collection of antique statues, gems, and coins to the Duke of Buckingham, the richest nobleman in England. More and more often now he traveled abroad, ostensibly to paint portraits in the royal courts, in fact as a roving ambassador and secret agent, frequently visiting London and Madrid, where he met Velázquez and was instrumental in arranging that the Spanish painter should be permitted to enjoy a prolonged tour of Italy at the King's expense. Both Charles I and Philip IV knighted him, and he was largely responsible for the signing of a peace treaty between England and Spain. He had the world at his feet, and he was still painting at the height of his powers.

In 1630, when he was fifty-three, he married Hélène Fourment, the sixteen-year-old niece of his first wife. She was plump and golden-skinned, with large doelike eyes and billowing golden hair. He painted her at least fifteen times: in a plumed hat with her children, or robed lightly in a fur, or holding a fan. Their happiness increased with the acquisition of a country house, the Château de Steen, some eighteen miles south of Antwerp, where he could paint the countryside and make studies of trees and flowers, and in these last years he painted some of his greatest landscapes. Hélène Fourment gave him ten years of renewed life, and when he died in the early summer of 1640 he could have had few regrets. He had lived fully, and no artist had ever received such tribute in his lifetime.

From Jan van Eyck to Rubens the wheel had turned full circle. From the divine light which bathes the works of Jan van Eyck to the luminous flesh painted by Rubens there were infinite distances, yet both derived from the light of the Flemish sky. The plains of Flanders, the colors of the Flemish earth, the sea and the wandering canals all played their part. The light over Flanders is richer, heavier, deeper, than the light over Holland, with the result that the Flemish had advantages denied to the Dutch. It is no accident that so many of the greatest paintings were produced on the seacoast or within a day's walk from the sea. Venice, Holland, and Flanders produced more than their fair share of the world's masterpieces.

The Flemish painters conquered so vast a territory in so short a space of time that they were like spiritual freebooters who plundered unmercifully and never had time enough to study their loot. It was a heroic venture, for they hurled back the frontiers of the human spirit and taught men more about themselves than they would otherwise have known. The great Dutch painters came later, to crown the edifice. They had the advantage of being able to study the works of the Flemish masters at their leisure.

From the beginning the Flemish were in command of their art, extraordinarily sure-footed. There is no awkwardness, no insecurity. Rubens might, and did, start a painting without knowing where it would lead him, with the result that he would sometimes have to add more canvas or more wooden panels—when he painted his most famous painting of the Château de Steen he started with a small wooden panel and added sixteen more before he was satisfied, the painting continually expanding, his art reaching out further and further to embrace new landscapes. Above all, the Flemish possessed an astounding boldness, and there was no atmosphere, no landscape whether in heaven or hell or on the earth, no person real or imaginary, no color or shadow or state of mind, which they could not reproduce to perfection on wood or canvas. Like heroes they traveled in unexplored regions.

Michelangelo, who was heroic in another tradition, never understood Flemish art and never penetrated the mystery. "They paint in Flanders only to deceive the external eye," he said. "Their painting is of stuff, bricks and mortar, the grass of the fields, the shadows of trees, and bridges and rivers, which they call landscapes, with little figures here and there; and all this is in truth done without reasoning or art, without symmetry or proportion." For once in his life Michelangelo was wrong.

The Magnificence of Venice

The visitor to Venice can only guess at the magnificence of the city in its glory. Today the churches, guild halls, palaces, and squares have been bleached by sun and age until they wear the color of ancient tombs, the frescoes that once decorated all the buildings along the Grand Canal have long since flaked away, and even the marble statues are slowly disintegrating: the angels are so ruined by industrial acids blown from neighboring factories that they may be taken for devils. Venice is drowning. Yet what remains is so palpably beautiful, so vivid and alive, that it is as though the city had the power to remain young even when suffering from the ravages of old age. In the days of the Bellinis and of Titian it was an open jewel box blazing with color, and even today it proclaims its delight in its own splendor.

The deep blue air above the lagoons, the light breaking on the sea walls, the sea flowing effortlessly along the canals, the intensity of the colors, the suddenness, the unexpectedness of so many domed and pinnacled buildings betraying their oriental origin, all these delight the eye, so that the whole city gives the impression of being designed by a painter; and just as the very air and atmosphere of Florence call for a sculptor to fill all the empty spaces, every piazza, every large room, with sculpture, so the air and atmosphere of Venice, already impregnated with rich colors, call for paintings in all the squares, on all the walls, and even in the smallest rooms. Color is the sovereign lord of Venice, and the painters are her priests, her servants, and her worshipers.

In the beginning there were only the low sandbanks and the lagoons. Gradually an artificial city arose on millions of piles of white poplar to form a skillfully camouflaged pirates' lair. It was never a very large city, and even when it became the inheritor of "one half and one quarter of the Roman empire," following the conquest of Constantinople by the Crusaders in A.D. 1204, with great wealth in its treasuries and vast territories at its disposal, it remained essentially a small community built around a shipyard and a palace. The power of the doge derived from his command of the sea, and since neither timber nor iron nor flax nor any of the things that went into the making of ships were to be found in Venice, it was necessary for the Venetians to capture the forests of Dalmatia and the iron mines of Croatia and to penetrate inland to ensure the possession of flax, vegetables, and even the earths from which the painters would make their paintings. At all costs the artificial city had to be defended, and though we think of it as a city of churches and palaces riding leisurely on the banks of canals, it was also a naval base and a military camp, powerfully fortified.

When the Venetians captured Constantinople, the pirates' lair became the capital of an empire, and more and more booty fell into the hands of the doge. The Basilica of St. Mark, the private chapel of the doge, had already been decorated with mosaics in the Byzantine manner. Now, not surprisingly, the victory brought a new strength and virtuosity in the designs, for although the mosaicists were largely imported from Constantinople and followed traditional forms, they had to reckon with the changed temper of their masters. The intricate, jeweled, rather squat figures, essentially linear, began to take on a three-dimensional quality, and Christ assumes a more commanding presence. The great wall of mosaics, showing the Agony in the Garden, in which Christ is represented many times over, belongs to the period when Venice was triumphant and aware of her triumph. The Byzantine influence was still present, but the tall, heroic, red-haired Christ who emerges from among the fierce rocks belongs to another dispensation. He rises above the sleeping disciples with a consciousness of power and heroic energy. There is a new freedom of movement, and an awareness of new urgencies. Something very similar happened when the brooding

Pantocrator of Monreale gave place to the urgent, heroic figure of the Pantocrator of Cefalù.

The historian Sansovino wrote that "painting came first to Venice," but this was to underestimate the importance of Venetian mosaics. At St. Mark's the fashioning of mosaics began in the ninth century, when the body of St. Mark was removed secretly from Alexandria to Venice, and continued well into the sixteenth century, when Tintoretto was employed to prepare cartoons of the stories of the saints to be reproduced in mosaic form. Tintoretto's saints in their voluminous draperies were free of Byzantine influence altogether and therefore at variance with the general design. The best of the mosaics at St. Mark's were those fashioned during the half-century following the rape of Constantinople, and this is exactly what we might expect. Venice was bathing in the glow of golden reliquaries, illuminated manuscripts, and jewel-studded crucifixes stolen from the treasuries of Constantinople. Enclosed in crystal vials were relics of the Holy Blood, the Nails, and the Crown of Thorns, and in the economy of the Middle Ages these also represented influence and power.

Venice in these early days was brilliantly served by its mosaicists, less brilliantly by its painters, who were imported from the mainland. Guariento's *Coronation of the Virgin*, painted in 1365, still glows in the Doge's Palace, though ruined by fire: the once vivid colors are now like dying embers, but there is the sense of spacious design, an intense feeling for color and little feeling for life. He painted as though Giotto had never existed. Forty years later Gentile de Fabriano, the Lombard painter, came to Venice and set in motion the long chain of events which was to produce in orderly sequence the great galaxy of Venetian painters. About the year 1400 Venetian painting begins, and for two hundred years it was to dazzle the world.

Gentile da Fabriano was one of those eclectic painters who are able to weld many influences into a single whole. The resilience of Florence, the spirituality of Siena, the solidity of Lombardy, the vigor of the Marches, where he was born, all these are visible in his paintings, but all curiously transformed into a style of great richness which presages the full glory of the Renaissance. He seemed to be a man out of his time, for he was born a generation before Masaccio. In Venice he painted a great fresco of a sea battle for the Doge's Palace, which vanished in one of the great fires that periodically swept through the palace. We know him best by his *Adoration of the Kings* in the Uffizi, where the richest gold and all the shades of blue are employed to suggest the crowded majesty of the occasion. His magnificent colors evidently pleased the Venetians, who paid him well, granted him a pension, and permitted him to wear patrician dress. Jacopo Bellini, a native Venetian, became his pupil, followed him to Florence, became a superb draftsman while remaining a mediocre colorist, and returning to Venice opened a school and founded a family. His two sons, Gentile and Giovanni, soon outstripped him. His eldest daughter married Andrea Mantegna. Scarcely ever has there been such a concentration of genius within a single family.

Like his father, Gentile was essentially a draftsman, with a profound delicacy of line. He painted *The Procession of the True Cross in St. Mark's Square,* now in the Accademia in Venice, and we are only too aware that those hundreds of celebrants have been drawn from the life, and the sketches were then reproduced in paint. When his brother Giovanni paints, we are never aware of line. The long-pent air comes rushing into the painting, the colors glow, the mouth opens and sings. Quite suddenly there is the quivering sense of life. For sixty years Giovanni Bellini painted Madonnas and Pietàs with an enthralled tenderness, and there is never any failing of energy or imagination. Venice had found her painter. He became "painter extraordinary to the lord," meaning the doge, and because he was also a magnificent portraitist every house in Venice vied to have a portrait from his hands. Vasari speaks of his geniality and kindness. Dürer, who met him when he was very old, thought him "the greatest painter of all." He died at the age of eighty-six, leaving a young wife who survived him by thirty years.

Of all painters known to us Giovanni Bellini seems to have lived the most charmed life. He gives the impression of effortless ease, emotion and intelligence in perfect balance, serene even when he is attempting the impossible, as when in *The Transfiguration* at Naples he paints a plowed field set against distant mountains, with a peasant driving an ox and two people stopping to talk along a country lane, and in the midst of all this he sets Christ between Elias and Moses with the disciples turning away in astonishment. In that perfectly natural setting he is able to represent Christ in his glory, as though glory was something you might expect to find in any field on a summer's day. Where other painters were concerned with the dramatic character of the Transfiguration, Giovanni Bellini is concerned to show its naturalness. When, as so often, he paints a Madonna worshiping her own Son in a field with some small sleeping town in the background, we do not ask ourselves why she is there, for we know she is everywhere. He painted no fiercely dramatic pictures: no Massacre of the Innocents, no Last Supper, no Kiss of Judas. When he painted a Pietà, we are made aware of the holiness of the dead Christ which transcends all agonies.

Andrea Mantegna, his brother-in-law, threw calm to the winds, reveled in violence, and was happiest when he was painting an execution or a triumphal march. Sometimes he seems to paint with the sharp edge of an ax. His clean incisive lines, his austere eloquence, and remorseless probing of pain suggest a man of ferocious intelligence with little sympathy for human failings, and indeed he was violent and quarrelsome. The famous *Dead Christ* at the Brera Gallery in Milan, with its skillful foreshortening, might be the dead Julius Caesar on a marble slab: when he painted a Crucifixion we are made aware of the intensity of agonizing pain; and when he paints St. Sebastian there are a multitude of arrows embedded in the flesh and all the wounds are spouting blood. When Giovanni Bellini painted St. Sebastian there was only a single arrow directed at his heart.

From a very early age Mantegna seems to have identified himself with the classical Roman past. With his friends he liked to go to Lake Garda, where there were some Roman ruins, and he would copy the ancient inscriptions and offer prayers to "the divine thunderer and his glorious mother." Not Roman *pietas* but Roman *gravitas* was his watchword. Together with his devotion to antiquity, his powerful identification with the Roman past, there went a deep feeling for rocks and carved stone, towering cliffs, shattered Corinthian columns, monumental arches, huge boulders. The aridity of stone, carved or uncarved, seemed to answer to some deep-felt need. Characteristically he painted a Crucifixion surrounded with towering rocks, and he had a way of painting rocks which made them unimaginably hard, sterile, and menacing.

Essentially he was a draftsman who painted the architecture with more care than the figures, who are at the mercy of his architectural design. His paintings are brilliantly conceived and laboriously constructed under the driving force of a relentless will. His last work was an immense series of canvases representing a Roman triumph, with a hundred figures riding or walking in procession. It was perhaps his most brilliant evocation of the antique world, resembling a frieze painted at some late period of the Silver Age of Rome. The triumph resembles an army on the march, destroying everything in its path.

Vittore Carpaccio was made of humbler stuff. A pupil of Gentile Bellini, he painted with an exquisite tenderness and generosity, and was as much at ease painting a girl asleep in her bedroom as painting the crowded scenes on the Grand Canal during a festival. Like Mantegna he delighted in processions; unlike Mantegna he gave them warmth and humanity. In *The Dream of St. Ursula* the sleeping girl is visited by an angel who announces her coming martyrdom; the girl, the angel, the room, and the very air are caught up in a strange dreamlike trance, and this is brought about by a mysterious fan of light which accompanies the angel and spreads across the room, leaving scarcely any shadow. The light of holiness shines on the sleeping face and on all the myriad objects in the room. So, too, when he paints *The Healing of the Obsessed* the act of healing takes place in a small corner of the picture, while the artist paints processions of gondolas along the Grand Canal and of people walking along its banks, and all of them seem to be lit with an inner flame. Sometimes he paints an angel with the quietness and repose which we associate with Giovanni Bellini's Madonnas. Carpaccio was the master of luminosity. When you see St. Stephen preaching or St. Ursula embarking on a ship or one of the oarsmen guiding his gondola or a fluffy dog looking up at St. Jerome, they seem to be very real and rather commonplace at first glance, and then you look again and find a special beauty in a revealing glance or in the way they hold their bodies, and then you realize that though they wear the airs of Venetians, they have never walked the streets of Venice: they are all in paradise.

This same inner flame glows within the faces of Giorgione's subjects. This shadowy genius, about whom almost nothing is known except that he came from Castelfranco and died of the plague in 1510, left upon Venice the memory of an indelible fame. Even when he was living, he appears to have been regarded with awe, for at a very early age—perhaps when he was about twenty-two— he invented a new kind of painting divorced from the Church and the State, without any narrative qualities whatsoever, and independent of the classics. He painted no portraits of eminent dignitaries, no Crucifixions, no Pietàs, no Resurrections. Since his paintings had no literal meaning and existed for their own sake, people were often puzzled by them. Vasari, who saw many of Giorgione's paintings about thirty years after his death, was as puzzled as everyone else. "I, for one, have never known what his pictures mean, and no one has ever been able to explain them to me," he wrote. "Here is a man, there a woman; one has the head of a lion beside him; near another is an angel that looks rather like a cupid—it is impossible to tell what it all means. On the whole, nevertheless, it is apparent that the work is well-composed, well designed, and colored with great animation. His works are highly extolled in Venice."

The man with the lion's head has vanished, and only seven completely authentic paintings by Giorgione have survived, one of them—a nude formerly painted on the German Warehouse in Vencie—so faded that it is scarcely possible to perceive the beauty of the original. There remain *The Tempest* in the Accademia in Venice, the *Three Philosophers* in the Kunsthistorisches Museum in Vienna, the *Fête Champêtre* in the Louvre, the *Sleeping Venus* in Dresden, the altarpiece of the *Virgin Enthroned* in Castelfranco, and the *Portrait of a Young Man* in Berlin. It is a very small collection, and there are perhaps five other paintings that could justifiably be credited to him, though without absolute conviction.

The Tempest has always troubled the critics, who were determined to wring some meaning out of it, even if it meant nothing more than a lyrical evocation of a thunderstorm. Obscure Latin

texts were consulted; the *Hypnerotomachia Poliphili* with its ornate
woodcuts was introduced as evidence; and the Neoplatonic philosophers were ransacked to explain why a man should be on one side
of a stream looking at a naked woman on the other. No one seems
to have concluded that no explanation was necessary.

Originally, where the man now stands, there was a woman
making her way into the stream, as we learn from X-ray photographs.
The composition changed in mid-passage. Giorgione, who had the
habit of painting straight on the canvas without preliminary sketches,
simply altered the composition to please himself. In its final form
the man was given a short crimson cape, a white shirt, embroidered
trunks and a long staff. The woman suckling an infant a few feet
away from him is naked except for a white cloth round her shoulders, and she gazes out of the painting. The colorful vagabond gazes
at her. In the distance lies the town of Castelfranco caught in the
light of the setting sun, ablaze and almost transparent, while the
high blue summer clouds roll menacingly across the lightning-lit
sky. Soon it will rain, and they will hurry back to their homes.

Clearly the painting means whatever Giorgione wants it to
mean. He is like a poet writing a poem which can be read on many
levels. Similarly the *Fête Champêtre* in the Louvre, with the two
shadowy musicians and the two naked women, one holding a flute,
the other pouring out water from a crystal goblet into an ancient
well, represents whatever the artist desires. Why does the woman
pour out the water? She leans against the edge of the well, and a
silvery white embroidery clings to one of her legs, leaving the rest
of her body bare, and in her nakedness and beauty there is a strange
peacefulness, as of one who demands nothing and is almost mind-
less because her flesh offers her all the satisfaction she needs. The
women of Giorgione are always glowing with an inner flame.
They belong to the earth, and the glow comes from themselves, not
from heaven.

Almost Giorgione is a pagan living in an enchanted golden age
of the imagination. The *Fête Champêtre*, so meditative, so compassionate toward the living flesh, seems to have come into existence
unplanned, without deliberation, as naturally as a tree or a flower.
The artist evidently luxuriated in the woodland setting, and just as

evidently painted his two superb nudes in the studio, before establishing them among trees and grasses under a cloudy, storm-laden sky. The mysterious light of a coming storm fascinated him. In that sultry light, akin to twilight, objects seem to acquire a greater density, stand out more boldly, and yet possess a dreamlike quality. There is no menace in the storm light: on the contrary, the coming of the storm is the promise that the earth will soon be refreshed. It is this calm, watery light softening into twilight that Giorgione made peculiarly his own.

Vasari, who was evidently enchanted by his paintings even though he found them incomprehensible, went to some pains to learn about the artist's life. We learn that Giorgione was born in very humble circumstances, was profoundly influenced by Leonardo da Vinci, who taught him the uses of chiaroscuro, and soon excelled Gentile and Giovanni Bellini to the extent that he was able to compete "with those who are the originators of the modern manner working in Tuscany." Vasari, being himself a Tuscan, was inclined to regard all Venetians as provincials, and this was his highest accolade. Giorgione's charm, intelligence, beautiful singing voice, and mastery of the lute soon brought him into contact with Venetian society, where he was in great demand at private entertainments. His polished manners pleased everyone, and women loved him. There was a story that he became infatuated with a woman whom he visited without knowing that she was suffering from the plague, and he died of the plague. Vasari found a drawing of Giorgione and this was reproduced as a woodcut in his book on the lives of eminent artists. In the woodcut he appears as a man of character and sensitivity, with something of the raw-boned peasant about him. It is a plausible portrait of a man who was to revolutionize Venetian painting.

Giorgione's originality lay in his power to take painting away from religion into a world of luminous forms, imaginary mythologies and dreamlike images. For him, the flesh of a woman was an object of veneration, and the earth was bathed in the divine light of the sun. In the greatest of his paintings, the *Sleeping Venus* at Dresden, we are presented with a woman who is far from being a goddess even though she possesses a superhuman beauty. Though she is sleeping, her whole body is glowing and quiveringly alive, bathed in a strong yellow light and with scarcely a shadow. Titian, who painted in the background left unfinished at Giorgione's death, made the mistake of placing her in the open fields, when it was evident that she should have been lying in bed in a richly appointed palace. In his own *Venus of Urbino* painted thirty years later he corrected the mistake and made handsome amends.

The *Sleeping Venus* shows Giorgione at the height of his powers; never was a painter's brush so amorous, nor flesh so desirable. Into his vision of sleeping beauty he has poured all his feeling for an ideal perfection transformed into living flesh. She is more vision than reality, therefore belonging to the instant and likely to vanish in an instant, but at least he has been able to capture the vision on the wing. She lies there like someone cast ashore from the seas of heaven, and one cannot imagine her ever waking from her sleep.

Giorgione came to maturity at a time when the young merchant princes of Venice were eagerly seeking for novelty. The exhausting war with the Ottoman Empire was over; Cyprus had become a Venetian possession; large areas of northern Italy were under her protection or dominion. Yet there was a growing sense of disquiet, a yearning for certainties in an age of anxiety. During the years from 1500 to 1510 Venice was under military attack from the Pope and the Emperor, while the Portuguese were threatening to acquire the monopoly of trade with the Orient. Bartholomew Díaz had rounded the Cape of Good Hope in 1488 and was busily establishing bases on the shores of the Indian Ocean. For two hundred years or more the Venetians had fought vigorously to retain the monopoly of trade; now it was slipping from their grasp. The young were in despair, while the old remained under the tutelage of the Church and the State. Giorgione, the friend and entertainer of the aristocracy, brilliantly reflected this period of quiet desperation when it was easier to escape into an imaginary world than to face reality. His visionary paradise could come about only in an age when paradise seemed to be lost.

In fact, Venice proved to be stronger than her best-informed citizens could have guessed. She survived the attacks by Emperor and Pope. Though she lost the monopoly of trade with the Orient, she was still a power to be reckoned with and her enemies still quailed before her. The brief period when Venice suffered a failure of nerve came to an end, and Giorgione entered into legend. Within thirty years of his death there was scarcely anyone who remembered him, but his fame was continually increasing. Within a hundred years of his death the noble family of Barbarelli was claiming him for its own, and every important collector claimed to possess at least one painting by him. The Church of San Rocco possessed a small miracle-working painting attributed to him, and acquired so much wealth from the possession of the picture that it was able to build the imposing Scuola of San Rocco, for which Tintoretto painted a dazzling series of masterpieces. The dead Giorgione became the creator of hitherto unknown harmonies, the inventor of a style, the founder of a new tradition; all who followed him were influenced by him. He was about thirty-three when he died.

Tiziano Vecellio, whom we know as Titian, was his pupil, friend, and sometime rival. He was descended from the nobility, a proud and somewhat arrogant man, who thought the world was made in order that he could create his paintings. He lived to an immense old age, and produced more paintings than Rembrandt and Goya combined.

Giorgione said of Titian that he was "a painter from his mother's womb," and his earliest works, even those in which he was clearly following in the master's footsteps, show an extraordinary maturity and assurance. For a generation after Giorgione's death Titian painted works which were scarcely distinguishable from the master's. It was not that he possessed no originality; it was simply that he was caught in the spell. The *Noli Me Tangere* in the National Gallery in London is recognizably by Titian, but concealed within it, like a flower in ice, there can be seen the haunting splendor of a work by Giorgione, and this is to be found in a certain reverence for the flesh and an elegance of gesture. The Magdalen, wrapped in a white gown and a crimson cape, sits at the feet of a nearly naked Christ, seeking assurance that he is indeed alive and indeed the Christ, and in her upward-turning face there is a look of such inquiry and innocence that it seems inconceivable that he will deny her. It is the hushed hour of the morning, when the fields and the distant towns are still asleep, and we hear the familiar note of music lingering on the air. Giorgione has cast his spell again, but Titian plays the role of the sorcerer's apprentice. Again and again he will echo the master, and even today we cannot be sure who painted some of the early paintings credited to Titian, with their sustained enchantment and aristocratic refinement.

Yet they were men of widely different temperaments, from widely different backgrounds, possessing different gifts. Where Giorgione is innocent, Titian is experienced in the ways of the world, and where Giorgione deliberately turns away from religion and invents a dreamlike world of his own, Titian accepts religion, as a man accepts food and sustenance from a friend, and he is at home in the world. Titian lived in a world that was finite, Giorgione in a world of infinite dreams.

Gradually, as the years passed, Titian escaped from the spell of Giorgione and established his own empire. The poetic contemplation remained, but there came a new energy, a new sense of drama, and an increasing delight in textures and colors. The change came perhaps from his profound study of portraiture. His portraits of Venetian noblemen have a sharp edge to them; he proclaims their magnificence, but also their lust for power. His noblewomen flaunt their beauty, but he knows them well enough to hint at their treacheries and unbridled lusts. When he painted women naked, he removed from them the last vestiges of character and presented them as instruments of pleasure. Sensual and splendid, they live only in their golden flesh. Some of his nudes, like the sumptuous *Danaë* in Madrid, have a palpable sexuality and seem to have been painted at white heat. This work was in fact painted while he was a guest in the papal apartments in the Vatican.

Though he painted many religious pictures, he seems to have possessed no genuine religious feeling until the last years of his life. His Madonnas are nudes wearing clothes. In the great *Assumption of the Virgin* at Santa Maria dei Frari in Venice the body of the Virgin is clothed in a heavy crimson robe, but we are left in no doubt about the sumptuous flesh beneath the robe; and if she were not the Virgin ascending to heaven, she might be Venus descending to earth. It is a vast canvas, more than twenty feet high, and he painted her life-size, as though to ensure that we would be made abundantly aware of her beauty, her corporeal presence, and the flow of her garments. Since the Virgin ascended corporeally to heaven, he was painting well within the established tradition, but as soon as the painting was hung on the walls of the church there was an outcry. Santa Maria dei Frari is a Franciscan church, designed to suggest severity and austerity. However, the father superior genuinely admired the painting, and after he had proclaimed his admiration from the pulpit the outcry stopped. Here and there in that vast church there is the glow of jeweled color in altarpieces by Bellini and Titian.

There were very few who raised their voices against his paintings, for it was generally recognized that no artist ever lived who possessed his gifts. He was the supreme colorist, the greatest of all portrait painters, the greatest painter of nudes. He reveled in sumptuousness and splendor, and all his works convey his electric excitement in portraying the flesh and the lineaments of the human face. An astute critic has observed that he gave special prominence to the eyes, nose, and mouth, and it may be added that he paid little attention to ears, which he painted indifferently, perhaps because they spoiled the perfect contour of a face. But it was the flesh which absorbed his closest attention. He painted it so that it glowed with a marvelously rich light, and so real that you felt it would bleed if touched with a knife. He lived in great state, but quietly and unostentatiously, with a mistress whom he later married, and he had very few pupils, for he detested teaching.

There are few authoritative accounts of Venetian painters at work. Marco Boschini, a contemporary art critic, visited Titian in his studio and reported what he saw:

> I myself saw the firm touches laid on with strokes of a thick brush, loaded with color, sometimes with a thin coating of pure earth red which served as a half tone, sometimes with a film of white lead. Then, with the same brush dipped in red, black or yellow, he formed a highlight, and following these rules he laid the foundation for a promising picture in four brushstrokes.
> Having laid the basis for his paintings, he would turn them

to the wall and leave them—sometimes for as long as several months—without looking at them; and when he returned to work on them, it was his habit to examine them with the utmost severity, as though they were his greatest enemies, in order to discover any faults or anything out of harmony with the delicacy of his intentions. Then, like a surgeon, he would reduce a swelling or remove a superfluity of flesh or straighten out an arm (if there was an error in the bone structure) or reset a leg (if it turned at a wrong angle), or make it longer without any thought of the pain he was inflicting. In this way, continually redesigning his figures, he brought them to that state of perfect harmony which reproduces both the beauty of art and nature.

Afterward he would work on some other painting until the first was dry, laboring in the same manner, and thus the essential outlines of his figures were covered with living flesh, so that they only lacked breath to be alive. He never finished a painting at the first attempt, and used to say that anyone who improvises his songs will never produce skillful and well-turned verses. He seasoned his final touches by making a scumble with the tips of his fingers on the light passages, drawing them closer to the half-tones and merging one tone with another. At other times, with a thin tone made with the tips of his fingers, he would put a spot of black in a corner of a shadow or reinforce it with a dab of red, like a drop of blood. In this way he brought his figures to life.

The man who painted with his fingers was famous for the greater part of his life. The Pope, the King of France, the Holy Roman Emperor, the Medicis, the D'Estes, the Della Roveres, all vied for his services, and being proud, he would sometimes keep them waiting. The Emperor Charles V was his most persistent patron, heaped honors upon him, went to great pains to satisfy his whims, and treated him as though he were the king of a friendly country. No painter ever received such tribute from a sovereign. Titian became Count of the Lateran Palace of Our Court and of the Imperial Consistory, with the rank of Knight of the Golden Spur. These honors came to him in 1533 when he was about forty-four. He lived on for another forty-four years, and might have lived to be a hundred if he had not insisted on remaining in Venice during the plague.

Throughout his long life, he never settled down to a life of cultivated ease. Each month there was a new painting, a new portrait or one of those mythological scenes which he called *poesie* or a *Christ Crowned with Thorns*. Toward the end of his life he painted a *Shepherd and Nymph* startlingly like Giorgione in style, and indeed the figure of the nymph was taken from one of Giorgione's paintings now lost. Once again the air is sultry with the light of a coming storm, and the naked nymph glows in the storm light, while the shepherd plays on his pipe and leans over her with an expression of grave tenderness. In the distance a goat is tearing off the last leaves of a blighted tree, and no doubt the goat and the tree are intended to possess symbolical significance: death, or the bitterness of defeat, or perhaps the inevitable hopelessness of the shepherd's love for the nymph. In this painting, where there are no outlines and every contour is a receding curve, there is a sense of finality, as though a vision which mysteriously embraces the ultimate meaning of life had been stated with an ultimate perfection. The nymph glows with an inner light, her golden body moving across the canvas like a golden wave, and the shadowy shepherd takes the form of a breaking wave. So, too, in the great *Deposition* which Titian intended for his own tomb and left unfinished at his death, the golden body of the dead Christ forms a wave breaking against the hollow rocks, and all the guardian statues, lion and pelican, Moses and Sibyl, are no more than the breaking of the wave. Once more Titian has encompassed a vision, but this time there is no trace of Giorgione's influence, nor is there any attempt to assert his own individual style. Like the *Shepherd and Nymph*, the *Deposition* seems to have escaped from the world of art and entered the world of pure contemplation.

It happens sometimes that an artist in his last years will abruptly change direction, and from moving outward into the world he will find himself moving inward toward God. So Michelangelo carved his last Pietàs as though he had broken finally with every joy the earth could offer him, and Beethoven wrote the posthumous quartets with every certainty that he was listening to the music of heaven. So, too, with Titian, whose last works were composed with a kind of brooding detachment, all passion spent and all hope renounced.

There is a sense in which Jacopo Robusti was his proclaimed successor, the inheritor of his gifts and the logical claimant to all the forms that flowered under Titian's brush. We know him as Tintoretto, from *tintore,* meaning "a dyer," his father having been a poor dyer from Lucca who lived in the slum quarters of Venice. A heavy, chunky, splenetic man, he did nothing to conceal his affection for ordinary humanity, for the common people are continually being represented in his paintings, and in appearance and manner he was the direct opposite of Titian. It was said that Tintoretto spent only ten days in Titian's studio and was then booted out, apparently for impudence. Yet he remained Titian's pupil, for he studied the master's paintings patiently, copied them endlessly, and showed in the works of his maturity that he had learned all the lessons the master could teach him. On the wall of his studio he wrote the inscription: *Il disegno di Michel Angelo e'l colorito di Titiano*—The drawing of Michelangelo and the coloring of Titian. These words resembled a battle flag with which a man charges into battle: the energy and fury belonged to Tintoretto alone.

Vasari, who visited Venice in 1566 and added an appreciation of Tintoretto in the second edition of his lives of the eminent artists of his time, credited him with extraordinary originality, rapidity and resolution, and perhaps the only fault was that he was too original, too rapid, too resolute—he painted straight onto the canvas without any preliminary working out of the design and often let rough sketches pass for finished work. He would have been one of the greatest painters Venice had known if only he had been more sparing in the use of his gifts. Vasari failed signally to understand the nature of those gifts. Tintoretto left nothing unfinished, for he knew when to stop, and if he painted rapidly, it was because his hand had difficulty keeping up with his imagination. "He had the finest intellect that painting has ever known," Vasari went on, as though to make amends for his strictures on the artist's lack of method, but in this too he was wrong. It was not intellect but the purest sensitivity to color and atmosphere that Tintoretto possessed in abundance.

Outside of Venice he is still the least known of Venetian painters, for most of his six hundred paintings are still in the city where he spent his entire life. Both Giorgione and Titian belonged to the mainland by birth; Tintoretto, being a native, possessed the characteristics of a native, exuberant, quick to anger, with a conqueror's dignity and lack of discipline. The poetry of exuberance and anger spills out over his canvases and was evident in his private life. He feared no one, not even the redoubtable Pietro Aretino, who once commissioned two paintings from him and ever afterward imagined that the artist owed him a profound debt which could only be remitted by a flow of drawings and paintings to be offered without payment. Aretino wrote venomously about the artists who failed to oblige him. Tintoretto decided to put an end to the blackmail by inviting Aretino to his studio, ostensibly for the purpose of making his portrait but actually in order to frighten him out of his wits. No sooner had Aretino sat down when Tintoretto produced a pistol. "Jacopo, what are you doing?" Aretino exclaimed, while Tintoretto calmly measured him out, using the pistol as his measuring rod. Suddenly Aretino bolted from the studio and Tintoretto was never bothered by him again.

Tintoretto made a living with his portraits, all executed hastily and sometimes brilliantly with a wonderful penetration of character, but his chief delight lay in large official paintings for churches and the residences of high officials. He saw himself as a monumental painter, the creator of images filling entire walls. He painted an immense *Last Judgment* for the Church of Madonna dell'Orto, which Vasari regarded as a joke, because it was even more obsessively filled with the tortured bodies of the damned than Michelangelo's *Last Judgment* and far more difficult to understand. Tintoretto's painting may have been too exuberant, but it was not a joke. He was deadly serious when he painted religious paintings and he was the inventor of the supernatural light which bathes his figures and landscapes in a strange electric fire. He could paint wonderful nudes, and never painted more seductively than when he showed Susanna preening herself before the prying elders, the woman's pearly flesh aglow in the sunlight. But his temperament was essentially austere and ascetic, and by far the greater number of his paintings was concerned with religious themes.

Like all painters Tintoretto dreamed of enormous walls to be painted at leisure and enough income to support him while he was painting them. Giotto had painted the Scrovegni Chapel, and Michelangelo the Sistine Chapel. But such gifts of walls were rare: at the best an artist could hope for the privilege of painting a small corner of a church, thus claiming it for his own, as Mantegna claimed his small corner of the Eremitani Church in Padua, and Masaccio shared with Masolini the honor of a small corner of the Church of the Carmine in Florence. Tintoretto possessed an insatiable appetite. He would have liked a whole church for himself. He received instead the palatial mansion of the Scuola of San Rocco. Here over a period of twenty-three years he painted some fifty major works on the walls and ceilings, receiving an annual stipend and the absolute freedom to interpret biblical subjects as he pleased. His contract called for three pictures a year until such time as the task was completed.

No artist was ever luckier or more deserving. The Scuola of San Rocco is crammed with masterpieces, from the great *Crucifixion*, full of human frenzy and the fierce light of divinity, to the *Mary of Egypt*, who wanders among moonlit lakes and lagoons as though entering paradise. The *Crucifixion* has an epic grandeur, *Mary of Egypt* resembles a lyrical poem. Since there were no overseers to tell him how to compose his paintings and he was under no necessity to paint according to the established conventions, he gave his imagination full rein. In *The Temptation of Christ*, for example, Christ was usually represented in the desert confronting a monstrous horned Satan. Tintoretto portrays Christ crouching on a rock beside the Jordan while from among the lush grasses below there emerges a youth of great power and beauty with rosy wings, and we know this is Satan only because his face seems to be bathed in the light of flames. So again when Tintoretto paints an *Annunciation*, there is no calm encounter between the Virgin and the Angel. Instead, the Angel bursts through the walls of the Virgin's house like an exploding bombshell, and his path is littered with earthly debris. It has been observed that artists painting the Annunciation will un-

consciously identify themselves with the Virgin or the Angel. Tintoretto clearly identified himself with the Angel. When Christ rises
from the tomb, there is another explosion. No one ever depicted
the Christian story with such excitement or such imaginative ferocity.

In the *Crucifixion* Tintoretto outdid himself, for just as Michelangelo painted figures in the *Last Judgment* which seem to go
beyond painting altogether because they involve subjects which are
almost beyond the power of any man to imagine, so in the *Crucifixion* Tintoretto portrays a vast landscape of rock and battlements
with some fifty or sixty figures crowding around Golgotha, and for
the first time we are presented with a credible panorama of the
event. Christ is already crucified. One of the thieves is being lifted
up, the other is still lying on the ground. The Roman soldiers are
pulling at ropes, sweating, shouting. Horsemen are riding up, and
one of them is patting his horse for fear that it will become unman-
ageable amid all the commotion. In the center, shimmering in a
fierce and lonely light, his head sunk on his chest, high above the
throng, Christ stands against the darkening sky.

The *Crucifixion* is a large canvas, perhaps the largest he ever
painted, and the most brilliant of all. The sense of excitement is
sustained throughout. All those crowds of Roman soldiers, onlookers,
and disciples are wonderfully integrated into the scene, so that there
is never a moment when we feel that any one of them is an inter-
loper, placed there simply to assist the general design. Here raging
humanity confronts the rage of God, and the shattered light shines
equally on saints and sinners, and Christ stands above all men.
Tintoretto's personal theology had always involved a devout compassion for men at work. On Golgotha we see them at work, their
muscles straining at the ropes and their bodies gleaming.

Tintoretto did not always reach these heights. On occasion his
imagination becomes strained, almost hysterical. Sometimes this
straining after effect becomes almost unendurable. Titian's verses
rhyme: they are calm and superbly literate. Tintoretto has the
romantic temper, his verses do not rhyme, and he shouts them at
the top of his lungs, declaiming visions he has seen as wonderfully as he declaims visions he has only guessed at.

What he enjoyed most was the rush and fury of things, the brilliant revelation of sudden colors, the confrontation of God and man. He liked to show his heroes in contorted flight, hurtling from one end of a room or of a street or of a church to another, never at rest. At the first sign that anyone is at rest, Tintoretto immediately breathes energy into him and catapults him out of his chair or sends him spinning through the air.

He painted altogether six versions of the *Last Supper*. In the first, painted in 1547, the scene is relatively calm. The disciples sit sedately around the table, at ease among themselves, only dimly aware that they will soon be caught up in a terrible drama. Then we observe that two women are rushing into the room from either side. They may be Mary and Martha, or Hope and Charity, or simply neighbors: no one knows. He evidently enjoyed painting these extraneous figures, as though it were not difficult enough to paint thirteen men sitting round a table.

Some ten years later he painted another version of the *Last Supper* for the Church of San Trovaso. Christ sits at a table cater-cornered to the spectator, in a room where everything is in confusion. There is one chair filled with a disorderly pile of books, another is overturned, cloaks have been tossed hastily over a stair rail leading to an upper room, and the disciples are leaning back, as though a hand grenade had been hurled at the table. A servant girl stares down from the top of the stairs and a young Venetian nobleman stands at the left of the painting, his head bowed, lost in meditation. It is all a brilliant confusion.

In 1594, the year of his death, Tintoretto painted the immense canvas that now hangs in the Church of San Giorgio Maggiore, and where previously the windows and doors were opening, and we saw the people in the street, now it all takes place amid the vast disorder of an underground cellar lit by a single flaring oil lamp. The table is so long that it seems to vanish into the depths of space. Half the disciples have jerked, trembling, to their feet, a storm of angels is swooping down on them, and only the cooks who fill the foreground go about their affairs as though nothing was happening. This *Last Supper* is dark, crepuscular, almost incoherent, with so many conflicting lines of force that the

eye has nowhere to rest. Tintoretto is one of the very few painters
who suggest sounds—we hear doors opening and closing, the squeak
of a chair sliding across the floor, and the slapping of bare feet on
the marble tiles—and from this painting there can be heard the
rolling of the thunder as it echoes and re-echoes through the vast
cavern, and more faintly the muffled shouts of the disciples and
the incongruous clatter of dishes. Though the painting corresponds
to nothing comprehensible, and is totally unbelievable, it remains
a stupendous achievement. Finally, on this sixth attempt, he has
said what he wanted to say about the Last Supper, which took
place in a cluttered cavern, in a state of wild disorder, the air thick
with legions of angels, in glory and misery.

All his life he had lived in a world of allegory filled with
tempestuous, tormented visions, and during his last years he depicted
them without restraint. He painted St. Catherine in her toils: the
naked Catherine as she falls backward into a pool of heavenly
light, a horseman galloping out of one corner of the painting, an
angel descending from another, and all the rest of the canvas filled
with three vast shattered wheels with murderously glinting iron
hubs, the spokes radiating fiercely in all directions. Catherine has
been torn to pieces by the wheels, and now in her immaculate
new body she ascends to heaven, casting the world, the wheels,
and the galloping horseman aside. Then in the very last days of his
life he painted an *Entombment,* the three crosses glowing in a
crepuscular sunset far in the distance while in the foreground
Christ lies in the arms of his disciples, neither dead nor alive, looking like some exhausted warrior on an abandoned battlefield.

Like Michelangelo, Tintoretto practiced a heroic art. He dared
immensely. There was almost no limit to the range of his imagination. He painted a *Paradiso* for the Doge's Palace eighty feet
long and twenty-five feet high, and that immense painting might
be a record of his own visionary confrontation with paradise. With
the same relish he painted a series of four allegorical scenes for
the same palace, in which he celebrated the transparent beauty of
women, giving to their nakedness a majestic luster. Paolo Veronese,
who was his contemporary, excelled him in the dramatic texture
of his colors and in his power to compose paintings filled with

vast assemblies of people going about their daily affairs, but he lacked Tintoretto's imagination and spiritual insight, and no air flows around his figures. Tintoretto lived in the tempest, while Paolo Veronese lived on the quiet shores.

After painting the *Paradiso* Tintoretto slackened his pace. The story was told that he refused to accept any money for the painting, which he offered as his supreme tribute to the Doge. Similarly he accepted little more than a pittance from the members of the Scuola of San Rocco. For him, it was enough that he should be allowed to paint, but during the last years of his life he painted only a few paintings. "His fury for work decreased," wrote the contemporary art historian Carlo Ridolfi, "and he gave himself up to the contemplation of heavenly things." In fact he had been contemplating heavenly things throughout the greater part of his life.

When Tintoretto died in 1594, the golden age of Venetian art died with him. Other painters would employ the same quivering liquid colors to depict the light of Venice, but without the glowing intensity of the great masters and without their sense of the inherent dignity of man. While the Florentines always resembled youths and were in love with youth, the Venetians were mature men in love with maturity. They achieved an astonishing plenitude in their art, and those who came after them walked in their shadows.

The Clarity of the Dutch

The traveler across the plains of Holland soon finds himself wondering at the immensity of the sky, so vast that even the clouds seem to be lost in it and the birds seem to be looking helplessly for somewhere to rest. From Amsterdam to the Hague there is only an endless plain, where the occasional trees stand like sovereigns gazing down at a conquered land. Even the gentlest and greenest of plains have a starkness about them, and the Dutch who live on these plains have iron in their souls.

In Holland, where the sea is always very near, where the sky is ever present, and where there is a sense of illimitable horizons, the people have long since acquired an inner fortitude in keeping with their landscape. They were, and are, a kindly, stubborn, sober people, generous and tight-pursed by turns, essentially pragmatic, anxious to maintain their dignity. Not for them the *kermesses héroïques* of Flanders, those passionate festivities at which the Flemish joyfully paraded the sins of the flesh under the watchful eyes of the priests. Calvinism suited the Dutch, as Catholicism suited the Flemish. Holland was a land at the mercy of the sea, and every Dutchman knew that a man must live cautiously if he was to safeguard the land reclaimed from the sea.

In the early years of the seventeenth century the Dutch threw caution to the winds. Quite suddenly, and apparently without any conscious plan, they began to assert their independence of their Spanish conquerors. There had been wars and rebellions; they had suffered appalling religious persecution from the soldiers of Philip II; they had often outfought and outmaneuvered the Spaniards, but they had never succeeded in removing the yoke from their necks.

The defeat of the Spanish Armada and the growing power of the Dutch fleet showed the way to independence. Under William the Silent, Prince of Orange, the Dutch finally succeeded in freeing themselves from Spanish tyranny, and with the signing of the Twelve Years Truce in 1609 the Golden Age of Holland began.

There appears to be a historical law by which all the great periods of artistic creation last for no more than fifty or sixty years, a single life-span. So it was in the age of Pericles and in the age of the Medici. All the great Dutch painters of the seventeenth century were born within a few years of one another. Frans Hals was born about 1580, Van Goyen in 1596, Saenredam in 1597, Rembrandt in 1606, Ter Borch in 1617, Cuyp in 1620, Kalf and Fabritius in 1622, and Ruisdael, Metsu, De Hooch and Vermeer between 1628 and 1632. A man living in Holland in 1666, the year of the Great Fire of London, would have seen such a blaze of artistic genius as had not appeared in Europe since the time of the Medicis. He could have talked to Frans Hals, Rembrandt, and Vermeer, and bought their paintings for a song. If he had known what he was about, he would have been able to amass a collection of the world's greatest masterpieces without taxing his budget. Unhappily there were not many people who knew that a Golden Age had come, and few of the artists could have guessed that their works would be acclaimed by posterity. The artists were too busy warding off poverty to care what happened to their paintings.

Frans Hals appears to have been fighting poverty for the greater part of his life. He received at least nine commissions for large group paintings and painted perhaps two hundred portraits in the course of his life, but he was rarely well paid. He was originally a refugee from Antwerp, and he seems to have had the habits of a refugee throughout his life. He was about seventy-two when a baker to whom he was indebted for bread and money forced him into bankruptcy. An inventory of his property lists his few remaining possessions: three mattresses, an armoire, a table, and five paintings. He had evidently sold his bed, chairs, curtains, blankets, and cooking utensils. There was nothing left. For the remaining years of his life—he lived to be eighty-four—he lived on the charity of the Haarlem municipality and was permitted to receive his share of the turf carted through the streets by municipal officers. The turf was the winter fuel of the poor. The municipality also paid for his lodgings and saw that he was decently clothed.

When he was young, they said he was "a great lover of life," and he appears to have possessed a quiet gusto that survived his protracted bouts with poverty. He fathered at least ten children, and we hear of an imbecile son and a daughter who was sent to a workhouse because she was uncontrollable; we also hear that seven of his sons became painters, though only one of them made a name for himself. Born a quarter of a century before Rembrandt, Frans Hals died only three years before Rembrandt's death.

He was the master of the slashing brushstroke, the stroke that conveys a finger or the curve of a cheek in a single throw. Examined closely, his paintings break up into meaningless ridges and troughs of color exactly like the paintings of the Impressionists, who admired and imitated him. His strength lay in his power to pour vivid life into a painting. He will paint an old woman from the slums with a dazzled delight in her humanity, and he will paint the rich burghers with almost the same glee. It is fashionable to pronounce him lacking in depth or psychological insight, but this is to underestimate his capacity to portray his characters with a staggering intensity. He painted burgomasters, preachers, tradesmen, brewers, fishwives, topers, strolling players, old shrews, swashbucklers, and devout old women with the same lusty warmheartedness, and he especially enjoyed painting them as though he had caught them unawares, obliquely, at a moment when they were leaning back in their chairs or following a half-formed thought. One of his most prestigious works, The Laughing Cavalier in the Wallace Collection in London, shows a young gallant dressed up in the most theatrical costume, with slashed embroidered sleeves and a coat of black silk and gold, all this surmounted by an enormous lace ruff, and the very theatricality of the costume suggests that he is taking part in an elaborate charade. The Laughing Cavalier is certainly not laughing, and he is scarcely smiling: he is absorbed in the contemplation of his own beauty, his indifference to all things except the revolving mirrors of the mind. The princes of Renaissance Italy were equally bemused by their own beauty, but their delight in themselves derived ultimately from their sense of power. *The Laughing Cavalier* is a young bourgeois from Haarlem who has no illusions about his own power: he was probably a clerk in the municipal office. So, too, when Frans Hals at the end of his life paints the superintendents of the poorhouse, those five frigid old women consumed with a devastating close-lipped pride, he sees them with a kind of desolate clarity, stripping bare their pretensions, knowing full well that they have no power at all, unless ordering the lives of a few old men can be called power. Meanness, cruelty, and insensitivity are the demonstrable signs of their profession, yet he grants them an appropriate grandeur. He was eighty-two when he painted them, but his brushstrokes were as firm as ever.

At least two of his pupils, Adriaen Brouwer and Johannes Verspronck, produced great and memorable works. Rubens admired Brouwer's landscapes and tavern scenes so much that he bought seventeen of them; Rembrandt, who also admired his work, bought seven paintings and a book of drawings. Brouwer led a wildly bohemian life, spent six months in prison, and died at the age of thirty-six, apparently of the plague. Verspronck was a gentler soul, more methodical than Frans Hals, with a gift for depicting serene young women. Serenity, indeed, had become endemic, and there were twenty artists painting the gentle fields and dunes of Holland with masterly precision. Jan van Goyen, who ruined himself by speculating in tulips, produced at least a thousand landscapes, and some thirty of them are masterpieces. Pieter Saenredam, who painted church interiors with a feeling for the silence and holiness of barren walls, possessed the same calm temperament. It was the calm after a great storm, for the Dutch knew at last that their borders were safe and though there would be more indecisive battles with the Spaniards, they had nothing to fear as long as their ships roamed the Atlantic and the Indian Ocean.

It was at this moment that Rembrandt appeared, throwing his shadow on all the Dutch painters who came before and after him. In his own time he was never regarded highly in fashionable circles: this honor was reserved for Bartholomeus van der Helst, now relegated to an undeserved obscurity, for he was a brilliant portraitist who could catch a likeness and paint the voluminous

silk gowns of the period with a feeling for their gleaming splendor.
Van der Helst was all elegance; Rembrandt was all the rawness
of flesh and spirit. Full-faced, with wrinkled brows, a putty nose, a
fleshy mouth, with broad shoulders and small legs, Rembrandt
looked like a barge captain; it was a face without refinement,
very vulnerable. He would invent a world of images and proclaim
his mastery over the art of painting, so that for ever afterward
people seeing his paintings would hold their breath in wonder.

The life of Rembrandt can be told briefly. He was born in
Leyden on July 15, 1606, his father a miller, his mother the
daughter of a baker. He was the eighth of nine children, of whom
only four survived their infancy. The family was moderately pros-
perous and they were able to send him to the local Latin school
and later to the university. At fourteen he had already announced
his determination to be a painter. Apprenticed to the landscape
painter Jacob van Swanenburgh, from whom he learned little or
nothing except some elementary techniques, he went on to spend
six months in the studio of Pieter Lastman in Amsterdam, and
then returned to Leyden, where he settled down for the next
six years, establishing himself as a professional painter.

He was only nineteen when he returned to Leyden, for his
studies at the university and his two apprenticeships were telescoped
into a phenomenally brief period. Already he seemed to know
everything he needed to know and had acquired a style which
was recognizably his own and which would not change in essentials
during the course of his life. From the beginning there was an
insistence on character, a love of darkness and chiaroscuro, a delight
in rich embroidered fabrics to offset the rich embroidery of the
human face. Michelangelo saw heroic form in the naked human
body; Rembrandt saw heroic form in the wrinkles of an aging face.
He had learned much during the six months he spent with Pieter
Lastman, who had studied in Italy under Adam Elsheimer, who
in turn had studied under Caravaggio. The strange, glittering,
feverish light of Caravaggio became diffused when it reached
Holland, but it was still strange, still glittering, still feverish.

By 1628, when he was twenty-two, Rembrandt had already
attracted the attention of Constantijn Huygens, the secretary of the

Prince of Orange, and an accomplished musician, poet, and linguist, a close friend of both Descartes and John Donne. Huygens was struck by Rembrandt's profound originality, but wondered whether he did not already possess the temperament of an old man who knows that all is vanity. He encouraged his protégé to do gymnastic exercises and to travel in Italy, where he had himself traveled in great state. Rembrandt felt that nothing would be gained by travel and he continued to live a quiet sedentary life without benefit of gymnastics. In fact he scarcely traveled at all, and was perfectly content to spend the whole of his life within the small triangle of Leyden–The Hague–Amsterdam.

He prospered, opened a school, refined his art, and when the surgeon's guild of Amsterdam offered him a commission to paint a group of distinguished surgeons, he went off to Amsterdam, which became his home for the rest of his life. The painting, known as *The Anatomy Lesson of Dr. Tulp*, had very little to do with anatomy lessons, for the seven surgeons crowded around Dr. Nicolaes Tulp, the president of the surgeon's guild, were in no need of lessons. Rembrandt had placed a dead, eviscerated body in the foreground and grouped the surgeons around it. They are all gazing at it with passionate attention, and it is their passion that gives so much life to the painting. He had broken the mold. Usually these group paintings simply showed the doctors sitting at a table, gazing glumly at the invisible audience. Rembrandt was concerned to charge his paintings with a kind of quivering excitement and he would accomplish this by deflecting the spectator's attention from the real subject of the painting. The body in *The Anatomy Lesson* has the effect of a flame lighting up the faces of the surgeons.

In 1632, the year he finished the painting, he met Saskia van Uylenburgh, the cousin of Hendrik van Uylenburgh, an art dealer and painter, belonging to the Dutch Protestant sect of the Mennonites, who refused to swear on oath, wear weapons, or enter military service. Rembrandt lived for two years in his house, and he seems to have had considerable sympathy for the Mennonites without ever joining the sect. Saskia was an orphan and an heiress with a large fortune. He was betrothed to her in June 1633 and three days later drew a portrait of her in silverpoint. She is wearing a straw hat wreathed with flowers and holds a single petal in her hand and leans forward, pensive and half smiling and a little uncertain of herself. They were married the following year and eight years later she was dead.

In various disguises Saskia appears in many of his paintings, drawings, and engravings, often wearing fantastical costumes. Delicate, slender, with pleasantly aristocratic features, she sometimes seems to enter his paintings like a stranger, as though she were not quite sure what she was doing there. In the famous Dresden painting showing Rembrandt as a laughing cavalier lifting a huge wineglass above his feathered cap, while the green-robed Saskia sits on his knees, we are aware that she feels out of place and is far from being at ease. He painted her as Flora, as Bellona, as the prophetess Hannah. There is always some strangeness in her, as though she were someone set apart, very precious, and perhaps not long for this life. She gave him four children, of whom three died in infancy. The last, Titus, was born in the autumn of 1641, and in the summer of the following year she died. In her will she stipulated that her husband was to receive half her wealth, the other half going to Titus. If Rembrandt remarried, then his share of the estate would go to her sister Hiskje.

He was in no need, being already a man of some substance, for he charged high fees to his sitters and in addition he was a dealer in paintings. In the year of Saskia's death he completed the huge painting known as *The Night Watch,* charging 100 guilders from each of the sixteen soldiers shown marching out under the command of Frans Banning Cocq, a captain of the civic guard. *The Night Watch* is a misnomer, for they are marching out of the shadows into the broad sunlight. The huge canvas, today one of the glories of the Rijksmuseum, was regarded with mixed feelings by the musketeers who paid for it. Rembrandt had fulfilled the task assigned to him: he had painted them all, but he had painted them in his own way, their features being merely the decorative elements of his composition. He painted them in disorderly array, in sumptuous uniforms, making expansive gestures. Among them he placed a dark urchin who fires off a burst of gunpowder in the direction of the youthful lieutenant extravagantly arrayed in daffodil yellow, and in addition there is a strange, scurrying girl who may be Saskia (for she has Saskia's golden hair and something of her delicate features), who is also attired in brilliant yellow. The girl is a mystery. Where she has come from, and what she is doing in the painting are never explained. There is something about her that suggests an apparition from another world who has come to haunt the musketeers at their masquerade; and at her waistband she carries a golden pestle, a golden purse, and a white cock.

By placing the mysterious girl in the yellow dress and the young lieutenant in blinding light, Rembrandt has demonstrated once again that he places the light where he pleases. Like Caravaggio he creates and models out of light, and what excites him are the surfaces of things where they catch the light. To explain how the light falls in *The Night Watch* one would have to imagine a roof fitted with round holes through which the sun comes slanting directly onto the face of each musketeer, but quite clearly no such roof was ever built. At all costs Rembrandt was determined to be the master of the flow of light, the supreme arbiter of every lit surface.

Critics have spoken of Rembrandt's artistic development, dividing his creative life into periods, but in the strict sense there was no development. At twenty-three, when he painted *The Tribute Money*, he was already the superb master of lights and shadows, and there is no essential difference between these early paintings and those he painted forty years later. Grief would work on him, so that the shadows would become more somber and menacing, or other women would enter his life, with the result that he found himself studying different textures of skin and different faces with passionate intensity, but there had never been any diminution of intensity. Once Carel Fabritius, his most gifted pupil, was asked the first rule in good composition, and answered that it was "to arrange and organize what is most noble in nature." It was a lesson he had evidently learned from Rembrandt, who possessed an unerring sense of nobility.

There are people for whom grief is a goad, and they work all the more ferociously because they are aware of the terrors of mortality. In the years immediately following Saskia's death Rembrandt worked with an increasing skill and what appears to be a greater awareness of his own potentialities. To this period belongs the etching called *The Three Trees*, which is no more than three beech trees under lowering skies, but he had invested them with such nobility and monumental grandeur that they dominate the scene; they are like three kings looking out over their possessions. There is scarcely a painting by Rembrandt which is not set against darkness, and scarcely an etching which is not set against the open skies. For him therefore etching was a kind of liberation from the immaculately closed, enchanted world of painting. Life flows free in the etchings; there are rivers and plains and the ordinary workaday people go about in carts or stroll down country lanes, as small as the people in a Chinese painting, and the peculiar concentration and power which he manifested as a painter are exchanged for the etcher's diffuse discovery of the world around him. The line sparkles, and there is a sense of joyous release.

The paintings of women made after Saskia's death show a curious coarsening of the texture of the flesh. Titus had inherited his mother's silken skin and refined features, so that he looked at all times, even when he was quite young, like a Renaissance prince. Rembrandt evidently doted on him and continually painted him, so that we have a complete record of him from childhood to the time of his death at the age of twenty-seven. He had auburn hair, dark expressive eyes, and finely chiseled lips, but sometimes there can be seen a gray scoring under the eyes indicating that he was never in robust health. For a while the boy's nurse was an ordinary working woman, Geertje Dircx, the widow of a trumpeter, who may have become Rembrandt's mistress, for there were quarrels and recriminations after she insisted that he had offered her marriage and given her a rose ring. Rembrandt denied that he had offered to marry her, and she went insane.

Her place was taken by Hendrickje Stoffels, the daughter of a sergeant from Bredevoort, a buxom woman, warmhearted, without elegance but possessing a natural nobility. We know her well because Rembrandt exulted in her flesh and painted her with a fine regard for the texture of her skin and her golden hair, which she sometimes wore with thin braids tightly wound around her head, like golden chains. She was a sensible, earthy woman who took care of him as long as she lived. He painted her even more often than he painted Titus, and if we add up his self-portraits and the portraits of Titus and Hendrickje they come to about a sixth of all his works.

His self-portraits, beginning when he was in his teens and ending in the last year of his life, were among his most formidable achievements. No other artist ever studied himself so minutely over so long a time. Van Gogh's self-portraits, which evidently arose from the same consuming desire to know himself, were painted over a very brief period; Rembrandt's were painted over a lifetime. A sensual, self-indulgent man, well aware of his genius, humble and proud by turns, he portrayed himself at least sixty times: so that we must imagine that he spent perhaps three or four years of his life in uninterrupted contemplation of his own features. Nearly always there is a hint of irony, as though he could not quite believe that this rather pudgy, heavyset man with a potato nose and ghostly mustache was indeed the great artist Rembrandt van Rijn. He paints himself in his painter's smock and house cap, or in the furs of a merchant, or wearing the turban and gold lace of an Eastern potentate, but there is always that curiously baffled look, as of a man who had asked a question and heard only an echo. If you compare a self-portrait by Van Dyke with one by Rembrandt, you see one opening himself out to reveal the whole of himself, while the other remains mute and reserved, lost in his thoughts. Rembrandt aims to accomplish the portrait of his dreams, of his inner life. The substantial flesh melts into meditation, and the meditations, continuing over the years, record a desperate yearning to understand. As he grew older, he became even more unsparing in his desire to see himself with all the veils stripped away, and in the Cologne portrait, painted shortly before his death, he shows himself old and broken, with a face like one of the golden leaves of autumn, all withered and turning into mold. He laughs toothlessly, cocks one eyebrow, points his maulstick at an uncompleted painting of one of his patrician sitters, and utters a jest. It is the perfect coda. There at last, in those fierce and unrelenting brushstrokes, he has found what he was looking for: the old peasant glorying in all the fields he has planted, and ready to go.

Long ago Constantijn Huygens had detected that he was an old man before his time. Now in these last paintings he seems to have caught up with himself.

The last years were difficult beyond any he had known. He was never a popular painter during his lifetime, and though he sometimes obtained important commissions he was not a wealthy man. He had apparently run through the greater part of Saskia's inheritance; his tastes were expensive, for he haunted the auction galleries and if there was anything he wanted, he would bid more than the fair price for it. In 1656, when he was fifty, he went bankrupt and an inventory was made of all his possessions. The inventory survives, and tells a good deal about his life and habits. It included seventy-five of his own paintings, which had not been sold. In addition there were sixty works by other masters, including a *Head of an Old Man* by Jan van Eyck and paintings by or attributed to Giorgione, Palma Vecchio, Raphael, Hercules Seghers, Adriaen Brouwer, and many of the contempory Dutch masters. There were drawings and etchings by Mantegna, Antonio Tempesta, Schongauer, Holbein, Titian, Michelangelo, Rubens, Van Dyke, Jordaens, Bruegel the Elder, and the three Carraccis. He possessed a small head by Michelangelo and busts of Homer, Heraclitus, Socrates, and Aristotle, together with busts of all the Roman emperors. It was a princely collection, and would be worth many fortunes in our own day. Even more illuminating was his collection of props. There were Indian robes, Spanish chairs, lions' skins, halberds, bows, arrows, a crossbow, assegais, swords, pistols, a small cannon, cuirasses, helmets, one fit for a giant, another made in Japan. There were stags' horns, sea shells, lumps of coral, a harp. There were surprisingly few books: an old Bible, the *Jewish Antiquities* of Flavius Josephus, the *Essays* of Montaigne, Dürer's book on proportions, and a tragedy by Jan Six. He was allowed to keep a few chairs, his palette and brushes, a few bottles of turpentine and varnish, and a stuffed figure which could be used as a model for flying angels.

Rembrandt's collection of paintings and engravings shows that he had one of the greatest collections ever amassed by a private collector. He had the advantage of being a dealer in art and the close friend of dealers, yet it was a collection which would have been regarded as princely in Italy. He thought nothing of beggaring himself for a painting. What was art for, except to be collected by men like himself? These paintings and engravings were the presences that filled his solitude.

His taste ranged over the whole world of art, as his imagination ranged over the world of life and legend. All that was strange, curious, and exotic pleased him. The paintings he acquired were studied until they had revealed their secrets, and he borrowed from them unashamedly: there is perhaps more of Jan van Eyck, Giorgione, and Titian in his paintings than he ever knew. When we think of him at work during the years of obscurity, living in genteel poverty, his fame forgotten, all his hopes dimmed by scandal and loss, we are inclined to see him as a lonely and despondent old man endlessly exploring the world within, but this is to mistake the temper of the man. To the end he lived strenuously. When his collection was sold, it is unlikely that he felt any prolonged regret. He possessed an intense visual imagination, and he could summon up the lost paintings at will. The real sorrows went deeper: grief, the coming of old age, the gradual lessening of his skill. He seemed to be haunted by shadows, but he still saw the world with an intense clarity.

The sale of Rembrandt's effects did not free him from bankruptcy, for he remained an undischarged bankrupt until 1660. In that year Titus became nineteen and an adult in the eyes of the Dutch law. A corporation was set up with Titus and Hendrickje as the painter's employers; whatever he produced belonged to the corporation, and in return he received board and lodging, food and drink. No money passed through his hands, and in theory he was owned by them, as one might own an old mule. He was ageing rapidly, but his genius remained undimmed and to this last period of his life belong some of his greatest paintings, among them *The Jewish Bride*, a marvel of tenderness, and *The Syndics*, depicting five cloth assayers sitting round a table in monumental tranquillity.

It was as though his private miseries gave a mysterious strength to his art. He had never painted better. Hendrickje died in 1663, leaving him for the second time a widower. One child, Cornelia, had been born to them, and the family now consisted of Rembrandt, Titus, and a small daughter. Six years later Titus died, and this time the shock was unendurable. A year later Rembrandt died, working to the very end. An unfinished canvas stood on the easel: it was a picture of an old bearded man with a child in his arms.

Rembrandt had no successors. He was like a man who invents a new language, then composes all the songs of which the language is capable, and thus exhausts it. His one pupil of genius, Carel Fabritius, remains a shadowy figure because most of his works are lost. He made no use of Rembrandt's characteristic deep shadows but instead set his figures against light-colored walls or open spaces, building up his planes with minute strokes. From Rembrandt he derived perhaps his bite, his sense of the radiating power of the human face, and his intensity. He could paint a goldfinch on a seedbox and make it more real than any goldfinch ever painted. Quite properly Fabritius's goldfinch hangs at the Mauritshuis in The Hague opposite Vermeer's *Young Girl in a Blue Turban*. Fabritius died at the age of thirty-two when a powder magazine blew up at Delft, causing the loss of many lives.

Jan Vermeer of Delft, who may have been a student of Fabritius, was the third of the great triumvirate of Dutch painters. He was the son of a silk weaver who kept a tavern and also dealt in works of art. He married, had eleven children, painted perhaps fifty pictures, and died at the age of forty-three. He has almost no biography: the artist's ghostly presence hovers over his paintings and then abruptly vanishes. Of all the great and enduring artists he is the one we know least. No letters in his handwriting survive, and there are only the briefest indications of his existence in loan books and registries. We know the date of his marriage and how much money he borrowed, and we can see his name inscribed in the register of painters belonging to the local guild of St. Luke, but we do not know how he lived and there is only one recorded instance of anyone paying the slightest attention to his paintings. Altogether some thirty-five of his paintings survive. Of these the lion's share has found its way to museums in the United States, with seven in

New York and four in Washington. Amsterdam and The Hague between them have seven, London has four, Paris and Edinburgh have one each, and the rest are scattered among the museums of Europe or remain in private hands.

The works of Vermeer cannot be dated with any accuracy. Almost from the beginning his mastery is complete. There are paintings that are demonstrably more successful than others, but there is scarcely any sense of growth, of advancement toward greater mastery. Like Titian, he seems to have set aside his half-finished paintings and returned to them many months or even years later. With the exception of two famous landscapes, both in Holland, he painted only interiors or portraits; and there is such a likeness among his portraits that it is easy to believe that his models were his wife and daughters. The scene is nearly always the same: a high-walled, tiled room, a window opening on the left, a woman meditating or caught in a moment of silent interrogation. Indeed, so pervasive is the silence of his paintings that it is possible to recognize a Vermeer by the quality of its silence.

There are paintings by Gerard Ter Borch and Gabriel Metsu which are almost indistinguishable from Vermeer. They painted credible interiors lit with a cool northern light, inhabited by men and women perfectly composed, silent amid their adornments, at ease in their homes. They too could paint cascading folds of silk and the porcelain features of women. What distinguishes Vermeer is a kind of adoration, as he paints rooms and people who are infinitely dear and familiar to him. The curving brass lamps, the heavy tapestries, the wrinkled maps, the clean white walls and checkered floors of Mechelen, his house on the market square of Delft, the very quality of the light streaming through the windows, sweetened by rains and cooled by spring winds, all these are held in the balance of his adoring love, and weighed, and found almost too good to be true. He loves quietly and patiently, and in his affections there is something that reminds us of the convalescent returning to the world of the living, seeing everything a little brighter than it is because it is lit with his own feverish expectation.

Although there are few documentary records, the man himself is revealed to us in his paintings and there is little mystery about him. A methodical, sedentary, housebound man, rarely in good health, often in debt, a practitioner of many trades—he was simultaneously a painter, an art dealer and a tavern keeper, the whole lower floor of the Mechelen house being given over to the tavern he had inherited from his father—he was one of those men who walk through life with a calm assurance, never for a moment departing from the course they have undertaken. He seems never to have left Delft, or even to have wandered more than half a mile from his house. Living on the town square in the shadow of the church, he had no need to leave his house: the world passed in front of his eyes, and sometimes it would enter his tavern. When the tavern was crowded, he would retreat to the quiet rooms upstairs and labor over his paintings. Just as he loved his house and family, so he loved his paintings, rarely attempting to sell them.

On August 11, 1663, Balthasar de Monconys, a French collector and alchemist, noted in his diary: "At Delft I saw the painter Vermeer who had none of his works to show me, but we found one at the baker's. He had paid 600 livres for it, although it had only one figure and I would have thought it overvalued at six pistoles." Balthasar de Monconys was not always reliable about the prices he was asked, and in general he found Dutch prices much higher than he had expected when he set out on a picture-collecting tour. Vermeer had not refused to sell a painting to the distinguished Frenchman; he had simply refused to show a single painting, thus obviating the necessity of any further discussion. These paintings, over which he had worked for so many months or years, were treasures to be cherished; they were not to be sold, but might serve at different times as collateral for loans, like jewels or diamond necklaces.

Most painters keep some of their best works for themselves: Vermeer differed from them by keeping nearly all his works for himself.

The reason was an obvious one: his art was private, his paintings intensely personal. Essentially they were portraits of his wife and daughters; sometimes he painted his own portrait, as in *The Geographer* and *The Astronomer*, where he is seen bending over a table and studying a globe of the heavens. We see him again in the *Lady and Gentleman at the Virginals*, *The Courtship*, and *The Procuress*. He has a low forehead, a prominent nose, a long upper lip, a sensitive mouth, and a woman's chin. It is not a particularly memorable face; its characteristics are a grave delicacy and refinement, which are exactly the characteristics we might expect to find in him. He wears his chestnut-colored hair very long, and on the evidence of the paintings it was very fine and well cared for, clustering in thick curls around his shoulders. Far from concealing himself, he rejoiced in studying himself, though without Rembrandt's passionate obsession with his own features. In *The Artist in his Studio* Vermeer painted a back view of himself, an effect easily achieved by the use of mirrors. On the table beside the artist there lies a plaster cast of a man with a low forehead, a prominent nose and a long upper lip.

Vermeer's genius lay in his power to render the light and the living air around the object with such clarity that they become his accomplices. The technique was essentially *pointilist*, with the millions of specks of light fusing together, and each speck will have three, four, or five specks beneath it to give it the intensity he demanded. The colors and the contrasts are deliberately heightened. Depth is achieved by a series of calculated maneuvers: in the foreground there is usually a thick-piled Persian carpet thrown over the edge of a table, then comes the neatly tiled floor, then a chair, then a table. With space measured out by the inch, he sets his figure within a geometrical construction so firm and well anchored that it is virtually unbreakable. A surprisingly large number of his paintings are constructed in this way, and even the small, almost postcard size *The Lacemaker* in the Louvre is constructed in the same manner. He needed wood, tiles, carpets, and windows to give substance to his figures; and every projection, every crust of bread, every finial, receives its tribute of glittering, glancing light. Not since the time of the Abbot Suger had there been an artist so in love with the purity of light.

This purity, this caressing power to make light reveal itself, were not acquired easily and were evidently achieved by prolonged and concentrated contemplation. Vermeer's finished paintings are deceptively simple in appearance; they are in fact immensely complex experiments in the mechanics of light. Sometimes he would give himself problems almost beyond solution, as when he painted *The Allegory of the New Testament,* where plump Virtue clothed in a blue blouse and a white satin skirt rests one foot triumphantly on a globe of the earth. A golden chalice and an open Bible lie by her side, a crystal ball is suspended on a blue cord above her head, and in front of her on the tiled floor lie Satan's apple and a serpent crushed by a stone, while the blood from the serpent's mouth seems to form the letters *Vermeer.* The painting is so weighed down with allegory that it is in danger of disintegrating. Soon Virtue will totter and crash down on the floor, the apple will roll away, the serpent will slither under the table, and there will be nothing left except the spinning globe. No doubt the painting was commissioned after the French invasion of Holland in 1672, when Vermeer was in danger of starving to death. The inevitable curtain in the foreground is painted lovingly, but all the rest gives the impression of having been painted while under constraint and against the grain. Vermeer's entire body of work had been a denial of allegory or symbolism: his objects existed in light, in the calm and pure benignity of a light that bathed all things equally, for in the economy of his paintings only light possessed value, and the more calm and gentle the light the more he valued it.

The Allegory of the New Testament was his only failure: in all his other paintings he achieves a strange and happy perfection. There are no anecdotes: there is only the luminous fact, the woman pouring milk, or reading a letter, or making lace, while absorbed in her timeless meditations—the milk, the letter, and the lace being no more than the necessary decorations of her beauty. Similarly, when the woman is seen sitting at the spinet, we are not conscious of music. She has not sat down at the spinet this very moment, she is not playing, she has not completed whatever she was playing: she is simply there, for he asks no more of her than that she should be there. She is inseparable from the objects around her, and at the same time she is the reason for their existence.

His affection for his family was indistinguishable from his affection for his city, and therefore when he painted the warm red stones of Delft he worked with the same precise, cool, luminous affection. Just as the Parthenon is an abstract portrait of the goddess Athena, so *The Little Street in Delft* and *View of Delft* are abstract portraits of his wife and daughters, aspects of their enduring presence. The *View of Delft* especially reminds us of a smiling face, the city basking in a quiet joy and separated from us by the moving waters of the canal. The sky is overcast but here and there the red roofs are touched with splashes of yellow sunlight—"those precious little patches" which so enraptured Marcel Proust. And though there are people standing on the nearby canal bank, the red walls give the impression of being more alive than the people. Happily the *View of Delft* has remained in Holland, and we see it today in the same wonderfully crystalline light in which it was composed. At the Mauritshuis in The Hague it dominates all the other paintings like a king surrounded by his attendants.

Until 1866, when the French art critic and journalist Etienne Joseph Théophile Thoré (William Bürger) saw the *View of Delft* and pronounced it a work of unalloyed genius, Vermeer was little known. For two hundred years his works had been forgotten, and except for a brief and erratic reference in a history of Dutch art published in 1816 his name was never mentioned. Until the time of Thoré no one collected Vermeer's works, compared them, studied them, or sought to discover the springs of his genius. What had happened was something that is familiar enough in the history of art. Thoré, who knew the work of the French Impressionists, saw in Vermeer the forerunner of the Impressionists: his eyes had been opened to those peculiar qualities of light which were the special studies of Monet, Manet, and Pissarro. His discovery of Vermeer was not made by chance. He had seen in Vermeer what he had seen in Argenteuil, where all the colors of the sunlight were being examined and reproduced by painters who had never heard of Vermeer or seen his paintings.

There was also another reason why Vermeer faded into obscurity. His oeuvre was so very small that it had almost assumed the dimensions of a vanishing point in space. Since no one had seen more than a handful of his works until Thoré began to collect them, no one could pronounce judgment on them. Twenty years passed before Vermeer was admitted into the ranks of great European painters, and the immensity of his genius was only recognized in the twentieth century.

There was still another reason why Vermeer was so long in achieving the fame he deserved. He was working within an established tradition, painting in a manner and a style not altogether different from that of his contemporaries. Gerard Ter Borch, Gabriel Metsu, and Pieter de Hooch also painted calm interiors where the light falls evenly on the marble tiles, and that same ethereal calm appears in the landscapes of Jacob von Ruisdael. He did not invent the silence and clarity we associate with his name. To a quite extraordinary degree he deepened the silence and gave to clarity a hitherto unknown brilliance. He was not so much an innovator as an artist who, coming at the end of a long tradition, concentrates all its energies in his own person. When he died in 1675 the Golden Age of Dutch painting was nearly over. For a few more years artists would produced admirable paintings. By 1700 the painters were merely imitating one another, and the Golden Age came to an end like a lamp blown out on a windy night.

The German Agony

The imagination of every people would appear to contain archetypal images that rarely change, just as the fundamental character of a people rarely changes. The forms of art continue down the centuries, the works of the most ancient artist being immediately intelligible to people living in the present day. So the small bronze dancing girl found in Mohenjo-daro and made in the third millennium B.C. communicates intense pleasure to the modern Indian, who recognizes a form which has descended through the ages. It is not simply that the girl is naked and therefore appealing, but she has a particular kind of nakedness which is essentially Indian and never appears in any other culture: those long slender limbs, that elaborate coiffure, and the provocative twist of the hips will be found again in countless temple carvings. In the same way we find Chinese forms first elaborated in the Shang Dynasty constantly recurring, the same dragons and the same birds continuing to haunt the Chinese imagination down the ages. In the Near East, Persia, and Japan the archetypal forms continue with a persistence that can only be explained by an enduring need. In some mysterious way these forms have taken up their habitation in men's minds and every new generation discovers them afresh.

In the West, too, these archetypal forms persist down the centuries. An Anglo-Saxon monk in the ninth century makes a pen drawing of Christ with a flamelike line, and a thousand years later William Blake will make a similar drawing with the same flamelike line, the same contours, the same volumes; and these contours and volumes can be observed throughout the history of English art, just as the contours and volumes of the *Avignon Pietà* can be observed

throughout the history of French art. Every culture has its characteristic lines and volumes, its characteristic language of images, and
continually explores them, subtly modifying them and enlarging on
them while leaving them virtually intact. It could hardly be otherwise, for the single most powerful force working on a culture is
tradition, and when a culture moves away from its traditional forms
it disintegrates.

German culture grew out of the customs and beliefs of barbaric
tribesmen isolated from one another by marshes, rivers, and deep
forests. They had no cities, no common laws, no art, no temples.
Roman civilization, which was imposed throughout southern Europe
from the Atlantic to the shores of the Black Sea, left no trace on
the huddled tribes of Germany. Conversion to Christianity came
late, for it was not until the ninth century that Charlemagne
sent his missionaries into Germany, giving them power to root out
the ancient pagan beliefs with fire and sword; and this forced conversion left wounds that never healed. Paganism survived, and
Christ was identified with Odin, god of thunder and war. The
titanic battles of the ancient divinities were vividly remembered, and
the German imagination fed eagerly on the *Götterdämmerung*, the
twilight of the gods, when the earth was given over to fire and
flood, night and mist. Doom, from the beginning, held its fascination for the Germans.

So we may expect to find in their art a preoccupation with
doom, the war in heaven, darkness sweeping over the land. It
would be a fragmentary art, deeply melancholy, in love with the
woodlands and the groves where they worshiped their tribal gods.
Space and time would not be the orderly space and time which the
Romans derived from the ancient Greeks. There would be an un-
easy traffic with space, time vanishing as though it had slipped round
a corner of the universe. Above all, there would be evidence of intense and irremediable strain, as the two cultures, pagan and Christian, wrestled interminably.

From the beginning German painting showed a remarkable insensitivity to spatial form. The painters known as Master Bertram
and Master Francke set down their figures haphazardly without
any feeling for the relationships between them. Master Bertram,

living at the end of the fourteenth century, paints a wonderfully colorful *Nativity,* with St. Joseph tossing the Christ child in the air, while the roof is about to collapse and the Virgin about to slide off her bed. Neither the figures nor the design are anchored. The German genius was more at ease with sculpture than with painting. Though the great heroic statues at Bamberg were carved by French sculptors from Reims, there was no lack of German sculpture in wood of the finest quality. Christ in agony was rendered with extraordinary power and with a total lack of realism: the open mouth becomes a cave, the thorns curve menacingly into the eyes, and even the nose is ridged and wrinkled with pain. In a hundred carvings they conveyed the agony on the face of the dying Christ, but they were less successful in conveying the Christ who walked the earth or the Christ enthroned in heaven.

Sculpture and painting followed divergent paths. An honor list of formidable sculptors could be compiled, but there would be no comparable honor list of painters. Tilman Riemenschneider, the greatest of the sculptors, worked exclusively in wood; his carvings are marked by a great tenderness and what can only be called "fluidity." There was no violence in him, and he therefore carved out of the strength of his pity and tenderness, so that his Virgins come to possess a very human beauty and we can believe that mercy springs from them. For his part in the Peasants' War Tilman Riemenschneider was thrown into prison and tortured. Released, he immediately went back to his studio and continued to carve magnificently for the remaining six years of his life. Veit Stoss carved even more brilliantly and more powerfully, driven by an inner turbulence, his tormented apostles and saints reflecting the torment of his improvident life. Sometimes he gives the impression of a man who carved with a hatchet, and he rejoiced in the sharp biting strokes which produced deep shadows.

While the painters proliferated, they left few memorable works. The greatest was Martin Schongauer, born in Colmar in 1430, a man of such superb ugliness that he was called "Handsome Martin." Like Tilman Riemenschneider he was the victim of his tenderness, and his most famous painting *The Virgin in the Rose Bower,* now exhibited outside the altar rail at St. Martin's Cathedral in Colmar, shows a Virgin who is only too well aware of the thorns in the rose bower and who therefore gazes into the distance with a look of calm despair. The Child clings to her gently, as though to remind her that despair will one day change to joy. The Virgin is robed in scarlet and vermilion, and over her head blue angels support a marvelously intricate golden crown. In reproductions the painting gives an impression of sentimentality, which is absent in the original. The tenderness is everywhere, but it is expressed in sharp, incisive lines and in glowing colors.

But Schongauer's chief claim to fame lies in his copper engravings. No one, not even Dürer, engraved with a purer line. He had evidently studied the mysterious Master E.S., whose engravings, though medieval in spirit, already suggest a Renaissance awareness of a wide range of emotions. Schongauer's engravings have a clean-cut splendor, a diamond-sharp clarity, which places them among the greatest engravings ever made, and it is not surprising that both Dürer and Michelangelo admired him. One day Dürer called at Schongauer's studio in Colmar to pay tribute to him, only to learn that he was dead. He had lived very quietly and scarcely anyone in Germany knew he had died.

Schongauer was the precursor. When he died in 1491, Grünewald was probably still in his teens and Dürer was only twenty. Between them they would lift German painting to its greatest heights.

Although scholars have labored to solve the mystery, very little is known about the career of Mathis Gothart, whom we know as Grünewald only because an art historian once misread his name. One of the few certain dates is 1515, which he wrote on an ointment jar set at the foot of the Cross on the *Isenheim Altarpiece,* the date thus marking the completion of his greatest surviving work. We know that he met Dürer on October 23, 1520, at the time of the coronation of Charles V, and Dürer records in his diary that he gave him two florins' worth of engravings and woodcuts. It was a generous gift, but there is no evidence that Dürer saw any of Grünewald's work. We find traces of Grünewald in Frankfurt in 1526. Here he painted for the monastery of the Dominicans a *Transfiguration,* which is lost. This is a serious loss, for such a subject would have excited his imagination to the uttermost. There were many other losses, including three altarpieces at Mainz removed by invading Swedes only to perish in a shipwreck in the Baltic.

That his works would eventually be lost was a fate he probably expected. He could not have painted the *Isenheim Altarpiece* unless he had known suffering and fear, and possessed a tragic vision of life. Although the Crucified Christ of the altarpiece would have impressed his contemporaries less than it impresses us—for the wood-carvers had made even more terrible versions of a dead man hanging on a cross—nevertheless Grünewald's paintings speak of vast sorrows and insurmountable fears, of endless agonies and terrors. "He led a lonely and melancholy life, and was unhappily married," wrote Sandrart. Loneliness, melancholy, and an unhappy marriage may have been the least of his sufferings.

What is known for certain is that he was invited to paint the altarpiece by Guido Guersi, a Sicilian who was preceptor of the Monastery of St. Anthony at Isenheim. In the normal course of events the preceptor would decide on the general form it would take, and the design would not be entirely of the artist's choosing. Inevitably St. Anthony would be given special prominence, and he appears three times in the painting. The entire altarpiece with its nine panels was so designed that it could be twice unfolded, and at the end the worshiper would see the gilt statue of St. Anthony himself with the events of his life painted on two side panels.

This intricate design was demanded by the nature of the monastery, which was also a hospital crowded with patients suffering from leprosy and the plague. As part of their cure they were brought before the altar to summon God's help against their afflictions. First, they would see the dead Christ nailed to a roughly formed cross, his mouth open like a suppurating wound, his green, emaciated, and festering body already in a state of corruption, his hands curling like thorns, his feet blackened, swollen, and shapeless. Beside him stood John the Baptist, a powerful figure swathed in a ragged robe of scarlet, pointing. What John the Baptist is saying is clearly indicated in writing above his massive hand: ILLVM OPORTET CRESCERE ME AVTEM MINVI. "He must increase but I must decrease." The sense was that Christ would be resurrected in the flesh and would mount to glory, while the Baptist, so vigorous in the painting, would become no more than one of the divine servants. Though the painting was filled with torment, it conveyed a message of hope, for just as the suppurating flesh of Christ would be cleansed by divine grace, so too would the flesh of the lepers and the plague-stricken.

When the outer panels were unfolded, an altogether different sight greeted the worshiper. In dazzling orange, yellow, rose, and scarlet, Grünewald portrayed the Incarnation from the moment when the Archangel appeared to the Virgin to the final moment when Christ ascended to heaven in a sunburst of divine light so blinding that we can discern only the faint outlines of his features. Just as the outer panel conveyed the colors of death, so this inner panel conveys the color of vivid life, earthly and divine. Quite deliberately Grünewald seems to have displayed colors that are physically exciting and heartwarming while at the same time inviting the worshiper to enter a visionary scene. We see the Virgin embracing the Child in a summer landscape, and mysteriously there is a small bed beside her, a wooden bathtub, and a chamber pot. An angel plays a viola da gamba, another plays a viol, while an archangel with green wings and a face of great power listens attentively. Not far from the Virgin is another Virgin kneeling and worshiping in a glow of incandescence so fierce, so burning that nothing is left of her except a white face, red lips, and red eyes. Beyond the Virgin an incandescent Christ leaps into the flame-lit air.

There is no order or logic in this visionary scene; everything takes place as in a dream. All the elements of the vision are put together with a quite extraordinary intensity, as though the artist had simply painted what he had seen and was still quivering and was still half blinded. He had painted the Crucifixion as though he were standing five feet away from the Cross, and he paints the Virgin and her celestial orchestra as though he were standing even closer.

Finally, this second panel is unfolded and the worshiper comes into the presence of a gilded wooden figure of St. Anthony attended by St. Jerome and St. Augustine, and on the side panels Grünewald has painted St. Anthony during a calm encounter with a hermit in the desert, and then again he has painted the saint in agony, assaulted by an army of demons which would have dismayed Hieronymus Bosch, for these owls with the carapaces of lizards, horned griffins, and venomous fish convince us of their reality. They, too, are visionary, and are seen with a terrible precision. Tucked in the right-hand corner of this outer panel is a pathetic strip of parchment bearing the words: VBI ERAS JESV BONE VBI ERAS QVARE NON AFFVISTI VT SANARES VUL-NERA MEA. "Where wert thou, good Jesus, where wert thou? Why didst thou not come to heal my wounds?" These words, which do not appear in the gospels, seem to have been forced out of Grünewald himself as he watched the saint being drowned in a sea of bestial monsters. High in the sky God, armed with the scepter of his power, sheds his beneficent light.

None of Grünewald's other works possess the power and visionary quality of the *Isenheim Altarpiece.* There survive two smaller *Crucifixions,* a *Virgin of the Snows,* a *Mocking of Christ,* a panel showing the saints Erasmus and Maurice, a *Christ Carrying the Cross,* and there are perhaps twelve surviving drawings which can safely be attributed to him. Somewhere in Germany there may still be paintings by his hand, for it is inconceivable that so much of a man's work should perish so completely.

Grünewald had no pupils and no followers, and since he fell quickly into obscurity he left no lasting impression on German painting. There are no letters, no diaries, no treatises on the nature of art. Scholars accounted themselves lucky when they found his name mentioned in a rate book and luckier still when they discovered the inventory of his estate. The inventory lists some valuable clothing, jewelry, rare colors, books on hydraulic engineering, some Lutheran pamphlets, and two paintings, one of them a *Crucifixion.* The estate was left to his adopted son, Andreas, who is otherwise unknown.

Grünewald, too, is unknown, yet scarcely any painter has so convincingly portrayed his own character. We know his features, for he provided us with a portrait of himself in the St. Sebastian riddled by arrows, a strong face weighed down with sorrow, tight-lipped and unshaven. He has the body of a peasant with broad shoulders and strong legs, and he has the look of yearning and at the same time of smoldering defiance. The inner man is even more deeply revealed in the great altarpiece. We see him in his hours of exaltation and in his hours of dejection, and we come to know him almost as well as we know our closest friends. He was a man apart from other men, and none of his contemporaries, not even Dürer, possessed his formidable power.

With his long narrow face, his sensitive lips, and large melting eyes, Albrecht Dürer gazes out of his self-portraits with the air of a man perpetually immersed in his Gothic dreams, troubled by the demon of self-consciousness. There was something faintly foreign about him—in the curve of the high cheekbones, in the jut of the chin, in the elaborate elegance of his clothes, and this perhaps was due to his Hungarian ancestry. He aged rapidly, for although he was only fifty-seven when he died, his friend Pirkheimer said "he was withered like a bundle of straw and could never be a happy man or mingle among people." Melancholy and pride were his companions, an unhappy marriage contributing to the melancholy, his early successes giving wings to his pride. There was very little that was gentle in him. A hard, controlled vigor was concealed in the delicacy of his line, as it was concealed in the delicacy of his features.

He was born in Nuremberg, the son of a goldsmith, who apprenticed him to the goldsmith's trade when he left school. At thirteen the boy had already demonstrated his skill in drawing with a mannered self-portrait, which showed that he was already absorbed in his own elegance and beauty and especially with the beauty of his hands, with their long, delicate, and slender fingers. Soon he was permitted to learn painting, and with his father's reluctant consent he was apprenticed to Michael Wohlgemut, a painter of altarpieces, who lived nearby. He was about nineteen when he set out on his *Wanderjahre*, and for four years little more is heard of him. He collected prints and studied Schongauer's *The Virgin in the Rose Bower* at Colmar, and soon he was off to Basel and Strasbourg for more study, more absorption in the techniques of engravers and painters until he had learned almost all he would ever know about them; for the rest of his life he would explore his own mastery. He returned to Nuremberg in 1494, married, and immediately set off alone to Italy, away from the Gothic north, visiting Venice and Padua, surrendering to the southern light and copying the works of Mantegna and Pollaiuolo, then returning to Germany and the young wife he had abandoned.

For the next twenty-three years there came from him an incessant stream of woodcuts, oil paintings, and watercolors on every subject under the sun. He would paint a blade of grass as unerringly as he painted the Heavenly Host, and no one ever rivaled him in the sleekness and sharpness of his line. When he draws the *Apocalypse,* you are made aware of heavenly fires and heavenly thunders, but always there is a sharpness in the line like thin threads of steel. What is surprising is the steadiness of hand, the springing curves drawn with a draftsman's precision, the stern outlines. He drank hugely and had a passion for wenching, but he was ruled by a steel-hard will. Though he belongs to the Renaissance, the shadows of medieval Germany hung over him; and he had the medieval delight in monsters, witches, the terrors of the night. He helped to design the triumphal arch which the Emperor Maximilian ordered for his own pleasure, an arch unlike any other that ever existed, since it was made entirely of paper and was in fact a vast compilation of woodcuts fitted together until they formed an arch eleven feet high and ten feet wide, and this was followed by an even more portentous folly, for the Emperor who won so few victories demanded that there should also be a triumphal procession made up of over two hundred woodcuts, which, when finally joined together, stretched for 180 feet. Dürer lent himself to these fantasies, prepared many of the woodcuts, and seems to have delighted in the opportunity of showing his skill in a new and hitherto unknown form. These giant woodcuts are among the more curious products of Maximilian's hapless reign, and the experiment was never repeated.

Dürer revealed himself in the vast range of his paintings, watercolors, engravings, woodcuts, and drawings, and also in his voluminous writings. He was the author of three books, on geometry and perspective, anatomy, and fortification. He seems to have kept a diary at intervals through his life, but there survives only the diary he wrote in 1520–21 during a journey to the Netherlands.

When he set out from Nuremberg with his wife Agnes and his maid Susanna, he was at the height of his fame. The diary records his triumphal progress and his expenditures. We learn how much he paid for bread, butter, pears, a whetstone, a haircut, and how much he received for his paintings and woodcuts. He makes careful note of the value of gifts received—an elk's foot, for example, was estimated at six florins. On the whole the diary is calm, unemotional, as precise and accurate as a laundry list, but on one famous occasion he burst into a passionate prayer to God on behalf of Martin Luther, who was reported to have been arrested. The report was untrue, but there was no doubting Dürer's reverence for Luther or his horror of Luther's enemies. He records a meeting with Erasmus and an audience with the King of Denmark, whose portrait he drew in charcoal. On one memorable day at Brussels he saw the treasures of Aztec gold sent by the conquistadors to the young Emperor Charles V, and he appears to have been one of the very few who recognized their superb artistic quality. He wrote:

> Today I have seen the objects brought to the King from the newfound land of gold. There was a sun made all of gold, six feet across, and a silver moon of the same size, and two rooms full of the armor of those people, and all kinds of wonderful weapons, harness and arrows, and some very strange clothing, and also beds, and every kind of utensil, and these things are more beautiful than miracles. They are all very precious and their value has been computed at 100,000 florins. Upon my life I have never seen anything that rejoiced me so much as these things, for I saw among them marvellous works of art, and I wondered at the subtle *Ingenia* of men in foreign lands.

There were many other things to marvel at during this journey. He met the Fuggers, the financial magnates whose power reached across the whole of Europe, admired paintings by Rogier van der Weyden and Hugo van der Goes, and paid tribute to the holy relics, the Virgin's shift and girdle, at Aachen, where he attended the coronation of Charles V. It was a busy time, but he reveled in the new sights, and was continually making drawings or paintings of the people he met and selling them. One day he went to Zeeland to see a six-hundred-foot whale that was cast ashore, and he was nearly drowned in his effort to come close to the whale. As a result of the drenching, he caught pleurisy and for the rest of his life he seems to have been a sick man.

Nuremberg had never treated him well, but it was his home and he wanted to round out his life in the city where he was born and had countless relatives, for he was the third child of eighteen children. He had seven more years to live, but produced very little except for two brilliant panels showing the four apostles Mark, John, Peter, and Paul. He seems to have lived obscurely, perhaps in poverty. In 1525 he recorded a strange nightmare—he had seen the waters falling on the earth, striking the ground with tremendous force, and he made a watercolor of this terrible vision. Thereafter we hear little more about him until his death on April 6, 1528, at the age of fifty-seven. The two greatest lights of German art died in the same year, for Grünewald died a few months later.

The range of Dürer's work is so vast that it is almost intimidating. No other artist ever commanded so many media, or showed such mastery in so many arts. Strangely, he produced no sculpture, though he possessed a sculptural imagination; and though he prided himself on his oil paintings and was an absolute master of the art, nevertheless he produced many inferior altarpieces, perhaps because he half-despised the rigid, formal designs required of him by the Church. Once, commenting on the occasion when he watched the triumphal entry of the Emperor into Antwerp, he wrote: "Being a painter I looked about me a little more boldly than the others." He was thinking about the beautiful girls who accompanied the procession, but he might have been referring to his visions.

Dürer's woodcuts and engravings have been ill served by modern processes of reproduction. His original work on paper has a bite, an intensity, a depth of field, and a luminosity which is totally lacking in photographic copies. To see a real Dürer engraving on a richly textured paper which has remained unblemished through the centuries is to see the art of engraving at its highest potential, wholly monumental. His men and horses and mythological creatures are set firmly in space, well anchored, thrusting upward, in firm control of their destinies. When he engraves St. Jerome in his study and places a human skull on the windowsill, then we are aware that he has chosen an exactly appropriate place for it, and when he portrays St. Eustace falling to his knees after seeing a stag bearing a crucifix, then he sets the scene in such a way that all the details—distant castle and blasted tree, curving bridge and tufts of grass—acquire a special appropriateness, as though they had existed for centuries and were therefore closely related to each other. He fills the whole foreground with hunting dogs, and they too have the quality of being exactly where we should expect to find them. Dürer's compositions are built up with an exquisite sense of order, and the whole is subordinated to the logic of the parts.

When he was traveling in the Netherlands, he would sometimes sell the two engravings *Knight, Death, and the Devil* and *Melencolia* as a pair. They were regarded as companion pieces, having in common an extraordinary intensity of feeling and resonance. Once seen, they echoed and re-echoed in the mind, and even if they were not entirely comprehensible, they spoke directly to the heart. *Knight, Death, and the Devil* is based on an earlier watercolor of a quite ordinary knight on a quite ordinary horse. But there is nothing in the least ordinary in the knight of the engraving. He has within him a somber divinity, and becomes wholly monumental, so much larger than life that he is more like the projection of the idea of Christian knighthood than a man. He has the vigor and resolution of Verrocchio's Colleoni advancing relentlessly upon the enemy. As he rides through the valley of the shadow of death yet with the heavenly Jerusalem in sight, he is accompanied by an unwelcome stranger, who is not exactly Death, for he wears a beard and his hair is twined with serpents and he holds an hourglass. He is Father Time reminding the knight of his approaching death. Hard on the knight's heels, as though to emphasize the presence of death, there comes a grotesque horned monster with hooves and bat's wings and the face of a wild boar, who may be the devil incarnate, but is perhaps a phantom of terror. Dürer himself called the engraving *The Knight.* The title *Knight, Death, and the Devil* was invented at a later time.

This engraving was made after his mother's death, when he

was grief-stricken and filled with forebodings. About the same time he drew *Melencolia,* where winged Melancholy like a fallen angel is seen gazing despondently over a rainbow-haunted sea, with all the tools of a builder's trade scattered around her. We see nails, a plane, a saw, a hammer, a ladder, a pair of dividers, a pair of scales. There is an hourglass over her head and touching one of her wings. She has reason enough for melancholy, and there is very little mystery about her. Dürer himself said that she must be understood as "looking through the eyes of Saturn." In those days Saturn was regarded as the father of profound philosophical speculations. In *The Knight* Dürer proclaimed his religious faith; in *Melencolia* he proclaimed his faith as an artist aware of the agonies of creation, the angelic tasks of the creator. He considered the artist as one who partakes of some of the powers of God, and he had no illusions about the nature of artistic gifts: they were God-given, and therefore divine.

The *annus mirabilis* of Dürer's artistic life was 1511, when he issued in a single year three superb sets of woodcuts: *The Life of the Virgin, The Large Passion,* and *The Apocalypse,* which had been published in a first edition some years earlier. Each of these sets had wonderfully memorable designs, and Dürer seems to have been well aware of the advantages of bringing them out simultaneously. Altogether they comprised forty-seven woodcuts, but there was scarcely one which did not show him at the height of his powers. While *The Apocalypse* showed the greatest originality, *The Life of the Virgin* showed him in full possession of a humble faith. *The Large Passion,* so called because the pages were of unusual size, contained some of the most complex designs he had ever attempted. They were made with such force, with such an air of absolute conviction, that they virtually introduced a new iconography. Henceforth the Germans would see God and Christ through Dürer's eyes.

These woodcuts were distributed in hundreds and perhaps thousands of copies at the local fairs, where they were sold singly or in sets. Sometimes his wife Agnes would sit at the stall and sell her husband's work. These woodcuts reached Italy, where they were especially admired by artists, who would use his designs for their own purposes. And no one seeing his Virgin suckling her child in a sunburst of glory, or the Four Horsemen of the Apocalypse thundering across broken skies, or Christ harrowing hell, ever forgot them. The woodcut can never achieve the delicacy of an engraving, but he was not searching for delicacy. The power—the God-given power of the artist—leaps impetuously over the page. If you turn the page upside down, it looks like an explosion.

But when Dürer seriously asked himself where he most excelled, he would answer that he was above all a painter. Long before he traveled in Italy, he had shown himself to be far more than an accomplished painter. At the age of twenty-two he painted his first self-portrait in oils, wearing a pleated Italianate shirt and a remarkable tasseled red cap; and in that face, so young and so irrepressibly self-regarding, so conscious of its own beauty, pride and sensuality seemed to be in league with each other. He painted many more portraits of himself. Five years later he painted himself in almost the same pose, but now he wore a thin golden beard, and golden ringlets flowed over his shoulders, and he was even more purposefully elegant than before. Two years later, at the age of twenty-nine, he painted himself full-face, ringleted, with slashed sleeves and a heavy fur collar, and there is not the least doubt that he is presenting himself as a Christ image, so compelling is the resemblance between himself and Christ. Once more he seems to be proclaiming the divinity that lies within the artist. In 1504 he painted an *Adoration of the Kings*, the most brilliantly successful of all his religious paintings, and Dürer appears squarely in the middle of the painting as the young king robed in a magnificent jeweled gown, bearded and ringleted, one hand clutching his crown, the other supporting a golden chalice, and there is perhaps some significance in the fact that he is turning away from the Christ child.

In these paintings Dürer portrays himself with sovereign delight and a fierce consciousness of his own excellence. He knew his worth, and was not unduly surprised when he received ovations during his tour of the Netherlands. He was the first artist to sign and date even his most occasional drawings, and he would usually place his powerful signature, the D enclosed within a majestic A, in a prominent place where it could not possibly fail to be observed. Like Leonardo da Vinci he was haunted by the demon of self-consciousness and he was able to make the demon work for him.

Those last years when he sank into a mysterious silence may be accounted for in the same way that we usually account for the long silence of Leonardo. He was exhausted by his long labors and his many illnesses. Fame had meant much to him when young; it meant less as he grew older. In his *Four Books on Human Proportion,* published shortly after his death, he wrote: "Occasionally God gives an artist the ability to learn and to create something good; and no one like him can be found in his own time, or perhaps ever existed before, or will soon come again." Long before he died he knew he had almost single-handedly created German painting.

His contemporaries and successors live in his shadow. None had his range, his energy, or his vision, and only Grünewald could be mentioned in the same breath. Melanchthon said that Dürer, Grünewald, and Cranach were the three glories of German painting, but Cranach for all his superb nudes lacks the authentic fire. In his long life—he was born a year after Dürer, whom he survived by a quarter of a century—he was pre-eminently the fashionable court painter who conformed to the demands made on him by a rich and influential public and was deaf to the demands of his own genius. He became fantastically successful. He was a rich landowner, the owner of a wine shop, a print shop, an apothecary's shop, and a well-attended studio, and by order of the Electors of Saxony he paid no taxes. On his tombstone he is described as *pictor celerrimus,* "the speediest painter," and that fatal ease and quickness of hand is evident in all his works. He painted over a hundred nudes, calling them, as the occasion demanded, Venus or Diana or Lucretia, but they are always the same. Luther, who knew him well, objected strongly to this mass production of provocative and experienced young women leering invitingly from his canvases. "Master Lucas is a coarse painter," he wrote in 1545. "He might have spared the female sex because they are God's creatures and because of our mothers." They had been close friends for more than twenty years when Luther wrote these words.

When Cranach painted a nude and set her against a dark

background, alone against infinite space, there is such a concentration on nubile flesh, such a delicate insistence on the curving outline encompassing a jellylike substance, that the spectator finds himself mesmerized, as though he were being wantonly pursued by a woman from the Elector's court. Cranach relishes the young flesh, exhibits it with extraordinary verve, and never tires of it. He will paint scenes of fifty young women disporting themselves in the nude, and though they all assume different attitudes and are all the same woman, it is impossible not to respect the virtuosity of the artist who could paint figures so admirably but could never set them in a real landscape. Dürer complained about the fragmented landscapes of his contemporaries, and Cranach was the worst offender. The ground tilts away, the rocks might be made of matchwood, and the trees are painted paper.

Dürer's generation saw the greatest concentration of artistic talent that Germany was ever to see. Within a few years of his birth Grünewald, Cranach, Hans Burgkmair, Hans Baldung Grien, Albrecht Altdorfer, and Tilman Riemenschneider were all born. Burgkmair, who studied under Martin Schongauer, painted with the same deliberate sweetness as his master, and there was more of the fiber of genius in Baldung's allegorical nudes than in any of Cranach's impatient nymphs. He painted deft and simple altarpieces and he had a way of emphasizing the comic expressions of his sitters. Albrecht Altdorfer was totally unaware of the comic possibilities of the human face. He painted landscapes, and if there were human figures he preferred to see them dwarfed by immense trees or lost within the vastness of a palatial building. When he painted a *Nativity*, he painted an intricate and capacious inn and permitted the Virgin and Child to hide behind a broken wall. When he painted St. George slaying the dragon, we see an immense forest of shimmering gold-green leaves, and St. George is sketched in lightly near the roots of the trees, and the dragon is scarcely visible among the tall grasses. Altdorfer was happiest when he painted landscapes where no human figures appear, and he would paint a lonely footbridge or a sunlit woodland with a quiet relish as though he were a seventeenth-century Dutch painter before his time. His curious canvas called *Alexander's Battle*, with a thousand minutely painted

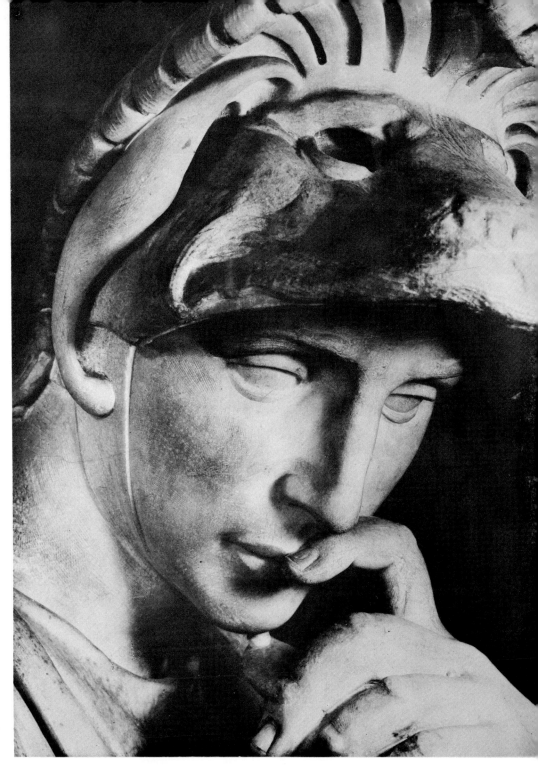

Head of Lorenzo de' Medici, Duke of Urbino, by Michelangelo.

David,
by Michelangelo.
ACCADEMIA, FLORENCE.
ALINARI.

The Christ of the Last Judgment, by Michelangelo.

SISTINE CHAPEL, ROME. ALINARI.

Portrait of the Artist's Father, by Albrecht Dürer.
NATIONAL GALLERY, LONDON.

The Tempest, by Giorgione.
ACCADEMIA, VENICE. AFI.

Abraham and Isaac, by Rembrandt.
PRIVATE COLLECTION. ALEXANDER ARTEMAKIS.

Self-portrait by Rembrandt.

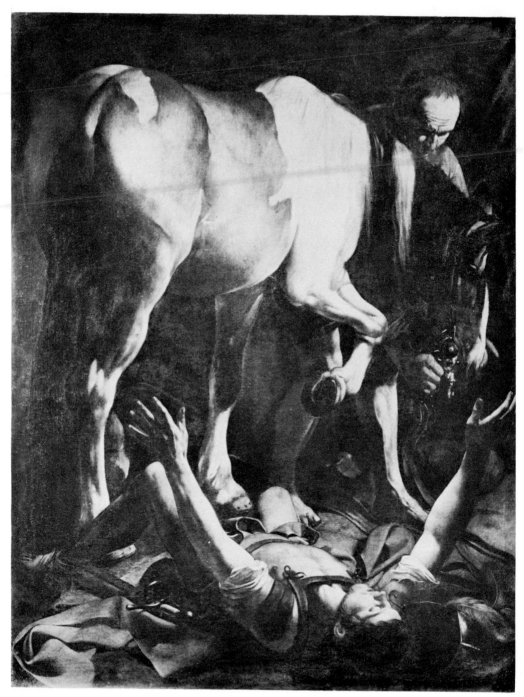

The Conversion of St. Paul, by Caravaggio.

Greeks and Persians in medieval armor, is a memorable tour de force more remarkable for the extraordinary brilliance of the sunset sky than for the battle taking place below. By profession an architect, he painted for his own pleasure, and his best works have a quality of grave intimacy with woods and growing things, as though the sunlight were about to fade from the sky and he would snatch them out of darkness; and we remember his enchanted forests more than we remember his knights in armor.

Dürer's generation died, and none came to replace them. The German genius for painting rose to its height in the early sixteenth century, and then sank away. Holbein, born sixteen years after Dürer, exiled himself from Germany and spent the greater part of his active life in England. Like a musician who can play only one piece of music and plays it superbly, he limited himself to portraits of the learned and the nobility. A fastidious draftsman, he was incapable of catching the inner life of his subjects, and if we set his best portraits against the self-portrait of the youthful Dürer we observe a strange reticence. It is as though Holbein possessed the power to fill his portraits with life but dared not do so.

One last small flame appeared in the work of Adam Elsheimer, born a hundred years after Dürer. Like Holbein he abandoned his homeland and settled abroad. Proud, nervous, weighed down with an incurable melancholy, he painted small figures against the vastness of landscapes, and the smallest of them possesses a feverish life of their own. He was a master after his time, for he belonged to the age of Altdorfer, whom he admired. The deepest shadows fascinated him, and since he lived in Rome and was a follower of Caravaggio, he had ample opportunities to study the shadow play of a great master. Finally the shadows engulfed him and he went mad and died miserably at the age of thirty-two.

Elsheimer did not live in vain, for he introduced a certain Pieter Lastman to the works of Caravaggio, and their meeting was to have a phenomenal influence on the history of art. Lastman studied all the available paintings by Caravaggio, the master of the directed light and the somber shadow. He also studied Elsheimer's paintings and after the young artist's death removed them to Amsterdam. Lastman became the teacher of Rembrandt. Elsheimer was the bridge between Caravaggio and Rembrandt.

Elsheimer deserves to be remembered, not only because he was a bridge between the two most powerful painters of the age. His small paintings on copper have a mysterious dreamlike intensity, which shows that he had become all the more German from long exile in Italy. The demons of pride and melancholy assailed him, as they assailed nearly all the German masters, but permitted him to pursue his art until he had found himself. There is a purity in his work which can only derive from processes of refinement. The glow of his night scenes is not spectral: the night is seen in all its mystery. In his hands night becomes an enchanted forest.

Elsheimer was the last of the German painters, and far from being the least. If Dürer and Grünewald are the great peaks, Altdorfer and Elsheimer are the high foothills.

Michelangelo

The story is told that when Michelangelo met Raphael accompanied by a flock of pupils, he could not contain himself and shouted angrily: "Where are you going—marching out like a general?" Raphael answered: "And you, alone like an executioner!"

Of Raphael no one ever used the word *terribilità*, the word which is always associated with Michelangelo to suggest his superhuman powers, his vast and dangerous accomplishments. Raphael belongs to a tradition; Michelangelo seems to break through the walls of tradition, composing his statues and paintings as though no one had ever painted or sculpted before. There was something elemental and titanic in him, as though the ordinary preoccupations of the human race were scarcely worthy of his regard, as though he was more familiar with the life of rocks than the lives of men. Born in a castle on a high crag not far from the place where St. Francis received the stigmata, he seemed always to live on the mountaintops, at one with the storms and the starlit night.

In his own lifetime Michelangelo was regarded with awe and something approaching terror. Men knew even then that he would be spoken about hundreds of years after his death, and they spoke of him as a necromancer, one who possessed powers so rare that millenniums might pass before another like him appeared. They called him *divino* while he was still living; it was a title formerly reserved for emperors. Seven popes and two emperors demanded the honor of being his patrons, and though he obeyed the popes and suffered them with ill humor, he paid scant attention to emperors or tyrants wherever they were found. His aim was to free himself of all bondage by creating his own world, and in this he succeeded more than any artist before or after him.

Michelangelo di Lodovico di Lionardo di Buonarroto Simoni was born in 1475, the son of the mayor of Caprese, who claimed descent from the ancient family of the Counts of Canossa. It appears that the claim was unfounded, but Michelangelo delighted in this connection with a rich and powerful family. According to Vasari, he delighted still more in the memory that he was put to nurse with the wife of a stonecutter. "I sucked in with my nurse's milk the chisels and hammers out of which I made my statues," he said, and he regarded this strange diet as the proper nourishment for a sculptor. His mother died when he was only six years old, and he received little affection from his father, who beat him unmercifully and despised him for his boyish infatuation with art. The early loss of the mother appears to have affected him deeply, and to have encouraged his natural melancholy. He never laughed easily, and his rare jokes are usually forced. He grew up to become a strangely silent man, reserved even with his intimates, and so devoted to his art that nothing else existed for him. His scorn for the works of other artists was as terrible as Dante's scorn of his Florentine persecutors, and sometimes Michelangelo will give the impression of a man in full flight from the avenging furies.

He was fourteen or fifteen when he first came to the attention of Lorenzo de' Medici, who was so impressed by the boy's skill that he gave him a room of his own in the Medici palace and permitted him to sit at table with the Medici children. In addition Michelangelo received a regular salary of five ducats a month, and for some particularly fine achievement he was presented with a purple cloak. But the four years he spent under Lorenzo's roof were not years of unrelieved pleasure. He continued to study under Domenico Ghirlandaio, who taught both painting and sculpture, but appears to have been an impatient pupil who thought little of his teacher and was not particularly popular with his fellow students. One day, when he was about fourteen, he was copying Masaccio's frescoes in the Carmine when a student called Torrigiano picked a quarrel with him. There was a savage fight and Michelangelo's nose was broken and crushed. For the rest of his life he was to bear the scars

of that desperate battle fought beneath the masterpieces that announced the coming of the Renaissance. News of the affair came
to the attention of Lorenzo de' Medici, and the young Torrigiano
was banished from Florence.

When Lorenzo de' Medici died three years later, Michelangelo
was left to his own resources, no longer the pensioner of a princely
court. He returned to his father's house, carved a heroic Hercules
and a wooden crucifix, both lost, and for a while entered the court
of Lorenzo's son Piero, who gave him no commissions, although it
is reported that during a hard winter he was ordered to carve
snowmen for the young prince's pleasure. A more rewarding occupation was provided by a friendly priest, who permitted him
secretly to dissect corpses in one of the buildings attached to the
Church of the Santo Spirito. Anatomy became his passion, and
there is some evidence of his proficiency in the best of his early
carvings, a small unfinished relief of naked warriors showing a
youthful Michelangelo rising superb above the tumult with one
arm bent behind his head as though about to hurl a stone or javelin.
The artist liked this relief so much that he kept it beside him for
the rest of his long life. No doubt he saw in this early relief many
of the preoccupations of his later years; and indeed these embattled youths engaged in naked warfare are to be found again and
again in his later works.

His art, however, was still unformed and uncertain when the
French army under Charles VIII entered Florence in November
1494. Like many others who feared the invaders, Michelangelo
took flight a few days before the army entered the city, and for a
year he seems to have wandered across northern Italy, a vagabond
in search of a master. Venice rebuffed him; he could find no employment there. In Bologna he was arrested, and only the intervention of a certain Giovan Francesco Aldovrandi, one of the leading
citizens, saved him from imprisonment. Aldovrandi was a cultivated
man, who enjoyed listening to the recital of the works of Dante,
Petrarch, and Boccaccio in the Tuscan pronunciation, and Michelangelo, who read well, possessing a sonorous voice and a deep feeling
for the Tuscan language, was employed as a reader. The tomb of
St. Dominic, designed by Niccolo dell' Arca, had been left un-

completed, and Michelangelo was given the task of adding some small figures. He performed the task faithfully, if without any great distinction, and seems to have been content to spend his days under the protection of a kindly master. Fifteenth-century Bologna could offer him little scope for his genius, and soon he wearied of the pleasant life in Aldovrandi's household and set out for Florence and thence to Rome.

He reached Rome in the summer of 1496, bearing letters of introduction from Lorenzo di Pierfrancesco de' Medici, who apparently gave him a small allowance. The most important of these letters of introduction was addressed to Cardinal di San Giorgio, who had accumulated a small collection of antique statues, which were housed in the Palazzo Riario. The cardinal invited Michelangelo to see the statues, asked him whether he could do as well, and when he was told that it was impossible for any modern sculptor to rival such excellence, he seems to have been pleased, and hinted at a commission. Nothing came of it. In despair Michelangelo bought a block of marble and began to carve a life-size figure, in the assurance that he could make a living as a sculptor without the patronage of the Church; and already possessing some small renown, he set about cultivating the dealers and wealthy patrons of Rome. The life-size figure became the *Bacchus*, bought by Jacopo Galli, a connoisseur who also possessed a collection of antique statues. The *Bacchus*, now in the Bargello in Florence, was given pride of place in Galli's collection, for it had all the appearance of an antique derived from Hellenistic models. It is a strange work, wholly decadent, excessively ornate and devoid of passion, for the naked Bacchus appears to be admiring himself in a mirror, chilled by the spectacle of his own beauty. The legs and thighs are carved with a springing elegance, but the torso remains flaccid and lifeless. The controlling hand was still unsure of itself. With his next composition Michelangelo showed himself to be a master.

The leap from the *Bacchus* to the *Pietà* encompasses centuries of experience and eternities of thought. Quite suddenly, with nothing in his past to suggest that he possessed formidable powers, he produced a masterpiece of such staggering proportions that even today we look upon it with awe and amazement. Commissioned by

Cardinal Jean de Bilhères de Lagraulas, the French ambassador to the Holy See, it seems originally to have been intended for the cardinal's tomb. Clad in a vast mantle, the Virgin rests on a rock and supports the dead Christ on her lap, gazing down at his nakedness with an expression of grave wonder and sadness. The theme of the *Pietà* was more appropriate to the Gothic North than to Italy, and it has been supposed that the dying cardinal—he died in 1499, the year after the contract was signed and two years before the sculpture was completed—must have shown Michelangelo one of those vivid Gothic paintings where the Virgin is seen lamenting over her son, her face white with tears, his body red with blood. But in Michelangelo's sculpture there are no tears and no blood. The Gothic vision is transformed into a singularly Florentine vision, and while the agony of the Virgin is wholly absent, and the son sleeps calmly, the sculptor has given such splendor and dignity to the conception of the mourning Mother of God that it seems that here for the first time there has been expressed the ultimate blessedness, the certainty of divine love.

Never again was Michelangelo to carve with such tenderness and compassion, and at the same time with such extraordinary command over his material. The proportions are heroic, for the dead Christ resembles a Greek warrior fallen in battle and the Virgin might be Athena mourning for her lost son. But while the influence of classical Greece is demonstrably present, the flowing robes of the Virgin are carved with a peculiarly Florentine luxuriance and nobility, fold melting into fold, so that the robes form as it were the setting in which the dead Christ lies, so weak and yet so handsome in death. Above him the face of the sorrowing Virgin broods like the moon.

Michelangelo's contemporaries wondered at her calm, her beauty, and her youth, for she seemed even younger than her son. To his biographer Ascanio Condivi he replied that the Virgin, being chaste and undefiled, was not subject to the laws of time, adding that the son, having assumed the physical body by God's decree, was subject to those laws. No doubt Michelangelo was deeply impressed by the Neoplatonic doctrine current in the court of Lorenzo de' Medici which recognized physical perfection as the earthly mirror and emblem of divinity, but it is not necessary to go to the Neoplatonic philosophers to discover why the Virgin should appear so radiant and so young. Michelangelo, who read Dante throughout his life, would have found the perfect description of the Virgin in the last canto of the *Paradiso,* where she appears in her utmost glory—*"Vergine madre, figlia del tuo figlio."* In the *Pietà* we see the Virgin Mother as daughter of her Son.

As it stands today in a small chapel at the entrance to St. Peter's, the *Pietà* is out of place. It was clearly intended to be seen from a distance and to be approached gradually, as one approaches an altar; light should bathe the body of Christ, and the Virgin should appear in the hovering shadows, and it should be low to the ground. None of these requirements demanded by the nature of the statue have been observed. The visitor who turns into that small chapel finds himself bewildered by the appearance of a shadowed masterpiece in an abrupt and irrelevant setting. From the beginning Michelangelo was ill served by the Church.

He was twenty-five or twenty-six when he completed the *Pietà,* and he was already the absolute master of his craft. Quite suddenly he had emerged as the most brilliant sculptor in Italy, and the authentic successor of Phidias and Praxiteles. His fame was assured; he had already become a legend. Yet no more commissions came from powerful cardinals, and in a mood of baffled incomprehension he returned to Florence to place his services before the youthful republic. More than fifty years were to pass before he created in the *Pietà* in the Duomo at Florence another sculpture so instinct with tenderness and Christian feeling.

Florence greeted him warmly, for his fame had preceded him. The city magistrates offered him a commission: a statue which would express the vigor and defiance of the republic beset by enemies. A gigantic block of wonderful creamy white marble, already worked by the sculptor Agostino di Duccio forty years earlier, was at hand, and Michelangelo was invited to rework the marble in his own way. Vasari tells us that as soon as he took possession of the block of marble, which reposed in the workshop of Santa Maria del Fiore, he built a high wooden fence around it, permitting no one to see him at work. The block was eighteen feet high. Agostino di Duccio had merely carved some draperies, and these were quickly removed. Thereupon, slowly, over a period of three years, Michelangelo carved the *David*, which stands today in the Accademia in Florence, after having stood at the gates of the Palazzo Vecchio for three hundred and seventy years.

While the *Pietà* expressed the Christian's longing for ultimate blessedness, the *David* expressed a pagan reliance on strength, cunning, and intelligence. A muscular youth, with thick curling hair falling over the nape of his neck, with an expression of great power and refinement, he stands there like a god who has descended to earth in order to chastise the mighty and to tear kings from their thrones. His brows are knit, his eyes are watchful, the youthful body stands in absolute composure, conscious of its own strength, its own power to accomplish whatever the intelligence demands. Authority and self-reliance have become so habitual that he scarcely knows they exist, and he wears his flesh with the same divine negligence. There is something in him of the impudent and repulsive *Bacchus*, but it is no more than a distant and half-forgotten memory. So he stands there in his arrogance and splendor, superbly defiant, celebrating his own humanity, beauty, and magnificence. He is more Apollo than David, and belongs more to Greece than to the Renaissance. Here Michelangelo stated once and for all, in a manner he would never surpass, the ideal inhabitant of the visionary earth.

Critics have commented unfavorably on the stance, on the large hands, and on the head, which they regard as too big for the body. A famous German art historian complained of "the obscene triangle formed by the legs," as though it were possible for a man to put one leg before another without forming a triangle. Sir Kenneth Clark has stated that Michelangelo made the mistake of deriving his portrait of David from a relief as a basis for a figure in the round, and he is appalled because the statue is sixteen feet high. Others have commented on those massive thickly veined hands, suggesting that they are out of all proportion to the figure, forgetting that the hands of heroes are likely to be large. In fact *David* is all of a piece; the parts are merely the decorations of the whole; and just as there is no Pietà to rival the *Pietà* in St. Peter's, so there exists no heroic youth to rival the *David*. We must go back to the heroic figures of the Parthenon pediment and the supremely authoritative Apollo of Olympia to see another youth so noble or so touched with divinity.

When Michelangelo threw down the wooden hoardings which concealed the *David* for three years, the Florentines realized that they had received a gift which would henceforth be counted among the greatest treasures of the republic. Accordingly the statue was removed from the workshop of Santa Maria del Fiore in a wooden cart and set up outside the Palazzo Vecchio as a warning to tyrants to remember that men, made in the image of God, found tyranny intolerable. And when the tyrants came back again and the effete Dukes of Tuscany sat in their thrones in the Palazzo Vecchio, the statue was still there, though it became weather-beaten and discolored over the centuries. Once on a day of uproar a heavy bench was thrown at it, and one of the arms was broken. It was quickly repaired, and the statue shows today little sign of damage. Set in the rotunda of the Accademia, at the end of a long avenue, brilliantly lit and placed on a pedestal of exactly the right height, it is one of the few statues of Michelangelo that are shown to advantage in an appropriate setting.

With the *David* and the *Pietà* Michelangelo showed that he was the master of both the Christian and pagan worlds. He could convey the most exquisite tenderness and charity, and he was equally proficient in conveying the fierce passion of unbridled youth. Youth indeed was his chief study, and henceforth he was to spend the greater part of his life depicting youths charged with ferocious energy. He would show them in their anguish and torment, wrestling heroically, struggling against the blind forces of destiny or taking heaven by storm, and it was all one to him whether they succeeded in their endeavors. It was enough that they should be shown in mortal combat, with the dew of fear on their faces and the light of triumph in their eyes.

The *terribilità* of Michelangelo is already announced in the *David*, who is more tyrannical than the tyranny he contemplates. Even today he inspires fear and awe, for he wears his nakedness like a sword. Michelangelo would go on to depict Samson smiting the Philistines with the jawbone of an ass, or Hercules in his labors, or a youthful Christ presiding fiercely over the world of the damned. He rarely shows men at rest. The Florentines called him *il terribile,* and sometimes they would make the sign against the evil eye when he passed.

After the triumph of the *David,* he was awarded two major public commissions. The first was for a painting along one of the great walls in the Great Council Chamber of the Palazzo Vecchio, to confront Leonardo's *Battle of Anghiari.* The second was for twelve large statues of the apostles to be set up in the nave of the Duomo. These were princely commissions for a young artist of twenty-nine, but neither commission was carried out. He seems to have had no desire to portray the apostles in stately contemplation, and succeeded only in scratching the surface of a block of marble with the outline of a heroic St. Matthew, who has the features of an Assyrian king and the limbs of a wrestler. The painting was never begun, although he completed the cartoon, which survives only in copies. In the copy made by Bastiano da Sangallo, preserved at Holkham Hall in England, we see eighteen naked soldiers who have been surprised while bathing by the appearance of the enemy. Clambering on the rocky shore, they hunt for their weapons and their armor, and in their haste fall upon one another and get in each other's way. One blows on a trumpet, another shouts and points in the direction of the advancing enemy, a third hurls himself impetuously forward as though he would embrace them all in a last protective gesture. The composition consists of interlacing nudes, and the cartoon resembles the relief of naked warriors he carved when he was very young. Though the copy only hints at the grandeur of the original, it conveys the urgency and terror of the soldiers. The Florentine artists of the time regarded it with the same awe as the *David,* for Michelangelo had depicted his naked warriors with unrivaled passion and intensity. Cellini called the cartoon "the school of the world." Completed in 1506, it disappeared ten years later, having apparently been cut into many pieces and distributed among his friends.

In 1506 two events occurred which deeply influenced the course of Michelangelo's life. Pope Julius II, the former cardinal-priest of the Church of San Pietro in Vincoli, laid the cornerstone for the new St. Peter's, and the *Laocoön* statue was unearthed from a vineyard in the center of Rome. Michelangelo was among the first who saw the statue with the earth still clinging to it, for he was staying not far away. He studied it with immense care, and henceforth many of his statues and paintings were to echo the turbulent shapes which he first saw in the vineyard. Pliny had pronounced the *Laocoön* the greatest single piece of statuary in the world, surpassing all others, and the Romans who flocked to see it were inclined to believe that it came as a messenger from the antique world, stupendous and terrible, but nevertheless worthy of admiration. Inevitably the statue came into the possession of the Pope; so too did Michelangelo.

Julius II was a man gripped with a passion for conquest. Old and infirm, suffering from gout and venereal disease, he coveted everything that was splendid, beautiful, and surprising. Magnificence was the world he walked in, and he permitted no one to refuse him anything. Although the old St. Peter's was to be torn down, the Sistine Chapel, built in 1473 by Pope Sixtus IV, the uncle of Julius II, was to remain intact. This vast chapel had been elegantly furnished with frescoes by Botticelli, Piero di Cosimo, Domenico Ghirlandaio and others, all painted in mannered, highly decorative styles, and in addition there was Perugino's *Assumption of the Blessed Virgin Mary* on the wall behind the altar. The ceiling was blue sprinkled with stars. This ornate and very feminine chapel was entirely out of keeping with the style of Julius II, who decided to give it a more impressively masculine appearance by the addition of twelve huge apostles at the pendentives of the low-slung barrel vault. Michelangelo, who had very little knowledge of painting and no knowledge whatsoever of the art of the fresco, was commanded to paint the apostles.

In obedience to the Pope, he made a preliminary sketch, which survives, but he seems to have had no more intention of painting the apostles for the Sistine Chapel than he had of carving the apostles for the Duomo in Florence. He regarded himself always as a sculptor and he had a particular distaste for painting. He quarreled bitterly with the Pope, who decided that Michelangelo was perversely creating difficulties for himself. And when finally Michelangelo offered to paint a vast design on the ceiling, which would include the Creation of the World, the Birth of Adam and the Expulsion from the Earthly Paradise, the Flood and the New Dispensation under Noah, the Pope reluctantly agreed. A frescoed ceiling could always be covered with a coat of whitewash, and there were many in the Pope's entourage who hoped for Michelangelo's downfall.

Michelangelo knew so little about fresco painting that he summoned friends from Florence to teach him. Once he had mastered the technique he mastered the art. The Sistine ceiling, which covers an area of 5,595 square feet, took four and a half years to paint. Sometimes the Pope would climb wearily up the scaffolding to watch him at work, and once when Michelangelo unwisely announced that he would finish the fresco when he could, the Pope struck him with a cane and bitterly mimicked him, saying: "Yes, when you can, when you can!" Michelangelo detested the task and luxuriated in it. With wild joy and inconsolable misery he worked day after day on the high scaffolding, the paint splashing on his ragged beard, his bones aching, his loins, as he said, "grinding into my belly," and all the while he was aware that he was accomplishing something never attempted before by a single man—a portrait of the entire history of the world up to the time of the Flood, and by implication, for all the prophets and Sibyls were in attendance, he was portraying all eternity. God appeared, but not Christ; yet Christ was present through the presence of the prophets. Just as the Byzantine cathedrals were transformed into picture galleries where the mosaics recounted all human and spiritual history, so the ceiling of the Sistine Chapel was a picture gallery of all human and spiritual history up to the coming of Christ, and it was not accomplished by an army of workers in mosaics but by a single man armed with a brush and attended by a solitary servant.

The ceiling of the Sistine Chapel is uneven, episodic, majestic, and preposterous. There is no way in which the observer may take in the whole sweep of it: to see it properly, one must lie on the floor and turn this way and that, while the attendants are not looking. Happily, the chapel is sometimes empty and it is possible to traverse considerable distances on one's back, gazing up at a ceiling which was not so much designed to be looked at as to be there, a numinous presence superintending the councils of the cardinals. A cardinal, wishing to be pope, may find himself gazing absentmindedly at Ezekiel upside down, or contemplating the classical beauty of the Delphic Sibyl. The ceiling was designed as a distraction for people looking heavenward.

Sometimes the genius of Michelangelo flagged, and some of the smaller scenes in the spandrels were unworthy of him. The dreaming Adam is wonderfully conceived, but the too plump Eve who emerges from his side to confront the Almighty is little more than a large fat grub, and Noah's Ark provides an unconvincing backdrop for the desperate crowds fleeing from the promise of the Flood. Michelangelo was the supreme master of the figure, but never painted a convincing landscape or interior. He would set his figures against the whole of space and make them credible; set inside a room, they look troubled and apprehensive like prisoners waiting for the moment when they are permitted to emerge into freedom.

The great panel showing God reaching out to touch the hand of Adam has an astonishing simplicity which conceals many complexities. Adam is a young Renaissance prince lying at his ease, and there is in God more than a hint of the features of Michelangelo himself; but even more remarkable is the shape of the billowing red cape surrounding God and the cluster of angels simultaneously supporting him and propelling him through the heavens, for the cape is shaped like an eagle's wing and the hand resembles an eagle's distended beak aimed at the heart and liver of Adam, another Prometheus on the mountains of the Caucasus. The pagan myth underlay the biblical story, and indeed paganism is celebrated on the Sistine ceiling not only by the presence of idealized youths of immaculate beauty and by the ancient Sibyls but also by a certain intoxication with muscular flesh. Half the figures on the ceiling are naked. They are splendid, but they have little enough to do with the Christian mystery.

When the Sistine ceiling was completed and solemnly unveiled by the Pope, Michelangelo was thirty-seven. Twenty-nine

years later he would be summoned back to Rome by the reigning
Pope to paint the *Last Judgment* on the west wall of the chapel.
There was little difference in his style, which was essentially the
massive and monumental style of a sculptor. Just as in the ceiling
he painted one unbelievably magnificent passage which stands out
above all the rest, so on the wall he painted Christ in Majesty,
summoning the blessed with one hand and invoking damnation on
sinners with the other, a figure of astonishing power and energy.
In the original sketch the Virgin, naked, kneels before him in
supplication for all sinners. In the final version she has abandoned
her role as mediator and intercessor, and simply huddles beside him,
turning her face away from the sinners to contemplate the blessed,
and she wears a blue gown.

Nowhere, not even in the great tympana of the Romanesque
churches, has Christ been rendered with such fierce authority or
such youthful energy. No doubt the pose owes much to the *Laocoön*,
which Michelangelo so assiduously admired, but the portrait ultimately derives from the *Rex tremendae majestatis* of the *Dies Irae*,
the Franciscan hymn written by Thomas of Celano to celebrate the
terrors of the Day of Judgment. Michelangelo's painting is at once
a commentary and an illustration of the hymn. This is the moment
when Christ dissolves the world and establishes his own kingdom;
history and time fade away, to be replaced by his eternal presence;
the dead awaken and the damned are consigned to their eternal
punishment amid the trumpeting of angels and the roaring of the
flames. He has painted the scene as though he were present, and it
is perhaps significant that he has depicted heaven perfunctorily and
employed his best energies in depicting Christ and the damned.

Even the saints who cluster around Christ are struck by the suddenness of the event, caught in strange attitudes of protest and consternation. They cling to one another, and some turn away as
though blinded by Christ's terrible beauty. Indeed, the entire composition resembles an explosion, the shock waves setting off secondary waves that have the effect of causing further explosions. The
mold is shattered, the universe splits asunder, the blessed rise to
the heights, the damned plunge downward into the depths, where
Charon, Minos, and the Skeleton await them. Never was there a

more disorderly composition, but the disorder is deliberately conceived and sytematically sustained. We are told that the Pope was thunderstruck when the painting was unveiled, and well he might be. There was little orthodoxy except in the lunettes, where muscular angels could be seen carrying the Cross and the Pillar in triumph. Michelangelo had imposed his own vision on Christianity, and his Christ was overwhelmingly his own, not the Christ of the Church.

Inevitably there were those who protested at the sea of naked bodies depicted in the painting, for the men were nude and of the women only the Virgin was fully clothed. Biagio da Cesena, the papal Master of Ceremonies, visited the chapel in the company of Pope Paul III, and when asked his opinion of the fresco, he answered that "it was more fit for a place of debauchery than the Pope's chapel." Michelangelo took his revenge by altering his portrait of the haggard, snake-entwined Minos to resemble the sharp-nosed Biagio da Cesena, who immediately implored the Pope to have it changed. "If the artist had banished you to Purgatory," the Pope replied, "I would have used my best efforts to get you released; but as it is, I exercise no influence in Hell."

So great was the outcry against the nakedness of the saints that the Pope, after consulting Michelangelo, commissioned Daniele da Volterra to paint draperies in the proper places. Mostly they take the form of colored handkerchiefs wafted in the appropriate directions by the winds of heaven. Later still, four more painters were commissioned to complete the works of modesty. The effect was to dissipate the deliberate rawness intended by Michelangelo, who saw the human figure in its fullness and had no use for colored handkerchiefs.

The *Last Judgment* was a vast projection of the painter's secret hopes, his fears and despairs. He cherished the vision of an Apollonian Christ, the Titan king who overthrew the established order and introduced a new dispensation; he had no faith in the intercessionary powers of the Virgin, who seems to be terrified by the appearance of her Son, averting her face and shrinking into the smallest possible space; he had respect for the heroic saints, though he crowded them haphazardly together. For him, there was no order in heaven, only the blaze of Christ's presence, the fire at the heart of the fire. Just as there were no hierarchies of the saints, so there were no hierarchies among the angels, who can scarcely be distinguished from one another. He had pity for the damned, and showed them rebelling against the avenging legions of angels. As for Death, a blackened skeleton on a rock, clutching his head in stupefaction, Michelangelo granted him no nobility, no majesty. In the *Last Judgment* he is represented as a giant insect.

But in fact Michelangelo had a healthy fear of death, and had long ago determined to outwit him. "Groans, terrors, agonies, death and horror," these were his companions. So he wrote in one of his death-haunted poems, and he told Vasari: "I never had any thoughts but death left its trace on them." In his paintings and statues death is always present.

Although he lived to be eighty-nine and was vigorous throughout most of his life, he was never a well man. Very early in his letters we find him complaining about his health, forgetting that his habits of work were not conducive to prolonging life. He would work till he dropped exhausted, and he would live for days on bread and cheese. He slept in his working clothes wherever he could find a corner to sleep in. He was so absorbed in his work that he lost all sense of time, and he grudged every moment he spent away from it. He knew everyone of importance but had few close friends, and when they died he took to his bed in grief.

With his profound humility went a towering pride, for he was well aware of his tremendous accomplishments. A catalogue of his work includes only masterpieces. In art he was incapable of error, just as in life he was capable of all the errors that afflict solitary men. He poured money and presents on his worthless nephew Lionardo, but took care never to divulge the full extent of his wealth for fear that Lionardo would wish him dead. Only in the last years of his life did he find in friendship an answer to his soul's needs. The friendship of Tommaso Cavalieri and Vittoria Colonna was like a benediction to him, and in their company he softened and became human again.

Sometimes he came to regard his own works with a kind of princely disdain. Quarreling with the Medicis, he simply abandoned Florence forever, leaving behind him the unfinished Medici

Chapel with its unfinished statues. Of the four reclining figures he made for the chapel—*Twilight, Night, Dawn,* and *Day*—only two were completed, and the face of *Day* was merely sketched out hurriedly, even though he knew that all the statues were intimately related to one another and that an imperfection in any of them would reflect on the others. The *Madonna and Child* carved for the chapel was also left uncompleted. Sometimes he seems to have deliberately avoided completing a statue when he felt he had already extracted the utmost power from the stone. The figures of the *Slaves*, intended for the tomb of Julius II and now in the Accademia in Florence, are still enclosed in the rock, and therefore all the more slavelike. In sculpture he seems to have worked first on the legs, then on the torso, then on the arms, and finally on the head. When he completed a work, it sometimes gives the impression of being too complete; and when we ask ourselves why this should be so, we discover that it is because he has taught us the supreme virtue of the unfinished statue. *Day,* the *Slaves,* and the last *Pietàs* work more powerfully on our imaginations than *Moses* in San Pietro in Vincoli or the two dreaming princes in the Medici Chapel. The unfinished statues are in a state of becoming, possessing these qualities of suddenness and springing life which he demanded in sculpture. *Moses* and the two princes have been worked so masterfully and with such extreme care that they chill the blood with their phenomenal dexterity and technical brilliance before they warm the blood again with their fire. They are indisputable masterpieces, but one does not have affection for them. For the three unfinished *Pietàs,* the two in Florence and the last in Milan, demand of us that we should finish them in our imaginations.

These three statues were all the work of his last years, when his infirmities made work increasingly difficult. Now at last in grief and agony and in the knowledge of his coming death he surpassed himself. Always, up to this time, he had delighted in his power to create powerful forms. In these *Pietàs* he observes Christ in the arms of his Mother after being taken down from the Cross in all the frailty of death, the body limp, the arms drooping and the legs buckling. Christ sinks downward into the earth, while the Mother upholds him. In the great *Pietà* now standing to the left of the altar in the Duomo in Florence, he carved a towering figure of Nicodemus, who also supports Christ, with the Mother on one side of him and Mary Magdalene on the other. Nicodemus wears a monk's cowl and bears a curious resemblance to Michelangelo himself, but this resemblance appears to be fortuitous: the *Pietà* was designed for his own tomb, and it is unlikely that he would portray himself as one supporting Christ. One night, working by candlelight, he accidentally cracked the Mother's arm with his chisel. In his eyes the sculpture was ruined, and he abandoned all work on it. Another *Pietà* was started. This time the pyramidal composition was abandoned for a purely vertical construction, with the Mother standing behind Christ, whose arms fall heavily as though all the weight of mortality was concentrated in them. For some reason this *Pietà* was never finished. During the last days of his life he was working on the third *Pietà*, now in the Castello Sforzesco in Milan. This time the figure of Christ was almost an abstraction, the masklike face and body sketched in roughly, the lower limbs carefully worked, for as usual he was carving upward, leaving the features to the last. And in this nearly abstract form, slender as a wing or a leaf, Christ stands in the embrace of his Mother. In the background a powerful isolated arm, the product of an earlier version carved from the same marble block, seems to hang suspended in the air. It is as though Michelangelo were saying: "Here at last I have made my most perfect work, and here is the arm that made it!"

He was still working on the *Pietà* on February 12, 1564, but he was already failing. Daniele da Volterra remembered afterward that he worked the whole day. Two days later he was found wandering aimlessly in the streets in the rain; his speech was impeded, for he had suffered a stroke. Returning to his house he lay on his iron bed with its straw and wool mattresses, but after a while he made his way to an armchair beside the fire and sat staring at the flames; and then he would return to his bed, and get up again, complaining that he could find no rest. He had never rested during his life and he was restless in his dying.

He died at dusk four days later in the presence of Tommaso Cavaleri and Daniele da Volterra. He left no will. In his walnut strongbox there were eight thousand gold ducats, a small fortune.

Since the Pope demanded that his body should be buried in St. Peter's although it was well known that he had always wanted to be buried in Florence, he was smuggled out of Rome by his closest friends, and three weeks later the body was borne in triumph through the streets of Florence. They knew even then that he was quite simply the greatest artist who had ever lived.

The Dark Ones

There are men who seem to have a dark knowledge of the world, a strange familiarity with the shadowy places of the soul. They make war against their own time, and drive themselves headlong in the direction of the nearest abysses. They are haunted by the ghosts of the past and by the horrors of the present, and find no relief in contemplating the absurdities of the civilization they live in. They hammer against the walls and it is all one to them whether they break through, for they know that beyond the walls of their own prisons there are more walls stretching to infinity. Such a man was Michelangelo Merisi, born in Caravaggio in the lowlands below Bergamo on September 28, 1573.

We know him as Caravaggio, for the rumbling syllables of his birthplace suggest the quality of the man better than his real name. A self-portrait, introduced slyly into his painting of *The Martyrdom of St. Matthew*, shows him dark-eyed and dark-visaged, looking calmly and determinedly at the back of the naked youth who is about to run a sword through St. Matthew. Small and ugly, with a flair for self-advertisement, an unruly temper, and a viperish tongue, he enjoyed painting himself, but the self-portraits follow an unchanging pattern: there is only the head. Usually he represents himself in the head of John the Baptist lying on a silver platter, or in the head of Goliath held up by a triumphant David, the agony still quivering in the eyes and the open mouth. As he portrays himself, uncouth and savage, with his short thick beard and enormous brown eyes, he shows no liking for himself. He sees himself as pitilessly as he sees the world.

He found his vocation early, for he was only eleven when he

was apprenticed to Simone Peterzano, an obscure minor painter in Milan. His father died when he was very young, and at the end of his apprenticeship, when he was fifteen, he seems to have led the wandering life of an itinerant painter in northern Italy. He was about eighteen when he came to Rome and eked out a precarious existence as a painter of flowers and fruit. Penniless and starving, he spent some time in hospital, and on his recovery joined the fashionable atelier of Giuseppe d'Arpino, whose empty frescoes cover acres of Roman walls. He quarreled with D'Arpino, as he quarreled with nearly everyone he met. From painting flowers and fruit he went on to paint effeminate youths crowned with garlands, their flesh glowing like warm peaches in the sun, and from effeminate youths it was only a short step to youthful John the Baptists robed negligently in sheepskins, insolent and debonair. His models were boys picked off the streets. He knew them well, and he could render them with feverish precision. He had no taste for the idealized portraits of the Mannerists. Asked to admire the statues of Phidias, he replied that they had nothing to tell him. "How many better masters nature has provided for me," he declared. "I do not need your statues." He then pointed to a gypsy girl in the street, took her to his lodgings, and painted her in the act of telling a young man his fortune. The painting became famous, and it became known that a new and surprising artist had descended on Rome with the gift of painting from the model untrammeled by academic form. He saw directly and painted directly. In his paintings there is always the shock of discovery.

His early paintings are bright with color minutely observed. Gradually he learned to tame his palette, abandoning the traditional cinnabar and azure for the more somber and livid blacks, browns, and yellows, rejoicing in the contrast produced by sudden gleams of crimson. He liked to paint in a darkened studio with a lamp hanging from the ceiling, above or a little to one side of the model, so that the light had the effect of a glancing blow, giving a particularly violent contrast of vivid, clear-cut shapes against the surrounding darkness, and he liked to place the highlights in the foreground, to give depth and urgency to the dimensions of the small enclosed space in which everything took place. Light was his plaything. Together with the light hanging from the ceiling, there might be another shooting directly into the face of the model and still another lighting some detail of a chair or a damask curtain. Always the light was designed to bring out the scene in high relief, so that his paintings possess a sculptural quality, hands and faces cleaving the air, while the shadows wheel away and lose themselves in the background.

All these were new techniques, but they were dictated by the logic of his theory that the task of the painter was to represent the reality he knew, not the academic forms of the past. His models were not the superb athletes of Michelangelo or the high-born women who people the canvases of Raphael, but the common people of Rome, who wore rumpled clothes or rags, sweated, caroused in the taverns, and slept together in filthy lodgings. He would paint a dead prostitute lying on a table not long after she had been fished out of the Tiber, surround her with despairing mourners, and hang a vast crimson curtain overhead to indicate the blood-lit solemnity of the occasion, and the finished canvas, entitled *The Death of the Virgin*, would be offered to a church to decorate the altar. In fact, the picture was refused, because the clergy recognized the models, but all Rome came to admire it when it was placed on exhibition after being bought by the Duke of Mantua on the advice of Rubens. Today this vast painting is among the chief glories of the Louvre.

While Caravaggio was painting *The Death of the Virgin*, he was deliberately bringing his talents to bear against the accepted canons of the Church. Intellectually he was closer to Luther than to the Counter-Reformation, then in full swing. His Christ walked through the streets of Rome, dust-stained and haggard, and his apostles were gnarled old men, the beggars and tavern keepers of the Piazza Navona. For Santa Maria del Popolo he painted *The Conversion of St. Paul* in a manner designed to shock the worshiper. At first glance the spectator sees only an enormous sleek piebald farm horse, the quivering flanks brilliantly lit with a glancing light from above. Paul, struck by the divine vision, lies in a crumpled heap in the foreground, and he is far from being the main character of the scene. Caravaggio has sought to suggest the majesty of the vision by the play of light on the majestic horse. In much the same way, forcing his own interpretation on sacred events, he paints *The Summoning of St. Matthew* in an ill-lit room where the elderly Matthew, wearing the robes of a majordomo, gambles among handsome youths dressed up in the costumes of page boys, while from a shadowy corner there emerges an imperious hand and a familiar face. Christ, as so often in Caravaggio's paintings, hovers in the darkness.

The genius of Caravaggio was soon recognized by cultivated ecclesiastics, who hung his paintings in their own palaces even when they officially forbade the paintings to hang in a church. Cardinal Francesco Maria del Monte, a Florentine of exquisite manners and highly developed taste, learned in alchemy and statecraft, lived in fabulous luxury in the Palazzo Madama, which overlooks the Piazza Navona. He became Caravaggio's protector and official patron, and for about three years the young artist wore his livery and lived in his palace. Commissions poured in on him. The princely families of Doria and Colonna vied for his services, while young painters and poets gathered around him and acknowledged him as the genius of an age in which little genius survived. Fashionable and popular, he took to wearing the uniform of a man about town, and after a day's exhausting work he would stalk the streets in the company of his page, looking for adventures and quarreling with anyone who crossed his path. He was quick with his dagger. A lawyer who offered to marry the beautiful young woman who served as the model for many of his Virgins nearly died of his wounds. There were tavern brawls, midnight encounters, passages of arms with the police. More than once he found himself in one of the rat-infested prison cells of the dreaded Tor di Nona, the prison tower overlooking the Tiber.

He seemed to be courting death, becoming more eccentric and more dangerous with every passing month. Cardinal del Monte quietly dismissed him from the palace, and he took up lodgings only a stone's throw away. He continued to produce masterpieces, his own violence filling his paintings until they seemed about to explode from the canvas. Then at last the inevitable happened: he was playing a ball game with some friends when a slighting remark aroused him to fury, and he killed his opponent, being himself wounded in the struggle. Though he had powerful protectors, there was none powerful enough to save him from a trial for murder except the Pope, who was in no mood to forgive him. He went into hiding and made his way secretly to Naples, which lay outside the papal dominion. The paintings made at Naples betray his uncertainty, the large conceptions giving way to crowded and dislocated figures, with here and there a portrait or a gesture recalling his former mastery. A hunted man, he sailed for Malta, where his fame had preceded him. There he was given a studio and treated honorably by Alof de Wignacourt, the Grand Master of the Knights of Malta, and his genius revived.

His superb portrait of the Grand Master, now in the Louvre, and his great canvas of *The Beheading of St. John,* painted for the Cathedral of St. John in Valletta, show him at the height of his powers. He would never penetrate more deeply into character than in the portrait of the arrogant and exacting Grand Master, and with *The Beheading of St. John* he demonstrated his power to paint a scriptural event with a fierce realism and a visionary intensity unequaled in his time. There is no longer any attempt to suggest relief in recessive planes; the singularities of his temperament are abandoned; he paints with the terrible calm of the visionary who has seen the agony of sanctity and contemplated it fearlessly. The youthful St. John lies in the prison courtyard with the executioner bending over him. Salome approaches with a golden salver, an old woman flings her hands to her face in horror, and an officer of the court, standing impassively by the prison gate, points to the salver, indicating to the executioner that nothing remains except that the head must be given to Salome. From the barred windows of the prison two condemned prisoners look on with expressions of complete disinterest. It is something they have seen before, and no doubt they will see it again.

In this painting the drama of the theme is heightened by understatement. So quiet and casual is the execution that it might be the slaughter of a lamb in an abandoned corner of a farmyard, and this is precisely the effect which Caravaggio intended to produce. Yet that prison yard, with its towering undifferentiated walls brooding over the lonely actors in the scene, is forever memorable. All

Caravaggio's devotion to the beauty of youth is expressed in the prone St. John with his hands tied behind his back. The executioner is a figure of formidable physical power, against whom no other power can prevail. There is no combat; only the remorseless acting-out of an ancient crime.

According to Pietro Bellori, the seventeenth-century chronicler of the lives of artists, the Grand Master was so pleased with the painting that he gave Caravaggio a collar of gold and two Turkish slaves. The artist had already been admitted into the Order of the Knights of Malta, being made a Knight of Grace. The distinctions conferred by the Grand Master proved ephemeral. An argument with a Knight of Justice, who belonged to a higher order of knighthood, led to a brawl, and Caravaggio was arrested and thrown into prison, stripped of his honors, and in danger of being sold into slavery—the usual punishment for those who offended the Grand Master.

Somehow he escaped from prison and found a boat sailing for Sicily, where he lived in hiding from the vengeance of the Grand Master. There, in an astonishingly short space of time, he produced three canvases which are comparable in their intensity and visionary power with *The Beheading of St. John*. At Syracuse he painted *The Burial of Santa Lucia* for the Church of Santa Lucia. Once again there is a huge, empty wall, a small prone figure, and powerfully built, remorseless executioners. A handful of people watch the burial, some agitated, some indifferent. Only a frail light shines on the saint, who will vanish in a moment when the earth is heaped over her. Yet this moment is seen with a grave calm and a relentless intelligence, as though the artist were exploring still deeper into the mystery of martyrdom beyond the point where prayers can reach the dead. The painting is at once a benediction and a cry for mercy.

The agents of the Grand Master made no secret of their determination to arrest him and bring him in chains to Malta, and soon he was again fleeing for his life. He went to Messina, where he painted *The Adoration of the Shepherds* and *The Raising of Lazarus;* and while the *Adoration* differs from similar paintings only by being more earthy, so that at last we see real peasants in a real stable littered with spiky straw, *The Raising of Lazarus* is one of the six or seven absolute masterpieces he created during the course of his unruly and unhappy life.

This huge painting—it measures twelve and a half by nine feet—shows Lazarus waking into the agony of life. The winding-sheet has been unwound, and he is naked, lying across the canvas at an angle, one hand falling, the other raised high in a gesture of perfect triumph; and all round him there gather in the half-darkness disciples and strangers, while his sisters stand at his head and Christ with outstretched arm continues to summon him into life. Christ towers. Darkness descends. As Lazarus rises into life—one hand catching a mysterious ray of sunrise—there is the sense of a mystery being performed in the shadows, and perhaps for the first time in history a painter has succeeded in representing a credible resurrection. The painting, which is cracked and discolored by age, hangs on one of the walls of the museum at Messina, where a visitor is likely to find himself in complete solitude. Yet, in its fearful beauty, this is one of the greatest of all masterpieces of Christian art.

Not long after completing *The Raising of Lazarus* Caravaggio fled to Naples. The agents of the Grand Master caught up with him and stabbed him within an inch of his life outside a German hostelry. When he recovered, he decided to take ship to Rome and throw himself on the Pope's mercy, but for some reason the felucca took him instead to Porto Ercole on the southern shore of Tuscany. Porto Ercole was a Spanish enclave, and the Spanish officials regarded him with suspicion. They arrested him and set him free only when the felucca had departed. Believing that his paintings were still on the ship, he staggered along the coast as though he hoped to reach the next port of call in time to collect his possessions, and he died of sunstroke a few hours later in the malarial swamps along the Tuscan shore. In fact, the Spanish customs officers had sequestered his possessions, which they kept under lock and key in the customs house. He died on July 18, 1610, at the age of thirty-six. Three days later, knowing nothing whatsoever about his death, the Pope granted him a free pardon.

The life of Caravaggio was one of unremitting despair and

brilliance, which he channeled into his strenuous art. There seems never to have been a time when he was not in complete command of his art, just as there was never a time when he was in full command of his life. He was one of the very few artists of the first rank—Hugo van der Goes was another—who went mad under the strain of painting. But there is never any trace of madness in his paintings. On the contrary, they are distinguished by a terrible sobriety, a dazzling sanity. Because he saw the world anew with fresh and sober vision he was to have an incalculable influence on future artists, and both Rembrandt and Vermeer were heavily in his debt. During the eighteenth century his works fell into obscurity, and it was only at the beginning of the present century that critics began to pay serious attention to him. In 1951 there was held in Milan a retrospective exhibition of his works. Then for the first time it was possible to recognize the stupendous energy of his imagination and the purity of his compositions.

El Greco, who was Caravaggio's contemporary, was another great artist who had to wait three centuries before fame caught up with him. Like Caravaggio he explored unknown regions of art and painted "on the very edge of painting," evolving a style which could have no imitators and creating images of such intensity that no one setting eyes on them can ever forget them. In a strange way he has come to personify the genius of Spanish painting, although he was a Cretan who spent his formative years in Italy.

He may have been born in Italy, the son of one of those Greek icon painters called *madonneri* who lived out their obscure lives in the Greek quarter of Venice. As a youth he studied under Titian and later under Tintoretto, whose *Christ Walking on the Sea of Galilee* in the National Gallery in Washington provides the clue to many mysteries. Livid skies and broken clouds, tormented flamelike figures, space cracking wide open or melting into flame, all these can be observed in Tintoretto's painting, which is like a foretaste of things to come.

We have our first glimpse of El Greco in a letter written in 1570 by Giulio Clovio, a well-known art collector and miniaturist from Croatia, to Cardinal Alessandro Farnese. "There has recently arrived in Rome a young Cretan, a disciple of Titian, who seems to me to be one of the greatest of painters," Clovio wrote. "Among other things he has painted a self-portrait which has caused a sensation among Roman artists." Clovio urged the cardinal to take the Cretan under his protection and to give him lodgings in the Farnese Palace. This was done, and in gratitude El Greco painted a vivid portrait of Clovio with a book of miniatures, while the storm gathers and the trees bend outside the window.

We know scarcely anything at all about El Greco's apprenticeship. He appears to have been a strange, reserved, solitary man, and one of the few anecdotes about him concerns his devotion to solitude and the inner light. Clovio, who tells the story in one of his letters, relates that he called on El Greco one spring day to invite him for a walk. "But when I reached the studio, I found the shades drawn and you could scarcely distinguish the objects in the room. Greco was sitting in a chair, neither working nor sleeping. He would not come with me, for he said that the sunlight blinded the light shining within him." The story rings true. Less convincing, but quite plausible, is a story related by Giulio Cesare Mancini, physician to Pope Urban VIII, in his memoirs published five years after El Greco's death. The doctor relates that when the Pope was contemplating painting out some of the less decorous figures in Michelangelo's *Last Judgment* in the Sistine Chapel, El Greco stepped forward and offered, if Michelangelo's work were demolished, to produce another *Last Judgment* which would be no less a work of genius but considerably more chaste and decorous. According to Mancini, the Roman artists and their patrons were so outraged by El Greco's contempt for Michelangelo that they made it impossible for him to remain in Rome and he fled to Spain. El Greco himself was secretive about the reasons which brought him to Spain. In the course of one of his lawsuits he declared: "I am neither bound to say why I came to this country nor to answer the other questions put to me." He was one of those who do not offer hostages to biographers.

Although he lived a long life and obviously met many people who could be expected to write their memoirs and remember what he said to them, only one conversation with him is recorded. Francisco Pacheco, the father-in-law of Velázquez, a painter and the author of a treatise called *Arte de la Pintura*, met El Greco in 1611 and asked which he regarded as more important, drawing or coloring. El Greco said "coloring," and Pacheco professed to be surprised by the answer and still more surprised when El Greco said Michelangelo was a good man but did not know how to paint. "Greco was a man," Pacheco comments, "who opposed the generally accepted opinion and in all things, as in his painting, he was singular."

Nevertheless El Greco owed much to Michelangelo, whose works he had evidently studied in Rome with great care, for he imitates forms that were never depicted until Michelangelo painted or sculpted them. The naked, sprawling, drastically foreshortened figures in his paintings derive from the *Last Judgment* and the frescoes in the Pauline Chapel. El Greco has altered them, bent them to his own purpose, colored them with the colors of flames, set them against lightning-lit skies, but they are recognizably derivative. Indeed he acknowledges his debt in a remarkable painting of *Christ Driving out the Traders from the Temple*, apparently made in Rome about 1572, where Michelangelo, Titian, and Giulio Clovio appear together in the lower right-hand corner beside a young red-haired man with drawn features who must be El Greco, for Clovio is pointing approvingly at him.

Suddenly in the spring of 1577 he is in Spain, at Toledo, working on paintings for the High Altar and side altars of the Church of San Domingo el Antiguo, and almost at once he is displaying a prodigious originality. The main altarpiece was an *Assumption of the Virgin,* who soars out of her tomb as though propelled by cannon fire. One red-robed angel, spinning around the Virgin with skirts lifted above her knees, seems about to explode. In characteristic El Greco fashion the faithful disciples gathered around the empty tomb seem not unduly disturbed, as though the Assumption was something they had long expected. Whenever he painted heaven and earth, the violence is always in heaven. The Virgin derives directly from Titian; the exploding angel belongs to El Greco alone.

In the same year he began work on *The Despoiling of Christ* for the sacristy of Toledo Cathedral. Christ, in a vast scarlet robe, is about to have the robe ripped from him, and all round him are gathered the onlookers who always appear when a public murder is about to be committed. They are such people as a man might meet on any Spanish street, but they are huddled close together, pressing against one another and against Christ, in such terrifying proximity that they resemble a machine about to crush him with its weight. In the foreground a carpenter is hammering a nail into a wooden beam, and the three Marys look apprehensively in the direction of the nail. The church authorities objected to the presence of the three Marys as being without scriptural authority, but El Greco insisted on keeping them there. He had his own iconography and would permit no one to change it.

The scarlet robe shines like an immense glowing ruby, dominating the whole painting, so that all the other figures, even those who are touched by a cold sunshine, seem to be in a shadow. Out of the robe comes a powerful neck and an upturned face of great power and beauty, the gaze already fixed on heaven, his thoughts far from the sullen mob congregated around him. The artist has created a silence around Christ, and beyond this silence there can be heard only the low hum of voices and the hammering of the nail.

The prodigious brilliance of the work owes very little to his Italian masters; the sharply contrasting planes, the strange disharmonies, the absence of any real perspective or verifiable space are characteristic of El Greco, and of El Greco alone. One can understand the spatial formation of the painting only by assuming that Christ is walking down a nearly vertical slope.

Often when El Greco painted crucifixions, he would paint Toledo in the background, for he evidently came to possess a great affection for the city. But Toledo is nearly always spectral and transparent, as though made of glass, a ghostly city seen in a lightning flash, set in a landscape charged with menace and curiously impermanent. It was as though he felt that at any moment his beloved city might be blown away by the winds of heaven, vanishing into the surrounding darkness.

He seems to have feared darkness and therefore filled his canvases with brilliant jewel-like colors, the richest reds, the ripest greens, the most succulent yellows. There was a mystical practice then common in Spain which sometimes permitted the devotees to enjoy visions. They would set up a candle in a dark room, gaze at it intently while reciting the name of Jesus, and they would see the face of Jesus in the candle flame. St. Theresa of Avila had no need to gaze at candle flames, for her visions came naturally. "What I see," she wrote, "is a white and red such as one finds nowhere in nature, which shine and glow more brightly than anything else one can perceive, and images which no artist has yet painted, the originals of which are nowhere to be found, and which nevertheless are nature itself and life itself and the loveliest beauty that can be imagined." In a spirit of mystical exaltation El Greco painted "the loveliest beauty that can be imagined."

So he went on year after year producing those extraordinary paintings which always tend to dissolve into flame. Yet there was often a hard masculine mastery in his paintings: his portraits are solid, three-dimensional, and when he wanted to, he could portray the world around him with a great awareness of its palpable existence, but more often he painted the visionary world within him. Sometimes, as in *The Burial of Count Orgaz*, we are permitted to see those two worlds simultaneously, in equilibrium.

This painting must be counted among the most dazzling of his achievements. According to the legend, the pious Count Orgaz, a fourteenth-century nobleman of Toledo, having died a most holy death, was welcomed at the graveyard by Saints Stephen and Augustine, who were his patrons. They descended from heaven for no other purpose than to lay him in the grave with their own hands. El Greco paints the two saints in their golden vestments in the foreground, the dead nobleman lying limp in their arms, and beyond the saints stand the mourners, the nobility of Toledo, in black silk and snow-white ruffles. Directly above them an angel carries the naked and transparent soul of the count through a strange passageway into the presence of Christ and the hosts of heaven, who are all represented as flamelike, while the stately mourners are represented in the dignity of their human flesh, solid and austere.

Simultaneously El Greco has contrived a sense of upward and downward movement. The body of the count sinks slowly into the earth, and at the very same moment his soul rises dizzily to heaven. The earth is a real earth, and heaven is made credible by all the tumult around the figure of Christ. About fifty figures are seen in heaven, and there are nearly thirty on earth. The boldest of all the earthly figures are Saints Stephen and Augustine in their heavily textured dalmatics contrasting brilliantly with the icy gleams from the dead man's armor. The saints indeed belong palpably to earth: their very weight has the effect of giving stability to a composition that would otherwise disintegrate. El Greco has anchored the painting with golden weights.

Never again would he demonstrate quite the same mastery in a complex design, nor would we ever again see earth and heaven in such close communion. When, for example, he paints an Ascension, where it might be expected that a flamelike Christ would arise from a solid tomb set among solid Roman legionaries, what we see is the direct opposite. Christ is palpable flesh, and the astonished soldiers tumbling in fright and horror assume the dimensions of flame with raking lights running up and down their naked bodies, and there is no tomb at all. When he paints an Adoration of the Shepherds, the Virgin, the Child, and the shepherds are as insubstantial as the angels flying overhead. As he grew older, El Greco plunged deeper into the mysterious world of flames and sometimes he seemed to lose himself in them, dazzled by the intensity of light he had himself created.

For thirty-seven years he lived quietly in Toledo in a vast twenty-four-roomed house in the Jewish quarter. The house belonged to the Marquis of Villena, who was long suspected by the Inquisition of being a practitioner of black magic. Here he lived with his wife, Doña Jerónima de las Cuevas, their son Jorge Manuel, and perhaps half a dozen pupils and assistants. Like Giulio Clovio he made many miniatures of his paintings to serve as reference works for future compositions, and like Tintoretto he made small clay models to study the effects of lighting and foreshortening; indeed, many of his later figures have the consistency of clay or wax and he must have painted directly from these models. He lived quietly, taking no part in the life of the city: in the records of Toledo he is mentioned only in connection with the lawsuits he fought against the ecclesiastical authorities who paid him insufficiently, but there is no reason to believe that he was unduly litigious. Like all mystics—like St. Theresa of Avila and William

Blake—he could be profoundly practical when he thought it necessary.

When he died in the summer of 1614, two years before Shakespeare, an inventory was made of his effects. He was evidently not selling all his paintings, for an astonishing number of them were still in his possession. Altogether there were 143 paintings, mostly finished, still lying in his studio. There were nearly fifty models in wax, clay, and plaster, filling an entire cupboard. There were 120 drawings, presumably his own sketches, of which only three or four have survived. He left over a hundred books, the greater part of them in Italian. There were only a few books in Spanish, and it is possible that he never learned to speak the language well. Among his books was the *Mystical Theology* of Dionysius the Aeropagite, a work of great beauty celebrating the divine light.

El Greco lived by the divine light, Caravaggio by the divine flesh. One painted exaltations, the other painted elegies for the living and the dead.

There is a sense in which Diego Velázquez was their spiritual descendant. Born in 1599, the son of a minor Portuguese nobleman living in Seville, Velázquez very early showed a remarkable gift for painting, and he was ten years old when he was apprenticed to Francisco Pacheco. It is possible that he was present during the famous interview with El Greco, and it is certain that he came under the influence of Caravaggio, whose works were especially admired by Pacheco. Indeed, all Velázquez's early works betray the influence of Caravaggio, although he subtly modifies the forms invented by the great Italian. He began by painting peasants, workers, tradesmen, ale boys, and ended by painting a long series of portraits of emperors and courtiers, princesses and court buffoons, and always he was seeking for an essential nobility. When he paints some topers applauding a half-naked boy garlanded like Bacchus, we are aware that he is depicting a charade and at the same time we are aware of the humanity of these men gathered together in a monumental tribute to Bacchus. We are also aware that the Bacchus derives directly from Caravaggio and at least one of the topers has already appeared in Caravaggio's *Supper at Emmaus*. Caravaggio's influence on him was so pervasive that he evidently found himself fighting against it. Velázquez's early paintings are proof that a surprisingly large number of Caravaggio's paintings were in the possession of Spanish collectors.

Velázquez was totally lacking in the tragic sense, and he had little interest in religious subjects. What interested him above all was the drama of nobility as it is observed in the human face. An ale boy or a girl at a loom, a cretinous dwarf, defeated soldiers, a young prince hardly old enough to walk, a poor water carrier, and the King himself all belonged in some mysterious way to the confraternity of nobility. Just as he never, or very rarely, painted for money but always insisted on painting for his own pleasure, so he never painted anyone or anything he did not admire. Having divested himself of religious scruples, he was free to devote himself to the contemplation of human personality. Riches and success came to him early, for he was appointed painter to the King at the age of twenty-three, and therefore the ordinary preoccupations of humanity meant very little to him. He was one of the few artists permitted to accomplish their work in sovereign ease, and he took full advantage of his singular good fortune.

Nevertheless Velázquez remains an enigmatic character in the history of painting. He possessed extraordinary talents but very little experience of life; and having no interest in mysticism, a subject which appeared to absorb El Greco, or in the spiritual dramas which absorbed Caravaggio, he could quite easily have developed into an indolent, cynical, and somewhat mechanical painter of royalty. There was no doubt that he was indolent, for the King sometimes complained about it. "I am well aware of his phlegm," the King wrote to the Spanish ambassador in Rome, when Velázquez was visiting Italy, giving himself up to an orgy of indolence. Nevertheless the King gave him high appointments, and during their long friendship, which lasted nearly forty years, scarcely a year passed without some new appointment or honor, and Velázquez must have painted Philip IV at least forty times.

Velázquez seems to have been a man without passion, except the passion to paint. He had the aloofness of a surgeon, the instincts of the aristocrat, the ignorance of a courtier. He lived at a time of unprecedented corruption, the Spanish Empire falling into

ruins, ruled by a succession of royal favorites who were incapable of
governing, but no one seeing Velázquez's paintings would ever
guess at the extent of the corruption or the viciousness of the court.
In this enclosed world he moved like a man in a dream, coming to
life only when he found himself confronted with the enigmas of
personality in a human face or with some problem connected with
the art of painting. He would unravel the enigma and solve the
problem with startling ease.

Of the seven or eight works which may be regarded as his
supreme masterpieces, *The Surrender of Breda* is the most trou-
bling. Technically, it is superb. All the problems of composition, perspective, and texture are triumphantly resolved, and we are brought
into immediate confrontation with the Spanish general, Ambrosio
de Spinola, and the defeated Dutch general, Maurice of Nassau,
who bends his head and offers the keys of the city to the victor;
and Spinola, placing one hand on Maurice's shoulder, as though in
commiseration, is presented as the magnanimous soldier who honors
the defeated and will assure them the most lenient terms; and indeed
he was a man of great nobility and courage, and truly magnanimous.

Although the scene is magnificently composed and gives an
impression of extraordinary credibility, with the staffs of the two
generals arranged behind them, the burning city in the misty blue
distance, two handsome chestnut horses vying with the soldiers for
our attention, and some thirty pikes belonging to the Spanish Guard
dramatically emphasizing the victory, something is missing. The
faces are painted with depth and penetration, the gestures are exactly
observed, the illusion of reality is sustained, but we find ourselves
disturbed by the knowledge that it could not possibly have happened
in this way, and what we are seeing is another charade, a stage
performance by living actors against a painted backcloth. The defeated, who have been starved for eleven months into surrender,
look wonderfully healthy. There is no blood, no wounds. The miseries of Breda are relegated to the remote blue distance, and we
might be observing the visit of two emperors accompanied by their
escorts. The scene is bathed in the light of a noble serenity.

The Surrender of Breda is so vivid and compelling a work that
scholars have gone to some pains to probe its sources. They dis-

covered that the composition derives from an engraving by Bernard Salomon showing the encounter between Abraham and Melchizedech, that the city of Breda is faithfully copied from an engraving by Hermannus Hugo, that the group of Spanish soldiers derives from El Greco's *Espolio,* and that almost every figure except the two superb chestnut horses, which belonged to Philip IV, was derivative. Although the composition was built up piecemeal, Velázquez succeeded in interpreting the event with a prodigious originality, powerfully impressing his own almost impressionist style over the whole painting so that it acquired a sense of unity. Proud of the painting, he deliberately omitted to sign it, although a blank piece of paper was painted in to receive his signature. Instead, immediately above the piece of paper, he painted a portrait of himself as one of the members of Spinola's staff.

He painted himself again even more presumptuously in his finest work, *Las Meninas,* showing the visit of the five-year-old Princess Margarita to his studio in the palace. He stands beside a huge canvas, on which he is painting portraits of Philip IV and Queen Mariana, and shows himself to be a tall, well-set, rather ponderous man with smoldering dark eyes and the look of one accustomed to command. He wears a costume of black silk with slashed sleeves revealing the silver lining, perhaps because black and silver were his favorite colors. It is a painter's portrait of a painter, sketched rapidly and convincingly, with absolute authority. Four brushstrokes, and he has made a hand. Another stroke of the brush, and he has made a collar. Everything about the painting suggests a dazzling self-assurance.

We see the King and Queen in a distant mirror; they are spectral presences. The radiant Margarita takes her place solidly in the middle of the canvas, her serving women around her, two dwarfs in attendance, a nun and a majordomo in the background, while in the distance another majordomo is seen descending a flight of steps leading to the studio, pausing as though in midair at the spectacle unfolding before him. The studio, usually so quiet, is bustling with activity. The young princess has just burst in to pay her respects to her royal parents, who are standing exactly where the spectator stands, and we are therefore seeing the scene through their eyes.

Once again we can detect the sources. There are details reminding us of Titian and Tintoretto, whose paintings he had copied during a prolonged visit to Italy, but no one else could have achieved such tumultuous magnificence, such an explosion of sunlit atmosphere. He has given the spectator the illusion of having entered by chance into his studio during a royal visit, but in fact the composition was built up from a multitude of separate studies minutely contrived and the element of chance is totally lacking. Like *The Surrender of Breda*, the painting disturbs by its theatricality, but it is all deliberately contrived. Velázquez was a painter of superb intelligence and he knew at all times exactly what he was doing.

But it was above all in his portraits that we are aware of his intelligence at work as he probes deeper and deeper into the mind of his subject. The surgeon's knife flashes in the air and cuts deep in the wound. His portrait of Pope Innocent X in scarlet and white, composed after a brief sitting, must be counted among his greatest accomplishments. Crafty, sullen, cruel, generous on occasion and sometimes compassionate, more imperial than any emperor, the Pope emerges into abundant life and still inspires a kind of terror in the hearts of those who come suddenly on the painting in the Doria Gallery in Rome. Philip IV inspires a different kind of terror, for Velázquez painted him always in such a way that his essential weaknesses become apparent. Arrayed in majestic costumes, his wrinkles smoothed out, his fading hair shining with a golden light, he nevertheless shows himself as a frightened, self-indulgent, and tyrannical man. Velázquez was kinder to the young princesses and the cretinous dwarfs employed by the court, perhaps because they were beyond the reach of his intelligence. He made numerous portraits of them—there are at least twelve portraits of dwarfs and buffoons and about fifteen portraits of princesses—and was evidently fascinated by them, although he could penetrate only a little way below the surface. He is known to have painted many nudes, but only one, the *Rokeby Venus* in the National Gallery in London, has survived. She lies on a black silken sheet superbly aware of her own beauty. She, too, derives from Titian, but where Titian is concerned to create a setting for her beauty, Velázquez concentrates on the pearly flesh, the luster of her youthful and careless body. Somewhere, in some deserted monastery attic in Spain, there may be an entire collection of Velázquez nudes sequestered by the Inquisition and since forgotten.

Velázquez eclipsed all his Spanish contemporaries. The patient Zurbarán, who loved to paint the folds of monkish gowns, "crisp as frozen snow, soft as cotton, heavy as cream," devoted his life to religious paintings of a curiously somber kind. Ribera, who spent most of his life in Naples, painted equally somber figures with no rippling gowns to conceal their suffering flesh. Like Caravaggio, whom he worshiped to the point of imitation, he could paint the withered flesh of an old peasant and make it holy. Murillo, born twenty years after Velázquez, living for most of his life in Seville and painting scenes out of picaresque novels and holy pictures, surrendered too easily to the charm of his models. On occasion he could paint a ragged peasant boy with a wonderful detachment which did not exclude affection. Zurbarán, Ribera, and Murillo were all magnificent painters, but they had the misfortune of being the contemporaries of Velázquez. He could have shaken them all out of his pocket handkerchief.

The dark intelligence of Velázquez, which revealed itself in every stroke of the brush, seems always poised for the kill. His superb arrogance did not prevent him from taking immense pains over paintings which seem to have been produced effortlessly; and indeed it was the mark of the aristocrat that he should do everything effortlessly, whatever the difficulty. Until the time of Goya no Spanish artist rivaled him; he was one of those giants who create deserts around them.

Caravaggio painted the griefs of the flesh and the spirit. El Greco painted the ecstasy of heaven. Velázquez painted the nobility of man. Between them they encompassed a whole universe.

RIPENESS AND DECAY

The Desperate Visionaries

The eighteenth century in Europe was a century of lost hopes and
the beginning of the modern age. When it began, Peter the Great
was on the throne of Russia, and when it ended Napoleon was on
the way to becoming Emperor of the French. We speak of it as an
age of enlightenment, and certainly there was increasing knowledge,
but there was also an increasing despair. The ancient traditional
patterns of life were breaking up in the face of the industrial
revolution and the failure of the Church to offer a way of life
suitable for an age of violent change. It was an age of tyranny, and
the tyrants benefited by the new weapons placed in their hands by
the scientists. Almost without exception the great painters of the
eighteenth century turned away from the present and lost themselves in unavailing dreams of the past.

The return to the imaginary past is a phenomenon often wit-
nessed in the history of art. Rome in the age of Augustus looked
back to Hellenistic Greece; the painters of the Sung Dynasty looked
back to the far greater painters of the T'ang Dynasty. There is
scarcely a Roman statue in existence which does not resemble a
distant copy of a statue made at the time of Alexander the Great,
and there is scarcely a painting by a Sung master which does not
proclaim its derivation from Wang Wei or Wu Tao-tzu. The masters
of the eighteenth century, at odds with their own time, looked
back to a golden age or took refuge in mythologies. Watteau,
Chardin, Fragonard, Canaletto, Guardi, Tiepolo, Piranesi, Goya,
and Blake—all in their various ways escaped from the age they
lived in and invented their own imaginary worlds. No one seeing
their work would ever have guessed that the age of enlightenment

had come. On the contrary, their paintings and engravings proclaim the supremacy of the senses and the ravaged nerve ends.

With Antoine Watteau the austere academism of the French seventeenth century comes to an end. Suddenly there is a voice speaking plainly and urgently about a strange predicament of the spirit, a *malaise* so terrible that it can scarcely be borne. The characters of his paintings are the gaily appareled men and women of the time, or the actors of the *Commedia dell' arte*. They are drawn with wonderful precision by an artist who had made innumerable careful studies after Rubens and who was in complete mastery of his craft, but those masked balls, *fêtes galantes,* and assemblies of courtiers are rarely what they seem to be. Watteau is always the stranger looking on, separated from his characters by his poverty and despair. His clowns have not come to amuse us. Like Rouault's clowns they have come to ask terrifying questions.

With Watteau we fall into the trap before we are aware that there is any trap at all. The gleaming silks, the baroque architecture of the gardens, the astonishing air of verisimilitude which he gives to these formal eighteenth-century gardens, all these suggest that he was well acquainted with the lives of the rich and the carefree as they paraded in their country estates. In fact, he knew very little about them. His most prestigious painting, known as *The Embarkment for Cythera* and usually regarded as a picture of young gallants and their women about to embark for the island of love, actually shows them about to leave the island. They are returning to the cold familiar world, all passion spent, and in their gestures there is the weariness and gentleness of despair. In the sky the light is fading, and soon darkness will have fallen on the island.

Watteau was the son of a master carpenter and roofer from Valenciennes, once an important city in Flanders but at the time of his birth merely an outpost of northern France. His ancestors were Flemish, and his masters were Rubens and the great Flemish painters of an earlier age. As a youth he came penniless to Paris and lived by painting religious pictures wholesale in a factory, where he earned an occasional bowl of soup and three livres a week. He was wretchedly poor, already suffering from the consumption that would kill him. A few connoisseurs who recognized his genius came to his rescue, and he was able to spend the last years of his brief life in comfortable poverty. He was a lively companion, sweet-tempered and intelligent, but difficult to help. He held the affection of his friends, who were drawn to him by his charm, his wit, his intelligence, and his obvious integrity.

The force of his intelligence can be seen in his studies of clowns and in his crayon drawings with the unerring sharpness of line. There is no frailty in them. When he painted his *fêtes galantes,* the outlines are blurred and everything is bathed in a blue diaphanous light. The figures are very small in comparison with the immense overarching trees, and it is therefore impossible to recognize the expressions of their faces. If we could see them more clearly, they would resemble clowns. They are all masqueraders in an indifferent world, where everything is transient, and even the most gallant of them will never stay long enough to receive his reward. It is high summer, and the leaves are heavy on the trees, or so it seems, until you remember that it is a painted backcloth and soon all the trees will roll away and the stage will be empty and a cold wind will scatter the masqueraders.

Baudelaire, who studied Watteau carefully and counted him among the greatest of painters, to be set beside Michelangelo, Rembrandt, Rubens, Goya, and Delacroix, spoke of his "fresh and gentle settings lit by chandeliers pouring madness on the swirling dance." But it was not madness so much as desperation which illuminated those scenes where the lovers are always remote from one another even when they are in one another's arms.

With his steady gaze, Watteau saw the world whole and found it terrifying. For him, art was salvation, the only salvation worth thinking about, and he could see no obvious connection between a work of art and the financial reward, with the result that he was continually giving his paintings away. Once he gave a wig maker two of his oil paintings in exchange for a wig, and reproached himself for not having given a third painting. When his friend the Comte de Caylus reproached him for taking so little care of his fortune, with hunger and illness awaiting him unless he spent some time acquiring wealth, he answered: "If the worse comes to worst, there is always the public hospital. They don't turn people away, do they?"

Watteau was a portent of the time, a man who seems to incarnate a whole age. He died with his work scarcely begun, in the summer of 1721. He was thirty-seven, a dangerous age for painters, for both Raphael and Van Gogh died at that age.

Jean-Baptiste-Siméon Chardin, who was born in 1699 and died eighty years later, was a man of very much the same spirit. He was gentle, improvident, casual in his dealings with his patrons, discreet to the point of silence, with no great faith in the providence that rewards artists. Like Watteau he was the son of a master carpenter, and like Watteau he was a superb technician, with a vast knowledge of his craft. Like no one else he painted the familiar objects of the kitchen: jugs, tables, chairs, bottles, loaves, grapes, pomegranates, a heap of oysters, a dead hare, a skate hanging from a hook on a wall—he painted them with the same enduring affection as he painted his occasional portraits. A stone-walled kitchen was his refuge: the bread still smoking, the fruit succulent, even the absurd and ugly skate melting in its juices. He could paint a copper water cistern set down on a three-legged stool as though it possessed the everlasting sobriety of a chair by Van Gogh. His world is Eden, never trivial, extraordinarily calm. "These things stand," he seems to be saying, "and all the rest is vanity."

All the rest included the age of enlightenment, through which he lived. He painted only the things he knew, and he had not the slightest interest in the world of the court, or of fashion, or of the marketplace. He never painted a nude or a silken dress or a pretty face. He never so much as raised his head to look out of a window to admire the passing crowds: people and the sky are rarely present in his paintings. He would paint a kitchen and put his wife or a maidservant in it, and this was enough. Paradise was a pomegranate on an earthenware plate.

In his own way Chardin was escaping from his own time into a golden age where jugs and roughhewn cups and all the bare necessities of life reigned in perfect silence, every object in harmony with every other object. The French called these paintings *natures mortes*, but in fact they were still lives. Such works of art were not regarded highly in an age of artifice: a rich man could hardly be expected to decorate his walls with scenes from Chardin's kitchen. Nevertheless his paintings were bought, often by other artists, who recognized his genius and hoped to discover how he achieved the intense luminosity of his colors. He was very reticent, and rarely spoke about his art. Once he told Diderot that he could see no purpose in academic training. What was the use of copying plaster casts? It was better that a man should paint the world around him.

He lived quietly and obscurely, married twice, and endured the grief of losing two daughters in their early childhood. His son by his second marriage grew to manhood, learned a little about painting, was captured by Barbary pirates, escaped, and finally died in Venice, apparently a suicide. Chardin went on painting. He was elected to the Academy, and in due course rose to become a councilor, then the treasurer, and finally the official *arrangeur* responsible for hanging the pictures in the salons. Toward the end he abandoned oils for pastels, perhaps because he could no longer tolerate the smell of oils. He died in the official apartment set aside for him in the Louvre, having outlived all his friends and leaving behind a small collection of unsold paintings.

Chardin was a giant, and not only because he could paint a loaf of bread or a jug of wine and give them more true dignity than anything that existed in the palace at Versailles. By exploring the simple shapes of things he was giving art a purpose, which was notably lacking in the age of enlightenment. He gave weight and density to color, and he seems to have invented the method of applying pure colors close to one another, so that an apple, for example, when viewed close up, vanishes in a rainbow of colors in the same way that a mosaic when viewed close up seems to have no relation at all to the subject depicted on the wall. An apple by Chardin is an exercise in consummate daring because it involves the recreation of an apple out of pure colors, soberly, tranquilly, with immense patience. When he was painting, he refused to let anyone watch him, for good reason. He was engaged on an appallingly difficult task which needed all his reserves of strength and concentration. By this heroic endeavor he enlarged the bounds of human sensibility.

No one would ever say of Fragonard, who was briefly Chardin's pupil, that he enlarged the bounds of human sensibility. He painted for the purest pleasure—his own and other people's. Gay, amusing, decorative, his paintings reflect the voluptuous proclivities of the dying monarchy, and no one ever painted elegant nudes with so much fervor. The tragedy was that he possessed great gifts, which he squandered in an effort to remain fashionable. The painter of amorous allegories lived to see the monarchy perish and a new monarchy arise, but long before the French Revolution he had outlived his usefulness. He died in 1806, and to the very end he was bewildered by the passing of his fame. Fifty years after his death he was remembered by the Impressionists, who delighted in his swift and nervous colors.

The Venetian Giovanni Battista Piranesi died in 1778, a few months before the death of Chardin. Their paths never crossed and they were totally unaware of each other's existence, but they had much in common. They were determined men who created their own universes. Their formidable art had nothing whatsoever to do with the age they lived in. Chardin could have been a contemporary of Vermeer, Piranesi a contemporary of Michelangelo. Just as Chardin throughout his lifetime studied only what he saw in his stone-walled kitchen, leaving to others the task of painting everything outside the kitchen, so Piranesi reserved for himself the small corner of the world which he called *Magnificènza*, meaning "the stupendous." He delighted in immense crumbling ruins, palaces and triumphal archways which he reproduced in a vast series of engravings. The ancient ruins of the Etruscans and Romans were invested with a majesty they had never possessed, and no one ever gave to massive blocks of crumbling stone such monumentality and intensity. Piranesi resurrected ancient Rome and magnified it until it assumed the shape of another city altogether—the city the artist had wanted to see, had hoped to see, and had to invent, because it no longer had any existence.

Like many Venetians he was a heavyset, broad-shouldered, powerfully built man with a ferocious temper and a sharp tongue.

He quarreled violently with Giuseppe Vasi, his first teacher, and very nearly murdered the doctor who attended his daughter. He was almost certainly thrown into prison when he was in his early twenties. He was about twenty-five, and at the height of his genius, when he began to draw the long series of prison scenes which are his greatest claim to fame. Those dark, terrifying prisons, with their endless stairways and galleries, their vast heraldic monuments left over from another age, their coldness and clamminess, are not entirely imaginary. These are prisons as seen by prisoners, when the full horror has only just dawned on them. Piranesi engraved his prisons as though he were engraving the features of someone he had known, hated, and loved, with a fierce and unyielding passion.

It is the modern vision: man lost in the immensity of his own prison, where there are stairways but no doors, and where the jailers have fled, so that no one knows what is demanded of him, what stairway he should climb, what cell he should occupy. In nearly all these engravings huge ropes hang on pulleys from the high ceilings. To us, living two centuries later, these ropes, though menacing, merely add an exciting decorative element by emphasizing the vast height of the building. For Piranesi they had a very different connotation. Prisoners were sometimes bundled into baskets attached to these ropes, then the baskets would be pulled up to the ceiling, and suddenly the rope would be spun out, the basket would be allowed to fall two hundred feet while still attached to the rope, and when the rope was completely played out and the basket was a few feet from the stone-flagged floor, it would jerk to a halt. At that moment the prisoners in the basket were exactly in the position of men who had been thrown two hundred feet off a wall, for all their bones would be broken. The softly waving ropes signified death.

These prison scenes, begun when Piranesi was about twenty-four and resumed when he was forty, were profoundly original, the product of an intensely personal vision. Here and there, in those cavernous halls, he would sketch in the shape of a ragged prisoner, or else, along a distant overhanging catwalk, there would be an insectlike prisoner making his way to an unknown destination. In the engraving illustrated in this book two immense battle flags, so old and threadbare that they are flaking away, loom over a giant stairway guarded by gigantic images of Roman trophies; and from every balcony men lean down to watch the passing scene, while on every slender, creaking ladder men make their perilous journeys, but what is chiefly notable is that nothing whatsoever is happening, there is no passing scene, there is only emptiness, *nada*, the tragic vision coming at last to its perfect expression.

In his engravings of the Roman ruins Piranesi followed the same method of pouring his own desolate romanticism into everything he saw. A Roman archway in his engravings is never an archway as seen by the naked human eye, never a photograph. Piranesi took the arch, reshaped it in his imagination, and then etched it on the copperplate as though it were twice as large and five times more magnificent, and he gave to the stone a luxuriant texture altogether different from the stone quarried by the ancient Romans. His engravings were published in editions of 4,000, and many of them reached England. Before embarking on the grand tour, young Englishmen would study the engravings carefully and look forward to the time when they would be standing among ruins as vast and as beautiful as Angkor Wat, and they would return a little dispirited, having seen only a few tawdry monuments which did not compare with the engravings.

Piranesi was an inventor of ruins, the creator of a new ancient Rome. In much the same way his contemporary Giovanni Battista Tiepolo invented entire mythologies and painted them with absolute conviction, filling the ceilings of ducal houses with sunlit heroes and goddesses set against soft ethereal skies. Like Piranesi he was a Venetian with astonishing powers of invention. Did the Prince-Bishop of Würzburg desire to have frescoes in his palace? Tiepolo invented the mythology, painted a heaven of unprecedented brilliance, and peopled it with his inventions. God appears among the clouds; Alexander the Great rides in a heavenly chariot; Apollo leads the German Emperor Barbarossa by the hand. He had a taste for scenes of martyrdom, while crowds watch silently from marble balconies; and he painted heavens filled with cascading angels and chariots with such assurance that he almost convinces us that these heavens exist. He worked with amazing rapidity, traveled all over Europe painting churches and palaces, and seems never to have

spent an idle moment. When he wearied of painting elegant eighteenth-century figures lolling among the clouds or naked martyrs
having their throats cut, he amused himself with brilliant wash
drawings of fantastic clowns and goblins, delighting as much in his
comic inventions as in his absurd and wonderfully colored heavens.

These comic drawings had a long history, and they were not
always comic. Thin, spidery, clownlike creatures had appeared in
Pompeian frescoes, where they could usually be observed prancing
menacingly in the foreground. No doubt they derived ultimately
from Greek origins, and were intended to represent men in a state
of nature, untamed and uncivilized. They were the sons of the
earth, *filii terrae*, hinting at sorceries. They reappear in the paintings of Magnasco, who cultivated a world peopled with tiny hermits,
debauched gamblers, and loose-living nuns seen in the flickering
light of the forest or of vast candle-lit rooms, where they gleam like
wax. Magnasco's world was valid and coherent, intensely personal,
menacing, strangely compelling, as far removed as possible from the
enormous rainbow-colored figures of Tiepolo's imagination. Yet they
shared a common affection for these little fantastical creatures. Indeed, these creatures had taken up their habitation in the eighteenth-
century imagination, and there was scarcely an artist who did not
amuse himself with them. Magnasco made them look like congealed
fumes from a sewer, Tiepolo made them fat and dumpy, while
Piranesi depicted them as the inhabitants of his imaginary prisons,
resembling dark ghosts wrapped in dank feathers. These strange
creatures were not grotesqueries or caricatures: they had a life of
their own, and they had come to stay.

Whether they came ultimately from Greece or from Pompeii
or from the medieval manuscripts on which the monks sometimes
drew the features of the familiar devils who haunted their lives,
they were surprisingly prevalent during the age of enlightenment.
They represented one aspect of the age, and not the least formidable
aspect. They had much to do with despair and death, and they were
the brothers of the succubi and the werewolves. The *capriccio*,
meaning a creature of pure fantasy (the word derived from *capra*,
a goat), was related in a roundabout way to the ever present Pan,
the wild creature of the woodland, who despised all the works of

civilization and held them to scorn. Jacques Callot, who had drawn these strange creatures with great skill in an earlier age, depicted them as though they were deadly insects in human form, and they were about an inch high. By the time of Piranesi they had grown to be three or four inches high. Goya would paint them on the walls of his house near Madrid, and they would be larger than life.

Francisco de Goya y Lucientes was born in the obscure Aragonese village of Fuendetodos in 1746, the son of a gilder and the grandson of a notary. His mother seems to have been descended from a noble family from Saragossa, and certainly came from a family which had once possessed considerable wealth. Francisco was born in a small, dark farmhouse built of massive stone such as might belong to a peasant. For some unknown reason the gilder had left Saragossa to live the life of a poor peasant. Goya came out of the impoverished bourgeoisie, and spent his boyhood in sullen poverty.

By the time he was thirteen, we find him apprenticed to the painter José Luzán y Martínez, who had learned from Tiepolo the use of bold colors and who had received from the Inquisition the title of "Corrector of Indecencies," which gave him the privilege of adding substantial loincloths to the paintings hanging in churches. He was a mediocre painter, a hard taskmaster, and a pleasant friend. Goya complained of his methods of teaching: a pupil was instructed to paint from plaster casts until he could almost cry out with horror at the sight of plaster. Goya preferred to paint what he saw in the streets. There is a story that when he was about seventeen he was involved in a bloody feud in the dead of night. When it was over, there were three people dying of knife wounds lying in the gutter. Goya fled to Madrid.

The story may not be true, but certainly he saw many bloody fights in his time. He knew the life of the city dwellers and of the peasants, he had a rich sense of color, and if he was deficient in design, this would be remedied later. By the end of 1763 he was in Madrid, competing for a scholarship awarded by the Society of San Fernando. He failed, lived miserably for a while, sailed for Naples, visited Rome, where he is said to have climbed the dome of St. Peter's and engaged in picaresque adventures among

Roman cutthroats. In Naples he entered a competition organized by the Parma Academy, and though he failed to win the prize he was awarded a commendation for his "warmth of expression" and the excellent technical qualities of his work. Then he returned to Saragossa, apparently without any great ambition to establish himself elsewhere. He was twenty-five, and he might reasonably expect to remain a provincial painter for the rest of his life.

For more than two years he painted the walls of neighboring monasteries. They were terrible paintings in the style of Tiepolo, with choirs of angels and deep-breasted female figures sunning themselves on banks of clouds. A fortunate marriage to Josefa Bayeu, the sister of a court painter, led to his employment as a designer of cartoons in the Royal Tapestry Manufactory in Madrid. In sixteen years he produced sixty-three cartoons for the manufactory. Some were magnificent, some pedestrian, some appalling, with the people looking like painted cardboard. He was beginning to move in fashionable circles, and his portraits of influential patrons were being noticed. He painted the Infante Don Luis de Bourbon, the younger brother of King Charles III, surrounded by his family. These portraits were always uneven, he still had trouble establishing relationships between the people in his paintings, and he had not yet mastered the art of painting groups. He was still the provincial lucky enough to have a few contacts at court.

If he had died at the age of forty, very little would ever have been heard of him. He was one of those who develop slowly, cautiously, and then by sudden leaps. The sixty-three cartoons for the Royal Tapestry Manufactory showed him to be a brilliant colorist, the paintings of courtly patrons showed him to be an uneven judge of character. There was no urgency, no wrestling with the angel. He was aware that time was running out. "I am grown old," he wrote to a friend when he was forty-one, "and there are so many wrinkles on my face that you would not recognize me except for my flat nose and sunken eyes." Half of his life was over, and the best was yet to come.

About this time a decisive change can be noticed in him. As he became more successful, he became more somber, more reflective, more daring. As court painter to the fat, amiable, and

wholly inept King Charles IV, he enjoyed the privileges of the
court, painted the King and his family brilliantly, with only the
faintest trace of sardonic amusement, and continued to refine his
skill. His figures begin to stand out, and the rococo influences derived
from an early admiration for Tiepolo begin to wither away. There
can be seen the first gleams of a swift intelligence, like light running
up and down a sword blade. It is as though he had spent his life
painting in a state of happy indifference, relying on his native skill,
and now quite suddenly he was determined to paint with the full
force of his intelligence.

In the autumn of 1792 he suffered a complete nervous and
physical collapse. The causes are unclear, and it is possible that
even Goya did not know what had brought about this rending of
his whole being. For nearly a year he remained prostrate, suffering
from delirium, giddiness, interminable hallucinations, robbed of
sight, speech, and hearing. When at last he recovered, he was
stone deaf, and for the rest of his life the only sound he heard was
a strange, high-pitched buzzing, which sometimes drove him to the
edge of delirium. This illness burned away the last vestiges of the
charming extrovert. In the place of the illustrator there emerged
the moralist.

Goya's change of direction was not brought about by the
terrible sickness that afflicted him. The change had begun before,
and when he left his sickbed he continued in the direction he had
already taken. His skill in portraiture was undiminished; nothing
had been lost, but much had been gained. There was now a cutting
edge to his brain: when he wrote or made known his opinions, we
are aware of the sharp play of the mind, and when he painted we are
aware that the brush is guided as much by his intelligence as
by his sensitivity. No one would have accused Watteau or Chardin
or Tiepolo of possessing intelligence: their virtues lay elsewhere.
With Goya, we are brought into the presence of a formidable
directing intelligence, all the keener because he was often in despair
and sometimes on the edge of madness.

Recovering, he set to work on a series of eleven small paintings
which he called *Popular Digressions,* saying that the subjects had
occupied his imagination ever since his sickness. "They would

enable me," he said, "to make some observations for which commissioned works generally give no room, and in which fantasy and
invention have no limit." Now, perhaps for the first time, he was
painting solely for his own pleasure. They were harsh compositions
intended to describe popular amusements, especially those amusements which he found depressing. A procession of half-naked
flagellants are seen slicing each other to ribbons beneath a serene
statue of the Virgin. In a madhouse he observes naked lunatics
at play, one crowned and thinking he is a king, another violently
attacking an invisible opponent, another praying vehemently over a
naked boy, who may be dead, but he may be pretending to be dead
in order to provide the old man with an excuse for his prayers. In
The Burial of the Sardine he paints a delirious, drunken mob dancing to honor the sardine, which can be seen in the outstretched hand
of a woman white as a sheet. These masquerades fascinated and hor-
rified him, and there were more to come.

Between painting the portraits of the aristocracy, he would
return again and again to this world of vulgarity and violence, the
only too familiar world he saw whenever he walked through the
streets of Madrid. In *Los Caprichos,* a series of eighty etchings produced between 1796 and 1798, he explored this world at his leisure.
It amused him to draw priests with asses' heads and politicians with
the faces of dogs. Others whom he detested were given the beaks
of rapacious birds, the snouts of wolves, the gaping mouths of the
damned. In one of the most carefully worked-out etchings he shows
himself asleep beside a table, his head buried in his hands, while
poisonous birds and bat wings fill the air, and there is the inscription:
"The sleep of reason produces nightmares." He had sketched out
many versions of this etching. In one variation he looks down at
himself with a mocking smile and the air is filled with the faces of
people laughing. In another a bat with a vast wingspread is about
to perch on his head. In the final version the air is dark with the
ghostly shapes of owls and bats all crowding round him and over
him, while a white cat looks on with studied nonchalance. It is a
portrait of a man at the mercy of the phantoms of his imagination,
and utterly cast down. For the rest of his life Goya would see these
phantoms in his waking dreams.

The sleep of reason also produces wars, and the Napoleonic invasion of Spain brought about the devastation of large areas of his homeland. His own safety was never in doubt, for he was court painter successively to Ferdinand VII, King Joseph Bonaparte, and the Duke of Wellington, but the eighty-two etchings comprising *The Disasters of War* show him in a state of absolute despair. There is no evidence that he ever saw the nightmares he depicted with such terrible accuracy: men choking in their own blood, or hanging like dead fruit from the trees. The horror was all the more horrible because it sprang from a tormented imagination and an overwhelming grief; a nihilistic fury and a hopeless abandonment to a vision of all-consuming evil. A dead man half rises from his grave and has just enough time to scrawl the world *"Nada"*—Nothingness—on a scrap of paper before the assembled demons thrust him back into the earth, and there is not the least doubt that Goya saw himself as the dead man. *The Disasters of War* are at once a document against war and its obscene works, and an intensely personal statement of his own helplessness in the face of a society which seemed to be composed of murderers. Never before or since has anyone conveyed the obscenity of war so brilliantly or so dispassionately.

One might have thought that *The Disasters of War* would have exhausted Goya's absorption in the evils around him, but he continued to plunge deeper and deeper into a world of terror. On the walls of his house, the Quinta del Sordo, the House of the Deaf Man, on the banks of the Manzanares River, he painted terrifying nightmares in broad, impressionistic, agonized strokes; and where previously he painted the terror that roams over the earth, he now painted terror robed in its metaphysical majesty. Giant Saturn devours his own daughter, the evil witches assemble for the mysterious Sabbath, the masklike murderess brandishes her sword, two men sinking in quicksand cudgel each other to death, and over the emptiness of space a giant dog glares menacingly, as though it wondered what had happened to all the decaying flesh in the vast nothingness of creation.

Goya's terrible understanding of terror increased with the years. It was no romantic filibustering with demons; he painted the terror at the heart of things, seeing man corrupt and evil, irremediably cast out from the regions of divine grace, because he is committed to evil as a moth is committed to a flame. In his etchings and drawings divine grace and human pity have no place; he is the detached artist concerned only with the exploration of a particular landscape. In *The Disparates, or Follies,* a series of twenty-two etchings which remained unpublished until after his death, he went still deeper into that landscape, but by this time he seems to have lost the thread of discernible meaning in the shapes of terror. Strange dolls cavort, hooded figures walk on stilts, ghostly shapes emerge out of the encompassing darkness—a man advances across a road with another man's head skewered on a pole, and people watch him slyly or turn away in despair. On a white horse the dazzling queen of the circus dances lightly, and the crowd watches happily, for the horse is poised perilously on a single rope. All things are falling, he says, and he records the fury of the fall, the stampede of the Gadarene swine.

Yet even during the periods when he was clinging to the edge of madness, the superb portraitist continued to paint those portraits which are a denial of madness. They are sober, earthbound, filled with human character and affection. He painted his grandson Mariano about the same time that he was painting his nightmare visions on the walls of the Quinta del Sordo, and the boy, in his velvet coat and frilly lace collar, is a masterpiece of demure innocence and impudence: in a moment he will have divested himself of coat, collar, and top hat, and he will be playing with all the other ragamuffins in the street. In Goya the human eye and the visionary eye were in curious equilibrium. He was seventy years old when he painted *The Third of May, 1808,* that visionary and at the same time only too earthly description of an execution of Spanish stalwarts by a French patrol outside the walls of Madrid. In a blaze of cadmium yellow a prisoner throws up his hands in a wild gesture of despair that embraces all his comrades, all Madrid, and the dark skies.

Goya lived to be eighty-two and was painting to the very end. His last painting, completed shortly before his death, was a portrait of a milkmaid of Bordeaux, where he had taken refuge. In her lightness and grace the milkmaid is a strangely prophetic figure, for she might have been painted by Renoir in the high tide of

Impressionism. Goya reached far back into the ancient past and far into the future, and he belongs among those rare artists—Titian was another—who come to maturity at a time of phenomenal change and thus reflect all the potentialities of the changing times.

William Blake, almost the exact contemporary of Goya, was poet, painter, and engraver. He, too, drew his sources from a distant past, his early poems being almost indistinguishable from Elizabethan lyrics, while his hard, wiry line derived ultimately from the medieval brasses in Westminster Abbey, and therefore from the time of the Crusades. Yet his imagination was not bound by lines: impulsive, willful, and exuberant, he painted and drew with visionary power, and no other English artist could rival him in depicting the shapes of heaven and hell.

He was born on November 28, 1757, the son of a London hosier, who sensibly permitted the boy to leave school at the age of ten to attend a drawing school. At fifteen he was apprenticed to James Basire, a master engraver, for a period of seven years: that long apprenticeship gave him a subtle mastery of the techniques of copperplate engraving, so that he was able to invent new processes to satisfy his needs. He was a technician as well as a mystic, and the elaborate engravings that accompany his poems testify to a prodigious skill. These engravings were later painted in watercolors of astonishing purity and brilliance.

Outwardly, he lived a life of calm obscurity always, close to poverty, with few friends and few supporters, little known, derided as a madman by people in high places who rarely troubled to take a second look at those illuminated books which are now the glory of the museums lucky enough to possess them. Unlike Goya, he had no instinct for advancing himself. It was a drab life, with starvation always waiting for him. Inwardly, it was a life of heroic activity and spendthrift expenditure of energy, of continuous conquests achieved with the utmost daring. He was one of those men so determined to live for their art that they are scarcely aware of the outside world, and he was happy in his poverty.

In letters to his friends, in proverbs and rules of art, Blake expressed his belief in art as the essential activity of the human soul. "Exuberance is Beauty," he wrote. "Think always on excess,"

pure gas-flame shading to silver and powdery white on the horizon. It is a rich and satisfying color, and the painters evidently rejoiced in it. They painted the sky as though it consisted of blue waves breaking on the deeper blue of heaven and throwing up golden wave crests. The sun rides in his four-wheeled chariot, and he has the face of Christ.

There are many mysteries about these illuminations, and the most insoluble is how anything so perfect could have been produced at a time of such misery. No doubt the Limbourg brothers came from Flanders, where all the conditions for the great Flemish revival in the arts were being prepared, and they were the contemporaries of the Master of Flémalle. Their art is not essentially French, but they were painting scenes in France with a peculiarly French gaiety and sensibility. These were the last real landscapes to be painted in France until the middle years of the nineteenth century.

After the Limbourg brothers the light went out of the French sky. The French painters of the Renaissance shut themselves up in their studios and resolutely refused to paint in the open air. Abbot Suger had opened the windows of the Gothic cathedral to the sunlight; the Sainte-Chapelle was a jewel box with only enough wall to support acres of colored glass; the French theologians and philosophers incessantly debated the nature of light and color. Lucidity, clarity, luminosity—these were the words most prized by the French intelligence, but they had vanished from the world of French art. The greatest painters of the eighteenth century seemed to fear the sunlight. Watteau painted his backgrounds as though he were painting stage sets; Chardin remained obstinately in his kitchen, while Ingres remained permanently in his drawing room. Not one of the painters of the age of the Roi Soleil gave any indication that he had looked at the sun, or walked down a country lane, or seen the peasants at their haymaking. The heavenly blue of the *Très Riches Heures du Duc de Berry* had vanished, it seemed, beyond recall.

During the middle years of the nineteenth century there emerged a group of great artists who broke through the studio walls and painted the earth and the sky as though they were drunk with light.

The age of Prince Louis Napoleon was not one that could be expected to produce masterpieces, and he was far from being another Lorenzo de' Medici. He objected strongly to the words Liberty, Fraternity, and Equality, and ordered them painted out wherever they appeared in the streets. It was the age of Offenbach and of Baron Haussmann, who carved long straight streets through Paris so that the artillery would have a clear field of fire against any insurgents. The French bourgeoisie was in the saddle and riding hard on all the forces that had produced the French Revolution.

The revolutionaries who suddenly appeared on the scene and changed the course of French painting were themselves members of the bourgeoisie. They were small shopkeepers or the sons of shopkeepers, judges, bankers, noblemen. They broke free from the constraints of academic painting and looked at the world as though no one had ever looked at it before. If they did not look with any penetrating depth and failed to produce a single artist who could rank with Michelangelo or Rembrandt, this was because they were concerned with the appearance of things, not with the dark depths. The eye opened wide, and the world was seen to be full of summer pools and clear, washed skies, of blazing cornfields and dappled woodlands. There was a soft, smoky texture to the air, and everyone was bathed in it, and the sun glinted off the wild poppies in the fields. The light of the sky and the light on water especially delighted them and they attempted to paint light as it was, not as the academic painters saw it. According to the academic tradition, if you painted someone walking in the woods, you stood him up in the studio and put in the sky and the trees later. It was not in the least necessary to look at a real sky or to examine a real tree, because everyone knew what they looked like.

In fact, everyone had forgotten that nature existed. Even Delacroix painted his wild seas in the studio, arranging his models on a raft supported on cushions: the sea was an academic sea, too blue and too strident. Corot made luminous sketches of landscapes in his sketchbook, but they were for his own eyes and few people were permitted to see them until after his death. The sketches were worked up in the studio, and the finished painting would be provided with an academic varnish for the benefit of the hanging committee. Nature was recorded in pencil, and the colors were added in the seclusion of the studio. Skyscapes were unheard of. This is all the more inexplicable because the skies of France have an incomparable richness and delicacy in the north and a ferocious savagery in the south, crying out to be painted.

The first man to paint the French sky was Eugène Boudin, a frame maker and the owner of a stationery store in Le Havre. In 1850, when he was twenty-six, he won a scholarship to Paris which enabled him to study for three years. When he returned to Le Havre, he was more perplexed than ever. He had learned nothing. He went on painting in his own way, using watercolor to record the immense reaches of space rising above the seashore. Baudelaire, who met him in Honfleur, was immensely attracted by those skyscapes and by the painter. He spoke about Boudin's extraordinary skill in painting fiery skies—"immensities of green and rose, suspended and piled one upon the other, gaping furnaces, firmaments of black and purple silk, crumpled, tossed, torn to fragments, horizons in mourning, horizons streaming with molten metal." Boudin himself was inclined to regard his skyscapes more coolly: he was a man who observed carefully and recorded what he saw. On the margin of his watercolors he inscribed the date, the time of day, and the direction of the wind, and as Baudelaire observed, it was quite unnecessary, for you could guess the time of day and the direction of the wind without looking at the inscription. Boudin spent the rest of his life—he lived to 1894—painting the seacoast and the towering skies. Sometimes he painted people walking along the beach.

Today Boudin is nearly forgotten, and perhaps he would have been forgotten completely if he had not chanced to peer into an ironmonger's window one day in 1858. Hung up in the window were a number of rather cruel caricatures drawn in pencil by the seventeen-year-old Claude Monet, whose father owned a local grocer's store. Amused by the caricatures, and recognizing a certain skill, Boudin sought out the boy and encouraged him to paint. The young Monet had very little interest in painting, and very soon he was called up for his period of service in the Army. He served in Algeria in the Chasseurs d'Afrique, and only took up painting seriously when he returned to Le Havre in 1862, spending the summer painting with Boudin. The lesson he learned from his friend came to him with all the force of a revelation.

For the rest of his life Monet was in love with color, all colors, but especially the brightest and those that shone with the gleam of metal or shimmered like fountains in sunlight. He liked to paint fields of flowers, seascapes, rivers, fleecy clouds, all dappled things, and was so intensely preoccupied with color that we are never quite sure whether the women he painted had bodies under their vivid clothes. In this he was unlike his friend Auguste Renoir—they had met at art school and subsequently joined forces to earn a living in Paris by painting portraits of merchants at fifty francs each. Renoir had a formidable sense of volume, and was happiest painting rather plump, smooth-fleshed nudes in sunlight, giving them a wonderfully rich glowing luster, which derived perhaps from the years of his apprenticeship in a porcelain factory, for his nudes have both the glow of porcelain and the glow of flesh. When Monet painted women, they gleamed like petals.

Renoir was deeply interested in the shapes of things and in the world around him. Monet had very little interest in the world, and he was absorbed in the study of light to the exclusion of almost everything else. There was an element of mysticism in him. He said once that he would like to paint like a blind man who has suddenly recovered his sight. In 1857, the year before Boudin encountered Monet in the ironmonger's shop, the same idea had been expressed more theoretically by John Ruskin in *The Elements of Drawing*. "The whole technical power of painting depends on our recovery of what may be called the *innocence of the eye,* that is to say of a sort of childish perception of those flat stains of colour, merely as such, without consciousness of what they signify, such as a blind man would see them if suddenly gifted with sight."

The image of the blind man overwhelmed by a sudden, startling visitation of light was profoundly appealing to Monet, who always painted as though he was seeing the world in a sun-drenched haze. He was solitary and aristocratic in manner, while Renoir was sociable and convivial. Renoir painted with his eyes and his mind, and we are aware of his immense skill and his delighted pleasure in his skill. Monet painted with his eyes alone, permitting them every licence, endowing them with powers of contemplation and thought: he was a mystic in tranced adoration of the colors of the earth. "Monet is only an eye," Cézanne said, "but what an eye!" That ambiguous tribute was no more than the truth.

Of all the painters who came to be known as the Impressionists Monet was the only one who consistently maintained an unchanging style. There was scarcely any sense of development; at the end of his long life he was still painting the dappled, formless shapes of sunlight. When he painted haystacks, he might have been painting the interior of a furnace: the hay becomes flame. When he painted Rouen Cathedral, he might have been painting a model of the cathedral made out of ice cream, for there is not the slightest suggestion of stone and only the faintest suggestion of structure. The light melts, glints, fuses, throws out streamers of brilliant color, falls back upon itself; and the cathedral vanishes in a tumultuous haze.

At Giverny, where he settled late in his life, he diverted the course of a small river and made it flow through his garden, and so arranged it that the overflow became a pool of water lilies. Willows grew on the bank, and nothing pleased him more than to meditate beside the silent pool. The meditation took the form of endless paintings without any composition whatsoever, blue lilies dissolving in blue water, the reflections of the willows pouring over the pool, and the gold speck may be a dragonfly pausing on the open petals of the lily or it may be a sun speck. His friend Georges Clemenceau commissioned vast panels of water lilies for the Louvre. The visitor to the Musée de l'Orangerie may see these paintings hanging in a circular room, covering the entire wall, and everywhere he looks, he sees the summer pool glowing with brilliant splashes of blue and green and yellow, a sun-drenched splendor.

Renoir was the son of a poor tailor; Monet was the son of a grocer. Edouard Manet, who was to bring the Impressionist movement to a sharp focus and receive more than his fair share of abuse from the critics, came from a considerably richer and more influential stratum of society. His father was chief of personnel in the Ministry of Justice, his mother was the daughter of a diplomat who was largely instrumental in elevating General Bernadotte to the Swedish throne. As a young man, he wanted to paint, but his father wanted him to become a lawyer or a naval officer. Since these were the only choices offered him, he chose to become a naval officer and in 1849, at the age of seventeen, he sailed to Rio de Janeiro as an apprentice pilot. The colors of Rio entranced him, and he was more than ever determined to become a painter. Returning to Paris, he argued that there was no alternative to painting and he proposed to study in the painting classes of Thomas Couture, an intelligent and kindly academic painter. Thereafter there were no more battles of will, and he spent the rest of his life painting. When his father died in 1862, he inherited a fortune.

Monet and Renoir knew poverty; Manet lived in state and kept a stable of servants. In 1852, when he was barely twenty, he had an affair with a pianist, Suzanne Leenhoff, by whom he had a son, known as Léon-Edouard Leenhoff. The boy officially passed as Suzanne Leenhoff's younger brother and was not legitimized until a month after the death of Manet's father, when Manet married the mother secretly in Holland. There were to be no more adventures. He lived quietly and placidly, dressed elegantly in frock coat, silk cravate, and top hat, held open house for his fellow artists, and enjoyed the company of fashionably dressed women and attended the more fashionable cafés. Yet there was something faintly spurious in his elegance. Monet, who sported a lace-frilled shirt and a gold-handled cane even when he was living in grotesque poverty, was the more naturally the dandy, because he was more naturally driven by the knowledge of his own genius. Manet was more self-critical, more skillful, more respectful before the masters, and totally incapable of those prolonged meditations, like prayers, which filled Monet's existence. They were both at odds with society, but for different reasons.

Manet's respect for the masters led him to make careful copies of the works of Titian, Rembrandt, Fra Angelico, and Goya, but he learned most from Velázquez, saying after a visit to Spain that he was overwhelmed by the genius of the Spanish painter. Like Velázquez, Manet painted with the objectivity that comes from seeing the world in a mirror, standing apart from it, never permitting himself to be caught up in its illusions because he was himself playing the part of an illusionist. He had only one thing in common with

Monet, but this was the most important thing. He rediscovered for himself the secret of painting with harsh, strong dabs of color. Unlike Monet, he was able to build up volume and thus give depth and perspective to his paintings.

His most famous paintings were deliberate exercises in transforming old masters into new masters. His *Déjeuner sur l'Herbe* was based on Giorgione's *Fête Champêtre*, with the nude women enjoying the countryside among clothed men, and in addition he borrowed a set of postures from an engraving of Raphael's *Judgment of Paris*. The painting was saturated with classicism even to the extent that he posed his sitters in his studio and added the unconvincing trees and their even less convincing foliage later, so that they exist in a dark vitreous green limbo. He succeeded in painting a nude as it had never been painted before, so assertive in its nudity, so harsh, so strong, that it seemed to leap out of the canvas altogether and take up an independent existence of its own. The French public was scandalized, and Manet was viciously attacked in the press. His *Olympia*, evidently modeled on Titian's *Venus of Urbino*, which he had copied during a trip to Italy, and perhaps also on Goya's *The Naked Maja,* was an even greater scandal. The elegant demimondaine, wearing a thin black ribbon round her neck, an orange-colored orchid in her hair, a richly ornamented gold bracelet, silk slippers, and nothing else, is being attended by a Negro maidservant, who carries a bouquet of flowers from an unknown admirer. At the foot of the bed there is a black cat with its tail flying in the air. The critics raged over it for weeks. Outraged propriety demanded a victim, and it was remembered that Baudelaire and Manet were close friends: clearly Manet had been influenced by Baudelaire to paint one of the flowers of evil, and had not Baudelaire been brought before the courts, publicly pilloried and heavily fined? Manet wrote to Baudelaire that "curses are raining down on me like hail." One angry critic described the nude as "a female gorilla." Very few people realized that Manet was using slashes of color in a totally new way to express a peculiarly modern attitude to the world. He was determined to introduce sweeping simplifications, violent contrasts, sudden alterations of tone, improbable and startling colors. The central figure is bathed in a fierce light, as though a spotlight had been directed on her, and all the rest of the painting vanishes in sporadic shadow.

In the last year of his life, when he was suddenly attacked by locomotor ataxia and could scarcely walk, a prematurely old man who leaned trembling on a cane, he painted *Le Bar aux Folies-Bergère*, his final act of homage to the joy of light. A barmaid stands at a bar with a curved mirror behind her, and the mirror has the effect of throwing her reflection far to the right, so that we see her twice and find ourselves wondering whether they are the same people. In the depths of the mirror we see the crowded tables, splinters of light falling from a heavy chandelier. The spotlight is thrown frontally on the barmaid, who stares straight out of the painting with an unseeing gaze full of thought and a certain bewilderment. She blocks the way into the picture in the same way that Velázquez so often blocks the way into his paintings by rooting his figures solidly in the foreground. Her lace-trimmed bodice reveals a wide expanse of breast; the face is pearly and pink; her black velvet coat and gray silk skirt resemble an exaggerated hourglass, and the sheer weight of the figure pulls the center of gravity down toward the marble-topped table. She is isolated from the rest of the painting, and all round her there is only a vast shimmer of broken lights, gleaming oranges, gold foil on champagne bottles, faces seen in the mirrorlike gleams of light from cut glass, and in one of the upper corners there appear the green boots of a trapeze artist, as though to suggest that somewhere in the remote heights some violent activity was still going on even though no one is paying any attention to it. But what the picture conveys is a moment of absolute stillness, the stillness that takes place when you see a girl coming toward you across a room and you are aware only of her presence and all the rest of the room fades into oblivion.

Into this painting Manet was pouring all he had ever learned. He was not painting what he saw, although the model came to his studio and stood endlessly behind a table. He was painting light and air and also the air which lies imprisoned in mirrors, and he was painting the intense emotions aroused in a dying man by the world of colors. In all this he was not very different from Monet, with his

Saturn Devouring One of His Children, by Francisco Goya.

From The Prisons, by Giovanni-Battista Piranesi.

Nada. Ello Dira (Nothing. We Shall See)
From The Disasters of War, by Francisco Goya.
PRIVATE COLLECTION.

When the Morning Stars Sang Together, by William Blake.

The Italian Woman, by Georges Rouault.
TATE GALLERY, LONDON.

Tahitian Women with Mango Blossoms, by Paul Gauguin.

Les Demoiselles d'Avignon, by Pablo Picasso.

Man Awaking, by Henry Moore.
JERUSALEM UNIVERSITY.
ROBERT PAYNE.

passion for rippling water, rippling skies, and the multitudinous fragments of color thrown up by the silent lilies in his silent pool.

Emile Zola spoke of a certain austerity in Manet, and it is true that he possessed an austere manner and a total devotion to his art; there was also a curious bitterness. With almost his last words as he lay dying—his left leg had been amputated, and his circulation and nervous system were in disarray—he spoke bitterly about the attacks on him, which had never ceased since the day when he first showed his paintings. Why had so few people understood him? Once Zola told him that the time would come when his paintings would hang in the Louvre, and he had only shaken his head in disbelief. He died at the age of fifty-one, his friend Monet surviving him by forty-three years.

Manet never regarded himself as an Impressionist and never exhibited with them. He regarded them with a certain impatience, as though they had embraced too many revolutionary concepts and he would have preferred them to advance more slowly. Yet he often painted with the same brazen indifference to form, the same intoxicated enthusiasm for sunlight. Monet had acquired a small studio boat, little more than a rowing boat with a blue cabin in which he could store his canvases and take shelter from the sun. One day Manet painted him sitting comfortably in the bow of the boat with his easel in front of him; and in this painting all form vanishes, there is only a brilliant scattering of light, the blue boat melting in the blue water, the sky melting in the misty shore, and the only fixed and stable thing in the whirl of colors is the bearded face of Monet seen in profile, looking exactly like one of those princes who appear in Indian miniatures. It was Manet's tribute to the man who was chiefly responsible for the break with the traditions of the past.

Historically, the break had come about at a period when French society was undergoing acute and terrible stresses. Prince Louis Napoleon had become Napoleon III, and the apparent stability of his regime concealed intolerable tensions. The industrial revolution was at its height, and there is a sense in which Impressionism can be understood as an escape from the overwhelming demands of an industrialized society. In hundreds of different ways the patterns of society were being changed. Portrait painting was no longer in demand: its place had been largely taken by photography. In the past a painter ground and mixed his own paints, but after 1861, with the invention of tube paints, this no longer became necessary. For the first time a painter could march out into the country with a dozen tubes of paint in his pocket and with his canvases strapped to his back, and he could sit down and paint wherever he pleased. Tube paints gave him mobility and freed him from the restrictions of the studio. Finally, Japanese wood-block prints were reaching France in increasing numbers and the French artists were astonished and delighted by the works of Utamaro, Hokusai, and Hiroshige, with their unconcern for formal balance and their extraordinary skill in suggesting a whole figure when presenting only a part.

The painter who was most deeply influenced by Japanese wood-block prints was Edgar Degas, the son of a banker. Like Manet he was born to wealth, and like most wealthy men he was coolly indifferent to the plight of humanity, with the result that there is little warmth in his paintings and pastels. Nor did he have any great respect for the Impressionists, although he was counted among them. He detested painting in the open air and he disliked their "spectrum palette" with its bright prismatic colors. "You know what I think of people who work out in the open," he said. "If I were the government I would have a special brigade of gendarmerie to keep an eye on artists who paint landscapes from nature. Oh, I don't mean to kill anyone, I would be quite content with a little birdshot now and then as a warning." Then he added: "Renoir is all right. He can do anything he likes."

Degas, who descended from the minor Italian nobility, was a man of firm opinions and strict loyalties, an anti-Dreyfusard, a stern moralist, conventional to the point of caricature. Yet in art he had an exquisite daring and a wonderful gift for unexpected color, although he liked to regard himself as a man pre-eminently talented in drawing. He had trained himself as a painter in Florence, and the swift, decisive Florentine line remained with him to the end. He lived near the Opera, frequented the racetracks and the racing stables, attended the theater, and knew all the right people, but permitted nothing to get in his way, protecting his talent by every subterfuge, pretending to detest the women he painted with so much affection for their flesh. In the end of his sight gave out and he suffered the cruelest fate that any painter can suffer. With his heavy white beard, and wearing an Inverness cape, he wandered through the streets of Paris nearly blind, tapping his cane. He died in 1917 at the age of eighty-three, having outlived all the Impressionists. "I want to be famous and unknown," he said once, and these words may well serve as his epitaph.

Between Degas and Henri de Toulouse-Lautrec there were strange similarities of style and temperament, of passion and aristocratic contempt, of elegance and delicacy. Lautrec descended from the ancient Counts of Toulouse, his father a rich landowner, the owner of many carriages and many mistresses, his mother a quiet and deeply religious woman of aristocratic descent. At fourteen Lautrec fell and broke his legs; they never grew again; and for the rest of his life he resembled a dwarf. The legend that his deformity embittered him and led him into a profligate existence dies hard. In fact, he had an angelic temper, laughed and sang while he painted, enjoyed all the pleasures of life, charmed all his friends, and never painted a portrait in which he did not honor the sitter. Unlike Degas, he possessed a gift for poetic fantasy and liked to present a scene slightly askew, deliberately emphasizing a bizarre detail, rejoicing in his power to suggest the whole by means of a significant part.

His genius lay in his humanity, his calm, his ironic gift for observing what no one else dared to observe. He sometimes spent days in brothels, observing that the prostitutes were considerably more alive than their clients. He painted them without compassion, for he honored them too much to pity them. "Those people are full of life," he observed. "Look how they stretch themselves on the divans like animals." In the same spirit he painted the circus, the racetrack, the theater, dance halls, cabarets, and he had the happy gift of being able to catch quick movement. His earliest paintings were of horses galloping swiftly, but as he grew older he preferred to paint in his studio with the model sitting in front of him, sometimes demanding as many as seventy sittings.

Absinthe killed him. In the last years of his life he fought a losing battle with alcohol with the help of a friendly "watchdog" installed by his mother. The watchdog drank as furiously as Lautrec, and soon Lautrec was committed to hospital for treatment. There, recovering from delirium tremens, he drew from memory a series of circus drawings which have the dry, mordant wit of Daumier at his best. Released from the hospital he continued to paint with immense skill, but without energy. He died in his mother's château in the south of France in 1901. He was younger than Raphael when he died, for he was only thirty-six.

Among the most startling of Lautrec's drawings is a portrait of his friend Vincent van Gogh seen in profile, seated at a café table, thin, nervous, evidently trembling as the result of some inner agitation. He leans forward a little, and one has the impression that at any moment he will be caught up by some invisible power. He does not seem to belong to this world.

When Van Gogh received the orders of his superiors commanding him to abandon preaching to the mine workers of the Borinage because it was thought that he was behaving eccentrically when he gave his possessions to the poor, he was only twenty-seven, but he had already failed in many other occupations. He had been a teacher of English in London, an apprentice art merchant, and a student of art. With the mine workers he felt he had found his vocation. Now, with a feeling of despair, still regarding himself as a priest possessing the care of souls, he turned to painting. He came to it with the fervor of an Old Testament prophet, and no worldly failure ever discouraged him from the belief that as a painter he was ministering to humanity, to the sick and the suffering. His power, his energy, were gifts placed at the service of mankind.

He began to paint when he was a schoolboy, but his paintings were no better or worse than those of any talented boy and he had long ago abandoned his gift. He began to paint seriously in 1880 after returning to Holland from Belgium. He received little encouragement, and was largely self-taught. In November 1885 he entered the Antwerp Academy because he wanted to draw from the living model, and was told that his drawing was so bad that he must enter the beginners' class. In the spring of that year he had completed his masterpiece *The Potato Eaters*.

When he came to Paris in February 1886 a new life opened out for him. Gradually he abandoned the dark earth colors of his palette and the somber portraits of peasants. He had seen his first Japanese prints and for the first time encountered the Impressionists; and he was never to forget the revelation of Japanese design or the sunlight drenching the paintings of the Impressionists. There were given to him four and a half miraculous years in which to explore the newly discovered landscape of art. During a period of twenty-seven months spent in the south of France he painted like a man possessed.

At first he had wanted to paint the peasants "like potatoes, with the skin on them, fresh from the earth," and *The Potato Eaters* was a triumphant vindication of his early style. Paris released him from his bondage to the peasants. He painted the houses and the wharfs, haunted the Louvre, met Toulouse-Lautrec and many other painters, and lived on the bounty of his younger brother Theo, an assistant in the Goupil Gallery. Then abruptly, having learned all that Paris could teach him, he took the train for the south of France, determined to paint in the sunlight. It was February 1888, and Arles, where he got off the train, was still under snow.

His friend Paul Gauguin once drew a caricature of Van Gogh sitting on an Alpine peak and busily painting the sun. It was a friendly caricature, and there was a good deal of truth in it. The dark earth colors were abandoned for lemon green, red ocher, and chrome yellow, which Van Gogh regarded as "the color of God," and when the spring came a few days later he gave himself up to a prolonged exaltation. He painted the orchards of flowering almond trees as though he could never exhaust their beauty—altogether he painted sixteen paintings of almond trees—and when the summer came he was out in the fields painting the cornfields in the sweltering heat. He still painted portraits, with brilliant red, blue, or green backgrounds, thus granting to a French soldier, a postman, or a local boy a curious hieratic character, so that they stood out in sharp relief with an extraordinary authority; and though they were painted indoors, they seem to be lit by the sun that blazed over the fields.

In the evenings, returning from work, he gave himself up to drinking bouts, which weakened his health. He was already a sick man when he invited Gauguin to come and stay with him in October. Gauguin possessed a tyrannical belief in the justice of his own theories of art, and took it upon himself to teach Van Gogh how to paint. Inevitably they quarreled, made up, and quarreled again. One day Gauguin was crossing a street when through the corner of his eye he saw that he was being following by Van Gogh with an open razor. He slipped away and spent the night in a hotel. The next day he learned that Van Gogh had cut off his ear during the night, placed it in an envelope, and handed the envelope to the doorman of a brothel. Absinthe, the southern sun, and the quarrels with Gauguin had driven Van Gogh over the edge of madness.

For the rest of his life Van Gogh was aware that he was living on borrowed time, with the knowledge that at any moment he might suffer another and more dangerous attack. He committed himself to a lunatic asylum at Saint-Remy, where he continued to paint, read Shakespeare, and submit to "the regimen which the incomparable Dickens prescribes against suicide"—a glass of wine, a piece of bread with cheese, and a pipe of tobacco. He had the same unbounded admiration for Shakespeare that he had for Rembrandt. "What Rembrandt has alone or almost alone among painters," he wrote to his brother Theo, "that tenderness of gaze, that heart-broken tenderness, that glimpse of a superhuman infinitude—in many places Shakespeare has it too. And then above all he is full of portraits, just like Rembrandt's *Jan Six* and his *Traveler* and his *Saskia.*"

The lunatic asylum was a converted thirteenth-century monastery lying at the foot of the Alpilles. He remained there for a year, hating his enforced incarceration, happy when he was permitted to paint in the nearby fields. For long intervals he was lucid and calm, and to this period belong the famous paintings of cypresses licking upward like flames with the tormented mountains behind them, and it is usually supposed that the frenzy of the cypresses and the exploding mountains reflect a deterioration in his condition. In fact, the Alpilles have the wildest and most improbable shapes, and cypress trees bend and twist voluptuously when the mistral is blowing. Van Gogh was recording the scene accurately. He had a passion for cypresses. "They are always occupying my thoughts," he wrote, "and it astonishes me that they have not yet been done as I see them—the cypress is as beautiful in line and proportion as an Egyptian obelisk."

He went on painting and dreaming, all the time aware that he was a prey to suicidal mania, at the mercy of forces beyond his control. "*Je grandirai dans la tempête,*" he said once, "I shall grow in the storm." But the storm was fiercer and more destructive than he realized, and a few weeks after being released from the asylum, while staying at Auvers-sur-Oise, just outside Paris, he shot himself. During his lifetime he had sold exactly one painting and a number of drawings.

Both Van Gogh and Gauguin were deeply learned men with a vast knowledge of the theory and practice of art. Gauguin made a special study of Memlinc, worked as a ceramicist, and was equally proficient in sculpture and wood-block engraving. They were both latecomers to painting: Gauguin took up painting at the age of thirty-five, abandoning a successful career as a stockbroker. He had hoped to make a living as a painter, but his savings disappeared in eight months and for the rest of his life except for a brief period when he enjoyed an inheritance he was immersed in poverty. He had married Mette Gad, who belonged to a prominent family in Copenhagen, and went to live with her in Denmark, sponging on her relatives. He abandoned his family and went to Brittany only because he had heard of a cheap lodging house at Pont-Aven, but even in Brittany he could scarcely afford to live, and he dreamed of escaping to Tahiti. When he was staying with Van Gogh in Arles, financial difficulties were just as exasperating as they had been before.

A violent and domineering man, he was determined to live for his art. Some of his violence came from his ancestry of mixed Inca, Spanish, and French blood. His grandmother Flora Tristan was a brilliant revolutionary, his grandfather André Chazal attempted to murder her and was sent to prison. Gauguin expressed his own inner violence in his paintings with their explosive colors. His *Vision after the Sermon* shows Jacob wrestling with the Angel in a field in Brittany, while the white-coiffed village girls look on in calm amazement. There is a purple tree cutting diagonally across the painting, and the field where Jacob wrestles with the Angel is ruby red. The technique might be called imaginative Impressionism, for he was not painting what he saw before his eyes: he was engaged in recreating what he had seen and deliberately distorting it until it assumed the shape of visions. Just as Van Gogh regarded painting as a sacramental and priestly art, so Gauguin regarded it as a visionary art: every painting should be a vision reduced to intelligible form. "A powerful sensation should be translated with immediacy," he wrote. "Dream about it, and seek its simplest form." By "simplest form" he meant the primitive and archetypal form which lay beyond civilized sensations. Naturalism was the enemy: Greek art was responsible for the slackening of vigor in the arts. "One should go far back, farther than the Parthenon horses—as far back as the *dada* from my childhood, that good old wooden rocking horse." And always there was the need to go back into the most ancient springs of a man's being. So in the *Vision after the Sermon* the wrestlers, though they occupy only a small portion of the canvas, possess an archaic vitality that threatens the existence of the village girls. What he wanted most from his painting was a certain rough and compelling music. "When my sabots fall on this granite earth," he wrote during his stay in Brittany, "I hear the muffled, deadened and powerful sound I seek in my paintings."

In 1891, at the age of forty-three, he abandoned France and sailed for Tahiti. Living in a small village some forty miles from Papeete, he trained himself to paint as though he were a Tahitian, with primitive wonder and a sense of the wholeness of the earth. It was an extraordinary adventure into unknown territory. He was well aware of its dangers and penalties. A new kind of painting, "the sound of the sabots," began to emerge, but often the colors seem to be restless, the background obtrudes, there is the sense of incoherence, as though he were trying to say something he could not fully express. But from time to time, as in *Vahine no te tiare*, the portrait of a Tahitian girl holding a gardenia, now in Copenhagen, and in *Aha oe feii*, which shows two naked women on the sands, now in the Hermitage in Leningrad, he demonstrated a new mastery of the figure, a dazzling self-assurance. The visionary eye was opening wide; and from those golden bodies there came the hint of even greater splendors.

"It took me almost a year to learn how to paint the Tahitians," he wrote. Once he had learned, there was no turning back. He returned to France in the hope of finding a dealer and settling his complicated affairs. Two years later he was back in Tahiti, where he spent the last eight years of his life. After months of terrible suffering, he died alone in his small hut on the island of Hiva-Oa on May 8, 1903.

To the very end he was making discoveries. He painted with savage energy, a fierce delicacy. In the year before his death he painted *The Summons, The Gold of their Bodies,* and *Barbaric Tales,* which were among his supreme achievements, during a period when he was sick and poverty-stricken and waging a hopeless war against the local authorities. In a letter to Daniel de Monfreid he wrote in October 1897: "The great error is the Greek, however beautiful it may be. Have always before you the Persians, the Cambodians and a bit of the Egyptians." Yet the Greeks haunted him, and though he sometimes employed the clear colors of Persian miniatures and admired the Cambodian sculptures and the human dignity of the Egyptians, he owed most to the sun of Tahiti and the strangely quiet Tahitian women who posed for him.

In one of his last letters he wrote that he wanted to establish the right to dare everything and that future generations of painters would owe a debt to him because he had opened the way. There was nothing in the least boastful about the claim. Like Van Gogh, he had thrown his own life into the scales and lost the wager, but gained the prize which meant most to him. He had won a posthumous life which would continue down the centuries.

The eye had opened wide; gradually it would close again.

High Noon and Darkest Night

The traveler walking along the Chemin des Lauves toward Cézanne's studio just outside the town of Aix-en-Provence soon finds himself gazing into the blue distance across the fields of summer wheat and the red-roofed houses. Through the trees bordering the road he sees a low mountain shaped like the crest of a wave, blue and yellow, hovering in the heat haze, so that it appears to advance and recede. It is not a particularly high mountain, or a particularly arresting one. Unlike the tormented lava-blue Alpilles, which fascinated Van Gogh at nearby Saint-Remy, it is lacking in dramatic grandeur. At some remote period in geological time it seems to have erupted through the crust of the earth very slowly and heavily, but also with a kind of inevitability, in order to look round and survey the landscape, and having seen the landscape, it closed its eyes.

For many years of his life Cézanne studied Mont Sainte-Victoire passionately, as though his life depended on it. He painted it over sixty times, and during his last years built the studio on the Chemin des Lauves so that he could study it more closely. Just as Monet found his chief inspiration in a shimmering stream filled with water lilies, the petals melting in the surface of the water, so Cézanne found it in rugged mountains, winter trees, square-shaped rocks, red roofs, houses stacked up on hillsides, ginger jars, skulls, apples, and pears. Against the evanescent world of Monet he proclaimed his own sturdy, incontrovertible world of solid forms arranged in space in such a way that their solidity was maintained. He scarcely ever painted a tree in flower and he disliked painting flowers, because they usually died before he could finish painting them. He feared the transitory, and went in search of permanence. He was obsessed with the enduring and the eternal, and he had the Provençal peasant's passion for the land, the only enduring thing under the sun.

The greater part of Cézanne's work consisted of landscapes and still lifes. When he painted portraits, he would regard the human face as though it were a roughhewn rock quarry, full of sharp splintered planes, and he would demand that his sitters remain motionless for days, for weeks, sometimes for months, as he grappled with the problems of reproducing the infinite variety of planes in paint. Ears troubled him; noses fascinated him, and he liked them to be sharp and prominent, like his own; and he labored untiringly over lips, which were nearly always too soft for his liking. His portraits therefore acquire a curious monumentality, and it is sometimes difficult to believe that blood pours through the sitters' veins or that any thoughts have ever filled their minds. His famous series of paintings called *The Card Players* shows solid peasants sitting at table; they are so solid, so monumental, that they might be generals planning a campaign to overthrow an empire. Not since Giotto had any painter exulted so much in the weight and solidity of the human body.

Cézanne was born in Aix-en-Provence and spent most of his life there or in the neighboring villages. Because he was the son of the most important banker in the town he was never in financial difficulties. His difficulties lay elsewhere: in the emotional instability which he controlled with an iron will, in his continual dissatisfaction with his work—he was always tearing up his canvases—and in his relations with other people, for he quarreled with most of his friends. A thickset, heavy man, nearly six feet tall, he had a way of walking like a man shouldering his way through a forest. Among people he did not know well, he could be alarmingly gauche and even silly, announcing opinions which he did not believe. He would say of himself one moment: "I am the only painter," and the next moment he would be celebrating the genius of painters whose works he had scarcely studied. He dismissed Gauguin, who admired him and collected his paintings, as "merely a maker of Chinese images," and when he met Van Gogh in Tanguy's shop in Paris, he said:

"In all sincerity, you paint like a madman." There were large areas of his mind which were completely insensitive to ideas and people. He was a man with only one passion: painting.

This stern, irascible, haunted man brought about a revolution in painting, a revolution so vast that its effects can still be felt. Like Giotto, and for very much the same reason, he set himself the task of depicting the tangible world, the world as it is, stripped bare of the imagination's adornments and of mystery. For Giotto, too, the world was finite and clear-cut. Cézanne found himself groping for definition, hardness, structure, fields of force. For him, fields, mountains, faces, apples were all equally impersonal and passionless. The task of the painter lay in a scrupulous avoidance of passion and an absolute determination to render what he saw cleanly, nakedly, giving every object its appropriate value, depth, and atmosphere.

Inevitably passion crept in. There were colors he enjoyed more than others, motifs which pleased him more than others, and he was especially fond of geometrical forms. "See in nature the cylinder, the sphere and the cone," he said in the most famous of his pronouncements, and sometimes, like Jacob wrestling with the Angel, he seems to be wrestling with nature until she reveals herself in cylinders, spheres, and cones. Since structure was all-important, linear perspective could be abandoned or so subordinated to structure that it became merely a weapon to be used at rare intervals. At all costs planes must be established, and at all costs the painting must present the weight and mass of the objects represented. It follows that a round jug may become angular, or one side of it may be permitted to swell out, or the handle may be placed in an impossible position, so long as the painter faithfully represents its weight within the composition. Fidelity to nature did not involve photographic fidelity. On rare occasions he painted from photographs, and the paintings and original photographs have survived. Comparing them, we see how he deliberately distorted, simplified, recreated the scene. When he painted trees from a photograph, we see that the branches were bent back, leaves and grasses were trimmed away, and the rocks, which are scarcely visible in the photograph, are given pride of place.

Cézanne's method derived from the Impressionists who employed dabs of brilliant contrasting colors to represent the intensity of sunlight, but Cézanne used the method for another, and more arduous purpose. He did not see color merely as an effect of sunlight; he saw it welling out of the earth, out of rocks and bark and the skins of faces and apples. When he paints Mont Sainte-Victoire we can never tell what time of the day it is: it might be dawn or dusk or high noon. When the Impressionists painted the boatmen on the Seine at Argenteuil, we can tell what time it is to a quarter of an hour.

Often wrongheaded and willful, sometimes wildly elated but more often sunk in despair, Cézanne thought of himself as a prophet leading future artists toward a promised land, though he had little hope of seeing it with his own eyes. His hard, austere paintings were tablets of the new law; he demanded that painters should produce paintings as austere as his own. A friend who watched him painting reported that he wore a look of despair and would sometimes groan and clench his fist at the unconquered enemy, while of Monet it was related that he would sometimes laugh like a drunkard in his joy at the progress of a painting. Happiness was not something Cézanne expected or hoped for.

What he hoped for was a final solution to the problem of reality, and he was well aware of the philosophical implications of his work. He had read Kant and Schopenhauer with profound interest; he knew Virgil and Baudelaire by heart, and was far more learned than the majority of painters. Though he wrote no extended treatise or commentary on painting, his letters show him wrestling fiercely with the problem of reality, and when he wrote that he was attempting to create "constructions after nature," he meant exactly what he said. These constructions were to be endowed with the reality of the physical world and to be as enduring as the physical world. When he painted apples, they look as hard as marble. One could bite into the apple which Memlinc's Virgin presents to her Child, but one could not bite into Cézanne's apples without breaking one's teeth.

Van Gogh, who knew Provence well, said that Cézanne painted "only the hard side of Provence," and this was true. He made the hard harder, insisted that everything should be well anchored, though Nature herself permits many loose anchorings, and sometimes he resembled Don Quixote attacking the colors of the air with a sledgehammer. Significantly he made few flower studies and those few were failures.

During the last year of his life he attempted a long series of paintings called collectively *The Bathers* in which he attempted to integrate nude bathers in the foreground with a scene of trees or rocks or Mont Sainte-Victoire in the distance. The problem obsessed him, and he resolved it as well as he could by giving his bathers the solidity of stone, so that they might have been carved out of the rock from the local quarry. He had trouble finding models, and to a German art collector who visited him he said: "An invalid posed for all these women." Although the foreground figures are scarcely more than sketches, he was able to give them an extraordinary monumentality and he succeeded in integrating them fully into the landscape. *The Great Bathers,* a canvas so large that a special slit had to be made in the studio wall to permit its entry, shows the bathers under an archway of towering trees with a river and fields in the distance. Although unfinished, the painting shows Cézanne at the height of his powers, at ease among the receding blue planes, the massive limbs and torsos of the bathers gleaming in the foreground, the dappled light of the leaves falling on them.

He had wanted to die painting, but this gift was not given to him. One day in the autumn of 1906 he painted his gardener outside his studio on the Chemin des Lauves and during the afternoon walked to Entremont nearby and set up his easel. He was still painting when a violent storm sprang up. He tried to return to his studio, but collapsed on the roadside. Some hours later the driver of a laundry cart found him lying on the road, drenched and suffering from fever. He was taken in the laundry cart to his apartment in Aix-en-Provence, and the next day, although obviously ill, he insisted on returning to his studio to do more work on the portrait of his gardener. It was his last visit to the studio. He was brought back to his apartment in a neighbor's carriage, and died a few days later of double pneumonia.

When Cézanne died on October 22, 1906, Pablo Picasso had

already established himself as a master, the blue and rose periods were over, and some of his most famous paintings, including *The Family of the Saltimbanques* and *The Boy Leading a Horse*, were already completed. While Cézanne lay dying, Picasso was at work on his formidable portrait of Gertrude Stein, one of the comparatively few portraits from his hand which are solidly anchored in space. The young Picasso—he was then only twenty-five—had already passed through at least six separate stages of development which future art historians would have no difficulty in recognizing.

Born in Málaga in 1881, the son of an art teacher, he showed very early a remarkable talent as a draftsman. He drew with a diamond-sharp line and with incredible facility and self-assurance, and all his subsequent works relied heavily on his mastery of line. He soaked up influences like a sponge, and in his early work especially he was often derivative, borrowing from Toulouse-Lautrec, Van Gogh, Manet, Gauguin, and many others, so that a single painting may contain reminiscences of three or four or even more painters. Yet his own peculiar characteristics are always visible: the firm outline, violently contrasted colors, figures set in a shallow and insubstantial space, while nevertheless possessing extraordinary vitality. His figures were usually set about eight inches from a nondescript wall or backcloth, and those problems of depth and perspective that preoccupied Cézanne almost to madness had no meaning for him. Nor was he concerned to anchor his figures or to build up contours with minutely observed striations of color. The impact of his paintings is always sharp, sudden, unequivocal, the thing seen being immediately reproduced on canvas by means of line and flat color. The primacy always belongs to line, for as Picasso has observed several times, "If I run out of blue, I put in red."

Only a virtuoso could speak in this way, and Picasso was always the virtuoso. He had no patience with conventional theories of reality, and he came to regard the physical universe as a springboard for his private transformation acts. "A green parrot is also a green salad *and* a green parrot," he declared. "A palm tree is also a horse." But these fictions were designed to give him the utmost license as a painter while scarcely affecting his drawings. When he drew a parrot or a horse, it was unmistakably a real parrot, a real horse. They were minutely observed and wonderfully expressed. But when he painted parrots and horses, they might become anything he pleased and were very likely to become flowers or rampaging bulls. Like Rubens, who would stand before a canvas without knowing where the design would lead him, Picasso operated on the principle that the design must be left to take care of itself and though he might consciously manipulate it, he could never completely control it. When the parrot was broken down into its essential components, it might decide to become a green leaf and it was not his task to prevent the transformation from taking place. In the same way, during his cubist period, a man's face might be transformed into broken fragments resembling a hundred gray shutters in a state of explosion.

The process of breaking down the elements of a figure he called "destruction." "A picture used to be a sum of additions," he wrote. "For me, a picture is a sum of destructions." Since Cézanne was above all the master of construction, Picasso was making his declaration of independence and embarking on a contrary philosophy. Cézanne saw a figure or a landscape as a whole; Picasso saw them in brilliant fragmentation. From the very beginning his artist's eye rejoiced in the anarchic and the unexpected. He intended to startle, and he nearly always succeeded.

The movement that came to be known as Cubism had obscure origins, which have never been satisfactorily investigated. While it derived ultimately from the age-old observation that all the shapes of the universe partake of the cylinder, the sphere, the cone, and the cube—an observation that strongly commended itself to Cézanne and was well-known to the ancient Greeks and no doubt to the Babylonians—yet these geometrical shapes had little enough to do with the movement when it finally emerged, and the word "Cubism" was essentially misleading. The Cubists were not attempting to rearrange their figures into elementary forms; they were attempting a revolution which would drastically change the nature of painting itself by means of "a sum of destructions."

Many influences were working to bring about the sum of destructions. In music, sculpture, literature, and the sciences there was the growing recognition that the old forms were outmoded and that new and more violent forms were becoming necessary in order to reflect the growing disorder of society. There was the realization that all the forms of European art were ultimately derived from classical Greece and that it was perfectly possible to imagine an art derived from a totally different source or even from a set of newly formed hypotheses. Traditional art had very little relation to life as it was being lived in Paris in 1907.

In the autumn of that year there had been an exhibition of African sculpture at the Palais du Trocadéro. Most of the painters working in Paris were already aware of African sculpture and admired it because the artists were attempting to produce works of great power by means of brutal simplifications, sharp planes, and deliberately heightened relief. African art was not representative art, because the images existed in their own right independent of anything observed in life. A face might be a simple disk with two eyes punched out of it, and the arms might come out of the face. Most of the African sculptures were fertility symbols or portraits of the dead, and were created for magical purposes. At the same time they were extremely sophisticated works charged with the energy of ancient traditions and firmly held beliefs.

The French painters who began to collect African sculptures at the turn of the century knew nothing about the magical intentions of the sculptors. They saw entirely new forms created with incomparable freedom. Picasso experimented with these harsh African forms in his preliminary sketches for his painting called Les Demoiselles d'Avignon, Avignon being the name of a brothel in Barcelona. Originally conceived as a set piece with the madame surrounded by her girls, it became a study of three naked women and two sailors. The face of one of the women derived from Gauguin, the faces of the sailors derived from African masks. There was no sensation of space; the figure of a squatting sailor was only minimally human; the flat colors clashed; and for once there was no evidence of Picasso's mastery of line. Matisse, who saw the work shortly after it was completed, intensely disliked it and thought it had set back the progress of modern painting.

Nevertheless Les Demoiselles d'Avignon was the beginning of

a revolution in painting which is still going on. The squatting sailor, descendant of African tribal ghosts, his face a mask, his body very nearly shapeless, had erupted with the force of an explosion, and for the rest of his life Picasso would be haunted by that broken iconic image, painting endless variations on it, while painters everywhere were forced to study this new visionary concept of an art which became increasingly remote from ordinary human preoccupations. From time to time, as one clearly defined period followed another, Picasso would return to a simpler, more representational painting, and the masklike faces would be temporarily abandoned. In 1917, ten years after *Les Demoiselles d'Avignon,* he visited Rome to design scenes for a ballet, and was so impressed by the monumental forms of ancient Roman sculpture that he began to paint representational figures of women with heavy limbs and stone faces, their bodies in violent movement. Simultaneously he would produce portraits like the *Seated Harlequin,* where there were no distortions at all, and at intervals he would return to the distorted, fragmented world of his ancient mariner in the brothel in Barcelona. He was Proteus, and he could assume any form he pleased.

The years immediately after World War I were so confused and disorganized that it might have seemed impossible to produce any great art, but in fact it was a period of towering artistic accomplishment. Matisse, Modigliani, Rouault, Braque, Klee, Kokoschka, Soutine, Miró were painting with a new exuberance and freedom. Klee and Miró invented new worlds, patiently constructing them out of non-representational forms and endowing them with a remarkable gaiety. Cubism, "the sum of destructions," had no decisive influence on them. What was chiefly remarkable about these painters was a certain purity, even a kind of innocence. The purity of Modigliani's line derived directly from Piero della Francesca, and he continued to paint with a kind of luminous intensity even when he was dying of tuberculosis, alcoholism, and starvation. It was an art of precise, formal outlines, and at the same time it was filled with an opulent energy. He was so poor that he was selling his drawings for the price of a drink in the cafés of Montmartre, and he could never have guessed that he would soon be counted among the masters.

In spite of the artists' manifestos and proclamations, and the proliferation of artistic "movements," there was never any concerted program. The manifestos written by their literary friends were disconcertingly literary and the "movements" were often motionless or else they split so quickly into their component parts that they vanished altogether. Fauves, Expressionists, Analytical Cubists, Futurists, Vorticists, Dadaists, Surrealists succeeded one another, but they had no clear boundaries. "Fauve" means "wild beast," but there was nothing wild or bestial about them, and even Soutine, with his prodigious display of chaotic forms and tormented colors, remained a representational painter to the end. The ancient mariner had proclaimed the end of tradition, but tradition insistently prevailed. When Picasso drew with a pen, he was following a tradition that derived from the drawings on Greek vases and the engravings on Etruscan mirrors. When Rouault painted his clowns, he followed the example of thirteenth-century artists in stained glass by enclosing them with heavy, ribbed outlines and giving to his colors the intense glow of stained glass. Matisse derived straight from the Impressionists and from Cézanne, and even Mondrian could claim descent from the Dutch masters. Only Brancusi seemed to have no ancestors and to have escaped from tradition altogether.

Brancusi was one of those rare artists who seemed never to have contemplated or studied the work of other artists. By birth a Rumanian peasant, he had spent his childhood as a shepherd in the Carpathians, carving his own shepherd's crook and whittling his own flute. Studying at the Bucharest Academy, he developed a prodigious but facile talent: he could model a finished portrait in clay in a single sitting and it would be acclaimed as a small masterpiece. When he came to Paris at the turn of the century he was already resolved "to kill the marionette." He was determined to begin again from the beginning. For the rest of his long life he created forms of such purity and innocence that they seemed to have escaped out of time and history.

In conversation he liked to present himself as the great iconoclast, heaping damnation on the artists who failed to see the world in all its freshness. "Michelangelo's paintings in the Sistine Chapel are a butcher's shop," he would say. Seeing an unpainted canvas, he would run his fingers over it and complain that paint would only spoil the immaculate linen. "Art is not the performance

of the appropriate movements," he said once. "It is not knowing how
to swim: it is swimming to the point where you become the whole
sea." That sense of wholeness permeated his work, and inevitably
it led him to the study of simple generative forms which at first
sight resembled abstractions. Eggs, fishes, columns of birds, tor-
toises, and swans—all these became in his hands powerful symbols
of life eternally renewing itself. He carved a column of birds, and
he was not entirely joking when he described it as a "project for
a column which, if enlarged, would support the vault of heaven."
Similarly, he would say of his *Bird in Space* that "it would fill
the whole universe," remembering perhaps the strange words of
Leonardo de Vinci about *il grande uccello*: "The great bird will
make the first flight mounted on a great swan, filling the universe
with stupor." But those graceful *Birds in Space* (for he made many
of them and continually refined them) did not so much fill the
whole of space as leap out of space altogether, becoming ideas, concepts, shining images of speed and conquest, the very apotheosis
of the bird in flight.

Brancusi made many portraits of women, not all of them
successful. But in *The Sleeping Muse,* a head without a body,
which lay in his studio like an egg within its nest, the features
only sketchily indicated and with faint blue shadows for eyes, he
succeeded wonderfully in conveying the portrait of a goddess; and
you have the feeling that if you put your hand on it, you would
find it warm with life. For Brancusi, life was movement, flight, the
stirrings of elemental life in the egg and in the fish poised in a
stream. He therefore liked to show his sculptures in movement,
and it pleased him to watch them rotating slowly. He had devised
his own ingenious system of turntables, and the visitor to the
studio in the Impasse Ronsin would suddenly discover that all the
sculptures were in motion, each of them spinning round at a
different speed, for he had calculated the exact speed needed by
each one.

In this way Brancusi pursued his genius, not turning aside,
like Picasso, at every breath of new fancy, but moving as birds
fly, directly, without equivocation. In that studio one could live
for ever in the calm of contemplation. For him the birds stood
poised on the branch, sang, and flew across snowy skies in the

same moment of time; the fish slept, hunted, floated, and swam, all in the same moment; and always *The Sleeping Muse* awakened from her sleep and fell into a trance—the trance from which the world began.

When he died in the spring of 1957, he gave his entire collection to the people of Paris and asked that his studio should be reconstructed in the Musée de l'Art Moderne. It was the supreme gift of himself to the people who had sheltered him throughout his long life, though he had scarcely seen them and scarcely spoke their language.

Matisse, who was seven years older than Brancusi, seems sometimes to speak in the same idiom. He possessed an extraordinary mastery of line and with a few threadlike lines he could enclose any space, real or imaginary. Like Brancusi, he preferred elemental forms, and in the great series of paintings of dancers he reduced the human body almost to an abstraction of movement, and in his illustrations for books there would be the same delight in pure form. When he grew very old and could no longer hold a brush, he made cutouts from colored paper which seemed to leap and dance with the life he had poured into them, so that the decorations formed out of scissors and paste seemed to be as urgent and as inevitable as his dancers.

Although Matisse was dominated by a sense of line, he was also a superb colorist who refused to obey any of the accepted laws of color but continually experimented. Gauguin had said once that the future of art would owe much to Persian color and Cambodian form, and while Cambodian form had no influence on Matisse whatsoever, the colors of the Persian miniaturists entered his canvases. Sometimes he would experiment with dazzling dissonances, and in *The Egyptian Curtain* he filled a window with a sunlit palm tree, all black and yellow and grass green, and placed beside it a black curtain with huge leaf shapes in emerald and dusky red, and below the window lay a bowl of orange fruit. The effect was to send vibrant colors shooting from one side of the canvas to the other. This youthful display of brilliantly successful pyrotechnics was performed by the artist when he was seventy-nine years old. He died ten years later, in the year following the

"Head of a Woman" by Henri Matisse.

death of Brancusi. Like most of the world's great artists he had
been granted a long life.

Rouault, a far more complex artist, with deeper resources of
feeling and sensibility, might seem to belong to a wholly different
tradition, but in fact his greatest works, those into which he poured
the abundance of his troubled spirit, were precisely those which
were based on elemental forms. He painted at least a hundred oval
faces: Christ, the Madonna, clowns, saints, prostitutes, all resting
in a nest of flaming colors, as Brancusi's *The Sleeping Muse*
rested on a polished stone. These portraits possess a ferocious energy
and a haunting clarity. As Matisse was the master of the pure
line, so Rouault was the master of the broken line: he jabs and
probes. His colors, too, were constructed from deliberate dissonances,
like the colors of stained-glass windows, and these oval-shaped icons
clearly had their place on the walls of a church. His clowns
bless; his saints accuse; even the prostitutes demand no pardon.

The twenties and thirties were a period of astonishing exploration in the arts. Picasso, Brancusi, Matisse, and Rouault were at

the height of their powers. So were perhaps fifty other artists possessing great gifts. Kokoschka and Bonnard were exploring the boundaries of Impressionism, Ernst van Leyden was producing monumental collages which glowed like a long afternoon in autumn, Miró was creating Spanish fairy tales, and Klee, one of the boldest of modern painters, was exploring a strange microcosmic world of fantasy, where nothing was what it seemed to be. The youthful Gaudier-Brzeska, who died in the First World War, sculpted with extraordinary force and made drawings of panthers and birds which live with the running fire of his line: he, too, came into his own between the two wars. Epstein experimented in massive forms derived from an immense knowledge of the history of art, but was remembered chiefly for his sharply delineated bronzes. Henry Moore simplified his sculptures almost to excess, but gave dignity to his primordial men and women. Through all these works there flowed the blood of health.

When Hitler seized power in 1933, the world entered a new dispensation. There were few who doubted that he intended to conquer the world at whatever the cost in lives; he would reduce the world to his own nihilistic image. He had no understanding of the arts, no desire that any monuments except his own should survive him. In Munich he established an exhibition of Decadent Art, where the visitor was permitted to see some of the very greatest of modern paintings. Storm troopers marched up and down the corridors, and if the visitor paused too long opposite Kokoschka's miraculous *Windbraut,* he was likely to be arrested.

Hitler declared war on the modern artist, as he declared war on all men. The terror he introduced deeply influenced the artists, and gradually a new art emerged, nihilistic, violent, strangely incoherent. In occupied Paris, Rouault continued to paint his saintly clowns, the line becoming more broken than ever, the color more dissonant, and Picasso continued to work on the edge of Cubism. They belonged to an old tradition and were no longer revolutionaries. A new art was brought into being by Jean Fautrier and Jean Dubuffet, who painted as though all Western civilization had fallen into ruins and they were hesitantly starting again in some abandoned railroad shed where the disemboweled engine still disgorged steam and the cesspools were green with slime. Fautrier's paintings took

the form of small shapeless slabs of plaster of paris painted with
trickles of blood. The series called *The Hostages* was undeniably
terrifying, for those small paintings suggested smashed skulls, the
remnants of a human body flattened by a tank, a face riddled with
machine-gun bullets. In a similar way he painted the naked torsos
of women with green and shapeless breasts and gelatinous buttocks.
Fautrier resembled Piero di Cosimo gazing at his famous damp
wall in the hospital, marveling at the terrible stains; unlike Piero
di Cosimo he refused to permit his imagination to see anything
more than the stains. Jean Dubuffet produced paintings deliberately
intended to be senseless and pronounced sentence of death on all
human values. "My apparatus functions as a machine for abolishing
the names of things," he wrote. "I break down the partitions
raised by the mind between different objects, between different
systems of objects, between different registers of facts and of things,
and the different levels of thought." He demanded that art should
be "impeccably raw, invested with all the fascination of the portraits
children make of themselves in the snow." His strange, ragged, calligraphic designs were lacking in any element of childishness. They
resembled acts of torture.

In the wake of Fautrier and Dubuffet the most talented artists
allied themselves with "the machine for abolishing the names of
things." It was as though the artistic nerve had been stunned
with an injection of poison and could no longer respond in any
human fashion. Abstraction was piled upon abstraction. Jackson
Pollock would simply pour paint on immense stretches of canvas
and wade over it in his thigh boots, and the finished painting
would solemnly be presented to collectors as a work of art. The
artists have gone over to the enemy.

We have fought great wars, and there are no memorials to
these wars worth a moment's attention. We have produced great
men, but we have designed no tombs worthy of them. Millions
have been tortured to death, and nowhere in the world are there
any sculptures which celebrate their deaths worthily; and the living
are also forgotten. The visitor to museums of modern art sees
paintings and sculptures made in derision and hatred of men,
gallery upon gallery filled with a fierce, intoxicated calligraphy de-

signed to remind men of their helplessness in the face of all the destructive forces created by the modern world. It is only a minute's walk from the Musée Guimet in Paris to the Musée de l'Art Moderne. In the Musée Guimet the Khmer statues proclaim the beauty and divinity of man, the subtlety of his mind, the joy of his handiwork. In the upstairs gallery of the Musée de l'Art Moderne the canvases stridently utter threats of all-encompassing doom.

For a few more years we may have to suffer the presence of a nihilist art, while the poison works its way out of the physical system of the artists. The world of art rests on unshakable foundations and will not be overthrown. From the cave paintings of Lascaux to the last works of Matisse, Rouault, and Brancusi the tradition was maintained in unbroken sequence, each artist following in the footsteps of those who went before him, and it is beyond belief that the tradition has come to an end. Art is the mystery that continually renews itself, our only safeguard against the darkness. Art glows like the sun, the stars, and the wheeling galaxies, and sheds the light by which man can live in an age of terror and conformity. Every man born on the earth receives the gifts of the artists, who come to him like the Magi offering their treasures. For the world of art is man's natural home, his appointed rest, his benediction and supreme consolation, a possession for everlasting.

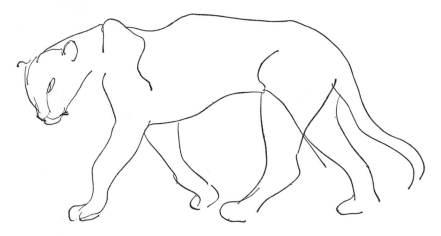

"Jaguar" by Gaudier-Brzeska. Tate Gallery, London.

Index

Aachen, 410
Abbé Breuil, 23
Abbot Suger, 188, 193–97, 198, 199, 341, 397, 481
Abd-al-Malik, Caliph, 212–13, 214
Abgar, King of Edessa, 164
Abraham, 213
Abstract art, 508, 511–12; Chinese, 267, 268, 269
Abu Simbel: Ramses II statues, 54–55
Abyssinia, 76
Achaemenids, 72–78; art, 11, 71ff., 223, origins, 73; destruction, 74, 79; empire, 72, 74; kings, 169; Luristans, 72. See Persepolis
Acheiropoietoi, 163
Acropolis. See under Athens
Actium, Battle of, 134, 135
Actors, prints of, 301
Adriatic Sea, 122, 128
Aegean islands, 161
Aeneas, 137
Aeschylus, 103
Afghanistan, 219, 241, 247, 248, 249; art, 248; Egypt, 218
Africa, 318; masks, 15, 16; sculpture, 505
Agatharchus of Samos, 103
Age of Enlightenment, 459–60, 462, 463, 467
Agincourt, Battle of, 479
Aisha (Mohammed's wife), 211
Aix-en-Provence, 498, 499, 502
Ajanta caves, 11, 236–39, 240, 242; Buddha figures, 250–51
Akhenaton (Pharaoh), 46, 47–52, 53, 54, 135, 478; art, 52, 53; death, 51, 52; Hymn to the Sun, 47–49; queen (see Nefertiti, Queen)
Al Aqsa Mosque, 317
Alaska, totem poles, 306
Albert the Great, 206
Alcamenes, 113
Aldovrandi, Giovan Francesco, 421
Alexander the Great, 56, 74, 78, 114, 136, 459; Persepolis, 78; personal sculptor, 117; portraits, 117; successors, 79, 248
Alexandria, 209, 210, 362
Alexandrine mosaics, 148

Al-Muayyad Shaykh, Caliph, 218–19
Al-Nasir Mohammed, Sultan, 219
Alsace, 339
Altamira, cave paintings, 30
Altarpieces, 176–77, 404–7
Altdorfer, Albrecht, 416–17, 418; Alexander's Battle, 416–17
Al Uqsur ("the palaces"), 46
Amazon, 305
Americas (Pre-Columbian): art, 303, 305, 314; gods, 305, 312–14. See also Aztecs; Chavín de Huántar; Cuzco; and Peru
Amiens Cathedral, 205, 206, 207
Amr ibn-al-As, 210
Amsterdam, 386, 387, 395; Rijksmuseum, 388
Ananda (Buddha's disciple), 252
Ananias, 164
Anatolia, 219, 220
Anavyssos (Attica), Apollo of, 99–100
Andes, 303, 304, 305
Angkor Wat, 466
Anhalt, Duke of, 224
Animals: Achaemenids, 72, 76; cave paintings, 19ff., 22; fanged jaguar, 303ff., 313; horses: Chinese paintings, 280, da Vinci, 332–33, 336; Luristanis, 72; medieval art, 181–82; sculpture, 66, 67, 303–4; Zoroastirianism, 76
Ankhesenaton (wife of Tutankhaton), 53
Anselm, St., of Canterbury, 166
Ansquitil, Abbot, 185
Anthemius of Thralles, 154
Antinoüs, 142
Antiquity, 422, 428, 459; devotion to, 364; ownership, 50; ruins, Piranesi engravings, 464, 465, 466
Antonello da Messina, 175, 328; Salvator Mundi, 175
Antwerp, 354, 357, 383, 411, 492
Apelles, 103
Apollo at Olympia, 115–16
Apollo of Anayssos, 99–100
Apollodorus, 103
Apostles, 158, 166, 167; Sleeping Apostle, ill. 190. See under name
Apulia, 132
Aquinas, St. Thomas, Summa, 206

Aquitaine, 193
Arabian Sea, 241
Arabs, 46, 82, 198, 209, 210, 211, 280;
  Egypt, 56; Persians, 82
Aral Sea, 248
Arca, Niccolo dell', 421
Archaeology (archaeologists), 21, 25, 50,
  52, 59, 60–61, 71, 74, 85, 86, 95, 101,
  122, 126, 212, 261
Architecture (architects), 40, 44, 86, 154;
  Aztec, 310; Chinese, 292; Florentine,
  321; Gothic, 202, 203, 204, 205; Greek,
  105; Inca, 308; Indian, 243; Islamic,
  214; Japanese, 292; Javanese, 256–57;
  Persian, 223–24; Roman, 142; Seljuk,
  215–16; Sumerian, 66. See also under
  country
Aretino, Pietro, 376
Arezzo, 126, 130, 172, 173, 329–30
Argenteuil, 399, 501
Aristocracy, art of, 191, 255
Aristotle, 125, 198, 392
Arles, 493, 495
Armenia, 164, 196, 272
Arno River, 121
Arpino, Giuseppe d', 438
Art, 4, 7, 55; abstractions, 508, 511–12;
  aristocratic, 191, 255; atmosphere,
  343–44, 352–53; characteristics, 3, 7,
  16, 126–27, 478, 507, 513; collections,
  10, 354, 392–93, 444, 479; conventions,
  15; critics, 372, 399, 425; dealers, 387,
  393, 396; fantasies, 347–48; fees, 357–
  88; feminine, 322 (see Siena); forms:
  African, 505, archetypal, 401–2, geometric, 504; genius, 383; great, characteristics, 11, 15, 30n, 33, 98, 119, 317ff.,
  339, 479–80; grotesque, 349, 351–52;
  heroic, 380; historians, 381, 404, 442,
  503; history, 14, 98, 459, 510ff.; innovations, 193, 298–99; laws of, 4, 15;
  masterpieces, 151, 326, 343, 358, 383,
  422, 425–26, 443; modern, 510ff.; naturalism, 343; nature of, 5–7; nihilistic,
  511ff.; ownership, 7, 12; paradoxes, 7;
  patrons, 354, 419 (see under artists);
  -place, relationship, 11, 43; production,
  causes, 248; purpose, 4, 5, 463; repeti-
  tion, 478; roots, 19–82: Egyptian, 35–
  56, prehistoric, 19–34, Persian, 69–82,
  Sumerian, 57–68; -science, 323, 324,
  328; sounds, suggestion of, 380; techniques: chiaroscuro, 90, 324, 368, 386,
  flesh, 358, 369, 372, 416, 450, pointilism, 397; time-place necessity, 11–12;
  tradition, 507; traditional, 505; war,
  339; wealth, 339, 479. See also Artist
Artist, 8–9; cave, 19ff.; court, 94, 169;
  dangerous age, 462; direction, change
  of, 374–75; exiles, 417, 418, 441–42,
  445; keeping own works, 396; madness,
  444, 470, 472, 473, 494; most prolific,
  301; position in society, 9; purpose of,
  5; relation to work, 7–8; signatures,

9, 25, 337–38, 414–15, 453; survival,
  336. See also under city and/or coun-
  try and name
Artistic creation, length of periods, 383
Artistic vision, aspects, 33. See Calli-
  graphic image and Eidetic image
Arwad, 219
Asia, 272, 304
Asia Minor, 74, 88, 115, 119, 121, 161,
  218, 318
Asoka, King, 235
Assisi, 319; Giotto frescoes, 321
Assurbanipal, King, 67
Assyria, 66–68, 73; art, 68, 76; legacy,
  68; Sumeria, influence of, 68
Aswan Dam, 55
Athenaeus, 75
Athens, 78, 85, 97, 104, 159–60, 317;
  Acropolis, 105–6, 107–8, 109–11, 147,
  museum, 12, 101, 112, Turks, 110–11;
  art: greatest single achievement, 108,
  as reflection of spirit, 105; fall of, 115;
  influences on, 97, 130, 161; National
  Museum, 99, 104; Parthenon (see
  Parthenon); treasury, 107. See Greece
Atlantic Ocean, 385
Attalus II, 119
Attalus III, 119
Attica, 99
Augustine, St., 166
Augustus Caesar, 10, 56, 130, 134–35,
  142, 317–18; Age of, 459; appearance,
  137; art, 134ff.; peace, 137
Autun, Honorius d', 188, 191
Avignon Pietà, 176
Azerbaijan, 73
Aztecs, 309–11, 410; Calendar Stone, ill.
  312

Baalbek, 154
Babylonia, 66, 74, 317, 504; art, 68;
  Sumerian influence, 68
Baghdad Museum, 61, 62
Bak (Egyptian artist), 52
Baldung Grien, Hans, 416
Baldwin II, King, 202
Balearic Islands, 122
Balkans, 76, 173
Banasura, King, 229
Bandello, Matteo, 336
Baptistery doors (Florence), 324–26
Barbarelli family, 370
Barcelona, 505
Barquq, 218
Basel, 408
Basire, James, 474
Basutoland, 30–31
Baths of Caracalla, 141–42
Baths of Diocletian, 142
Battle of Alexander (mosaic), 103, 148
Baudelaire, Pierre Charles, 461, 483, 487,
  501
Bayeu, Josefa, 469
Baysunghur, 220

of Liebana: *A Commentary on
ook of Revelation,* 186
, 188
Cathedral, 205
ins, 54
ethoven, Ludwig van, 374
Belgium: Borinage, 492; Brabant, 339,
340
Bellini, Gentile, 363, 365, 368; *Proces-
sion of the True Cross in St. Mark's
Square,* 363
Bellini, Giovanni, 14, 177, 360, 363–64,
365, 368, 372; *Transfiguration,* 363–64
Bellini, Jacopo, 363
Bellori, Pietro, 442
Beneventum, triumphal arch, 141
Bergamo, 437
Berlin, 366; Museum, 50
Bernadotte, General, 485
Berry, Jean, Duc de, 479–80
Bertram, Master, 402–3; *Nativity,* 403
Bhagiratha, 240
Biagio da Cesena, 432
Bihzad (Persian artist), 221–22
Black Sea, 272
Blake, William, 401, 449–50, 459, 474–
76; art, belief in, 474–75; engravings,
474–76; mysticism, 474. *See* Dante Ali-
ghieri
Boccaccio, 421
Bodhisattvas, 260; Indian, 282; stone rub-
bing (Chinese), 276, *ill.* 277. *See under*
Buddhas
Bokhara, 220; mausoleum of Ismail Sam-
anid, 215
Bolivia, 306
Bologna, 421–22
Bonaparte, Joseph, 472
Bonaparte. *See* Napoleon Bonaparte
Bonaventura, St., 206
Boniface VIII, Pope, 319
Bonnard, Pierre, 511
Book of Kells, 182
Books, 182, 300; Chinese, 269–70, 274n;
Rembrandt collection, 392; *Tale of
Genji,* 295–96; world's oldest, 263–64.
See Literature
Bordeaux, archbishop of, 197
Borgia, Cesare, 336
Borgo San Sepolcro, 328; Pinaoteca Com-
munale, 329
Borobudur: Buddhist sculpture, 265; tem-
ple (Java), 256–58
Bosch, Hieronymus, 347–50, 351, 407;
four triptychs, 348; *Garden of Earthly
Delights,* 348, 349; self-portrait, 350
Boschini, Marco, 372
Boston: Museum of Fine Arts, 273
Botticelli, 9, 328–29, 331, 428, *ill.* 330;
Birth of Venus, 329
Boudin, Eugène, 483–84
Bouts, Dieric, 344, 345
Brancusi, 507–9, 510, 513; *Birds in Space,*
508; *The Sleeping Muse,* 508, 509, 510
Brandt, Isabella, 355

Braque, Georges, 506
British Museum, 10, 111, 112, 168, 270
Brittany, 485–86
Bronze Age, 147
Bronzes: Chinese, 70–71, 267, 268; *cire
perdue* process, 69; Luristan, 69–70;
patina, 334
Brouwer, Adriaen, 385, 392
Bruegel, Jan, 353
Bruegel, Pieter the Elder, 351–53, 392;
The Seasons, 352–53; successors, 353
Bruegel, Pieter the Younger, 353
Bruges, 340, 345, 346, 348; Memlinc dip-
tych, 345
Brunelleschi, 317, 322, 324, 326
Brussels, 340, 347, 410
Bucharest Academy, 507
Buckingham, Duke of, 357
Buddha, 7; appearance, 163, 254; birth-
place, 247; conceptions of, 265; crema-
tion (Kusinagara), 247; disciples, 252
(Ananda); divinity, insignia of, 255;
enlightenment (Bodh Gaya), 242, 247;
future (Maitreya), 260, 274n; greatest
painting of, 251; history, 257; images,
235, 244; messianic hope, 260–61; relics, 235, 236, 252–53; son (Rahula),
250; "Udayana portrait," 247; wife
(Princess Yasodhara), 250
Buddhas: Apollonian (Gandhara), 248–
49, 250; Bodh Gaya, 242; Bodhisattvas,
260, 262–63; Borobudur temple, 256–
57; Cambodia, 265, 266; Ceylon, 251–
53; *Chakravarti,* 248; China, 253, 258,
259–60, 279, 282; Coming Buddha
(Maitreya), 187; *Dasa Dhamma Sutta,*
247; face of, 246–66; Greece, 248;
Gupta period, 255–56; Indian, 282;
Jataka stories, 235; Jetavana Garden,
279; Kamakura, 55; Korea, 265–66;
Nepal, 265, 266; Parinirvana, 279; portraits, 14, 15, 162ff.; Sarnath (seated
Buddha), 250, 258, 262; statues, 248–
49; Sukhothai, 253–54; symbols, in
early sculptures, 247; T'ang Dynasty,
262, 330; Thailand, 253–55; T'ien
Lung Shan, 262–63; walking statue,
253
Buddhism, 169, 219, 246, 251, 287, 295;
China, 272–73, 274 *and* n, 290–91;
gods, 235; Hinayana, 251, -Mahayana
schism, 235; India, 235; Japan, 290–
91, 294–95; Mahayana, 237, 251, 291;
missionaries, 289–90; pilgrimages, 261;
spread of, 162, 255, 265
Buddhist art, 266; achievements, 257;
Borobudur statues, 265; cave-temples
(China), 11; Egypt, influence, 55;
heights, 265; paintings, 264–65
Burgkmair, Hans, 416
Burgundy, Duchy of, 339, 340: Duke of
(*see* Philip the Good)
Bushmen (Basutoland), 30–31
Byzantine art, 160–61, 213, 319; char-

acteristics, 161, 165, 173; Christ, 148, 176, 246; churches, 148, 169–70, 429; humanism, 159; icons, 175; influence of, 161, 361, 362; masterpieces, 157; mosaics, 149–50, 200; origins, 165
Byzantium, 12, 13, 144, 202, 280, 317; Christ, representation of, 162; Christianity, 168; court, 169; empire, 155, 164, 209, end of, 160–61; icons, 322; rulers, 5, 164, 209; splendor, 154; Yeats' tribute, 152–53

Caesar, Julius, 134
Cairo, 45; Mosque of Ibn Tulun, 215; Museum, 40, 51; slave market, 218
Calendar: Aztec stone, *ill.* 312
Caliph Hisham, 211, 212
Caliph of Islam, 212
Caliph Umar, 82, 210
Callicrates, 105
Calligraphy, 29–30, 284–85; Chinese, 269; eidetic, 30, 31
Callot, Jacques, 4, 468
Calvinism, 382
Cambodia, 497, 509; Buddhas, 265, 266
Canaletto, 459
Canossa, counts of, 420
Canterbury, archbishop of, 197
Cape Artemision, 104
Cape of Good Hope, 369
Capitoline Museum, 126, 127
Caravaggio, 9, 12, 346, 355, 386, 417, 418, 437–44, 451; exile, 441–42; influence, 444, 450–51; masterpieces, 143; patron, 440; self-portrait, 437; style, 438–39, 451, 455; *works:* 437, 439, 440, 441, 442–43, 450, *Beheading of St. John,* 441–42, *Death of the Virgin,* 354, 439
Caravan routes, 272
Carnarvon, Lord, 52
Carpaccio, Vittore, 365–66; *Dream of St. Ursula,* 365; *Healing of the Obsessed,* 365
Carpets: Anhalt, 224–25; Ardebil, 224, 225; Ctesiphon palace, 82; Persian, 224; signatures, 224
Carrey, Jacques (of Troyes), 110
Carter, Howard, 52
Carthage, 122
Carthaginians, 127
Cassel (Germany) museum, 10
Castelfranco, 366, 367
Castiglione, Baldassare, 337
Catacombs, 166–67; Christ portraits, 170, 177, 183, 246
Cathedrals, 256, 347; Cefalù, 4. *See also* under name
Catholicism, 382
Cavalieri, Tommaso, 433, 435
Cave of the Trois Frères (France), 27, 33; painting, *ill.* 27–28; "Sorcerer," 33
Cave paintings, 19ff., 25, *ill.* 26, 27, 29, 31, 32; characteristics, 22–23, 24, 25,

29; meaning of, 25–26, 28; s[...] 23; themes, 20, 25, 28
Caves, 11, 23; Buddhist, 7; ten[...] 261. *See under* country
Caylus, Comte de, 461
Cefalù, Christ of, 171–72; Pantocr[...] 362
Central Asia, 209, 251, 272; Silk Road, 272
Ceramics: China, 282
Ceylon: art, 252; Buddhism, 236, 251, 252–53
Cézanne, Paul, 12, 13, 159, 485, 498–502, 503, 504, 507; *The Bathers,* 502; *The Card Players,* 499; *The Great Bathers,* 502
Ch'an Buddhist sect, 287
Ch'ang-an, 271–72, 274, 275, 279, 282, 294
Chang Yen-yuan, 278
Chao Meng-fu, 13, 287
Chardin, Jean-Baptiste, 12, 459, 462–64, 470, 481
Charioteer at Delphi, 104, 109
Charlemagne, 194, 402
Charles I, King of England, 357
Charles III, King of Spain, 469
Charles IV, King of Spain, 469–70
Charles V, Holy Roman Emperor, 373, 404, 410
Charles VI, King of France, 479
Charles VIII, King of France, 421
Chartres Cathedral, 192, 199–202, 205, 206; fire, 199, 200; rebuilding, 199–200; Royal Portal, 11, 207–8; stained-glass windows, 200–1, 203, *ill.* 201
Château de Steen, 357, 358
Chavín de Huántar, 304, 305, 306; Great Image, 305–6, *ill.* 307
Chazal, André, 495
Chialing River, 275
Chiaroscuro, 90, 324, 368, 386
Chimu art, 13, 308, 309
China, 16, 56, 220, 225, 251, 267–88; -America (Pre-Columbian), 304–5; archaeologists, 261; archetypal forms, 401; art, 12–13, 220, 248, 282, 292, 294, 299, 304, characteristics, 267–69, 271, 274–75, 278: forms, 267, 268, 269–71, horses, 281, 284, 287, influences on, 270, 280–82, materials, 274, "Mi-dot" technique, 283, purpose, 271, tombs, 281, 287 (*see* T'ang Dynasty); artists, 7, 270–71, 273, 274–76, 278–79, 280, 296, greatest, 275, 279; Bodhisattvas, 260, 262; books, 269–70; bronzes (Yellow River Valley), 70–71; Buddhas, 253, 258, 259–60, 261, 282, Lung Men, 262, Maitreya, 260–61; Buddhism, 236, 258–59, 264, 272–73, 274 *and* n, 290–91; calligraphy, 30, 269; capital (*see* Ch'ang-an); caravans, 272; cave-temples, 11, 22, 260–61; Ch'ang-an, 271–72; characteristics, 267, 272, 274, 282, 288, 291,

303; Ch'in Dynasty, 270, 478; Chou Dynasty, 269, 304; Communist, 303; court, 262, 271–72, 285; frescoes, 7, 264; Goddess Kuanyin, 242; gods, 267; greatest dynasty (see Han Dynasty); Gupta art, 258, 262; Han Dynasty, 259, 270, 273, art, 270–71, 287; India, 280–82; influences on, 280; jade, 282; Japan, cultural contrast, 291–92, 294, 296, 297; Kansu, 248; landscapes, 264, 275, 288; Lung Men caves, 260–61, 262; Mai Chi Shan caves, 261; Ming Huang, Emperor, 275, 278; monasteries, 273, 278, 287; Mongols, 219, 287; Ning, Prince, 275; paintings (painters), 9, 15, 270–71, 274–80, 282–83, 285–88, 296, 390, 459, cave, 11, 22, 260–61; pilgrimages, 261; poets, 271, 278, 279, 284, 301; power, 270; religion, 7, 287 (see Buddhism); scholars, 253; sculpture, 261, 304 (see Buddhas); Shang Dynasty, 288, 303, 401, bronzes, 267–69, 270; Sui Dynasty, 273; Sung Dynasty, 276, 278, 282–85, 296, 459; Szechuan, 275; T'ai Tsung, Emperor, 273–74; T'ang Dynasty, 262, 264, 271–72, 273, 280–82, 284, 288, 299, 330, 339, 459, 478, art, 262, colors, 264, masterpieces, 283; t'ao-t'ieh (dragon), 268–69, 270, 304, ill. 269; temples, 294; T'ien Lung Shan Buddhas, 262; tomb figures, 281; T'o-pa emperors, 259; travelers, 253; Tun-huang caves, frescoes, 264; Wei Dynasty, 187, 259–60, 261, 264; Wu, Empress, 262, 274n; yang and yin, 267–68, ill. 268; Yüan Dynasty, 280; Yün Kang caves, 261–62
Chios: Nea Moni mosaics, 159
Ch'i Pai-shih, 13, 288
Chosroes II, 81, 82
Christ, 104, 147; appearance, 151, 163, 165–66, 246; catacombs, 166–67; of Cefalù, 171–72; Crucifixion, 172–74, 184; Dead Christ, 176; divinity, concept of, 171; Edessa portrait, 163–65, 169; glorification (medieval), 181; halo, 169; icons, 163; Pietàs, 177 (see Michelangelo); portraits, 15, 162–78, Byzantine, 171, 172, 176, 183, evolution, 170–73, 176, Flemish, 176, Gothic, 176, medieval sculptures, 180, mosaic, 169–70, 174, oils, 174–75, Renaissance, 175–77, Romanesque, 183, 191, third century, ill. 168, veneration of, 169; Salvator Mundi, 175; Second Coming, 165, 166, 246; symbols, 246, 247; walking statue, 253; youthful tradition, 167–68
Christian art, 165, 225
Christianity, 8, 157, 165, 246; cemeteries, 124; Constantine, 143, 168; gateways, 181, 185; Germany, 402; relics, 479; Resurrection (see under Caravaggio); Roman Empire, 167; Romanesque art, 182–83; spread of, 162ff.

Christus, Petrus, 344
Chuang Tzu, 270
Churches, 7, 147, 152, 169; -artist, relationship, 7–8; Byzantine, 148, 169–70; Christian, 147–48; Gothic, 191–92; Romanesque, 183, 191, 195, 198, 205. See Hagia Sophia
Cicero, 130
Cimabue, 172, 173, 174, 319, 322
Circassian slaves, 218
Cities, as works of art, 317–18
Civilizations, 33, 68, 124
Clark, Kenneth, 425
Clemenceau, Georges, 485
Clement of Alexandria, 166
Clouet, François, 334
Clovio, Giulio, 444–45, 446, 449
Clovis, King, 185
Clowns, 460, 461. See Rouault, Georges
Cluny, tympanum, 191
Coatlícue, 310–11, 312
Coins, 115, 121, 134, 143, 247–48, 318
Collages, 511
Collections (art), 10, 12, 392–93
Colleoni, Verrocchio statue, 332
Colman: St. Martin's Cathedral, 403, 408
Colonies, 122
Colonna, Vittoria, 433, 435
Colonna family, 440
Color, 289; Bosch, 350; Chardin, 463; laws, 509; nature of, 481, 482, 487 (see Impressionism); Time and, 334; Tintoretto, 375, 376; Titian, 372, 375; Venice, 360; Veronese, 380
Comic drawings, 467–68
Communication, tools of, 30
Condivi, Ascanio, 423
Confucius (Confucianism), 270, 271, 287
Conquerors, monuments, 219
Constantina, baptistery, 149
Constantine, 143–44, 147, 149, 168; Arch of, 143–44; Christ, portrayal of, 169; court, 169
Constantinople, 111, 155, 160, 202; Crusaders, 361; fall of, 8, 160–61; mosaics, 151, 153, 154–55 (see Hagia Sophia); Nika riots, 152; relics, 199; Venetians, 160, 361, 362
Convent of San Marco, 25
Copenhagen, 496
Corot, Jean Baptiste, 482
Correggio, 475
Corsica, 122
Cortés, Hernán, 309, 310
Counter-Reformation, 439
Court: -artist relationship, 7–8 (see painters); Byzantine, 169; caliphs, 215; Chinese, 271–72, 285; Crete, 94; Flemish, 340; Japanese, 294; painters, 173, 191, 250, 340, 354–55, 415, 451, 469, 470; Spanish, 453, 454
Coutances Cathedral, 205
Couture, Thomas, 486
Cranach, Lucas, 415–16
Crete, 85–97, 444; arts, 85–90, 93; char-

acteristics, 85, 88, 93–94; court, 94; dates, 85; Egypt, 93–94; frescoes, 89–90; gods, 95; Greeks, 85, 88. *See* Knossos

Croatia, 444

Croesus, King, 122

Crown of Thorns, 202, 204

Crucifix, 124, 172

Crusades (Crusaders), 198, 199, 204, 213, 216, 219, 361, 474

Ctesiphon, 209; palace, 81–82, 209

Cubism, 504, 506, 507, 511

Cult objects, 147, 305–6

Culture: indestructibility of, 130; -tradition, relationship, 402

Cuyp, Jacob, 383

Cuzco, 308

Cycladic statues, 100

Cylinder seals, 58–59

Cyprus, 369

Cyrus the Great, 68, 74

Dacia, 139, 140

Dadaists, 507

Damascus, 209, 212, 219; Great Umayyad Mosque, 212, 213

Daniele da Volterra, 432, 435

Dante Alighieri, 320, 420, 421, 424; *Divine Comedy*, Blake illustrations, 475, 476; *Inferno*, Blake illustrations, 476–77; *Paradiso*, 424

Daphni, church of, 159–60

Daphni Pantocrator, 171, 172, 173, 175

Darius I, King, 68, 74, 77, 78, 79

Daumier, Honoré, 492

David (Michelangelo), 8, 104, 327, 425–26, 427

Da Vinci. *See* Vinci, Leonardo da

Death: abstract forms, 95–96; Etruscans, 125–26; Japanese, 292; masks (Roman), 133, 136

Degas, Edgar, 490–91

Deir el Bahri, 44, 45

Delacroix, Eugène, 461, 482

Delft, 394, 395, 396, 398–99

Delhi, Mongols in, 219

Della Roveres, 373

Del Monte, Cardinal Francesco Maria, 440

Denmark, 495

Descartes, René, 387

Diamond Sutra, The, 263–64, *ill.* 263

Díaz, Bartholomew, 369

Díaz del Castillo, Bernal, 310

Dickens, Charles, 494

Diderot, 463

Dignity of man, 78–79, 341, 381

Dijon, 340

Dio Chrysostom, 168

Diocletian, 150

Diodorus Siculus, 122

Dionysius the Aeropagite, 450

Divine Comedy: Blake illustrations, 475, 476; Botticelli illustrations, 330, 331

Divinity, 14–15, 330–31, 343; artist creation of, 7; emblem of, 423–24; image of, 162; Indian, 232; nature of, 177–78; within the artist, 414. *See* Coatlícue

"Divine repositories," 115; classical example, 114–15

Dome of the Rock, 213–14, 218

Dominic, St., 205

Donatello, 322, 323, 326–28; *David* (Bargello), 326; *Gattamelata*, 327, 328; influence, 327, 329; *St. John the Baptist* (Duomo), 326, 327

Donne, John, 387

Dono, Paoli di. *See* Uccello, Paolo

Doria family, 440

Dorian invasions, 85, 96–97

Dresden, 366, 368

Dreyfus, Alfred, 490

Dubuffet, Jean, 511, 512

Duccio, Agostino di, 12, 173–74, 322, 424–25

Dürer, Agnes, 409, 410, 413

Dürer, Albrecht, 177, 363, 392, 404, 408–17, 475; *Apocalypse*, 409, 413; death, 411; paintings, 414; self-portraits, 408, 414, 417; signature, 414–15; woodcuts, 413–14; writings, 409–10, 415

Dutch art, 358, 507; interiors, 395ff., 400; landscapes, 385, 400; light, 397; painting, 383ff.

East, the, 198, 230, 232

East Berlin Museum, 119

Eastern Church, Fathers, 166

East Indies: Buddhism, 251, 255

Ebro River, 28

Edessa portrait (icon), 163–65, 169

Edfu (Egypt), 37

Edinburgh, 395

Egypt, 35–56, 57, 68, 72, 74, 288, 303; Arabs, 210; art, 37, 38, 39–40, 43, 44, 46, 52, 53ff., 57, 63, 64, 65, 86, 100, 218, 478, 497, endurance, 55–56, influence of, 44, 55, inventions, 43, 56, masterpieces, 45, 50–51, 56; civilization, 35, 37, 56; Cretans, contrast, 93–94; death, 95; Eighteenth Dynasty, 37, 45, 78–79; Eleventh Dynasty, 44; gods, 38, 39, 40, 41–42, 45, 50; griffin, 90; Herodotus, 121; hieroglyphics, 30, 37; invasions, 56; Islamic rulers, 215; kingship, 38, 41–42; Mamluk (slave) Dynasty, 218–19; murals, 63; mythology, 42; Nineteenth Dynasty, 37; Old Kingdom, 43, 44, 45; pharaohs, 44, 45, 54–55, 65, 72, 87, 95, 122, 314, 478; portraiture, 86; priesthood (Amon), 46, 51, abolition, 47, 49; pyramids, 41, 42, 313 (*see under* name) reliefs, 64; Romans, 131; sculpture, 39–40, 43, 44, 65, 100; Sixth Dynasty, 56; State Department of Antiquities, 50; Sun worship, 47; temples, 45–46; Third Dynasty, 40; tombs, 44, 52, 92; wall painting, 37, *ill.* 36. *See* Akhenaton

Eidetic images, 30, 31, 33
Elba, 122
Eleanor of Aquitaine, 193, 197
Elephanta, 229; caves, 229, 232, 242; *Trimurti*, 305
Elgin, Lord, 111
El Greco, 12, 444–50, 455, 475; influences on, 446; inventory, 450; Michelangelo, 445, 446; mysticism, 449, 451; patron, 445; self-portrait, 445, 446; style, 444, 445, 447, 449, 450; teachers, 444; Toledo, 447–49; *works: Assumption of the Virgin*, 446, *Burial of Count Orgaz*, 448–49, *Christ*, 13, *Christ Driving Out the Traders from the Temple*, 446, *Despoiling of Christ*, 446–47, *Espolio*, 453
El Karnak ("the fortress"), 46
Ellora caves, 233, 235, 236
Elsheimer, Adam, 355, 386, 417, 418
Emperors, first, 72
Empires, death of, 94
England, 318, 357, 427; art, 183, 197, 205, 207, 401, 417, 474; royal collection, 10 (*see* Blake, William); empire, end of, 94; France, 207; Gothic cathedrals, 197, 205, 207; Holbein, 417; India, 236; Piranesi engravings, 466; poets, 387; Romanesque, 183; Spain, 357. *See* London *and* British Museum
Engravings: Blake, 474ff.; Dürer, 408, 411–12; eighteenth century, 460; German, 404, 475; Italian, 475; painted (*see* Blake, William); Piranesi prison scenes, 465–66
Epstein, Jacob, 511
Equestrian portraits, 322
Equestrian statues, 327–28, 332
Erasmus, 410
Erechtheion (Greek temple), 107, 114–15
Estes family, 373
Etchings: Goya: *Disasters of War*, 472; Rembrandt, 390
Eternity: eidetic images, 30, 33
Ethiopia, 56
Etruria, 121, 129, 174. *See* Etruscans
Etruscans, 121–30, 135; *Apollo of Veii*, 127; art, 125, 126–28, 507; Greek influence, 128–29; Chimaera, 126; culture, 122; decline (date), 124; Greeks, 125; language, 130; Museum (Florence), 126; origin, 121; Romans, 125, 129–30, 132; ruins, 464; tombs, 123, 124, 128, 132–33
Euphrates River, 57
Euphronios, *ill.* 102
Europe, 80, 93, 198, 219, 318, 410; twelfth century, 478; fifteenth century, 339–40; eighteenth century, 459–60; Arabic influence, 198; artistic capital, 130 (*see* Florence); arts, 119, 303, 321, 505; Byzantine influence, 161; Greece, 282; modern age, beginning, 459
Eusebius: *Ecclesiastical History*, 164

Evagrius, 161
Evans, Sir Arthur, 86–91, 94
Expressionists, 507
Eyck, Hubert van, 341; *Ghent Altarpiece*, 341–43
Eyck, Jan van, 174, 340–44, 346, 347, 351, 358; characteristics, 343–44, 358; Rembrandt, 392, 393; *works: Adoration of the Lamb*, 342, 346, *Arnolfini and wife*, 343, 350, *Head of an Old Man*, 392, *Rolin Madonna*, 342–43

Fabergé, 63
Fabritius, Carel, 383, 389, 394
Fa Hsien, 253
Family (human), representation of, 56
Far East: sculpture, 55
Farnese, Cardinal Alessandro, 444–45
Fautrier, Jean, 511–12; *The Hostages*, 512
Fauves, 507
Ferdinand VII, King of Spain, 472
Ferghana, 76
Fertility emblems, 62, 242–43
Fiesole, 130
Flanders, 328, 339, 340, 358, 359, 382, 460; art revival, 481; *kermesses héroiques*, 382; light, 319
Flémalle, Master of, 344, 481
Flemish art, 15, 174, 176, 351, 358, 460; golden age, 339–40; greatest painters, 353; masterpieces, 345, 346; modern man, 347; sky, light of, 358
Florence, 8, 104, 130, 321, 335–36, 337, 347, 377, 421; Accademia, 425, 426, 434; art, 130, 174, 258, 319, 320, 323ff., 329, 331, 338, 490; artists, 321ff. (*see under* name); atmosphere, 360; Baptistery, 115, 324–26; Bargello, 326, 422; Black Death, 176; Byzantine influence, 161; characteristics, 360, 362, 381; coinage, 318; Duomo, 326, 424, 435; Etruscans, 122, 127, Museum, 126; France, 421; medieval banners, 132; Michelangelo, 433 (*see under* name); museums, 10, 126, 363; *Orator* (Etruscan), 127; painters, 319ff.; Palazzo Vecchio, 332, 425, 426; Pisa, 332; power, 318–19; Renaissance, 317–38; Rome, 319; Santa Croce, 329; sculptors, 319ff.; Uffizi, 10, 363; wealth, 318
Florentia, 130
Flowers, painting, 353, 498–99
Focillon, Henri, 180, 205
Font-de-Gaume (France), cave paintings, 22
Formosa: Palace Collection, 297
Fountains (Islamic), 214
Fourment, Hélène, 357, 358
Fra Angelico (Giovanni da Fiesole), 25, 322, 323, 328, 486
Fragonard, Jean Honoré, 459, 464
France, 94, 110, 181, 459, 480–81, 483,

501; fifteenth century, 479ff.; eighteenth century, 481; nineteenth century, 481–82, 489–90; twentieth century, 502ff., 506; Academy, 463; Arabic artisans, 216; archetypal forms, 401–2; Army, 483; arts: painting: seventeenth century, 460, eighteenth century, 459ff., cave, 19, 21, 25, *natures mortes*, 462–63: Impressionists, 12, 13, 14, 384, 399, 464, 474, 485ff., 489, 490, 491, 493, 496, 501, 507, 511: sculptors, 403; *Avignon Pietà*, 401; Brittany, 485–86; cave paintings, 19, 21, 25; China, 261; England, 207; Florence, 421; Gothic cathedrals, 188, 205, 207, 339; Holland, 398; Italy, 332; Japan, 490, 493; mistral, 494; museums, 10 (*see under* Paris); *pater patriae*, 193; poets, 483; Provence, 499, 501; Revolution, 204, 464, 482; Romanesque, 183; Spain, 472

Francesca, Piero della, 12, 328, 329–30, 506; Madonnas, 337; *The Risen Christ*, 329

Francis, St., of Assisi, 205

Francke, Master, 402

Frankfurt, 404

Frescoes: Ajanta caves, 238, 240; Chinese, 7, 263–65; da Vinci, 333; Etruscan, 123–24; Francesca, 329–30; Giotto, 183, 320–21; Italian, 132, 428; Michelangelo, 429; Minoan, 89–90; monasteries, 263–64; mosaics, 160; Pompeiian, 467

Fugger family, 410

Funeral mounds: Lydian, 121–22

Funeral steles: Greek, 117, 124

Futurists, 507

Gad, Mette, 495

Galerius, Emperor, 149

Galileo, 354

Galla Placidia, Empress, 157–58

Galli, Jacopo, 422

Gandharan art, 14, 169

Ganges River, 241, 242, 248

Gardens, hanging, 59, 60

"Gateway of the Sun," 306

Gateways, 181, 185

Gaudier-Brzeska, 511; *ill.* 513

Gauffrage, 299

Gauguin, Paul, 493, 494, 495–97, 499, 503, 505, 509; fame, 497; *works*, 495–97

Genghis Khan, 219

Genji, Prince, 295–96

Genoa, 354; Church of St. Bartholomew of the Armenians, 165

Gentile da Fabriano, 362–63; *Adoration of the Kings*, 363

Germany, 176, 402–18; art, 402ff., 418, Dürer contribution, 415, greatest figures, 411, 418, height, 417, 418, painting, 402ff., 408, 415, sculpture, 403;

Christianity, 402; culture, 402ff.; Gothic cathedrals, 207; *Götterdämmerung*, 402; landscapes, 416; medieval, 409; museums, 10 (*see under* city); Nefertiti statue, 50; philosophers, 501

Ghent, 340; Altarpiece, 341–43, 346

Ghiberti, Lorenzo, 322, 323, 324; Baptistery doors, 324–26

Ghirlandaio, Domenico, 420, 428; *Last Supper*, 335–36

Giacometti, 128

Gill, Robert, 236–37

Giocando, Lisa del, 333. *See* Mona Lisa

Giorgione, Il, 14, 366–70, 371, 374, 376, 392; *Fêtes Champêtre*, 366, 367–68, 487; *Sleeping Venus*, 366, 368–69; *works*, 366–67. *See* Titian

Giotto, 173, 174, 317, 319, 320–21, 322, 323, 324, 362, 499, 500; assistants, 321; frescoes, 183, 320–21; Scrovegni Chapel, 377; *works: Crucifixion* (Padua), 173, *Ognissanti Madonna*, 321

Gislebertus of Autun, 188–89, 191, 192

Gods: androgynous, 232; East-West contrast, 230. *See under* country or civilization

Goes, Hugo van der, 345–47, 410, 444; *Adoration of the Shepherds*, 346–47

Goldsmiths, 95–96, 339; Ghiberti, 325–26

Goldwork, Sumerians and, 68

Gonzaga, Vincenzo (Duke of Mantua), 354–55

Gothic art, 191, 192, 196ff., 203, 204–5, 207–8; architects, 202, 203, 204, 205; cathedrals, 191–92, 205, 207–8, 339, 481; cost, 204, creation, 341, first, 188; Christ, 176; demise, 207; *Gothic,* term, 198; innovator, 193, 198 (*see* Abbot Suger); *lux continua*, 196, 197, 202; origin, 216; Romanesque, 192; supreme achievement, 202 (*see* Chartres Cathedral); tombstones, 126

Goths, 155, 179, 181, 198

Government: medieval Christian concept, 157

Goya, Francisco de, 12, 370, 455, 459, 468–74, 475, 477, 486; court painter, 469–70, 472; madness, 470, 472, 473; patrons, 469; reputation, 461; signature, 9; teacher, 468; *works*, 470, 471, 472, 473, 476, *The Naked Maja*, 487

Goyen, Jan van, 383, 385

Grave robbers, 280

Great Cloud Sutra, The, 274n

Great Goose Monastery, 273

Greece (Ancient), 56, 72, 74, 103, 124, 207, 288, 318, 459, 504; Achaemenids, 74; architects, 105; art, 7–8, 60, 497, 507, abstract hieratic element, 99, characteristics, 115, 126, 181, 478, dominance of forms, 119, end of, 119, endurance, 119–20, influence, 248, 258,

423, 505; Byzantine art, 159; colonies, 115, 128; Crete, 85, 88; Dorian invasions, 96–97; Egypt, influence, 44, 55; Etruscans, 125, 127, influence on art, 128–29; Florence, 174; gods, 40, 100–1, 104, 110, 115–16, 233; historians, 122, 124; India, 232; Islam, 215; *kouroi*, 44; Minoan influence, 95; mosaics, 103; museums, 10; mythology, 99; orators, 168; painting, 6, 101, 102–3; Periclean Age, 339; Persepolis, 78; Persians, 78, 104, 105; philosophy, 100–1, 332; pottery, 9, 306; revival of learning, 8; Rome, 68, conquest, 119; sculpture (sculptors), 12, 98–101, 105, 113, 116–18, 168, heroic theme, 101, 104–5, Rome, 133–34, 136–37, signatures, 9; temples, atmosphere, 147; vases, 102–3, 128; wall painting, 103. *See also* Athens; Mycenae; *and* Parthenon
Griffins, 89–90
Grünewald, Andreas, 407
Grünewald, Matthias, 404–8, 415, 416, 475; death, 411; self-portrait, 407–8; *works*, 404, 407, *Altarpiece at Colmar*, 176, *Isenheim Altarpiece*, 176–77, 404, 405–7
Crylli, 349
Guardi, Francesco, 459
Guariento: *Coronation of the Virgin*, 362
Guatemala, 311
Gudea statues, 65–66
Guersi, Guido, 405
Gunadharma (Javanese architect), 256–57
Gupta art, 14. *See under* India

Haarlem, 383
Hadith, 209, 211
Hadrian, 142, 143, 144; villa, 142, 144
Hagia Sophia, 153–56, 160–61, 169
Hagia Triada sarcophagus, 91–94; *ill.* 92
Hague, The, 387, 395; Mauritshuis, 394, 399
Halicarnassus, 121
Halo, 169
Hals, Frans, 383–85; imitators, 384; *Laughing Cavalier*, 384–85; pupils, 385
Han Dynasty, 259, 270–71, 273; emperors, 259
Han Fei Tzu, 270
Hanging gardens, 59, 60
Hankan, 280, 284; *Training Horses*, 283
Harunobu, 298–99
Harvester Vase (Cretan), 9, 93–94
Hatshepsut, Queen, 44, 79
Haussmann, Baron, 482
Heliopolis, 47
Hellenistic art, 133; China, 280; influence, 162. *See* Greece
Henri IV, King of France, 356
Henry V, King of England, 479
Heraclitus, 392

Heraklion (Crete) museum, 86
Herat, 220
Herculaneum mosaics, 148–59
Hermitage (Leningrad), 496
Herodotus, 121
Heroic age, mark of, 105
Hierakonpolis, 43; wall paintings, 37, *ill.* 36
Hieroglyphics, 30, 37
Hildesheim Cathedral, 181
Himalayas, 232, 233, 236
Hinduism, 232, 235
Hiroshige, 301–2, 353, 490
Historians, 121, 122, 124, 132, 164, 251, 259, 362, 392, 428; art, 381, 404, 442, 503 (*see* Vasari, Giorgio)
History of art, 37; calligraphy, 29–30; milestones, 64. *See* Art
Hitler, Adolf, 50, 511
Hittites, 54, 71
Hokusai, 300–1, 490; *Hundred Views of Mount Fuji*, 300
Holbein, Hans, 392, 417
Holland, 339, 358, 382–83, 492; France, 398; Golden Age, 383, 400; Guilds, 387; landscape, 382, 385; law, 393; painters, 383ff., 394; religion, 382, 387; Spain, 382–83, 385. *See* Dutch art
Holy See, 193
Homer, 96, 392
Honfleur, 483
Hooch, Pieter de, 383, 400
Horace, 131, 135
Horyu-ji (temple), 264–65, 290, 293
Hosios Lucas (near Delphi), 171; mosaics, 159
Hsüan Tsang (monk), 236, 253, 272–73, 274 *and* n
Hsü Hsi, 283
Hugo, Hermannus, 453
Human dignity, 78–79, 341, 381
Humanism, 177, 328, 355; twelfth century, 159
Human relationships, 56
Hundred Views of Mount Fuji, 300
Hundred Years' War, 207
Hunting scenes, 67–68; Persian, 80–81
Huygens, Constantijn, 386–87, 392
Hymn to the Sun, 47–49
Hypnerotomachia Poliphili, 367

Ibn Tulun, 215
Iconoclasts, 5
Iconography, 158, 183, 184; Buddhist, 260, 273; Dürer, 413; Thais, 254
Icons, 510; Byzantine, 175, 322; Christ, face of, 163, 165 (*see Edessa portrait*); Greek, 444
Ictinus (Greek architect), 105
Illuminated manuscripts, 174, 220–21, 479–80
Images, 163–64; Buddhism, 235, 246; calligraphic-eidetic distinctions, 30; Hinduism, 244; Islamic, 211, 212, 244

Imagination, influencing factors, 289. *See under* country
Imhotep, 40–41
Immortality, beliefs in, 95
Impressionism (Impressionists), 12, 13, 14, 384, 399, 464, 474, 485ff., 489, 490, 491, 493, 496, 501, 507, 511. *See under* name
Incas, 13, 308–9
India, 12, 14, 72, 76, 211, 229–45, 272, 292, 339; Ajanta caves, 11, 236–40, 242, 250–51; archetypal forms, 401; architects, 243; art, 220, 230–33, 234, 236ff., 244–45, 248, 255, contributions, 244–45, Gupta, 232, 240, 251, 252, 257, 258, height, 239, 249, 251, masterpieces, 231: miniatures, 16, painting, 319, portraits, 230, 237–38, rock carvings, 240–41, sculpture, 229–31, 233, 241–42, 243, 249; Bengalis, 242; Buddha Padmapani, 237–38, 239; Buddhism, 235, 236, 242, 251, 291, art, 236, end, 236, 265, Hindu conflict, 236; Ceylon, 239; Chandellas, 242; China, 272, 273, 280–81; dancing, 242, 244–45; Deccan, 241; Elephanta caves, 229, 232; Ellora cave-temples, 233, 235, 236; fertility theme, 242–43; Gandharan art, 232; gods, 229–35, 239–40, 241, 243–45 (*see* Siva); Gupta era, 231, 239, 288, 478, art (*see under* art); Hindu temples, 242; Hoysala kings, 242; imagination, 234, 267; influence, 251; Kailasa temple, 233–35, 236; Khajuraho, 242, 244; Kupta emperors, 249; Kushans, 248; *lingam*, 234–35; Lion Rock at Sigiriya, 239–40; Mahendra I, 241; Mamallapuram rock carving, 240–41, 242; missionaries, 262; Narasimha I, 241; Pallava rulers, 240, 241; Rajput princes, 242; religion, official, 235; Sena Dynasty, 241; Siva, 229–31, 232, 240, birthplace, 233, Nataraja, 244–45; *stupas*, 235, 236; Sun Temple of Konarak, 243–44; Tara, 241–42; temples, 235, 242–44, 245; *Trimurti*, 230, 231–32, 233. *See* Buddha *and* Buddhist art
Indian Ocean, 251, 369, 385
Indochina, 272, 274
Indonesia, 249
Industrial Revolution, 459, 489
Ingres, Jean, 481
Innocent X, Pope: Velázquez portrait, 454
Ionian Sea, 122
Ireland, 182
Irenaeus, 166
Isaiah, 187
Isenheim: Monastery of St. Anthony, 405
Isfahan, 215, 220, 223–24, 317; Masjid-i-Jami, 216, 217
Islam, 186, 213; extent of empire, 212; history, 218; India, 243, 244; religion, 212, 219, 225; rulers, 212–13, 215. *See* Islamic art
Islamic art, 5, 211–12, 213, 214, 215, 218, 225–26; death of, 226. *See also* Persia
Isodorus of Miletus, 154
Israelites, 204
Italy, 121, 155, 181, 317, 354, 369, 409; art, 12, 131ff., 183, 207, frescoes, 132, 428, sculpture, most brilliant, 424; Byzantine influence, 161; Dürer woodcuts, 413–14; Etruscans, 123; Lombardy, 362; Spain, 355; Tuscany, 10, 336, 368. *See* Florence; Renaissance; Rome (Ancient); Rome (city) *and under* names of artists

Ja'afar Baysungkuri, 221
Jade, 282
Japan, 289–302, 311, 392; archetypal forms, 401; art, 289ff., 292–93, 294, 295–96, 297ff., 490, 493, *gauffrage,* 299, painting, 264–65, 293, 295–97, prints, 16, 297–302, sculpture, 12, 293–94, "splashed ink" technique, 297, *ukiyo-e,* 297, 299, 300; artists, 296, 297, 298, 299, 300, 301; Buddha statues, 249, 251, 293–94; Buddhism, 290–91, 294–95; capital (*see* Kyoto); characteristics, 289, 291, 293, 311; China, 311, cultural contrast, 291–92, 294, 296, 297; collections, 297; color, 289; court, 294; *Daibutsu* (Nara), 294; Fujiwara clan, 294, 295; gods, 294; Gupta art, 258; *haniwa* figures, 290; Heian era, 478; history, 289–90; Horyu-ji monastery, 264–65; Kamakura period, 293; Meiji Restoration, 302; *mono no aware,* 292; prostitutes, 298–99; religion, 290; temples, 290, 294; tombs, 290; *ukiyo-e,* 297, 299; United States, 302; woodblock prints, 281, 490, 493; Zen, 297
Java, 256
Jeremiah, 186, 187
Jericho, 211
Jerome, 166
Jerusalem, 317; Crusaders, 213–14; Dome of the Rock, 213–14, 218; Fountain of Qait Bey, 214; Wailing Wall, 317
Jewelry, Etruscan, 128
Jews, 272
John, St., of Damascus, 163–64, 169
John the Baptist, 212
Jordaens, Jacob, 392
Josephus, Flavius: *Jewish Antiquities,* 392
Judas, 167
Judea, 131, 165
Julius II, Pope, 153, 427–28; Michelangelo, 428–29, 434; tomb, 434
Justinian, Emperor, 152, 153–54, 155–56, 158, 169–70; appearance, 156, 157; mosaics, 153ff.

Kadesh, 54
Kalf (Dutch painter), 383
Kant, Immanuel, 501
Karnak (temple complex), 46, 51-52, 54; Akhenaton statues, 51
Kashans, pottery, 217
Kassites, 71
Kavvadias, Panagiotis, 101
Kesh: Timur Palace, 219-20
Khmer art, 12, 13, 513
Khotanese, 272
Kingship, 41-42, 56, 87
Kiyonaga, 299
Klee, Paul, 506, 511
Knossos, 85, 88, 89, 90, 91, 94, 95; art, 100, 239; excavations, 86ff., 94; "throne room," 89
Koran, 209, 211
Korea, 270; Buddhas, 265-66; Gupta art, 258; Japan, 289
Kokoschka, Oskar, 506, 511; *Windbraut*, 511
Kouroi, 44
Kuchanese, 272
Ku K'ai-chih (Han artist), 270-71, 283; *Admonitions of the Imperial Instructress*, 270-71
Kung Hsien, 288
Kunsthistoriches Museum (Vienna), 366
Kuo Hsi, 285-87
Kurush. *See* Cyrus the Great
Kushans, 248-49; art, 248, 251; Gandhara (Apollonian Buddha), 248, 249; Mathura, 249
Kyoto (Japan), 12, 294, 301, 317

Lachares, 114
Lagash statues, 65
Lagraulas, Jean de Bilhères de, 423
Lake Baikal, 259
Lake Garda, 364
Landscapes, 8, 350; Cézanne, 499; Chinese, 264, 275, 279-80; Dutch, 385, 400; French, 480-81; German, 416; Japanese, 301; painting from nature, 490; Rubens, 357
Language: calligraphic art, 30; Chinese, 267; Cretan, 86; Etruscan, 130; Minoan, 95; Mycenae, 95; Paleolithic, 28; Sanskrit, 264
Laocoön, 428, 431
Lascaux cave paintings, 21, 22, 25-26, 27, 30, 513, *ill.* 26; date, 37
Last Judgment (Michelangelo), 117, 376, 378, 431-33, 445, 446
Lastman, Pieter, 386, 417-18
Last Supper (da Vinci), 177, 334-36
La Tzu, 269-70
Leenhoff, Léon-Edouard, 486
Leenhoff, Suzanne, 486
Le Havre, 483
Leningrad: Hermitage, 496
Lentulus, 165
Leo III (Byzantine emperor), 163
Lerma, Duke of, 355

Leyden, Ernst van, 511
Lhote, Henri, 31
Liang K'ai, 296, 297
Libraries, 119
Libya, 56
Light, 409; Caravaggio, 417; Dutch, 395, 397-99; El Greco, 450; Flanders, 319; Florence, 319; nature of, 481, 482, 484, 487-89; Rembrandt, 389; Van Eyck, 343, 344, 358; Venice, 381
Li Lung-mien, 283, 284
Limbourg, Herman, 479-81
Limbourg, Jehanequin, 479-81
Limbourg, Pol, 479-81
Lion Rock at Sigiriya, 239-40
Li Ssu-hsün, 274-76
Literature, 450, 479-80, 484, 504-5. *See also* Books
Liu Pang, 270
Livy, 132
Lodovica, Anna Maria, 10
Lombardy, 362
London, 357, 395; British Museum, 10, 111, 112, 168, 270; Crystal Palace, 237; Great Fire, 383; National Gallery, 175, 331, 343, 345, 370, 454; Tate Gallery, 513; Victoria and Albert Museum, 224; Wallace Collection, 384; Westminster Abbey, 474
Lorenzetti, Pietro, 322
Lorraine, 339
Louis VI, King of France, 193, 197
Louis IX, King of France (St. Louis), 200, 202-4, 205
Louvre (Paris), 10, 118, 333, 342, 366, 369, 397, 439, 441, 463, 485, 489, 493
Ludovisi Sarcophagus, 180
Luristan, 71; bronzes, 69-73, -Chinese, compared, 70-71; Sumerian influence, 71
Luther, Martin, 410, 415, 439
Luxembourg, 339; Palace, 356-57
Luxor (temple complex), 46, 54, 74, 317
Luzán y Martínez, 468
Lydians, 121, 154
Lysippus, 117-18

Macedonia, 161
Madonneri, 444
Madrid, 357, 371, 468, 471; Prado, 344, 348; Royal Tapestry Manufactory, 469
Magic: cave paintings, 21
Magnasco, Alessandro, 467
Mainz, 405
Málaga, Spain, 503
Malta, 441, 442; Cathedral of St. John (Valetta), 441
Mamallapuram (India) rock carving, 240-41
Mamluks, 218-19
Man: dignity of, 78-79, 341, 381; Greek philosophy, 100-1; modern, 33, 65
Mancini, Giulio Cesare, 445
Manet, Edouard, 399, 485-89, 490, 503;

Déjeuner sur l'Herbe, 487; *Le Bar aux Folies-Bergère*, 488; *Olympia*, 487
Mantegna, Andrea, 354, 363, 364–65, 377, 392, 409; *Dead Christ*, 364
Mantua, court of, 354–55
Maqsud Kashani, 224
Marcus Agrippa, 10, 11, 142
Marcus Aurelius, 114, 139, 143; Column, 140–41
Mariana, Queen of Spain, 453
Martini, Simone, 322, *Annunciation*, 322
Martyrs, portrayal of, 140
Masaccio, 322–23, 326, 328, 363, 377; frescoes, 420; *The Tribute Money*, 323–24; *The Trinity*, 324
Mashhad, mosque, 215
Masks, 15; African, 505; Chimu, 308; Chinese, 304; Mycenae, 95; oceanic, 15, Roman, 133
Masolini, 377
Matisse, Henri, 505, 506, 507, 509–10, 513; *The Egyptian Curtain*, 509; *Head of a Woman, ill.* 510
Mauretania, 131
Maximilian, Emperor, 144, 347, 409
Mayans, 311, 313
Mecca, 212, 214; fall of, 210–11
Medici, Cosimo de', 328
Medici, Lorenzo de', 8, 65, 161, 328, 329, 482; court, 423–24; death, 337; Michelangelo, 420–21
Medici, Marie de', Queen of France, 356, 357
Medici, Piero de', 328; Michelangelo, 421
Medici family, 258, 336, 345, 346, 373, 383; Age of, 383; Chapel, 433–34; last, 10; Michelangelo, 433–34
Medieval art, 180, 181–82; manuscripts, 467; Roman influence 180–81
Medina, 82
Mediterranean, 88, 209; Roman conquest, 131
Meiji Restoration, 302
Melanchthon, Philipp, 415
Memlinc, Hans (*or* Memling), 344–45, 495, 501
Memphis (Egypt), 41
Mencius, 270
Mennonites, 387
Mentuhotep III, 44
Mes-kalam-dug (Sumerian general), gold helmet, *ill.* 61
Mesopotamia, 57, 58, 71; Mongols, 219. *See* Sumerians
Messara, plain of, 94
Messina, 442
Metalsmiths, 308
Metropolitan Museum (New York City), 12, 73
Metsu, Gabriel, 383, 395, 400
Mexico, 13, 311–13; Aztecs, 309–10
Mexico City, 303, 310, 311; Anthropological Museum, 312
Michael VIII Palaeologus, 160

Michelangelo, 8, 113, 119, 140, 326, 338, 375, 392, 404, 419–36, 439, 461, 464, 475, 482, 507; biographer, 423; birth, 420; characteristics, 275, 419–20, 424–426, 433; the Church, 424; death, 317, 435–36; *"divino,"* 419; El Greco, 445, 446; Flemish art, 358–59; Florence, 424ff.; friends, 433; heroic art, 380, 386; influences on, 327, 423; patrons, 419, 420, 422, 423, 433; poems, 433; Raphael, 419; reputation, 275, 424, 436; Rome, 422–24; signature, 9; sculpture, 428, 431, 434–35; teacher, 420; *terribilità*, 419, 426; themes, 432, 433; wealth, 433, 436; youth, 426; *works: Bacchus*, 422, 425; *David*, 8, 104, 327, 425–26, 427; *Last Judgment*, 177, 376, 378, 431–33, 445, 446; Medici Chapel, 434; *Moses*, 106, 327, 434; *Pietà*, 9, 15, 422–24, 425; *Pietàs*, 177, 374, 434–35; Sistine Chapel, 342, 377, 429–30, 431, 445
Middle Ages, 302
Middle East, 78, 162
Mi Fei, 278, 283–84, 285; *Gathering of Scholars in the Western Garden*, 283–84
Milan, 332, 434, 444; Brera Gallery, 364; Castello Sforzesco, 435; Convent of Santa Maria della Grazie (*Last Supper*), 334, 336
Miletus, 100
Ming Huang, Emperor, 13
Ming Ti, Emperor, 259
Miniatures (miniaturists), 274, 328, 351; Belgian, 479–80; Italian, 444; Persian, 220–21, 322, 497, 509. *See* Breugel, Jan
Minoan civilization, 85, 94, 97, 478; art, 95, 97, 100; capital, 94; colonies, 94–95; end of, 86, 94–95; Greece, influence on, 95; Hagia Triada sarcophagus, 91–94, *ill.* 92; Mycenae, 95, 130; palaces (*see* Knossos *and* Phaestos). *See* Crete
Minos, "priest-king," 87
Minotaur, 85
Miró, Joan, 506, 511
Missionaries, 259, 262, 289, 290, 402
Mixtec, 311
Moche, Peru, 306, 308, 314
Mochica ware, 306, 308
Modigliani, Amedeo, 506
Mohammed (prophet), 213, 214, 225; death, 209, 210; sayings (*see* Hadith); successor, 210; wife, 211
Mohenjo-daro, 401
Moissac (France) tympanum, 185ff., 189, 192, 207
Mona Lisa (da Vinci), 333–34
Monasteries, 263–64, 405; Buddhist, 278, 280; Chinese, 273, 278; frescoes, 263–64; Horyu-ji, 264–65
Monconys, Balthasar de, 396
Mondrian, Piet, 507
Monet, Claude, 399, 483–85, 486, 487, 488–89, 498, 501

Monfreid, Daniel de, 497
Mongols, 217, 219, 259, 270, 272, 287;
    invasions, 218; Mamluks, 219
Monks, 467. See Hsüan Tsang and Mon-
    asteries
Monreale, 171, 177; Pantocrator, 362
Montaigne: Essays, 392
Monte Albán, 313
Monterchi: Madonna in Childbirth, 329
Montespan (France) cave paintings, 21
Monteverdi, 354
Montmorillon, Virgin at, 183–84, 191
Montreuil, Pierre de, 202
Mont Sainte-Victoire, 498, 501, 502
Moore, Henry, 511
Morella la Vieja (Spain), 28–29, ill. 29
Morosini, Francesco, 110–11
Mosaicists, 150–51
Mosaics, 158; Alexandrine, 148; ancestry,
    148; Battle of Alexander, 148; Byzan-
    tine, 429; of Christ, 177; Christian,
    earliest, 149; Christ's portrait, 169–70;
    church, 169; cost of making, 152; de-
    velopment, 158–60; expense, 153, 158;
    Greek, 103; largest sheet, 144; master-
    works (see Salonica); rediscovery, 160;
    revolutionary invention, 174; Roman,
    144; Sumerians, 68; Umayyad, 211–12;
    Venice, 361–62; Virgin, 200; wall,
    148; Western churches, 257. See Ra-
    venna
Moses (Michelangelo), 106, 327, 434
Moses, staff, 203
Moses of Khorem, 164
Mosques, 82, 317; general plan, 214–15;
    Great Umayyad (Damascus), 212; lux-
    ury, 215; Masjid-i-Shah, 223; Persian,
    215; Seljuk, 215–16; Taj Mahal, 223
Mo Tzu, 270
Mount Kailasa, 233, 234
Muawiya, Caliph, 212
Mu Ch'i, 287, 288, 296, 297
Muhammed the Prophet, 82
Mumtaz Mahal, Empress, 223
Munich, 511
Muraski, Lady, 291, 295; Tales of Genji,
    295–96
Murillo, 455
Musashi, 297
Museums, 10–11, 61, 62, 73, 77, 86, 99,
    101, 104, 111, 112, 118, 119, 126, 127,
    132, 136, 142, 148, 168, 175, 224, 269,
    273, 297, 311, 331, 333, 342, 343, 344,
    345, 348, 363, 364, 366, 370, 371, 384,
    388, 394–95, 397, 399, 439, 441, 444,
    454, 463, 485, 489, 493, 496, 509, 513;
    concept of, 9–10; misleading character-
    istic, 11; most prestigious, 12; public,
    first, 10. See under name and/or city
Music, 21, 431, 482, 504–5
Mutawakkil, Caliph, 215
Mycenae, 96, 97; art, 95–96, 100,
    -Minoan, differences, 95; court, 95;
    end of, 95, 96; -Minoan culture, 130
Mycerinus, 44, 100

Myron, 113
Mystical Theology, 450
Mysticism (mystics), 449–50, 451, 474,
    484, 485
Mythology, 85, 459; Egyptian, 42; Greek,
    99; Tiepolo, 466

Naples, 104, 441, 443; National Museum,
    132, 148; Parma Academy, 469
Napoleon, Prince Louis, 482, 489. See
    Napoleon III
Napoleon Bonaparte, 459
Napoleon III, 489
Napoleonic Wars, 472
Nara (Japan), 12, 290, 293, 294, 317
Nara (Korea): Chugu-ji nunnery, 265–
    66
Narasimha, King, 243
Narmer, King, 38–40
Nasca, Peru, 306
National Gallery (London), 175, 331,
    343, 345, 370, 454
Naturalism, 478–79
Nature, 482–83, 500
Natures mortes, 462–63
Near East, 69, 155, 272, 280, 281; arche-
    typal forms, 401; Egypt, 218; Islam,
    219
Nefertiti, Queen, 47; portrait bust, 50–
    51, 52
Neolithic Age, 147
Nepal, 242, 265, 266
Nero, 139
New York, 352, 395
Nika riots, 152
Nile River, 35, 37, 57
Nineveh, 67
Nointel, Marquis de, 110
Nomads, 72
Noort, Adam van, 354
Normans, 172
North Africa, 155, 179, 181, 212
Nôtre Dame Cathedral (Paris), 202, 204,
    205, 206
Nubians, 54
Nudes: Cranach, 415–16; greatest painter
    of, 372; Tintoretto, 376; Velázquez,
    454–55. See also flesh under Art, tech-
    niques
Numidia, 154
Nuremberg, 408, 409, 410, 411

Oaxaca, 313
Oceanic masks, 15
Offenbach, Jacques, 482
Olmecs, 305
Olympic games, 8
On (ancient city), 47
Orient, 227–314, 369, 370; art, 12, 253,
    303; Buddha, face of, 246–66; China,
    267–88; color, 289; emperors, 224; In-
    dia, 229–45
Ottoman Turks, 218; Constantinople,
    160–61; Mongols, 219; Venice, 369

Pacheco, Francisco, 445–46, 450
Padua, 320, 409; Arena Chapel, 320–21; *Crucifixion* (Scrovegni Chapel), 173; Eremitani Church, 377; *Gattamelata* (Donatello), 327, 328; *St. Francis,* 327
Pagodas, 292
Painting (painters): academic, 482; Chinese, 274, 282–83, 285–87, 459; color, 274; Cubism, 504; Dutch, 383ff., 394; eighteenth century, 459ff.; Florence, 319ff.; flowers, 498–99; foreshortening, 324; France, 481–82; Germany, 402ff., 408, 414, 415–18; greatest, 461; Greek, 101, 102–3; Indian, 236ff., height, 239; intelligence, 321, 322; Japanese, 293, 295–97; landscape, 264, 275, 288; materials, 490; media, 174; modern, 510–11; "movements," 507; to music, 21; nature, 482–83; nature of, treatises on, 328; oils, 174–75; outside, 490; post-World War I, 506; primitives, 496; reality, 323, 501; Rembrandt, 386; Renaissance, 323ff.; revolution in, 500; Roman, 103; Romanesque, 183–84; royal honors, 221–22; science, 323, 324, 328; secularization, 8; silk, 15; Spanish, 444, 455; "spectrum palette," 490; techniques, 324; tempera, 174; tradition, 507; turning point, 321 (*see* Giotto); Venice, 360, 362–63, 368, 370. *See also under* country, painter *and/or* movement
Pakistan, 248
Palaces 74; Gothic, 192, 197–208; Persian, 81–82; Phaestos, 94. *See* Knossos
Paleolithic era, 21, 25
Palestine, 169; Arabs, 209
Palma Vecchio, 392
Palmer, Samuel, 475
Panoply, 169, 313; China, 272–73; Etruscans, 122, 129; Persia, 169
Pantheon (Rome), 142–43, 180
Pantocrator at Daphni, 171, 172, 173, 175
Paris, 69, 193, 395, 460, 493; Bastille, 479; Goupil Gallery, 493; Ile de la Cité, 202; Louvre, 10, 118, 333, 342, 366, 369, 397, 439, 441, 463, 485, 489, 493; Luxembourg Palace (Rubens), 356–57; Montmartre, 506; Musée de l'Art Moderne, 509, 513; Musée de l'Orangerie, 485; Musée Guimet, 513; Nôtre Dame, 202, 204, 205, 206; Occupied, 511; Opéra, 490; Palais du Trocadéro, 505; Sainte-Chapelle, 202–4, 481; Saint-Germain-des-Prés, 202; streets, 482; Tanguy's, 499
"Parisienne, la," 90, 91
Parthenon (Athens), 75, 97, 105, 106–14, 138, 313, 334, 399, 426; drawings of, 110; goddesses, 101; most precious figures, 110–11
Parthians, 79
Pa-ta Shan-jen, 287–88

Patrons, 336, 339, 354; royal, 373. *See under* artist
Paul III, Pope, 431, 432, 436
Paul, St., 151, 155, 158, 186, 187
Paulus Silentarius, 154, 155
Pausanias, 114
Pax Romana, 339
Peasants' War, 403
Peking, 317
Peloponnesian War, 107, 114, 115
Pepin the Short, tomb, 194
Peplos Kore, 101
Pergamon, 141; Great Altar, 118–19
Pericles, 105, 114, 339; Age of, 383
Persepolis, 11, 72, 77, 78, 81; Alexander the Great, 78; palace, 74–77
Persia, 11, 56, 101, 179, 196, 212, 272, 274, 339; Arab conquest of, 82; archetypal forms, 401; architecture, 216, 223–24; art, 68, 80, 82, 220, 222–23, 225, 226, 248, 497; influence, 220 (*see* Achaemenids, art); carpets, 224–25; China, 280; Egypt, 218; empire, 76–77; gods, 77, 79; Greece, 104, 105, 114; Luristan, 69, bronzes, 70, 71; Mervdasht Plain, 78; miniatures, 220–21, 322, 509; Mongols, 219; mosques, 215, 223; panoply, 169; religion, 76, 226; rulers, 209, 221; Safavid Dynasty, 222–24; Scythian invasion, 71; seat of power, 78 (*see* Persepolis); Seljuks, 215–16; symbol of royalty, 77; time (*zurvan*), obsession with, 81
Persian Gulf, 57
Peru, 304, 306, 308; pottery, 306, 308
Perugino, 354; *Assumption of the Blessed Virgin Mary,* 428
Peter, St., 155, 158
Peter the Great, 459
Peterzano, Simone, 438
Petrarch, 421
Phaestos, palace, 94
Phaidimos, 101
Phidias, 9, 104, 105–6, 110, 113–14, 116, 168, 256, 424, 438; signature, 9
Philip II, King of Spain, 382
Philip IV, King of Spain, 357, 451, 453; Velázquez portrait, 454
Philip the Good, 339–41, 343
Philosophers, 140, 198, 387, 501; French, 481; Neoplatonic, 367, 423–24; *School of Athens* (Raphael), 337
Photography, 490, 500
Picardy, 339
Picasso, Pablo, 502–6, 507, 508, 510, 511; characteristics, 503–4; influences on, 503; *works: Boy Leading a Horse,* 503, *Les Demoiselles d'Avignon,* 505–6, *Family of the Saltimbanques,* 503, *Gertrude Stein* (portrait), 503, *Seated Harlequin,* 506
Pictographs, 28, 38, *ill.* 36; antecedents, 58; Chinese, 267–68
Piero di Cosimo, 6, 428, 512

Pietà (Michelangelo), 9, 15, 422–24, 425
Pilgrimages: Buddhist, 261
Piraeus, 116
Piranesi, Giovanni, 459, 464–66, 467, 468; engravings, 465–66; teacher, 465
Pirkheimer, 408
Pisa, 332
Pisano, Giovanni, 319–20, 321
Pisano, Nicola, 320
Pissarro, Camille, 399
Pistoia: Church of San Andrea, 320
Pitti Palace (museum), 10
Pizarro, Francisco, 309
Plataea, 104
Platonism, 8
Pliny, 103, 428
Plutarch, 78, 106, 113
Po Chü-i, 291
Poets: Chinese, 278, 279, 284, 291, 301; English (*see* Blake, William); French, 483; Japanese, 291. *See under* name
Pointilism, 397
Pollaiuolo, 327, 409
Pollock, Jackson, 512
Pompeii, 103, 467
Popes, 139, 319, 369, 427–28, 445, 454
Portable art, 59
Portinari, Tommaso, 346, 347
Porto Ercole, 443
Portraiture (portraits), 8; bronze (Azerbaijan), 73; Buddha, 162ff.; Chinese, 273–74; Christ, 162ff., 172, 175–76; Cretan, 86–87; death masks, 133, 136; Dutch, 385–86; Egyptian, 86; equestrian (first in West), 322; Goya, 470; greatest, 372; imperial (mosaics), 156–57; Indian, 230, 237–38; Islamic, 215; Roman, 79; -self (Rembrandt), 391, 397; Sumerian, 64; Velázquez, 454; Venice, 363, 371 (*see* Titian). *See* name of artist
Portugal, 369
Pottery: Greece, 7–8, 306; *haniwa*, 290; Kashans, 217; Mochica, 306, 308; Peru, 306, 308; Rayy, 217; Seljuk, 217
Prado (Madrid), 344, 348
Prague, 352
Praxiteles of Athens, 116–17, 424
Prehistoric artist, 23. *See* Cave paintings
Priest-kings, 122
Primitive societies, 9, 30, 33
Prints, 297–302; *ukiyo-e,* 297, 299, 300
Procopius, 155, 164
Prostitution: Etruscans, 121–22; Japanese, 298–99
Proust, Marcel, 399
Punt, expedition to, 45
Pyramids: Giza (Gizeh), 42, 313; Saqqara, 41, 43; stepped, 59, 312 (*see* Ziggurats); Teotihuacán, 311–13; Zoser, 42, 43
Pyrenees, 27
Pythagoras, 143

Qait Bey, 218

Quetzalcóatl, 13, 310, 312
Quirino Nicola, 202

Ramessid pharaohs, 54
Rampin Horseman, 101
Ramses II, 37, 46, 54–55; statuary, influence of, 55, 56
Raphael, 12, 177, 198, 336–38, 354, 392, 439, 475, 492; da Vinci, 336; death, 462; Madonnas, 337, 338; Michelangelo, 419; *works:* 337–38, *Judgment of Paris,* 487, *School of Athens,* 337, *Sistine Madonna,* 337
Ravenna: Byzantine influence, 161; Church of San Vitale (mosaics), 155–57; Galla Placidia mausoleum, 157–58, 167
Rayy pottery, 217
Reims, 403; archbishop of, 97; Cathedral, 205, 206, 207
Relics, 195, 199, 202, 203, 204; purchase of, 202
Reliefs: Borobudur Temple, 257
Religions, 382; androgynous gods, 232; "divine repositories," 115, classical example, 114–15; mathematics, 143. *See under* name
Religious art, 7, 8
Reliquary, 256
Rembrandt, 12, 15, 51, 370, 383, 384, 385–94, 461, 475, 482, 486; Caravaggio, 418; collection, 392–93; etchings, 390; Hendrickje, 390, 391, 393, 394; influence, 385; influences on, 444; pupils, 389, 394; Saskia, 387–88, 389, 390, 392; self-portraits, 391–92, 397; son (Titus), 388, 390, 391, 393, 394; style, 386, 389, 394; successors, 394; teacher, 418; Van Gogh, 494; *works:* 356, 387–90, 393, 494, *Anatomy Lesson of Dr. Tulp,* 387, *The Jewish Bride,* 393, *Night Watch,* 388–89, *Titus,* 356
Renaissance, 7, 8, 180, 362, 404, 409; artists, 9, 12, 13, 336; Christ, portraits of, 175–76; divinity, end of, 175; Florence, 317–38 (*see* Florence); France, 481; height, 126; Italy, 384–85; mosaics, 159
Renoir, Auguste, 355, 473, 483, 485, 486, 490
Retouching, 334, 335
Ribera, 455
Ridolfi, Carlo, 381
Riemenschneider, Tilman, 403, 416
Rio de Janeiro, 486
Robbia, Luca della, 322, 323
Robusti, Jacopo, 375. *See* Tintoretto
Rock carvings: Sassanian, 80
Rock paintings, 31, 33, *ill.* 33. *See* Cave paintings
Rolin, Chancellor, 339, *Rolin Madonna,* 342–43
Roman de la Rose, 205–6
Romanesque art, 159, 179–92; cathedrals, 347; characteristics, 182, 183, 184, 185,

189, 191–92, 195, 196, 198, 205; Christ, 183; churches, 127, 191, 431; sculpture, 184–88, 261, masterpieces, 185–87
Romanus I Lecapenus, Emperor, 164
Rome (Ancient), 56, 79, 80, 119, 131–44, 337; architecture, 142; art, 131, 133, 135–36ff., 142–43, beginning, 133, characteristics, 141, 180, 478, conqueror theme, 140, 141, masterpieces, 180, survival, 179–80, triumphal arches, 180; Augustan Age, 317–18, 339, 459; basilica, 148; Baths of Caracalla, 141–42; Baths of Diocletian, 142; Campus Martius, 137–38; catacombs, 166–67; characteristics, 129, 130, 131, 132, 198; Christ, portraits, 172; Christianity, 167; Church of Santa Constanza, 149; civilization, extent of, 402; coins, 134, 143; conquest of, 122, 123; emperors, 139, 141, 143; Empire: end of, 179, 198, extent, 179; Etruscans, 122, 125, 129–30; Farnese Palace, 445; founding, 137; gods, 233; Goths, 198; Greece, 68, 117, 119, 133–35; imperial, 142, 161 (see Empire); Jubilee (1300), 319; legions, 130, 132, 140; Marcus Aurelius Column, 140–41; museums, 10; paintings, 103, 143; Pantheon, 142–43, 180; Piazza Navona, 439, 440; Republic, 133; ruins, 364, Piranesi engravings, 464, 465, 466; Samnium, 132; sculpture, 136–40, 143, 326 (see Trajan, Column); Senate, 165; stained-glass windows, 195; Tor di Nona (prison), 440. See Augustus Caesar and Rome (city)
Rome (city), 354, 417; Byzantine influence, 161; Church of San Pietro in Vincoli, 428; dedication to Apollo, 135; Doria Gallery, 454; National Museum, 142; Palatine, 135, 136; St. Peter's, 9, 424, 428; Sistine Chapel, 11, 342, 377, 428–30, 431, 445, 507; Villa Giulia Museum, 127
Rouault, Georges, 506, 510, 513; clowns, 460, 507, 510, 511; Man of Sorrow, 177
Rouen: archbishop of, 197; Cathedral, 485
Rubens, Jan, 353–54
Rubens, Peter Paul, 353–58, 385, 392, 439, 504; Breugel, 353; commissions, 356–57; fees, 357; reputation, 358, 461; style, 355–56, 358; Watteau, 460; works: Fall of the Rebel Angels, 355, Three Graces, 355
Ruisdael, Jacob van, 383, 400
Rumania, 507
Ruskin, John: The Elements of Drawing, 484
Russia, 72, 459; Byzantine influence, 161; Mongols, 219; peasant art, 181

Sacsaihuamán, 308
Saenredam, Pieter, 383, 385

St. Anne, 199, 202
Sainte-Chapelle (Paris), 202–4, 481
Saint-Denis (France), 188, 193, 194–95, 197; Abbot Suger, 194; Carolingian Church, 193, 194–95, 197, 199
St. Mark, 362
St. Peter's (Rome), 9, 424, 428
Saint-Remy, 494, 498
Saints. See St. listings and also under name
St. Sophia. See Hagia Sophia
St. Theresa of Avila, 449
Saladin, 214
Salisbury Cathedral, 205
Salomon, Bernard, 453
Salonica, 149–52; Byzantine influence, 161; Church of Hagia Sophia, 152, 153; mosaics, 151, 159
Salvers, silver, 80
Samarkand, 219, 220; Timur mausoleum, 220
Samarra: Great Mosque, 214–15
Samnites, 131–32, Rome, 132
Sangallo, Bastiano, 427
Sanskrit, 264
Sansovino, Andreas, 362
Santorini, volcano, 94
Saqqara pyramid, 41, 43, 49
Saracens, 198
Sarcophagus: Etruscan, 125; Hagia Triada, 91–94, ill. 92; Ludovisi, 180
Sardinia, Etruscans and, 122
Sargon II, 66
Sassanians, 78, 79–82, 169, 260; art, 79–81, 223, 280
Saulieu, 191
Scandinavia, 181
Scenery: stage (Greek), 103
Schematic drawings, ill. 26, 27, 31, 32, 33, 36
Schliemann, Heinrich, 60, 95
Scholars, Chinese, 272–73
Schongauer, Martin, 392, 403, 416; Virgin in the Rose Bower, 403–4, 408
Schools (art): cave artists, 23
Schopenhauer, Arthur, 501
Science, 323, 324, 328, 459, 504–5
Scotland, 179
Scrovegni, Enrico, 320
Sculpture (sculptors), 7, 11, 127, 189, 328, 504–5; Achaemenid, 72–73; African, 505; Aztec, 310–11; Brancusi, 508–9; Cambodia, 497, 509; cave art, 23; Christ, 176; cliff, 55; Egypt, 43, 100; Etruscan, 126–28; Far East, 55; Florence, 319ff.; Germany, 403; Greece, 98–1, 113, 116–18, heroic theme, 101, 104–5; Gudea statues, 65–66; heroic figures, 327; India, 229–31, 233, 241–42, 243, 249; Japan (Buddha), 293–94; Lagash, 65; Laocoön, 428, 431; largest human figures, 54–55; life casts, 117; Luristan bronzes, 70; masterpieces, 258; medieval, 181; Michelan-

gelo, 424; modern, 511; Olmec, 305; Persian, 80; Pre-Columbian, 305; Roman, 136, 140, 143, 326; Romanesque, 184–87, 192, 261, masterpieces, 185–87; settings, 118, 119; Sumerian, 65–66; time-place necessity, 12; turning point, 321 (*see* Pisano Giovanni). *See also under* name of sculptor *and* country
Scythia, 70, 73, 248
Seal stones: Cretan, 86
Seascapes, 358, 483
Secular art, 8
Sefar (North Africa), schematic drawing (nude), 31, *ill.* 32
Seghers, Hercules, 392
Seljuks, 215, 216–17; appearance, 217; architecture, 215–16; art, 215–18, 223; empire in Persia, end, 217
Semites, 281
Senmut, 44–45
Sens, archbishop of, 197
Sesshu (Zen priest), 297
Seville, 450
Sex: Etruscans, 124–25
Sforza, Francesco: da Vinci statue, 332
Sforzas, 336
Shaft graves: Mycenae, 95, 96
Shah Abbas, 223, 225
Shah Isma'il, 221–22
Shah Jehan, 223
Shah Rukh, 220
Shakespeare, William M., 450; Van Gogh, 494
Shang Dynasty: bronzes, 9; signatures, 9
Shantipore (the city of gold), 229
Shapur I, 80
Sharaku, 301
Shih Huang Ti, 270
Shiraz, 220, mosque, 215
Shomu, Emperor, 294
Shotoku, Prince, 290
Shub-Ad, Queen, 62, 63–64; gold cup, 62, 63, 68, 96
Siamese Buddha, 12, 14–15
Sibai Santra, 243
Siberia, 271
Sibylline Oracles, 129
Sicily, 115, 144, 442; Byzantine influence, 161
Siddhartha, Prince, 250, 257. *See* Buddha
Siena, 174, 322, 362; medieval banners, 132
Signatures, artists', 9, 25, 224, 337–38, 414–15, 453
Silk paintings, 15
Silk Road, 272, 280
Silks: Seljuks, 217
Simon, James, 50
Sistine Chapel, 11, 342, 377, 428–30, 431, 445, 507; Michelangelo, 429–30, 431
Sistine Madonna (Raphael), 337
Siva, 229–31, 232, 240; birthplace, 233
Siva Nataraja, 244–45

Six, Jan, 392
Sixtus IV, Pope, 428
Skyscapes, 483
Slaves, 218; states, 131
Sloane, Hans, 10
Smenkhkare (Pharaoh), 52
Smyrna, 121
Socrates, 392
Soghdians, 272
Somaliland, 45
Sotatsu, 296
Souillac, Abbey, 187
South America, 308. *See* Americas (Pre-Columbian)
South China, 272
South China Sea, 251, 271
Southeast Asia: Buddhism, 236
Soutine, Chaim, 506, 507
Spain, 28, 131, 179, 181, 211, 225, 318, 451–52, 486, 503; cave paintings, 19; conquistadors, 410; court, 355, 453, 454; England, 357; France, 472; Holland, 382–83, 385; Inquisition, 449, 455, 468; Italy, 355; painting, 444, 455; Romanesque, 183; title: "Corrector of Indecencies," 468. *See* El Greco
Spanish Armada, defeat of, 383
Spanish Conquest, 303, 309
Sparta, 107, 154
Spina (Italy), 122, 128, 129
Stained-glass windows, 195, 197, 203, 339, 507, 510; Chartres, 200–1, *ill.* 201; greatest, 200; Sainte-Chapelle, 203–4
Standard of Ur, 63
Stein, Gertrude: Picasso portrait, 503
Still lifes, 462–63, 499
Stoffels, Hendrickje, 390–91
Stone rubbings, 276, *ill.* 277
Stoss, Veit, 403
Strasbourg, 207, 408
Subhuti, 263–64
Sultan Mohammed II, 161
Sumerians, 56, 57, 60, 62–63, 69, 70, 73, 288; architecture, 60, 66; art, 61ff., 68, portraiture, 64; sculpture, 65, 66; conquest of, 66; cylinder seals, 58; Egyptian art: relationship, 63, 64, 65; gold helmet, *ill.* 61; legacy, 68; Luristan, 71; temples, 59; tombs, 62–63; *ziggurats,* 59–60, 68
Sung Dynasty, 6
Sun Temple of Konarak, 243–44
Surrealists, 507
Surya, 243; images, 244
Su Tung-p'o, 278, 279, 283, 284, 285
Swanenburgh, Jacob van, 386
Sweden, 405, 485
Symbolism: Christian, 181
Syria, 56, 165, 219, 272; art, 220; icons, 169; Mongols, 219

Tabriz: carpets, 224
Tahiti, 495, 496–97
T'ai Tsung, Emperor, 273

Taj Mahal, 223
Tale of Genji, 295–96
Tanagra figurines, 12
T'ang Dynasty, 7, 13, 16, 217, 251
Taoism, 287
T'ao-t'ieh mask, 304
Tao Yuan-ming, 271
Tapestries, 155
Taq-i-Bustan, 81
Taq-i-Kisra, palace, 81–82
Tarquinia (Italy), 123; winged horses, 127
Tassili N'Ajjer Mountains, 31
Tasso, 354
Tate Gallery (London), 513
Teheran, 11, 217; Museum, 77
Tell-el-Amarna, 317; Akhenaton's capital, 50
Tempesta, Antonio, 392
Temple-caves (T'ien Lung Shan), 12
Temple of Amon (Thebes), 46
Temple of Zeus (Olympia), 104
Temples: Aztec, 310; Borobudur, 256–58; pagan, atmosphere, 147; Pre-Columbian, 313–14; Thai, 255
Tenochtitlán, 309, 310
Teotihuacán, 311–13
Ter Borch, Gerard, 383, 395, 400
Teruel (Spain): carved warrior rock painting, 31, 33, *ill.* 33
Thailand, 255; Buddha image, 253–55
Thasos (island), 119
Thebes, 45–46; Akhenaton statue, 50
Theodora, Empress, 154, 156–57
Theodosius the Great, 149, 168
Theologians, 198
Theopompus, 124–25
Theseus, 85
Thessaly, 154
Thomas of Celano, 431
Thoré, Théophile, 399
Tiahuanaco, 306
Tiber River, 121
Tibet, 270, 272; Buddhism, 236; goddess (Tara), 241–42; silk paintings, 15
T'ien Lung Shan: Buddha, 12, 13; temple-caves, 12
Tiepolo, Giovanni Battista, 459, 466–67, 469, 470
Tigris River, 57, 82
Timur the Lame, 219–20, 221; successors, 220
Tintoretto, 14, 159, 173, 362, 370, 375–81; heroic art, 380; influences, 454; pupils, 444; Scuola di San Rocco, 377; style, 449; *works:* 376, 377, 378, *Christ Walking on the Sea of Galilee,* 444, *Paradiso,* 380, 381
Titian, 11, 12, 13, 14, 159, 354, 360, 369, 370–75, 376, 378, 392, 395, 474, 486; copies of, 355; El Greco, 444, 446; honors, 373; influences, 454, 455; patron, 373; pupils, 372, 375, 444; Rembrandt, 393; technique, 373; *works:* 370–72, 374, *Venus of Urbino,* 369, 487

Tohaku, 297
Tokyo, 297, 298, 301
Toledo: Cathedral, 446; El Greco, 447–49
Toltec, 311
Tombs: chambers, 43 (*see* Pyramids); Chinese: figures, 281, Han, 270; Egypt, 123; Etruscan, 125–26, 128, frescoes, 123–24, paintings, 132–33; Gothic, 126; Hagia Triada, 91–94, *ill.* 92–93; Italic tribes, paintings, 131ff.; Japanese, 290; Ludovisi Sarcophagus, 180; paintings, 37, *ill.* 36; T'ai Tsung, 273; Tutankhaton, 52–53
T'o-pa tribesmen, 259, 260
Torcello, 171
Torrigiano, 420–21
Totem poles, 306
Toulouse, Counts of, 491
Toulouse-Lautrec, Henri de, 491–92, 493, 503
Tower of Qabus, 217
Trade, 121, 128, 251, 280, 281, 318, 339, 340, 369, 370; -art relationship, 479
Trajan, 139, 141, 143; Column, 139–40, 179, 180–81, 182
Transoxiana, 215
Travel (travelers), 198, 253, 259, 387
Très Riches Heures du Duc de Berry, 479–80, 481
Trianon Press, 475
Tribute bearers, 92; Achaemenid, 76–77; China, 270
Triptychs, 348
Tristan, Flora, 495
True Cross, 202
Tu Fu, 301
Tulp, Dr. Nicolaes, 387
Turkestan, 270; Chinese, 280
Turks, 110, 160, 164, 259, 272; Seljuk, 215
Tuscany, 10, 336, 368
Tutankhamon. *See* Tutankhaton
Tutankhaton (pharaoh), tomb, 52–54
Tuthmosis III, 37, 46, 54, 79
Tyrrhenian Sea, 122

Uccello, Paolo, 322, 323, 324, 328
Udayana, King of Kosambi, 273
Uffizi Gallery (Florence), 10, 363
Uighurs, 272
Ukiyo-e "Floating World Picture," 297, 299, 300
Umayyad Caliph Abd-al-Malik, 163
Umayyad kings, 211
Umayyad mosaics, 211–12
Underwood, Dr. Paul, 160
United States: -Japan, 302
Universe: concepts of, 192; Hindu conception, 230; history of (Western Churches), 257
Ur: royal cemetery, 61; Standard, 63–64
Urban VIII, Pope, 445
Ur-Nammu: *ziggurat,* 60
Utamaro, 299–300, 301, 490

Uylenburgh, Hendrik van, 387
Uylenburgh, Saskia van, 387–88, 389, 390, 392

Valenciennes, 460
Valerian, Emperor, 80
Valley of the Kings, 52
Vandals, 179, 181
Van der Helst, Bartholomeus, 385–86
Van Dyke, Anthony, 392; self-portrait, 391
Van Eyck, Jan. See Eyck, Jan van
Van Gogh, Theo, 493, 494
Van Gogh, Vincent, 12, 283, 462, 492–95, 496, 497, 498, 499–500, 501, 503; death, 462, 495; madness, 494–95; self-portraits, 391; signature, 9; Toulouse-Lautrec portrait, 492; works: Potato Eaters, 492, 493
Vaphio (Laconia), gold cup, 96, 97
Vasari, Giorgio, 6, 173, 323, 327, 333, 363, 366, 368, 375, 376, 420, 424, 433
Vases: Cretan, 9, 93–94; Greek, 102–3, 128
Vasi, Giuseppe, 465
Vatican, 117, 371; frescoes, 337; Museum, 136; papal art collection, 10
Velázquez, Diego, 445, 450–55, 486, 488; influences on, 450–51, 454, 455; nudes, 454–55; patron, 451; portraits, 454; Rubens, 357; self-portrait, 453; signature, 9, 453; themes, 451; works: 453–55, Surrender of Breda, 452–53, 454
Venice, 11, 14, 110, 202, 317, 318, 354, 358, 360–81, 409, 421, 463; Accademia, 363, 366; art: colors, 360, golden age, 381, light, 381, mosaics, 158–59, 177, 361–62, painters, 362ff.; Byzantine influence, 161; Church of Madonna dell' Orto, 376; Church of San Giorgio Maggiore, 379; Constantinople, 160, 361, 362; doges, 361, 363, palace, 362, 363, 380; Greek quarter, 444; Piazza of San Marco, 224; plague, 368, 373; St. Mark's, 110, 361, 362, mosaics, 158–59; Santa Maria dei Frari, 371–72; Scuola of San Rocco, 370, 377, 381; trade, 369–70
Ventris, Michael, 86, 89
Vermeer, Jan, 12, 383, 394–400, 464; fame, 399–400; influences on, 444; self-portraits, 396–97; style, 397–98; works: 394, 396, 397, 398, 399, The Lacemaker, 397, View of Delft, 399, Young Girl in a Blue Turban, 394
Veronese, Paolo, 380–81
Verrocchio, 327, 412; da Vinci, 332
Versailles, 463
Verspronck, Johannes, 385
Vézelay, 191; Christ, 191; tympanum, 191
Victoria, Queen of England, 88
Victoria and Albert Museum (London), 224
Victory of Samothrace, 118

Vienna, 348, 352; Kunsthistoriches Museum, 366
Villa Giulia Museum (Rome), 127
Villard de Honnecourt, 190
Villena, Marquis of, 449
Vincent of Beauvais: Speculum, 206
Vinci, Leonardo da, 6, 12, 159, 177, 331, 508; aims, 332, 336; characteristics, 331–32, 336, 415; horses, 332–33, 336; influences on, 327, 368; music, 21; notebooks, 286, 332, 336; pupils, 336; teacher, 332; works: 332–35, greatest, 332, Last Supper, 177, 334–36, Mona Lisa, 333–34
Virgil, 501
Virgin, 206–7, 242; Van Eyck, 344; veil, 199, 202; veneration of, 80
Vishnu images, 244
Volsinii (Etruscan city), 129
Volterra, 130
Vorticists, 507

Wallace Collection (London), 384
Wall paintings: Ajanta caves, 238; Buddhist monasteries, 264–65; Chinese: Han, 270; earliest on man-made surface, 37–38; Egypt, 37, ill. 36; Greek, 103; Hindu, 230; Romanesque, 183
Wang Shen, Prince, 283
Wang Wei, 279–80, 283, 459
War-art, relationship, 339; Disasters of War, 472
Washington, D.C., 395; Freer Gallery, 269; National Gallery, 444
Watteau, Antoine, 459, 460–62, 470, 481; reputation, 461; The Embarkment for Cythera, 460
Wealth-art, relationship, 339, 479. See also Court
"Weeper holes," 60
Wellington, Duke of, 472
Western art, 257; archetypal forms, 401; color, 289; masterpieces, 177; Michelangelo, 275; most beautiful architectural form, 207
Weyden, Rogier van der, 344, 410; Dead Christ (Bruges), 176; Descent from the Cross, 344
Whittemore, Dr. Thomas, 160
Wignacourt, Alof de, 441, 442, 443
William VIII (Hesse), 10
William the Silent, Prince of Orange, 383
Winchester Cathedral: Crucifixion, 184
Winter scenes: Hiroshige, 301–2
Wohlgemut, Michael, 408
Women: Etruscan, 125; female form presentation, 206; Greek sculpture, 117; Japanese, 298–300
Wood-block prints, 263–64, ill. 263; Japanese, 297–98, 490, 493
Woodcuts, 176, 367, 368; Dürer, 409, 411, 413–14; Japanese (see Hiroshige)
Woolley, Sir Leonard, 60–61, 62, 63
World War I, 506, 511
World War II, 511

Writing, antecedents, 58
Wu, Empress, 274n
Wu Tao-tzu, 264, 275–79, 299, 459, 475,
    ill. 277

Xerxes, King, 74

Yangtze River, 275
Yeats, W. B., 152–53
Yen Li-pen, 273–74
Yoshiwara, 298, 300
Yucatan, 313–14

Yunan, 270

Zapotec, 313
Zen, 297
Zeuxis, 103
Ziggurats, 59–60, 68; "weeper holes," 60
Zola, Emile, 489
Zoroaster, 76
Zoroastrianism, 77, 226
Zoser: pyramid, 42, 43; statue of, 40
Zubarán, 455
Zurvan ("endless Time"), 81